WRITING OF TODAY

WRITING OF TODAY:

MODELS OF JOURNALISTIC PROSE

Selected and Discussed by

J. W. CUNLIFFE, D.Lit.

*Professor of English and Associate Director of
The School of Journalism, Columbia
University*

and

GERHARD R. LOMER, Ph.D.

*Instructor in English, The School of Journalism,
Columbia University*

NEW YORK
THE CENTURY CO.
1918

PREFACE

Why does the teaching of English composition, to which modern schools and colleges give so much time and energy, yield unsatisfactory results? The main reason is, in our judgment, that it seems to be out of touch with reality; the pupil sees in his appointed tasks no connection with his life as it is or as it is likely to be. Accordingly he treats his themes as intellectual 'stunts' that have to be gone through simply because they are part of the course, and he fails to apply in his every day speech and writing the lessons he has learnt in the classroom. This sense of artificiality is partly due to the subjects he is asked to write about and the literary models set before him for imitation. Stevenson acknowledges that he 'played the sedulous ape' to Hazlitt, Lamb, Sir Thomas Browne, Montaigne, and other great writers of prose, but it does not follow that the average American youth can learn to write by the study of Newman, Pater, and Stevenson, even when their essays are elaborately analyzed and interpreted for him. He finds the subjects outside of his everyday interests and the mode of treatment altogether beyond his reach. The result is lassitude and discouragement.

Enterprising teachers have striven to overcome these difficulties by setting exercises on subjects of immediate interest and by the use of current periodicals as models of style. The present volume is an effort in the same direction, with the additional advantage of carefully selected examples, classified for ease of reference under general headings, with such comments on the separate types as seem likely to be of advantage in class room instruction or private study. The technique of news reporting having been adequately discussed in more than one recent text book, we have given the space at our disposal to those forms of newspaper and magazine writing which offer more opportunity for individual treatment. A youth who cannot be sent out to gather news may be interested in the discussion of some present day issue, and willing to observe how the masters of the craft exercise their art. The first step in the problem is to win the student's attention and good will. With this in mind we have endeavored to choose papers which from their subject or mode of presentation are likely to attract and stimulate intelligent young people. To disregard the element of literary charm would be even more absurd than to offer the youthful mind the subtleties of the skilled dialectician or the last refinements of a mannered style.

We wish to acknowledge most gratefully the generosity with which authors and publishers have granted us permission to reprint. Some of the articles have been already republished in book form, and in such cases we have adopted the revised text when the author has requested it; in the other cases, the original form of the article as it appeared in newspaper or magazine has been retained, save for an occasional correction, again at the author's request. The complete text of the selections is reprinted, except in a very few instances, where omissions are indicated by asterisks. Where the author's name is given below the title in square brackets, the article was originally published anonymously, and the name of the writer is now added by authority.

Our first aim has been to select examples likely to be of service to the young student of the art of writing; but the volume will, we hope, also interest the general public as an illustration of the variety and excellence of the articles published day by day in the newspapers and periodicals of the United States and Great Britain.

CONTENTS

A. Descriptive Articles

B. Narrative Articles

E. Humorous and Occasional Articles

H. Dramatic Criticism

I. Musical Criticism

J. Art Criticism

WRITING OF TODAY

WRITING OF TODAY

A. DESCRIPTIVE ARTICLES

The essential merits of descriptive writing are (1) accuracy; (2) clearness; (3) vividness. The first depends upon the writer's power of observation, the last upon his power of presentation, and the second on both. A good piece of description should put the ordinary reader in a position to see things not merely with his own eyes, but with the keener eyes of the skilled observer. It is therefore necessary that young people who are learning to write should be trained to observe, and that they should cultivate their faculties of observation by practice. The ambitious student should look with understanding eyes upon the district in which he lives and the country through which he travels. Whether his home is in a great city or in a country town, in a village or on a farm, the place has individual characteristics which he should not fail to note, salient features which the majority of the inhabitants pass with unseeing eyes. It is a useful exercise for him to endeavor to put down in writing his impressions of what he has seen, and to compare his efforts with those of the craftsmen whose work is included in this section. If he has traveled, abroad or in his own country, let him compare the record of his memories with Viscount Bryce's account of Palestine. If he has lived almost continuously in one place, let him strive to emulate Mr. Will Irwin's description of San Francisco. The result will probably be somewhat disheartening, but it will be salutary if it convinces him that his undertaking involves qualities in addition to the skill of the ready writer. This last is of obvious importance, and there is no need to stress it. The young student is more likely to overlook the importance of an orderly arrangement of his material and the selection for his picture of those features, which, presented in due proportion, will give the impression he is seeking to convey. The ability to do these things is seldom innate, and often needs to be cultivated by assiduous practice, but the task is not an impossible one, granted a sufficient degree of native intelligence to start with, and an education which has enabled the student to master the rudiments of English composition. At first, he can only admire from a distance the vivid color with which Mr. Hichens recalls the beauty of Athens or the skill and power with which Mr. Huneker reproduces the experiences of a summer night at Coney Island. If he realizes appreciatively that the thing is done, he may come to understand how, and, according to his own capacity, and in his own way, learn to describe for others life as he sees it himself — but he must first see it.

The same principles apply to the description of a building or a ship, a bridge or a canal, a manufacturing process or a scientific discovery. These may appear simpler on account of their limited scope, but they demand perhaps greater skill on account of their restricted interest, and they present special difficulties from the technical knowledge which is often required. In dealing with them the student should be careful not to try to describe what he does not understand, and he should also avoid attempting to take his readers beyond the limits of their comprehension. In such descriptions the main virtues are simplicity and clearness, and the various examples here presented have been chosen from that point of view.

I

IMPRESSIONS OF PALESTINE

JAMES BRYCE

[*National Geographic Magazine*, Washington, D. C. — Copyright, 1915. By special permission.]

No country has been so often described or so minutely described by travelers of all sorts of tastes and interest as Palestine has been; and this is natural, for none has excited so keen an interest for so long a time and in so many nations.

5 As we have all at some time or other read much about the country, it may well be thought that nothing now remains to be said about Palestine, except by archeologists, whose explorations of the sites of ancient cities are always bringing 10 fresh facts to light. But if all of us have read a good deal about the Holy Land,

3

most of us have also forgotten a good
deal, and our ideas of the country — ideas
colored by sentiments of reverence and romance — are often vague and not always
correct.

It may therefore be worth while to set
down in a plain and brief way the salient
impressions which the country makes on
a Western traveler who passes quickly
through it. The broad impressions are
the things that remain in memory when
most of the details have vanished, and
broad impressions are just what an elaborate description sometimes fails to convey, because they are smothered under an
infinitude of details.

A SMALL COUNTRY

Palestine is a tiny little country.
Though the traveler's handbooks prepare
him to find it small, it surprises him by
being smaller than he expected. Taking
it as the region between the Mediterranean on the west and the Jordan and
Dead Sea on the east, from the spurs of
Lebanon and Hermon on the north to the
desert at Beersheba on the south, it is
only 110 miles long and from 50 to 60
broad — that is to say, it is smaller than
New Jersey, whose area is 7500 square
miles.

Of this region large parts did not really
belong to ancient Israel. Their hold on
the southern and northern districts was
but slight, while in the southwest a wide
and rich plain along the Mediterranean
was occupied by the warlike Philistines,
who were sometimes more than a match
for the Hebrew armies. Israel had, in
fact, little more than the hill country,
which lay between the Jordan on the east
and the maritime plain on the west.
King David, in the days of his power,
looked down from the hill cities of Benjamin, just north of Jerusalem, upon
Philistine enemies only twenty-five miles
off, on the one side, and looked across the
Jordan to Moabite enemies about as far
off, on the other.

Nearly all the events in the history of
Israel that are recorded in the Old Testament happened within a territory no bigger than the State of Connecticut, whose
area is 4800 square miles; and into
hardly any other country has there been
crowded from the days of Abraham till
our own so much history — that is to say
so many events that have been recorded

and deserve to be recorded in the annals
of mankind. To history, however, I shall
return later.

FEELING PALESTINE'S SMALLNESS

Nor is it only that Palestine is really
a small country. The traveler constantly
feels as he moves about that it is a small
country. From the heights a few miles
north of Jerusalem he sees, looking northward, a far-off summit carrying snow for
eight months in the year. It is Hermon,
nearly 10,000 feet high — Hermon, whose
fountains feed the rivers of Damascus.
But Hermon is outside the territory of
Israel altogether, standing in the land of
the Syrians; so, too, it is of Lebanon.
We are apt to think of that mountain
mass as within the country, because it
also is frequently mentioned in the Psalms
and the Prophets; but the two ranges of
Lebanon also rise beyond the frontiers of
Israel, lying between the Syrians of
Damascus and the Phœnicians of the
West.

Perhaps it is because the maps from
which children used to learn Bible geography were on a large scale that most of
us have failed to realize how narrow were
the limits within which took place all
those great doings that fill the books of
Samuel and Kings. Just in the same way
the classical scholar who visits Greece is
surprised to find that so small a territory
sufficed for so many striking incidents
and for the careers of so many famous
men.

LITTLE NATURAL WEALTH

Palestine is a country poor in any natural resources. There are practically no
minerals, no coal, no iron, no copper, no
silver, though recently some oil wells
have been discovered in the Jordan Valley. Neither are there any large forests,
and though the land may have been better
wooded in the days of Joshua than it is
now, there is little reason to think that
the woods were of trees sufficiently large
to constitute a source of wealth. A comparatively small area is fit for tillage.

To an Arab tribe that had wandered
through a barren wilderness for forty
weary years, Canaan may well have
seemed a delightful possession; but many
a county in Iowa, many a department in
France, could raise more grain or wine
than all the Holy Land.

PLAIN OF ESDRAELON

There is one stretch of fertile, level land 20 miles long and from 3 to 6 miles wide — the Plain of Esdraelon. But with this exception it is only in the bottoms and on the lower slopes of a few valleys, chiefly in the territory of Ephraim from Bethel northward and along the shores of the Bay of Acre, that one sees cornfields and olive yards and orchards. Little wine is now grown.

Such wealth as the country has consists in its pastures, and the expression 'a land flowing with milk and honey' appropriately describes the best it has to offer, for sheep and goats can thrive on the thin herbage that covers the hills, and the numerous aromatic plants furnish plenty of excellent food for the bees; but it is nearly all thin pasture, for the land is dry and the soil mostly shallow. The sheep and goats vastly outnumber the oxen. Woody Bashan, on the east side of Jordan, is still the region where one must look for the strong bulls.

SEEN THROUGH A GOLDEN HAZE

Palestine is not a beautiful country. The classical scholar finds charms everywhere in Greece, a land consecrated to him by the genius of poets and philosophers, although a great part of Greece is painfully dry and bare. So, too, the traveler who brings a mind suffused by reverence and piety to spots hallowed by religious associations sees the landscapes of the Holy Land through a golden haze that makes them lovely. But the scenery of the Holy Land, taken as a whole (for there are exceptions presently to be noticed), is inferior, both in form and in color, to that of northern and middle Italy, to that of Norway and Scotland, to that of the coasts of Asia Minor, to that of many parts of California and Washington.

The hills are flat-topped ridges, with a monotonous skyline, very few of them showing any distinctive shape. Not a peak anywhere, and Tabor the only summit recognizable by its form. They are all composed of gray or reddish-gray limestone, bare of wood, and often too stony for tillage. Between the stones or piles of rock there are low shrubs, and in the few weeks of spring masses of brilliant flowers give rich hues to the landscape; but for the rest of the year all is gray or brown. The grass is withered away or is scorched brown, and scarcely any foliage is seen on the tops or upper slopes of the rolling hills. It is only in some of the valleys that one finds villages nestling among olive groves and orchards where plum and peach and almond blossoms make spring lovely.

Arid indeed is the land. The traveler says with the Psalmist: 'My soul longs in a dry, parched land, wherein no water is.' Wells are few, springs still fewer, and of brooks there are practically none, for the stony channels at the bottom of the glens have no water except after a winter rainstorm. There may probably have been a more copious rainfall twenty or thirty centuries ago, when more wood clothed the hillsides, and the country would then have been more pleasing to Northern eyes, to which mountains are dear because rills make music and green boughs wave in the wind.

THE RIVER KISHON

To this general description there are certain exceptions which must not be forgotten. The high ridge of Mount Carmel rises grandly from the sea, and on its land side breaks down in bold declivities and deep glens upon the valley through which the Kishon, an almost perennial stream, finds its way to the Bay of Acre. Here, upon the slopes of a long ridge, on the other side of the Kishon, there is a wildering forest of ancient holm-oaks, all the more beautiful because it is the one considerable stretch of natural wood in the whole country west of Jordan.

On the other side of that river the slopes of the plateau which runs eastward into the desert, the Bashan and Gilead of the Old Testament, have also patches of woodland left, and in the canyons that cut deep through these slopes there is many a picturesque scene where the brooks, Jabbok and Yarmuk, leap in tiny waterfalls from ledge to ledge of the cliffs. These are the only brooks in all the country, these and the Kishon, which itself is reduced in late summer to a line of pools.

VIEW FROM TABOR

Of the wider views there are two that ought to be noted. One is beautiful. It is the prospect from the top of Mount

Tabor, a few miles east of Nazareth, over the wide plain of Esdraelon, specially charming in April, when the green of the upspringing wheat and barley contrasts with the rich red of the strips of newly plowed land that lie between.

The other is grand and solemn. From the Mount of Olives, and indeed from the higher parts of Jerusalem itself, one looks across the deep hollow where the Jordan, a little below Jericho, pours its turbid waters into the Dead Sea, and sees beyond this hollow the long, steep wall of the mountains of Moab.

These mountains are the edge of the great plateau, 3000 feet higher than the Dead Sea, which extends into the Great Desert of Northern Arabia. Among them is conspicuous the projecting ridge of Nebo, or Pisgah, from which Moses looked out upon that Promised Land which he was not permitted to enter. These mountains are the background of every eastward view from the heights of Judea. Always impressive, they become weirdly beautiful toward sunset, when the level light turns their stern gray to exquisite purples and a tender lilac that deepens into violet as the night begins to fall.

PROSPECTS THAT PLEASE

In eastern Galilee also there are noble prospects of distant Hermon; nor is there any coast scenery anywhere finer than that of the seaward slopes of Lebanon behind Sidon and Beirut. But Hermon and Lebanon (as already remarked) lie outside Palestine and would need a description to themselves. Damascus, seen from the heights above, its glittering white embosomed in orchards, is a marvel of beauty — a pearl set in emeralds, say the Muslims. Petra, far off in the Arabian Desert to the south, is a marvel of wild grandeur, with its deep, dark gorges and towering crags; but these also lie outside Palestine.

THE SEA OF GALILEE

Though not comparable in beauty either to the lakes of Britain or to those that lie among the Alps, or to Lake George in New York and Lake Tahoe in California, the Sea of Galilee has a quiet charm of its own.

The shores are bare of wood and the encircling mountains show no bold peaks; yet the slopes of the hills, sometimes falling abruptly, sometimes in soft and graceful lines, have a pleasing variety, and from several points a glimpse may be caught of the snowy top of Hermon rising beyond the nearer ranges. A great sadness broods over the silent waters. The cities that decked it like a necklace have, all but Tiberias, vanished so utterly that archeologists dispute over their sites. There is little cultivation, and where half a million of people are said to have lived at the beginning of our era, not 5000 are now to be found. Many a devastating war and the misgovernment of fourteen centuries have done their fatal work.

PALESTINE SUMMED UP

If Palestine is not a land of natural wealth nor a land of natural beauty, what is it? What are the impressions which the traveler who tries to see it exactly as it is carries away with him? Roughly summed up, they are these: stones, caves, tombs, ruins, battle-fields, sites hallowed by traditions — all bathed in an atmosphere of legend and marvel.

Never was there a country, not being an absolute desert, so stony. The hillsides seem one mass of loose rocks, larger or smaller. The olive yards and vineyards are full of stones. Even the cornfields (except in the alluvial soil of the plain of Esdraelon and along the sandy coast) seem to have more pebbles than earth, so that one wonders how crops so good as one sometimes sees can spring up. Caves are everywhere, for limestone is the prevailing rock, and it is the rock in which the percolation of rain makes clefts and hollows and caverns most frequent.

HISTORIC CAVES

Many of the incidents of Bible history are associated with caverns, from the cave of Machpelah, at Hebron, where Abraham buried Sarah and in which he is supposed to have been himself interred, down to the sepulchre hewn in rock in which the body of Christ was laid and over which the Church of the Holy Sepulchre was built by Helena, the mother of the Emperor Constantine.

Tradition points out many other sacred caves. It places the Annunciation by the Angel Gabriel to the Virgin at Nazareth in one cavern and the birth of Christ at Bethlehem in another, and assigns others to Samson, to David, to Elijah, and to various prophets. All over the country one finds tombs hewn in the solid rocks and pillars or piles of stone marking a burial place. Many of these rock tombs may be the work of races that dwelt here before Israel came. In a rocky land, where natural cavities are common, this becomes the obvious mode of interment. Thus here, as in Egypt, one seems to be in a land rather of the dead than of the living.

The impression of melancholy which this brooding shadow of death gives is heightened by the abundance of ruins. From very early times men built here in stone because there were, even then, few large trees, and though the dwellings of the poor were mostly of sun-baked mud and have long since vanished, the ease with which the limestone could be quarried and used for building made those who sought defense surround even small towns with walls, whose foundations at least have remained. The larger among the surviving ruins date from Roman or from Crusading times. These are still numerous, though Muslim vandalism and the habit of finding in the old erections material for new have left comparatively little of architectural interest.

GRECO-ROMAN RUINS

The best preserved remains are those of the Greco-Roman towns east of the Jordan, and these cities, singularly good specimens of the work of their age, are being rapidly destroyed by the Circassians whom the Turks have placed in that region. Be the ruins great or small, they are so numerous that in the course of a day's ride one is everywhere sure to pass far more of them than the traveler could find in even those parts of Europe that have been longest inhabited, and of many the ancient names are lost.

One is amazed at the energy the Crusaders showed in building castles, not a few of them large and all of them solid strongholds, as well as churches. But none of the fortresses are perfect, and of the churches only four or five have been spared sufficiently to show their beauty. Several, among these the most beautiful and best preserved, have been turned into mosques. Of these ruins few are cared for except by the archeologist and the historian.

RELIGIOUS MEMORIALS

But there are other memorials of the past that have lived on into the present. In no country are there so many shrines of ancient worship, so many spots held sacred — some sacred to Jews, some to Christians, some to Mussulmans. Neither has any other country spots that still draw a multitude of pilgrims, not even Belgium and Lombardy, each a profusion of battlefields. It is a land of ancient strife and seldom-interrupted slaughter.

Before Israel came, the tribes of Canaan warred with one another, and against those tribes Israel had to fight for its life. Along its western border ran the great line of march from Egypt to northern Syria and Mesopotamia, the highway of war trodden by the armies of Assyria and Babylon when they passed south to attack Egypt, and by the armies of Egypt when the great Pharaohs, Rameses, Thothmes, and Necho, led them north against Assyria.

In later days the Seleucid kings of Babylon and Antioch had fight after fight for the possession of the country with the Egyptian Ptolemies. Then appeared the legions of Rome, first under Pompey, then many a campaign to quell the revolt of the Jews. Still later came those fiercest enemies of Rome, the Sassanid kings of Persia, whose great invasion of A. D. 614 laid waste Jerusalem and spread ruin over the land.

THE ARAB INVASION

Just after that invasion the Arabs, then in the first flush of their swift conquest, descended on the enfeebled province and set up that Muslim rule which has often changed hands from race to race and dynasty to dynasty, but has never disappeared. When the Mohammedan princes had fought among themselves for four centuries they were suddenly attacked by a host of Crusaders from western Europe, and the soil of Palestine was drenched afresh with blood. The chronicle of more recent wars, which includes Napoleon's irruption, stopped at Acre in 1799, comes down to the Egyptian invasion in the days of Mehemet Ali.

From the top of Mount Tabor one looks down on six famous battlefields — the first, that of the victory of Deborah and Barak over Sisera, commemorated in the oldest

of Hebrew war songs (Judges, Chapters
IV-V), and the latest, that of the victory
of the French over the Turks in 1799.
And in this plain, near the spot where
Barak overcame Sisera and Pharaoh
Necho overcame Josiah, is to be fought
the mysterious Armageddon (Revelation,
Chapter XVI).

DOMINION OF THE PAST

Caves and tombs, ruins and battlefields,
and ancient seats of worship are the visible signs of that dominion of the past,
overweighting and almost effacing the
present, which one feels constantly and
everywhere in Palestine. For us English-
speaking men and women, who read the
Bible in our youth and followed the
stream of history down through antiquity
and the Middle Ages, no country is so
steeped in historical associations.

It could not be otherwise, for in no
other country (save Egypt) did history
begin so early; none has seen such an unending clash of races and creeds; none
has been the theater of so many events
touching the mind of so large a part of
mankind. The interest which Nature,
taken alone, fails to give is given in un-
equaled profusion by history, and by legend even more than by history.

THE ATMOSPHERE OF LEGEND AND MARVEL

The Holy Land is steeped also in an
atmosphere of legend and marvel. As the
traveler steps ashore at Jaffa he is shown
the rock to which Andromeda was chained
when Perseus rescued her from the sea
monster. (It is the only Greek story lo-
calized on these shores.) Till recent
years he was also shown the remains of
the ribs of another sea monster, the ' great
fish' that swallowed and disgorged the
prophet Jonah, whose tomb he will see on
the coast near Sidon. When he proceeds
toward Jerusalem he passes Lydda, the
birthplace of St. George, where that youthful hero slew the dragon. A little farther
comes the spot where another young champion, Samson, the Danite, had in earlier
days killed a thousand Philistines with
the jaw-bone of an ass.

Still farther along the railway line he is
pointed to the opening of the Valley of
Ajalon, where, according to the Book of
Joshua, the sun and moon stood still while
Israel pursued their enemies. An hour
later, as the train approaches Jerusalem,
he looks down on the rocky gorge in which
St. Sabas, himself a historical character,
famous and influential in the sixth century, dwelt in a cave where a friendly lion
came to bear him company; and from Jerusalem he can note the spot at which the
host of Israel passed dry-shod over Jordan,
following the Ark of the Covenant, and
near which Elisha made the iron swim and
turned bitter waters to sweet. Thence,
too, he can descry, far off among the blue
hills of Moab, the mountain top to which
Balaam was brought to curse Israel, and
where ' the dumb ass, speaking with man's
voice, forbade the madness of the prophet'
(Numbers, Chapter XX; II Peter, Chapter I).

WILD MUSLIM LEGENDS

These scenes of marvel, all passing before the eye in a single afternoon, are but
a few examples of the beliefs associated
with ancient sites over the length and
breadth of the country. All sorts of legends have sprung up among Muslims, as
well as Jews and Christians, the Muslim
legends being indeed the wildest. For
nearly every incident mentioned in the
Old or New Testament a local site has
been found, often one highly improbable,
perhaps plainly impossible, which nevertheless the devout are ready to accept.

The process of site-finding had begun
before the days of the Empress Helena,
and it goes on still. (Quite recently the
Muslims have begun to honor a cave at the
base of Mount Carmel, which they hold to
have sheltered Elijah.) Nothing is more
natural, for the number of pilgrims goes
on increasing with the increased ease and
cheapness of transportation, and sites have
to be found for the pilgrims.

CHRISTIAN PILGRIMS

The Roman Catholics come chiefly from
France, but they are few compared with
the multitude of Russians, nearly all simple peasants, ready to kiss the stones of
every spot which they are told that the
presence of the Virgin or a saint has hallowed.

To accommodate these pilgrim swarms,
for besides the Catholics and the Orthodox, the other ancient churches of the
East, such as the Armenians, the Copts,
and the Abyssinians, are also represented,
countless monasteries and hospices have
been erected at and around Jerusalem,

Bethlehem, Nazareth, and other sacred spots; and thus the aspect of these places has been so modernized that it is all the more difficult to realize what they were like in ancient days.

Jews have come in large numbers; they have settled in farm colonies; they have built up almost a new quarter on the north side of old Jerusalem. But even they are not so much in evidence as the Christian pilgrims. The pilgrim is now, especially at the times of festival, the dominant feature of Palestine. It is the only country, save Egypt, perhaps even more than Egypt, to which men flock for the sake of the past; and it is here that the philosophic student can best learn to appreciate the part which tradition and marvel have played in molding the minds and stimulating the religious fervor of mankind.

WHAT PALESTINE MIGHT BE

Under a better government — a government which should give honest administration, repress brigandage, diffuse education, irrigate the now desolate, because sun-scorched, valley of the lower Jordan by water drawn from the upper course of the river — Palestine might become a prosperous and even populous country and have its place in the civilization of the present.

The inhabitants, mostly Muslims, are a strong and often handsome race, naturally equal to the races of Southern Europe; but as Palestine stands to-day, it is a land of the past, a land of memories — memories of religion, but chiefly of religious war, and always rather of war than of peace. The only work ever done in it for peace was done by the preaching, nineteen centuries ago, of One whose teaching His followers have never put in practice.

The strife of Israel against the Amorites and of the Crusaders against the Muslims pale to insignificance compared with the conflict between five great nations to-day who bear the Christian name, and some of whom are claiming the Almighty as their special patron and protector.

Of one other kind of impression something remains to be said. Does travel in the Holy Land give a clearer comprehension of the narratives of the Old and New Testament? Does it give a livelier sense of their reality? This question must be answered separately for the two divisions of the Bible.

ISRAEL'S NEIGHBORS

On the Old Testament the traveler gets an abundance of fresh light from visiting the spots it mentions. The history of Israel from the time of Joshua — indeed, from the time of Abraham — stands out vividly. One realizes the position of the chosen people in the midst of hostile tribes — some tribes close to them: the Philistines at the western part of the Judean hills; the Tyrians almost within sight of Carmel, to the north; Amalek in the desert to the south, raiding as far as Hebron; Moab and the Beni Ammon on the plateau that lies beyond Jordan to the east, while the Syrian kingdom of Benhadad and Hazael threatens from behind the ridges of Galilee.

One sees the track along which the hosts of Egypt and Assyria marched. One feels the breath of the desert upon the prophets, for the desert comes into Palestine itself. One traverses it descending from Jerusalem to the Dead Sea. It lies in bare, brown cliffs above the gardens of Jericho. One understands what the foe of Israel meant when he said that the gods of Israel were gods of the hills, and his own gods of the valleys.

HOW NEAR WAS ENDOR!

One sees how near to the Gilboan Mountains was Endor, where Saul went to consult the witch the night before the fatal battle (I Samuel, Chapter XXVIII), and how near also the wall of Bethshan, to which the Philistines fixed his body and that of the gallant Jonathan. Samaria, the stronghold of Omri, and long afterward of Herod, frowns upon the plain beneath, and at Jezreel the slope is seen up which Jehu drove his steeds so furiously to the slaughter of Jezebel (II Kings, Chapter IX).

One can feel it all to be real. Elijah runs before the chariot of Ahab while the thunder is pealing above, and Naaman is bathing in Jordan on his way back to Damascus from the visit to Elisha. The historical books of the Old Testament are so full of references to localities that one uses them almost as a handbook. Napoleon, they say, had them read aloud to him in the evenings in his camp on the Syrian expedition of 1799.

And though the aspect of things has been greatly changed since those days by the disappearance of ancient forests, the introduction of some new trees and new kinds of buildings, not to speak of two railways and a few macadamized roads, still the natural features of hill and valley remain, and there is much in the ways and customs of the people that remains the same. The shepherd leads the same life, except that he has no longer to fear the lion, who has long since vanished, nor the bear, who survives only in the recesses of the northern hills.

NEW TESTAMENT PALESTINE

When one turns to the New Testament, how great is the difference. Except as regards Jerusalem and the Sea of Galilee, there are scarcely any references to localities in the Gospel narratives, and in those few references little or nothing turns upon the features of the place.

We can identify some of the spots where miracles are related, such as Nain and Cana of Galilee, but the events are not connected with any special feature of the locality. Journeys are mentioned, but not the route along which Christ passed, except Sychar, in the Samaritan territory, where was Jacob's well, one of the few sacred spots which can be positively identified. (The Crusaders erected a church over it which is now being restored by Franciscan monks.) The cities round the Sea of Galilee have, all except Tiberias, vanished from the earth, and the sites of most of them are doubtful.

The town now called Nazareth has been accepted for many centuries as the home of Christ's parents, but the evidence to prove it so is by no means clear, and it is hard to identify the cliff on which the city was built. The Mount of Olives, in particular, and the height on its slope, where Christ, following the path from Bethany, looked down on Jerusalem, and the temple in all its beauty, are the spots at which one seems to get into the closest touch with the Gospel narrative; and it is just here that the scene has been most changed by new buildings, high walls, villas and convents and chapels. Even the scenic conditions and whatever we may call 'the setting' of the parables belong rather to the eastern world than to Palestine. You do not feel the incidents to be the more real because they are placed in this particular part of the East.

THE ACTUAL AND THE IDEAL

All this makes the traveler realize afresh and from a new side that while the Old Testament is about and for Israel, as well as composed in the land of Israel, the Gospel, though the narrative is placed in the land and the preaching was delivered to the people of Israel, is addressed to the world.

The Old Testament books, or at least the legal and historical books, are concerned with one people, with the words and deeds of its kings and prophets and warriors, whereas the New Testament is concerned with the inner life of all mankind. The one is of the concrete, the other of the abstract; the one of the actual, the other of the ideal. The actual is rooted in time and place; the ideal is independent of both. It is only in parts of the poetical and prophetic books that the teaching becomes ideal and universal, like that of the New Testament.

It ought perhaps to be added that the incidents of Chronicles in the Old Testament belong (except, of course, when the element of marvel comes in) to what may be called normal history, and can therefore be realized just as easily as we realize the wars of the Crusaders and the deeds of Sultan Saladin.

THE GOSPEL AND PALESTINE

We picture to ourselves the battle of Saul and the Philistines at Gilboa as we picture the battle of Napoleon against the Turks, a few miles farther north. It is much harder to fit the Gospel with the framework of Jerusalem or Galilee, because its contents are unlike anything else in history. An Indian Mussulman scholar or a thoughtful Buddhist from Japan might not feel this, but it is hard for a European or American Christian not to feel it.

Whether these explanations be true or not, it is the fact that to some travelers the sight of the places that are mentioned in the Gospel seems to bring no further comprehension of its meaning, no heightened emotion, except that which the thought that they are looking upon the very hills, perhaps treading the very paths that were trodden by the feet of Christ and the Apostles, naturally arouses. The narrative remains to them in just the same ideal, non-local atmosphere which surrounded it in their childhood. It still belongs to the realm of the abstract, to the world of the soul rather than to the world of physical nature. It is robed not in the noonday glare of Palestine, as they see it to-day, nor even in the rich purple which her sunsets shed upon the far-off hills, but in a celestial light that never was on sea or land.

TYPICAL PILGRIM'S VIEWPOINT

These persons, however, mostly Protestants, are the few exceptions. The typical pilgrim, be he or she a Roman Catholic Legitimist from France or an unlettered peasant from Russia, accepts everything and is edified by everything. The Virgin and the saints have always been so real to these devout persons, the sense of their reality heightened by constant prayers before the Catholic image or the Russian icon, that it is natural for the pilgrim to think of them as dwelling in the very spots which the guide points out, and the marvelous parts of the legends present to them no difficulty.

The French Catholic has probably been on a pilgrimage to Lourdes and drawn health from the holy spring in its sacred cavern. The Russian peasant has near his home some wonder-working picture. The world to him is still full of religious miracles, and Palestine is but the land in which the figures who consecrate the spots are the most sacred of all those whom Christianity knows. To him to die in it is happiness, for death is the portal to heaven. Nowhere else does one see a faith so touching in its simplicity.

A ROMANTIC JOURNEY

To all travelers who have anything of poetry in their hearts, be they pilgrims or tourists, or critical archeologists and historians, there is, and there will always be, an inexpressible romance in this journey. Palestine is preëminently the Land of the Past — a land whose very air is charged with the human emotions and the memories of human action, reaching far back into the dim twilight of prehistoric centuries.

No one who is in any degree susceptible to the impressions of nature or of history can help feeling the glamour of the country. The colors of distant hills, seen at morn or even through this clear, keen air, seem rich and sad with pathos of ages of human effort and human passion. The imagination is always trying to body forth the men and women who lived beneath these skies, the heroes of war and the saints of suffering, the nameless poets, and the prophets who live on in their burning words, and to give them visible form and life.

Imagination always fails, but it never desists from the attempt, and though it cannot visualize the scenes, it feels the constant presence of these shadowy figures. In them, shadowy as they are, in the twilight of far-off ages, the primal forces of humanity were embodied — in them its passionate aspirations seem to have their earliest, simplest, and most moving expression.

II

IN AND NEAR ATHENS

ROBERT HICHENS

[*Century Magazine*, April, 1913. By permission.]

What Greece is like in spring, I do not know, when rains have fallen round Athens and the country is green, when the white dust perhaps does not whirl through Constitution Square and over the garden about the Zappeion, when the intensity of the sun is not fierce on the road to the bare Acropolis, and the guardians of the Parthenon, in their long coats the color of a dervish's hat, do not fall asleep in the patches of shade cast on the hot ground by Doric columns. I was there at the end of the summer, and many said to me, 'You should come in spring, when it is green.'

Greece must be very different then, but can it be much more beautiful?

Disembark at the Piræus at dawn, take a carriage, and drive by Phalerum, the bathing-place of the Athenians, to Athens at the end of the summer, and though for just six months no rain has fallen, you will enter a bath of dew. The road is dry and dusty, but there is no wind, and the dust lies still. The atmosphere is marvelously clear, as it is, say, at Ismailia in the early morning. The Hellenes, when they are talking quite naturally, if they speak of Europe, always speak of it as a continent in which Greece is not included. They talk of 'going to Europe.' They say to the English stranger, 'You come to us fresh from Europe.' And as you drive toward Athens you understand.

This country is part of the East, although the Greeks were the people who saved Europe from being dominated by the races of Asia. All about you — you have not yet reached Phalerum — you see country that looks like the beginning of a desert, that holds a fascination of the desert. The few trees stand up like carved things. The small, Eastern-looking houses, many of them with flat roofs, earth-colored, white, or tinted with mauve and pale colors, scattered casually and apparently without any plan over the absolutely bare and tawny ground, look from a distance as if they, too, were carved, as if they were actually a part of the substance of their environment, not imposed upon it by an outside force. The moving figure of a man, wearing the white fustanelle, has the strange beauty of an Arab moving alone in the vast sands. And yet there is something here that is certainly not of Europe, but that is not wholly of the East — something very delicate, very pure, very sensitive, very individual, free from the Eastern drowsiness, from the heavy Eastern perfume which disposes the soul of man to inertia.

It is the exquisite, vital, one might almost say intellectual, freshness of Greece which, between Europe and Asia, preserves its eternal dewdrops — those dewdrops which still make it the land of the early morning.

Your carriage turns to the right, and in a moment you are driving along the shore of a sea without wave or even ripple. In the distance, across the purple water, is the calm mountain of the island of Ægina. Over there, along the curve of the sandy bay, are the clustering houses of old Phalerum. This is new Phalerum, with its wooden bath-houses, its one great hotel, its kiosks and cafés, its shadeless plage, deserted now except for one old gentleman who, like almost every Greek all over the country, is at this moment reading a newspaper in the sun.

Is there any special charm in new Phalerum, bare of trees, a little cockney of aspect, any exceptional beauty in this bay? When you have bathed there a few times, when you have walked along the shore in the quiet evening, breathing the exquisite air, when you have dined in a café of old Phalerum built out into the sea, and come back by boat through the silver of a moon to the little tram station whence you return to Athens, you will probably find that there is. And from what other bay can you see the temple of the Parthenon as you see it from the bay of Phalerum?

You have your first vision of it now, as you look away from the sea, lifted very high on its great rock of the Acropolis as on a throne. Though far off, nevertheless its majesty is essentially the same, casts the same tremendous influence upon you here as it does when you stand at the very feet of its mighty columns. At once you know, not because of the legend of greatness attaching to it, or because of the historical associations clinging about it, but simply because of the feeling in your own soul roused by its white silhouette in this morning hour, that the soul of Greece — eternal majesty, supreme greatness, divine calm, and that remoteness from which, perhaps, no perfect thing, either God-made or, because of God's breath in him, man-made, is wholly exempt — is lifted high before you under the cloudless heaven of dawn.

You may even realize at once and forever, as you send on your carriage and stand for a while quite alone on the sands, gazing, that to you the soul of Greece must always seem to be Doric. From afar the Doric conquers.

The ancient Hellenes, divided, at enmity, incessantly warring among themselves, were united in one sentiment: they called all the rest of the nations 'barbarians.' The Parthenon gives them reason. 'Unintelligible folk' to this day must acknowledge it, using the word 'barbarian' strictly in our modern sense.

But the sun is higher, the morning draws on; you must be gone to Athens. Down the long, straight, new road, between rows of pepper-trees, passing a little church which marks the spot where a miscreant tried to assassinate King George, and always through beautiful, bare country like the desert, you drive. And presently you see a few houses, like the houses of a quiet village; a few great

Corinthian columns rising up in a lonely place beyond an arch tawny with old gold; a public garden looking new but pleasant — not unlike a desert garden at the edge of the Suez Canal,— with a white statue (it is the statue of Byron) before it; then a long, thick tangle of trees stretching far, and separated from the road and a line of large apartment-houses only by an old and slight wooden paling; a big square with a garden sunken below the level you are on, and on your right a huge, bare white building rather like a barracks. You are in Athens, and you have seen already the Olympieion, the Arch of Hadrian, the Zappeion garden, Constitution Square, and the garden and the palace of the king.

Coming to Athens for the first time by this route, it is difficult to believe one is in the famous capital, even though one has seen the Acropolis. And I never quite lost the feeling there that I was in a delightful village, containing a cheery, bustling life, some fine modern buildings, and many wonders of the past. Yet Athens is large and is continually growing. One of the best and most complete views of it is obtained from the terrace near the Acropolis Museum, behind the Parthenon. Other fine views can be had from Lycabettus, the solitary and fierce-looking hill against whose rocks the town seems almost to surge, like a wave striving to overwhelm it, and from that other hill, immediately facing the Acropolis, on which stands the monument of Philopappos.

It is easy to ascend to the summit of the Acropolis, even in the fierce heat of a summer day. A stroll up a curving road, the mounting of some steps, and you are there, five hundred and ten feet only above the level of the sea. But on account of the solitary situation of the plateau of rock on which the temples are grouped and of its precipitous sides, it seems very much higher than it is. Whenever I stood on the summit of the Acropolis I felt as if I were on the peak of a mountain, as if from there one must be able to see all the kingdoms of the world and the glory of them.

What one does see is marvelously, almost ineffably beautiful. Herodotus called this land, with its stony soil and its multitudes of bare mountains, the 'rugged nurse of liberty.' Though rugged, and often naked, nevertheless its loveliness — and that soft word must be used — is so great and so pure that, as we give to

Greek art the crown of wild olive, so we must give it surely also to the scenery of Greece. It is a loveliness of outline, of color, and above all of light.

Almost everywhere in Greece you see mountains, range upon range, closing about you or, more often, melting away into far distances, into outlines of shadows and dreams. Almost everywhere, or so it seemed to me, you look upon the sea. And as the outlines of the mountains of Greece are nearly always divinely calm, so the colors of the seas of Greece are magically deep and radiant and varied. And over mountains and seas fall changing wonders of light, giving to outline eternal meanings, to color the depth of a soul.

When you stand upon the Acropolis you see not only ruins which, taking everything into consideration, are perhaps the most wonderful in the world, but also one of the most beautiful views of the world. It is asserted as a fact by authorities that the ancient Greeks had little or no feeling for beauty of landscape. One famous writer on things Greek states that 'a fine view as such had little attraction for them,' that is, the Greeks. It is very difficult for those who are familiar with the sites the Greeks selected for their great temples and theaters, such as the rock of the Acropolis, the heights at Sunium and at Argos, the hill at Taormina in Sicily, etc., to feel assured of this, however lacking in allusion to the beauty of nature, unless in connection with supposed animating intelligences, Greek literature may be. It is almost impossible to believe it as you stand on the Acropolis.

All Athens lies beneath you, pale, almost white, with hints of mauve and yellow, gray and brown, with its dominating palace, its tiny Byzantine churches, its tiled and flat roofs, its solitary cypress-trees and gardens. Lycabettus stands out, small, but bold, almost defiant. Beyond, and on every side, stretches the calm plain of Attica. That winding river of dust marks the Via Sacra, along which great processions used to pass to Eleusis by the water. There are the dark groves of Academe, a place of rest in a bare land. The marble quarries gleam white on the long flanks of Mount Pentelicus, and the great range of Parnes leads on to Ægaleos. Near you are the Hill of the Nymphs, with its observatory; the rocky plateau from which the apostle Paul spoke of Christ to the doubting Athenians; the new plantation at the foot of Philopappos which surrounds the so-called 'Prison of Socrates.' Honey-famed Hymettus, gray and patient, stretches toward the sea — toward the shining Saronic Gulf and the bay of Phalerum. And there, beyond Phalerum, are the Piræus and Salamis. Mount Elias rules over the midmost isle of Ægina. Beneath the height of Sunium, where the Temple of Poseidon still lifts blanched columns above the passing mariners who have no care for the sea-god's glory, lies the islet of Gaidaronisi, and the mountains of Megara and of Argolis lie like dreaming shadows in the sunlight. Very pure, very perfect, is this great view. Nature here seems purged of all excesses, and even nature in certain places can look almost theatrical, though never in Greece. The sea shines with gold, is decked with marvelous purple, glimmers afar with silver, fades into the color of shadow. The shapes of the mountains are as serene as the shapes of Greek statues. Though bare, these mountains are not savage, are not desolate or sad. Nor is there here any suggestion of that 'oppressive beauty' against which the American painter-poet Frederic Crowninshield cries out in a recent poem — of that beauty which weighs upon, rather than releases, the heart of man.

From this view you turn to behold the Parthenon. A writer who loved Greece more than all other countries, who was steeped in Greek knowledge, and who was deeply learned in archeology, has left it on record that on his first visit to the Acropolis he was aware of a feeling of disappointment. His heart bled over the ravages wrought by man in this sacred place — that Turkish powder-magazine in the Parthenon which a shell from Venetians blew up, the stolen lions which saw Italy, the marbles carried to an English museum, the statues by Phidias which clumsy workmen destroyed.

But so incomparably noble, so majestically grand is this sublime ruin, that the first near view of it must surely fill many hearts with an awe which can leave no room for any other feeling. It is incomplete, but not the impression it creates.

The Parthenon, as it exists to-day, shattered, almost entirely roofless, deprived of its gilding and color, its glorious statues, its elaborate and wonderful friezes, its lions, its golden oil-jars, its Athene Parthenos of gold and ivory, the mere naked shell of what it once was, is stupendous. No memory of the gigantic ruins of Egypt, however familiarly known, can live in the mind, can make even the puniest fight for existence, before this Doric front of Pentelic marble, simple, even plain, but still in its devastation supreme. The size is great, but one has seen far greater ruins. The fluted columns, lifted up on the marble stylobate which has been trodden by the feet of Pericles and Phidias, are huge in girth, and rise to a height of between thirty and forty feet. The architrave above their plain capitals, with its projecting molding, is tremendously massive. The walls of the cella, or sanctuary of the temple, where they still remain, are immense. But now, where dimness reigned,— for in the days when the temple was complete no light could enter it except through the doorway,— the sunlight has full possession. And from what was once a hidden place the passing traveler can look out over land and sea.

Some learned men have called the Parthenon severe. It is wonderfully simple, so simple that it is not easy to say exactly why it produces such an overpowering impression of sublimity and grandeur. But it is not severe, for in severity there is something repellent, something that frowns. It seems to me that the impression created by the Parthenon as a building is akin to that created by the Sphinx as a statue. It suggests — seems actually to send out like an atmosphere — a tremendous calm, far beyond the limits of any severity.

The whole of the Parthenon, except the foundations, is of Pentelic marble. And this marble is so beautiful a substance now after centuries of exposure on a bare height to the fires of the sun, to the seawinds and the rains of winter, that it is impossible to wish it gilded, and painted with blue and crimson. From below in the plain, and from a long distance, the temple looks very pale in color, often indeed white. But when you stand on the Acropolis, you find that the marble holds many hues, among others pale yellow, cocoa color, honey color, and old gold. I have seen the columns at noonday, when they were bathed by the rays of the sun, glow with something of the luster of amber, and look almost transparent. I have seen them, when evening was falling, look almost black.

The temple, which is approached through the colossal marble Propylæa, or state entrance, with Doric colonnades and steps of marble and black and deep-blue Eleusinian stone, is placed on the very summit of the Acropolis, at the top of a slope, now covered with fragments of ruin, scattered blocks of stone and marble, sections of columns, slabs which once formed parts of altars, and broken bits of painted ceiling, but which was once a place of shrines and of splendid statues, among them the great statue of Athena Promachos, in armor, and holding the lance whose glittering point was visible from the sea. The columns are all fluted, and all taper gradually as they rise to the architrave. And the flutes narrow as they draw nearer and nearer to the capitals of the columns. The architrave was once hung with wreaths and decorated with shields. The famous frieze of the cella, which represented in marble a great procession, and which ran round the external wall of the sanctuary, is now in pieces, some of which are in the British Museum, and some in Athens. A portion of this frieze may still be seen on the west front of the temple. The cella had a ceiling of painted wood. On one of its inner walls I saw traces of red Byzantine figures, one apparently a figure of the Virgin. These date from the period when the Parthenon was used as a Christian church, and was dedicated to Mary the mother of God, before it became a mosque, and, later, a Turkish powder-magazine. The white marble floor, which is composed of great blocks perfectly fitted together, and without any joining substance, contrasts strongly with the warm hues of the inner flutes of the Doric columns. Here and there in the marble walls may be seen fragments of red and of yellow brick. From within the Parthenon, looking out between the columns, you can see magnificent views of country and sea.

Two other temples form part of the Acropolis, with the Propylæa and the Parthenon, the Temple of Athene Nike and the Erechtheum. They are absolutely different from the profoundly masculine Parthenon, and almost resemble two beautiful female attendants upon it, accentuating by their delicate grace its majesty.

The Temple of Nike is very small. It stands on a jutting bastion just outside the Propylæa, and has been rebuilt from the original materials, which were dug up out of masses of accumulated rubbish. It is Ionic, has a colonnade, is made of Pentelic marble, and was once adorned with a series of winged victories in bas-relief.

Ionic like the Temple of Nike, but much larger, the Erechtheum stands beyond the Propylæa, and not far from the Parthenon, at the edge of the precipice beneath which lies the greater part of Athens. A marvelously personal element attaches to it and makes it unique, giving it a charm which sets it apart from all other buildings. To find this you must go to the southwest, to the beautiful Porch of the Caryatids, which looks toward the Parthenon.

There are six of these caryatids, or maidens, standing upon a high parapet of marble and supporting a marble roof. Five of them are white, and one is a sort of yellowish black in color, as if she had once been black, but, having been singled out from her fellows, had been kissed for so many years by the rays of the sun that her original hue had become changed, brightened by his fires. Four of the maidens stand in a line. Two stand behind, on each side of the portico. They wear flowing draperies, their hair flows down over their shoulders, and they support their burden of marble with a sort of exquisite submissiveness, like maidens choosing to perform a grateful and an easy task that brings with it no loss of self-respect.

I once saw a great English actress play the part of a slave girl. By her imaginative genius she succeeded in being more than a slave: she became a poem of slavery. Everything ugly in slavery was eliminated from her performance. Only the beauty of devoted service, the willing service of love,— and slaves have been devoted to their masters,— was shown in her face, her gestures, her attitudes. Much of what she imagined and reproduced is suggested by these matchlessly tender and touching figures; so soft that it is almost incredible that they are made of marble, so strong that no burden, surely, would be too great for their simple, yet almost divine, courage. They are watchers, these maidens, not alertly, but calmly watchful of something far beyond our seeing. They are alive, but with a restrained life such as we are not worthy to know, neither fully human nor completely divine. They have something of our wistfulness and something also of that attainment toward which we strive. They are full of that strange and eternal beauty that is in all the greatest things of Greece, from which the momentary is banished, in which the perpetual is enshrined. Contemplation of them only seems to make more deep their simplicity, more patient their strength, and more touching their endurance. Retirement from them does not lessen, but almost increases, the enchantment of their very quiet, very delicate spell. Even when their faces can no longer be distinguished and only their outlines can be seen, they do not lose one ray of their soft and tender vitality. They are among the eternal things in art, lifting up more than marble, setting free from bondage, if only for a moment, many that are slaves by their submission.

About two years ago this temple was carefully cleaned, and it is very white, and looks almost like a lovely new building not yet completed. Here and there the white surface is stained with the glorious golden hue which beautifies the Parthenon, the Propylæa, the Odeum of Herodes, the Temple of Theseus, the Arch of Hadrian, and the Olympieion. The interior of the temple is full of scattered blocks of marble. In the midst of them, and as it were faithfully protected by them, I found a tiny tree carefully and solemnly growing, with an air of self-respect. Above the doorway of the north front is some very beautiful and delicate carving. This temple was once adorned with a frieze of Eleusinian stone and with white marble sculpture. Its Ionic columns are finely carved, and look almost strangely slender, if you come to them immediately after you have been among the columns of the Parthenon. Majesty and charm are supremely expressed in these two temples, the Erechtheum and the Parthenon, the smaller of which is on a lower level than the greater. One thinks again of the happy slave who loves her master.

The group of magnificent, gold-colored Greco-Roman columns which is called the Olympieion stands in splendid isolation on a bare terrace at the edge of the charming Zappeion garden. In this garden, full of firs and pepper-trees, acacias, palms, convolvulus, and pink oleanders, I saw many Greek soldiers, wearied out with preparations for the Balkan war against Turkey, which was declared while I was in Athens, sleeping on the wooden seats, or even stretched out at full-length on the light, yellow soil. For there is no grass there. Beyond the Olympieion there is a stone trough in which I never saw one drop of water. This trough is the river-bed of the famous Ilissus!

The columns are very splendid, immense in height, singularly beautiful in color,— they are made of Pentelic marble, — and with Corinthian capitals, nobly carved. Those which are grouped closely together are raised on a platform of stone. But there are two isolated columns which look even grander and more colossal than those which are united by a heavy architrave. The temple of which they are the remnant was erected in the reign of Hadrian to the glory of Zeus, and was one of the most gigantic buildings in the world.

From the Zappeion garden you can see in the distance the snow-white marble Stadium where the modern Olympic and Pan-Hellenic games take place. It is gigantic. When full, it can hold over fifty thousand people. The seats, the staircases, the pavements are all of dazzling-white marble, and as there is of course no roof, the effect of this vastness of white, under a bright-blue sky, and bathed in golden fires, is almost blinding. All round the Stadium cypress-trees have been planted, and their dark-green heads rise above the outer walls, like long lines of spearheads guarding a sacred inclosure. Two comfortable arm-chairs for the king and queen face two stelæ of marble and the far-off entrance. The earthen track where the sports take place is divided from the spectators by a marble barrier about five feet high, and till you descend into it, it looks small, though it is really very large. The entrance is a propylæum. It is a great pity that immediately outside this splendid building the hideous panorama should be allowed to remain, cheap, vulgar, dusty, and despicable. I could not help saying this to a Greek acquaintance. He thoroughly agreed with me, but told me that the Athenians were very fond of their panorama.

In a straight line with the beautiful Arch of Hadrian, and not far off, is the small and terribly defaced, but very graceful, Monument of Lysicrates, a circular chamber of marble, with small Corinthian columns, an architrave, and a frieze. It is surrounded by a railing, and stands rather forlornly in the midst of modern houses.

The Temple of Theseus, or more properly of Hercules, on the other side of the town, is a beautifully preserved building, lovely in color, very simple, very complete. It is small, and is strictly Doric and very massive. Many people have called it tremendously impressive, and have even compared it with the Parthenon. It seems to me that to do this is to exaggerate, to compare the very much less with the very much greater. There really is something severe in great massiveness combined with small proportions, and I find this temple, noble though it is, severe.

Athens contains several very handsome modern buildings, and one that I think really beautiful, especially on a day of fierce sunshine or by moonlight. This is the Academy, which stands in the broad and airy University Street, at whose mouth are the two cafés which Athenians call 'the Dardanelles.' It is in a line with the university and the national library, is made of pure white marble from Pentelicus, and is very delicately and discreetly adorned with a little bright gold, the brilliance of which seems to add to the virginal luster of the marble. The central section is flanked by two tall and slender detached columns crowned with statues. Ionic colonnades relieve the classical simplicity of the façade, with some marble and terra-cotta groups of statuary. The general effect is very calm, pure, and dignified, and very satisfying. The Athenians are proud, and with reason, of this beautiful building, which they owe to the generosity of one of their countrymen.

*   *   *   *   *   *

III

THE BLACK FOG

HERMAN SCHEFFAUER

[*Atlantic Monthly*, February, 1908. By permission of author and publisher.]

The black fog has come. Over all the city it lies intact and deep. An absolute midnight reigns. Almost material, almost tangible, almost massive, seems this envelope of sulphurous gloom. It invests the city like a flood; within the streets, within the houses, and within the lungs of all its denizens, it lies intrenched and pitiless. The chimneys pour forth their smoke, but the leaden air oppresses and repels it, and it sinks to the ground, making the darkness denser. The gloom seems to have risen from the shores of those streams of wailing and lamentation, baleful Acheron and Cocytus environing Tartarus, where the thin shades cluster and move, like those who are now pent in this city on the Thames.

The darkness is not black, but of a deep brown. It is as though one walked at the bottom of a muddy sea. The farther wall of this chamber is almost invisible — at ten o'clock in the morning. Above this dreadful pall that hides his rays, the life-giving sun, bursting with useless fire, now beats upon the surface of the sea of shadow, but his baffled light is repelled or smothered in the misty deeps. Difficult is it for him who walks in an unlifted night to believe that the sun still shines.

Let us forth into the streets so still and sorrowful. With our hands we grope our way past garden-railings, feeling with adventurous foot for the steps or curbs. A glowing patch appears above us; it seems incredibly far away. We put forth our hand and touch the dank iron of a lamp-post. Not even fire and light avail against the almighty fog. Footsteps resound about us, but they are the footsteps of ghosts, for one beholds no body. Now and then some human being brushes by — a woman, announced, perhaps, by rustling skirts or by some perfume cast from her clothes; perhaps a man, declared by the thud of a cane on the flagstones or the dull glow of a cigar.

Upon the main thoroughfares, a weird and muffled pandemonium prevails. From out the heart of the yellow-reddish murk resounds the beat of horses' hoofs; now and then a spark flies close from their iron shoes. Hoarse warning cries are heard from everywhere, and sometimes, where the fog for a moment is thinned, exaggerated shapes and monstrous figures loom up and creep along, great trucks, wains, and omnibuses with lanterns lit and the drivers leading the horses. Then again strange man-shaped spots appear, like demons come from infernal corridors; they swell out of the darkness surrounded by faint red haloes. These are pedestrians preceded by link-boys, bearing their flaming torches to guide their patrons on their way. The lofty and powerful electric arc-lights, so keenly radiant when the air is clear, now sputter dismally, invisible save at a few yards. From directly below the iron standards, the fierce white arc is dimmed to the luminosity of a red-hot ember. Before some of the railway stations wave great gasoline flambeaux, and fires in iron cressets struggle with the fog — like beacons before the sea-castle of some medieval robber-lord. The detonators, placed upon the railway tracks in place of light signals, incessantly rend the air. The curbs are cumbered with useless hackney and hansom cabs, the horses unharnessed, the drivers disconsolate. The crawling omnibuses, blundering along the indistinguishable streets, often meet or mount upon the sidewalks amidst cries and wild confusion, and there they remain, like ships becalmed at night. Those huge Behemoths and cars of Juggernaut, the gigantic, double-decked motor-omnibuses, with their two lurid yellow eyes and little sparks of red and green, stand trembling and snorting with impatience, immersed and obliterated in the fog. Universal night enthralls the world-metropolis; its currents of commerce stagnate in its veins, its mighty plans and purposes are frustrated or delayed, and this central heart of the trade of the whole earth is standing still in a dark paralysis.

Onward into the night, into the mists, into the unknown! We see not and are not seen. We pass and repass, all of us shrouded in the all-enveloping gloom, along the daily walks where life roared in the sunlight of yesterday; we pass,— lovers may almost touch each other, each unknown to each, wives may pass their husbands and mothers their sons, mortal enemies may walk side by side and feel no stir of rage, the outcast and pariah may jostle with the peer of golden millions, for all are blind, helplessly blind! Eerie is this fog-life; London lies beneath its spectral pall like a doomed state whose hope and whose daylight are wrecked by the thick shadows of war or insurrection.

Swiftly we move along beside a stone wall surmounted by an iron rail which serves as a guide. We recoil as a vast apparition looms up before us and our hands touch its cold, graven sides. It is the Marble Arch, rising like a pale transparent stain out of the dunnest blankness of the fog. One might imagine it the vision of a cyclopean tomb of some long-buried Cæsar lifted up out of the vistas of fading time.

A great policeman stands before us not a yard away, yet ghostly and insubstantial to the eye. To him there comes a little girl, terror-stricken and in tears, who, straying from her mother, has been swallowed up in the mists.

'I've lost my mother, where is my mother?' she cries.

'Where do you live, little girl?' asks the tall specter of the constable.

'I live in Fulham, sir,' she replies. 'Please, sir, which is the way to Fulham?'

The policeman points into the darkening wastes.

'You cannot find it now,' he says. 'Better wait here, then come to the station with me.'

'Where are you, little girl?' says a voice, and a bent figure with outstretched hands emerges through the walls of obscurity. 'Where are you? I'll show you the way to Fulham. Come with me.'

It is an old man; his beard is white as snow; a placard glimmers faintly on his breast. He is blind. The little maid places her hand in his; they make two steps and the next instant are effaced in the fog. Only the blind know the way through this city that is blind.

Does the sun still move on overhead and the hours with him, or are time and the earth standing still? After a long time we at last wander along the Strand, which is smitten with an unusual silence. The close current of its traffic is stayed and disorganized; its thousands of pedestrians have shrunk to hundreds groping through the choking miasma and the channels of tenebrous smoke.

How in the blindness that encompasses them do these dark-flitting shapes of men and women hurry on! They are as shadows lost and dissolved in night. They are the searchers and the symbols of the never-ending quest for light, for happiness, for peace. Something of the same feeling comes upon me as once came upon me when I walked through the empty streets of the dead Pompeii and only my footfall echoed on its sunswept stones. Here each is by and to himself complete, a little animated fire in the heart, a little light in the brain, in the veins a little warm red blood that keeps the breathing mechanism astir so long as the fire burns. Out of the darkness they came, in darkness they walk, into the darkness they shall go. The Black Fog, like Death it-self, is a great leveler. All these beings are but phantoms to the eye, phantoms of human lives, dusky moths storm-driven to and fro on the gusts of existence, each on its own quest, which is that dream of the unattainable that will not come to pass.

Now we are close to Saint Paul's Churchyard. Here the mausolean night is lifted for a space, and out of the blankness of an umber-tinted vast swells forth a vague and mystic bulk of gray, a shadow without shading or relief. It is the im-mense cupola of the cathedral rising like a mountain above the streets. The sun does battle with the flying mists about the dome and melts them to a dull and sullen gold, wherein the star of day hangs like a quivering globe of blood. It is a spec-tacle of soft yet somber sublimity, such as only the towering imaginations of a Turner, a Doré, or a John Martin, ex-pressed by brushes of opulent wealth and daring power, could conceive or execute. The drifting scud grows thinner and ever thinner in the upper air, and unfolds to him who gazes upward from the deep streets the gilded symbol of Christianity glowing softly in the golden haze, invested with a mild irradiance from the feeble light of the sun. There it lifts and gleams above the shadows like the sweet smile of the gentle Galilean whose sorrow and burthen it was and whose symbol it has remained. Below rolls the world, swart-black with its crime and misery; above, the titanic cross stretches wide its golden arms as with an imploring appeal from the Son of Man to the Love of Man. Pillars and cornices and angles of carven stone emerge faintly from the turbid chaos, like dim suggestions in a dream, or half-heard whispers out of midnight, all under the towering rood throbbing to the sky. It is high noon; a burst of bells suddenly breaks forth from the gossamer towers, a clanging chorus, loud, vibrant, and me-tallic. These violent voices are the chimes that utter every day with their iron tongues the beloved national hymn, 'God Save the King.' Now the strong glooms darken about the dome once more; the luster fades, and the great cross blurs dimly back into the crowding ocean of fog that overpowers it. Few of the thou-sands pressing along the paves have seen it, and had their eyes beheld it for a space, this apparition of the sign of human love, it would but have called forth ideas of the olden agony or a slight, subcon-scious tremble of reverence in those of re-ligious blood. We repeat again the eternal interrogations: What is Truth? and — Where may Peace be found?

Is it here, perchance, where we now stand, upon the cold stone arches of Lon-don Bridge, above the ghostly rushing Thames whose clashing waves lap and swish against the stolid stone? Whence comes or goes this river, plunging out of darkness into darkness, broad and vast with the mystery of existence, and the con-stant cry of ever-recurrent life? Down from the hills to the sea, we say, up from the sea to the cloud, then down to the hills again, and again onward to the sea. It is the known and visible obedience to some iron law. But seldom we venture to pierce beneath the surfaces of semblance, lest we alight upon truths unknown, hor-rors negative to Hope, and see the old guides through life, blind and decrepit now, fall dead at our feet, or lest, cower-ing in our creeds, we fear, like savages in the storm-swept woods, that the hand that lifts the veil will be withered by some bolt from the furious heavens. Mantled in the palls of this everlasting ig-norance, we stalk upon the highways of life like shadows drowned in shadow. Upon this ignorance the human heart builds its dreams as with inspiration, and draws hope from the very truth that this life seems so ill a recompense for all that tears and torments the baffled mind, adrift on the desert seas of mere conjecture. Yet all nature about us is content, and the sojourn in the sunshine of all other liv-ing things is full of beauty and joy. But to-day the city mourns in sackcloth and ashes.

Darkly the waters gurgle through this murky night-in-day. Perhaps Peace is there, upon their bosom or within their depths, to be borne onward in some oar-less, rudderless boat, past the muffled thun-der of the metropolis, past fields filled with the mystery of things that live and grow and die, past the river's mouth where its lips of land speak a great farewell, out into the wastes of the infinite sea. Lov-ingly its breast would open and merge

one again into the elements of its mighty
vase, to be formed anew in the unceasing
ferment of processes of creation.

Over the bridge the breathing specters
move; below, indistinct and long-drawn
shapes fare by, silent and immense, past
all the pride of the city,— bearing what
burthens? steered by what ghostly helms-
man? So the barge of dolor must cross
the lamenting currents of the infernal
river. The shadow of another boat, with
sweeps groaning in their locks, glides by
beneath. Within its ribs lie piled

What merchandise? whence, whither, and for
   whom?
Perchance it is a fate-appointed hearse,
Bearing away to some mysterious tomb
   Or Limbo of the scornful universe
The joy, the peace, the life-hope, the abor-
   tions
Of all things good which should have been
   our portions
But have been strangled by that City's
   curse.

IV

THE CITY THAT WAS

WILL IRWIN

[This is a recast of a newspaper article of the
same title published in the *Sun*, April 21, 1906,
three days after the Visitation came upon San
Francisco. It is here reprinted by permission of
the *Sun* and of Mr. B. W. Huebsch, who republished the revised article in book form. Two omitted passages are indicated by asterisks.]

The old San Francisco is dead. The
gayest, lightest hearted, most pleasure loving city of the Western Continent, and in
many ways the most interesting and romantic, is a horde of refugees living among
ruins. It may rebuild; it probably will;
but those who have known that peculiar
city by the Golden Gate, have caught its
flavor of the Arabian Nights, feel that it
can never be the same. It is as though a
pretty, frivolous woman had passed
through a great tragedy. She survives,
but she is sobered and different. If it
rises out of the ashes it must be a modern
city, much like other cities and without
its old atmosphere.

San Francisco lay on a series of hills
and the lowlands between. These hills
are really the end of the Coast Range of
mountains, which stretch southward between the interior valleys and the Pacific

Ocean. Behind it is the ocean; but the
greater part of the town fronts on two
sides on San Francisco Bay, a body of
water always tinged with gold from the
great washings of the mountain, usually
overhung with a haze, and of magnificent
color changes. Across the Bay to the
north lies Mount Tamalpais, about 3000
feet high, and so close that ferries from
the waterfront take one in less than half
an hour to the little towns of Sausalito
and Belvidere, at its foot.

Tamalpais is a wooded mountain, with
ample slopes, and from it on the north
stretch away ridges of forest land, the
outposts of the great Northern woods of
Sequoia sempervirens. This mountain
and the mountainous country to the south
bring the real forest closer to San Francisco than to any other American city.
Within the last few years men have killed
deer on the slopes of Tamalpais and
looked down to see the cable cars crawling up the hills of San Francisco to the
south. In the suburbs coyotes still stole
in and robbed hen roosts by night. The
people lived much out of doors. There is
no time of the year, except a short part
of the rainy season, when the weather
keeps one from the fields. The slopes of
Tamalpais are crowded with little villas
dotted through the woods, and these minor
estates run far up into the redwood country. The deep coves of Belvidere, sheltered by the wind from Tamalpais, held
a colony of 'arks' or houseboats, where
people lived in the rather disagreeable
summer months, coming over to business
every day by ferry. Everything there invites out of doors.

The climate of California is peculiar;
it is hard to give an impression of it. In
the region about San Francisco, all the
forces of nature work on their own laws.
There is no thunder and lightning; there
is no snow, except a flurry once in five
or six years; there are perhaps half a
dozen nights in the winter when the thermometer drops low enough so that in the
morning there is a little film of ice on exposed water. Neither is there any hot
weather. Yet most Easterners remaining
in San Francisco for a few days remember that they were always chilly.

*   *   *   *   *   *

So much for the strange climate, which
invites out of doors and which has played
its part in making the character of the

people. The externals of the city are — or were, for they are no more — just as curious. One usually entered San Francisco by way of the Bay. Across its yellow flood, covered with the fleets from the strange seas of the Pacific, San Francisco presented itself in a hill panorama. Probably no other city of the world, excepting perhaps Naples, could be so viewed at first sight. It rose above the passenger, as he reached dockage, in a succession of hill terraces. At one side was Telegraph Hill, the end of the peninsula, a height so abrupt that it had a one hundred and fifty foot sheer cliff on its seaward frontage. Further along lay Nob Hill, crowned with the Mark Hopkins mansion, which had the effect of a citadel, and in later years by the great, white Fairmount. Further along was Russian Hill, the highest point. Below was the business district, whose low site caused all the trouble.

Except for the modern buildings, the fruit of the last ten years, the town presented at first sight a disreputable appearance. Most of the buildings were low and of wood. In the middle period of the '70's, when a great part of San Francisco was building, the newly-rich perpetrated some atrocious architecture. In that time, too, every one put bow windows on his house to catch all of the morning sunlight that was coming through the fog; and those little houses, with bow windows and fancy work all down their fronts, were characteristic of the middle class residence districts.

Then the Italians, who tumbled over Telegraph Hill, had built as they listed and with little regard for streets, and their houses hung crazily on a side hill which was little less than a precipice. The Chinese, although they occupied an abandoned business district, had remade their dwellings Chinese fashion, and the Mexicans and Spaniards had added to their houses those little balconies without which life is not life to a Spaniard.

Yet the most characteristic thing after all was the coloring. The sea fog had a trick of painting every exposed object a sea gray which had a tinge of dull green in it. This, under the leaden sky of a San Francisco morning, had a depressing effect on first sight and afterward became a delight to the eye. For the color was soft, gentle and infinitely attractive in mass.

The hills are steep beyond conception. Where Vallejo Street ran up Russian Hill it progressed for four blocks by regular steps like a flight of stairs. It is unnecessary to say that no teams ever came up this street or any other like it, and grass grew long among the paving stones until the Italians who live thereabouts took advantage of this herbage to pasture a cow or two. At the end of four blocks, the pavers had given it up and the last stage to the summit was a winding path. On the very top, a colony of artists lived in little villas of houses whose windows got the whole panorama of the bay. Luckily for these people, a cable car scaled the hill on the other side, so that it was not much of a climb to home.

With these hills, with the strangeness of the architecture and with the greengray tinge over everything, the city fell always into vistas and pictures, a setting for the romance which hung over everything, which has always hung over life in San Francisco since the padres came and gathered the Indians about Mission Dolores.

And it was a city of romance and a gateway to adventure. It opened out on the mysterious Pacific, the untamed ocean; and through the Golden Gate entered China, Japan, the South Sea Islands, Lower California, the west coast of Central America, Australia. There was a sprinkling, too, of Alaska and Siberia. From his windows on Russian Hill one saw always something strange and suggestive creeping through the mists of the Bay. It would be a South Sea Island brig, bringing in copra, to take out cottons and idols; a Chinese junk after sharks' livers; an old whaler, which seemed to drip oil, home from a year of cruising in the Arctic. Even the tramp windjammers were deep-chested craft, capable of rounding the Horn or of circumnavigating the globe; and they came in streaked and picturesque from their long voyaging.

In the orange colored dawn which always comes through the mists of that Bay, the fishing fleet would crawl in under triangular lateen sails; for the fishermen of San Francisco Bay are all Neapolitans who have brought their customs and sail with lateen rigs stained an orange brown and shaped, when the wind fills them, like the ear of a horse.

Along the waterfront the people of these craft met. 'The smelting pot of the races,' Stevenson called it; and this was always the city of his soul. There were black Gilbert Islanders, almost indistinguishable from negroes; lighter Kanakas from Hawaii or Samoa; Lascars in turbans; thickset Russian sailors; wild Chinese with unbraided hair; Italian fishermen in tam o' shanters, loud shirts and blue sashes; Greeks, Alaska Indians, little bay Spanish-Americans, together with men of all the European races. These came in and out from among the queer craft, to lose themselves in the disreputable, tumble-down, but always mysterious shanties and small saloons. In the back rooms of these saloons South Sea Island traders and captains, fresh from the lands of romance, whaling masters, people who were trying to get up treasure expeditions, filibusters, Alaskan miners, used to meet and trade adventures.

There was another element, less picturesque and equally characteristic, along the waterfront. San Francisco was the back eddy of European civilization — one end of the world. The drifters came there and stopped, lingered a while to live by their wits in a country where living after a fashion has always been marvelously cheap. These people haunted the waterfront and the Barbary Coast by night, and lay by day on the grass in Portsmouth Square.

The square, the old plaza about which the city was built, Spanish fashion, had seen many things. There in the first burst of the early days the vigilance committee used to hold its hangings. There, in the time of the sand lot troubles, Dennis Kearney, who nearly pulled the town down about his ears, used to make his orations which set the unruly to rioting. In later years Chinatown lay on one side of it and the Latin quarter and the 'Barbary Coast' on the other.

On this square the drifters lay all day long and told strange yarns. Stevenson lounged there with them in his time and learned the things which he wove into The Wrecker and his South Sea stories; and now in the center of the square there stands the beautiful Stevenson monument. In later years the authorities put up a municipal building on one side of this square and prevented the loungers, for decency's sake, from lying on the grass.

Since then some of the peculiar character of the old plaza has gone.

The Barbary Coast was a loud bit of hell. No one knows who coined the name. The place was simply three blocks of solid dance halls, there for the delight of the sailors of the world. On a fine busy night every door blared loud dance music from orchestras, steam pianos and gramaphones, and the cumulative effect of the sound which reached the street was chaos and pandemonium. Almost anything might be happening behind the swinging doors. For a fine and picturesque bundle of names characteristic of the place, a police story of three or four years ago is typical. Hell broke out in the Eye Wink Dance Hall. The trouble was started by a sailor known as Kanaka Pete, who lived in the What Cheer House, over a woman known as Iodoform Kate. Kanaka Pete chased the man he had marked to the Little Silver Dollar, where he halted and punctured him. The by-product of his gun made some holes in the front of the Eye Wink, which were proudly kept as souvenirs, and were probably there until it went out in the fire. This was low life, the lowest of the low.

Until the last decade almost anything except the commonplace and the expected might happen to a man on the waterfront. The cheerful industry of shanghaing was reduced to a science. A citizen taking a drink in one of the saloons which hung out over the water might be dropped through the floor into a boat, or he might drink with a stranger and wake in the forecastle of a whaler bound for the Arctic. Such an incident is the basis of Frank Norris's novel, Moran of the Lady Letty, and although the novel draws it pretty strong, it is not exaggerated. Ten years ago the police, the Sailors' Union, and the foreign consuls, working together, stopped all this.

Kearney Street, a wilder and stranger Bowery, was the main thoroughfare of these people. An exiled Californian, mourning over the city of his heart, has said:

'In a half an hour of Kearney Street I could raise a dozen men for any wild adventure, from pulling down a statue to searching for the Cocos Island treasure.' This is hardly an exaggeration. It was the Rialto of the desperate, Street of the Adventurers.

These are a few of the elements which made the city strange and gave it the glamour of romance which has so strongly attracted such men as Stevenson, Frank Norris, and Kipling. This life of the floating population lay apart from the regular life of the city, which was distinctive in itself.

The Californian is the second generation of a picked and mixed ancestry. The merry, the adventurous, often the desperate, always the brave, deserted the South and New England in 1849 to rush around the Horn or to try the perils of the plains. They found there a land already grown old in the hands of the Spaniards — younger sons of hidalgo and many of them of the best blood of Spain. To a great extent the pioneers intermarried with Spanish women; in fact, except for a proud little colony here and there, the old, aristocratic Spanish blood is sunk in that of the conquering race. Then there was an influx of intellectual French people, largely overlooked in the histories of the early days; and this Latin leaven has had its influence.

Brought up in a bountiful country, where no one really has to work very hard to live, nurtured on adventure, scion of a free and merry stock, the real, native Californian is a distinctive type; as far from the Easterner in psychology as the extreme Southerner is from the Yankee. He is easy going, witty, hospitable, lovable, inclined to be unmoral rather than immoral in his personal habits, and easy to meet and to know.

Above all there is an art sense all through the populace which sets it off from any other population of the country. This sense is almost Latin in its strength, and the Californian owes it to the leaven of Latin blood. The true Californian lingers in the north; for southern California has been built up by 'lungers' from the East and Middle West and is Eastern in character and feeling.

Almost has the Californian developed a racial physiology. He tends to size, to smooth symmetry of limb and trunk, to an erect, free carriage; and the beauty of his women is not a myth. The pioneers were all men of good body; they had to be to live and leave descendants. The bones of the weaklings who started for El Dorado in 1849 lie on the plains or in the hill-cemeteries of the mining camps.

Heredity began it; climate has carried it on. All things that grow in California tend to become large, plump, luscious. Fruit trees, grown from cuttings of Eastern stock, produce fruit larger and finer, if coarser in flavor, than that of the parent tree. As the fruits grow, so the children grow. A normal, healthy, Californian woman plays out-of-doors from babyhood to old age. The mixed stock has given her that regularity of features which goes with a blend of bloods; the climate has perfected and rounded her figure; out-of-doors exercise from earliest youth has given her a deep bosom; the cosmetic mists have made her complexion soft and brilliant. At the University of California, where the student body is nearly all native, the gymnasium measurements show that the girls are a little more than two inches taller than their sisters of Vassar and Michigan.

The greatest beauty-show on the continent was the Saturday afternoon matinée parade in San Francisco. Women in so-called 'society' took no part in this function. It belonged to the middle class, but the 'upper classes' have no monopoly of beauty anywhere in the world. It had grown to be independent of the matinées. From two o'clock to half-past five, a solid procession of Dianas, Hebes, and Junos passed and repassed along the five blocks between Market and Powell and Sutter and Kearney — the 'line' of San Francisco slang. Along the open-front cigar stores, characteristic of the town, gilded youth of the cocktail route gathered in knots to watch them. There was something Latin in the spirit of this ceremony — it resembled church parade in Buenos Ayres. Latin, too, were the gay costumes of the women, who dressed brightly in accord with the city and the climate. This gaiety of costume was the first thing which the Eastern woman noticed — and disapproved. Give her a year, and she, too, would be caught by the infection of daring dress.

In this parade of tall, deep bosomed, gleaming women, one caught the type and longed, sometimes, for the sight of a more ethereal beauty — for the suggestion of soul within which belongs to a New England woman on whom a hard soil has bestowed a grudged beauty — for the mobility, the fire, which belongs to the Frenchwoman. The second generation of

France was in this crowd, it is true; but climate and exercise had grown above their spiritual charm a cover of brilliant flesh. It was the beauty of Greece.

With such a people, life was always gay. If the fairly Parisian gaiety did not display itself on the streets, except in the matinée parade, it was because the winds made open-air cafés disagreeable at all seasons of the year. The life careless went on indoors or in the hundreds of pretty estates — 'ranches' the Californians called them — which fringe the city.

San Francisco was famous for its restaurants and cafés. Probably they were lacking at the top; probably the very best, for people who do not care how they spend their money, was not to be had. But they gave the best fare on earth, for the price, at a dollar, seventy-five cents, a half a dollar, or even fifteen cents.

If one should tell exactly what could be had at Coppa's for fifty cents or at the Fashion for, say thirty-five, no New Yorker who has not been there would believe it. The San Francisco French dinner and the San Francisco free lunch were as the Public Library to Boston or the stockyards to Chicago. A number of causes contributed to this. The country all about produced everything that a cook needs and that in abundance — the bay was an almost untapped fishing pound, the fruit farms came up to the very edge of the town, and the surrounding country produced in abundance fine meats, game, all cereals, and all vegetables.

But the chefs who came from France in the early days and stayed because they liked this land of plenty were the head and front of it. They passed on their art to other Frenchmen or to the clever Chinese. Most of the French chefs at the biggest restaurants were born in Canton, China. Later the Italians, learning of this country where good food is appreciated, came and brought their own style. Householders always dined out one or two nights of the week, and boarding houses were scarce, for the unattached preferred the restaurants.

*   *   *   *   *   *

The city never went to bed. There was no closing law, so that the saloons kept open nights and Sundays at their own sweet will. Most of the cafés elected to remain open until two o'clock in the morning at least.

This restaurant life, however, does not express exactly the careless, pleasure-loving character of the people. In great part their pleasures were simple, inexpensive, and out of doors. No people were fonder of expeditions into the country, of picnics — which might be brought off at almost any season of the year — and of long tours in the great mountains and forests.

Hospitality was nearly a vice. As in the early mining days, if they liked the stranger the people took him in. At the first meeting the San Francisco man had him put up at the club; at the second, he invited him home to dinner. As long as the stranger stayed he was being invited to week end parties at ranches, to little dinners in this or that restaurant and to the houses of his new acquaintances, until his engagements grew beyond hope of fulfilment. Perhaps there was rather too much of this kind of thing. At the end of a fortnight a visitor with a pleasant smile and a good story left the place a wreck. This tendency ran through all grades of society — except, perhaps, the sporting people who kept the tracks and the fighting game alive. These also met the stranger — and also took him in.

Centers of man hospitality were the clubs, especially the famous Bohemian and the Family. The latter was an off-shoot of the Bohemian; and it had been growing fast and vying with the older organization for the honor of entertaining pleasing and distinguished visitors.

The Bohemian Club, whose real founder is said to have been the late Henry George, was formed in the '70's by newspaper writers and men working in the arts or interested in them. It had grown to a membership of 750. It still kept for its nucleus painters, writers, musicians, and actors, amateur and professional. They were a gay group of men, and hospitality was their avocation. Yet the thing which set this club off from all others in the world was the midsummer High Jinks.

The club owns a fine tract of redwood forest fifty miles north of San Francisco on the Russian River. There are two varieties of big trees in California: the Sequoia gigantea, and the Sequoia sempervirens. The great trees of the Mariposa grove belong to the gigantea species. The sempervirens, however, reaches the diameter of sixteen feet, and some of the greatest trees of this species are in the Bohemian Club grove. It lies in a cleft of the mountains; and up one hillside there runs a natural out of doors stage of remarkable acoustic properties.

In August the whole Bohemian Club, or such as could get away from business, went up to this grove and camped out for two weeks. On the last night they put on the Jinks proper, a great spectacle in praise of the forest with poetic words, music, and effects done by the club. In late years this has been practically a masque or an opera. It cost about $10,-000. It took the spare time of scores of men for weeks; yet these 750 business men, professional men, artists, newspaper workers, struggled for the honor of helping out on the Jinks; and the whole thing was done naturally and with reverence. It would not be possible anywhere else in this country; the thing which made it possible was the art spirit which is in the Californian. It runs in the blood.

Who's Who in America is long on the arts and on learning and comparatively weak in business and the professions. Now some one who has taken the trouble has found that more persons mentioned in *Who's Who* by the thousand of the population were born in Massachusetts, than in any other State; but that Massachusetts is crowded closely by California, with the rest nowhere. The institutions of learning in Massachusetts account for her preeminence; the art spirit does it for California. The really big men nurtured on California influence are few, perhaps; but she has sent out an amazing number of good workers in painting, in authorship, in music, and especially in acting.

'High society' in San Francisco had settled down from the rather wild spirit of the middle period; it had come to be there a good deal as it is elsewhere. There was much wealth; and the hills of the western addition were growing up with fine mansions. Outside of the city, at Burlingame, there was a fine country club centering a region of country estates which stretched out to Menlo Park. This club had a good polo team, which played every year with teams of Englishmen from southern California and even with teams from Honolulu.

The foreign quarters are worth an article in themselves. Chief of these was, of course, Chinatown, of which every one has heard who ever heard of San Francisco. A district six blocks long and two blocks wide, housed 30,000 Chinese when the quarter was full. The dwellings were old business blocks of the early days; but the Chinese had added to them, had rebuilt them, had run out their own balconies and entrances, and had given the quarter that feeling of huddled irregularity which makes all Chinese built dwellings fall naturally into pictures. Not only this; they had burrowed to a depth of a story or two under the ground, and through this ran passages in which the Chinese transacted their dark and devious affairs — as the smuggling of opium, the traffic in slave girls, and the settlement of their difficulties.

In the last five years there was less of this underground life than formerly, for the Board of Health had a cleanup some time ago; but it was still possible to go from one end of Chinatown to the other through secret underground passages. The tourist, who always included Chinatown in his itinerary, saw little of the real quarter. The guides gave him a show by actors hired for his benefit. In reality the place amounted to a great deal in a financial way. There were clothing and cigar factories of importance, and much of the Pacific rice, tea, and silk importing was in the hands of the merchants, who numbered several millionaires. Mainly, however, it was a Tenderloin for the house servants of the city — for the San Francisco Chinaman was seldom a laundryman; he was too much in demand at fancy prices as a servant.

The Chinese lived their own lives in their own way and settled their own quarrels with the revolvers of their highbinders. There were two theaters in the quarter, a number of rich joss houses, three newspapers, and a Chinese telephone exchange. There is a race feeling against the Chinese among the working people of San Francisco, and no white man, except the very lowest outcasts, lived in the quarter.

On the slopes of Telegraph Hill dwelt the Mexicans and Spanish, in low houses, which they had transformed by balconies into a semblance of Spain. Above, and streaming over the hill, were the Italians. The tenement quarter of San Francisco shone by contrast with those of Chicago and New York, for while these people lived in old and humble houses they had room to breathe and an eminence for light and air. Their shanties clung to the side of the hill or hung on the very edge of the precipice overlooking the Bay, on the verge of which a wall kept their babies from falling. The effect was picturesque, and this hill was the delight of painters. It was all more like Italy than anything in the Italian quarter of New York and Chicago — the very climate and surroundings, the wine country close at hand, the Bay for their lateen boats, helped them.

Over by the ocean and surrounded by cemeteries in which there are no more burials, there is an eminence which is topped by two peaks and which the Spanish of the early days named after the breasts of a woman. The unpoetic Americans had renamed it Twin Peaks. At its foot was Mission Dolores, the last mission planted by the Spanish padres in their march up the coast, and from these hills the Spanish looked for the first time upon the golden bay.

Many years ago some one set up at the summit of this peak a sixty foot cross of timber. Once a high wind blew it down, and the women of the Fair family then had it restored so firmly that it would resist anything. It has risen for fifty years above the gay, careless, luxuriant, and lovable city, in full view from every eminence and from every valley. It stands to-night, above the desolation of ruins.

The bonny, merry city — the good, gray city — O that one who has mingled the wine of her bounding life with the wine of his youth should live to write the obituary of Old San Francisco!

V

THE STREET

SIMEON STRUNSKY

[*Atlantic Monthly*, February, 1914. Republished in *Belshazzar Court* (Henry Holt and Co.), 1914. Reprinted by permission of the author and publishers.]

It is two short blocks from my office near Park Row to the Subway station where I take the express for Belshazzar Court. Eight months in the year it is my endeavor to traverse this distance as quickly as I can. This is done by cut-

ting diagonally across the street traffic. By virtue of the law governing right-angled triangles I thus save as much as fifty feet and one-fifth of a minute of time. In the course of a year this saving amounts to sixty minutes, which may be profitably spent over a two-reel presentation of *The Moonshiner's Bride,* supplemented by an intimate picture of *Lumbering in Saskatchewan.* But with the coming of warm weather my habits change. It grows more difficult to plunge into the murk of the Subway.

A foretaste of the languor of June is in the air. The turnstile storm-doors in our office building, which have been put aside for brief periods during the first deceptive approaches of spring, only to come back triumphant from Elba, have been definitely removed. The steel-workers pace their girders twenty floors high almost in mid-season form, and their pneumatic hammers scold and chatter through the sultry hours. The soda-fountains are bright with new compounds whose names ingeniously reflect the world's progress from day to day in politics, science, and the arts. From my window I can see the long black steamships pushing down to the sea, and they raise vague speculations in my mind about the cost of living in the vicinity of Sorrento and Fontainebleau. On such a day I am reminded of my physician's orders, issued last December, to walk a mile every afternoon on leaving my office. So I stroll up Broadway with the intention of taking my train farther up-town, at Fourteenth Street.

The doctor did not say stroll. He said a brisk walk with head erect, chest thrown out, diaphragm well contracted, and a general aspect of money in the bank. But here enters human perversity. The only place where I am in the mood to walk after the prescribed military fashion is in the open country. Just where by all accounts I ought to be sauntering without heed to time, studying the lovely texts which Nature has set down in the modest type-forms selected from her inexhaustible fonts, — in the minion of ripening berries, in the nonpareil of crawling insect life, the agate of tendril and filament, and the 12-point diamond of the dust, — there I stride along and see little.

And in the city, where I should swing along briskly, I lounge. What is there on Broadway to linger over? On Broadway, Nature has used her biggest, fattest type-forms. Tall, flat, building fronts, brazen with many windows and ribbed with commercial gilt lettering six feet high; shrieking proclamations of auction sales written in letters of fire on vast canvasses; railway posters in scarlet and blue and green; rotatory barber-poles striving at the national colors and producing vertigo; banners, escutcheons, crests, in all the primary colors — surely none of these things needs poring over. And I know them with my eyes closed. I know the windows where lithe youths in gymnasium dress demonstrate the virtue of home exercises; the windows where other young men do nothing but put on and take off patent reversible near-linen collars; where young women deftly roll cigarettes; where other young women whittle at sticks with miraculously stropped razors. I know these things by heart, yet I linger over them in flagrantly unhygienic attitudes, my shoulders bent forward and my chest and diaphragm in a position precisely the reverse of that prescribed by the doctor.

Perhaps the thing that makes me linger before these familiar sights is the odd circumstance that in Broadway's shop-windows Nature is almost never herself, but is either supernatural or artificial. Nature, for instance, never intended that razors should cut wood and remain sharp; that linen collars should keep on getting cleaner the longer they are worn; that glass should not break; that ink should not stain; that gauze should not tear; that an object worth five dollars should sell for $1.39; but all these things happen in Broadway windows. Williams, whom I meet now and then, who sometimes turns and walks up with me to Fourteenth Street, pointed out to me the other day how strange a thing it was that the one street which has become a synonym for 'real life' to all good suburban Americans is not real at all, but is crowded either with miracles or with imitations.

The windows on Broadway glow with wax fruits and with flowers of muslin and taffeta drawn by bounteous Nature from her storehouses in Parisian garret workshops. Broadway's ostrich feathers have been plucked in East Side tenements. The huge cigars in the tobacconist's windows are of wood. The enormous bottles of champagne in the saloons are of cardboard, and empty. The tall scaffoldings of proprietary medicine bottles in the drug shops are of paper. 'Why,' said Williams, 'even the jewelry sold in the Japanese auction stores is not genuine, and the sellers are not Japanese.'

This bustling mart of commerce, as the generation after the Civil War used to say, is only a world of illusion. Artificial flowers, artificial fruits, artificial limbs, tobacco, rubber, silks, woolens, straws, gold, silver. The young men and women who manipulate razors and elastic cords are real, but not always. Williams and I once stood for a long while and gazed at a young woman posing in a drug-shop window, and argued whether she was alive. Ultimately she winked and Williams gloated over me. But how do I know her wink was real? At any rate the great mass of human life in the windows is artificial. The ladies who smile out of charming morning costumes are obviously of lining and plaster. Their smug herculean husbands in pajamas preserve their equanimity in the severest winter weather only because of their wire-and-plaster constitution. The baby reposing in its beribboned crib is china and excelsior. Illusion everywhere.

But the Broadway crowd is real. You only have to buffet it for five minutes to feel, in eyes and arms and shoulders, how real it is. When I was a boy and was taken to the circus it was always an amazing thing to me that there should be so many people in the street moving in a direction away from the circus. Something of this sensation still besets me whenever we go down in the Subway from Belshazzar Court to hear Caruso. The presence of all the other people on our train is simple enough. They are all on their way to hear Caruso. But what of the crowds in the trains that flash by in the opposite direction? It is not a question of feeling sorry for them. I try to understand and I fail. But on Broadway on a late summer afternoon the obverse is true. The natural thing is that the living tide as it presses south shall beat me back, halt me, eddy around me. I know that there are people moving north with me, but I am not acutely aware of them. This onrush of faces converges on me alone. It is I against half the world.

And then suddenly out of the surge of faces one leaps out at me. It is Williams, whose doctor has told him that the surest way of fighting down the lust for tobacco is to walk down from his office to the ferry every afternoon. Williams and I salute each other after the fashion of Broadway, which is to exchange greetings backward over the shoulder. This is the first step in an elaborate minuet. Because we have passed each other before recognition came, our hands fly out backward. Now we whirl half around, so that I who have been moving north face the west, while Williams, who has been traveling south, now looks east. Our clasped hands strain at each other as we stand there poised for flight after the first greeting. A quarter of a minute perhaps, and we have said good-by.

But if the critical quarter of a minute passes, there ensues a change of geographical position which corresponds to a change of soul within us. I suddenly say to myself that there are plenty of trains to be had at Fourteenth Street. Williams recalls that another boat will leave Battery Place shortly after the one he is bound for. So the tension of our outstretched arms relaxes. I, who have been facing west, complete the half circle and swing south. Williams veers due north, and we two men stand face to face. The beat and clamor of the crowd fall away from us like a well-trained stage mob. We are in Broadway, but not of it.

'Well, what's the good word?' says Williams.

When two men meet on Broadway the spirit of optimism strikes fire. We begin by asking each other what the good word is. We take it for granted that neither of us has anything but a chronicle of victory and courage to relate. What other word but the good word is tolerable in the lexicon of living, upstanding men? Failure is only for the dead. Surrender is for the man with yellow in his nature. So Williams and I pay our acknowledgments to this best of possible worlds. I give Williams the good word. I make no allusion to the fact that I have spent a miserable night in communion with neuralgia; how can that possibly concern him? Another manuscript came back this morning from an editor who regretted that his is the most unintelligent body of readers in the country. The third cook in three weeks left us last night after making vigorous reflections on my wife's good nature and my own appearance. Only an hour ago, as I was watching the long, black steamers bound for Sorrento and Fontainebleau, the monotony of one's treadmill work, the flat unprofitableness of scribbling endlessly on sheets of paper, had become almost a nausea. But Williams will know nothing of this from me. Why should he? He may have been sitting up all night with a sick child. At this very moment the thought of the little parched lips, the moan, the unseeing eyes, may be tearing at his entrails; but he in turn gives me the good word, and many others after that, and we pass on.

But sometimes I doubt. This splendid optimism of people on Broadway, in the Subway, and in the shops and offices — is it really a sign of high spiritual courage, or is it just lack of sensibility? Do we find it easy to keep a stiff upper lip, to buck up, to never say die, because we are brave men, or simply because we lack the sensitiveness and the imagination to react to pain? It may be even worse than that. It may be part of our commercial gift for window-dressing, for putting up a good front.

Sometimes I feel that Williams has no right to be walking down Broadway on business when there is a stricken child at home. The world cannot possibly need him at that moment as much as his own flesh and blood does. It is not courage; it is brutish indifference. At such times I am tempted to dismiss as mythical all this fine talk about feelings that run deep beneath the surface, and bruised hearts that ache under the smile. If a man really suffers he will show it. If a man cultivates the habit of not showing emotion he will end by having none to show. How much of Broadway's optimism is — But here I am paraphrasing William James's *Principles of Psychology,* which the reader can just as well consult for himself in the latest revised edition of 1907.

Also, I am exaggerating. Most likely Williams's children are all in perfect health, and my envelope from the editor has brought a check instead of a rejection slip. It is on such occasions that Williams and I, after shaking hands the way a locomotive takes on water on the run, wheel around, halt, and proceed to buy something at the rate of two for a quarter. If any one is ever inclined to doubt the spirit of American fraternity, it is only necessary to recall the number of commodities for men that sell two for twenty-five cents. In theory, the two cigars which Williams and I buy for twenty-five cents are worth fifteen cents apiece. As a matter of fact they are probably ten-cent cigars. But the shopkeeper is welcome to his extra nickel. It is a small price to pay for the seal of comradeship that stamps his pair of cigars selling for a single quarter. Two men who have concluded a business deal in which each has commendably tried to get the better of the other may call for twenty-five cent perfectos or for half-dollar Dreadnoughts. I understand there are such. But friends sitting down together will always demand cigars that go for a round sum, two for a quarter or three for fifty (if the editor's check is what it ought to be).

When people speak of the want of real comradeship among women, I sometimes wonder if one of the reasons may not be that the prices which women are accustomed to pay are individualistic instead of fraternal. The soda fountains and the street cars do not dispense goods at the rate of two items for a single coin. It is infinitely worse in the department stores. Treating a friend to something that costs $2.79 is inconceivable. But I have really wandered from my point.

'Well, be good,' says Williams, and rushes off to catch his boat.

The point I wish to make is that on Broadway people pay tribute to the principle of goodness that rules this world, both in the way they greet and in the way they part. We salute by asking each other what the good word is. When we say good-by we enjoin each other to be good. The humorous assumption is that gay devils like Williams and me need to be constantly warned against straying off into the primrose paths that run out of Broadway.

Simple, humorous, average American man! You have left your suburban couch in time to walk half a mile to the station and catch the 7.59 for the city. You have read your morning paper; discussed the weather, the tariff, and the prospects for lettuce with your neighbor; and made the office only a minute late. You have been fastened to your desk from nine o'clock to five, with half an hour for lunch, which you have eaten in a clamorous, overheated restaurant while you watched your hat and

coat. At odd moments during the day the thought of doctor's bills, rent bills, school bills, has insisted on receiving attention. At the end of the day, laden with parcels from the market, from the hardware store, from the seedman, you are bound for the ferry to catch the 5.43, when you meet Smith, who, having passed the good word, sends you on your way with the injunction to be good — not to play roulette, not to open wine, not to turkey-trot, not to joy-ride, not to haunt the stage door. Be good, O simple, humorous, average suburban American!

I take back that word suburban. The Sunday Supplement has given it a meaning which is not mine. I am speaking only of the suburban in spirit, of a simplicity, a meekness which is of the soul only. Outwardly there is nothing suburban about the crowd on lower Broadway. The man in the street is not at all the diminutive, apologetic creature with side whiskers whom Mr. F. B. Opper brought forth and named Common People, who begat the Strap-Hanger, who begat the Rent-Payer, and the Ultimate Consumer. The crowd on lower Broadway is alert and well set up. Yes, though one hates to do it, I must say 'clean-cut.' The men on the sidewalk are young, limber, sharp-faced, almost insolent young men. There are not very many old men in the crowd, though I see any number of gray-haired young men. Seldom do you detect the traditional signs of age, the sagging lines of the face, the relaxed abdominal contour, the tamed spirit. The young, the young-old, the old-young, but rarely quite the old.

I am speaking only of externals. Clean-cut, eager faces are very frequently disappointing. A very ordinary mind may be working behind that clear sweep of brow and nose and chin. I have known the shock of young men who look like kings of Wall Street and speak like shoe clerks. They are shoe clerks. But the appearance is there, that athletic carriage which is helped out by our triumphant, ready-made clothing. I suppose I ought to detest the tailor's tricks which iron out all ages and all stations into a uniformity of padded shoulders and trim waistlines and hips. I imagine I ought to despise our habit of wearing elegant shoddy where the European chooses honest, clumsy woolens. But I am concerned only with externals, and in outward appearances a Broadway crowd beats the world. Æsthetically we simply are in a class by ourselves when compared with the Englishman and the Teuton in their skimpy, ill-cut garments. Let the British and German ambassadors at Washington do their worst. This is my firm belief and I will maintain it against the world. The truth must out. *Ruat cœlum. Ich kann nicht anders. J'y suis, j'y reste.*

Williams laughs at my lyrical outbursts. But I am not yet through. I still have to speak of the women in the crowd. What an infinitely finer thing is a woman than a man of her class! To see this for yourself you have only to walk up Broadway until the southward-bearing stream breaks off and the tide begins to run from west to east. You have passed out of the commercial district into the region of factories. It is well on toward dark, and the barracks that go by the unlovely name of loft buildings, are pouring out their battalions of needle-workers. The crowd has become a mass. The nervous pace of lower Broadway slackens to the steady, patient tramp of a host. It is an army of women, with here and there a flying detachment of the male.

On the faces of the men the day's toil has written its record even as on the women, but in a much coarser hand. Fatigue has beaten down the soul of these men into brutish indifference, but in the women it has drawn fine the flesh only to make it more eloquent of the soul. Instead of listlessness, there is wistfulness. Instead of vacuity you read mystery. Innate grace rises above the vulgarity of the dress. Cheap, tawdry blouse and imitation willow-plume walk shoulder to shoulder with the shoddy coat of the male, copying Fifth Avenue as fifty cents may attain to five dollars. But the men's shoddy is merely a horror, whereas woman transfigures and subtilizes the cheap material. The spirit of grace which is the birthright of her sex cannot be killed — not even by the presence of her best young man in Sunday clothes. She is finer by the heritage of her sex, and America has accentuated her title. This America which drains her youthful vigor with overwork, which takes from her cheeks the color she has brought from her Slavic or Italian peasant home, makes restitution by remolding her in more delicate, more alluring lines, gives her the high privilege of charm — and neurosis.

Williams and I pause at the Subway entrances and watch the earth suck in the crowd. It lets itself be swallowed up with meek good-nature. Our amazing good-nature! Political philosophers have deplored the fact. They have urged us to be quicker-tempered, more resentful of being stepped upon, more inclined to write letters to the editor. I agree that only in that way can we be rid of political bosses, of brutal policemen, of ticket-speculators, of taxicab extortioners, of insolent waiters, of janitors, of indecent congestion in travel, of unheated cars in the winter and barred-up windows in summer. I am at heart with the social philosophers. But then I am not typical of the crowd. When my neighbor's elbow injects itself into the small of my back, I twist around and glower at him. I forget that his elbow is the innocent mechanical result of a whole series of elbows and backs extending the length of the car, to where the first cause operates in the form of a station-guard's shoulder ramming the human cattle into their stalls. In the faces about me there is no resentment. Instead of smashing windows, instead of raising barricades in the Subway and hanging the train-guards with their own lanterns about their necks, the crowd sways and bends to the lurching of the train, and young voices call out cheerfully, ' Plenty of room ahead.'

Horribly good-natured! We have taken a phrase which is the badge of our shame and turned it into a jest. Plenty of room ahead! If this were a squat, ill-formed proletarian race obviously predestined to subjection, one might understand. But that a crowd of trim, well-cut, self-reliant Americans, sharp-featured, alert, insolent as I have called them, that they should submit is a puzzle. Perhaps it is because of the fierce democracy of it all. The crush, the enforced intimacies of physical contact, the feeling that a man's natural condition is to push and be pushed, to shove ahead when the opportunity offers and to take it like a man when no chance presents itself — that is equality. A seat in the Subway is like the prizes of life for which men have fought in these United States. You struggle, you win or lose. If the other man wins there is no envy; admiration rather, provided he has not shouldered and elbowed out of reason. That godlike freedom from envy is passing today, and perhaps the good nature of the crowd in the Subway will pass. I see signs of the approaching change. People do not call out, ' Plenty of room ahead,' so frequently as they used to.

Good-natured when dangling from the strap in the Subway, good-natured in front of baseball bulletins on Park Row, good-natured in the face of so much oppression and injustice, where is the supposed cruelty of the ' mob '? I am ready to affirm on oath that the mob is not vindictive, that it is not cruel. It may be a bit sharp-tongued, fickle, a bit mischievous, but in the heart of the crowd there is no evil passion. The evil comes from the leaders, the demagogues, the professional distorters of right thinking and right feeling. The crowd in the bleachers is not the clamorous, brute mob of tradition. I have watched faces in the bleachers and in the grand-stand and seen little of that fury which is supposed to animate the fan. For the most part he sits there with folded arms, thin-lipped, eager, but after all conscious that there are other things in life besides baseball. No, it is the leaders, the baseball editors, the cartoonists, the humorists, the professional stimulators of ' local pride,' with their exaggerated gloatings over a game won, their poisonous attacks upon a losing team, who are responsible. It is these demagogues who drill the crowd in the gospel of loving only a winner — but if I keep on I shall be in politics before I know it.

If you see in the homeward crowd in the Subway a face over which the pall of depression has settled, that face very likely is bent over the comic pictures in the evening paper. I cannot recall seeing any one smile over these long serials of humorous adventure which run from day to day and from year to year. I have seen readers turn mechanically to these lurid comics and pore over them, foreheads puckered into a frown, lips unconsciously spelling out the long legends which issue in the form of little balloons and lozenges from that amazing portrait gallery of dwarfs, giants, shrilling viragos and their diminutive husbands, devil-children, quadrupeds, insects,— an entire zoölogy. If any stimulus rises from these pages to the puzzled brain, the effect is not visible. I imagine that by dint of repetition through the years

these grotesque creations have become a reality to millions of readers. It is no longer a question of humor, it is a vice. The Desperate Desmonds, the Newlyweds, and the Dingbats, have acquired a horrible fascination. Otherwise I cannot see why readers of the funny page should appear to be memorizing pages from Euclid.

This by way of anticipation. What the doctor has said of exercise being a habit which grows easy with time is true. It is the first five minutes of walking that are wearisome. I find myself strolling past Fourteenth Street, where I was to take my train for Belshazzar Court. Never mind, Forty-second Street will do as well. I am now on a different Broadway. The crowd is no longer north and south, but flows in every direction. It is churned up at every corner and spreads itself across the squares and open places. Its appearance has changed. It is no longer a factory population. Women still predominate, but they are the women of the professions and trades which center about Madison Square — business women of independent standing, women from the magazine offices, the publishing houses, the insurance offices. You detect the bachelor girl in the current which sets in toward the home quarters of the undomesticated, the little Bohemias, the foreign eating-places whose fixed *table d'hôte* prices flash out in illumined signs from the side streets. Still farther north and the crowd becomes tinged with the current of that Broadway which the outside world knows best. The idlers begin to mingle with the workers, men in English clothes with canes, women with plumes and jeweled reticules. You catch the first heart-beat of Little Old New York.

The first stirrings of this gayer Broadway die down as quickly almost as they manifested themselves. The idlers and those who minister to them have heard the call of the dinner hour and have vanished, into hotel doors, into shabbier quarters by no means in keeping with the cut of their garments and their apparent indifference to useful employment. Soon the street is almost empty. It is not a beautiful Broadway in this garish interval between the last of the matinée and shopping crowd and the vanguard of the night crowd. The monster electric sign-boards have not begun to gleam and flash and revolve and confound the eye and the senses. At night the electric Niagara hides the squalid fronts of ugly brick, the dark doorways, the clutter of fire-escapes, the rickety wooden hoardings. Not an imperial street this Broadway at 6.30 of a summer's afternoon. Cheap jewelry shops, cheap tobacconist's shops, cheap haberdasheries, cheap restaurants, grimy little newspaper agencies and ticket-offices, and 'demonstration' stores for patent foods, patent waters, patent razors.

O Gay White Way, you are far from gay in the fast-fading light, before the magic hand of Edison wipes the wrinkles from your face and galvanizes you into hectic vitality; far from alluring with your tinsel shop-windows, with your puffy-faced, unshaven men leaning against door-posts and chewing pessimistic toothpicks, your sharp-eyed newsboys wise with the wisdom of the Tenderloin, and your itinerant women whose eyes wander from side to side. It is not in this guise that you draw the hearts of millions to yourself, O dingy, Gay White Way, O Via Lobsteria Dolorosa!

Well, when a man begins to moralize it is time to go home. I have walked farther than I intended, and I am soft from lack of exercise, and tired. The romance of the crowd has disappeared. Romance cannot survive that short passage of Long-acre Square, where the art of the theater and of the picture-postcard flourish in an atmosphere impregnated with gasoline. As I glance into the windows of the automobile salesrooms and catch my own reflection in the enamel of Babylonian limousines I find myself thinking all at once of the children at home. They expand and fill up the horizon. Broadway disappears. I smile into the face of a painted promenader, but how is she to know that it is not at her I smile but at the sudden recollection of what the baby said at the breakfast-table that morning? Like all good New Yorkers when they enter the Subway, I proceed to choke up all my senses against contact with the external world, and thus resolving myself into a state of coma, I dip down into the bowels of the earth, whence in due time I am spewed out two short blocks from Belshazzar Court.

VI

CONEY ISLAND AT NIGHT

JAMES HUNEKER

[New York Herald, August 19, 1906. Republished in New Cosmopolis (Chas. Scribner's Sons) 1915. Reprinted by permission of the author and publishers.]

It was the hottest night of the summer at Coney Island. All day a steaming curtain of mist hid the sun from the eyes of men and women and children; yet proved no shield against the blasting heat. Humidity and not the sun-rays had been the enemy. And when a claret-colored disk showed dully through the nacreous vapors just before setting, we knew that the night would bring little respite from the horror of the waking hours. It was a time to try men's nerves. The average obligations of life had faded into the abyss of general indifference, one that had absorbed the exactions of daily behavior — politeness, order, sobriety, and decency. Add a few notches upward on the thermometer, and mankind soon reverts to the habits and conditions of his primitive ancestors. The ape, the tiger, and the jackal in all of us come to the surface with shocking rapidity. We are, in a reasonable analysis, the victims of our environment, the slaves of temperature. Heat and cold could have produced the African and the Laplander. At Coney Island during a torrid spell we are very near the soil; we cast to the winds modesty, prudence, and dignity. Then, life is worth living only when stripped to the skin.

Three seasons had I passed without a visit to this astonishing bedlam, yet I found the place well-nigh unrecognizable. Knowing old Coney Island, the magnitude of its changes did not so much amaze and terrify me. One should never be amazed in America. After an hour's hasty survey, Atlantic City seemed a normal spot. Broad stretches of board walk, long, sweeping beaches, space to turn about — these and other items might be added. But at Coney Island the cramped positions one must assume to stand or move, the fierce warfare of humanity as it forces its way along the streets or into the crazy shows — surely conceived by madmen for madmen — the indescribable and hideous symphony of noise running the gamut from shrill steam-whistles to the diapasonic roar of machinery; decidedly the entire place produced the sensation of abnormality, of horrible joys grabbed at by a savage horde of barbarians, incapable of repose even in their moments of leisure. Some one has said that the Englishman takes his pleasures sadly; then we must take ours by rude assault. All Coney Island reminded me of a disturbed antheap, the human ants ferocious in their efforts to make confusion thrice confounded, to heap up horrors of sound and of sight.

There must be in every one, no matter how phlegmatic, a residuum of energy which may boil over when some exciting event knocks at the door of our being. It is, psychologists assure us, the play-instinct of the animal in us that delights in games innocent and dangerous. If forty thousand people assemble to see a game of baseball, how many more would gather with feverish gaiety if there were a surety of the umpire's death at every game? The Romans daily witnessed men and women destroyed in the arena of their circus — witnessed it with a satisfaction æsthetic and profound. The reason was not that they were less civilized than the moderns, but only more frank. Their play-instinct was more fully developed and the classical world was not hampered by our moral prejudices.

As cruelty is proscribed among highly civilized nations to-day — the game of life being so vilely cruel that the arena with its bulls and tigers is unnecessary — our play-instinct finds vent in a species of diversion that must not be examined too closely, as it verges perilously on idiocy. Coney Island is only another name for topsyturvydom. There the true becomes the grotesque, the vision of a maniac. Else why those nerve-racking entertainments, ends of the world, creations, hells, heavens, fantastic trips to ugly lands, panoramas of sheer madness, flights through the air in boats, through water in sleds, on the earth in toy trains! Unreality is as greedily craved by the mob as alcohol by the dipsomaniac; indeed, the jumbled nightmares of a morphine eater are actually realized at Luna Park. Every angle reveals some new horror. Mechanical waterfalls, with women and children racing around curving, tumbling floods; elephants tramping ponderously

through streets that are a bewildering muddle of many nations, many architectures; deeds of Western violence and robbery, illustrated with a realism that is positively enthralling; Japanese and Irish, Germans and Indians, Hindus and Italians, cats and girls and ponies and — the list sets whirring the wheels of the biggest of dictionaries.

In Dreamland there is a white tower that might rear itself in Seville and cause no comment.[1] Hemming it about are walls of monstrosities — laughable, shocking, sinister, and desperately depressing. In the center flying boats cleave the air; from the top of a crimson lighthouse flat, sled-like barges plunge down a liquid railroad, while from every cavern issue screams of tortured and delighted humans and the hoarse barking of men with megaphones. They assault your ears with their invitations, protestations, and blasphemies. You are conjured to 'go to Hell-gate'; you are singled out by some brawny individual with threatening intonations and bade enter the animal show where a lion or a tiger is warranted to claw a keeper at least once a day. The glare is appalling, the sky a metallic blue, the sun a slayer.

And then the innumerable distractions of the animated walks, the dwarfs and the dogs, the horses and the miniature railway. Inside the various buildings you may see the cosmos in the act of formation, or San Francisco destroyed by fire and quake; the end of life, organic and inorganic, is displayed for a modest pittance; you may sleigh in Switzerland or take a lulling ride in Venetian gondolas. But nothing is real. Doubtless the crowd would be disappointed by a glimpse of the real Venice, the real Switzerland, the real hell, the real heaven. Everything is the reflection of a cracked mirror held in the hand of the clever showman, who, knowing us as children of a larger growth, compounds his mess, bizarre and ridiculous, accordingly. There is little need to ponder the whys and wherefores of our aberrancy. Once en masse, humanity sheds its civilization and becomes half child, half savage. In the theaters the gentlest are swayed by a sort of mob mania and delight in scenes of cruelty and bloodshed — though at home the sight of a canary with a broken wing sets stirring in us tender sympathy. A crowd seldom reasons. It

[1] This was so before fire destroyed the place.

will lynch an innocent man or glorify a scamp politician with equal facility. Hence the monstrous debauch of the fancy at Coney Island, where New York chases its chimera of pleasure.

Nevertheless, with all its perversion, its oblique image of life, is Coney Island much madder than the Stock Exchange, the prize-ring, roller-skating, a fashionable cotillion, a political mass-meeting, or some theatrical performances? Again I must bid you to remember that everything is relative; that the morals of one age are the crimes of another; that I am, comparatively speaking, a stranger to our summer cities and perhaps not peculiarly well fitted to judge of such an astounding institution as Coney Island.

The madness converges below Brighton, reaching its apex on Surf Avenue, jammed with pleasure-seekers, fringed by 'fakers' and their utterly abominable wares. Farther up the beach order reigns, men and women are clothed in their right mind, walk, talk, and act rationally. At the Oriental dignity prevails. Few people are to be seen. The place slumbers. You feel that in such a hotel you may live as you wish. Manhattan, no longer queen of the beaches, has its interest. The bathing attracts. The wide porches and the dining couples are pleasing to see. A theater there is for those to whom the ocean is not a stimulating spectacle. Walk farther. We reach Brighton. There the pot begins to bubble. A smaller Coney confronts you. You pass on. Stopping before what was once Anton Seidl's music pavilion, you indulge, more sadly than sentimentally, in memories of those evenings, over two decades ago, when the sound of the waves formed a background for the dead master's music-making — Beethoven and Wagner and Liszt.

Instead of Brünhilde and her sisters' wild ride, we hear the wooden horse orchestrion screeching 'Meet Me at the Church.' Move on? Has public musical taste moved with the years? Meet me at the madhouse! We reach the Boulevard and note its agreeable vastness. The sun has set and the world is become suddenly afire.

Then Coney Island, with its vulgarity, its babble and tumult, is a glorified city of flame. But don't go too near it; your wings will easily singe on the broad avenue where beer, sausage, fruit, pop-corn, candy, flapjacks, green corn, and again beer, rule the appetites of the multitude. After seeing the aerial magic of that great pyrotechnic artist Pain, a man who could, if he so desired, create a new species of art, and his nocturnes of jeweled fire, you wonder why the entire beach is not called Fire Island. The view of Luna Park from Sheepshead Bay suggests a cemetery of fire, the tombs, turrets, and towers, illuminated, and mortuary shafts of flame. At Dreamland the little lighthouse is a scarlet incandescence. The big building stands a dazzling apparition for men on ships and steamers out at sea. Everything is fretted with fire. Fire delicately etches some fairy structure; fire outlines an Oriental gateway; fire runs like a musical scale through many octaves, the darkness crowding it, the mist blurring it. Fire is the god of Coney Island after sundown, and fire was its god this night, the hottest of the summer.

At ten o'clock the crowds had not abated. Noise still reigned over the Bowery, and the cafés, restaurants, dens, and shows were full of gabbling, eating, drinking, cursing, and laughing folk. I had intended to return either to my hotel or to New York, but the heat pinioned my will. In company with thousands, I strolled the beach near the Boulevard. An amiable policeman told me that few people would go back to the city, that, hot as it was at Coney, the East Side was more stifling. The sight of cars coming down crowded at eleven o'clock and returning half-full at midnight determined my plan of action. I went to my hotel, put on a sweater and a cap, changed a bill into silver, and with a stick for company I returned to the West End. There were more people than before, though it was nearly one o'clock and the lights were beginning to dim. I searched for the friendly policeman, but instead found a surly one, who warned me that it would be a risk to venture upon the beach if I had a watch or money. I longed for a Josiah Flynt who would pilot me through this jungle of humanity. The heat was depressing and mosquitoes made us miserable. They knew me for a fresh comer and exacted a sorry toll from my hands, neck, and face. I wavered in my resolution to spend the night on the beach. I had left my rake at home, and as I am not a socialist I could not emulate the performances of the 'white mice,' as the East Side names the good, well-dressed young men and women of means who make sociological calls on them, notebooks in their hands, curiosity in their eyes, and burning enthusiasm in their hearts.

All the lights of the pleasure palaces were extinguished. Across at Riccadonna's there was still a light, and peering over the Brighton pavilion there was a pillar of luminosity that looked a cross between a corn-cob and a thermometer afire. I sat down on the sand. I would stay out the night. And then I began to look about me. In Hyde Park, London, I had seen hundreds of vagabonds huddled in the grass, their clothes mere rags, their attitudes those of death, but nothing in England or America can match what I saw this particular night. While the poorer classes predominated, there was little suggestion of abject pauperism. Many seemed gay. The white dresses of the women and children relieved the somber masses of black men, who, though coatless for the most part, made black splotches on the sand. In serried array they lay; there was no order in their position, yet a short distance away they gave the impression of an army at rest. The entire beach was thick with humanity. At close range it resolved itself in groups, sweethearts in pairs, families of three or four, six or seven, planted close together. With care, hesitation, and difficulty I navigated around these islets of flesh and blood. Sometimes I stumbled over a foot or an arm. Once I kicked a head, and I was cursed many times and vigorously cursed. But I persisted. Like the 'white mice,' I was there to see. Policemen plodded through the crowds, and if there was undue hilarity warned the offenders in a low voice. But it was impossible for such a large body of people to be more orderly, more decent. I determined to prowl down the lower beach, between the Boulevard and Sea Gate.

My sporting instinct came to the surface. Here was game. Not in the immemorial mob, joking and snoring, shrieking and buzzing, would I find what I sought. I tried to pass under the bathing-houses, but so densely packed were the paths that I was threatened by a dozen harsh voices. So I pursued a safer way, down Surf Avenue. It was still filled with people — men and women, battered, bleary, drunk or tired, dragged their weary paces, regarding each other as do wolves, ready to spring. We all felt like sticky August salt. Reaching the beach again, I was too fatigued to walk farther. I propped my head against the wooden pillar of an old bath-house and my eyes began to droop. I heard without a quiver of interest the sudden scream of a woman followed by ominous bass laughter. Some one plucked a banjo. Dogs barked. A hymn rose on the hot air. Around me it was like a battle-field of the slain. A curious drone was in the air; it was the monster breathing. A muggy moon shone intermittently over us, its bleached rays painting in one ghastly tone the upturned faces of the sleepers. The stale, sour, rank smell of wretched mankind poisoned the atmosphere, thick with sultry vapors. I wished myself home.

Then a gentle voice said — the accent was slightly foreign:

'What a sight the poor make in the moonlight!' I did not turn, but answered that I had thought that same thing. The voice proceeded. It was not strong, though a resonant baritone:

'You are alone, good sir; but look at my brood, and don't wonder at people dying without asking the world's permission.'

I half arose, expecting that it was a beggar who addressed me. A child began whimpering. I saw a woman on her side holding with relaxed grasp this crying infant — the wail was hardly perceptible above the swish of the surf. Near her were two older children. The man who had spoken to me was sitting, his head plunged almost between his knees, his skinny hands supporting his head. He was exceedingly poor, wearing only a ragged shirt and trousers. His head was large and curly with thick hair. He could not have been more than forty. When he lifted his head his eyes in the moonshine were like two red cinders. A wild beast — and with a gentle, even cultivated, voice. I went over to him. The child still moaned as the fingers of the exhausted woman opened farther. I forgot sociology and wondered if here was a case of starvation — a hungry family in all the Gargantuan feast of Coney Island. The idea was horrible.

'What's the matter, Batiushka?' I

asked, adopting a familiar form of Russian salutation. He fell on his knees.

'Brother,' he panted, 'are you a Russian? A Jew? Help us. We have not eaten since yesterday morning.' I confess I shuddered. I confess also that I didn't believe him. A man, a Jewish man with a family, in New York and starving! New York, with its rich charitable institutions! And this fellow tried to make me think that he needed food; that his wife and children needed food! I had eaten my dinner at the Manhattan, and I enjoyed that selfish credulity which an able-bodied gourmand feels when he is approached by some one who has tasted no food for days.

And this miserable being came nearer to me, feebly, supplicatingly. His eyes were like red dots in the head of a famished animal. His hot breath issued as from an open grave. The child sobbed louder, and the mother, half awake, clutched it. She sat up. The other two children arose, alarmed, silent. It was too much for my pampered nerves. Bidding the man remain where he was, I ran across the beach to the Bowery and into a little saloon full of half-drunken, vicious people. Ten minutes later we sat at an improvised supper of pretzels, cold fish, and beer. I knew this family wouldn't touch anything else. Starvation itself would not force them to break their tribal law. I have an idea that I was thirsty myself, for I enjoyed the flat beer, and I enjoyed the subdued ferocity with which the family ate and drank. The baby did not stir. It had fallen asleep. The mother, a worn-out woman, still young, mechanically put the food into her mouth, not looking at us, not speaking to the two girls. She was numbed by hunger and heat.

'See here, what's your name?' I asked.

'My name,' he stammered, 'is Hyman.'

'I mean your family name,' I demanded; 'Hyman is your first name.'

He gave me a keen glance. Then he quietly replied: 'You are right. My full name is Hyman Levin.'

'Have you a home?' I pursued. I felt my importance. I was playing the rôle of benefactor, and what philanthropist, great or small, does not desire the worth of his money? Besides, it is good policy to cross-examine a starving man. He appreciates your interest at such a time. (Oh, what smiling villains are we all!)

'I live in an alley near Oliver Street. Usually we go to the recreation pier near Peck Slip, but the child was so sick that I came down here last night.'

'Last night?'

'Yes, I pawned my coat to get the car fare.'

This is a truthful report of the man's conversation. He was out of work — sickness — and he had pawned, piece by piece, bit by bit, everything in the house. His wife went to the pawnhouse, while he, scarcely able to hold up his head, watched the baby. The children lived in the streets, feeding at the garbage cans, thankful for such a chance. Is this exaggeration? If you think so, then you don't know your own city. Such things happen every day. The neighbors were kind, especially the Irish. But they, too, could scarcely boast more than one meal a day. Hyman coughed; he evidently was marked for the death of a consumptive. Yet he fought on. The charities were available — for a time. But funds ran low; public interest also ran low. The Levins found themselves within five days of rent time in their room, a musty, dirty garret. Life from heat and insufficient food became intolerable, and, half crazed with fever, on that hot Monday, they contrived to reach the seashore. With only a few pennies, yet they were happier; they could at least breathe fresh air, see the water. But so forbidding was the appearance of this unhappy family that they were warned off the board walk and frightened away from the crowd of pleasure-seekers. We do not care to see these death's-heads at our feasts. Finally they found refuge under the bathhouse, and there I met them.

Worse remains. When the dawn came up softly like the vanguard of an army without banners I shook the sleeping Hyman. I awoke the woman. I had heard queer sounds in the throat of the child, noises like water slowly dripping into a well. Why should I go on? The child was dead, and I was not surprised. Nor were the parents. They made no outcry, but covered the little thing with the mother's old pelisse. Stunned by their cumulative misfortunes, this death was accepted with the fatalism of a Russian. I told a policeman the story, and a half-hour later the entire family was carted away with the promise that they would be given food and shelter.

There was a bitter taste in my mouth. If a poor devil of a tramp or a working man had met me then I should not have been able to look either one in the eye. Oh, how cheap is charity! The silver I spent did not relieve the Levins. They had scarcely bade me good-by, so oppressed were they by their sorrow, their shame. They must have hated me. The man was not ignorant. His English betrayed a reader. He had conversed well about Gorky and Tolstoy, had read Karl Marx, and knew the names of all his saints of anarchy. A socialist? I do not know. I only know that your bookish theories go to smash when you hear a man's voice thrill with anguish. A pauper, you say, a lazy good-for-nothing? Ay, perhaps he was — perhaps they all are; but drunkard, thief, even murderer, must they starve? Anarchs and infidels? So were the Americans of 1776, according to the English.

Remember what Richard Jeffries wrote: 'Food and drink, roof and clothes are the inalienable right of every child born into the light. If the world does not provide it freely — not as a grudging gift, but as a right, as a son of the house sits down to breakfast — then is the world mad. . . . I verily believe that the earth in one year produces enough food to last for thirty. Why, then, have we not enough? . . . It is not the pauper — oh, inexpressibly wicked word! — it is the well-to-do who are the criminal classes.' Grant Allen said that all men are born free and unequal. True. But should they be allowed to want for bread?

Don't ask me the remedy. I am neither a professional prophet nor a socialist. Don't throw socialism at my head. Ready-made prophylactics smell suspiciously. The 'dismal science' scares me. Before the fatal words 'unearned increment' I retreat. And the socialist's conception of the state approaches singularly close to the old conception of monarchy. I know that there are many Levins in New York, of many nationalities. Starve in New York, the abundant city, where 'God's in the world to-day'? Impossible! cry the sentimentalists. I didn't believe it, either, until I met the Levins. That adventure has cured me of all foolish optimistic boasting. I have told the story plainly. I realized of how little account to people in such awful straits is the clangor of contending political parties. Of what interest to a man, his belly pinched by starvation, whether one Jack in office is ousted by another Jack who desires the place; whether this one is president, that one is governor? A flare of fireworks, a river of beer, on the East Side for a night, and the people are forgotten by their masters. It has been so always; for eternity it will endure. Does not Campanella's sonnet sing:

The people is a beast of muddy brain
That knows not its own strength, and therefore stands
Loaded with wood and stone;

.   .   .   .   .   .

Its own are all things between earth and Heaven;
But this it knows not, and if one arise
To tell this truth it kills him unforgiven.

Grunting, growling, spitting, coughing, the huge army of thousands began in maelstrom fashion to move cityward. Some stopped at the half-way house of whisky; many breakfasted, but the main body made a dash for the cars. The night had been a trying one, the new day did not promise; yet it was a new day, and with it a flock of fresh hopes was born. The crowd seemed rested; in its eyes was the lust of life, and it was absolutely good-humored. I heard a vague tale about a man-hunt during the night — how a thief had been chased with stones and clubs until, reaching Sea Gate, he had boldly plunged into the water and disappeared. His hawk-like features, the color of clay from fright, had impressed the old man who related the story. In return I told the Levins' heart-breaking tale, and he did not appear much interested. What signified to all those strong, bustling men and women the death of a tiny girl baby — dead and hardly clad in a wisp of blackened canvas?

'Better dead!' The mobs thickened. Policemen fought them into line. The hot sun arose, in company with the penetrating odors of bad coffee and greasy crullers. Another day's labor was arrived. Soon would appear the first detachment of women and children sick from the night in the city. Soon would be heard the howling of the fakers: 'Go to Hell, go to Hell-gate!'

I felt that I had been very near it, that I had seen a new Coney Island. I went home, after this, the most miserable night of my life — miserable because my nerves were out of gear. I was once more the normal, selfish man, thinking of his bed, of his breakfast. I had, of course, quite forgotten the Levins.

VII

THE NEW YORK PUBLIC LIBRARY

A. C. DAVID

[*Architectural Record*, September, 1910.
By permission.]

An architectural commentator cannot well approach such a building as the New York Public Library without a feeling of grave responsibility. In attempting to put some sort of an estimate upon it, he is confronted both by a large and important public edifice, and by a formidable array of incidental, but imposing, claims to consideration. The building is not merely spacious and important, but it is the most important building erected, since the American architectural revival began, in the largest city in the country. It has been designed by a firm of architects who, according to general consent, stand at the head of their profession. The library building they have presented to New York is undeniably popular. It has already taken its place in the public mind as a building of which every New Yorker may be proud, and this opinion of the building is shared by the architectural profession of the country. Of course, it does not please everybody; but if American architects in good standing were asked to name the one building which embodied most of what was good in contemporary American architecture, the New York Public Library would be the choice of a handsome majority. In criticizing it, consequently, a merely individual judgment, no matter how well considered it might be, would at the present time scarcely count. It is far more important to understand exactly why the building meets with such widespread popular and professional approval.

Perhaps some justification may be needed for the statement that the New York Public Library is the most impor-

tant building erected since the American architectural revival began. A little consideration will show that the foregoing claim is not in any way excessive. In the first place, in any modern American city the public library is the institution which is most representative of the aspirations of the community. The City Hall and the County Court House have become less representative of popular aspirations than they should be, because our local governments and our local courts have deservedly suffered a good deal in popular estimation, and the churches are the spiritual habitations merely of only fragments of the community. But the typical American aspiration is embodied in the word 'education'; and of all the organs of education, the one which belongs to the whole community is the public library. Partly owing to the generosity of a single individual, they have been built in enormous numbers all over the country; and almost universally they have assumed an institutional character. The old idea of the library as a secluded room, in which a few scholars could browse at leisure among dusty volumes, has given way to the idea that it is essentially a vehicle of popular education — one which should be in some measure supported by public funds and managed chiefly for the purpose of giving the widest possible circulation to its accumulated and accumulating store of books.

The American public library, consequently, has, like all institutional buildings, usually been designed for the purpose of imposing itself upon the public. It has not attempted to solicit patronage by a suggestion of studious detachment. It has announced to the public from some colonnaded portico that it was a great educational institution, and that the public must, for its own good, come in and get educated; and the designers have never felt it necessary to invite patronage by retaining in the building any flavor of domesticity, which in Europe has always been associated with such edifices.

The public libraries in the smaller American cities, whose dimensions were not well adapted to monumental treatment, have suffered from being treated too much as educational institutions and not enough merely as the shell of a reading-room and a book-stack. But in the larger cities, whose libraries are large, well equipped and fully capable of becoming valuable agencies for the dissemination of knowledge and ideas among a large number of people, the institutional idea has a much better chance of effective architectural expression. Such was particularly the case with the New York Public Library. No other library in the country represented such a combination of private and public endowment. The collection itself was the result of the generosity of three private donors, while the site for the new building and its cost was supplied by the city; and the city had been even more generous than Messrs. Astor, Lenox and Tilden. It had given a site in the heart of the city, whose market value at the present time must be between $7,000,000 and $8,000,000; and it had erected on this site an edifice almost regardless of expense. No public library in the world, unless it be that of Boston, occupies such a superb site, and on no other library building has anything like as much money been lavished. It is, consequently, a veritable institution — the result both of individual and of public aspiration and of individual and public sacrifices, and one which, when completed, will constitute a most efficient piece of machinery for converting a collection of books into a means of popular instruction. The building becomes the most important building of its kind in the country, because it will provide a fitting habitation for the most useful existing library in the largest American city.

There is one difficulty, however, which confronts almost every American architect who has to design a monumental public building. The really great monumental buildings have usually been simple in plan. They have been built usually around a comparatively few rooms of considerable area and height, which were also capable of large and simple treatment, and whose dimensions could be adapted to the scale of the exterior. But in all American monumental buildings, except, perhaps, tombs, the plan is necessarily very complicated. A few large rooms are required, together with a multitude of insignificant ones; and these rooms are required for certain practical purposes, which makes good lighting and a certain arrangement essential. A conflict almost certainly ensues between the plan and the design; and this conflict almost inevitably results in a compromise, in which either

certain important ingredients of a perfect plan or a perfect design, or both, are sacrificed. The consequence is that the finest achievements of the American architectural revival are not to be found in monumental buildings; and edifices such as the Columbia College Library and the Pennsylvania Station in New York, which are most imposing and effective as a matter of pure architectural form, are usually wasteful in plan.

In the case of a library, the difficulties which the necessities of the plan impose upon the architect are harder to solve even than they are in the case of a courthouse or a state capitol. The chief requirements are a spacious and perfectly lighted reading-room, an arrangement of the stacks, so that the books are easily accessible and their titles easily read, and a large number of small apartments for particular purposes of all kinds, ranging from galleries to small rooms for special collections of books. It is a well-known fact that in such buildings as the Columbia, the Boston and the Congressional libraries, these practical requirements have been met only in a very inferior manner; and while we have never seen the building, we understand that they are being most completely satisfied in the new library which has been built for the University of California.

Messrs. Carrère & Hastings have always been most conscientious about arranging the plans of their buildings so as to meet every reasonable practical requirement; and the New York Public Library is no exception to the rule. Its arrangements for storing and handling the books are said to be entirely satisfactory to the management of the library. The main reading-room is one of the most spacious rooms in the world — beautifully proportioned, lighted by a series of windows on both the long sides of the room, and entirely accessible to the stacks. To have obtained a room of these dimensions, so excellently adapted to its purpose in every respect, was a great triumph for the architects. The smaller rooms, also, particularly those like the gallery, whose practical requirements are severe, are also admirably planned for their purposes. These rooms have been supplied with a good light by avoiding anything like a heavy colonnade on the façade; and while most of them (all of them except those situated on the corners) obtain light from

only one direction, the light is, in all except a few cases, all that is needed. The
corridors, which run parallel to the outer
lines of the building between two rows of
rooms, one lighted from the street and
the other from a court, have to be arti-
ficially lighted, but that is as it should
be.

It is an interesting fact, however, that
the superbly dimensioned reading-room —
an apartment 395 feet long, over 75 feet
wide and 50 feet high — has practically no
salient effect on the exterior of the building. It stretches along the rear of the
structure, and this façade is very plainly
treated, without any pretence to architectural effect. It is, indeed, designed
frankly as the rear of a structure which is
not meant to be looked at except on the
other sides. Any attempt, consequently,
at monumental treatment has been abandoned. The building is designed to be
seen from Fifth Avenue and from the
side streets. The rear, on Bryant Park,
merely takes care of itself; and one of the
largest apartments in any edifice in the
United States is practically concealed, so
far as any positive exterior result is concerned.

The striking fact mentioned in the preceding paragraph is a sufficient characterization of the purpose of the architects.
They recognized that they could not plan
a room of the required dimensions and
light it properly without destroying its
value as the primary motive of a monumental building; and in obedience to their
settled policy of being loyal primarily to
the needs of the plan, they deliberately
sacrificed the monumental to the practical
aspect of the edifice. What is more, they
sacrificed the architectural effect of the
interior of the reading-room to the convenience of the management in the handling of the books. This superb apartment
is cut in two by an elaborate wooden
screen, from which the books contained in
the stacks are to be distributed; and it is,
consequently, almost impossible to get the
full architectural effect of the reading-
room, except from some point along the
balcony.

The New York Public Library is not,
then, intended to be a great monumental
building, which would look almost as well
from one point of view as another, and
which would be fundamentally an example
of pure architectural form. It is designed
rather to face on the avenue of a city, and
not to seem out of place on such a site.
It is essentially and frankly an instance of
street architecture; and as an instance of
street architecture it is distinguished in
its appearance rather than imposing. Not,
indeed, that it is lacking in dignity. The
façade on Fifth Avenue has poise, as well
as distinction; character, as well as good
manners. But still it does not insist upon
its own peculiar importance, as every
monumental building must do. It is content with a somewhat humbler rôle, but
one which is probably more appropriate.
It looks ingratiating rather than imposing, and that is probably one reason for
its popularity. It is intended for popular
rather than for official use, and the building issues to the people an invitation to
enter rather than a command.

From a strictly architectural point of
view, there are many criticisms which can
be passed upon the design. The niches and
fountains on either side of the entrance
— the one monumental feature of the
building — are a not very happy and appropriate device to ornament the stretches
of blank wall which flank the entrance
porch. The treatment of the two ends of
the façade is weak. The scale of the engaged colonnade looks too contracted.
The fact has not been sufficiently considered in the design that one sees the building not when one is walking west through
Forty-first Street, but when one is walking up or down Fifth Avenue. But blem-
ishes such as those mentioned are not of
sufficient importance seriously to attenu-
ate the fundamental impressiveness and at-
tractiveness of the façade. The architects
have succeeded in making the library sufficiently imposing and dignified in character to satisfy the prevailing idea that a
library is a great educational institution,
while, at the same time, they have awakened popular interest by making it look
like a pleasant place to enter and use.
And this is a great triumph, because there
is a real and sometimes an apparently irreconcilable conflict between the monumental and practical aspects of such buildings.

The final judgment on the New York
Public Library will be, consequently, that
it is not a great monument, because considerations of architectural form have in

several conspicuous instances been deliberately subordinated to the needs of the plan. In this respect it resembles the new Museum of Fine Arts in Boston. The building is at bottom a compromise between two groups of partly antagonistic demands, and a compromise can hardly ever become a consummate example of architectural form. But, on the other hand, Messrs. Carrère & Hastings have, as in so many other cases, made their compromise successful. Faithful as they have been to the fundamental requirement of adapting the building to its purpose as a library, they have also succeeded in making it look well; and they have succeeded in making it look well partly because the design is appropriate to its function as a building in which books are stored, read and distributed. A merely monumental library always appears somewhat forbidding and remote. The New York Public Library looks attractive, and so far as a large building can, even intimate. And in this respect it differs from the Boston Museum of Fine Arts, which, excellently planned as it may be, presents a dull and rigid architectural mask to the public.

The popularity of the New York Public Library has, consequently, been well earned. The public has reason to like it, because it offers them a smiling countenance; and the welcome it gives is merely the outward and visible sign of an inward grace. When people enter they will find a building which has been ingeniously and carefully adapted to their use. Professional architects like it, because they recognize the skill, the good taste and the abundant resources of which the building, as a whole, is the result; and while many of them doubtless cherish a secret thought that they would have done it better, they are obliged to recognize that in order to have done it better they would have been obliged to exhibit a high degree of architectural intelligence. In the realism of its plan and in the mixture of dignity and distinction in the design, the New York Public Library is typical of that which is best in the contemporary American architectural movement; and New York is fortunate, indeed, that such a statement can be made of the most important public building erected in the city during several generations.

VIII

THE TALLEST OFFICE BUILDING IN THE WORLD

[*Scientific American*, March 8, 1913. By permission.]

For the present at least the tallest office building in the world will be found on the western side of City Hall Park, where the towering Woolworth Building lifts its glittering steel-and-terra-cotta structure through a sheer height of 785 feet above the sidewalk. This is not only the loftiest office building, but, if we except the Eiffel Tower, it is the tallest structure of any kind as yet erected by man. Two other notable buildings in this city vie with the Woolworth tower in altitude, its nearest competitor being the Metropolitan tower at Madison Square with a total height of just over 700 feet, and the Singer tower, built like the Woolworth structure, on Broadway, and only a few city blocks to the south of it, which has a total height above the sidewalk of 612 feet. Mention should also be made of that remarkable structure on the opposite side of City Hall Park, the New Municipal Building; the top of the bronze figure with which it is now being crowned will be 560 feet above the sidewalk.

As the eye ranges up through the multitudinous stories of the Woolworth Building to the pyramidal structure at its top, the question arises as to what is the limit of height to which a habitable building can be carried. The answer can be found in a certain restriction laid down by the Building Code of New York City, which states that on a rock foundation the load may reach but not exceed fifteen tons to the square foot. It will surprise some of our readers to learn that on this basis, it would be possible on a plot of ground 200 feet square to erect an office building 2000 feet in height, and to build it, moreover, so that it would be perfectly secure against the fiercest hurricane, and, because of its elasticity, even against the altogether improbable event of an earthquake shock.

SOME DIMENSIONS AND QUANTITIES

The Woolworth Building is taller than it looks. To reach its lowest foundation, we must go down in one place to a depth of 120 feet beneath the sidewalk — for that was the depth to which it was necessary to sink the pneumatic caisson in that particular spot before the solid rock of Manhattan Island was reached. This would make the total height of the building from lowest foundation to summit 905 feet. Just here, while touching on the question of dimensions and quantities, we may state that the building contains 23,-000 tons of structural steel, 17,000,000 common brick, 7500 tons of terra cotta, 1,800,000 square feet of floor tiles, 1,800,-000 square feet of partition tiles, and 2500 square feet of cut stone.

The construction of the foundation, etc., involved 60,000 yards excavation, the use of 24,000 yards of concrete, 300 tons of reinforcement steel and 350 tons of steel sheet-piling. Finally, the building which, with its furniture, etc., will weigh more than 125,000 tons, will have cost, when complete, some $12,000,000.

The building covers a plot 155 feet by 200 feet. It is U-shaped in plan, with two wings, 60 by 95 feet, facing on Barclay Street and Park Place. The shorter side of the plot is that on Broadway. There are thirty stories in the main building, the roof of which stands 400 feet above the street. From the center of the Broadway façade and flush with it, rises a tower measuring 85 by 86 feet, which extends for an additional 25 stories above the roof. The building is carried on 66 concrete piers, sunk through gravel, sand and hardpan, everywhere to solid rock, which was found at an average depth of about 80 feet below the ground-water level. These foundation piers are of solid concrete. The majority are circular and vary in diameter from 8 to 19 feet. A few of them are of rectangular cross-section.

Until the hardpan was reached, the sinking of the caissons was quickly and rapidly done, and one, 6½ feet in diameter, went down 80 feet in less than a single day.

ERECTING THE STEEL FRAME

Although the vertical axes of the majority of the columns coincide with the axes of the concrete piers below them, this is not always the case. Several of the columns are supported upon two piers, the piers being spanned by girders with the columns resting at about their center. Thus, in one column the load of nearly 5000 tons is carried at a center of a girder, 8 feet deep, 6 feet 9 inches wide, and 23 feet long, which itself weighs over 100 tons. Ordinarily between the piers and the foot of the columns is a grillage of several tiers of 24-inch I-beams.

Naturally, the columns in a building of this height ran up enormous dimensions and weights in the lower stories. Usually they were built in two story lengths, and were of entirely inclosed box-section, consisting usually of two channels with cover plates on both flanges. The largest column measures 34 inches by 30 inches, and its cross-sectional area is 660 square inches; that is to say, the metal in it, if compressed into a solid square bar, would measure 25 inches on each side. It is easy to understand from these dimensions that the total weight of the structural steel reaches 23,000 tons.

TO RESIST WIND PRESSURE

When it is borne in mind that the storms which sweep across Manhattan Island, chiefly from the west and southwest, rise at times to cyclonic force and blow at a velocity of between eighty and ninety miles an hour, it can be understood readily that special provision had to be made, in designing so lofty a tower, to safeguard it against overturning or against failure in its steel frame, due to the enormous bending stresses engendered. It is considered that for a building of this magnitude it is sufficient to estimate the average wind pressure, at maximum velocity, as thirty pounds upon every square foot of surface exposed. If we disregard the shelter afforded by the low buildings at its base, we find that the total wind pressure from top of tower to sidewalk over the whole surface facing a westerly wind is 1300 tons, and this pressure may be considered as concentrated at a level of say about 300 feet above the sidewalk. It is evident, at once, that in order adequately to take care of this wind-load, special features had to be introduced into the design of the steel framework. The inclined steel rafters of the spire-like roof of the tower take care of the horizontal thrust of the wind. Below the roof at the forty-second floor, the wind stresses are provided for by the wall girders and the columns, which are connected by deep gusset plates at their intersection. From the forty-second to the twenty-eighth floors, deep wall girders, made especially heavy for the purpose, are connected to the columns by double knee-braces. From the twenty-eighth floor to the street, heavy solid plates of steel, or 'portals' as they are called, are constructed on the two sides and top of each opening or panel in the steel work. It was these portals that gave an appearance of enormous width to the columns before they were closed in by the terra cotta and stone work. On the Broadway front the portal girders are double as far up as the fourth floor, and they are no less than four feet in depth.

FIREPROOF CONSTRUCTION

The floors of the basement and first story are built of reinforced concrete slabs, and the floors above of hollow terra cotta. The structural steel is protected against fire by a coating of concrete not less than one inch in thickness, or else by three inches of terra cotta. Wood as a material of construction is entirely excluded; the windows, the trim, the doors, are of pressed steel, and furthermore, the exterior windows where exposed are glazed with wire glass. In addition to the twenty-six elevators there are four wide stairways. A description of the installation of steam heat, ventilation apparatus, plumbing, drainage, gas and electric light, pneumatic service, etc., would make a long story in itself.

The building was commenced in September, 1910, and it is to-day practically ready for occupation. The rate at which the building was carried up is shown in the accompanying set of illustrations, which were taken from a lofty building on the opposite side of City Hall Park.

SAFEGUARDING THE WORKMEN AND THE PUBLIC

An interesting feature of the construction of the Woolworth Building was the fact that the advanced ideas that underlie modern liability insurance were exemplified in an interesting manner, the inspection service rendered during the work being particularly worthy of note. The insurance company that carried the liability kept two inspectors on duty continuously, and immediately upon noting a condition which was likely to result in an accident, they notified the proper foreman or superintendent, and saw that the danger was removed. Their recommendations were also reported to the office of the engineering and inspection division of the insurance company, and written copies were then sent to the contractors.

Patent scaffolds were used for the bricklaying throughout the work, and these were covered, so far as possible, with substantial wire-mesh roofs, to protect the men at work upon the platforms from tools and materials that might fall from above. The sides of all the scaffold platforms were also protected by guard rails and by wire-mesh screens. Substantial bridges for the protection of pedestrians and others were built over the sidewalks, and these were made stout enough to resist the impact of any material that might fall upon them. Platforms twenty feet wide were also built out from the building at four different heights, to catch any material that might fall, and prevent it from descending into the street. Wire-mesh screens were arranged along their outer edges to give still further security.

All the hoisting apparatus was examined frequently and thoroughly by expert elevator inspectors; employees were not allowed to ride on material hoists, and the maximum number of persons who might be permitted to ride on a passenger hoist was definitely specified in each case. All hoists, whether used for the transportation of men or of materials, were covered overhead, to prevent accidents from falling objects. The hoist openings were effectively fenced, and were guarded by rails where the materials were loaded or unloaded. Openings in the floors were thoroughly guarded by rails or fences or otherwise. All stairways, whether temporary or permanent, were required to be rail-guarded. Proper lighting was insisted upon, particularly at work places, along gangways and passages, and at every other important point. Warning signs were put up at all dangerous places. Laborers engaged in cutting concrete and other similar substances were obliged to use chisels fitted with protective handles, so that their own hands would not be injured if the strikers should miss the heads of the chisels. An effective watch was kept for nails and other similar sharp metal points projecting from the woodwork or from loose planks or boards or elsewhere. These are prolific sources of injury, and the men were required to remove them at once. First-aid cabinets were also provided, at the suggestion of the liability inspectors.

It will be apparent that the comparative freedom from accident that characterized the erection of the Woolworth Building was not the result of chance, but that it was the logical outcome of the practical system of inspection that was adopted.

A REMARKABLE ELEVATOR TEST

The express elevators of the Woolworth Building have a vertical travel of 676 feet, and Mr. F. T. Ellithorpe, who is responsible for the safety system provided for the twenty-eight elevators, will make that 15 sheer drop to demonstrate that his apparatus is equal to the maximum stress to which it may by possible mishap be subjected in service. What is technically known as an 'air cushion' will first check 20 the car and then bring it to a gentle halt. From the bottom of each shaft upward for a distance of 137 feet the passageway is enclosed, forming the envelope of the so-called 'cushion.' Of course, there are 25 doors at each floor, but these are closed mechanically as the elevators pass onward. The broad essential is that the surrounding casing shall be substantially air tight and that there shall be no escape for the air 30 except upward past the sides of the descending vehicle. For the major part of its travel down this inclosed shaft, the space between the elevator and the envelope is just enough to permit the in- 35 creasingly compressed air to gradually slow up the car and finally to bring it to a standstill.

The falling elevator is substantially a loosely-fitting piston, but even so, it would 40 be stopped with a violent jar after entering the inclosed shaft if some provision were not made for regulating the initial compression of the confined air. A jar of this sort would be enough to throw the 45 occupants to the floor of the elevator, and might easily be the means of breaking their bones, if not hurting them more gravely. But the air pressure will be controlled by automatic valves. The designer has two 50 other ways of regulating the air pressure, which are illustrated herewith.

Mr. Ellithorpe has already dropped more than 300 feet without injury, and the car has been so gently restrained and halted 55 that water was not spilled from a brimming tumbler. In the test in the Woolworth Building, Mr. Ellithorpe will drop

in the car a sheer distance of 539 feet, and in that interval the elevator will attain a maximum velocity of two miles a minute — that fall will be made in less than six seconds; and the remaining 137 feet of confined air will be counted upon to overcome that momentum and to stop the car progressively. For the test, the ordinary cables will be detached, and a single rope with a tripper, subject to Mr. Ellithorpe's control, will be substituted.

By means of a large number of gauges, which will be fitted for the first time in tests of this sort, records will be taken of the air pressures at each stage of the drop within the limits of the air cushion, and engineers are much interested in the data which will be obtained in this way.

It is interesting to note that as the falling distance is four times the stopping interval, Mr. Ellithorpe will, during the latter interval, have his weight increased fourfold. Some time ago, during a test of this sort, the occupant of the car was seated in a chair. When his weight was increased by the retardation of the car, the chair was crushed, and the passenger was fatally injured by a splinter.

Our thanks are due to Mr. Cass Gilbert, the architect; W. Gunvald Aus, the structural engineer; and the Thompson-Starrett Company, the contractors, for courtesies rendered during the preparation of this article.

IX

MOTORIZING AMERICA

BRONSON BATCHELOR

[*Independent*, March 1, 1915. By permission.]

A little more than a decade ago men discovered for a second time in history how much of the world lay outside the narrow confines of their everyday lives.

Just as communities and peoples had brought home to them, with the coming of the locomotive a century before, the isolation of the little world in which they had previously dwelt, so now more acutely than ever before men realized the closeness with which for ages their individual inter-relations had been restricted. They grew impatient of the halting, crowded street-cars, by which their homes were connected with their businesses or their pleasures. They grew intolerant of the painful slowness of the horse, though it had been man's faithful servitor for centuries. The flat-dweller became discontented with the closeness of the city from which he could only escape by horse or by rail, and the farmer began to grow restive at his own isolation.

It was the automobile that brought the new vision of the widening horizons of life. With the discovery began a new revolution: the motorization of America.

Today one person out of every eighty in the United States possesses an automobile.

This year nearly 500,000 motor cars, with a value exceeding $450,000,000, will be produced in America.

Familiar as we are with tremendous figures, with the severing of continents and the leveling of mountains, more marvelous still has been the creation during the past decade and a half of the vast industry which is the outgrowth of that coughing, wheezing, rattling contraption that twenty years ago set forth on an adventure at the perilous rate of seven miles an hour!

What a far cry it is from New York's first automobile demonstration in 1896 when the Park Commissioner, 'for fear it might scare the horses,' forbade to the strange vehicle the right to go through Central Park!

Yet to-day involved in the making of those vehicles is invested millions of dollars, estimated variously at from two hundred million dollars up — pouring in so rapidly that the manufacturers themselves scarcely know what the amount is. In ten years, from one hundred and fiftieth in the list of American industries, the manufacture of motor cars has risen to a position among the first dozen, and to leadership in at least one state.

Not many years ago Michigan was largely an agricultural State; Detroit little more than a huge, sprawling, mid-Western town. Now the Wolverine State produces no less than 75 per cent. of that half a million cars. In Detroit are to be found a large proportion of the world's most efficient and scientific factories, running night and day in their effort to put an impatient earth on pneumatic-tired wheels. Twenty-two per cent. of the industrial workers of Michigan are employed in the automobile and allied trades. Motor cars have almost replaced Grand Rapids furniture as the trade-mark of the State.

If the story of Pennsylvania is the history of steel, then the later chapters of Michigan's annals are the story of the automobile. Pittsburgh has been called the 'city of a thousand millionaires'— made by steel; Detroit differs from Pittsburgh in that its millionaires are still in the making.

Now when men first discovered that the horse was an antiquated institution, and proceeded to retire it over-night, as it were, to the place where all antiquated things belong, they did it neither from a sudden inspiration nor from a dawning sense of reason. Economic revolutions as a rule do not happen that way. Some do occasionally, such as the sewing machine, the telephone, the electric light, which had advantages that could not be overlooked. They were simple, they were cheap, and their uses were almost imperative.

Not so with the automobile, the purchase price of which alone was equal to the cost of a fair-sized house and lot.

The motor car revolution has been due not so much to economic utility as to other causes; not to the machine so much as to the daring methods which the makers pursued in manufacture and salesmanship.

And the triumph they have achieved is but another tribute to the genius of the American business man. Nowhere else in the world is the automobile so generally used as in the United States; the American car, like farming machinery, adding machines, and any number of articles, has become the standard the world over.

Where the American manufacturer surpassed his European competitor is that he saw in the automobile something more than a luxury, a plaything for the very rich. In every class except the poorest, he visioned it as the necessity, while in Europe, except where the American lower-priced car has begun to compete, it is still the extravagance for the few. It is American daring that has made the motor car democratic and useful.

That the men in charge of the development of the automobile were men of genius is proved by two things. And those things were the two ideas of advertising and large scale production — with which the inventors of the automobile must share the credit for the Aladdin-like development of this newest of the Big Businesses.

Manufacturers as a rule are keen-eyed, long-headed gentlemen who pride themselves on knowing what the public wants, and then providing it. But the makers of automobiles were a little keener than the rest and they went a step further. They were not content merely to satisfy a public demand; they wanted to create it.

So they set about to show the public what a good thing the motor car was. Theirs was an expensive commodity, which was looked upon as luxury's last word, and its normal growth they knew would be slow and hazardous. The automobile companies began to talk its comforts and advantages, they began to preach the automobile as a *necessity*. By advertisements alluding to the great out-of-doors or the mystery of unseen places, by the romance of the race and endurance contests, they succeeded in creating a demand for motor cars. Factories sprung up like mushrooms over night.

Automobile manufacturers were among the first to appreciate the psychology of modern advertising. They were among the first to set aside regularly a portion of their earnings, amounting today to between 4 and 7 per cent. of the gross revenue, to the stimulation and development of the markets which the printed word made potential.

But to the second idea more than to the first has the present motor saturation been due.

Certain of the more far-seeing manufacturers began to perceive that the markets they were then cultivating had their limits. They saw that at the prices for which cars were selling, and with the tendency toward the still more luxurious machine, the people who could afford to buy them would soon be supplied.

One of the manufacturers, pursuing this idea, was curious to know how many persons there were in the United States who could afford automobiles. He wanted to know definitely how large the motor market was. The figures he found ran something like this. That 7000 families had incomes over $60,000 a year; 40,000 families had incomes between $15,000 and $60,000 a year; 253,000 families had incomes between $6000 and $15,000 a year; 700,000 families had incomes between $3000 and $6000 a year; 1,500,000 families had incomes between $1800 and $3000 a year; 2,138,000 families had incomes between $1200 and $1800 a year.

Then instead of conducting motor fashion shops with a dozen different models some of these makers decided to concentrate their entire energy on one design. That design was to be the best and cheapest in the world for the money. The lower they could bring the price of their product, they calculated, the more of the income groups of America would become potential purchasers of motor cars. As the next step began the study how to lessen costs of production without cheapening the quality. First the unessentials were eliminated: not an ounce of excess weight over the strength required, nor two bolts where one would do; not even was there a concession to ornament when it was at the expense of utility. In the factory everything was planned from the same scientific viewpoint of maximum efficiency from given effort. Statistics best tell the story of the revolution in production which followed.

From 1896 to 1904 the number of cars produced had reached only 12,000 annually, but in the next year alone, the number almost doubled, with 22,500. By 1907 the production had touched 39,000; in 1908 it was 50,000, with a second hundred per cent. jump the next year to 108,000. The figures of the following years sound almost like a fairy tale: 173,000 in 1910; 200,000 in 1911; 340,000 in 1912; 430,000 in 1913, culminating with the half million of the past year.

A like expansion has followed in the number of producers. To-day there are some four hundred and fifty American factories engaged in making a score of different varieties of gasoline and electric, pleasure and commercial motor cars. By far the greater number — two hundred and forty-five — are building gasoline vehicles for business, where competition has not yet weeded out the weak. In the older and more fully developed touring car field no less than one hundred and sixteen well established trade-marks coupled with constantly decreasing margins of profit unite to discourage the formation of new companies. Future progress will largely show the concentration of present numbers more than the addition of new competitors.

Another valuable lesson afforded to the

world by the automobile industry has been the keen race for the reduction of production costs. Within five years the average price of the motor car has dropped from nearly $3000 to less than $1000, and in every way each year's product is the superior of those that have gone before. The explanation is *scientific* industry.

In the automobile industry more than in others, the scientist has had full control of both the product and the plant. No longer is there room here for the hit-and-miss methods masqueraded for so many years under the name of Yankee shrewdness; no longer any scorning of 'scientific methods,' long synonymous in popular estimation with near-sighted eyes and absent-minded professors. Modern automobile manufacture is scientific and — what has not always followed the introduction of economics in manufacture — it is the consumer who has largely had the benefit. For factory buildings modern in every detail of light and air, for maximum efficiency in men and machines, for its wage level and the loyalty and morale of its workers, the automobile industry comes close — very close — to being the best in America.

The use of machinery and labor-saving devices has always been one of the main characteristics of American industry. If anything it is of their machines that our manufacturers have been proudest. Here, too, has the motor builder surpassed himself. More nearly does a modern automobile plant resemble a huge experimental laboratory than a factory. And the tens of thousands of cars which are the annual output of any one of many American companies suggest rather the product of these giant perfected frankensteins than that of human hands.

Watch, for instance, a gang of these machines in one of the large Detroit factories, set and controlled by a single hand, engaged in stamping out cylinder heads for engines fifteen at a time, as though no more than copper cents, milling at the same operation the top and two sides of each casting. Or, in another of the laboratory-shops, follow the work of a huge multiple drilling machine, which is the successor of twelve operators and as many drills. It bores in the frame sides of a motor car at one operation all the holes necessary for the assembling of the body and the chassis.

At another plant, in Cleveland, powerful machines mill out of solid steel wheels for the heaviest motor trucks. From the 900 pound casting they cut, in two and a half hours, 250 pounds of excess material, machining at the same time both sides of the wheel, the edges of all the spokes, the center and bores of the hub, even to cutting the threads for the ball-bearings and the dust caps. In the automobile industry, for the heaviest part of the work, man is now largely a supervisory intelligence.

The general organization of the motor factories is no less remarkable. The mere ability to turn out, complete, an average of a thousand cars a day, means organization, needless to say, which eliminates the second and expedites every possible operation.

The departments in one factory, for instance, have been arranged not in any arbitrary way, but as the particular part made in each contributed to the completed car. Thus literally, as well as in the advertising literature, raw material goes in at one end and comes out at the other a finished product.

One manufacturer, with an aerial monorailway, likewise has effected as much of a revolution in the shop as the automobile he makes has helped effect in the world. Instead of trundling material from department to department, or from floor to floor, in the time-honored and archaic way, he installed throughout his shop a miniature railway system transporting its burdens over to workmen and machines, thus saving both minutes and valuable floor space.

The complicated operation of assembling a car has been reduced to these simple elements:

Over a pair of 'horses' a rear axle is laid, to which the side frames are added, followed by the front axle. Wheels, with their tires already inflated, are then applied and the frame rolls to where an engine is fitted into position. At the third advance the dashboard and steering gear are bolted fast; at the next stop the radiator; then the gasoline tank is mounted filled with fuel.

The same efficiency obtains even to the testing of the mechanism. The engine is cranked by pressing the rear wheels of the car to revolving pulleys in the floor. A rubber hose connected with the exhaust pipe carries the gases outside the building.

A lever is thrown, and off through the door starts the chassis, wrenching itself loose from the hose as it goes. After a trial around the testing ground, the car returns to another point in the factory where down an inclined chute from an upper floor the body slides and is clamped rapidly to the chassis by men who have become experts in this one simple operation.

In less than a minute after a car has left any one position, another has taken its place.

It still remains to apply the motor car in commerce. Exploited as a toy, a huge plaything, as it were, for grown-ups, it must now be made to do the work of the nation.

Thus when a conservative dealer or stockholder gets alarmed at the present rate of automobile production and foresees the exhaustion of markets and closing of factories, it is to the future of the commercial car that the optimistic manufacturer points. And the immensity of this future he sees in that but a scant thirty thousand of last year's half million cars went into business use.

In every field where the horse is employed our enthusiastic maker knows that his truck has proved its superior economy and utility. He points as proof of his contention to the scores of businesses to-day where it is already indispensable. And in replacing the horses alone he sees a future market for more than three million trucks. After that, or along with it, if the conservative stockholder is still intractable, there is the export trade, now only in its beginnings, to be counted.

From exports of $150,000 in 1910 the total has risen to more than $33,000,000 the past year, excluding the immense numbers of war automobiles we are supplying to Europe. With any one of a dozen American companies exceeding in a month the entire year's output of the largest foreign factory, an optimistic maker visions a whole world supplied with American automobiles.

And the motor truck already promises to fulfil its expectations. Its growth thus far has exceeded even the corresponding period in the elder branch of the industry. In the department store, dairy, coal and express delivery business, the horse is in a fair way of soon being altogether eliminated. Cheaper to maintain, with a greater radius of action, capable of longer hours of service, and requiring but a small part of the same housing space, the motor truck is the horse's superior in every particular.

A big metropolitan dairy company well demonstrates this efficiency by doing with six ten-ton trucks the work for which it formerly employed a hundred horses. Instead of half-day service from its teams, the company by using two shifts of drivers, now gets twenty hours' work out of each of its motors. During the remaining four hours the trucks are overhauled and made ready for the next day's task. During the blizzard which last winter tied up all the horse and surface car transportation in New York City these trucks remained steadily in operation.

A Chicago coal dealer with one five-ton truck has been able to haul as high as two hundred and thirty-four tons of coal in a day. Thirty tons was his best day's record with a three-horse truck. By using motor cars an express company in another city has reduced the average cost of its parcel delivery from 11.68 cents each to the record figure of 3.16 cents. So economical and reliable has this form of delivery proved that one of the largest express companies of Philadelphia and one of the largest of the New York department stores have not a single horse in service.

The one hundred and ten motor cars of another New York store last year did no less than 75 per cent. of its delivery business, distributing in the city and surrounding country more than 3,375,000 packages. Horses are still used by the company, but in a lessened degree yearly, while their radius of action has constantly shortened. Formerly, to serve its suburban customers, the store sent its delivery wagon once a week by relays of horses to the outlying towns. Now, no horse vehicle goes above Sixtieth Street, and instead of weekly, the towns and their outlying districts are served daily from their delivery sub-stations, while increased territory has been brought under the store's influence.

In the estimation of the motor truck manufacturer one truck on the average can displace four horses. If he did not he would feel that he was making a poor product. Every horse is to him a direct challenge. And the census reminds him that there are in the country still some twenty-five millions of the animals.

Wherefore, if a motor maker gets the 'blues'— which conceivably may happen if the accustomed orders from Zanzibar, Siam, Terra del Fuego, or any other far corner of the earth fail to show up in the morning's mail; which may happen if some year his engineers fail to bring out a single new feature for his next model; which may happen if he is compelled to forego his annual custom of doubling the plant's capacity — in any one of these contingencies, I repeat, all the aforesaid manufacturer has to do to be blissfully happy is to think of those twenty-five million horses against which it is his duty to wage unceasing war.

X

EDISON LESSENS SUBMARINE PERIL

[*New York Times,* April 18, 1915. By permission.]

The announcement made last week that Thomas A. Edison had perfected a battery which is to be submitted to drastic tests in the newest of American submarine craft now building, the L-8, at the Portsmouth, N. H., Navy Yard, is the first authoritative information that the inventor is interested in solving the health and power problems of underwater fighting machines.

Much has been said connecting Mr. Edison with the submarine by officials in Washington and elsewhere, but until last week the inventor himself steadily declined to say a word. Now the announcement has been made by Miller Reese Hutchison, Mr. Edison's chief engineer and personal representative, that a superior style of submarine storage battery has been evolved.

So it may be said that Edison, the man opposed to war and its implements, has perfected a battery which will not only make the submarine habitable by preventing asphyxiation of a crew in the event of a prolonged enforced submersion, but will practically double the strategic efficiency of a submarine craft by providing it with a storage battery which will extend the undersea cruising range to 150 miles, the present radius being less than 100 miles.

Although the submarine has been steadily developed during the past fifteen years by countless inventions increasing its efficiency as a fighting machine, little good has been accomplished in making it habitable. Great sums have been spent to secure an adequate ventilation of the vessel when submerged. The heated air of the engine room and the exhaled air of the crew have been drawn off, filtered, oxygenated, cooled, and returned to the interior, but even this intricate process has failed to rid the boat of poisonous gases. Mr. Edison has attempted since 1910 to improve these conditions by getting at the exact source of trouble — the batteries.

Secretary Daniels of the navy gave the public the first intimation that Mr. Edison was lending his genius toward the submarine when he said last December, before the House Naval Committee:

Submarines have given us more trouble than anything else in the navy. Submarines are fickle — getting out of order any time — and we have yet to find a successful type of battery and engine. The lead casings around the battery are liable to be eaten out by the sulphuric acid in the batteries. Then the steel surrounding the lead is eaten through and the salt water from the submerging tanks gets in and chlorine gas is generated, which is very dangerous to the crew. . . . Mr. Edison proposes to use an alkaline solution in the cells of his battery and thus eliminate the danger to the lead casings and the steel partitions.

So imminent, indeed, is the danger to life from these lead-sulphuric acid batteries now in use in all our submarines that an ex-navy officer, when asked recently if he would volunteer his services in the event of hostilities, said:

'That would depend entirely upon the nature of the duty. If I could be reasonably sure either of complete annihilation or absolute safety, I would go. The probability of "passing out" does not worry me, but I do draw the line on becoming an invalid or a cripple — a burden to myself and family for the remainder of my days.'

No other problem of the submarine has so persistently asserted itself as the battery. If the battery is not in good working order, the submarine cannot be operated beneath the surface. The battery is the heart of a submarine, just as the periscope is the eye. When running on the surface the vessel is propelled by an ordinary gasoline engine, and running thus, with the conning tower open and the ventilators at work, air is forced into the boat, which, mixing with the gasoline, engenders the necessary combustion to run the ship. But when submerged the boat must necessarily be sealed. Access to the outside air is accordingly shut off, and the ordinary gasoline engine cannot be used. At this time, therefore, an entirely different source of power is called into use, namely, electric motors, deriving their energy from electric storage batteries.

Only last year the submarine E-2 was running from Newport News to New York when the commander smelled the familiar odor of chlorine. This gas is to the commander of a submarine exactly what fire-damp is to a miner. Instantly the commander gave orders for the tanks to be emptied, that the submarine might rise. Upon reaching the surface — and luckily enough the sea was calm — the hatches were opened and the crew ordered on deck. Despite the despatch of these relief measures the gas had got in its deadly work, and two of the crew had hemorrhages from the lungs. A call by wireless was sent out and the boat was towed back to port, where an examination of the ship's batteries revealed a typical condition of affairs.

In the type of battery employed on the E-2, a type employed on all our submarines, sheets of lead are suspended in sulphuric acid, within a hard rubber jar, hence the name lead-sulphuric acid batteries. These jars are in a compartment surrounded on all sides by the ship's main ballast tanks into which salt water is admitted and expelled. Once this sea water is mixed with sulphuric acid, hydrochloric acid fumes are formed. When the salt water finds its way to the interior of a lead storage battery and combines with the material on the lead plates, chlorine gas — one of the deadliest known gases — is generated.

This is exactly what had happened on the E-2. By some means, a slight crack, perhaps, or unusual strain, sulphuric acid had escaped from one of the jars, and, attacking the steel of the ballast tank, had eaten through, so that when the tank was filled the battery itself was flooded.

The dangers from chlorine gas are even yet more serious. Just before the submarine D-1 was going out for a cruise an inspection was held, which disclosed the fact that the acid had eaten its way to the gasoline tank and that the batteries were flooded with gasoline. Had the vessel been under way at the time it would have taken but a single spark to ignite the gasoline and cause an explosion.

All these dangers are at once done away with by Mr. Edison's new battery. It not only prevents asphyxiation, but it acts as a disinfectant because of the affinity of its solution — potash — for carbonic acid gas. There is enough potash solution in the batteries alone, says Mr. Hutchison, to purify the air for one hundred days or more.

It is a fact of peculiar significance that Mr. Edison's first visit aboard a warship occurred in December last at the Brooklyn Navy Yard, when he visited the battleship *New York* in company with Rear Admiral Fletcher and Secretary Daniels. At this particular time one of the inventor's new batteries was being put to a severe test in the basement of the Administration Building. The battery was placed on a specially designed cradle and was rocked to and fro, in imitation of the rolling motion of a submarine. When Mr. Edison saw the battery going through its rolling motions he turned to the man in charge of the test.

'Make her rock faster!' he shouted. 'Give her a big tip. Bump her. Do anything you want with her. I've tried everything and you can't faze her!'

Shortly thereafter Secretary Daniels announced from Washington that Mr. Edison was busy with his new battery for the submarine.

Before the inventor allowed his battery to be sent to the navy yard, or before he even considered the manufacture of it, he sent it to Mr. Bachmann, the General Superintendent of the laboratories, with these instructions:

1. Mount cell in cage of apparatus. No cushioning whatsoever between the cell and cage. Run the apparatus continuously until the cell has been raised three quarters of an inch and dropped on a solid block two million times.

2. There must be no sediment in the bottom of the can after this test and the cell must have as great electrical capacity as before.

3. Secure cell to truck and project truck against a brick or stone abutment five hundred times at a speed of fifteen miles an hour at moment of impact.

His battery met these tests as easily as it met the one later on at the navy yard. The navy officials found out, as did the inventor himself, that 'you can't faze her.'

But to go back still further. The new submarine storage battery is an adaptation of the commercial type of Edison battery now in world-wide use. It cost him seven years of labor and the expenditure of over $2,000,000 to perfect this battery. He started with the idea well fixed in mind that nature could certainly afford one more reaction for the production of electric current without the use of dangerous acids. The enormous, almost unsurmountable, detail which had to be carried through is almost beyond belief. Over 50,000 separate experiments were made, and the results of each carefully tabulated and plotted as curves before the final battery was evolved. The curve sheets alone, if placed end to end, would be sixteen miles long, or they would cover two acres of ground.

After innumerable experiments he at last struck upon a reaction, which, although it appeared weak at the beginning, was very promising. This one reaction was followed with most intense persistency for fully three years, before even the first unimproved type of nickel-iron-alkaline battery was produced. Any storage battery consists of a positive and a negative plate submerged in a jar in a liquid known as the electrolyte. Its value is dependent upon the fact that the elements of this combination are changed chemically by passing a current through them, but in such a way that the attempts of nature to bring back these elements to their original condition produces electricity.

The greater the surface presented by the plates, the greater the current produced. The positive plate of the Edison cell is composed of vertical rows of thin, perforated steel tubes, filled with nickel hydrate, these tubes being supported by a very light steel frame. The electrolyte is a solution of potash. At this point it can be said that the Edison battery differs from all other batteries; in fact, it is the only battery the elements of which are not attacked by the solution in which they are submerged when left standing in a charged or discharged condition for an indefinite period.

The battery, stated simply and concisely, is composed of but four things — nickel, iron oxide, and steel, in a solution of potash — and surprising as it may seem, the potash is a preservative of all the elements entering into the combination; thus the battery elements do not destroy each other. Sulphuric acid attacks steel; potash preserves it. The acid battery is a generator of noxious and, at times, deadly fumes. The Edison battery is fumeproof, gasproof — a hermetically sealed containing can making it so. Even if the potash gases could escape they would do no harm. Potash is an excellent disinfectant. Mr. Edison has explained this as follows:

When a storage battery is charged, hydrogen gas forms on the negative plates and oxygen gas on the positives. These gases, in the form of minute bubbles, rise to the surface of the solution and, being lighter than air, float away. Being formed in and subsequently passing through the electrolytes these minute bubbles convey each a small quantity of whatever chemical the solution is composed of; if they are formed in a lead-sulphuric acid type battery, sulphuric acid is the cargo; if in an Edison battery, potash.

When these bubbles rise from the surface of the electrolyte and come into contact with an object they either remain until evaporation disintegrates them and deposits their charge of acid or alkali, or they burst and accomplish the same result. The gas vent of a lead type cell is open and the bubbles may therefore pass through freely and away. The vent of the Edison cell is a check valve. To get out, the gases must lift this valve by pressure formed within the otherwise hermetically sealed containing can. If these potash gases were allowed to get out they would do no harm, for they purify the air.

No better proof of the healthfulness of the Edison battery is afforded than at the West Orange works, where several thousand cells are charged and recharged with hundreds of workmen around them. The executive offices of the plant, and in fact, Mr. Edison's library, are but a few yards from the storage battery building. Not so with lead-sulphuric acid batteries, however. They are manufactured as far away from the main works as possible, and powerful electric fans are used to remove the fumes.

Navy specifications covering the installation of lead-acid batteries stipulate lead-lined rooms to retain them, and lead-lined ventilating pipes with specially constructed and installed motors to operate the exhaust fans. In specifications covering the installation of Edison's new battery no mention need be made of lead-lined rooms or exhaust fans.

Of all fears which beset the submarine volunteer chlorine gas is the greatest. Five months after an inhalation of this deadly gas a cold may develop into pneumonia; the lungs seldom gain their previous healthy condition. If Mr. Edison's battery 'comes up to scratch,' as they say in the navy, it will solve those two great problems of life and power which, up to the present time, have made the submergible as dangerous in peace as in war, and as perilous to its crew as to its enemy. It will not only stimulate enlistment, but it will make American underwater craft the safest and most powerful fighting unit in the world.

Several weeks ago the electrical class of the Brooklyn Navy Yard visited Mr. Edison's plant. During their visit he gave them a talk on his new battery.

'Keep it clean, and give it water,' said he, 'and at the end of four years it will give its full capacity.'

'Four years?' they asked in wonder.

'Yes,' replied Mr. Edison, 'four years, eight years; it will outwear the submarine itself.'

XI

THE WRIGHT BROTHERS AËROPLANE

ORVILLE AND WILBUR WRIGHT

[*Century Magazine,* September, 1908.
By permission.]

Though the subject of aërial navigation is generally considered new, it has occupied the minds of men more or less from the earliest ages. Our personal interest in it dates from our childhood days. Late in the autumn of 1878, our father came into the house one evening with some object partly concealed in his hands, and before we could see what it was, he tossed it into the air. Instead of falling to the floor, as we expected, it flew across the room till it struck the ceiling, where it fluttered awhile, and finally sank to the floor. It was a little toy, known to scientists as a 'hélicoptère,' but which we, with sublime disregard for science, at once dubbed a 'bat.' It was a light frame of cork and bamboo, covered with paper, which formed two screws, driven in opposite directions by rubber bands under torsion. A toy so delicate lasted only a short time in the hands of small boys, but its memory was abiding.

Several years later we began building these hélicoptères for ourselves, making each one larger than that preceding. But, to our astonishment, we found that the larger the 'bat,' the less it flew. We did not know that a machine having only twice the linear dimensions of another would require eight times the power. We finally became discouraged, and returned to kite-flying, a sport to which we had devoted so much attention that we were regarded as experts. But as we became older, we had to give up this fascinating sport as unbecoming to boys of our ages.

It was not till the news of the sad death of Lilienthal reached America in the summer of 1896 that we again gave more than passing attention to the subject of flying. We then studied with great interest Chanute's *Progress in Flying Machines,* Langley's *Experiments in Aërodynamics,* the *Aëronautical Annuals* of 1905, 1906, and 1907, and several pamphlets published by the Smithsonian Institution, especially articles by Lilienthal and extracts from Mouillard's *Empire of the Air.* The larger works gave us a good understanding of the nature of the flying problem, and the difficulties in past attempts to solve it, while Mouillard and Lilienthal, the great missionaries of the flying cause, infected us with their own unquenchable enthusiasm, and transformed idle curiosity into the active zeal of workers.

In the field of aviation there were two 'schools. The first, represented by such men as Professor Langley and Sir Hiram Maxim, gave chief attention to power flight; the second, represented by Lilienthal, Mouillard, and Chanute, to soaring flight. Our sympathies were with the latter school, partly from impatience at the wasteful extravagance of mounting delicate and costly machinery on wings which no one knew how to manage, and partly, no doubt, from the extraordinary charm and enthusiasm with which the apostles of soaring flight set forth the beauties of sailing through the air on fixed wings, deriving the motive power from the wind itself.

The balancing of a flyer may seem, at first thought, to be a very simple matter, yet almost every experimenter had found in this the one point which he could not satisfactorily master. Many different methods were tried. Some experimenters placed the center of gravity far below the wings, in the belief that the weight would naturally seek to remain at the lowest point. It was true, that, like the pendulum, it tended to seek the lowest point; but also, like the pendulum, it tended to oscillate in a manner destructive of all stability. A more satisfactory system, especially for lateral balance, was that of arranging the wings in the shape of a broad **V**, to form a dihedral angle, with the center low and the wing-tips elevated. In theory this was an automatic system, but in practice it had two serious defects: first, it tended to keep the machine oscillating; and, second, its usefulness was restricted to calm air.

In a slightly modified form the same system was applied to the fore-and-aft balance. The main aëroplane was set at a positive angle, and a horizontal tail at a negative angle, while the center of gravity was placed far forward. As in the case of lateral control, there was a tendency to constant undulation, and the very forces which caused a restoration of balance in calms, caused a disturbance of the balance in winds. Notwithstanding the known limitations of this principle, it had been embodied in almost every prominent flying-machine which had been built.

After considering the practical effect of the dihedral principle, we reached the conclusion that a flyer founded upon it might be of interest from a scientific point of view, but could be of no value in a practical way. We therefore resolved to try a fundamentally different principle. We would arrange the machine so that it would not tend to right itself. We would make it as inert as possible to the effects of change of direction or speed, and thus reduce the effects of wind-gusts to a minimum. We would do this in the fore-and-aft stability by giving the aëroplanes a peculiar shape; and in the lateral balance, by arching the surfaces from tip to tip, just the reverse of what our predecessors had done. Then by some suitable contrivance, actuated by the operator, forces should be brought into play to regulate the balance.

Lilienthal and Chanute had guided and balanced their machines by shifting the weight of the operator's body. But this method seemed to us incapable of expansion to meet large conditions, because the weight to be moved and the distance of possible motion were limited, while the disturbing forces steadily increased, both with wing area and with wind velocity. In order to meet the needs of large machines, we wished to employ some system whereby the operator could vary at will the inclination of different parts of the wings, and thus obtain from the wind forces to restore the balance which the wind itself had disturbed. This could easily be done by using wings capable of being warped, and by supplementary adjustable surfaces in the shape of rudders. As the forces obtainable for control would necessarily increase in the same ratio as the disturbing forces, the method seemed capable of expansion to an almost unlimited extent. A happy device was discovered whereby the apparently rigid system of superposed surfaces, invented by Wenham, and improved by Stringfellow and Chanute, could be warped in a most unexpected way, so that the aëroplanes could be presented on the right and left sides at different angles to the wind. This, with an adjustable, horizontal front rudder, formed the main feature of our first glider.

The period from 1885 to 1900 was one of unexampled activity in aëronautics, and for a time there was high hope that the age of flying was at hand. But Maxim, after spending $100,000, abandoned the work; the Ader machine, built at the expense of the French Government, was a failure; Lilienthal and Pilcher were killed in experiments; and Chanute and many others, from one cause or another, had relaxed their efforts, though it subsequently became known that Professor Langley was still secretly at work on a machine for the United States Government. The public, discouraged by the failures and tragedies just witnessed, considered flight beyond the reach of man, and classed its adherents with the inventors of perpetual motion.

We began our active experiments at the close of this period, in October, 1900, at Kitty Hawk, North Carolina. Our machine was designed to be flown as a kite, with a man on board, in winds of from fifteen to twenty miles an hour. But, upon trial, it was found that much stronger winds were required to lift it. Suitable winds not being plentiful, we found it necessary, in order to test the new balancing system, to fly the machine as a kite without a man on board, operating the levers through cords from the ground. This did not give the practice anticipated, but it inspired confidence in the new system of balance.

In the summer of 1901 we became personally acquainted with Mr. Chanute. When he learned that we were interested in flying as a sport, and not with any expectation of recovering the money we were expending on it, he gave us much encouragement. At our invitation, he spent several weeks with us at our camp at Kill Devil Hill, four miles south of Kitty Hawk, during our experiments of that and the two succeeding years. He also witnessed one flight of the power machine near Dayton, Ohio, in October, 1904.

The machine of 1901 was built with the shape of surface used by Lilienthal, curved from front to rear like the segment of a parabola, with a curvature 1/12 the depth of its cord; but to make doubly sure that it would have sufficient lifting capacity when flown as a kite in fifteen- or twenty-mile winds, we increased the area from 165 square feet, used in 1900, to 308 square feet — a size much larger than Lilienthal, Pilcher, or Chanute had deemed safe. Upon trial, however, the lifting capacity again fell very far short of calculation, so that the idea of securing practice while flying as a kite, had to be abandoned. Mr. Chanute, who witnessed the experiments, told us that the trouble was not due to poor construction of the machine. We saw only one other explanation — that the tables of air-pressures in general use were incorrect.

We then turned to gliding — coasting down hill on the air — as the only method of getting the desired practice in balancing a machine. After a few minutes' practice we were able to make glides of over 300 feet, and in a few days were safely operating in twenty-seven-mile[1] winds. In these experiments we met with several unexpected phenomena. We found that, contrary to the teachings of the books, the center of pressure on a curved surface traveled backward when the surface was inclined, at small angles, more and more edgewise to the wind. We also discovered

[1] The gliding flights were all made against the wind. The difficulty in high winds is in maintaining balance, not in traveling against the wind.

that in free flight, when the wing on one side of the machine was presented to the wind at a greater angle than the one on the other side, the wing with the greater angle descended, and the machine turned in a direction just the reverse of what we were led to expect when flying the machine as a kite. The larger angle gave more resistance to forward motion, and reduced the speed of the wing on that side. The decrease in speed more than counterbalanced the effect of the larger angle. The addition of a fixed vertical vane in the rear increased the trouble, and made the machine absolutely dangerous. It was some time before a remedy was discovered. This consisted of movable rudders working in conjunction with the twisting of the wings. The details of this arrangement are given in our patent specifications, published several years ago.

The experiments of 1901 were far from encouraging. Although Mr. Chanute assured us that, both in control and in weight carried per horse-power, the results obtained were better than those of any of our predecessors, yet we saw that the calculations upon which all flying-machines had been based were unreliable, and that all were simply groping in the dark. Having set out with absolute faith in the existing scientific data, we were driven to doubt one thing after another, till finally, after two years of experiment, we cast it all aside, and decided to rely entirely upon our own investigations. Truth and error were everywhere so intimately mixed as to be undistinguishable. Nevertheless, the time expended in preliminary study of books was not misspent, for they gave us a good general understanding of the subject, and enabled us at the outset to avoid effort in many directions in which results would have been hopeless.

The standard for measurements of wind-pressures is the force produced by a current of air of one mile per hour velocity striking square against a plane of one square-foot area. The practical difficulties of obtaining an exact measurement of this force have been great. The measurements by different recognized authorities vary 50 per cent. When this simplest of measurements presents so great difficulties, what shall be said of the troubles encountered by those who attempt to find the pressure at each angle as the plane is inclined more and more edgewise to the wind? In the eighteenth century the French Academy prepared tables giving such information, and at a later date the Aëronautical Society of Great Britain made similar experiments. Many persons likewise published measurements and formulas; but the results were so discordant that Professor Langley undertook a new series of measurements, the results of which form the basis of his celebrated work, *Experiments in Aërodynamics*. Yet a critical examination of the data upon which he based his conclusions as to the pressures at small angles shows results so various as to make many of his conclusions little better than guess-work.

To work intelligently, one needs to know the effects of a multitude of variations that could be incorporated in the surfaces of flying-machines. The pressures on squares are different from those on rectangles, circles, triangles, or ellipses; arched surfaces differ from planes, and vary among themselves according to the depth of curvature; true arcs differ from parabolas, and the latter differ among themselves; thick surfaces differ from thin, and surfaces thicker in one place than another vary in pressure when the positions of maximum thickness are different; some surfaces are most efficient at one angle, others at other angles. The shape of the edge also makes a difference, so that thousands of combinations are possible in so simple a thing as a wing.

We had taken up aëronautics merely as a sport. We reluctantly entered upon the scientific side of it. But we soon found the work so fascinating that we were drawn into it deeper and deeper. Two testing-machines were built, which we believed would avoid the errors to which the measurements of others had been subject. After making preliminary measurements on a great number of different-shaped surfaces, to secure a general understanding of the subject, we began systematic measurements of standard surfaces, so varied in design as to bring out the underlying causes of differences noted in their pressures. Measurements were tabulated on nearly fifty of these at all angles from zero to 45 degrees, at intervals of 2½ degrees. Measurements were also secured showing the effects on each other when surfaces are superposed, or when they follow one another.

Some strange results were obtained. One surface, with a heavy roll at the front edge, showed the same lift for all angles from 7½ to 45 degrees. A square plane, contrary to the measurements of all our predecessors, gave a greater pressure at 30 degrees than at 45 degrees. This seemed so anomalous that we were almost ready to doubt our own measurements, when a simple test was suggested. A weather-vane, with two planes attached to the pointer at an angle of 80 degrees with each other, was made. According to our tables, such a vane would be in unstable equilibrium when pointing directly into the wind; for if by chance the wind should happen to strike one plane at 39 degrees and the other at 41 degrees, the plane with the smaller angle would have the greater pressure, and the pointer would be turned still farther out of the course of the wind until the two vanes again secured equal pressures, which would be at approximately 30 and 50 degrees. But the vane performed in this very manner. Further corroboration of the tables was obtained in experiments with a new glider at Kill Devil Hill the next season.

In September and October, 1902, nearly one thousand gliding flights were made, several of which covered distances of over 600 feet. Some, made against a wind of thirty-six miles an hour, gave proof of the effectiveness of the devices for control. With this machine, in the autumn of 1903, we made a number of flights in which we remained in the air for over a minute, often soaring for a considerable time in one spot, without any descent at all. Little wonder that our unscientific assistant should think the only thing needed to keep it indefinitely in the air would be a coat of feathers to make it light!

With accurate data for making calculations, and a system of balance effective in winds as well as in calms, we were now in a position, we thought, to build a successful power-flyer. The first designs provided for a total weight of 600 pounds, including the operator and an eight horse-power motor. But, upon completion, the motor gave more power than had been estimated, and this allowed 150 pounds to be added for strengthening the wings and other parts.

Our tables made the designing of the wings an easy matter; and as screw-propellers are simply wings traveling in a

9678

spiral course, we anticipated no trouble from this source. We had thought of getting the theory of the screw-propeller from the marine engineers, and then, by applying our tables of air-pressures to their formulas of designing air-propellers suitable for our purpose. But so far as we could learn, the marine engineers possessed only empirical formulas, and the exact action of the screw-propeller, after a century of use, was still very obscure. As we were not in a position to undertake a long series of practical experiments to discover a propeller suitable for our machine, it seemed necessary to obtain such a thorough understanding of the theory of its reactions as would enable us to design them from calculation alone. What at first seemed a simple problem became more complex the longer we studied it. With the machine moving forward, the air flying backward, the propellers turning sidewise, and nothing standing still, it seemed impossible to find a starting-point from which to trace the various simultaneous reactions. Contemplation of it was confusing. After long arguments, we often found ourselves in the ludicrous position of each having been converted to the other's side, with no more agreement than when the discussion began.

It was not till several months had passed, and every phase of the problem had been thrashed over and over, that the various reactions began to untangle themselves. When once a clear understanding had been obtained, there was no difficulty in designing suitable propellers, with proper diameter, pitch, and area of blade, to meet the requirements of the flyer. High efficiency in a screw-propeller is not dependent upon any particular or peculiar shape, and there is no such thing as a 'best' screw. A propeller giving a high dynamic efficiency when used upon one machine, may be almost worthless when used upon another. The propeller should in every case be designed to meet the particular conditions of the machine to which it is to be applied. Our first propellers, built entirely from calculation, gave in useful work 66 per cent. of the power expended. This was about one third more than had been secured by Maxim or Langley.

The first flights with the power-machine were made on the 17th of December, 1903. Only five persons besides ourselves were present. These were Messrs. John T. Daniels, W. S. Dough, and A. D. Etheridge of the Kill Devil Life Saving Station; Mr. W. C. Brinkley of Manteo, and Mr. John Ward of Naghead. Although a general invitation had been extended to the people living within five or six miles, not many were willing to face the rigors of a cold December wind in order to see, as they no doubt thought, another flying-machine *not* fly. The first flight lasted only twelve seconds, a flight very modest compared with that of birds, but it was, nevertheless, the first in the history of the world in which a machine carrying a man had raised itself by its own power into the air in free flight, had sailed forward on a level course without reduction of speed, and had finally landed without being wrecked. The second and third flights were a little longer, and the fourth lasted fifty-nine seconds, covering a distance of 852 feet over the ground against a twenty-mile wind.

After the last flight, the machine was carried back to camp and set down in what was thought to be a safe place. But a few minutes later, while we were engaged in conversation about the flights, a sudden gust of wind struck the machine, and started to turn it over. All made a rush to stop it, but we were too late. Mr. Daniels, a giant in stature and strength, was lifted off his feet, and falling inside, between the surfaces, was shaken about like a rattle in a box as the machine rolled over and over. He finally fell out upon the sand with nothing worse than painful bruises, but the damage to the machine caused a discontinuance of experiments.

In the spring of 1904, through the kindness of Mr. Torrence Huffman of Dayton, Ohio, we were permitted to erect a shed, and to continue experiments, on what is known as the Huffman Prairie, at Simms Station, eight miles east of Dayton. The new machine was heavier and stronger, but similar to the one flown at Kill Devil Hill. When it was ready for its first trial, every newspaper in Dayton was notified, and about a dozen representatives of the press were present. Our only request was that no pictures be taken, and that the reports be unsensational, so as not to attract crowds to our experiment-grounds. There were probably fifty persons altogether on the ground. When preparations had been completed, a wind of only three or four miles was blowing,— insufficient for starting on so short a track,— but since many had come a long way to see the machine in action, an attempt was made. To add to the other difficulty, the engine refused to work properly. The machine, after running the length of the track, slid off the end without rising into the air at all. Several of the newspaper men returned the next day, but were again disappointed. The engine performed badly, and after a glide of only sixty feet, the machine came to the ground. Further trial was postponed till the motor could be put in better running condition. The reporters had now, no doubt, lost confidence in the machine, though their reports, in kindness, concealed it. Later, when they heard that we were making flights of several minutes' duration, knowing that longer flights had been made with airships, and not knowing any essential difference between air-ships and flying-machines, they were but little interested.

We had not been flying long in 1904 before we found that the problem of equilibrium had not as yet been entirely solved. Sometimes, in making a circle, the machine would turn over sidewise despite anything the operator could do, although, under the same conditions in ordinary straight flight, it could have been righted in an instant. In one flight, in 1905, while circling around a honey locust-tree at a height of about fifty feet, the machine suddenly began to turn up on one wing, and took a course toward the tree. The operator, not relishing the idea of landing in a thorn-tree, attempted to reach the ground. The left wing, however, struck the tree at a height of ten or twelve feet from the ground, and carried away several branches; but the flight, which had already covered a distance of six miles, was continued to the starting-point.

The causes of these troubles — too technical for explanation here — were not entirely overcome till the end of September, 1905. The flights then rapidly increased in length, till experiments were discontinued after the 5th of October, on account of the number of people attracted to the field. Although made on a ground open on every side, and bordered on two sides by much traveled thoroughfares, with electric cars passing every hour, and seen by all the people living in the neighborhood for miles around, and by several hundred others, yet these flights have been made by some newspapers the subject of a great 'mystery.'

A practical flyer having been finally realized, we spent the years 1906 and 1907 in constructing new machines and in business negotiations. It was not till May of this year that experiments (discontinued in October, 1905) were resumed at Kill Devil Hill, North Carolina. The recent flights were made to test the ability of our machine to meet the requirements of a contract with the United States Government to furnish a flyer capable of carrying two men and sufficient fuel supplies for a flight of 125 miles, with a speed of forty miles an hour. The machine used in these tests was the same one with which the flights were made at Simms Station in 1905, though several changes had been made to meet present requirements. The operator assumed a sitting position, instead of lying prone, as in 1905, and a seat was added for a passenger. A larger motor was installed, and radiators and gasoline reservoirs of larger capacity replaced those previously used. No attempt was made to make high or long flights.

In order to show the general reader the way in which the machine operates, let us fancy ourselves ready for the start. The machine is placed upon a single rail track facing the wind, and is securely fastened with a cable. The engine is put in motion, and the propellers in the rear whir. You take your seat at the center of the machine beside the operator. He slips the cable, and you shoot forward. An assistant who has been holding the machine in balance on the rail, starts forward with you, but before you have gone fifty feet the speed is too great for him, and he lets go. Before reaching the end of the track the operator moves the front rudder, and the machine lifts from the rail like a kite supported by the pressure of the air underneath it. The ground under you is at first a perfect blur, but as you rise the objects become clearer. At a height of one hundred feet you feel hardly any motion at all, except for the wind which strikes your face. If you did not take the precaution to fasten your hat before starting, you have probably lost it by this time. The operator moves a lever: the right wing rises, and the machine swings about to the left. You make a very short turn, yet you do not feel the sensation of being thrown from your seat, so often experienced in automobile and railway travel. You find yourself facing toward the point from which you started. The objects on the ground now seem to be moving at much higher speed, though you perceive no change in the pressure of the wind on your face. You know then that you are traveling with the wind. When you near the starting-point, the operator stops the motor while still high in the air. The machine coasts down at an oblique angle to the ground, and after sliding fifty or a hundred feet comes to rest. Although the machine often lands when traveling at a speed of a mile a minute, you feel no shock whatever, and cannot, in fact, tell the exact moment at which it first touched the ground. The motor close beside you kept up an almost deafening roar during the whole flight, yet in your excitement, you did not notice it till it stopped!

Our experiments have been conducted entirely at our own expense. In the beginning we had no thought of recovering what we were expending, which was not great, and was limited to what we could afford for recreation. Later, when a successful flight had been made with a motor, we gave up the business in which we were engaged, to devote our entire time and capital to the development of a machine for practical uses. As soon as our condition is such that constant attention to business is not required, we expect to prepare for publication the results of our laboratory experiments, which alone made an early solution of the flying problem possible.

XII

THE MIRACLE OF THE MOVIE

W. P. LAWSON

[*Harper's Weekly*, January 2, 1915. By permission of author and publisher.]

A canny citizen annoyed by prate of the power and majesty of the law remarked once that if they 'd only let him make the songs of the people he should worry, or words to that effect. If he were with us now it is probable that he would stand back of his statement still — with the substitution of 'movies' for 'songs.' And he would not be far wrong. For however you figure it there is no dodging the fact that while laws are always in the long run the product of public opinion, public opinion itself is created by various humble but effective influences of which the movie, as we know it to-day, is invariably 'among those present.' Excepting the home, the press, and the schoolroom the movie has been called the most potent existing factor in the shaping of the national mind and morals.

For the last five and a half years the moral incidence of the motion picture has been guided by the National Board of Censorship, an organization founded upon a voluntary coöperative agreement between film manufacturers and the People's Institute of New York. The continued effectiveness of the arrangement, which has been more than once held up as a gratifying example of a great business working with real representatives of the people to the people's undoubted advantage, is threatened by the activities of various state and city boards of censors created under the police power of the communities in which they exist.

In *Harper's Weekly* for December nineteenth the situation was summed up editorially and the desirability of an immediate and uncompromising expression of public opinion on the subject indicated. It was stated that a test case would come up in Ohio during the 1915 session of the Ohio Legislature, when the repeal of the existing law providing for a state board of censors is voted upon.

Perhaps the greatest obstacle in the way of fully realizing the true importance of the film story as a social force and the consequent need of an adequate and uniform system of regulation is the overnight, mushroom growth of the industry. Any one old enough to vote is old enough to remember when the movie was not. As a business we may say that the film is scarcely adolescent; fourteen going on fifteen might be termed its age.

This does not mean that men were not working on the problem for years before this. Since 1829, when Ferdinand Pleateau proudly exhibited his Phenokistoscope (it's a safe bet he had no publicity or advertising manager) to an admiring world inventors have amused themselves in spare moments by experimenting with the physiological phenomenon called 'the persistence of human vision.' The fact that the retina of the eye has the property of retaining for the tenth of a second the impression of an image after the object which has produced it has disappeared makes it evident that when an image is placed before our eyes ten times in a second the idea of discontinuity is lost and the images appear to be in continual evidence. That was the fundamental principle of the whole business. And the pleasant dalliance of inventors with its various phenomena was for a long time looked upon as a mere scientific pastime unworthy the notice of practical men.

Even when in 1893 Edison exhibited his Kinetograph and for the first time in history demonstrated the possibility of a commercial exploitation of the principle, capital did not get over-excited. And while individuals and small companies gradually took up the idea and crude picture shows held in barns and lofts and old stores became fairly popular, it was not until 1905 that some inkling of the possibilities of the new business filtered through the brains of more than a few men. And not until 1907, when Edison established his patents and licensed a number of other companies, did the industry break into the rapid forward rush that is as yet unexhausted and that has made it the marvel of the new century.

The development of the movie during the past eight years is a phenomenon which should impel ancient Aladdin — if he knows about it — to turn over in his grave. It is without parallel or comparison. It would challenge the elasticity of the imagination were there not the facts to chain us to actuality. In 1914, up to the beginning of December, American manufacturers have turned out no less than ten thousand separate reels of negative film from each of which reels thirty-five 'positive' copies, on an average, are made. The standard reel is 1000 feet long, which makes 360,000,000 feet of film all told, including both the originals and copies! About 68,000 miles of motion pictures — enough to go round the globe a little less than three times. In one year less a month!

The cost of producing the ordinary sort of originals is at least $2 a foot. This means $20,000,000 spent in making the negative reels alone. The 350,000,000 of copies cost four cents a foot, which totals $17,000,000 for these. Altogether $37,000,000 spent in the manufacture of films in eleven months. Some figures! Yes, and they are not all. For this estimate does not take into account the special feature projects recently become an important factor in the film industry, on a single one of which may be spent, as in the case of a much advertised seven reel drama now playing, as high as $300,000.

It is estimated that there are to-day between seventeen and eighteen thousand motion picture theaters in the United States, to which more than ten million people go daily. A commission appointed by the Mayor of Cleveland in 1913 reported that one-sixth of the population of that city went to movie shows at least once a day. During the summer months of 1914 the National Board of Censorship estimated that in New York City between 850,000 and 900,000 people — one-seventh of the total population — attended the motion picture theaters daily. Admission receipts total in 1914 (to December first) approximately $319,000,000 for the movie theaters of the country.

Over $500,000,000 of actual capital has been invested in the business of making and exhibiting films in the United States. Two hundred and fifty thousand employees find in it a means of livelihood. Including all its ramifications and affiliations the industry is called the fifth largest in the land, and the total value of the property and good will of it all is practically inestimable.

The best known actors and actresses and the most famous writers serve beneath its standard. It ransacks the corners of the earth for sensations, it digs into the grave of the buried past, it searches every nook and cranny of life for new and interesting material. Its scope is as broad as the interests and occupations of mankind. Nature, art, history, science, industry, education, sociology — no subject is too great or too small, too simple or too abstruse to be caught and fixed upon the greedy screen.

Is it a flower shown growing, or the clash and roar of fighting armies, or a diver on the ocean's bed, or an aëroplane in the clouds, or a giant crane depicted in action to catch the trade of foreign buyers, or the cholera germ isolated and shown, or the delicate finger movements of some world-famous surgeon performing an operation that will be studied by students around the world! All men and all matter pays tribute to the new genius.

In the movie game all the world's a stage and a considerable part of the world is a daily audience. Is it any wonder that this ubiquitous visitor to all homes and all minds and all hearts should be credited by the discerning with a vast actual and potential power for good or evil, with a supreme influence upon public sentiment and public morality?

That much is now generally conceded. But just how vital and far-reaching this power is and in exactly what manner it may ultimately best be directed toward constructive social ends, are things more difficult to agree upon. Even the National Board of Censorship, which has been working on the subject for nearly six years, admits that it is only on the threshold of its ideal of analyzing the character and extent of the movie's influence in all its phases and formulating permanent standards for the constructive direction of this force.

'We have always been tolerant in censoring films,' said a member of the board. 'We reject or cut only when we are certain that the effect of a picture would be to offend public morality. The picture always gets the benefit of the doubt. In judging films we want first of all to be sure of our ground. Yet all the time we are working on the broader analytical and constructive aspects of our problem. We are adding yearly to our store of knowledge in the philosophy of criticism. We are beginning to appreciate some of the more subtle effects of the different classes of motion pictures on the individual.

'I'll tell you an incident that came under my notice not long ago, because it seems to me typical of a certain kind of constructive spiritual influence of the film whose importance we are just beginning to appreciate. I was sitting in a motion picture theater in Toledo, Ohio, waiting for the first reel of *Les Miserables* to begin. I noticed two couples directly in front of me, one a middle aged man and his wife talking about their neighbors, the other a boy and girl talking about themselves. They would have been flirting, I suppose, except that the ring on the girl's third finger which both examined now and again with much interest showed that their emotions had been standardized, so to

speak. So I did not frown disapproval as I might have otherwise.

'"Who is this Jean Valjean?" said the man after a pause.

'"I don't know, John," said his wife, "but Sarah told me it was a swell release."

'What the younger couple said need not be repeated. Suddenly the play began. The great dream of Victor Hugo lived again before their eyes. They were caught up in the sweeping movement of the story and carried along like leaves on the wind by the emotions the living shadows before them so vividly delineated.

'The old bishop forgave the felon and let him keep the stolen silver. The eyes of the four in front of me were wet. They entered the death chamber of Fantine with Father Madaline. They watched poor Cosette struggling with her load of water. They helped Father Madaline carry the little drudge from the home of the Thenadiers. Their hearts were wrung with pity as the pathos of Jean Valjean's life grew. Yet as the last reel ended the vision of Jean's real development, the ultimate glory of his life, shone from their faces and mirrored its own high colors in their eyes. The story got across.

'"I gotta do more reading," mumbled John as he groped for his hat. "I would n't have missed this — not for a coupla bucks!"

'The younger couple said nothing as they left. The girl hid her sober, tear streaked face in her muff. And on the boy's face, as he walked out with head erect, was an expression of faint awe, while his chin had a resolute tilt that spoke well for the fitness of his spirit at that moment.

'Now there is nothing here tangible, nothing that you can measure and weigh any more than you can measure emotion or weigh the breath of life. But if we could follow the thought planted in the minds of the four that night during its germination and development we might discover that its eventual results would prove extremely tangible. That is the sort of influence we know as yet very little about but which I believe in time we will understand and direct for ethical ends. We can deal now in practice with only the more obvious effects of the motion picture in the field of morality, but our standards are dynamic and we are trying all the time to learn more and do more.'

That is an interesting statement. It suggests a scope for the influence of the movie wider than is generally allowed. As to the more common cases of the direct and apparent sort, every one can cite any number from his own experience and observation to show how real and pervasive a thing is the movie's power as a moral agent. Those who are educated by the movies are educated through their hearts and through their sense impressions, and that sort of education sticks. Every person in an audience has paid admission and for that reason gives his attention willingly. He knows he is not to be lectured for his soul's good, or patronized in any way. He knows that the movie seeks his suffrage and lives or dies by the motion of his imperial thumb. Therefore he gives it his confidence and opens the windows of his mind. And what the movie says sinks in.

We know that the education dispensed by the movies directly or through suggestion may be of a sort the public considers moral or immoral. The function of the censor is to make certain, in so far as he can, that films which foster morality — or at least those which do not tend to immorality — are the only kind of films to appear on the screen. A delicate and difficult task, truly, and one which may well be the subject of study and of standardization of ideals and of policy. And a task for the very best and ablest men and women the nation boasts — provided they can be prevailed upon to undertake it.

B.   NARRATIVE ARTICLES

The narrative article seeks above all else to give a vivid, accurate, and interesting account of a series of incidents. It is frequently set off by a background and it often involves a personality as its motive force. Hence the narrative article usually includes a variable amount of description of places and persons, and by this combination it gains in interest and universality of appeal. The ordinary 'newspaper story' has been omitted from consideration here because its technique has become so specialised as to be unsuitable for general narrative writing. The mechanical restrictions of the average newspaper 'lead' are unnecessary in the freer writing of the longer narrative article, though both strive to answer as far as possible the five fundamental questions involved in this type of article: Who? What? Where? When? and Why?

The chief structural qualities which the narrative article should possess are: (1) Orderly sequence in the successive steps of the series of actions or incidents; this relation may be either causal, where one step depends upon a required antecedent condition or upon a state of mind, or else mechanical, where the article consists largely of a coherent account of steps in a process already completely determined. (2) Unity of the subject as a whole, which meets the Aristotelian demand that there be a beginning in which the action of the narrative is really started, a middle in which the action is developed and consistently carried on, and an end in which the various actions involved in the narration are brought to a satisfactory and complete conclusion.

The qualities of treatment and style which the narrative article demands are: (1) Interest arising partly from the nature of the actions related and partly from the interest which the writer himself takes in his subject, as well as from the professional desire to arouse interest, enthusiasm, or emotion in as many readers as possible. (2) Fidelity to fact, which allows no accessible source of information to go unregarded, and which permits no slovenliness of statement and no unjustified implication to pass uncensored, much less any actual misstatement of fact knowingly to be made. (3) Craftsmanship in method, which comes partly through constant practice and continuous effort, and partly from the careful and intelligent analysis of the masterpieces of those who have been conspicuously successful in writing stories that are compelling in interest, trustworthy in every detail, and noteworthy examples of the writer's craft.

In the selections which follow the student will find a descriptive narrative of the taking of Louvain written by Richard Harding Davis and of the occupation of Antwerp from the pen of Arthur Ruhl, which not only show the war correspondent with a thorough command of his material and an effective method of attacking his subject, but which also possess a literary quality which makes general interest in them more than merely ephemeral. The anonymous account of the Messina earthquake has all the vividness of the intimate letter colored with the emotion aroused by great and unforeseen disaster. The story of the sinking of the *Titanic*, related by the ship's wireless operator, shows the journalistic eye for detail and for sequence of that detail among distracting and distressing circumstances; while Mr. Stoddart's account shows in orderly fashion how the same story was handled by a metropolitan paper when the news 'broke.' Amundsen's narrative of the discovery of the South Pole has in it something of the quality and of the permanent appeal of the adventurous voyagers of Hakluyt's pages. With it may be compared the moving account of the work done by the expedition which gave to the world the news of the disastrous success of Captain Scott, whose memorable message to the English nation is now honorably preserved in the Library of the British Museum. Belmore Browne in his description of the ascent of Mt. McKinley and H. G. Wells' account of his trip in an aëroplane show skill in narrating human experiences in the upper air and succeed in giving a personal touch to subjects which are primarily of scientific interest.

I

HAROLD BRIDE'S STORY OF THE SINKING OF THE TITANIC

[*New York Times*, April 28, 1912. By permission.]

To begin at the beginning, I was born at Nunhead, England, twenty-two years ago, and joined the Marconi forces last July. I first worked on the *Haverford,* and then on the *Lusitania.* I joined the *Titanic* at Belfast.

ASLEEP WHEN CRASH CAME

I didn't have much to do aboard the *Titanic* except to relieve Phillips from midnight until some time in the morning, when he should be through sleeping. On the night of the accident I was not sending, but was asleep. I was due to be up and relieve Phillips earlier than usual. And that reminds me — if it hadn't been for a lucky thing, we never could have sent any call for help.

The lucky thing was that the wireless broke down early enough for us to fix it before the accident. We noticed something wrong on Sunday, and Phillips and I worked seven hours to find it. We found a 'secretary' burned out, at last, and repaired it just a few hours before the iceberg was struck.

Phillips said to me as he took the night shift, 'You turn in, boy, and get some sleep, and go up as soon as you can and give me a chance. I'm all done for with this work of making repairs.'

There were three rooms in the wireless cabin. One was a sleeping room, one a dynamo room, and one an operating room. I took off my clothes and went to sleep in bed. Then I was conscious of waking up and hearing Phillips sending to Cape Race. I read what he was sending. It was traffic matter.

I remembered how tired he was, and I got out of bed without my clothes on to relieve him. I didn't even feel the shock. I hardly knew it had happened until the captain had come to us. There was no jolt whatever.

I was standing by Phillips, telling him to go to bed, when the captain put his head in the cabin.

'We've struck an iceberg,' the captain said, 'and I'm having an inspection made to tell what it has done for us. You better get ready to send out a call for assistance. But don't send it until I tell you.'

The captain went away and in ten minutes, I should estimate the time, he came back. We could hear a terrible confusion outside, but there was not the least thing to indicate that there was any trouble. The wireless was working perfectly.

'Send the call for assistance,' ordered the captain, barely putting his head in the door.

'What call should I send?' Phillips asked.

'The regulation international call for help. Just that.'

Then the captain was gone. Phillips began to send 'C. Q. D.' He flashed away at it and we joked while he did so. All of us made light of the disaster.

JOKED AT DISTRESS CALL

We joked that way while he flashed signals for about five minutes. Then the captain came back.

'What are you sending?' he asked.

'C. Q. D.,' Phillips replied.

The humor of the situation appealed to me. I cut in with a little remark that made us all laugh, including the captain.

'Send "S. O. S.,"' I said. 'It's the new call, and it may be your last chance to send it.'

Phillips with a laugh changed the signal to 'S. O. S.' The captain told us we had been struck amidships, or just back of amidships. It was ten minutes, Phillips told me, after he had noticed the iceberg that the slight jolt that was the collision's only signal to us occurred. We thought we were a good distance away.

We said lots of funny things to each other in the next few minutes. We picked up first the steamship *Frankfurd.* We gave her our position and said we had struck an iceberg and needed assistance. The *Frankfurd* operator went away to tell his captain.

He came back, and we told him we were sinking by the head. By that time we could observe a distinct list forward.

The *Carpathia* answered our signal. We told her our position and said we were sinking by the head. The operator went to tell the captain, and in five minutes returned and told us that the captain of the *Carpathia* was putting about and heading for us.

GREAT SCRAMBLE ON DECK

Our captain had left us at this time and Phillips told me to run and tell him what the *Carpathia* had answered. I did so, and I went through an awful mass of people to his cabin. The decks were full of scrambling men and women. I saw no fighting, but I heard tell of it.

I came back and heard Phillips giving the *Carpathia* fuller directions. Phillips told me to put on my clothes. Until that moment I forgot that I was not dressed.

I went to my cabin and dressed. I brought an overcoat to Phillips. It was very cold. I slipped the overcoat upon him while he worked.

Every few minutes Phillips would send me to the captain with little messages. They were merely telling how the *Carpathia* was coming our way and gave her speed.

I noticed as I came back from one trip that they were putting off women and children in lifeboats. I noticed that the list forward was increasing.

Phillips told me the wireless was growing weaker. The captain came and told us our engine rooms were taking water and that the dynamos might not last much longer. We sent that word to the *Carpathia*.

I went out on deck and looked around. The water was pretty close up to the boat deck. There was a great scramble aft, and how poor Phillips worked through it I don't know.

He was a brave man. I learned to love him that night, and I suddenly felt for him a great reverence to see him standing there sticking to his work while everybody else was raging about. I will never live to forget the work of Phillips for the last awful fifteen minutes.

I thought it was about time to look about and see if there was anything detached that would float. I remembered that every member of the crew had a special lifebelt and ought to know where it was. I remembered mine was under my bunk. I went and got it. Then I thought how cold the water was.

I remembered I had some boots, and I put those on, and an extra jacket and I put that on. I saw Phillips standing out there still sending away, giving the *Carpathia* details of just how we were doing.

We picked up the *Olympic* and told her we were sinking by the head and were about all down. As Phillips was sending the message I strapped his lifebelt to his back. I had already put on his overcoat.

I wondered if I could get him into his boots. He suggested with a sort of laugh that I look out and see if all the people were off in the boats, or if any boats were left, or how things were.

I saw a collapsible boat near a funnel and went over to it. Twelve men were trying to boost it down to the boat deck. They were having an awful time. It was the last boat left. I looked at it longingly a few minutes. Then I gave them a hand, and over she went. They all started to scramble in on the boat deck, and I walked back to Phillips. I said the last raft had gone.

Then came the captain's voice: 'Men, you have done your full duty. You can do no more. Abandon your cabin. Now it's every man for himself. You look out for yourselves. I release you. That's the way of it at this kind of a time. Every man for himself.'

I looked out. The boat deck was awash. Phillips clung on sending and sending. He clung on for about ten minutes, or maybe fifteen minutes, after the captain had released him. The water was then coming into our cabin.

While he worked something happened I hate to tell about. I was back in my room getting Phillips' money for him, and as I looked out the door I saw a stoker, or somebody from below decks, leaning over Phillips from behind. He was too busy to notice what the man was doing. The man was slipping the lifebelt off Phillips' back.

He was a big man, too. As you can see, I am very small. I don't know what it was I got hold of. I remembered in a flash the way Phillips had clung on — how I had to fix that lifebelt in place because he was too busy to do it.

I knew that man from below decks had his own lifebelt and should have known where to get it.

I suddenly felt a passion not to let that man die a decent sailor's death. I wished he might have stretched rope or walked a plank. I did my duty. I hope I finished him. I don't know. We left him on the cabin floor of the wireless room, and he was not moving.

BAND PLAYS IN RAG-TIME

From aft came the tunes of the band. It was a rag-time tune, I don't know what. Then there was 'Autumn.' Phillips ran aft, and that was the last I ever saw of him alive.

I went to the place I had seen the collapsible boat on the boat deck, and to my surprise I saw the boat and the men still trying to push it off. I guess there wasn't a sailor in the crowd. They could n't do it. I went up to them and was just lending a hand when a large wave came awash of the deck.

The big wave carried the boat off. I had hold of an oarlock, and I went off with it. The next I knew I was in the boat.

But that was not all. I was in the boat, and the boat was upside down, and I was under it. And I remember realizing that I was wet through, and that whatever happened I must not breathe, for I was under water.

I know I had to fight for it, and I did. How I got out from under the boat I do not know, but I felt a breath of air at last.

There were men all around me — hundreds of them. The sea was dotted with them, all depending on their life-belts. I felt I simply had to get away from the ship. She was a beautiful sight then.

Smoke and sparks were rushing out of her funnel. There must have been an explosion, but we had heard none. We only saw the big stream of sparks. The ship was gradually turning on her nose — just like a duck does that goes down for a dive. I had only one thing on my mind — to get away from the suction. The band was still playing. I guess all of the band went down.

They were playing 'Autumn' then. I swam with all my might. I suppose I was 150 feet away when the *Titanic*, on her nose, with her after-quarter sticking straight up in the air, began to settle — slowly.

PULLED INTO A BOAT

When at last the waves washed over her rudder there was n't the least bit of suction I could feel. She must have kept going just as slowly as she had been.

I forgot to mention that, besides the *Olympic* and *Carpathia,* we spoke some German boat, I don't know which, and told them how we were. We also spoke the *Baltic.* I remembered those things as I began to figure what ships would be coming toward us.

I felt, after a little while, like sinking. I was very cold. I saw a boat of some kind near me and put all my strength into an effort to swim to it. It was hard work. I was all done when a hand reached out from the boat and pulled me aboard. It was our same collapsible. The same crowd was on it.

There was just room for me to roll on the edge. I lay there, not caring what happened. Somebody sat on my legs. They were wedged in between slats and were being wrenched. I had not the heart left to ask the man to move. It was a terrible sight all around — men swimming and sinking.

I lay where I was, letting the man wrench my feet out of shape. Others came near. Nobody gave them a hand. The bottom-up boat already had more men than it would hold and it was sinking.

At first the larger waves splashed over my clothing. Then they began to splash over my head, and I had to breathe when I could.

As we floated around on our capsized boat, and I kept straining my eyes for a ship's light, somebody said, 'Don't the rest of you think we ought to pray?' The man who made the suggestion asked what the religion of the others was. Each man called out his religion. One was a Catholic, one a Methodist, one a Presbyterian.

It was decided the most appropriate prayer for all was the Lord's Prayer. We spoke it over in chorus with the man who first suggested that we pray as the leader.

Some splendid people saved us. They had a right-side-up boat, and it was full to its capacity. Yet they came to us and loaded us all into it. I saw some lights off in the distance and knew a steamship was coming to our aid.

I did n't care what happened. I just lay and gasped when I could and felt the pain in my feet. At last the *Carpathia* was alongside and the people were being taken up a rope ladder. Our boat drew near and one by one the men were taken off of it.

ONE DEAD ON THE RAFT

One man was dead. I passed him and went to the ladder, although my feet pained terribly. The dead man was Phillips. He had died on the raft from exposure and cold, I guess. He had been all in from work before the wreck came. He stood his ground until the crisis had passed, and then he had collapsed, I guess.

But I hardly thought that then. I did n't think much of anything. I tried the rope ladder. My feet pained terribly, but I got to the top and felt hands reaching out to me. The next I knew a woman was leaning over me in a cabin, and I felt her hand waving back my hair and rubbing my face.

I felt somebody at my feet and felt the warmth of a jolt of liquor. Somebody got me under the arms. Then I was hustled down below to the hospital. That was early in the day, I guess. I lay in the hospital until near night, and they told me the *Carpathia's* wireless man was getting 'queer,' and would I help.

After that I never was out of the wireless room, so I don't know what happened among the passengers. I saw nothing of Mrs. Astor or any of them. I just worked wireless. The splutter never died down. I knew it soothed the hurt and felt like a tie to the world of friends and home.

II

TELLING THE TALE OF THE TITANIC

ALEX. McD. STODDART

[*Independent*, May 2, 1912. By permission.]

At 1.20 A.M., Monday, April 15, the cable editor opened an envelope of the Associated Press that had stamped on its face 'Bulletin.' This is what he read:

Cape Race, N. F., Sunday night, April 14. — At 10.25 o'clock to-night the White Star Line steamship *Titanic* called 'C. Q. D.' to the Marconi station here, and reported having struck an iceberg. The steamer said that immediate assistance was required.

The cable editor looked at his watch. It was 1.20 and lacked just five minutes of the hour when the mail edition goes to press.

'Boy!' he called sharply.

An office boy was at his side in a moment.

'Send this upstairs; tell them the head is to come; double column and tell the night editor to rip open two columns on the first page for a one-stick despatch of the *Titanic* striking an iceberg and sinking.'

Every one in the office was astir in a moment and came over to see the cable editor write on a sheet of copy paper:

Set across two columns.
Titanic Sinking
in Mid-Ocean; Hit
Great Iceberg.

'Boy!' he called again; but it was not necessary — a boy in a newspaper office knows news the first time he sees it.

'Tell them that 's the head for the *Titanic*.'

Then he wrote briefly this telegraphic despatch, and as he did so he said to another office boy at his side: 'Tell the operator to shut off that story he is taking and get me a clear wire to Montreal.'

This is what he wrote to the Montreal correspondent, probably at work at his desk in a Montreal newspaper office at that hour:

Cape Race says White Star Liner *Titanic* struck iceberg, is sinking and wants immediate assistance. Rush every line you can get. We will hold open for you until 3.30.

'Give that to the operator and find out if we caught the mail on that *Titanic* despatch,' he said quickly to the boy.

In a moment the boy returned.

'O. K. on both,' he said.

These night office boys can carry a message to Garcia.

The city editor, who had just put on his coat previous to going away for the night, took it off. At the copy desk where all the local copy (as the reporter's story is called) is collected, the night city editor and the telegraph editor stood together, joined later by the night editor, for the mail edition had left the composing room for the stereotypers and then to the pressroom, and from thence to be scattered wherever on the globe newspapers find readers.

The *Titanic* staff was immediately organized, for at that hour most of the staff were still at work. The city editor took the helm.

'Get the papers for April 11 — all of them,' he said to the head office boy, 'and then send word to the art department to quit everything to make three cuts, which I shall send right down.'

Then to the night city editor: 'Get up a story of the vessel itself; some of the stuff they sent us the other day we did not use and I ordered it put in the envelope.' (Morgue, obituary, call it what you will, are cabinets that contain envelopes filled with newspaper, magazine and other clippings on every conceivable subject, alphabetically arranged for immediate call.) 'Play up her mishap at the start. Get up a passenger list story and an obituary of Smith, her commander.'

There was no mention of Smith in the despatch, but city editors retain such things in their heads for immediate use, and this probably explains in a measure why they hold down their jobs; also having, it might be added, executive judgment, which is sometimes right.

'Assign somebody to the White Star Line and see what they've got.'

The night city editor went back to the circular table where the seven or eight men who read the reporters' copy were gathered.

'Get up as much as you can of the passenger list of the *Titanic*. She's sinking off Newfoundland,' he said briefly to one.

And to another: 'Write me a story of the *Titanic*, the new White Star liner, on her maiden trip, telling of her mishap with the *New York* at the start.'

And to another: 'Write me a story of Captain E. J. Smith.'

Then to a reporter, sitting idly about: 'Get your hat and coat quick; go down to the White Star Line office and telephone all you can get about the *Titanic* sinking off Newfoundland.'

Then to another reporter: 'Get the White Star Line on the 'phone and find out what they have got of the sinking of the *Titanic*. Find out who is the executive head in New York, his address and his telephone number.'

And in another part of the room the city editor was saying to the office boys: 'Get me all the *Titanic* pictures you have and a photo or cut of Captain E. J. Smith.'

Two boys instantly went to work, for the photos of men are kept separate from the photographs of inanimate things. The city editor selected three:

'Tell the art department to make a three-column cut of the *Titanic*, a two-column of the interior, and a two-column of Smith.'

In the meantime the Associated Press bulletins came in briefly. Stripped of their date lines they read:

Half an hour afterward another message came, reporting that they were sinking by the head and that women were being put off in the life-boats.

The weather was calm and clear, the *Titanic's* wireless operator reported, and gave the position of the vessel as 41.46 north latitude and 50.14 west longitude.

The Marconi station at Cape Race notified the Allan liner *Virginian*, the captain of which immediately advised that he was proceeding to the scene of the disaster.

The *Virginian* at midnight was about 170 miles distant from the *Titanic* and expected to reach that vessel about 10 A.M. Monday.

2 A.M. Monday.— The *Olympic* at an early hour this (Monday) morning was in latitude 40.32 north and longitude 61.18 west. She was in direct communication with the *Titanic*, and is now making all haste toward her.

The steamship *Baltic* also reported herself about 200 miles east of the *Titanic* and, was making all possible speed toward her.

The last signals from the *Titanic* were heard by the *Virginian* at 12.27 A.M.

The wireless operator on the *Virginian* says these signals were blurred and ended abruptly.

Paragraph by paragraph the cable editor was sending the story to the composing room. What was going on upstairs every one knew. They were side-tracking everything else and the copy-cutter in the composing room was sending out the story in 'takes,' as they are called, of a single paragraph to each compositor. His blue pencil marked each individual piece of copy with a letter and number, so that when the dozen or so men setting up the story had their work finished the story might be put together consecutively.

'Tell the operator,' said the cable editor again to the office boy, 'to duplicate that despatch I gave him to our Halifax man. Get his name out of the correspondents' book.'

'Who wrote that story of the "Carmania in the Icefield"?' said the night city editor to the copy reader who 'handled' the homecoming of the Carmania, which arrived Sunday night, and the story of which was already in the mail edition of the paper before him. The copy reader told him. He called the reporter to his desk.

'Take that story,' said the night city editor, 'and give us a column on it. Don't rewrite the story. Add paragraphs here and there to show the vast extent of the ice field. Make it straight copy, so that nothing in that story will have to be reset. You have just thirty minutes to catch the edition. Write it in twenty.'

'Get the passenger lists of the Olympic and the Baltic,' was the assignment given to another reporter, all alert waiting for their names to be called, every man awake at the switch.

In the meantime the story from the Montreal man was being ticked off, and on another wire Halifax was coming to life.

'Men,' said the city editor, 'we have just five minutes left to make the city. Jam it down tight.'

Already the three cuts had been made, the telegraph editor was handling the Montreal story, his assistant the Halifax end, and the cable editor was still editing the Associated Press bulletins and writing a new head to tell the rest of the story the additional details brought. The White Star Line man had a list of names of passengers of the Titanic and found that they numbered 1300 and carried a crew of 860.

In the meantime the proofs of all the Titanic matter that had been set were coming to the desk of the managing editor, in charge over all, but giving his special attention to the editorial matter. All his suggestions went through the city editor and on down the line, but he himself went from desk to desk overlooking the work.

'Time's up,' said the city editor, but before he finished the cable editor cried to the boy: 'Let the two-column head stand and tell them to add this head':

Titanic Sinking
in Mid-Ocean; Hit
Great Iceberg.

And to this was added:

At 12.27 this Morning Blurred Signals by Wireless Told of Women Being Put Off in Lifeboats — Three Liners Rushing to Aid of 1300 Imperiled Passengers and Crew of 860 Men.

'Did we catch it?' asked the cable editor of the boy standing at the composing room tube.

'We did," he said, triumphantly.

'One big pull for the last, men,' said the city editor. 'We're going in at 3.20. Let's beat the town with a complete paper.'

The enthusiasm was catching fire. Throughout the office it was a bedlam of noise — clicking typewriters, clicking telegraph instruments and telephone bells ringing added to the whistle of the tubes that lead from the city room to the composing room, the press room, the stereotype room and the business office, the latter, happily, not in use. But throughout the office men worked; nobody shouted, no one lost his head, men were flushed, but the cool, calm, deliberate way in which the managing editor smoked his cigar helped much to relieve the tension.

'Three-fifteen, men,' said the city editor, admonishingly. 'Every line must be up by 3.20. Five minutes more.'

The city editor walked rapidly from desk to desk.

'All up,' said the night city editor, 'and three minutes to the good.'

At the big table stood the city editor, cable editor, night city editor and managing editor. They were looking over the completed headline that should tell the story to the world. It read:

(Across three columns.)
New Liner Titanic Hits An Iceberg;
Sinking by the Bow at Midnight;
Women Put off in Lifeboats;
Last Wireless at 12.27 A.M. Blurred.

(Single column.)

Allan Liner *Virginian*
Now Speeding Toward
the Big Ship.

Baltic to the Rescue, Too.
The *Olympic* Also Rushing to
Give Aid — Other Ships
Within Call.

Carmania Dodged Bergs.
Reports French Liner *Niagara*
Injured and Several Ships
Caught.

Big *Titantic's* First Trip. Bringing Many
Prominent Americans, and Was Due
in New York Tomorrow.

Mishap at very Start. Narrowly Escaped
Collision with the American Liner
New York when Leaving Port.

'That will hold 'em, I guess,' said the
city editor, and the head went upstairs.

The men waited about and talked and
smoked. Bulletins came in, but with no
important details. Going to press at 3.20
meant a wide circulation. At 4.30 the
Associated Press sent 'Good-night,' but
at that hour the presses had been running uninterruptedly for almost an hour.

On Monday morning, at twelve o'clock,
the city editor was at his desk half an
hour earlier than usual. His assistant
already had read the morning papers
and the first editions of the afternoon
papers, known as the 'bulldog edition,'
which is really the morning papers re-
written, with just a new angle on the
news. In a poker way, the 'bulldog'
goes the morning paper one better.

'We got out a corker this morning,'
said the assistant city editor, although he
himself had been fast asleep and knew
nothing and did nothing until he picked
up his morning paper at the railway station, for assistant city editors, having day
jobs, can live in the suburbs. But before noon the assistant city editor had dug
out of the morning papers such events as
would take place during the day as the
city editor might care to 'cover,' the
'beats' the other papers had, the treatment of a story that was so different
from the others as the city editor might
be interested in, and anything that might
interest him generally, all of the clippings
clasped together and the schedule neatly
typewritten telling in a line the time, the
place and the thing.

As he handed it over he remarked to
his chief: 'Practically nothing new on
the disaster; all the passengers were taken
off in lifeboats and are now on their way
to Halifax, says Franklin of the White
Star Line. By the way, I had a letter
from Hitchens to-day. He's at St.
John's. Don't you think it would be a
good plan to send him over to Halifax
even if it does break up his vacation?'

'Yes; and tell him to get a private
wire when he reaches there.'

'Get this off quick,' he said, and he
handed the following telegrams to his assistant. 'Better have the boy take them
to the Marconi Wireless himself — 27
William Street,' he added.

These were the Marconigrams — in
duplicate to W. T. Stead, Major Archibald Butt and Jacques Futrelle:

Please send wireless exclusive *Titanic*
sinking; your own rates.

It was signed by different names, not
by the paper, because these men were
known to the individuals and were
friends. To Butt's telegram was left off
'Your own rates' and it was signed by
the name of the Washington correspondent, a personal friend of many years'
standing.

'Skipper wants to talk to you,' said
the assistant to the city editor, and he
pushed the bracket 'phone that both used
toward his chief. 'Skipper' is the title
in this office, and usually in all other
offices, that is given to the ship news man.

'He says Franklin is not telling the
truth, he believes, about the *Titanic*.
Write this name and address down,' said
the city editor, 'and rush this despatch:'

Can you get me the truth, for private information, about the *Titanic?*

The despatch was sent to the head of
one of Canada's great railways.

Meanwhile the city editor was perus-
ing the schedule of suggestions of his
assistant, to which he added his own, in
more terse language. This is what it
looked like:

Scenes at White Star Office ....Burnet
Passenger List ....Howard
First Steamer to Use Wireless ......Horry
Cape Race a Graveyard ....Wall
Description of *Titanic* ....Lynah

And so the morning work was started. The other local news, however, must not be neglected, and there was no disappointment when, in looking over the assignment book, it was found that, at least for the present, the following men were out of it:

And so the staff separated, all to turn in by five o'clock, when the copy readers should begin their work, the stories assigned to them earlier in the day. The organization must never go to pieces, no matter how big the news, the paper must always take care of the other news, no matter how greatly it is overshadowed.

'My God!' said the city editor, as he read a despatch at seven o'clock that night, 'the skipper's right. The White Star Line and Franklin have lied to us.'

'Here,' he said, calling to Burnet to come to his desk, 'go back to the White Star Line and tell Franklin he is a liar! The *Titanic* sank at 2.20 this morning and not more than 700 were taken off in the boats. Tell it to him with my compliments, too.'

Every one looked up, for the voice of the city editor was pitched high and he was angry clear through. 'Here's a private despatch,' he said, 'I have just received from a friend in Canada, who says that the *Titanic* went down at 2.20 and the only ones saved are practically women and children.'

And then was begun the story telling the world Tuesday morning of the *Titanic* sinking four hours after hitting an iceberg, 866 being rescued by the *Carpathia*, with probably 1250 perishing in the sea; with Ismay safe, and probably Butt, Astor, Smith, Stead, Guggenheim, Millet, Harris, Futrelle, Straus and others less prominent sinking with the *Titanic*.

When the city editor arrived on Tuesday morning, again at noon, showing practically no wear of the eighteen-hour stretch he had gone through, he recalled Hitchens, now in Halifax, telling him to 'never mind' and proceed on his vacation, etc., for the *Carpathia*, 'the hospital ship,' was bound for New York where everything would center.

No reply came from Butt, Stead or Futrelle. Naturally. But what bothered the city editor was that the offer made by wireless to the wireless man aboard the *Carpathia* brought no response, not a word came in answer to the message to Captain Rostrom, of the *Carpathia*, not a word from any passenger of the three women who, it had been suggested to him, might be able 'to write the story.'

The ship news man was sent early to find out about the *Carpathia*, when she would arrive, what men would board her, what and when the revenue cutter would leave, how many men each paper might be permitted to have on board, and arrangements on the pier. This, some of it for publication and some of it for office information, was hard to get because 'everything up in the air,' he reported. Tuesday brought by wireless the passenger list, but not a scrap of information. Nevertheless there were half a dozen pages to fill, and this is the way the city editor mapped out his story for certain things were evident: That the *Titanic* knew of the ice ahead (because she was warned by the *America*); Astor, Straus, Stead and Butt were given up for lost; there were not enough lifeboats; the *Titanic* was not 'unsinkable'; these were 'leads,' and so the staff got busy again.

There were the old stories to be covered again: the scenes at the White Star Line offices, *Titanic* accident, and life insurance of men and women lost, and these additional stories that the news reports suggested: Criticism of the northern route; young Astor to send ship to seek his father; customs men to pass the Carpathia without delay; American regulations compared with British regulations as to lifeboat capacity; big Atlantic liners that are now lacking in lifeboats; sea patrol suggested for the ice-region; vessels not built that will not sink; scout cruisers rushed to scene of wreck; care of survivors when they arrive; steerage survivors to find aid; sea traffic not hurt by the disaster; facts about those on the Titanic; people from afar off coming to New York; Congress likely to say 'more lifeboats'; triumph for wireless and why was false news given out Monday night, when it was known that the Titanic foundered at 2.20 A.M. Monday.

Tuesday midnight came. This query was handed to the city editor:

'Have story that wreck was caused by high speed and panic,' wired St. John correspondent. 'Shall I send?'

'Wire "Let it come,"' said the city editor.

Five hundred words came. The city editor read it carefully, balanced it in the scales, as it were, and then, reluctantly, as if still in doubt, he said to the telegraph editor:

'Doublelead it; across two columns; put a four-column head on it and say in the head that the tale is discredited.'

The city editor was taking no chances. And so Wednesday morning brought six, seven and eight pages of the Titanic matter when the only news was the list of passengers reported by wireless.

Wednesday — another day with no news and with the plan of many engaged to thwart the newspapers and keep what news of the disaster they could from leaking out. The Carpathia, it was figured, would be in late Thursday night or possibly Friday morning. Absolutely no news was received, even her position being six, eight and ten hours behind. It was definitely stated, however, that no newspaper man would be permitted to board the vessel on her way up New York Bay, or at her pier in the Hudson River. Quick work was required and the aid of President Taft, Mayor Gaynor and Secretary McVeagh was sought both by the newspapers and those desiring to stop publicity. The newspapers won, and Secretary Nagel received instructions from the President to see that at least reporters were permitted to tell the world what had happened. Every newspaper would have been glad to have assigned twenty-four reporters to interview survivors, but at last it was decided that the press associations should be represented by six men each, the morning newspapers by four men each, and the evening newspapers by two men each. Photographers were barred. Admission to the pier only was given. Previous to this newspapers were given a number of pier passes; these, however, were canceled, and special tickets of the number quoted were to take their place.

How Thursday's paper was got out is merely a repetition of Tuesday. The great story was Thursday night, when the Carpathia should arrive. For the Carpathia absolutely refused to give out anything by wireless which should tell in advance what had happened on that Sunday midnight and when 1595 men, women and children perished off Newfoundland. The whole of America wanted to know, the whole civilized world wanted information, but this is what the Associated Press had to send to its clients, the newspapers of America:

'We have no assurance that we will get any wireless news from the Carpathia, as this vessel studiously refuses to answer all queries. Even President Taft's requests for information, addressed to the Carpathia, have been ignored.'

How the city editor laid his plans to get the Carpathia's story of the Titanic disaster, with only four men to go on the pier, is interesting. First, as near to the pier as he could get it, he arranged for four private wires, direct wires, that would lead into the editorial rooms. These four wires were for the four men, the main men on whom he depended to get the great story of the Titanic's foundering. They were picked men, no better, probably, than the rest, but luck is always on the side of the man who is a worker and is alert. In the office were four men, with typewriters, with an instrument held in place to the ear. Whether the Carpathia got in at nine o'clock, or ten, or eleven, or twelve, or even one, the story would, must, be told. Time alone would give more opportunity as to whether the story could be told in two, four, six, eight, ten or twelve pages. The *Carpathia* docked at 9.35 o'clock, but that is getting ahead of the story.

Where the four private telephones were installed was the headquarters of the staff. Two blocks away, out of the way of the great crowd that should gather, were automobiles stationed to carry men to the office, the men who should write the advance stories of the crowds, the ambulances and other aid, the scenes on the pier, before the *Carpathia* came in.

The moment the *Carpathia* docked the real story would begin. Before six o'clock that night the four pier passes were distributed to the four men selected; the additional pier passes that were said to be of no use were also passed out, and in addition every member of the staff had his police card, which permits the reporter to go within the police lines.

At six o'clock that night sixteen men gathered around the city editor. By telephone or otherwise the men who were to gather the story were told to report promptly. They did. These sixteen men were the flying squadron, upon whom devolved the great task of the night. Outside the group, as it were, was the managing editor, who ordinarily is in entire charge of the paper. The night city editor, who is at the head of men who edit the reporters' copy, was near him. And near by were the telegraph and cable editors, whose *Titanic* work was practically finished, their work having been done on the nights when news really did come. Near by stood the four men who were assigned to take the stories over the telephone and write them on the typewriting machines. Other members of the staff stood by to hear how 'the chief,' as the city editor is sometimes called, intended to outline the story.

He began in a leisurely tone, as if telling a story. And this is what he said:
'When the *Carpathia* docks to-night which, as closely as I can figure it, will be between 9 and 9.15, there will probably be thirty thousand people held back by the police. The arrangements may go to pieces; but I imagine Waldo's men will not let the crowd break loose. But whatever happens, you will be up against a stiff game to get through the lines. We have established four telephones, which are direct wires between this office and the building on the northeast corner of Fourteenth Street and Eleventh Avenue.

'The four special passes which I have already given out will admit within the pier lines. The pier passes, which the customs people say now are not good, I have already given out. You may be able to break through lines here and there, but at any rate your police cards will be recognized. As you know, the main story is the arrival of the *Carpathia*, and the tales told by survivors and passengers who witnessed the rescues. The men with the special pier passes will get the story of the four officers who were saved and particularly the story of the second Marconi operator who came through alive. It may be another Jack Binns story and it may not, but we've got to get it. Also the story of the wireless operator of the *Carpathia* must be had. These men ought to have thrilling stories. Captain Rostrom's story should tell from the time he turned his vessel toward the *Titanic* till he reached the pier. Bruce Ismay must be seen. He will give out a formal statement. It won't be worth the paper it is written on, but we'll print whatever he says. Ask him how he came to be saved when Astor, Butt, Straus and Guggenheim went down. That's the story we want — no statement.

'Mr. Burnet will see the second Marconi wireless man; and, if possible, the first officer.

'Mr. Howard will see the wireless man of the *Carpathia* and if possible the second officer.

'Mr. Horry will see Ismay and the third officer, if possible.

'Mr. Wall will see Captain Rostrom and incidentally ask him why Taft's message was ignored.

'In charge of the story will be Mr. Burnet; you may have to ignore some of these assignments; you men on the ground will be the better judge. If you want me, I'll be right here at my telephone.'

All the men were listening intently, for an unusual scene like this is rarely witnessed in a newspaper office.

'You four men upon whom I am depending for the main story will see as many survivors as you can; get as many stories as you can and don't be afraid of duplicating. I'll take care of that.

'Every man will get survivors' stories; I repeat, don't be afraid of duplicating. I'll take care of that.

'Mr. Lynah will write the story on the arrival of the ship at the pier and interviews with survivors.

'Mr. Glover will write the story of the Senate committee that is on its way here, and which will arrive at eight o'clock, and interviews with survivors.

'Mr. Griffen will write the story of the tugs that will go out to intercept the *Carpathia* and interviews.

'Mr. Bush will write the story of the relief extended to survivors and get interviews.

'Mr. Payne will write the story of the crowd at the Battery and then follow the boat to the pier and get interviews.

'Mr. Kimpton will write the story of the distribution of the money sent by the stock exchange, and get interviews.

'Mr. Brewster will write the story of the autos and get interviews.

'Mr. Elmendorf will get the story of the crowds that will not get near the scene, and get interviews.

'Mr. Whitten will see Franklin and get what the White Star Line has to say, and get interviews.

'Mr. Moors will get interviews and then cover the hotels on Broadway between Twenty-seventh Street and Thirty-fourth Street.

'Mr. Bromiley will get interviews and cover the hotels between Thirty-fourth Street and Forty-fifth Street.

'Mr. McDonald will get interviews and cover the Fifth Avenue hotels, from the Holland House to the Plaza, and including the Ritz-Carlton.

'The autos for the men who are doing these hotels will be parked at Eighteenth Street and Eleventh Avenue. The chauffeurs of these machines will have a piece of white paper in their hats and will take instructions from any man who presents his police card. Mr. Payne, who will do the Battery first, will find his machine at the door.

'In getting the story of survivors and of those on the *Carpathia* to whom the survivors told their story, find out how Astor, Stead, Straus, Millet, Harris, Butt, Futrelle, Guggenheim and Smith died. Get every one to tell any story of heroism or cowardice he or she witnessed. Find out how the crew acted and the panic in the steerage, if there was one.

'The men who do the theaters will first send their stories over the telephone from the headquarters. If there is any jam on telephone we have arranged for three more wires at Twenty-third Street and Eleventh Avenue, the building on the southwest corner. But I don't expect any great jam. Then these men will do the hotels and telephone their story from whichever hotel they are in. The operator has been instructed to use every switch except one for the *Titanic* story, so there will be lots of wires, with men at each end to take stories. But it will help if the stories can come over the four special wires.

'The way the telephones will be cared for is this: When a man comes into headquarters, he will be told which telephone to use, so that the men at this end of the wire will not be interrupted. That is to say, over one wire will come the story of the arrival of the *Carpathia*.

'Over another wire will come the story of the wreck of the *Titanic*.

'Over a third telephone will come the story of the rescue work by the *Carpathia*.

'And over the fourth will come the story of survivors.

'As soon as a man gets into the office he will write down the name of the person he has interviewed. This list will be posted over each wire. If a reporter sees that the man he has interviewed is already posted, pass up the story.'

The city editor stopped talking.

'Are there any questions?' he asked. 'Have I made it clear what each man is to do?'

'You're the goods!' said the youngest of the group, marveling at this master mind that could see the whole scene long before it should be put into cold type and placed before a million readers.

'Then go to it!' said the city editor.

III

A LETTER WRITTEN AFTER THE MESSINA DISASTER

[*McClure's Magazine,* May, 1909. By permission.]

I had gone to Messina on the 26th, to visit my friends, the Levis. I spent the day of the 27th with them, visiting the city, a most beautiful one. Toward evening a heavy thunder-storm came up, and we went home, where Madame Gina Levi was seized with sudden illness. The doctor was called in. We spent the first part of the night around her bed, tending her, trying to quiet her in her nervous paroxysms. Finally we went to bed.

I, lying on a cot near her, had no more than a few minutes' unconsciousness at a time; I would doze, wake up, toss, cry out; I would speak to her, in the effort to soothe her. At last, after a terrifying dream, which I do not remember, I started up, broad awake. The others were all up, standing about my sick friend's bed. Impelled by some mysterious force I jumped out of bed; I seized a dress and hurriedly put it on. Madame Levi said to me, 'Put on your shoes and stockings.' I sat on the edge of the bed and put them on. Who would have believed that in that moment, by that act, I was saving my life?

We could already hear the tinkling, out in the street, of the goat-bells. The servant-girl opened the window; she bought milk. At that instant I was seized with a strange dizziness and violent nausea. The servant-girl offered me a cup of coffee. I went into the room where Gina was lying, and took the coffee. At the last swallow, I felt myself lifted from the floor to the ceiling. The ceiling dipped, the bed rose, and the horrible shaking began. We were tossed up and down for several seconds; then the earthquake changed its motion, hurled the sick woman from her bed, clove the walls, and the downfall began.

I heard a sound as if of countless paper tearing, stuff burning with crackling and explosions, and a deafening roar, a terrific crashing. They were balconies falling, steeples, chimneys, towers crumbling. I remember clearly that I was clutching my coffee-cup, trying to set it safely on the washstand, demented already, but calm. I thought, 'I will open the balcony door.' I could not do it; the ceiling gaped above my head.

I made a spring for the windows. Impossible to get them open. I was suffocating. The air was charged with thick dust which stopped respiration. I found the door. Behind me came the Levis, with a little girl, Melina, who habitually spent the day and sometimes the night at their house. On the right there had been, in its time, a balcony. The stairway, the house, were in ruins; the other wing of the house, too, was in ruins.

We all jumped from the balcony. We were on the second story; the heaped debris diminished the height of our jump. I fell. It was dark; it was white all around; beyond that, nothing. Ruins and the cries of the dying. Cries, cries, shrieks. Who was shrieking? We could not see. Had the heavens fallen? What had happened? My lips were tight shut in a spasm of agony. I ran. Where was I running? Perhaps it was not I running, but the earth running under my feet.

Then everything stood still, and for a moment there was silence. Then what was it? The cries began anew, the shrieking, the mad attempts at flight. I said over the names of all those I love; I cried them out aloud to the heavens, choking with the bloody froth that ran from my mouth and nostrils. I said them all over, the names of those, living and dead, whom I love; and my wits came back, and I did not lose them again until the moment when I found myself on the train for Catania.

I thought, 'Now I am going to escape from this!' But I did not know the way.

I found a man and said to him, 'Where are we?'

'In Piazza Spirito Santo,' he answered.

'Can we escape?'

'Stay where you are. We are blocked. We are safe here as long as God pleases.'

And the earthquake began again. The houses finished crumbling; they showered forth furniture, mirrors, wounded men, dead bodies. Yells and infernal panic. All suddenly caved in. We dropped face downward, and lay awaiting death. But before long we got up again, and in the dense dust found one another. Melina was trembling in the Professor's arms.

What joy, in all that anguish, to ascertain that we were all there — what joy! And joy over what? There were two hundred of us, injured and whole, in that small space. At our right was a convent, the walls of which had dropped in, but whose front, still standing, was a menace to us. At our left was a house, burst open fanwise, ready to fall at the next shock. Behind us the church of the Spirito Santo, tilting forward, with a great triangular crack down its façade. Before us the houses of the Porta Imperiale, in fragments; broken and torn bodies dumped into the square among gravel, blood, and wreckage. 'Let us stay where we are,' we said, 'all close clasped together, let us wait.' For what? For death?

A light broke above us, beyond the ruins which we could dimly distinguish, because an occasional street-lamp, impossible as it seems, had remained alight. 'The dawn! The dawn!' we shouted. No; it was Messina burning.

Then we were seized with desperate madness to flee. But whither? Oh, to the sea, to be drowned in it, to be buried in the depths of the sea! But fire, to die by fire? Oh, God, what anguish! I dumbly gazed at the heavens. I had never seen them of so deep a purple-blue; and how many stars were falling! A shower of stars, thick and shining. A benediction upon the ruins? Behind a house, whose front wall alone was standing, the sky opened, somewhat suddenly, and there poured down light, cold and pallid, like moonlight. Daybreak! Daybreak! 'Adduma! Adduma!' they cried, mad with the desire for light.

And never was the sun so worshiped, so prayed to, so invoked, as in that tragic hour. Day broke, but, alas! what a scene of sorrow it brought into view!

We looked at one another, to make sure it was ourselves, to make sure we were alive. We were white with mortar; we looked like ghosts, with hugely dilated eyes staring like madmen's. Oh, the dreadful ruin on every hand, the desolation, the horror! I believed that Catania too had been destroyed. I supposed that the disaster came to us from Ætna, and I prayed that Bruno, my husband, who was there, might have died at once, without knowing, without seeing. I made the reflection that possibly Erminia, my maid,

had been able to escape; she slept in a small chamber which I imagined was safe.

And there passed before my eyes all the beloved faces 'that I shall never see again, never again!' I said.

How, from what profound abysms of the soul, was faith born again in me? I felt that some one had worked that miracle for my sake, and I knelt down before the church, which no longer was there, but whose door stood sealed and intact, still guarding its mystery. What did I say? For whom did I pray? For myself, for Bruno, for my dear ones far away? I do not remember; I know that while I was praying two priests passed by. One had an august, aged face, haggard with grief. He looked at me; I told him everything in a look. He spoke over me the blessing for those about to die. He went about among the dying — how many of them! He blessed them, and went his way through the wreckage with his companion, who was weeping, to bless other dead, calmly, without haste, walking under the toppling walls, and we saw him no more.

When I rose to my feet I felt light, rested, strong, well, ready for everything. We began to work for the injured. What endless numbers of them! What slaughter, what mutilations, what horrors! A woman was delivered of twins there in the square: one was dead, one alive; she died later, of hemorrhage.

A father, almost completely naked, tore his face with his nails, desperate at having left his children behind among the ruins.

Meanwhile the miracles of life-saving had begun. Two children slid down a table, placed slantwise, between a stump of house and a heap of rubbish; then came the mother, then the father last. When he had reached the bottom, he saw that two were still missing. What weeping, what shrieks! Oh, God, and who could comfort them? There were some standing by who had no one, no one left. Little children, totally naked, or with nothing on but a little shirt, all blood, all mud; girls and women, gone quite mad, calling out strange pet names and terms of endearment: 'Catù! Vita! [My breath! My life!] Catuzza e mamma bedda!' Meant for whom? Alas! for sons, husbands, scattered, dismembered, or perhaps still alive beneath huge mountains of masonry.

I saw a father searching among the

wreckage for his children. He pulled out one of them, dead. One of them, whose head only projected from the horrible rubbish-heap, cried, ' Papà, papà, sete aio, sete aio!' [I am thirsty! I am thirsty!] And there was no water. The father bent over the dying child and gave him his saliva and all his soul in a kiss. The son closed his eyes and died.

The earthquake continued. The walls continued falling, mountains on top of mountains of stone and plaster. Precipices gaped and engulfed the surviving, who had hoped perhaps to reach safety. All that had been left standing after the first horrible, unending shock now went to pieces.

The instinct of life, however, love of that miserable gift which misfortune had left us, sprang up again within us, and we bethought us, poor wretches! that night would be coming on; we bethought us of the morrow. We rummaged among the ruins in search of food; we tested the earth, and trusted it, poor fools, to uphold the tables which were to shelter us during the night that was closing down — last, immeasurable calamity. We made a hut. And suddenly, as if a malign breath of insanity had overturned their reasons,— whilst, all equally unhappy, all equally poor, naked, wounded, weeping, we were awaiting death,— a small band of men, for a loaf of bread found among the broken masonry, wrenched bars from an iron gate and began whirling them among the crowd, to kill. Where could we flee?

Two or three dropped down, felled; they afterward died. That horrible danger passed, too. Some went searching among the ruins for bread, food, clothing, all that could keep off death — death which we notwithstanding were calling upon to come quickly, and which came not. Ah, the savage scenes over a chunk of bread, over a sup of putrid water, gathered as it dripped from the ruins, yellow, fetid, which was drunken after the dying had refused to taste it. What struggles for a nut, for a chocolate drop (a ruined sweet-shop had been found, which saved us by a few bottles, a few pots of preserve), for a bone gnawed by dogs, picked out of the refuse, for a mouthful of anything that could keep us from starvation! I saw what the human brute is like when, all restraint removed, all shame cast off, every law forgotten, he stands forth without disguise.

Horrible! Horrible! All the most bestial instincts, swarming up from the dregs of the soul, all the unbridled appetites, every baseness, every cowardice! But I saw likewise what treasures of self-renunciation, sacrifice, human brotherliness, generosity, what heroism, are in the depths of the human soul.

A young man, whom I shall never forget, a cripple, with only one leg, clambering with a crutch among the ruins, saved scores of people. Untiringly he searched among the wreckage, he brought back to us everything he could find; he took bits of chocolate out of his mouth to put into the mouths, forever open, of the crying children.

A marvel, in truth, was the forethought of this man. Where did he unearth a crate of apples? He hid them, he defended them from the violence of the greedy; and through the night he went among the huts, distributing quarters of apple to each one of us in his turn, with calculating parsimony, with implacable justice. I shall remember him as long as I live, that fragment of a man among the fragments of a city. He explored the ruined city in every direction, to find a way of escape, to open a road for us. We could see him hanging like a mountain goat over the edge of frightful precipices. At night he never rested, unless it were to make a pillow of himself for those who did not know where to lay their heads, amid the mire, the blood, and the ruin. The name of this hero is Salvatore Stellario. What became of him when the anguished fight for the preservation of life had ceased, and we saw the fire close at hand, after a night spent under the rain, dreadful scourge, amid continual earthquakes, the horrors of darkness, cold, fear, the ever fainter moaning of the hurt? They told me he sought safety in the direction of the railway. Perhaps I shall see him again.

There is another whom I remember for unparalleled self-control and equanimity — Nicola Sclepis, who could impose quiet by a gesture, who wore a look of fatalism, yet had words of encouragement, of hope. Cold, apparently unfeeling, he could stop a frenzied mob by a shout; he could smile while others were inquiring breathlessly, ' When, where, how are we doomed to die?' Oh, how well I remember him! I supposed him a skeptic; I thought him heartless. Later, I saw him clasp his friends to his breast; I saw tears filling his eyes while I told him my last will and testament of love for those who would come to look for me. Shall I ever forget him? He was saved, I know. He could not die; I felt that, and for that reason intrusted my last messages to him. He listened to me, serious, kind. He bade me not to move, when I wanted to go and try to find some way out of that horrible inclosure; he prevented me by a look. Men like Nicola Sclepis are rare indeed. One possessed of such moral strength and courage is worthy, truly, of the name of hero.

Evening came on again; it grew dark early: the light shrank away from the horrors of the catastrophe.

I had eaten a handful of oats, found I do not remember where. I had an egg which a lady had refused. As I was eating it, a woman came running, crying that she had no more milk for her baby. I put out the egg which I had so nearly swallowed; she caught it in her hands and fed it to her infant. Water had been found; it was yellow, thick; it tasted, alas! of decay, of death, of putrefaction: but I drank it. I was mad with thirst, with hunger. I had in my hands a jar of marmalade, but succeeded in no more than touching my lips with it. I distributed it among the injured, feeding them with a hollow cane, split in two. And so came the evening, and the rain fell, and for hours and hours earthquake and rain and weeping; sighs of the dying, howls of desperate grief. Oh, that tragic night! How we wept and how we prayed! Some were seen barbarously beating themselves, to punish themselves for being alive while their beloved were dead; and we wept in chorus, and sang in chorus.

I remember those lamentable chants: the passion of Jesus sung in Sicilian dialect, the sorrows of Mary, the praises of the Child Jesus,— all the Christian legends, all the songs of infancy. And it rained, it rained, and the earth continued to shake, implacably, and the day was slow in coming.

Oh, what eternal, what cruel waiting! When we were worn out with praying, there was deathly silence; but every little while a groan would bring us back to dreadful consciousness, and we would start up and begin rushing about. But to what purpose, for whose sake? The in-

jured would ask for a mattress, a pillow, and water, water, water! And we had nothing to give them but a few nuts, an apple, a morsel of bread. And those who had fractured jaws, teeth which they spat out with bloody foam, or injuries to their throats, they merely must die of hunger!

We heard a whistle or two in the distance. We supposed it must be some steamer coming to help us; but no one came. The thought crossed my mind that a dirigible balloon might have gotten cognizance of the condition of Messina, but that hope, too, was vain. We spent another night in the mud; at daybreak the rain stopped. As soon as the first light appeared in the sky, there reawakened in all the mad desire to flee. Whither, in what direction, with what hope?

On this side the conflagration, on that, mountains of masonry. The sea had withdrawn. The steamers would take on no more; people had killed one another to get aboard. Where could we go? But go we must.

I had in a little hand-bag, saved I know not how, my provisions for the days that must pass before help came, or death. Two walnuts, a few filberts, a nibbled bit of nougat, and a chocolate watch, such as we buy for children, which was presented to me by a little boy whom I do not remember. He handed it to me unasked, and ran away. I had with me my railway-book. I placed it in the bosom of my dress, thinking that perhaps by means of it I might be identified when they found my body. That was my great preoccupation — to be found, to be identified, to shorten the anxiety of my husband, who was perhaps already looking for me, desperate, among the ruins.

Nicola Sclepis told me to follow him and his caravan, headed for the mountains; he offered me his house, all he had, — at Santa Lucia, I think it was. There I would certainly have been out of danger, but I would have had to wait to send news.

I hesitated for an instant. Then I reflected that by way of the sea I would soonest reach Catania. Death was perhaps lying in wait for me in that direction; but go I must, and I went. My companions followed me a short way, then we separated.

I lost my reason again, and I do not know where I went. I was quite alone,

alone among the ruins, the dead, the fallen houses. Where was I? Near the cemetery, they told me. Some told me near the sea, others near the railroad; they did not understand what I said. Some who were crazy, some who were dazed, some who were wicked, misdirected me, sent me vainly wandering among the ruins, alone, forsaken, desperate.

I reached a place where the ruins had caught fire; I was forced to turn back. That had been a street, the handsomest in Messina; now the houses had fallen in, and the dead lay under them. Walking was easy there; but I could not bear to step on the wreckage; I knew of the human flesh throbbing beneath it; I caught glimpses of clothing, scraps of black. Oh, the horror of it!

I ran, I fell, I picked myself up; it began to rain again, but there were no more earthquakes. I came to an open place. Perhaps there had once been a church. I shall never know.

In the middle, a bronze Christ, maimed, wept, with his head bowed toward the right. In front of him a taper was burning. There were before me three roads. I took the one toward which the Christ was looking. Some one told me that was the right road. But what a road! How many crumbled houses, what destruction! I reached a place that was all like a marsh. I walked into it nearly to my knees. When I came out I could no longer walk: my clothes clung to me. I thought of taking them off, then I went down on my hands and knees, and crawled along like an animal. . . .

IV

HOW I FOUND THE SOUTH POLE

ROALD AMUNDSEN

[*Hearst's Magazine*, November, 1912. By permission.]

On April 21 the sun disappeared. The longest night any man had known in the Antarctic regions had begun. Old campaigners as we were, everything was well prepared for it. There was the hut, stout and strong. No storm, no matter how it blew, could hurt it. Light and warm it was inside, dry and airy. The large, roomy caverns we had excavated in the ice barrier and connected directly with the hut, gave us space sufficient for our workshops; we did not need to use our hut to work in.

We were amply supplied with provisions. Seven hundred yards from the hut was our chief store, containing enough for several years. We had killed and laid by 120,000 lbs. of seal meat, enough for ourselves and our dogs for our whole stay. Fuel and light we had in abundance, the best Welsh coal and dryest Norwegian birchwood. Barrel upon barrel of petroleum lay in our cellars.

All was thoroughly provided for, and we could apply ourselves to our winter work without a care.

The winter work consisted in preparing our outfit and getting everything ready for our march to the South. Our tours in the months of February, March and April, to form depots in latitude 80, 81 and 82 degrees, had taught us that we must make many alterations in our outfit. This had been prepared in Christiania, at a time when I only knew the Barrier by description, and I had had the things made as massive and strong as possible. The Barrier plains, we had now become acquainted with, did not in any way require this heavy equipment. On the contrary, they needed the lightest gear. To obtain this, the work was distributed amongst the members of the expedition, in such wise, that the special abilities of the various members were utilized to the utmost and the best guarantees for good workmanship obtained.

Thus, Bjaaland, ski and sledge maker, was set to make the necessary parts for four new sledges, weighing about fifty pounds apiece. The original sledges weighed a hundred and fifty pounds. Wisting and Hanssen, both good sailors and the latter an experienced polar explorer, had to fasten the parts together as strongly as could be done. Stubberud, a carpenter and joiner by trade, was assigned the unenviable task of reducing the weight of our sledge provision boxes. The packing of sledge provisions was a matter of the very utmost importance. Space was small and needs great, so quite an exceptional amount of thought and attention had to be devoted to the subject. This was intrusted to Johansen. Praesterud was occupied with the scientific arrangements for the expedition: pendulum and astronomical observations. Thus, each had his hands full and the winter set in.

Now a word about our supplies and equipment. The tent which we took with us was a double one. The inner was the actual tent, made of white linen cloth, such as is used for feather beds, pillows, etc. This was thin and quite light. Over this was an outer covering of thin red material, that had at one time adorned our bunks at Framheim in the shape of bed curtains, but as we considered it more useful as a polar tent, all the curtains were requisitioned and transformed by Wisting's able hand. We had much comfort from this double tent, it being unusually warm and at the same time dark. And a tent should be dark on such an expedition, so that one may get the eyes rested after the long march on the white snow. It was, moreover, easy to put up, had an exceedingly good shape, like a snow hut or beehive, thus not offering any flat surfaces to the wind. The floor of the tent was sewn in with the sides. I have always found that the best patent. If one forgets anything in the morning, one finds it again in the evening when erecting the tent. The tent had but one pole, of light, strong bamboo. The door was of the usual bag shape, and absolutely wind tight.

Our provisions were not rich in varieties of courses, but were the most nourishing and most concentrated obtainable. They consisted of pemmican, biscuits, chocolate, and dried milk. The pemmican was made in Norway and was somewhat different from that which is generally used, being mixed with oatmeal and vegetables as well as meat and fat. The biscuits were made expressly, and possessed a very high degree of nourishment. They consisted of oatmeal, milkmeal or dried milk and sugar. The chocolate was an ordinary kind. The milkmeal proved a splendid thing, and as much as possible should be taken on all such expeditions. It is light, packs well and keeps good under all circumstances. We brought dried new milk with us, the manufacturer assuring us it would keep through the tropics we had to traverse. Despite the treatment it received it kept perfectly good the whole time. We could make ourselves a cup of new milk at any time, and

that is a great advantage on such a long expedition.

We used the Swedish 'Primus,' which excels all such cooking lamps. It is easy to handle and never fails as long as one is reasonably careful with it. We used merely quite an ordinary pot to cook in.

On the first part of the journey we used double sleeping bags. The outer one of the skin of reindeer buck. The inner one of light skin of reindeer doe or reindeer calf. Both had the hairy side in. Outside the two, we had a cover of light linen cloth, somewhat longer than the bags. This cover was always kept on, both in the tent and on the march. In the tent, it protected the bags from damp, while on the march it kept the driven snow entirely out.

Our foot-coverings had necessitated much consideration, and were of the very best. The great thing for us was to combine sufficient rigidity with softness. They must be soft, to keep our feet warm, but stiff if our skis were to sit firmly. I used the following myself: outside of all, a boot, the sole of which was of solid leather, the outer covering strong, green, wind-proof cloth. Inside these, I had a pair of reindeerskin boots. As for stockings: next the foot I wore a little woolen sock lined with 'sennegrass' (a kind of soft grass used by Laplanders in their moccasins). I wore this sock, not so much for warmth as to keep the sennegrass in position. Then a stocking of dog's hair. Then an ordinary woolen stocking, and then two pairs of gabardine stockings. With these, my feet were never cold.

Otherwise we were lightly clad with light clothing under gabardine outer garments. Our fur clothing, which we took for use on the plateau, we never had much use for. As long as we had them, we used them under our sleeping-bags at night.

Of snow-spectacles, several kinds were used — each thought he had discovered the best. Personally, I used a pair of ordinary spectacles with light yellow glass. It may seem unheard of, to go on an expedition of 1500 miles in these surroundings, with only a pair of ordinary unprotected spectacles, in which the light can enter everywhere — but I did it, and, what is more, without so much as suffering once from snow blindness. That speaks for the excellence of the glass in them. Dr. Schantz, in Berlin, is the inventor. By a process the glasses have undergone, they are able to keep out the injurious rays.

On my hands, I used, from our winter quarters to the Pole and back, a pair of ordinary walking woolen mittens with the four fingers together in one compartment. One pair lasted the whole way.

Our sledges were of the ordinary Nansen pattern, but of unusually light build. Two were shod with steel, the others not. All four had spare runners. The sledges were as strong on our return as when we set out. Our provision boxes were made of ash, and had only a round opening on top, into which a lid of aluminum fitted, just as into ordinary milk cans. These were attached to the sledges with fixed wire fastenings in such a way that it was not necessary to undo them to get into the boxes. Thus we avoided unloading and reloading every evening and morning, which is no pleasurable work in cold weather. These lids also afforded protection from the dogs stealing,— but, as a matter of fact, the dogs never did attempt to attack the provision boxes. Our dog harness was also somewhat of a new kind and brilliantly proved its superiority. It was a combination of Alaskan and Greenland harness, very easy on our dogs.

Of instruments: we had two sextants, three artificial horizons, two of glass, one of mercury. We also used a theodolite on the shorter journeys, but I fancied I could work with quicker and greater accuracy with a sextant. We had also a hypsometer, and an aneroid to determine heights, and four ordinary thermometers. We carried a little sledge medicine chest presented by Boroughs, Wellcome & Co. It was splendid in every way. We had also some extra bandages, a pair of dentist's forceps, and a beard-clipping machine.

On August 23 all was ready, and at noon we drove our laden sledges up to the starting place on the other side of the bay, about three miles from our establishment, 'Framheim.' We had won in our race with the sun, which reappeared on the following day. Owing to the low temperature, 50 to 70 degrees below zero, Fahrenheit, we were obliged to wait some days. At last, on September 8, at 12.30 noon, we were able to get off.

The journey that followed I shall pass over quickly. It was terrifically cold, ranging from 60 to 75 degrees below zero; the dogs suffered greatly at night and three of the men had frozen heels. We had to be satisfied with reaching the depot, at 80 degrees, that we had built five months before, leaving stores there and returning to ' Framheim.'

This trip, however, taught us much. I saw we could without risk divide ourselves into two parties and thus accomplish more work. It was then determined that one party, under Lieutenant Praesterud, should go to King Edward's Land and do what they could there, while we others should follow the main plan — the march to the South.

The time was now spent in 'healing heels' and in sewing our outfit. I do not think any one will ever get an outfit that does n't want something done to it. If we were out one day, we had work enough on our things to keep us busy for a week. The heels began to mend a little in October, and the prospects of getting away again approached.

One great advantage we all, both men and dogs, gained by this delay was, that we all were well fed on fresh seal meat. Before our departure spring had come, the first signs of which is that the seals come up and lie on the ice. In our neighborhood they were not allowed to remain long before they were shot and subsequently eaten.

At length the 20th of October arrived — time seems long to those who wait. The weather was a little uncertain in the morning — squally. But at 8.30 o'clock it cleared from the east with a light breeze, and off we went. There were five of us: Hanssen, Wisting, Hassel, Bjaaland, and myself, with four sledges and fifty-two dogs — thirteen to each sledge. As we had all our provisions at 80 degrees, sledges were very light and we went along at a gallop. We did twenty miles a day those days, reaching our depot at 80 degrees at 1.30 P.M., on the 23d of October, in the densest fog. This gave us convincing proof of the accuracy of our compasses and of our distance meters.

After leaving the depot of October, we made fifteen miles a day, giving the dogs a chance to eat their fill at the depots. Soon we began erecting snow beacons to serve to guide us on returning. Such a beacon was somewhat more than a man's height, built of about sixty blocks of hard snow cut from the surface. We put up about 150, necessitating 9000 blocks. At first one was built every seventh and eighth mile — subsequently every fifth — and at last, near the Pole, every second mile. In each of these beacons a note was left stating the number of the beacon, its position, the direction and distance of the nearest beacon. In this manner we always kept a control of our march.

MOUNTAIN CLIMBING

On the morning of the 9th of November, when we got outside our tent, we found the air clear, and on examining the patches of cloud, which were still in the same place, we saw they were the tops of huge mountains. This sight wrought in us quite a curious sensation. There we had, before us, the mighty continent covered with ice and snow and barring our way to the Pole.

It must be the southern portion of the chain of mountains Shackleton has marked on his chart, which runs in a southeasterly direction from Beardmore Glacier. From our winter quarters we had followed the meridian as closely as we were able, and now found ourselves about 200 miles east from that glacier, which Shackleton ascended to the plateau.

I was much surprised when I returned to the outer world, to find that people imagined we would make use of the same ascent. I cannot imagine what could have created such an idea. It had never entered my mind or the minds of my companions. Never during the whole of the long winter, never during the whole of our sledge journeys, had any one of us for a moment thought of such a thing. We had come there to compete for the Pole, certainly. But we intended to find a way for ourselves.

We established depots built of hard snow at 83, 84 and 85 degrees and left provisions at each. The land unfolded itself more and more as we advanced, and displayed the most magnificent scenery.

Some mountains were more bare than snow-covered. Thus, that part of the mighty 'Fridtjof Nansen's' mountain, which faced the Barrier, was almost entirely bare. It stood like a dark, dreary sentinel, guarding the entrance to the mystic regions. Its head was capped by a magnificent dazzlingly white, glittering helmet at an elevation of 15,000 feet.

The 17th of November was a red-letter day. We climbed an undulating ridge of ice 300 feet high and then descended to the 'beach.' We encamped here at 85.5 degrees and prepared for the next stage. We five pedestrians were about to be transformed into Alpine climbers.

The story of the ascent to the plateau is one of almost constant adventure, of narrow escapes from death, from falling into crevices in the glaciers or off of bleak, slippery precipices. At times the faces of the men were swollen almost beyond recognition in the merciless Antarctic gales. Once men and dogs suffered from the heat with a blazing sun and the temperature at 15 degrees above zero. We were constantly sacrificing the dogs — once we had to despatch twenty-four of our brave, four-footed comrades at one time. Several times we camped over 9000 feet above the sea. At times we traversed snow bridges, eerie and dangerous, at others polished, wind-swept ice. But at last we forced our way and reached the level plateau.

I shall never forget the day we reached Shackleton's Farthest South. It was my turn to be pioneer. Hassel and I took turns. It is tiresome work thus going on in front. No one to talk to, nothing to see. The plain spreads out in all directions till it loses itself in the horizon. I had now gone on for a couple of hours and was deeply immersed in my own thoughts, when I was aroused by ringing cheers.

SHACKLETON OUTSTRIPPED

I turned sharp round and remained still. The scene was so engrossing that all description fails. The Norwegian flag — my own dear country's flag — unfolded itself from the foremost sledge and fluttered in the gentle southerly breeze — 88.23 degrees had been passed.

We gathered round the flag and pressed one another's hands. It was a wonderfully solemn moment. It may well be believed that we sent him who had reached thus far, and his faithful, brave companions, a thought full of admiration and respect for their manly courage and the perseverance they displayed during their long, severe struggle. There will ever be honor and renown for what Sir Ernest Shackleton has accomplished.

The rest of the journey was exhausting

because of the altitude, but we made good speed.

On the 11th of December we were at 89.15 degrees. Dead reckoning and observation again agreed exactly. We were nearing our goal with rapid strides. The next three days were spent under precisely the same conditions as the previous ones. Temperature continued even, at about —15 degrees, and the sun was out the whole time. On the 12th, by reckoning and observation, 89.30 degrees. On the 13th, the observation at noon gave 89.37 degrees. That evening we pitched our tent at 89.45 degrees by reckoning.

And then came The Great Day. Personally, perhaps, I slept less soundly that night and was more eager to get off in the morning than usual, but otherwise we felt much the same as we generally did. We had now seen so much of this high plateau, that we were sure its appearance would not alter. The only thing that brought our blood to circulate a little more rapidly than it was wont, was the thought, which often occurred to us and made us strain our eyes southward across the endless plain: 'Are we the first to get here, or not?' After ten o'clock there came a change in the sky, and it blew a little from the southeast, so we did not get the meridian that day. At 3 P.M., the distance meters announced that our goal was reached.

AT THE SOUTH POLE

We had got our silk flag ready in the morning. We gathered around it now, each man took hold, and together we planted it here — at the same time naming the plateau, on which the Pole is situated, 'King Haakon the Seventh's Wilds.'

We had reached the Pole with three sledges and seventeen dogs.

As soon as the business was all over, we went into our tent for our feast. It was not a very grand meal; a small piece of seal meat for each. Then we had a chat and a little nap. The sun had long since shone clear again, and we intended to take a midnight observation. So at 11.30 P.M. we turned out and took the altitude. The result gave us 89.56 degrees. This was good enough. We had probably of late got a little off the meridian, which made us four miles short. But that was of no importance. In order to make certain, I sent three men out to encircle the spot with a radius of ten miles. Wisting, Has-

sel, and Bjaaland started off just after midnight and were back again at 10 A.M. Meanwhile Hanssen and I had commenced a series of observations for each hour. We began at 6 A.M., Framheim time, and finished at 7 P.M. These observations gave us 89.55 degrees, and the meridian by our compasses in N. W. ¼ W. to S. E. ¼ E. I had not contemplated, after this, spending any more time here. The Pole had been ringed and the beacon set up. That ought to be sufficient. But I saw that my companions would like to try to get some observations from the very Pole itself. So, as we had food enough and the weather was fine, we resolved to make the experiment. Next morning, instead of turning our faces homeward, as I really would have preferred, we continued our march in the direction of the meridian. Before setting out, we left one of our sledges on the spot. We set it on end to make it more easily seen. We also left one of our distance meters. We now tried to march these five miles as straight as possible, and that we succeeded can best be understood from the fact that when we reached the end we found the sledge we had left exactly in the meridian.

We now made ourselves as comfortable as possible. Built up a substantial snow pillar for the artificial horizon, and set to work at once with the observations. For twenty-five hours we took the altitude of the sun, each hour. There were four of us, well accustomed to use a sextant. The sun's motion was very uneven. The atmosphere must have been greatly disturbed. For hours the sun could maintain exactly the same altitude, then make a little jump and again stop still. On the 7th of December at noon, Framheim time, we had finished. We had done all that could be accomplished with our instruments. For safety's sake, we went yet another four and a half miles in the direction of the meridian. Here we erected a small tent we had brought with us, with a flag and a pennant on top. 'Polheim' it was christened, and it will, probably, if the weather is always as we found it, remain there long.

In the tent we left some letters, a few clothes and a sextant, an artificial glass horizon and a hypsometer. At 7.30 P.M., Framheim time, we left Polheim. How often we turned and sent it a last farewell, it is not easy to tell.

V

THE DEATH OF CAPTAIN SCOTT

LIEUT. E. R. G. R. EVANS, R.N.

[*New York Times,* February 11, 1913.— Copyright. By permission.]

CHRISTCHURCH, New Zealand, February 10.— Capt. Robert F. Scott's Antarctic ship, the *Terra Nova,* on January 18, this year, arrived at Cape Evans, the base on McMurdo Sound, where it was to meet the explorers on their return from the expedition in search of the South Pole and bring them back, if they were ready. It was learned from the shore party found at this base that Captain Scott and the four men with him had reached the Pole on January 18, 1912, but all had perished on the return journey, about the end of March. Their bodies were not found until a searching party discovered them on November 12, nearly eight months after the disaster.

Captain Scott, Dr. Edward A. Wilson, chief of the scientific staff, and Lieut. H. R. Bowers had made their way back to within 155 miles of Cape Evans, when they were caught in a blizzard and were overcome about March 29. They were then within eleven miles of One Ton Depot, where they would have found shelter and supplies.

* * * * * *

THE SEARCH PARTY'S JOURNEY

The search party left Cape Evans after the winter on October 30 last. The party, which was organized by Surgeon Atkinson, consisted of two divisions, Atkinson taking the dog teams with Garrard and Demetri, and Mr. Wright being in charge of a party including Nelson, Gran, Lashley, Crean, Williamson, Keohane, and Hooper, with seven Indian mules. They were provisioned for three months, as they expected an extended search.

One Ton Camp was found in order, and all provisioned.

Proceeding along the old southern route, Wright's party sighted Captain Scott's tent on November 12. Within it were found the bodies of Captain Scott, Dr. Wilson, and Lieutenant Bowers. They had saved their records, hard pressed as they were.

From these papers the following information was gleaned:—

The first death was that of Seaman Edgar Evans, petty officer of the Royal Navy, official number 160,225, who died on February 17 at the foot of the Beardmore Glacier. His death was accelerated by a concussion of the brain sustained while traveling over the rough ice some time before.

Capt. L. E. G. Oates of the Sixth Inniskillen Dragoons was the next lost. His feet and hands had been badly frostbitten from exposure on the march. Although he struggled on heroically, on March 16 his comrades knew that his end was approaching. He had borne his intense suffering for weeks without complaint, and he did not give up hope to the very end.

OATES WENT OUT TO DIE

Captain Scott wrote in his diary this tribute to Captain Oates:

'He was a brave soul. He slept through the night, hoping not to wake, but he awoke in the morning. It was blowing a blizzard. Oates said, "I am just going outside and may be some time." He went out into the blizzard, and we have not seen him since.'

Another passage read: 'We knew that Oates was walking to his death, but, though we tried to dissuade him, we knew it was the act of a brave man and an English gentleman.'

On March 16 Oates was really unable to travel, but the others could not leave him and he would not hold them back. After his gallant death, Scott, Wilson, and Bowers pushed on northward when the abnormally bad weather would permit them to proceed. They were forced to camp on March 1, in latitude 79° 40' S., longitude 169° 23' E., eleven miles south of the big depot at One Ton Camp.

This refuge they never reached, owing to a blizzard, which is known from the records of the party at Cape Evans to have lasted nine days, overtaking them. Their food and fuel gave out and they succumbed to exposure.

In Captain Scott's diary, Surgeon Atkinson found the following, which is quoted verbatim:

MESSAGE TO THE PUBLIC

The causes of the disaster are not due to faulty organization, but to misfortune in all risks which had to be undertaken.

1. The loss of the pony transport in March, 1911, obliged me to start later than I had intended, and obliged the limits of stuff transported to be narrowed.

2. The weather throughout the outward journey, and especially the long gale in 83° S., stopped us.

3. The soft snow in lower reaches of glacier again reduced pace.

We fought these untoward events with a will and conquered, but it cut into our provision reserve.

Every detail of our food supplies, clothing, and depots made on the interior ice-sheet and over that long stretch of 700 miles to the Pole and back, worked out to perfection. The advance party would have returned to the glacier in fine form and with surplus of food, but for the astonishing failure of the man whom we had least expected to fail. Edgar Evans was thought the strongest man of the party.

The Beardmore Glacier is not difficult in fine weather, but on our return we did not get a single completely fine day; this with a sick companion enormously increased our anxieties.

As I have said elsewhere we got into frightfully rough ice and Edgar Evans received a concussion of the brain — he died a natural death, but left us a shaken party with the season unduly advanced.

But all the facts above enumerated were as nothing to the surprise which awaited us on the Barrier. I maintain that our arrangements for returning were quite adequate, and that no one in the world would have expected the temperatures and surfaces which we encountered at this time of the year. On the summit in lat. 85°, 86° we had –20°, –30°. On the Barrier in lat. 82°, 10,000 feet lower, we had –30° in the day, –47° at night pretty regularly, with continuous head wind during our day marches. It is clear that these circumstances come on very suddenly, and our wreck is certainly due to this sudden advent of severe weather, which does not seem to have any satisfactory cause. I do not think human beings ever came through such a month as we have come through, and we should have got through in spite of the weather but for the sickening of a second companion, Captain Oates, and for a

shortage of fuel in our depots for which I cannot account, and finally, but for the storm which has fallen on us within eleven miles of the depot at which we hoped to secure our final supplies. Surely misfortune could scarcely have exceeded this last blow. We arrived within eleven miles of our old One Ton Camp with fuel for one last meal and food for two days. For four days we have been unable to leave the tent — the gale howling about us. We are weak, writing is difficult, but for my own sake I do not regret this journey, which has shown that Englishmen can endure hardships, help one another, and meet death with as great a fortitude as ever in the past. We took risks, we knew we took them; things have come out against us, and therefore we have no cause for complaint, but bow to the will of Providence, determined still to do our best to the last. But if we have been willing to give our lives to this enterprise, which is for the honor of our country, I appeal to our countrymen to see that those who depend on us are properly cared for.

Had we lived, I should have had a tale to tell of the hardihood, endurance, and courage of my companions which would have stirred the heart of every Englishman. These rough notes and our dead bodies must tell the tale, but surely, surely, a great rich country like ours will see that those who are dependent on us are properly provided for.

(Signed) R. SCOTT.

March 25, 1912.

Surgeon Atkinson and his party gathered the records and effects of the dead men and read the burial service over their bodies and erected a cairn and cross to their memory over the inner tent in which they buried them. A record of the finding of their bodies was left attached to the cross.

The party then searched for twenty miles south, endeavoring to discover the body of Captain Oates. It was not found, but another cairn and record were left in the vicinity to his memory.

It should here most certainly be noted that the southern party nobly stood by their sick companions to the end, and in spite of their distressing condition they had retained every record and thirty-five pounds of geological specimens which proved to be of the greatest scientific value. This emphasizes the nature of their journey.

VI

THE CONQUERING OF MT. McKINLEY

BELMORE BROWNE

[*Hearst's Magazine*, December, 1912.
By permission.]

There is only one workmanlike way to reach the northern face of Mt. McKinley — in the winter time with dog sleds.

Professor Herschel C. Parker and the writer had exhausted every other promising approach. In 1906 we had studied the western and southwestern ridges, and in 1910 we had explored the excessively rugged glaciers and mountains of the southern approach. During the latter explorations we had tried the mountain at several different points between the southwestern, southern, and southeastern ridges, and on one of these attempts we reached our highest altitude of 10,300 feet. The problem of telling whether or not any particular route to the summit of this great peak is feasible, is far more simple than one would suppose. For Mt. McKinley rises to such a high altitude that unless the climbers find a route where they can camp and transport their food and shelter, their efforts would fail at the beginning.

Almost every high mountain in the world rises from a high base. In South America, for instance, the actual climbing of a 20,000 foot peak generally begins at an altitude of 16,000 feet or over. Whereas Mt. McKinley rises from a base of from four to five thousand feet, leaving 15,000 feet of snow and ice to be negotiated. This fact makes Mt. McKinley the highest peak in the world above the line of perpetual snow.

No possible route to the summit existed on any of the slopes seen by Professor Parker and the writer in 1906 and 1910. We decided, therefore, to make a third attack from the northeastern side of the big peak.

We were actuated by two especial motives: the ascent of Mt. McKinley, and the crossing and exploration of the rugged and unknown portion of the Alaskan Range lying just east of Mt. McKinley. To accomplish both ends we were forced to begin our travels at some seacoast town on the southern side of the Alaskan Range. As Cook's Inlet is closed to navigation during the winter, we began our journey at Seward, more than four hundred miles from the northern side of McKinley, and over the greater part of this distance we broke our own trail through the silent, snow-smothered wilderness.

Our party was composed of four men: Professor Parker, Arthur Aten, Merl La Voy, and the writer. All our supplies were drawn by two dog teams, and the greater part of our freight was a dead weight as we could not use it until we reached the mountain. Every mile that we advanced cost us at least five extra miles of travel, as we made an average of three relays during the entire trip.

Nothing that I know of can approach the fascination of traveling with dog teams through the Alaskan wilderness in the winter time, and our search for an unknown pass added tremendously to the excitement of our journey.

Space will not permit of the recounting of our adventures in breaking through the range, suffice it to say that we were seventeen days without seeing any vegetation, and were a rough looking crew when we reached the north side. By our journey we added a new glacier to the southern slope of the range and tied on a glacier system some sixty miles in extent to the northeastern face of Mt. McKinley.

We arrived at the base of Mt. McKinley on April 25, after nearly three months of continuous travel. We had studied the country carefully as we advanced, and I had made a long reconnaissance trip ahead, locating a camping spot, and finding a route to the glacier that forms a roadway to the eastern face of the big mountain. This route led through a deep gash that we called 'Glacier Pass,' which lay at the head of the valley in which our base camp was located. Going up this pass I came to a large glacier which, to my surprise, I found to be the Muldrow Glacier.

This glacier was put on the map in 1902 by Alfred H. Brooks and D. L. Reakburn of the United States Geological Survey, who mapped it for a distance of about ten miles from its snout. From the rugged mountains where I was standing I could see the glacier from a point near its snout to where its two large branches drained the ice and snow from Mt. McKinley. The main branch headed at the base of the eastern cliffs, but the second branch came from the basin between McKinley's two peaks. We spoke of the glacier that fell from the 'big basin' as 'McKinley Glacier.'

On the 29th of April Professor Parker, Merl La Voy, and the writer began our advance on the mountain. Arthur Aten remained at base camp to look out for our dogs and belongings, and to read the barometer. Our advance was really a reconnaissance as we took one dog team and heavily loaded sleds.

Following the 'McKinley Glacier' we reached the cliffs of McKinley at an altitude of 11,000 feet. One glance at the northeast ridge convinced us that it was climbable. It now became necessary to return to base camp to leave the dogs with Aten, as there was no way of feeding them while we were on the big mountain. Before leaving we cached a sled loaded with about 300 pounds of mountain food and equipment, against our return. We reached base camp after an absence of two weeks.

On our arrival we were beset by villainous weather. The 'bad spell' lasted for about three weeks, and then La Voy cut his knee badly while trying to photograph a caribou. We could take these misadventures philosophically, however, as we were confident that the lengthening days would improve the climbing conditions on the big mountain.

June 4 dawned partly clear and the barometer as well as La Voy's knee was promising, so we got our mountain equipment in order, and the night of June 5 found us camped at the base of the first sérac on McKinley Glacier. Aten had given us a hand with a dog team and intended to return at once to base camp, but we were pretty well played out by the long tramp and he stayed with us all night, sharing my wolf robe. The next morning we awoke to find a heavy snowstorm raging and we were forced to give up all thought of traveling. Aten, fearing that his trail would soon be covered, started immediately after breakfast. Lying full length on the light sled, he whistled to the eager dogs and shot away into the gray mist. On the 6th, 7th, and 8th of June the storm continued and we lay storm-bound in our little tent. We were dumfounded by the turn the weather had taken; all the mountains that were practically free of their winter mantles in May were now buried deep in snow.

We couldn't understand it, but since then we have found that the bad weather was general, and old settlers in the lowlands told us later that they had never seen so stormy a summer.

On the following day, paradoxical as it may seem, we were held by good weather, for the sun blazing down on the masses of new snow that clung to the cliffs made it dangerous to venture near. Even where we were camped — some 400 yards from the base of the cliffs — we did not feel any too secure, although there was a low moraine to guard us.

The temperature on this day was the highest recorded by us while we were on the ice. It was 46 degrees in the sun at 1 P.M., and 26 degrees in the shade! About noon a great avalanche fell, throwing a snow cloud about 1000 feet high. It was so close to us that we had to lower our tent or the tremendous wind caused by the falling snow, would have done us damage. The avalanche swept across the part of the sérac we had to cross and was finally stopped by the large crevasses. The thunder of snowslides was continuous during the day.

Our enforced wait had lowered our food supply and after the sun had settled the snow, La Voy and I snowshoed six miles to a cache we had made in Glacier Pass and returned with alcohol, pemmican, hardtack, and sugar.

Our second ascent of the glacier was accomplished without any unusual adventures. La Voy hurt his 'game' knee by falling into a crevasse, but our being roped averted a tragedy. Avalanches fell regularly but where we had to pass under the cliffs, we chose the safest time of day — either early morning or late evening. The trail breaking was excessively hard work, and our eyes suffered accordingly, as the glare on the snow made us snow-blind; but liberal doses of eye 'dope' allowed us to continue.

Our sled was reached on June 13, and a great weight was taken from our minds. Besides a liberal supply of food and fuel, we recovered many luxuries, such as caribou and mountain sheep skins to sleep on, and some pocket editions of well-known authors, and a pocket chessboard made life more worth living.

We were now at an altitude of 11,000 feet. The average cloud level was below us, and while we still had storms to contend with, we suffered less from delays than we had on the lower glaciers. On June 14 we packed all our duffle to the base of the northeast ridge. Just above us the ridge was broken by a low coll, and above us a steep but climbable snow slope led to the top.

While we were relaying up our packs, great masses of mist came rolling over the range from the south. The lowlands on the north were soon covered with as dense a mass of clouds as I have ever seen, that rose higher and higher until we were enveloped in mist and snow. We dug a deep hole for our tent, and shoveled the blocks of snow into a wall, so that we were well sheltered. The storm continued for two days and we lay in our fur bags listening to the howling of the wind and the sound of snow slithering across our frozen tent. Late on the afternoon of June 16, it cleared a little and we moved up the glacier to the point where we could climb the ridge. Removing our snowshoes, we toiled upward, pounding big foot holes as we went. We found a fairly flat place near the top of the ridge that with a little shoveling would make a good camp site.

The view from the coll was beyond words! We looked straight down into a grim amphitheater; the walls were as savage as I have ever seen. About a thousand feet below us lay a floor of cold gray clouds that hid the bottom of the great hollow, and as we looked a shaft of sunlight broke through the western peaks, and turned the clouds to fire.

On June 17 we relayed all our belongings 800 feet in the air to the top of the coll. Our altitude was 11,800 feet and the 'Coll Camp,' as we called it, was our climbing base during our attack on Mt. McKinley. We shoveled far into the snow and set the tent back so that it was absolutely protected from any gale. I reorganized our outfit, and found that we had ample rations for one month.

On June 18 I made the following entry in my diary: 'It looks as if it will be a good day to-morrow, and if it is, we will try to take a load of food and necessities up to the big basin between the two peaks.'

This entry expresses the optimism with which we planned the ascent of the ridge. As a matter of fact it took us four days to reach the edge of the big basin at an altitude of 15,150 feet. Once we were forced to return to the Coll Camp for ten days' rations, as we were beginning to realize the difficulties that confronted us. Our actual climbing time between our Coll Camp at 11,000 feet and our 'Fifteen Thousand Camp,' was fifteen hours of constant toil. It required seven hours of the hardest labor to climb to our 'Ridge Camp' at 13,600 feet, and eight hours climbing from the 'Ridge Camp' to the 'Fifteen Thousand Camp.' While relaying, after the steps were made we climbed faster. Deep, soft snow lying at a dangerous angle was the principal cause of our slow time.

On the 24th of June we had packed our complete equipment to 15,150 feet, and we were glad to find a level spot in the lee of some great granite slabs where we could pitch our tent. We were now on the very edge of the 'Big Basin' and from our tent door we could see the ice séracing down between Mt. McKinley's two peaks. Between the séracs lay smooth snow slopes, and all we had to do to enter the basin was to make an easy 'traverse' under the cliffs of the northeast ridge.

I went through an experience at this camp that gave us all the deepest cause for worry. Both Professor Parker and La Voy had had difficulty in digesting our pemmican. They thought that the pemmican was not good, and I scoffed at the idea until we reached the 15,000-foot camp and then I was attacked by severe cramps. Now pemmican was the foundation on which we had builded our hopes of reaching the summit, and if we found that we could not use it at high altitudes, we would be in a serious predicament. We decided to cook it at our next camp in the hope that it would be more digestible. During the night the wind began to moan among the rocks, and soon a gale was shrieking down between the two peaks. Mingled with the rattle of the gale we heard the lash of wind-driven snow. When we awoke next morning, the snow was still falling and as we lay blissfully dozing in our fur bags, avalanches began to roar down into the glacial amphitheaters below us, until the very mountain seemed to tremble, and the sound swelled to the steady rumble of thunder. We were stormbound all day.

June 26 dawned clear, and when night had come we were camped, bag and baggage, in the center of the 'Big Basin,' at an altitude of 16,000 feet. A sérac about 800 feet high broke across the basin above us, but on its northern end we could see good slopes of avalanche snow that promised an easy route to the top.

The temperature inside of our tent at 8.30 p.m. was 5 degrees below zero. Our vitality was low on account of the altitude and we suffered severely from the cold, and got little sleep. On June 27 we advanced in two relays to an altitude of 17,150 feet. This camp was situated about halfway up the 'big basin' in a flat that lay between the two séracs.

The last and highest sérac rose about 800 feet above us, but it came principally from the south peak, and there was an easy route that led around the north end to the very top of the 'Big Basin.' The main northeast ridge rose directly south of our camp, and while its side was steep in places, we saw that we could reach the top easily and follow it to the final summit of the south peak. We all got thoroughly chilled while making camp, but the thermometer only registered 8 degrees below zero — a great improvement over our last camp.

On June 28 we rested and reorganized. It blew a gale all day and we devoted ourselves to preparing for the final climb. The clouds were all below us and a clear sunset in the evening promised a good climbing day. Professor Parker boiled a hypsometer as a check on our aneroids. The temperature at 3.45 p.m. in the sun, was 8 degrees by one thermometer and 9 degrees by another. We ate sparingly of pemmican pudding.

At 6.30 on the morning of June 29 we started for the summit. It was a wonderful morning, clear and cold; the great snow slopes of the two peaks were still in shadow and the only sound was the grating of our ice creepers on the hard crust. As it was light all night we did not give a thought to the speed we should make, but plodded slowly and steadily upward. Our course was directly up the side of the northeast ridge. About 200 feet above camp we crossed a little bench, but from there on to the top, the grade was steep and we were forced to zigzag and chop steps.

Not a single difficulty confronted us. In places we encountered soft snow that kept us from making better time, but the difficult climbing was all behind us on the lower ridge. We reached the top of the ridge in about two hours and a half. According to our two barometers, we were now at an elevation of 18,250 feet. This placed our climbing at about 400 feet an hour. The altitude was in part responsible for our slow progress, but I feel that our light diet of raisins, sugar and hardtack was as important a factor; for while it was our rule to climb slowly but steadily, I know that if we had been well fed, we could have made faster time with the same expense of energy.

At the point where we reached the summit of the ridge we wound back and forth between great blocks of granite. As a keen wind was blowing from the south we munched our second breakfast in the lee of the rocks. The views looking down from this ridge were beyond words. We could see the whole eastern sweep of the great Alaskan Range spread out like a map below us. On the northern side of the range there was not one cloud. The tangled mountain chains blended into the rolling foothills, which in turn melted into the dim blue of the timbered lowlands that rolled away to the northward, growing bluer and bluer until they were lost at the end of the world.

On the humid south side, a sea of clouds was rolling against the main range like surf on a rocky shore. The clouds rose as we watched. At one point a cloud would break through between two guarding peaks; beyond, a serpentine mass would creep northward along a glacier gap in the range; soon every pass was filled with cloud battalions that joined forces on the northern side, and swept downward like a triumphant army over the northern foothills. It was a striking and impressive illustration of the war that the elements are constantly waging along the Alaskan Range.

On the southern side hang the humid clouds of the Pacific Slope; on the north is the clear, dry climate of the interior, while between, like a giant earthwork between two hostile armies, stands the Alaskan Range. From our eerie we could look down onto our 1910 battleground.

Through deep blue chasms in the clouds the well-remembered contours of the rugged peaks that we had explored in that eventful summer seemed like the faces of old friends. As we advanced upward along the arête we noticed that we were short of breath, but the altitude did not affect us in any other way. At a little less than 19,000 feet we got our first near view of the summit. The rocks ended and the ridge broadened into the first swell of the final summit. While climbing the ridge the wind had increased, and now the southern sky had darkened and the wind was blowing a small gale. Ahead of us was a round dome some 300 feet in altitude that we must climb before reaching the snow of the final summit. The footing was good and we made better time.

By the time we had reached the foot of the summit, the wind was laden with dry snow, and from this point upward every landmark was wiped out and we faced an ever-increasing blizzard. We had taken careful bearings, however, and as long as we were going uphill we had no fear as far as our ability to reach the final ridge was concerned. But several other facts *did* worry us. When I ended my turn of step chopping at 20,000 feet I found that my hands were beginning to freeze. La Voy's and my hands had become coated with ice in the making of steps, and from using the axes our leather-covered mittens had, in turn, become covered. The storm was so severe and the cold so pitiless that I was actually afraid to get new mittens out of my *ruck-sack* for fear that my hands would be frozen during the operation. In the lashing sheets of dry snow I could no longer see La Voy, and Parker who was only twenty feet ahead, was a dim blur. Realizing our desperate position, I concentrated my mind on getting blood back into my hands. During the process we were rising slowly foot by foot as La Voy finished the steps. At times I could no longer see Parker, and I had to feel for the steps with my ice creepers. At last I heard La Voy's hail above the roar of the wind, and knew that my turn to chop had come. Professor Parker advanced to the steps where La Voy stood, and when I joined them we stood braced against the storm and talked the situation over. Our hard work had come to an end; for just above me I could see between the clouds of snow a small *bergschrund,* or crack, that marked the shoulder of the ridge. I advanced to the lee of this point and as I rose above it I was met by a frozen gale that drove the breath from my body — I could n't face it. Quickly returning to my companions I told them that we could do nothing at present on the summit. We were in a dangerous place. The summit of the mountain was a horseshoe-shaped ridge about one-third of a mile in length, with the opening facing east. It was uneven on top and from clear views that we had obtained from below, we knew that there was a hummock or small dome rising from the northern bend of the horseshoe summit. This small dome is, in all probability, the highest point on Mt. McKinley. Now we were stormbound on the northern end of the horseshoe curve, where the mountain fell away to join the northeast ridge. According to our traveling time we were 250 feet above the point where Professor Parker's 20,000-foot barometer had ceased to register.

On reaching 19,000 feet my barometer had agreed within 100 feet with Professor Parker's. But as we rose higher my instrument — probably due to false compensation — *had dropped with great rapidity to 17,200 feet, or the same altitude as our camp between the two peaks!* From then until I returned to our 17,000-foot camp it was useless, but on the following day it regained its composure and registered the same as Professor Parker's. Professor Parker's barometer behaved with absolute regularity throughout, and as we knew that the final summit rose about 200 feet above us, the summit, according to our calculations, would be 20,450 feet above sea level.

The United States Government places the summit — by triangulation — at 20,300 feet, a small difference indeed. On leaving from, and returning to, our base camp, both our barometers and a third that Aten had read twice daily during our absence, closely agreed; and furthermore, all three agreed closely with Brooks' contour lines.

On returning to my companions, we held a council of war. While we could probably have reached the summit in a half-hour in clear weather, we were afraid to face the present gale. With our glasses covered with ice and fearing to remove them on account of the cold, we were helpless, and could not see each other even when only separated by a few feet. The fact that our steps were completely wiped out added to our concern, for we realized how difficult it would be to find the narrow ridge where it joined the smooth dome a thousand feet below us. After looking over our position, we decided to take the odds offered and try to ride out the storm.

Having once decided on this course we set to work and soon chopped a small shelter in the hard snow. Our hopes were soon blasted, however, for after a few minutes of inaction we began to feel the numbing effect of the cold. The gale was driving the dry snow into every seam and pore of our clothing, and the heat of our bodies was turning the snow to ice. Our parkas were becoming stiff and the wolverine fur on our parkahoods was frozen stiff from the moisture of our breath; our mittens were hard with ice, and we held our ice axes with difficulty. Our position was an unique one as I do not believe there is a parallel case in the history of mountaineering. Had Mt. McKinley's summit been a peak we would have swung to the leeward snow slopes and claimed a first ascent. As it was, we were on the summit's edge and but for the extent and formations of this 'ridge-summit' we should have claimed the first ascent. We were in the position of a ship that had traveled thousands of miles to reach a certain city and had then been fog-bound at the harbor's mouth. This much remains to console us: as far as the climbing was concerned we conquered Mt. McKinley — and when some day a party stands on the highest snow they will have followed our trail to the last dome. If it were not for this thought we would have to try again. The storm had now grown to a point where to face it required all our strength.

As I felt the cold creeping upward from my numbed hands and feet, I knew that it was dangerous to remain on the peak an instant longer, so I yelled to Parker and La Voy that we must get off the peak and get off quickly and that I would lead. The descent through the storm was the most exciting experience of my life. Everything depended on our finding and following the steps we had chopped, and the only way I could find them was by feeling for the soft spots in the snow. After what seemed hours, we arrived at a level spot above the first swell above the ridge, and a half-hour later we saw dim rock shapes through the storm and realized that the ridge was found.

With thankful hearts we halted to leeward of the highest rocks to rest, and as we continued downward to our camp the ridge protected us from the gale. Soon after our return the wind began to moderate but the *tourmente* on the summit continued for some hours.

The following day dawned as clear as crystal, and all day long the summit stood clear cut against the sky. We could not climb, however, for our moccasins, gloves, and outer clothing were impregnated with ice dust of the storm, and all day long we kept our alcohol stove going and dried our duffle. We spent hours talking of the causes of mountain storms, and we all held fast to the theory that it was the effect of the sun on the atmosphere that caused the sudden savage gales that lashed the peaks until night dispelled them. Acting on this theory, we determined that our next attempt would be made before the sun had had a chance to warm the lower strata of air.

Our inability to eat pemmican was a tremendous blow to us. It was not alone the weakening effect of our light diet that worried us, as added to this was the great waste of energy from having packed a food we could not eat, to a height of 17,000 feet, where everything in the food line was worth its weight in gold. Under our restricted diet we found that we were reduced to four days' rations, whereas if we had been able to eat pemmican, we possibly could have remained in the big basin a week longer. During our day of rest La Voy and I suffered acutely from snow-blindness, but thanks to a liberal supply of boracic acid and zinc sulphate, we got our eyes into fair condition for our second attempt to reach the summit.

Professor Parker was not affected by this painful malady, although his snow glasses gave less protection than the type La Voy and I used. We attributed all our eye trouble to step chopping and trail breaking, as in this work a man has nothing of a dark color on which to rest his eyes, and, what is worse, he is forced to keep his eyes focused on the white, glaring surface of the snow.

On the first of July we arose at 1.30 A.M. The weather as far as I could tell by looking down from the big basin on to the northern foothills, was beautifully clear. Not a cloud was visible and from the tent door the distant land, 15,000 feet below me stretched away like a great blue sea. We left camp at 3 A.M. and in two hours and a half we had climbed to 18,250 feet, and put the most difficult part of the ascent behind us.

On reaching the top of the ridge, we looked down onto a dense mass of clouds that were sweeping up from the Susitua Valley. Without waiting to rest, we turned and made the best speed we could up the ridge. As we advanced the clouds came rolling after us, until at 19,500 feet we were enveloped in a cold wind-driven mist that stopped our progress. Just before the wind caught us, we stopped above the last rocks at the base of the final peak, and we could trace our wind-blown steps to a point just below the little *bergschrund* on the edge of the crest where we had tried to weather the storm two days before. From where we stood we estimated that the north peak rose about 500 feet above us. As far as we could tell, the south peak was only 500 feet higher than the north peak.

Now we were stormbound again. We held on for more than an hour walking back and forth to fight the frost, and then, as the roar of the wind grew louder, we turned without a word, and fought our way back over the ground we had given so much to gain. We left a minimum thermometer in a crack on the western side of the highest boulder of the northeast ridge. On reaching camp, we held an inventory, and finding that we did not have enough food to allow of another attempt on the peak, we took time by the forelock, and descended to our 15,000-foot camp. We left our high camp after lunch, and it presented a lonesome sight as we turned our faces toward the lowlands. We descended in about three hours and our old trail still held. The following day we reached our 'Coll Camp' after some trying experiences. I was snow-blind again, and while leading I broke through a snow cornice on a knife-edge arête, but sunk my ax into the snow before the rope became taut. We organized at the Coll and at 8.30 that night we were camped among some crevasses at the head of the big sérac. We came down easily as far as the traveling was concerned, but our long absence had made a great difference in the snow, and great crevasses had appeared in all directions. These and a heavy fog kept us busy until finally the fog won and we made camp.

We were greatly worried about the séracs below us as we feared that some of the *bergschrunds* might have opened and blocked our path, but we finally wormed our way through, and after traveling all night, we reached 'Glacier Pass.'

I will never forget the joy we felt at having earth and rock beneath our feet. It was the first time in twenty-eight days that our feet had rested on anything but snow and ice. On the 4th of July, we staggered down the snow-filled pass on our way to base camp. La Voy and I were carrying packs of over eighty pounds, and in our weakened condition we made rough weather of it. But the joy of smelling green grass and flowers, and resting our aching eyes on the green mountain pastures repaid us for all our work. Where the snow melted into crystal streams, we entered the green lowlands and a herd of fifty caribou welcomed us to their country. The sun was going down in a sea of crimson when we neared our base camp. As we stumbled on, overcome with excitement, I kept wondering if Aten was safe, for much can happen in twenty-eight wilderness days.

Above our camp on a round hill stood a large rock that overlooked the surrounding country, and as we strained our eyes ahead, we saw a figure against the sky, then a smaller shape — a dog, appeared, and our yells echoed down the valley! We were a happy crew that night!

For several days we ate and rested, enjoying to the full the beauties of our wilderness home. But as the tender caribou meat brought back our strength, we began to long for the trail again, and on a sunny morning, we sadly bade good-by to our old camp and turned our faces northward — toward the Yukon.

VII

MY FIRST FLIGHT

H. G. WELLS

[*American Magazine*, December, 1912.
By permission.]

Hitherto my only flights have been [10] flights of imagination, but this morning [1] I flew. I spent about ten or fifteen minutes in the air; we went out to sea, soared up, came back over the land, circled higher, planed steeply down to the water, and [15] I landed with the conviction that I had had only the foretaste of a great store of hitherto unsuspected pleasures. At the first chance I will go up again, and I will go higher and further.

This experience has restored all the keenness of my ancient interest in flying, which had become a little fagged and flat by too much hearing and reading about the thing and not enough participation. Fifteen years ago, in the days of Langley and Lilienthal, I was one of the few journalists who believed and wrote that flying was possible — it affected my reputation unfavorably, and produced [30] in the few discouraged pioneers of those days a quite touching gratitude. Over my mantel as I write hangs a very blurred and bad but interesting photograph that Professor Langley sent me thirteen years [35] ago. It shows the flight of the first piece of human machinery heavier than air that ever kept itself up for any length of time. It was a model, a little affair that would not have lifted a cat; [40] it went up in a spiral and came down unsmashed, bringing back, like Noah's dove, the promise of tremendous things.

SOME EXPLODED PROPHECIES

That was only thirteen years ago, and it is amusing to recall how cautiously even we out-and-out believers did our prophesying. I was quite a desperate fellow; I said outright that in my lifetime [50] we should see men flying. But I qualified that by repeating that for many years to come it would be an enterprise only for quite fantastic daring and skill. We conjured up stupendous difficulties [55] and risks. I was deeply impressed and greatly discouraged by a paper a dis-

[1] Friday, August 2, 1912.

tinguished Cambridge mathematician produced to show that a flying-machine was bound to pitch fearfully, that as it flew on its pitching *must* increase, until up [5] went its nose, down went its tail, and it fell like a knife. We exaggerated every possibility of instability. We imagined that when the aëroplane was n't 'kicking up ahind and afore' it would be heeling [10] over to the lightest side wind. A sneeze might upset it. We contrasted our poor human equipment with the instinctive balance of a bird, which has had ten million years of evolution by way of a start. . . .

(The waterplane in which I soared over [15] Eastbourne this morning with Mr. Grahame White was as steady as a motorcar running on asphalt.)

Then we went on from those anticipations of swaying insecurity to speculations [20] about the psychological and physiological effects of flying. Most people who look down from the top of a cliff or high tower feel some slight qualms of dread, many feel a quite sickening dread. Even if men [25] struggled high into the air, we asked, would n't they be smitten up there by such a lonely and reeling dismay as to lose all self-control? And, above all, would n't [30] the pitching and tossing make them quite horribly seasick?

I have always been a little haunted by that last dread. It gave a little undertow of funk to the mood of lively curiosity [35] with which I got aboard the waterplane this morning — that sort of faint, thin funk that so readily invades one on the verge of any new experience; when one tries one's first dive, for example, or [40] pushes off for the first time down an ice-run. I thought I should very probably be seasick — or, to be more precise, airsick; I thought also that I might be very giddy, and that I might get thoroughly cold and [45] uncomfortable. None of those things happened.

I am still in a state of amazement at the smooth steadfastness of the motion. There is nothing on earth to compare with that, unless — and that I can't judge — it [50] is an ice-yacht traveling on perfect ice. The finest motor-car in the world on the best road would be a joggling, quivering thing beside it.

To begin with, we went out to sea before [55] the wind, and the plane would not readily rise. We went with an undulating movement, leaping with a light splashing pat upon the water, from wave to wave. Then we came about into the wind, and rose; and looking over I saw that there were no longer those periodic flashes of white foam. I was flying. And it was

AS STILL AND STEADY AS DREAMING

I watched the widening distance between our floats and the waves. It was n't by any means a windless day — there was a brisk fluctuating breeze blowing out of the north over the downs. It seemed hardly to affect our flight at all.

And as for the giddiness of looking down, one does not feel it at all. It is difficult to explain why this should be so, but it is so. I suppose in such matters I am neither exceptionally steady-headed, nor is my head exceptionally given to swimming. I can stand on the edge of cliffs of a thousand feet or so and look down, but I can never bring myself right up to the edge, nor crane over to look to the very bottom. I should want to lie down to do that. And the other day I was on that Belvedere place at the top of the Rotterdam skyscraper, a rather high wind was blowing, and one looks down through the chinks between the boards one stands on upon the heads of the people in the streets below; I did n't like it. But I looked directly down on a little fleet of fishing-boats over which we passed, and on the crowds assembling on the beach, and on the bathers who stared up at us from the breaking surf with an entirely agreeable exaltation. And Eastbourne in the early morning sunshine had all the brightly detailed littleness of a town viewed from high up on the side of a great mountain.

THAT GOING-DOWN SENSATION

When Mr. Grahame White told me we were going to plane down, I will confess I tightened my hold on the sides of the car, and prepared for something like the down-going sensation of a switchback railway on a larger scale. Just for a moment there was that familiar feeling of something pressing one's heart up towards one's shoulders and one's lower jaw up into its socket, and of grinding one's lower teeth against the upper, and then it passed. The nose of the car and all the machine was slanting downward, we were gliding quickly down, and yet there was no feeling that one rushed, not even as one rushes in coasting a hill on a bicycle. It was n't a tithe of the thrill of those three descents one gets on the great mountain railway in the White City. There one gets a disagreeable quiver up one's backbone from the wheels, and a real sense of falling.

It is quite peculiar to flying that one is incredulous of any collision. Some time ago I was in a motor-car that ran over and killed a small dog, and this wretched little incident has left an open wound upon my nerves. I am never quite happy in a car now; I can't help keeping an apprehensive eye ahead. But you fly with an exhilarating assurance that you cannot possibly run over anything or run into anything — except the land or the sea, and even those large essentials seem a beautifully safe distance away.

THE NOISE OF THE PROPELLER

I had heard a great deal of talk about the deafening uproar of the engine. I counted a headache among my chances. There again reason reinforced conjecture. When in the early morning Mr. Travers came from Brighton in this Farman in which I flew, I could hear the hum of the great insect when it still seemed abreast of Beachey Head, and a good two miles away. If one can hear a thing at two miles, how much the more will one not hear it at a distance of two yards. But at the risk of seeming too contented for anything I will assert I heard that noise no more than one hears the drone of an electric ventilator upon one's table. It was only when I came to speak to Mr. Grahame White, or he to me, that I discovered that our voices had become almost infinitesimally small.

WE SHALL ALL BE FLYING

And so it was that I went up into the air at Eastbourne with the impression that flying was still an uncomfortable, experimental, and slightly heroic thing to do, and came down to the cheerful gathering crowd upon the sands again with the knowledge that it is a thing achieved for every one. It will get much cheaper no doubt, and much swifter, and be improved in a dozen ways,— we *must* get self-starting engines, for example, for both our aëroplanes and motor-cars,— but it is available to-day for any one who can reach it. An invalid lady of seventy could have enjoyed all that I did if only one could have got her into the passenger's seat. Getting there was a little difficult, it is true; the waterplane was out in the surf, and I was carried to it on a boatman's back, and then had to clamber carefully through the wires, but that is a matter of detail.

This flying is indeed so certain to become a general experience that I am sure that this description will in a few years seem almost as quaint as if I had set myself to record the fears and sensations of my First Ride in a Wheeled Vehicle. And I suspect that learning to control a Farman waterplane now is probably not much more difficult than, let us say, twice the difficulty in learning the control and management of a motor bicycle. I cannot understand the sort of young man who won't learn how to do it if he gets half a chance.

The development of these waterplanes is an important step towards the huge and swarming popularization of flying which is now certainly imminent. We ancient survivors of those who believed in and wrote about flying before there was any flying, used to make a great fuss about the dangers and difficulties of landing and getting up. We wrote with vast gravity about ' starting rails ' and ' landing stages,' and it is still true that landing an aëroplane, except upon a well-known and quite level expanse, is a risky and uncomfortable business. But getting up and landing upon fairly smooth water is easier than getting into bed. This alone is likely to determine the aëroplane routes along the line of the world's coast-lines and lake groups and water-ways.

The airmen will go to and fro over water as the midges do. Wherever there is a square mile of water the waterplanes will come and go like hornets at the mouth of their nest. But there are much stronger reasons than this convenience for keeping over water. Over water the air, it seems, lies in great level expanses; even when there are gales it moves in great uniform masses, like the swift still rush of a deep river. The airman, in Mr. Grahame White's phrase, can go to sleep on it.

But over the land, and for thousands of feet up into the sky, the air is more irregular than a torrent among rocks; it is — if only we could see it — a waving, whirling, eddying, flamboyant confusion.

A slight hill, a plowed field, the streets of a town, create riotous, rolling, invisible streams and cataracts of air, that catch the aviator unawares, make him drop disconcertingly, try his nerve. With a powerful enough engine he climbs at once again, but these sudden downfalls are the least pleasant and most dangerous experience in aviation. They exact a tiring vigilance. Over lake or sea, in sunshine, within sight of land — this is the perfect way of the flying tourist.. Gladly would I have set out for France this morning instead of returning to Eastbourne. And then coasted round to Spain and into the Mediterranean. And so by leisurely stages to India. And the East Indies. . . .

I find my study unattractive to-day.

VIII

THE HORRORS OF LOUVAIN

RICHARD HARDING DAVIS

[*New York Tribune*, August 31, 1914. By permission.]

LONDON, August 30.— I left Brussels on Thursday afternoon and have just arrived in London. For two hours on Thursday night I was in what for six hundred years had been the City of Louvain. The Germans were burning it, and to hide their work kept us locked in the railroad carriages. But the story was written against the sky, was told to us by German soldiers incoherent with excesses; and we could read it in the faces of women and children being led to concentration camps and of citizens on their way to be shot.

The Germans sentenced Louvain on Wednesday to become a wilderness, and with the German system and love of thoroughness they left Louvain an empty, blackened shell. The reason for this appeal to the torch and the execution of non-combatants, as given to me on Thursday morning by General von Lutwitz, military governor of Brussels, was this: On Wednesday while the German military commander of the troops in Louvain was at the Hotel de Ville talking to the burgomaster a son of the burgomaster with an automatic pistol shot the chief of staff and German staff surgeons.

Lutwitz claims this was the signal for the civil guard, in civilian clothes on roofs, to fire upon the German soldiers in the open square below. He said also the Belgians had quick-firing guns, brought from Antwerp. As for a week the Germans had occupied Louvain and closely guarded all approaches, the story that there was any gunrunning is absurd.

Fifty Germans were killed and wounded. For that, said Lutwitz, Louvain must be wiped out. So in pantomime with his fist he swept the papers across his table.

'The Hotel de Ville,' he added, 'was a beautiful building; it is a pity it must be destroyed.'

EDUCATED MANY AMERICAN PRIESTS

Ten days ago I was in Louvain when it was occupied by Belgian troops and King Albert and his staff. The city dates from the eleventh century and the population was 42,000. The citizens were brewers, lacemakers and manufacturers of ornaments for churches. The university once was the most celebrated in European cities, and still is, or was, headquarters of the Jesuits.

In the Louvain college many priests now in America have been educated, and ten days ago over the great yellow walls of the college, I saw hanging two American flags. I found the city clean, sleepy and pretty, with narrow, twisting streets and smart shops and cafés set in flower gardens of the houses, with red roofs, green shutters and white walls.

Over those that faced south had been trained pear trees, their branches heavy with fruit spread out against the walls like branches of candelabra. The Town Hall was very old and very beautiful, an example of Gothic architecture, in detail and design more celebrated even than the Town Hall of Bruges or Brussels. It was five hundred years old, and lately had been repaired with great taste and at great cost.

Opposite was the Church of St. Pierre, dating from the fifteenth century, a very noble building, with many chapels filled with carvings of the time of the Renaissance in wood, stone and iron. In the university were 150,000 volumes.

Near it was the bronze statue of Father Damien, priest of the leper colony in the South Pacific, of which Robert Louis Stevenson wrote. All these buildings now are empty, exploded cartridges. Statues, pictures, carvings, parchments, archives — all are gone.

COMPARED WITH UNITED STATES IN MEXICO

No one defends the sniper. But because ignorant Mexicans when their city was invaded fired upon our sailors, we did not destroy Vera Cruz. Even had we bombarded Vera Cruz, money could have restored it. Money can never restore Louvain. Great architects and artists, dead these six hundred years, made it beautiful, and their handiwork belonged to the world. With torch and dynamite the Germans have turned these masterpieces into ashes, and all the Kaiser's horses and all his men cannot bring them back again.

When by troop train we reached Louvain, the entire heart of the city was destroyed and fire had reached the Boulevard Tirlemont, which faces the railroad station. The night was windless, and the sparks rose in steady, leisurely pillars, falling back into the furnace from which they sprang. In their work the soldiers were moving from the heart of the city to the outskirts, street by street, from house to house.

In each building, so German soldiers told me, they began at the first floor, and when that was burning steadily passed to the one next. There were no exceptions — whether it was a store, chapel or private residence it was destroyed. The occupants had been warned to go, and in each deserted shop or house the furniture was piled, the torch was stuck under it, and into the air went the savings of years, souvenirs of children, of parents, heirlooms that had passed from generation to generation.

The people had time only to fill a pillowcase and fly. Some were not so fortunate, and by thousands, like flocks of sheep, they were rounded up and marched through the night to concentration camps. We were not allowed to speak to any citizen of Louvain, but the Germans crowded the windows, boastful, gloating, eager to interpret.

WAR ON THE DEFENSELESS

We were free to move from one end of the train to the other, and in the two hours during which it circled the burning city war was before us in its most hateful aspect.

In other wars I have watched men on one hilltop, without haste, without heat, fire at men on another hill, and in consequence on both sides good men were wasted. But in those fights there were no women or children, and the shells struck only vacant stretches of veldt or uninhabited mountainsides.

At Louvain it was war upon the defenseless, war upon churches, colleges, shops of milliners and lacemakers; war brought to the bedside and the fireside; against women harvesting in the fields, against children in wooden shoes at play in the streets.

At Louvain that night the Germans were like men after an orgy.

There were fifty English prisoners, erect and soldierly. In the ocean of gray the little patch of khaki looked pitifully lonely, but they regarded the men who had outnumbered but not defeated them with calm but uncurious eyes. In one way I was glad to see them there. Later they will bear witness as to how the enemy makes a wilderness and calls it war. It was a most weird picture.

On the high ground rose the broken spires of the Church of St. Pierre and the Hotel de Ville, and descending like steps were row beneath row of houses, roofless with windows like blind eyes. The fire had reached the last row of houses, those on the Boulevard de Jodigne. Some of these were already cold, but others sent up steady, straight columns of flame. In others at the third and fourth stories the window curtains still hung, flowers still filled the window boxes, while on the first floor the torch had just passed and the flames were leaping. Fire had destroyed the electric plant, but at times the flames made the station so light that you could see the second hand of your watch, and again all was darkness, lit only by candles.

MEN TO BE SHOT MARCHED PAST

You could tell when an officer passed by the electric torch he carried strapped to his chest. In the darkness the gray uniforms filled the station with an army of ghosts. You distinguished men only when pipes hanging from their teeth glowed red or their bayonets flashed.

Outside the station in the public square the people of Louvain passed in an unending procession, women bareheaded, weeping, men carrying the children asleep on their shoulders, all hemmed in by the shadowy army of gray wolves. Once they were halted, and among them were marched a line of men. They well knew their fellow townsmen. These were on their way to be shot. And better to point the moral an officer halted both processions and, climbing to a cart, explained why the men were to die. He warned others not to bring down upon themselves a like vengeance.

As those being led to spend the night in the fields looked across to those marked for death they saw old friends, neighbors of long standing, men of their own household. The officer bellowing at them from the cart was illuminated by the headlights of an automobile. He looked like an actor held in a spotlight on a darkened stage.

It was all like a scene upon the stage, so unreal, so inhuman, you felt it could not be true that the curtain of fire, purring and crackling and sending up hot sparks to meet the kind, calm stars, was only a painted backdrop; that the reports of rifles from the dark rooms came from blank cartridges, and that these trembling shopkeepers and peasants ringed in bayonets would not in a few minutes really die, but that they themselves and their homes would be restored to their wives and children.

You felt it was only a nightmare, cruel and uncivilized. And then you remembered that the German Emperor has told us what it is. It is his Holy War.

IX

THE FALL OF ANTWERP

ARTHUR RUHL

[Collier's, November 14, 1914.— Copyright.
By permission.]

The storm which was to burst over Antwerp the following night was gathering fast when we arrived on Tuesday morning. Army motor trucks loaded with dismantled aëroplanes and the less essential impedimenta screamed through the streets bound away from, not toward, the front. The Queen, that afternoon, was seen in the Hotel St. Antoine receiving the good-bys of various friends. Consuls suddenly locked their doors and fled. And the cannon, rumbling along the eastern horizon as they had rumbled, nearer and nearer, for a fortnight, were now beyond the outer line of forts and within striking distance of the town.

That night, an hour or two after midnight, in my hotel by the water front, I awoke to the steady clatter of hoofs on cobblestones and the rumble of wheels. I went to the window, on the narrow side street, black as all streets had been in Antwerp since the night that the Zeppelin threw its first bombs, and looked out. It was a moonlight night, clear and cold, and there along the Quai St. Michael, at the end of the street, was an army in retreat. They were Belgians, battered and worn out with their unbroken weeks of hopeless fighting; cavalrymen on their tired horses, artillerymen, heads sunk on their chests, drowsing on their lurching caissons; the patient little foot soldiers, rifles slung across their shoulders, scuffling along in their heavy overcoats.

In the dark shadow of the tall old houses a few people came out and stood there watching silently and, as one felt, in a sort of despair. All night long men were marching by — and in London they were still reading that it was but a 'demonstration' the Germans were engaged in — down the quay and across the pontoon bridge — the only way over the Scheldt — over to the Tête de Flandre and the road to Ghent. They were strung along the street next morning, boots mud-covered, mud-stained, intrenching shovels hanging to their belts, faces unshaven for weeks just as they had come from the trenches; yet still patient and cheerful, with that unshakable Flemish good cheer. Perhaps, after all, it was not a retreat; they might be swinging round to the south and St. Nicholas to attack the German flank. . . .

But before they had crossed, another army, a civilian army, flowed down on and over the quay. For a week people had been leaving Antwerp, now the general flight began. From villages to the east and southeast, from the city itself, people came pouring down. In wagons drawn by huge Belgian draft horses, in carts pulled by the captivating Belgian work dogs, panting mightily and digging their paws into the slippery cobbles; on foot, leading little children and carrying babies and dolls and canaries and great bundles of clothes and household things wrapped in sheets, they surged toward that one narrow bridge and the crowded ferryboats. I saw one old woman, gray-haired and tanned like an Indian squaw with work in the fields, yet with a fine, well-made face, pushing a groaning wheelbarrow. A strap went from the handles over her shoulders, and, stopping now and then to ask the news, she would slip off this harness, gossip for a time, then push on again. That afternoon under my window there was a tall wagon, a sort of hay wagon, in which there were twenty-two little tow-headed children, none more than eight or ten, and several almost babies in arms. By the side of the wagon a man, evidently father of some of them, stood buttering the end of a huge round loaf of bread and cutting off slice after slice, which the older children broke and distributed to the little ones. Two cows were tied to the back of the wagon and the man's wife squatted there milking them. All along the quay and in the streets leading into it were people like this — harmless, helpless, hard-working people, going they knew not where. The entrance to the bridge was soon choked. One went away and returned an hour later and found the same people waiting almost in the same spot, and, with that wonderful calm and patience of theirs, feeding their children or giving a little of their precious hay to the horses, quietly waiting their turn while the cannon which had driven them from their homes kept on thundering behind them.

That afternoon I walked uptown through the shuttered, silent streets — silent but for that incessant rumbling in the southeast and the occasional honking flight of some military automobile — to two of the hospitals. In one, a British hospital on the Boulevard Léopold, the doctor in charge was absent for the moment, and there was no one to answer my offer of occasional help if an outsider could be of use. As I sat waiting a tall, brisk Englishwoman, in nurse's uniform, came up and asked what I wanted. I told her.

'Oh,' she said, and in her crisp English voice, without further ado, 'will you help me with a leg?'

She led the way into her ward, and there we contrived between us to bandage and slip a board and pillow under a fractured thigh. Between whispers of '*Courage! Courage!*' to the Belgian soldier, she said that she was the wife of a British general and had two sons in the army, and a third —'Poor boy!' she murmured, more to him than to me—on one of the ships in the North Sea. I arranged to come back next morning to help with the lifting, and went on to another hospital in the Rue Nerviens, to find that little English lady who crossed with us in the Ostend boat in August on the way to her sister's hospital in Antwerp.

CHEERFUL LOSERS

Here in the quiet wards she had been working while the Germans swept down on Paris and were rolled back again, and while the little nation which she and her sister loved so well was being clubbed to its knees. Louvain, Liège, Malines, Namur—chapters in all the long, pitiless story were lying there in the narrow iron beds. There were men with faces chewed by shrapnel, men burned in the explosion of the powder magazine at Fort Waelhem, when the attack on Antwerp began—dragged out from the underground passage in which the garrison had sought momentary refuge and where most of them were killed, burned, and blackened. One strong, good-looking young fellow, able to eat and live apparently, was shot through the temples and blind in both eyes. It was the hour for carrying those well enough to stand it out into the court and giving them their afternoon's airing and smoke. One had lost an arm, another, a whimsical young Belgian, had only the stump of a left leg. When we started to lift him back into his bed, he said he had a better way than that. So he put his arms round my neck and showed me how to take him by the back and the well leg.

'*Bon!*' he said, and again '*Bon!*' when I let him down, and then reaching out and patting me on the back, '*Bon!*' he smiled again.

That night, behind drawn curtains which admitted no light to the street, we dined peacefully and well, and, except for this unwonted seclusion, just outside which were the black streets and still the endless procession of carts and wagons and shivering people, one might have forgotten, in that cheerfully lighted room, that we were not in times of peace. We even loitered over a grate fire before going to bed, and talked in drowsy and almost indifferent fashion of whether it was absolutely sure that the Germans were trying to take the town.

THE FLYING DEATH

It was almost exactly midnight that I found myself listening, half awake, to the familiar sound of distant cannon. One had come to think of it, almost, as nothing but a sound; and to listen with a detached and not unpleasant interest as a man tucked comfortably in bed follows a roll of thunder to its end or listens to the fall of rain.

It struck me suddenly that there was something new about this sound; I sat up in bed to listen, and at that instant a far-off, sullen 'Boom!' was followed by a crash as if lightning had struck a house a little way down the street. As I hurried to the window there came another far-off detonation, a curious wailing whistle swept across the sky, and over behind the roofs to the left there was another crash.

One after another they came, at intervals of half a minute, or screaming on each other's heels as if racing to their goal. And then the crash or, if farther away, muffled explosion as another roof toppled in, or cornice dropped off, as a house made of canvas drops to pieces in a play.

The effect of those unearthly wails, suddenly singing in across country in the dead of night from six—eight—ten miles away—heaven knows where—was, as the Germans intended it to be, tremendous. It was not easy to describe nor to be imagined by those who had not lived in that threatened city—the last Belgian stronghold—and felt that vast, unseen power rolling nearer and nearer. And now, all at once, it was here, materialized, demoniacal, a flying death, swooping across the dark into your very room.

It was like one of those dreams in which you cannot stir from your tracks, and meanwhile 'Boom! . . . *Tzee-ee-ee-ee!*' —is this one meant for you?

Already there was a patter of feet in the dark, and people with white bundles on their backs went stumbling by toward the river and the bridge. Motors came honking down from the inner streets, and the quay, which had begun to clear by this time, was again jammed. I threw on some clothes, hurried to the street. A rank smell of kerosene hung in the air; presently a petrol shell burst to the southward, lighting up the sky for an instant like the flare from a blast furnace, and a few moments later there showed over the roofs the flames of the first fire.

Although we could hear the wail of shells flying across their wide parabola both into the town and out from the first ring of forts, few burst in our part of the city that night, and we walked up as far as the cathedral without seeing anything but black and silent streets. Every one in the hotel was up and dressed by this time. Some were for leaving at once; one family, piloted by the comfortable Belgian servants — far cooler than any one else — went to the cellar, some gathered about the grate in the writing room to watch the night out; the rest of us went back to bed.

POURING OUT OF ANTWERP

There wasn't much sleep for any one that night. The bombardment kept on until morning, lulled slightly as if the enemy might be taking breakfast, then it continued into the next day. And now the city — a busy city of near 400,000 people — emptied itself in earnest. Citizens and soldiers, field guns, motor trucks, wheelbarrows, dogcarts, hayricks, baby carriages, droves of people on foot, all flowing down to the Scheldt, the ferries, and the bridge. They poured into coal barges, filling the yawning black holes as Africans used to fill slave ships, into launches and tugs, and along the roads leading down the river and southwestward toward Ostend.

One thought with a shudder of what would happen if the Germans dropped a few of their high-explosive shells into that helpless mob, and it is only fair to remember that they did not, although retreating Belgian soldiers were a part of it, and one of the German aeroplanes, a mere speck against the blue, was looking calmly down overhead. Nor did they touch the cathedral, and their agreement not to shell any of the buildings previously pointed out on a map delivered to them through the American Legation seemed to be observed.

Down through that mass of fugitives pushed a London motor-bus ambulance with several wounded British soldiers, one of them sitting upright, supporting with his right hand a left arm, the biceps, bound in a blood-soaked tourniquet, half torn away. They had come in from the trenches, where their comrades were now waiting, with their helpless little rifles, for an enemy miles away, who lay back at his ease and swept them with shrapnel. I asked them how things were going, and they said not very well. They could only wait until the German aeroplanes had given the range and the trenches became too hot, then fall back, dig themselves in, and play the same game over again.

TOWARD THE CANNON

Following them was a hospital-service motor car, driven by a Belgian soldier and in charge of a clean-cut, soldierlike-appearing young British officer. It was his present duty to motor from trench to trench across the zone of fire, with the London bus trailing behind, and pick up wounded. It wasn't a particularly pleasant job, he said, jerking his head toward the distant firing, and frankly he wasn't keen about it. We talked for some time, every one talked to every one else in Antwerp that morning, and when he started out again I asked him to give me a lift to the edge of town.

Quickly we raced through the Place de Meir and the deserted streets of the politer part of Antwerp, where, the night before, most of the shells had fallen. We went crackling over broken glass, past gaping cornices and holes in the pavement, five feet across and three feet deep, and once passed a house quietly burning away with none to so much as watch the fire. The city wall, along which are the first line of forts, drew near, then the tunnel passing under it, and we went through without pausing and on down the road to Malines. We were beyond the town now, bowling rapidly out into the flat Belgian country, and clinging there to the running board with the October wind blowing quite through a thin flannel suit, it suddenly came over me that things had moved very fast in the last five minutes, and that all at once, in some unexpected fashion, all that elaborate barrier of *laissez-passers, sauf conduits,* and so on, had been swept aside, and, quite as if it were the most ordinary thing in the world, I was spinning out to that almost mythical ' front.'

THE GUNNERS' CHORUS

Front, indeed! It was two fronts. There was an explosion just behind us, a hideous noise overhead, as if the whole zenith had somehow been ripped across like a tightly stretched piece of silk, and a shell from the Belgian fort under which we had just passed went hurtling down long aisles of air — further — further — to end in a faint detonation miles away.

Out of sight in front of us, there was an answering thud, and —'*Tzee-ee-ee-er-r-r-BONG!*'— a German shell had gone over us and burst behind the Belgian fort. Under this gigantic antiphony the motor car raced along, curiously small and ir-relevant on that empty country road.

We passed great holes freshly made — craters five or six feet across and three feet deep, neatly blown out of the mac-adam, then a dead horse. There were plenty of dead horses along the roads in France, but they had been so for days. This one's blood was not yet dry, and the shell that had torn the great rip in its chest must have struck here this morning.

We turned into the avenue of trees lead-ing up to an empty château, a field hos-pital until a few hours before. Mattresses and bandages littered the deserted room, and an electric chandelier was still burn-ing. The young officer pointed to some trenches in the garden. 'I had those dug to put the wounded in in case we had to hold the place,' he said. 'It was getting pretty hot.'

WHILE THE SHELLS BURST

There was nothing here now, however, and, followed by the London bus with its obedient enlisted men doing duty as am-bulance orderlies, we motored a mile or so further on to the nearest trench. It was in an orchard beside a brick farmhouse with a vista in front of barbed-wire en-tanglement and a carefully cleaned firing field stretching out to a village and trees about half a mile away. They had looked very interesting and difficult, those barbed-wire mazes and suburbs, ruthlessly swept of trees and houses, when I had seen the Belgians preparing for the siege six weeks before, and they were to be of about as much practical use now as pictures on a wall.

There are, it will be recalled, three lines of forts about Antwerp — the inner one, corresponding to the city's wall; a middle one a few miles further out, where the British now were, and the outer line, which the enemy had already passed. Their artillery was hidden far over behind the horizon trees, and the British marines and naval reserve men who manned these trenches could only wait there, rifle in hand, for an enemy that would not come, while a captive balloon a mile or two away to the eastward and an aeroplane sailing far overhead gave the ranges, and they waited for the shrapnel to burst. The trenches were narrow and shoulder deep, very like trenches for gas or water pipes, and reasonably safe except when a shell burst directly overhead. One had struck that morning just on the inner rim of the trench, blown out one of those craterlike holes, and discharged all its shrapnel back-ward across the trench and into one of the heavy timbers supporting a bomb-proof roof. A raincoat hanging to a nail in this timber was literally shot to shreds. 'That's where I was standing,' said the young lieutenant in command, pointing with a dry smile to a spot not more than a yard away from where the shell had burst.

Half a dozen young fellows, crouched there in the bombproof, looked out at us and grinned. They were brand-new sol-diers, some of them boys from the Lon-don streets who had answered the thrill-ing posters and signs, 'Your King and Country Need You,' and been sent on this ill-fated expedition for their first sight of war. The London papers are talking about it as I am writing this — how this handful of 9000 men, part of them recruits who scarcely knew one end of a rifle from another, were flung across the Channel on Sunday night and rushed up to the front to be shot at and rushed back again. I did not know this then, but wondered if this was what they had dreamed of — squatting helplessly in a ditch until an-other order came to retire — when they swung through the London streets singing 'It's a long, long way to Tipperary' two months ago.

WHAT A PICNIC IT WAS

Yet not one of the youngest and the greenest showed the least nervousness as they waited there in that melancholy little orchard under the incessant scream of shells. That unshakable British coolness, part sheer pluck, part a sort of lack of imagination, perhaps, or at least of 'nerves,' left them as calm and casual as if they were but drilling on the turf of Hyde Park. And with it persisted that almost equally unshakable sense of class, that touching confidence in one's superiors — the young clerk's or mechanic's inborn conviction that whatever that smart, clean-cut, imperturbable young officer does and says must inevitably be right — at least that if he is cool and serene you must, if the skies fall, be cool and serene too.

We met one young fellow as we walked through an empty lateral leading to a bombproof prepared for wounded, and the ambulance officer asked him sharply how things had been going that morning.

'Oh, very well, sir,' he said with the most respectful good humor, though a shell bursting just then a stone's throw beyond the orchard made both of us duck our heads. 'A bit hot, sir, about nine o'clock, but only one man hurt. They do seem to know just where we are, sir; but wait till their infantry comes up — we'll clean them out right enough, sir."

And if he had been ordered to stay there and hold the trench alone, one could imagine him saying in that same tone of deference and chipper good humor: 'Yes, sir; thank you, sir,' and staying, too, till the cows came home.

RIGHT AT OUR FEET

We motored down the line to another trench — this one along a road with fields in front and about a couple of hundred yards behind a clump of trees which masked a Belgian battery. The officer here, a tall, upstanding, gravely handsome young man, with a deep, strong, slightly humorous voice, and the air of one both born to and used to command — the best type of navy man — came over to meet us, rather glad, it seemed, to see some one. The ambulance officer had just started to speak when there was a roar from the clump of trees, at the same instant an explosion directly overhead, and an ugly chunk of iron — a bit of broken casing from a shrapnel shell — plunged at our very feet. The shell had been wrongly timed and exploded prematurely.

'I say!' the lieutenant called out to a Belgian officer standing not far away, 'can't you telephone over to your people to stop that? That's the third time we've been nearly hit by their shrapnel this morning. After all '— he turned to us with the air of apologizing somewhat for his display of irritation —'it's quite annoying enough here without that, you know.'

It was, indeed, annoying — very. The trenches were not under fire in the sense that the enemy were making a persistent effort to clear them out, but they were in the zone of fire, their range was known, and there was no telling when that distant boom thudded across the fields whether that particular shell might be intended for them or for somebody's house in town. We could see in the distance their captive balloon, and there were a couple of scouts, the officer said, in a tower in the village, not much more than half a mile away. He pointed to the spot across the barbed wire. 'We've been trying to pick them off with our rifles for the last half hour.'

THE DESIRE TO BE SOMEWHERE ELSE

We left them engaged in this interesting distraction, the little rifle snaps in all that mighty thundering seeming only to accept the loneliness and helplessness of their position, and spun on down the transverse road, toward another trench on the left. The progress of the motor seemed slow and disappointing. Not that the spot a quarter of a mile off was at all less likely to be hit, yet one felt conscious of a growing desire to be somewhere else. And though I took off my hat to keep it from blowing off, I found that every time a shell went over I promptly put it on again, indicating, one suspected, a decline in what the military experts call *morale*.

As we bowled down the road toward a group of brick houses on the left, a shell passed not more than fifty yards in front of us and through the side of one of these houses as easily as a circus rider pops through a tissue-paper hoop. Almost at the same instant another exploded — where I have n't the least idea, except that the dust from it hit us in the face. The motor rolled smoothly along meanwhile, and the Belgian soldier driving it stared as imperturbably ahead of him as if he were back at Antwerp on the seat of his taxi-cab.

You get used to shells in time, it seems, and, deciding that you either are or are not going to be hit, dismiss responsibility and leave it all to fate. I must admit that in my brief experience I was not able to arrive at this restful state. We reached at last the city gate through which we had left Antwerp, and the motor came to a stop just at the inner edge of the passage under the fort, and I said good-by to the young Englishman ere he started back for the trenches again.

'Well,' he called after me as I started across the open space between the gate and the houses, a stone's throw away, ' you 've had an experience anyway.'

DISCREETLY ZIGZAGGING

I was just about to answer that undoubtedly I had when—'*Tzee-ee-ee-er-r*' —a shell just cleared the ramparts over our heads and disappeared in the side of a house directly in front of us with a roar and a geyser of dust. Neither the motor nor a guest's duty now detained me, and, waving him good-by, I turned at right angles and made with true civilian speed for the shelter of a side street.

The shells all appeared to be coming from a southeast direction, and in the lee of houses on the south side of the street one was reasonably protected. Keeping close to the house fronts and dodging — rather absurdly no doubt — into doorways when that wailing whistle came up from behind, I went zigzagging through the deserted city toward the hotel on the other side of town.

It was such a progress as one might make in some fantastic nightmare — as the hero of some eerie piece of fiction about the Last Man in the World. Street after street, with doors locked, shutters closed, sandbags, mattresses, or little heaps of earth piled over cellar windows; streets in which the only sound was that of one's own feet, where the loneliness was made more lonely by some forgotten dog cringing against the closed door and barking nervously as one hurried past.

Here, where most of the shells had fallen the preceding night, nearly all the houses were empty. Yet occasionally one caught sight of faces peering up from basement windows or of some stubborn householder standing in his southern doorway staring into space. Once I passed a woman bound away from, instead of toward, the river with her big bundle; and once an open carriage with a family in it driving, with peculiarly Flemish composure, toward the quay, and as I hurried past the park, along the Avenue Van Dyck — where fresh craters made by exploding shells had been dug in the turf — the swans, still floating on the little lake, placidly dipped their white necks under water as if it were a quiet morning in May.

WORK FOR A SAMARITAN

Now and then, as the shell's wail swung over its long parabola, there came with the detonation, across the roofs, the rumble of falling masonry. Once I passed a house quietly burning, and on the pavement were lopped-off trees. The impartiality with which those far-off gunners distributed their attentions was disconcerting. Peering down one of the up-and-down streets before crossing it, as if a shell were an automobile which you might see and dodge, you would shoot across and, turning into a cozy little side street, think to yourself that here at least they had not come, and then promptly see, squarely in front, another of those craters blown down through the Belgian blocks.

Presently I found myself under the trees of the Boulevard Léopold, not far from the British hospital, and recalled that it was about time that promise was made good. It was time indeed, and help with lifting they needed very literally. The order had just come to leave the building, bringing the wounded and such equipment as they could pack into half a dozen motor busses and retire — just where, I did not hear — in the direction of Ghent. As I entered the porte-cochère two poor wrecks of war were being led out by their nurses — more men burned in the powder explosion at Waelhem, their seared faces and hands covered with oil and cotton just as they had been lifted from bed.

PARADE OF THE WOUNDED

The phrase 'whistle of shells' had taken on a new reality since midnight. Now one was to learn something of the meaning of those equally familiar words, 'they succeeded in saving their wounded, although under heavy fire.'

None of the wounded could walk, none dress himself; most of them in ordinary times would have lain where they were for weeks. There were fractured legs not yet set, men with faces half shot away, men half out of their heads, and all these had to be dressed somehow, covered up, crowded into or on top of the busses and started off through a city under bombardment toward open country which might already be occupied by the enemy.

Bundles of uniforms, mud-stained, blood-stained, just as they had come from the trenches, were dumped out of the storeroom and distributed, hit or miss.

British 'Tommies' went out as Belgians, Belgians in British khaki; the man whose broken leg I had lifted the day before we simply bundled in his bed blankets and set up in the corner of a bus. One healthy-looking Belgian boy, on whom I was trying to pull a pair of British trousers, seemed to have nothing at all the matter with him, until it presently appeared that he was speechless and paralyzed in both left arm and left leg. And while we were working, an English soldier shot through the jaw and throat sat on the edge of his bed, shaking with a hideous rattling cough.

The hospital was in a handsome stone building, in ordinary times a club, perhaps, or a school; a wide stone stairway led up the center, and above it was a glass skylight. This central well would have been a charming place for a shell to drop into, and one did drop not more than fifty feet or so away, in or close to the rear court. A few yards down the avenue another shell hit a cornice and sent a ton or so of masonry crashing down on the sidewalk. Under conditions like these the nurses kept running up and down that staircase during the endless hour or two in which the wounded were being dressed and carried on stretchers to the street. They stood by the busses making their men comfortable, and when the first busses were filled they sat in the open street on top of them, patiently waiting, as calm and smiling as circus queens on their gilt chariots. The behavior of the men in the trenches was cool enough, but they at least were fighting men and but taking the chance of war. These were civilian volunteers, they had not even trenches to shelter them, and it took a rather unforeseen and difficult sort of courage to leave that fairly safe masonry building and sit smiling and helpful on top of a motor bus during a wait of half an hour or so, any second of which might be one's last.

NO TEARS

There was an American nurse there, a tall, radiant girl, whom they called, and rightly, 'Morning Glory,' who had been introduced to me the day before because we both belonged to that curious foreign race of Americans. What her name was I have n't the least idea, and if we were to meet to-morrow, doubtless we should have to be carefully presented over again, but I remember calling out to her: 'Good-by, American girl!' as we passed in the hall during the last minute or two, and she said good-by, and suddenly reached out and put her hand on my shoulder and added, 'Good luck!' or 'God bless you!' or something like that. And these seemed at the moment quite the usual things to do and say. The doctor in charge and the general's wife apologized for running away, as they called it, and the last I saw of the latter was as she waved back to me from the top of a bus, with just that look of concern over the desperate ride they were beginning which a slightly preoccupied hostess casts over a dinner table about which are seated a number of oddly assorted guests.

The strange procession got away safely at last, and safely, too, so I was told later, across the river; but where they finally spent the night I never heard.

ANYTHING BUT CAPTURE

I hurried down the street and into the Rue Nerviens. It must have been about four o'clock by that time. The bright October morning had changed to a chill and dismal afternoon, and up the western sky in the direction of the river a vast curtain of greasy black smoke was rolling. The petrol tanks which stretched for half a mile or so along the Scheldt had been set afire. It looked at the moment as if the whole city might be going, but there was no time then to think of possibilities, and I slipped down the lee side of the street to the door with the Red Cross flag. The front of the hospital was shut tight. It took several pulls at the bell to bring any one, and inside I found a Belgian family who had left their own house for the thicker ceilings of the hospital, and the nuns back in the wards with their nervous men.

Their servants had left that morning, the three or four sisters in charge had had to do all the cooking and housework as well as look after their patients, and now they were keeping calm and smiling to subdue as best they could the fears of the Belgian wounded, who were ready to jump out of bed, whatever their condition, rather than fall into the hands of the enemy. Each one had no doubt that if he were not murdered outright he would be taken to Germany and forced to fight in the east against the Russians.

Several, who knew very well what was going on outside, had been found by the nurses that morning out of bed and all ready to take to the street.

YET THEY REMAIN

Lest they should hear that their comrades in the Boulevard Léopold had been moved, the lay sister — the English lady — and I withdrew to the operating room, closed the door, and in that curious retreat talked over the situation. No orders had come to leave; in fact, they had been told to stay. They did have a man now in the shape of the Belgian gentleman, and from the same source an able-bodied servant, but how long these would stay, where food was to be found in that desolate city, when the bombardment would cease, and what the Germans would do with them — well, it was not a pleasant situation for a handful of women. But it was not of themselves she was thinking, but of their wounded and of Belgium, and of what both had suffered already and of what might yet be in store. It was of that this frail little sister talked that hopeless afternoon, while the smoke in the west spread farther up the sky, and she would now and then pause in the middle of a syllable while a shell sang overhead, then take it up again.

Meanwhile the light was going, and before it became quite dark and my hotel deserted, perhaps, as the rest of Antwerp, it seemed best to be getting across town. I could not believe that the Germans could treat such a place and people with anything but consideration and told the little nurse so. She came to the edge of the glass-covered court, laughingly saying I had best run across it, and wondering where we, who had met twice now under such curious circumstances, would meet again. Then she turned back to the ward — to wait with that roomful of more or less panicky men for the tramp of German soldiers and the knock on the door which meant that they were prisoners.

FLIGHT OR THE GERMANS?

Hurrying across town, I passed, not far from the Hotel St. Antoine, a blazing four-story building, nearly burned out now, and, like the other Antwerp fires, not spreading beyond its four walls. The cathedral was not touched, and indeed, in spite of the noise and terror, the material damage was comparatively slight. Soldiers were clearing the quay and setting a guard directly in front of our hotel — one of the few places in Antwerp that night where one could get so much as a crust of bread — and behind drawn curtains as usual we made what cheer we could. There were two American photographers and a correspondent who had spent the night before in the cellar of a house, the upper story of which had been wrecked by a shell; a British intelligence officer, with the most bewildering way of hopping back and forth between a brown civilian suit and a spick-and-span new uniform, and several Belgian families hoping to get a boat downstream in the morning.

We sat round the great fire in the hall, above which the architect, building for happier times, had had the bad grace to place a skylight, and discussed the time and means of getting away. The intelligence officer, not wishing to be made a prisoner, was for getting a boat of some sort at the first crack of dawn, and the photographers, who had had the roof blown off over their heads, heartily agreed with him. I did not like to leave without at least a glimpse of those spiked helmets nor to desert my friends in the Rue Nerviens, and yet there was the likelihood, if one remained, of being marooned indefinitely in the midst of the conquering army.

EVEN THE BRITISH

Meanwhile the flight of shells continued, a dozen or more fires could be seen from the upper windows of the hotel, and billows of red flame from the burning petrol tanks rolled up the southern sky. It had been what might be called a rather full day, and the wail of approaching projectiles began to get a bit on one's nerves. One started at the slamming of a door, took every dull thump for a distant explosion, and when we finally turned in, I carried the mattress from my room, which faced the south, over to the other side of the building and laid it on the floor beside another man's bed. Before a shell could reach me it would have to traverse at least three partitions and possibly him as well.

After midnight the bombardment quieted, but shells continued to visit us from time to time all night. All night the Belgians were retreating across the pontoon bridge, and once — it must have been about two or three o'clock — I heard a sound which meant that all was over. It was the crisp tramp — different from the Belgian shuffle — of British soldiers, and up from the street came an English voice: 'Best foot forward, boys!' and a little farther on: 'Look alive, men; they've just picked up our range!'

I went to the window and watched them tramp by — the same men we had seen that morning. The petrol fire was still flaming across the south, a steamer of some sort was burning at her wharf beside the bridge — Napoleon's veterans retreating from Moscow could scarcely have left behind a more complete picture of war than did those young recruits.

THE FRENZY OF RETREAT

Morning came dragging up out of that dreadful night, smoky, damp, and chill. It was almost a London fog that lay over the abandoned town. I had just packed up and was walking through one of the upper halls when there was a crash that shook the whole building, the sound of falling glass, and out in the river a geyser of water shot up, timbers and boards flew from the bridge, and there were dozens of smaller splashes as if from a shower of shot. I thought that the hotel was hit at last and that the Germans, having let civilians escape over the bridge, were turning everything loose, determined to make an end of the business. It was, as a matter of fact, the Belgians blowing up the bridge to cover their retreat. In any case it seemed useless to stay longer, and within an hour, on a tug jammed with the last refugees, we were starting downstream.

Behind us, up the river, a vast curtain of lead-colored smoke from the petrol tanks had climbed up the sky and spread out mushroom-wise, as smoke and ashes sometimes spread out from a volcano. This smoke, merging with the fog and the smoke from the Antwerp fires, seemed to cover the whole sky. And under that sullen mantle the dark flames of the petrol still glowed; to the left was the blazing skeleton of the ship, and on the right Antwerp itself, the rich, old, beautiful, comfortable city, all but hidden, and now and then sending forth the boom of an exploding shell like a groan.

A large empty German steamer, the *Gneisenau*, marooned here since the war, came swinging slowly out into the river, pushed by two or three nervous little tugs — to be sunk there, apparently, in midstream. From the pontoon bridge, which stubbornly refused to yield, came explosion after explosion, and up and down the river fires sprang up, and there were other explosions, as the crushed Belgians, in a sort of rage of devastation, became their own destroyers.

WHAT TO THINK OF

By following the adventures of one individual I have endeavored to suggest what the bombardment of a modern city was like — what you might expect if an invading army came to-morrow to New York or Chicago or San Francisco. I have only coasted along the edges of Belgium's tragedy, and the rest of the story, of which we were a part for the next two days — the flight of those hundreds of thousands of homeless people — is something that can scarcely be told — you must follow it out in imagination into its countless uprooted, disorganized lives. You must imagine old people struggling along over miles and miles of country roads; young girls, under burdens a man might not care to bear, tramping until they had to carry their shoes in their hands and go barefoot to rest their unaccustomed feet. You must imagine the pathetic efforts of hundreds of people to keep clean by washing in wayside streams or ditches; imagine babies going without milk because there was no milk to be had; families shivering in damp hedgerows or against haystacks where darkness overtook them; and you must imagine this not on one road, but on every road, for mile after mile over a whole countryside. What was to become of these people when their little supply of food was exhausted? Where could they go? Even if back to their homes, it would be but to lift their hats to their conquerors, never to know but that the next week or month would sweep the tide of war back over them again.

Never in modern times, not in our generation at least, has the world seen anything like that flight — nothing so strange, so overwhelming, so pitiful. And when I say pitiful, you must not think of hysterical women, desperate, trampling men, tears and screams. In all those miles one saw neither complaining nor protestation — at times one might almost have thought it was some vast eccentric picnic. No, it was their orderliness, their thrift and kindness, their unmistakable usefulness, which made the waste and irony of it all so colossal and hideous. Each family had its big round loaves of bread and its pile of hay for the horses, the bags of pears and potatoes; the children had their little dolls, and you would see some tired mother with her big bundle under one arm and some fluffy little puppy in the other. You could not associate them with forty-centimeter shells or burned churches and libraries or anything but quiet homes and peaceable, helpful lives. You could not be swept along by that endless stream of exiles and retain at the end of the day any particular enthusiasm for the red glory of war. And when we crossed the Dutch border that afternoon and came on a village street full of Belgian soldiers, cut off and forced to cross the line, to be interned here, presumably until the war was over, one could not mourn very deeply their lost chances of martial glory as they unslung their rifles and turned them over to the good-natured Dutch guard. They had held back that avalanche long enough, these Belgians, and one felt as one would to see lost children get home again or some one dragged from under the wheels.

X

A NIGHT IN A RUSSIAN OUTPOST

The following vivid sketch of war scenes appeared in the *Russkoye Slovo:*

The master — a small, shriveled old man — can hardly get up from his filthy bed; and the mistress — a wrinkled, ill old woman — weeps unceasingly. Somewhere far away are her children — for she does not know where they are. There is nothing to eat, and she is ashamed to have to beg from the soldiers, who are so willing to share with her. Besides this, there is the ever-present terror that from the trenches, which are so very, very close, there may appear a German to fire the last remainders of her once-prosperous farm.

And with these two in their half of the hut, there are billeted eight orderlies; in the other half, in which there are two low, minute bunks like those in a ship's cabin, there are living five doctors and three organizers of an ambulance unit. In these rooms are two offices — a kitchen and a store of provisions — and here is carried on the business interwoven with the life of every day.

Towards the evening it becomes hot and stuffy in the hut from the number of persons gathered in it, the tobacco smoke, and the stove on which the evening meal is being cooked. So every one goes out for a walk in the road by the woods.

There is a moon, and the evening is bright and quiet. From here can be seen troops advancing, orderlies galloping to and fro, and a long line of field-kitchens on its way to the front stretched over the surface of the sparkling snow.

Now is a strange time, when everything along the front is quiet and the war ceases for an hour or two; for the men must rest and eat to be able afterwards to carry on as before.

At nine o'clock everything is as it was; shrapnel bursts close by, and the heavy boom of artillery can once more be heard. Sometimes rifle-firing will start, to continue intermittently throughout the night.

Having returned to the farm, where a lamp is burning and newly arrived papers are lying on the table, we drink tea with lemon juice. A young Caucasian doctor smokes now and then to deaden the numerous smells. Then we all begin to get ready to go to sleep. Some lie on their narrow folding camp beds, some on crates which once held provisions, and the rest simply on the beaten earth floor. The conversation is of the war, of our birthplaces, and of the possibility of a night attack by the enemy. Soon all are asleep. In the little hut it is warm, quiet, and snug, and only occasionally it shakes from the force of the exploding shells. It seems that here there is and can be no danger.

Close on three o'clock we are awakened by a series of shocks which by the rattling of the furniture seem to be so great that the flimsy hut is having great difficulty in keeping to one spot. Some one speaks excitedly: 'Do you hear it? It must be a night attack.'

An incessant artillery battle now begins. The bursts of shells come one on top of another, they are quite close, next to us, almost upon us, right under the walls of the hut, surely it must fall. And now we can hear a sound as of a person tapping persistently, untiringly, irritably at the wall with an enormous dry hard fist. This is the rifle firing beginning.

We hurriedly dress and go out.

It is terrible, but wonderfully beautiful.

Short red flames burst out one after another; the searchlight throws its strange, long pale beams as far as the horizon, and the screaming shrapnel falls on the ground in bright, meteor-like sparks, and in the air there is the ceaseless crack of rifle fire, bursting of shells, and clatter of shrapnel, the constant, untiring business of a battle.

Then everything begins to quiet down, like a storm that has exhausted its fury. But hardly have we started towards the hut when again ... it starts slowly, quietly, far away. Then nearer, clearer, more persistently, shriller. Rifles, quick-firers, howitzers, all once more enter the lists. The farther away the fiercer it seems. Now it becomes hard to distinguish one sound from the other, for the rifles and the big guns seem to make the same amount of noise.

I have an unconquerable craving to go and see what is happening a verst or two away, where the battle is being fought. But from the peat bog on which the hut stands a fog has risen, and, in spite of the bright moon, it is impossible to see anything in the damp mist.

And then suddenly a drawling, low, distant roar arises, grows, approaches. I can clearly hear amid this tornado of sounds the tones of many men's voices. Afar away, 'A!—a!—a!' getting louder every moment, 'Again, again!' Here it is quite close to me, then farther off again, from this side, then from the other.

My heart beats with excitement and agitation. I imagine — as I cannot see anything in the cold, dank mist — that something is approaching, that in a minute out of that darkness there may appear foreign soldiers. And again, although I am encircled by a blanket of fog, I imagine I can see something. But that is impossible.

Then again the long-drawn-out 'A!—a!—a!' Now somewhat louder, more convincing, more triumphant. But suddenly everything almost at the same moment grows calm. One or two more shots are fired by rifles and guns. ... And by seven o'clock in the morning, when a slow, dull, drowsy dawn comes up from the north, there is complete silence all along our front.

The day in the trenches begins. Baggage carts make their way along the road, orderlies hurry hither and thither. On the plain and in the woods the artillery fire at intervals. Some wounded are being brought in to the bandaging point, and some one says that last night there was a night attack on our trenches, but by the strong, well-aimed thrusts of our brave men's bayonets it was repulsed.

XI

SAVING 27,000 LIVES IN ONE STATE

CHARLES FREDERICK CARTER

[*Technical World*, February, 1912. By permission.]

Nobody can be expected to believe that a state health department worthy of the second decade of the twentieth century exists in America. We have been turning our streams into sewers and our lakes into cesspools, scattering pollution everywhere, treating contagious diseases as jokes, violating every law of hygiene, outraging every dictate of common sense, and blaming Providence instead of our own criminal incompetence for the resultant untimely deaths, with all their mournful train of sorrow and suffering, for so many years that the country seemed beyond hope.

To say, therefore, that a legislature has had the wisdom to provide a state health department with ample funds and authority is to make the improbable seem preposterous. To add that the operations of this properly organized and equipped health department have reduced the annual death rate of the State enough to save twenty-seven thousand lives in the last four years is to put the finishing touch to a story that only sounds fit to tell the marines. Having now strained credulity to the uttermost we may as well go the limit by naming the State that enjoys the beneficent activities of an enlightened and efficient health department.

It's Pennsylvania!

Yes, there are some things that seem too good to be true. This is one of them. Pennsylvania, the favorite hunting ground of the muckraker and the surveyor, actually has a health department with 4000 employees, every one of whom is holding his job, not by order of the 'organization,' but solely by the saving grace of fitness and industry, which is disbursing millions of dollars and receiving full value for every nickel. And the results that the four thousand have accomplished and are still achieving are impressive and inspiring.

Pennsylvania was no worse than its neighbors, but natural conditions were such that the punishment for its sanitary sins fell a little more harshly upon the Keystone State than upon some others. The death rate from typhoid fever grew to the proportions of a national scandal. To be sure there was a so-called health department, just as there are to-day in so many other States; but it had no authority, no funds, no staff, no power to do anything but to issue an annual report. It was a grim joke at the taxpayers' expense. There were also health boards in the cities and some of the towns; but they were little, if any, better off than the state health department, while even the feeble power they may have had did not extend beyond the boundaries of their respective municipalities. To try to safeguard the lives and health of people on one side of an imaginary line while the people on the other side were free to lead the lives of hygienic anarchists or cavemen — in other words, the lives of free-born American citizens, was worse than futile.

When manufacturing establishments began to move out of the State because so many of their employees were sick all the time that the plants could not be operated profitably, it was realized that something had to be done. To clean up an entire State that had been accumulating filth and foulness for generations was an undertaking that made the fabled job of Hercules in the Augean stables seem petty; but when there is a big task to be done a big man is always at hand to do it.

Dr. Charles B. Penrose, a retired physician of Philadelphia, a member of one of Pennsylvania's prominent families, embodied his ideas of what a health department's powers should be in three bills. He appeared before various legislative committees to advocate his ideas, and it is just possible that he may have interested his brother, Boies Penrose, member of the United States Senate, who is popularly supposed to have some political influence in Pennsylvania, in them. At all events the bills were enacted into laws in the form that Dr. Penrose drew them. The next step was to find the right man for commissioner of health, or rather to persuade him to accept the position; for no one had any doubt about who the right man was.

Unfortunately, the salary of $10,000 a year was no inducement whatever to Dr. Samuel G. Dixon, for he is wealthy. A public office was still less to his taste. He had taken up the practice of law in his younger days just for the sake of having something to do, until he had too much to do and thus caused his health to break down. Upon recovering he studied medicine, graduated with honors from the University of Pennsylvania, pursued post graduate studies in London and Munich, then returned to practise his profession in Philadelphia. To kill time he accepted the chair of hygiene in medicine at the University of Pennsylvania, made a hobby of bacteriology, became professor of bacteriology and microscopic technology at the University and discovered tuberculin, a culture made from the bacilli of tuberculosis, a year before the great Koch announced it as a cure for consumption. That it is not a cure, but is now used chiefly in discovering tuberculosis in cattle does not reflect upon the scientific skill or work of these men. There can be no doubt about Dr. Dixon's priority of discovery, for the announcement of it was published in a medical journal a year before Koch made his announcement. Dr. Dixon also became president of the Academy of Natural Sciences of Philadelphia, the oldest scientific body in America, a member of the Philadelphia Board of Education, a trustee of the Wistar Institute of Anatomy, a councilor of the American Philosophical Society, a director of the Zoölogical Society of Philadelphia, and an active member of a dozen other scientific societies at home and abroad. He published a work on physiology and was a frequent contributor to medical and scientific journals.

With such an insatiable appetite for work, backed by so notable a career, Dr. Dixon was obviously the man for the place. Being finally persuaded that he need never suffer from ennui if he accepted the appointment, Dr. Dixon became commissioner of health of Pennsylvania in 1905. He took so much time in organizing his department and in preparatory work that he was unable to spend all of the first appropriation of $400,000 within the time limit, which unheard-of conduct caused his political friends no little anxiety. Their worry proved to be supererogatory, for when the legislature met in 1907 it appropriated $1,059,312 to fight tuberculosis and $441,288 for the general work of the department without a murmur just because Dr. Dixon said he needed that much.

After an outbreak of smallpox at Waynesboro was taken in hand by the new department, there was no lack of the picturesque in its activities. Some outraged citizens who found for the first time that they were no longer free to spread disease and death at their own sweet will hanged Dr. Dixon in effigy, while others denounced him as a 'czar,' and a 'dictator,' and worried greatly over the peril of placing so much power in the hands of one man. The commissioner's mail began to be burdened with threatening letters. One man in the smallpox belt, whose fears were wrought upon by the anti-vaccinationists until he became convinced that the health department was seeking to kill his seven children by vaccinating them, lay in wait one night to shoot Dr. Dixon. The commissioner, by the merest chance, took an unusual route home that night and so escaped. The would-be assassin upon being discovered acknowledged that he had intended to kill Dr. Dixon and explained why. Thereupon the doctor wrote him a kindly letter which so filled his whilom enemy with remorse that he went into hysterics in the prosecuting attorney's office. Then he went home a convert to vaccination and a faithful admirer of Dr. Dixon.

Employees of the health department, too, found no lack of excitement. A stream inspector, for example, upon going to examine some premises suspected of polluting a brook which emptied into a stream from which the city of Reading drew its water supply, was ordered off by the irate owner, who did not propose to have his right to empty his sewage where he pleased abridged. The inspector tried to pacify the farmer, but was answered with a blow from a club which fractured his skull. On another occasion the occupants of a house in which there had been a case

of measles put out a health officer's eye by way of expressing their disapproval of his attempt to disinfect the premises.

While some folk thought a health department was a good thing to make other people behave themselves, they resented any attempt to interfere with their own liberty to do as they pleased. Thus, when twenty hogs died of cholera their owner refused to bury them. When the department of health notified him to abate the nuisance he allowed that he would do as he darn pleased on his own land. It required a fine of $25 to induce him to revise his opinion.

This was bad enough for an uneducated farmer; but what is to be said of a manufacturing town which, upon being ordered to make certain changes in its water supply, engaged a lawyer to fight the department's order, then sent a deputation accompanied by the lawyer to protest to the commissioner. Dr. Dixon waited until the deputation was out of breath, then produced data from his own engineers, who had measured the flow of the stream that supplied the town with water. The intake of the water works was just above a little dam on one side of the stream while a sewer discharged on the opposite bank. The engineers' measurements proved that the stream did not furnish water enough to supply the town if it had not been reinforced by the sewage poured into the pond. The deputation turned pale and wobbled at the knees upon receiving this disquieting information. They had not another word to say. Dr. Dixon thereupon dismissed his callers with a funny story; but somehow, though the laugh came at the proper place, it seemed to lack spontaneity and sprightliness. The changes ordered were made with alacrity.

These are but samples of the opposition which the department encountered in almost everything it undertook at first. However, that is only the dark side of the story. While bills were repeatedly introduced in the legislature to abolish the department of health or to restrict its powers they all died a sudden death. Then some foolish candidates in the campaign of 1910 thought to make political capital out of the supposed opposition to the department. With fine sarcasm they alleged that the next move of the health department would be to compel farmers to filter water for their ducks to swim in.

and to Pasteurize the swill for the hogs. The sarcastic ones suffered the usual fate of those who interfere in family quarrels; which is to say, both parties turned on them and rended them limb from limb, politically speaking. In other words, the voters didn't do a thing to them. The next legislature appropriated $3,657,248 for the use of the department of health in 1911 and 1912, as its way of saying that Pennsylvania had entire confidence in Dr. Dixon and that he might go as far as he liked. All this seems to bear out Dr. Dixon's theory that sanitary sins are committed through ignorance; and that most people are willing to do right when shown how.

Since the department of health was created in 1905 a grand total of $8,558,048 has been appropriated for its use up to the end of 1912. Never before has money been so freely spent for the conservation of human life. The results have more than justified the expenditure, for the work of the department has been a spectacular success.

The decrease in the annual death rate brought about by the measures initiated by the department of health means that in round numbers 27,000 persons who under former conditions would have died within the State within the four years ending with 1911 are alive today. Prof. Irving Fisher, of Yale University, one of the foremost of American economists, has estimated the worth to society of the average life lost by preventable diseases at $1700. Taking this as a basis, the economic value of the lives saved by the Pennsylvania department of health so far reaches the impressive total of $45,900,-000. Deducting the total expenditures of the department, $6,719,424 (one-half the current appropriation being for the year 1912) gives a net profit of $39,180,576, which is 583 per cent. on the investment.

Or, to figure it another way, the average cost of saving one life has been $199.19. Frederick Hoffman, statistician of the Prudential Insurance Company, estimates the average net economic value of a man, that is, the selling value of his product less the cost of materials, the wear of machinery, and the cost of living for the man and his family, at $300 a year for the normal period of industrial activity, which is from the fifteenth to the sixty-fifth year. On this basis the State of Pennsylvania is enriching itself by a net profit of 50 per cent. per year on every $200 invested in saving life through its department of health. The actual profit is much greater, for part of the appropriations have been invested in permanent improvements; and, besides, the effect of all sanitary work is cumulative. The longer the work is continued the greater the benefits and the less the average cost per life saved.

These figures are fascinating so long as they apply to others. But what man is willing to consider his own life from the standpoint of his economic value to society? He wants to live, and he expects the State to protect his inalienable right to life, liberty, and the pursuit of happiness, regardless of any question of cost or economic value. And how is the human suffering and sorrow averted by the prevention of sickness and death to be computed? The better way is to leave questions of economic value out of consideration and to judge the department of health by the reductions in the sick rate and death rate it has brought about.

In 1906, 56.5 persons out of every 100,-000 in Pennsylvania died of typhoid fever; in 1907, 50.3; in 1908, 34.4; in 1910, 24.5. This means that there are now living more than 2400 persons who, had the death rate of 1906 prevailed in 1910, would have died of typhoid. In the same time the death rate from pulmonary tuberculosis fell from 129.6 per 100,000 to 117.4. This means the saving of about 1000 lives annually. From October, 1905, when the health department began the free distribution of diphtheria antitoxin among the poor, down to December, 1910, 27,318 cases of this dread disease, mostly little children, were treated with the life-saving serum. Statistics show that without antitoxin 42 out of every 100 of these children would probably have died; but with the aid of the State's antitoxin the deaths were reduced to 2324, and the death rate was reduced to 8.50. Free antitoxin was also given for immunization purposes in 20,294 cases that had been exposed to the disease. All but 335 of these were absolutely protected against diphtheria. The actual saving of child life resulting from the State's free distribution of diphtheria antitoxin to the end of 1910 was 9152 lives. The death rate from measles has been reduced from 21 per 100,000 in 1906, to 11 in 1910; the death rate from whooping cough has been reduced from 22 to 16, and so on through the whole long list of contagious diseases.

In 1906 the Pennsylvania death rate per 1000 was 16.5; in 1908 it had dropped to 15.7. At first glance this does not seem a remarkable reduction; but it means that had the death rate of 1906 prevailed in 1908, 5914 more persons would have died than actually succumbed. In 1910 the death rate was 15.6. Had the 1906 rate prevailed in that year 6898 more men, women, and children now living and presumably in good health and spirits, would have died.

These splendid results have been made possible in the first place by laws which give the commissioner of health the necessary authority to do things, and that means practically unlimited power. It is made 'The duty of the commissioner of health to protect the health of the people of the State and to determine and to employ the most efficient and practical means for the prevention and suppression of disease.' The commissioner is given power, without any qualifications or restrictions, to abate nuisances. His agents are empowered to enter and examine any premises in the State. He may issue warrants for the arrest of those who disobey his rules and regulations and he can subpœna witnesses and 'compel' them to testify in any matter relating to the work of his department. To disobey any order or regulation of the department of health is a misdemeanor punishable by fine or imprisonment or both.

The organization under which the autocratic powers of the commissioner are exercised is an intricate network, the wires of which designedly cross each other at so many points that there are ample checks on everything done by employees of the department and upon everything that in any way may affect the public health. The department takes no chances, and nothing has been overlooked.

For instance, many physicians thought the law requiring them to report births and deaths didn't mean them. After sixty doctors had been arrested and fined in one day in Philadelphia for neglecting their duty in this regard, a batch of sixteen in Scranton on another day, and large batches in other cities, the doctors reached the unanimous conclusion that at least some laws in Pennsylvania mean exactly what they say. Since this conclusion was reached Pennsylvania mortuary statistics have so improved that the United States census bureau has found them within 1 per cent. of absolute accuracy.

One of the nine bureaus into which the department of health is divided is called the division of medical inspection. It consists of a chief medical inspector with an office staff and a field staff made up of a medical inspector in each county and as many health officers and visiting nurses as may be required. The county medical inspector directs all quarantine measures, is frequently called to see those sick with communicable diseases, enforces the department's regulations for the sale of milk in premises infected with diphtheria, scarlet fever, typhoid and other diseases and supervises the sanitary conditions of his county in general. The division of medical inspection conducts a campaign of sanitary education reaching dairy farms and public schools. Twice a year health officers visit all premises which market milk, and there are some seventy-five thousand of them. Twice a year the health officers visit all the thirteen thousand public schools in the State and make full reports on the sanitary condition of school room, grounds, outbuildings and water supply.

One of the newest tasks of the division of medical inspection is the examination of pupils in public schools, an undertaking which will keep a thousand inspectors busy. A trial test in three counties to ascertain whether such an inspection was needed or not revealed the astonishing fact that more than half the pupils were abnormal in some way. Numerous incipient cases of contagious disease were discovered by this means in time to prevent epidemics.

Whenever a case of contagious disease is reported the house is immediately placed under quarantine by a health officer who explains the necessity therefor, gives instructions for caring for the patient and preventing the spread of the disease and leaves a circular of printed directions couched in simple language. Librarians of public libraries, school teachers and Sunday school teachers are at once notified of the quarantine that they may be on their guard against any possible violation. If the patient is too poor to pay for medical treatment the medical inspector attends the case and if necessary a visiting nurse also calls. In certain cases the wage earner of the family is given a permit to work provided he agrees not to come in contact with the patient or any one attending him. If the family sells milk the health officer sees that an outsider attends to the milking or that the cows are sent away to be cared for. Great pains are taken to safeguard the public health without interrupting the family income whenever that is possible and never to try to enforce a rule without first explaining the necessity for it. By this policy the department secures the coöperation that makes for effectiveness.

When the patient recovers or dies the house is thoroughly disinfected by a health officer. Great stress is laid on disinfection. A horrible example discovered by the department is a house that was occupied by three different families in ten years in which twenty cases of tuberculosis developed. Nine died in the house, while several others have died since leaving. All this might have been prevented by disinfecting the house after the first case. So strongly has the public been impressed with the importance of disinfection by the educational campaign of the health department that they tell of one farmer who walked twenty miles to get a health officer to disinfect his house after a death from tuberculosis.

Even yet, though, there are some who do not appreciate the importance of disinfection. A member of the legislature made a special trip to Harrisburg to have the regulations regarding disinfection suspended or modified for a constituent whose family included an aged grandmother. The chief medical inspector refused to relax the rules but he did instruct the health officer to consult the convenience of the householder in disinfecting and to make as many trips as might be necessary to do the work without causing the grandmother any discomfort.

In the frequent typhoid epidemics the department either assumes control of the situation, drawing upon an ample emergency fund for whatever sums may be needed, or it coöperates with the local health board if that body gives sufficient evidences of its ability, as circumstances may seem to require. Some twenty-three such epidemics, some of which were of large proportions, have been handled in whole or in part by the department of health. When an epidemic broke out in

Nanticoke, a mining town of fourteen thousand inhabitants, for example, the health department took charge. The source of infection was traced to a single case two months earlier which had contaminated the creek that furnished the water supply. An emergency hospital was organized, visiting nurses were sent from house to house to instruct in exact methods of disinfection, the water supply was disinfected with sulphate of copper, every premise in the entire community was visited and revisited until it was certain that every menace to health had been abolished and sewage disposal on individual estates was supervised. Warning placards were posted everywhere urging the boiling of water and the Pasteurizing of milk. The most rigid sanitary measures were enforced from the source of the water supply to the ultimate disposal of sewage. When the disease was under control the reservoir which supplied Nanticoke and other towns was emptied, cleaned and disinfected.

Every watershed in the State is being gone over by employees of the division of sanitary engineering. Every house is visited. Up to August 1, 1911, 34,481 private sources of stream pollution have been abated, while thousands more have been stopped through the moral influence of this work. Eighty-nine modern sewage disposal plants have been built or are under construction under plans approved by the department. Two hundred and eighty-four municipalities and private sewerage corporations are building comprehensive sewerage systems in accordance with plans approved by the department. No town can extend its sewerage system without the approval of the department of health. Already eighty-six modern water filtration plants have been approved by the department.

Pennsylvania has some forty thousand cases of tuberculosis within its borders. To stamp out this plague the department of health uses two and a half times as much money as is spent on its other work. A tuberculosis sanitarium with a thousand patients is maintained at Mont Alto in the southern part of the State while two others with a capacity of 350 each have just been completed. To supplement these sanitariums there are 115 free dispensaries scattered throughout the State, where 222 medical men and 110 nurses look after those who are too poor to care for themselves. Up to June 30, 1911, 41,792 poor patients have received attention at the free dispensaries. Milk and oil, paper handkerchiefs and sputum boxes which can be burned after use are provided by the State for tubercular patients who are unable to provide such things for themselves.

Free diphtheria antitoxin can be obtained at 656 stations throughout the State, tetanus antitoxin from 67 stations. The diphtheria remedy can be obtained in a few hours at most in any part of the State, while the tetanus antitoxin is accessible from any locality within twenty-four hours.

For efficiency and enthusiasm the Pennsylvania department of health is a wonder. The commissioner sets the pace by working an average of fourteen hours a day. That means fourteen hours' work, and not four hours' work and ten hours ' out to lunch,' for Dr. Dixon usually eats his luncheon and his dinner at his desk. His example seems to be contagious. They tell a story of a health officer who worked until midnight during a smallpox epidemic, then arose at three o'clock in the morning to run down a ' contact ' away out in the mountains, thus checking the further spread of the epidemic.

It is such a spirit as this everywhere in the department which is spreading the gospel of health into the remotest corners of darkest Pennsylvania. Perhaps in time some of that gospel may be carried beyond the boundaries of the State.

C.   PERSONAL SKETCHES AND INTERVIEWS

Description may be said to deal with persons or things at rest; narration recounts events as they happen, usually in order of succession. The personal sketch may employ either or both of these methods, according as one's object is to enable the reader to realize an individual from what he has done or from what he is. The first article on our list in this section employs the former method, for we understand best what Bismarck was from what he accomplished — the achievement of the German Empire, doubtless the most significant fact of his time. Signor Cortesi's account of the Pope uses both expedients, and so does the admirably balanced estimate of Taft and Roosevelt by Mr. Leupp, written, it will be remembered, in 1910, before the time when both became candidates for the Presidency.

The interview generally deals with a particular moment rather than with a succession of events — a personality rather than a life history. For the particular individuality concerned, it aims at showing 'the very age and body of the time his form and pressure.' The two interviews from the *New York Times*, that with Mr. Henry James and that with Sir J. M. Barrie, are both masterpieces of craftsmanship in their presentation of those subtle and delicate differences which distinguish the speech and gesture of the exceptional man from the hosts of his fellows; Mr. James's intellectual finesse is caught and rendered as skilfully as Sir J. M. Barrie's elusive whimsicality. Indeed it has been suggested of the latter interview that none but Barrie himself could have written it.

Mr. Alleyne Ireland relies chiefly on narrative, but he is no less successful in the presentation of the extraordinarily vigorous and striking personality of Joseph Pulitzer. The subjects in the other cases hardly afford equal opportunity, but the articles are all excellent after their own manner, and afford the young student many salutary hints of what he should strive for in this kind of work — the complete effacement of himself, and the clear and vivid realization of the person whom the readers must see for themselves 'in his habit, as he lived' so that they are endowed for the moment, all unconsciously, with the cunningly concealed insight and sympathy of the biographer or interviewer.

I

BISMARCK

[*Evening Post* (New York), April 1, 1915. By permission.]

One hundred years ago to-day was born the man to whose influence, more than to that of any other, historians trace the causes of the war which is now torturing Europe and testing the relations of all the great nations of the world — Bismarck, the first German Imperial Chancellor, who as a statesman found his nation an outstretched hand and who left it a clenched fist.

When he began the career which ended in his becoming the strongest force in the state, Germany was hardly even a loose confederacy of individual states, torn by conflicting interests and revolutionary tendencies, held together practically by the one mutual bond of race, based upon industrialism and inviting by free trade the commerce of the world. When he had finished his work, Germany was a compact empire, dominated by Prussian autocracy, single in aim, protectionist, in concentrating and developing its own commerce, and based upon militarism.

What would Bismarck have done, had he been alive in the present crisis? That he foresaw it, and that he tried to plan against it, the record of his own acts and statements leaves no question. If he had been at the helm from which he was separated by the break with the present Emperor, pictured in the now famous cartoon of the London *Punch,* 'Dropping the Pilot,' would he have allowed Germany to steer into the dangers of antagonism with all but one of the great Powers of

Europe? That is the question which students of the events of to-day have repeatedly asked themselves. As a comparison with the present diplomacy of his country, an analysis of the principles of Bismarck is suggestive.

BISMARCK'S IDEALS FOR GERMANY

Bismarck's leading thought was that Germany should be an invincible and self-sufficient empire, controlled by the central authority of Prussia. Immediate satisfactions and temporary gains he was always ready to sacrifice to this end. He stimulated and used the spirit of national unity to extend and consolidate Prussian supremacy; and it has been said that in his statecraft the new philosophy of Germany, the doctrine of triumphant energy, was exemplified.

Nevertheless, he saw with perfect clearness that supremacy must be based upon security; and this realization shaped the foreign policy which he made famous. It is significant to note how at every turn in the expansion of the power of his state, whenever he could control the desire of his ruler and people, he avoided taking from a defeated adversary territory whose loss would provide an enduring cause for hatred and the spirit of revenge. It was by this wise principle that he was able to maintain the possibility of a natural alliance with Austria, even through the crisis of a decisive defeat in war.

A second principle was the cultivation of friendly relations and alliances, even apparent sacrifice to avoid bad feeling, wherever this was possible. Often he opposed a strong national sentiment to accomplish this aim; and it was only when events had reached a point where he believed that war with a certain nation was necessary that he deliberately accepted a course which would lead to hostility. His offer of German aid to Russia in the Polish revolt of 1863 was an example of this policy, by which he gained an advantage over France, Austria, and England, and secured Russian neutrality in the conflicts that were to come. Again, in 1863, upon the death of King Frederick VII in Denmark, when Prince Frederick of Augustenburg claimed the duchies of Schleswig and Holstein, hitherto attached to the Danish crown, and was strongly supported by the German nation, he refused to break the London treaty of 1852 guaranteeing the integrity of Denmark; and so avoided a coalition of Powers against his state. Later, he brought on war with Denmark on a charge of oppression of German subjects, unifying German sentiment behind him, gaining the alliance of Austria, and paving the way for the annexation of the duchies by Prussia instead of Augustenburg.

EARLY DAYS AND RISE TO POWER

Born at Schönhausen on April 1, 1815, into an old manorial family, and educated at the Graue Kloster School in Berlin and the University of Göttingen, Otto Edouard Leopold von Bismarck is first seen as an exuberant and radical young landlord, who, after qualifying for public service in 1835, developed a distaste for it, resorted to travel and study of European countries, then to private life and the management of his estate, and flirted with Socialism and liberal ideas generally. A vital change of thought as a result of the religious revival in the early years of the reign of Frederick William IV developed the strong conviction of the divine right of kings and monarchy as the true expression of the Christian state which always afterward distinguished him, and brought him back again into public life.

In 1847, the year of his marriage to Johanna von Puttkamer, which strengthened his deep religious beliefs, he represented the lower nobility of his district in the Estates-General at Berlin. He became a leader of the early monarchical Junkers, favoring Prussian militarism and conservatism against the liberal trend toward revolution and republicanism, as member for Brandenburg in the new Parliament of 1849; and after the quelling of revolution was a strong Prussian representative appointed by the King in the restored Diet of Frankfurt. Here he discovered the intention of Austria to humble Prussia, and accepted the idea of conflict and the strengthening of Prussia by foreign alliance. He urged alliance with Russia in the Crimean War; strengthened friendship with Russia as Ambassador for four years from 1858, and later at Paris renewed the understanding of 1857 with Napoleon, thus gaining freedom for action against Austria as the first great rival to be met.

Events now pushed him rapidly into power. His letter to Manteuffel in July,

1857, showed that he felt the necessity of the coming conflict with Austria for Prussian existence. Soon, with the support of Roon as Minister of War, he gained the offices of Foreign Minister and Minister-president.

'BLOOD AND IRON'

Boldly he began his ministry with the phrase most closely associated with his name, in the enunciation of the policy he believed inevitable for the establishment of the empire: 'It is not by parliamentary speeches and majority votes that these great problems will be settled, but by blood and iron.' The words resounded through Germany, startling the people into a new attention; and brought a clanging echo from every great nation of Europe. From that time forth it was certain that the imperial development was to be characterized by the spirit which other races have come to call the worship of force, and by the words which followed the successful settlement of the issue of 1871 with France: 'We must keep our powder dry and our sword sharp.'

The early years of his ministry were occupied with procuring the neutrality of Russia and France, and an alliance with Italy, in preparing for war with Austria. A cause which would unite German sentiment in the fight he found in a charge of provoking disloyal action in the southern Duchies in 1866, and announcing full Prussian control. The people were reluctant; but by delays, Bismarck made incensed Austria seem to provoke war. Then, after victory, he assured south German friendship by blocking his ruler's desire for invasion and annexation, by the granting of universal male suffrage and by publishing Napoleon's offer of an alliance in 1866 in return for control of the Palatinate and western Hesse. In the spring he completed the union of the north German states; and with the practical control of both southern and northern Teutonic action, began to look toward the campaign to crush France.

The conflict was foreshadowed in the refusal to countenance French rule and the insistence on the neutralization of Luxemburg in 1867, in the treaty of London; and in 1868 Moltke began to formulate his plans of campaign. Bismarck allowed the rumors of possible war to be judiciously spread. Then, in 1870, came the offer that Prince Leopold of Hohenzollern be made king of the disrupted Spanish nation, the enthusiasm of the German people for the proposal which furnished Bismarck the popular feeling he desired, the opposition of France, and the famous Ems telegrams in which France demanded that the candidature never be resumed, and in which the German King rejected the proposal. Bismarck had already roused antipathy to France by his publication of the relations with Napoleon as mediator in the settlement with Austria, in which there was an implied attempt to dictate terms, and of the suggestion of aid in South Germany in return for Luxemburg and Belgium. The publication of the Ems telegrams was the spark which set national spirit aflame.

GERMANY AN EMPIRE

The peace with France was gained with the King signing the agreements as acknowledged Emperor, rather than as the representative of a confederacy of German states, and with the cession of the most of Alsace and a fifth of Lorraine and the imposition of heavy indemnities upon France. The establishment of the new Imperial order of government in Germany followed rapidly. Bismarck became a prince and the first Imperial chancellor, with a rooted belief in the divine right of the monarchy, a hatred of revolutionary forces and of the mob, and a ruling passion for power for himself, his party, his Prussia, his Empire, and his people.

His efforts to establish the union took many forms. He had early recognized the new power of the press by founding the *Kreuzzeitung* in 1847; and later he attempted to subordinate it to the ends of the state by stern limitation of freedom and by laws against public agitation.

His policy on trade was also significant. Up to the great war of 1870 he had been the guardian and favorite of the free-trade party, and Germany remained open to the world. Afterward, however, in 1878, he definitely abandoned this stand; and began by gradual imposition of duties to transform Germany into a protectionist state, forcing its own industries and concentrating wealth.

Socialism was a force he greatly feared, and he attempted to combat it by his notable experiments in identifying its principles with the monarchical power of the state, recognizing the principle of man's right to labor, of the duty of the state to aid in giving it, and of the protection of workers through insurance and compensation laws.

The church he succeeded in controlling, after a long conflict, by legislation which produced a relation safeguarding the rights of the state, while reconciling and satisfying the ecclesiastical power.

Colonization he favored upon the discovery of the fallacy in the theory of equality for Germans in British colonies. It is recorded that he distrusted colonial enterprise, and was most concerned over intact power for the Empire; but that he was forced by the national demand first into an attempt to satisfy it by favoring the development of colonies by private enterprise, and then by circumstances into admission of the necessity of protectorates.

DREAM OF DREIKAISERBUND

Bismarck's great hope was for an alliance of Germany, Austria, and Russia; and if it had been realized, it is probable that the union of natural and political forces would have established an impregnable position, which would have forestalled the wars which Bismarck feared for his country. Russia, however, he failed fully to gain, and he was forced into the Triple Alliance with Austria and Italy. He dreaded the Russian-French alliance which followed, and desired an understanding with England, which was prevented by the destruction of free-trade good will through the protective tariff. Thus, with the practical certainty of the ultimate action of these countries against his, he turned to Turkey even as early as 1884, and sent an agent to induce Abdul Hamid to arm against Russia, and procure his armament in Germany. His famous break with the present Emperor, which ended in his resignation, came over the question of the Russian occupation of Bulgaria, which he was ready to allow on account of his fear of the Russian-French alliance, but which the Emperor insisted upon preventing on the ground of loyalty to Austria. The result was the dismissal from office in 1890. He died at Friedrichsruh on July 31, 1898.

His attitude toward foreign relations was summed up in his remark upon treaties that 'no people could sacrifice its interest on the altar of fidelity to treaty; but would go only as far as suited its own interests.' However, in pursuing the opportunist policy, he was remarkable for the success, which the student of comparisons with modern German statecraft must observe, with which he always managed adroitly to make his people seem to be attacked by the nation with which he had prepared war.

The inevitable fallacy to which he appears to have been forced, in common with most of the great builders of empire, was the fallacy of compromise, of inability to push through an unmodified program.

'Universal suffrage is the necessary sugar coating of the conscription pill,' he is reputed to have said. He opposed the Prussian love of monarchy supported by arms to a maimed liberalism, while on the other hand he was forced to arm with votes a stimulated spirit of democracy. He attempted to use an efficient army as the subordinate force of diplomacy, intelligence justifying force. Would he have had faith or fear, asks the student of to-day, for militarism in the ascendant, force justifying itself?

Let him speak, in the words of a letter written to his wife, in final comment upon his own career and upon his ultimate convictions regarding the world in which he had tried to build an enduring structure: 'Peoples and individuals, folly and wisdom, war and peace — all comes and goes like wave upon wave; and only the sea remains.'

II

BENEDICT XV—POLITICAL POPE

SALVATORE CORTESI

[*Independent*, October 12, 1914. By permission.]

The most surprised person at the election of Giacomo della Chiesa as head of the Catholic Church was Benedict XV himself, for he knew his disqualifications as well as did his colleagues, and so had not contemplated the supreme dignity — for the present. To begin with he is only sixty years old, which is quite young for a pope, and means a probable pontificate of fifteen or twenty years; he has only been a cardinal three months, and he was sent to his Archdiocese of Bologna, if not as a disgrace, at least to remove him from the Vatican, where, as Cardinal Rampolla's most faithful disciple, he was not *persona grata*. These were the disqualifications; the qualifications were less on the surface. Certainly the policy of Pius X was not looked upon with favor by many of the cardinals nor was his easily influenced character considered the best for the head of the church in a crisis, and in turning to della Chiesa they found one who supposedly will follow Rampolla's policy, and who is strong and firm in whatever he does, while having a thorough knowledge of church affairs through his training in the time of Leo XIII.

The new pope is small in stature even for an Italian (so much so that the tailor had to be called immediately after his election, to make smaller the smallest of the three suits which are always prepared beforehand for the new pontiff). He is sallow, with a thin, keen face; gesticulates freely with nervous movements of the hands; wears spectacles and is full of energy and life; and with it all has the indefinable 'something' which is popularly supposed to denote refinement and a long line of ancestors.

The della Chiesa is a noble family of Genoa originally from Milan, and dates back to the time of St. Ambrose, who, having the temporal as well as the spiritual government of most of northern Italy, created some captains, with the object of defending the church from the Arian attack. Some of these captains through their acts of valor were called 'Champions of the Church,' in Italian 'Campioni della Chiesa,' and the founder of the pope's family was one of these soldiers. The della Chiesa family distinguished themselves in the church, counting two saints, a cardinal, several bishops, and now a pope, but not showing great capacity in other fields. The father of Benedict XV was Marquis Giuseppe, while he has a brother who is an admiral on the retired list of the Italian navy, and is related to many well known families of Rome and Italy.

Although noble, the della Chiesa family is quite poor, so that the many acts of charity of Benedict XV are all the more to his credit, as they manifest a large generosity, and to this he adds faithfulness and gratitude. He undoubtedly owed the first steps in his career to Cardinal Rampolla, who took him to Madrid when he was nuncio there, and had him as his substitute when he himself was secretary of state.

Della Chiesa witnessed the fall of his patron, saw the sycophants drop away, even friends finding too little to be got out of it to make it worth while to visit the lonely recluse. But the loyalty and affection of della Chiesa never wavered. No matter what his cares or fatigue he paid his daily visit to Cardinal Rampolla, bringing a wave of affairs with him and brightening the declining years of his old friend and master, while on his part receiving counsel, and, more remarkable, acting on it. When Cardinal Rampolla died, Archbishop della Chiesa was in Bologna. He rushed to Rome and showed such violent and sincere grief that the saying, 'like della Chiesa's love for Rampolla,' became the symbol of fidelity at the Vatican.

So much has happened since Giacomo della Chiesa was a comparatively young man at the Vatican that looking back it seems thirty instead of fifteen years ago. It seems only the other day that I climbed the innumerable stairs (at that time the only elevator in the Vatican was forbidden to outsiders and especially to journalists) leading to the Secretaryship of State in the Apostolic Palace. Once arrived one had the impression of being in a garret transformed into a photographer's gallery, as the corridor out of which the rooms of the office open takes its light from a skylight. In these modest and small, but historic rooms, where the celebrated Consalvi worked at the time of Napoleon, and Cardinal Antonelli under Pius IX; where Gioacchino Pecci, the greatest pope of modern times, began his career, and where his powerful Secretary of State, Cardinal Rampolla, had made his mark, there the young Monsignor della Chiesa was then supreme. Those rooms, which seem to be camped in the sky, so high they stand at the top of the Vatican, are the same which have produced the present generation of papal diplomatists; Merry del Val, perhaps the chief, who had his first mission in Canada; Sbaretti, who went to Cuba, and Ceretti, who after having been in Washington has recently been appointed to be the first apostolic delegate to Australia, and so on. Monsignor della Chiesa was always to be found there, or walking in the upper loggia, on which his own apartment opened, with the Eternal City at his feet. Even then, over fifteen years ago, one could scarcely call him 'young,' for he is one of those people who are never young and never old, this appearance being emphasized by a slight inequality in his shoulders, the habit of wearing his spectacles crooked, and using his hands continually in arranging the sash about his waist. I cannot say that he liked newspaper men, but at a time when the suave and kind Monsignor Bisleti, now cardinal, had not yet risen to be majordomo, and his place was then occupied by men like della Volpe and Cagiano de Azevedo, who detested journalists, journalism and writers, and took no trouble to conceal their feelings, Monsignor della Chiesa seemed an anchor of refuge. He was indeed most affable, very witty and sarcastic when in a good humor, as he usually was, *but* if something had gone wrong, although it had nothing to do with the person he was receiving, he was one of the most brusque men that I have ever come across. I remember that his face was entirely transformed and it seemed as though a dark, threatening cloud had descended upon it. We knew the signs portending the storm, and when we saw him thus at a distance we quickly turned and literally ran, waiting for a more propitious moment, which always came, and, as is usual with men of his nature, the sunshine repaid for the preceding squall. The worst time to approach him was in the last years of the pontificate of Leo XIII, when the trouble with France began and the policy of the great Secretary of State, to which Monsignor della Chiesa had contributed such strenuous labor, threatened to fail.

Such is the man at sixty years of age.

At ten he was much the same — impatient of control and given to fits of stormy temper, which a loving mother was helpless or careless of controlling, followed by the sunshine of a most attractive repentance. At thirteen he turned his thoughts toward the church and developed a love of study which has remained through life. His mother became so worried that on one occasion she presented him with a spade and insisted upon his digging up the garden. At that time he planted a palm in a pot which became his chief treasure. It grew so great that it was eventually set out in the garden, and will now, of course, be the chief sight of his home. His father insisted upon his taking his degree as a lawyer, which was an extreme penance to him, as his talents did not lie in that direction, but he persevered and took a high place in his class. The day that he received his degree he went to his father and said, 'I have obeyed you about my studies, and now wish my reward. I must enter the church.' This he was allowed to do by his parents, but reluctantly.

Like his predecessor, Benedict XV is most abstemious in his habits and a very early riser. Half past five or six sees him at his altar, and at seven he has already breakfasted; at eight he is at his desk, and woe to the clerk who is not in his place.

It remains to be seen if Benedict XV will restore the pomp of the papacy, so much relied upon and appreciated by Leo XIII, and so much reduced by Pius X. His traditions and training must have taught him the usefulness of pomp, while his personal wishes would be for simplicity — time will tell. Time will also reveal his policy, of which it can now only be said that it will not be conspicuously Germanophile; but he will certainly be a political Pope, belonging to that school of churchmen who think that it is the duty of the Holy See to make itself felt in all possible ways and directions for the good of humanity, and therefore it is impossible to ignore the influence which the Vatican traditionally and historically has exercised over the destinies of the peoples by dealing with the different governments, Catholic and non-Catholic alike.

III

TAFT AND ROOSEVELT: A COMPOSITE STUDY

FRANCIS E. LEUPP

[*Atlantic Monthly*, November, 1910. By permission of author and publisher.]

President Roosevelt regretted deeply the resignation of Elihu Root as Secretary of War in 1903. 'As an adviser,' said he, ' Root gives me just what I need — candid opposition when he thinks I am wrong. Shall I ever find any one to take his place?' To a suggestion of Mr. Taft's name he responded, ' Of course, Taft is the only man possible. I am very fond of him, and he will make an ideal member of the Cabinet. The only trouble with him is,'— and he ended the sentence with his whimsical smile and in his semi-falsetto, —' he is too much like me!'

Mr. Taft came, and in due course was chosen by Mr. Roosevelt for his successor. The President pressed his candidacy on the ground of their sympathetic agreement on questions of policy, intimating that the Taft administration would be, in effect, only a more polished continuation of the Roosevelt administration. Mr. Taft's popular majority therefore contained a mixture of voters who wished to see the Roosevelt administration carried through a few more chapters, and of voters whom nothing but the promised polish reconciled to the threatened prolongation.

The outcome astonished both groups. President Taft was not slow in letting it be known that the contrasts between himself and his predecessor were going to be emphasized quite as strongly as their likenesses. His reorganization of the Cabinet, his demand that Congress address itself immediately to a revision of the tariff, his preparations for indiscriminate prosecutions under the anti-trust law, were among the plainest evidences that a new day had dawned. What one element read in the change was a reversal and rebuke of Rooseveltism; what the opposing element read was the out-Rooseveltism of Roosevelt. Unbiased observers saw in it merely the spectacle of two men aiming at the same ends, but differing radically in their manner of reaching these. A brief review of their dissimilarities, which are partly temperamental and partly the effect of training, may explain some phenomena that seem to have mystified the bulk of the newspaper-reading public.

We may set out with the assertion that both men are genuinely patriotic. Both are highly educated, the one on technical lines, the other in general scholarship. Neither began his public career with the Presidency in view. Taft's ambitions pointed in the direction of the Federal Supreme Court; Roosevelt's toward diplomacy, looking to the erection of the United States into a great World Power.

Circumstances which could not have been foreseen deflected the currents of their lives. Each is a living force after his kind: Taft static, Roosevelt dynamic. Taft takes advantage of opportunity when it comes his way, and strives to shape it for the public good; Roosevelt goes hunting it, and consequently gets a larger choice. Inertia, for Taft, means rest; for Roosevelt, incessant activity.

To recognize visually the temperamental difference between the two men, we need only see them at their equestrian exercise. Mr. Taft's horse must be one which can be depended on to carry him a given distance over a specified course, in a stated time and at a certain gait; Mr. Roosevelt's must be one which will not balk at leaving the beaten trail and plunging into a thicket, a jumper which will refuse no bar, a mettlesome animal which taxes continually its rider's vigilance. Both men are laughing philosophers; but Taft laughs at the world, Roosevelt with it. The Taft smile has passed into a proverb; it is always there, shining even through the mists of conventional sobriety. The Roosevelt smile comes and goes; it emerges from his nearsighted scowl and disappears again behind it, as the sun plays with an opaque cloud.

Both men have vigorous tempers. When Taft gives way to his, it is to inflict a merciless lashing upon its victim, for whom thereafter he has no use whatever. With Roosevelt it is a case of powder and spark; there is a vivid flash and a deafening roar, but when the smoke has blown away, that is the end, and the author of the explosion of January may become a boon companion by June, if accident have meanwhile invested him with new interest.

Both men have strong wills; Roosevelt's

is aggressive to the verge of tyranny, Taft's obstinate to the point of perverseness. So marked are these characteristics that it is not difficult to fancy what either man would do in a fateful crisis. Had Taft been in Stoessel's place at Port Arthur, for instance, he might have starved rather than surrender; Roosevelt would have headed a forlorn hope and tried to cut his way through the besiegers, taking as many lives as he could before giving up his own.

Their theories of administration are fundamentally diverse. Mr. Taft's is the more dignified, Mr. Roosevelt's the more human. Mr. Taft's conception of the government is of a gigantic machine, its many parts so articulated as to be moved from a single source of energy; and as engineer he confines his attention to this central distributing point. As Mr. Roosevelt sees it, the government is an organization of live men, each engaged in doing something which, if not well done, diminishes the efficiency of the rest; hence, when he was in command of this legion, he had his eye on the corporals not less than on the captains. Technically speaking, Mr. Taft follows the more orderly method when he communicates only with his Cabinet officers, and leaves to them the direction of their subordinates.

Setting aside the question of orderliness, however, and considering rather the accomplishment of results, there is good reason for thinking that a president who takes a personal hand in everything will loom larger in history than one who sticks closely to a prescribed task. His example vitalizes the whole working force. His meddling may occasionally make discipline difficult in the higher places, but it inspires the rank and file with a sense of individual responsibility and encourages them to think as well as work. Only a brain and body of uncommon endurance could stand such drafts, and not one president in a dozen is equipped for undertaking more than the laws demand of him. This is a beneficent provision of nature to avert chaos in our governmental affairs; but it should not blind us to the fact that the country's debt to some of its masterspirits of the past has grown out of their idiosyncrasies rather than their conformity to rule.

Volunteer criticism brings into view another variance between the two men.

Taft, shut in as he was for the first year of his presidency, knew virtually nothing of what the newspapers were saying about him and his official family. He never cared for such reading himself, and others decided for him how much, and what, he should see. Those adverse opinions which did get past them and reach his eye, excited only his contempt, as either founded on misinformation or instigated by the 'conspirators' whom he suspected of constantly plotting harm to his administration. He rarely noticed such things publicly; when he did, he dealt with his critics at arm's length, and in terms which, though distinct, were fairly moderate.

Roosevelt, on the other hand, has always kept track of the newspapers, a practice in which he has had the aid of an enormous personal acquaintance. As the result of a particularly abusive screed there is apt to be a jarring of the elements till he has published to the world his opinion of the writer, in which the neutral tints of rhetoric are conspicuous by their absence. Were not his store of vital energy inexhaustible, he would long ago have worn himself out with the explosive force he puts into his retorts. His best friends regret that he does not reserve his artillery fire for the big foes who are worthy of it, instead of wasting so much ammunition on ground-moles and jackrabbits. Besides, it loses a good deal of its potency by too frequent use. No public man can take up every quarrel thrust at him, save at the expense of other and larger warfare. Half the calumniators of a really fine fellow would go unheeded by the multitude but for the free advertising he gives them; and one deplorable effect of his condescension is to encourage them to bait him whenever they are short of legitimate excitement from other sources.

A certain kind of criticism, nevertheless, is accepted without resentment by the self-assertive Roosevelt. During his presidency he hardly ever put forth an important manifesto without first submitting it to a council in which the several elements likely to be affected by it were represented, with a request that every one speak his mind unreservedly. I have seen at such gatherings, clergymen, lawyers, editors, college presidents, merchants, members of the administration, and subordinates in the civil service. All took their host at his word, and voiced their views when called upon. Often he made changes suggested by the least distinguished of his guests, but he was equally frank in holding to his first notions if unconvinced by argument. This was his means of getting into touch with public opinion on matters which he could not go out and discuss directly with his fellow citizens in mass. One can hardly imagine President Taft calling together such a miscellaneous company from the four corners of the country, and submitting his judgments for their approval or dissent. The reason is not far to seek.

Passing reference has been made to the education of the two men. In its broader sense the term includes, not only their academic studies, but their training in the everyday work of the world. Taft's brief but admirable service on the bench proved his fitness for a career there. It also fixed upon him the judicial habit of thought and action, which is utterly unlike the executive habit. The former means equipoise, deliberation, and carefully revised conclusions; the latter means prompt decision and swift reinforcement, followed by the stroke that counts. Coming to the presidency, Mr. Taft moved from a somewhat secluded domain in which he was at home, into an open one in which he was a stranger. The offices which had fallen to Roosevelt, from the day he entered public life, had, on the contrary, been legislative or executive, never judicial; they had kept him constantly leading somebody and hammering at something, instead of calmly analyzing evidence and formulating principles.

It is true that Taft had some experience nominally executive, for a few years as Governor of the Philippines, and later as Secretary of War; but his colonial work was chiefly in the way of determining rights and administering justice among a dependent people, and in the Cabinet his functions were more advisory than constructive. It is not wonderful, therefore, that as President he approached his problems by the judicial rather than the executive route. Indifference to criticism was a feature of his judicial training; so was the weighing of all the pros and cons of a proposition before acting on it. Contrasted with Roosevelt's rapid despatch of business, this often aroused the impatience of non-official spectators, who set down Taft's conservatism as mere stubbornness. For the best enterprise proposed to him,

Taft must find an affirmative sanction in the statutes and digests, or he will have none of it; Roosevelt, in a like situation, used to say, 'Is there any law against it? No? Then go ahead!'

In short, Taft interprets the Constitution in the light of its tenth amendment, Roosevelt in the light of its preamble. Both are equally sincere in their desire to serve the people. Taft takes for his guide the written law, and the platform pledges on which he was elected, as the latest recorded expressions of the popular will; Roosevelt mingles with the people themselves, and, if in thought and feeling they have run ahead of the written record, he also runs ahead, trusting that the formal expression will in due season catch up with the sentiment. This leads, now and then, to unexpected results. For example, when he started for Africa last year the present 'Insurgent' movement was unknown, and he was still figuring as a champion of Speaker Cannon; but no sooner does he return and take his bearings than he discerns in the revolt a real uprising of the people, and accordingly throws the weight of his influence rather toward its side than toward the other. The Old-Liners denounce his action as sheer demagogy; the Insurgents applaud it as true democracy.

As for President Taft, he seems to have reasoned like a magistrate up to the time of Mr. Roosevelt's return, and since then like an executive. Not many months elapsed between his exculpation of the Payne-Aldrich tariff because its accusers had not proved their case beyond a reasonable doubt, and his appearance as the sponsor for an entirely dissimilar scheme. This is not cowardice, or mere wanton tergiversation, but a sign of an awakening sense that the President sits, not on a bench, but in a chair of state.

Or, take the Pinchot-Ballinger controversy as an illustration of the difference between judicial and executive methods. The new administration was like an army just put into the field to attain certain ends for the common welfare. The effectiveness of its campaign depended on the concentration, not the diffusion, of its energies; yet two of the officers, having a disagreement, halted and undertook to settle it by a duel.

How would Commander Roosevelt have handled such a situation? He would have notified the disputants that they were there to destroy the enemy, not each other; that it was his business to lead the column, not to compose personal quarrels; and that, no matter what theirs was about, they must 'drop it'— his familiar phrase — or one of them must go outside of the public service to do his further fighting. Had his order been disregarded, he would summarily have cut off the official head of the combatant he deemed most at fault, and moved along.

Commander Taft's course, equally characteristic, was the very reverse of this. He patiently listened to both parties, said as pleasant things as he could to both, and urged an investigation by Congress, very much as the trial judge turns over to a jury the issues of fact as a preliminary to applying the law. Even Mr. Pinchot's dismissal came not as a decision of the controversy, but as an incident, the forester having committed what the judge was pleased to regard as contempt of court. But for that, affairs might have remained till to-day where they stood last December.

The contrast here indicated is borne out in the attitudes of the two Presidents toward the bench itself. When President Taft looks for a new judge, he aims to find one whose past activities convey little assurance as to his individual trend of thought on the questions of the day. President Roosevelt, believing that a policy is essential to all progress in government, and that the courts are part of the machinery of government, preferred men whose personal views on certain important subjects were well known. This was not with the purpose of influencing the courts unduly in the direction in which he thought civic welfare lay, but of preventing their being influenced in the opposite direction. No other President has so freely criticized the judiciary, and thereby provoked censure for himself from those who regard the courts as sacred because they hold the seals of ultimate authority; but to Mr. Roosevelt's mind they are human institutions, subject to human shortcomings, and to be kept pure only by exposure to the candid comment of the people to whom they owe their existence.

Though not strictly within the purview of this article, it might have been interesting to compare the respective ideals of the President and the ex-President as to party politics and management; but space limitations warn me that I must pass to the last phase of my topic, the mutual relations of the two men. This may be condensed into the simple statement that there is not now, and has not been, any misapprehension in the mind of either as to the other. In spite of the gossips, Mr. Taft has wasted no time in wondering 'where Roosevelt stands,' nor has Mr. Roosevelt agonized over the alternative of 'going to Taft's rescue or leaving him in the mire.' Mr. Taft has done many things which Mr. Roosevelt would not have done, and left undone many more which Mr. Roosevelt would have done; but this is Mr. Taft's administration, and no one realizes the fact better than Mr. Roosevelt. The 'Return from Elba' fol-de-rol has already dissolved into the thin air from which it was conjured, and the 'Roosevelt for 1912' hurrah still belongs in the same category with the familiar abridgement of *Hamlet*. No American publicist believes more implicitly in party solidarity than the ex-President; and when the test of the ballot-box shall have demonstrated the relative strength of the Progressive and the Old-Style Republicans, he expects to see the minority fall in, with true sportsmanlike spirit, behind the majority, and vote the same ticket at the next national election.

Without pretending to be a prophet or the son of a prophet, I will stake my all as a political weather-observer on the proposition that, however serious may be their factional differences, the Republicans will renominate President Taft in 1912 if he wishes it. This is not a guess, but a sober thesis in the psychology of practical politics. The party that has elected its candidate President by vouching for him unconditionally to the American people would be ashamed to confess, at the end of his term, that it had misled the voters. Look back over the last fifty years. No power under heaven, except his own disinclination, could have prevented Lincoln's second nomination, or Grant's, or Garfield's, if he had lived; or Cleveland's, or Harrison's, or McKinley's. As neither Johnson nor Arthur had reached the presidency by election, and Hayes had publicly declared that he would not stand for a second term, their cases are not precedents.

But, albeit Mr. Taft will be the arbiter of his own fortunes as regards a renomination, a reëlection is of course quite another matter. That depends, not on the pride of a party, but on the satisfaction of the people; and no prediction of the result at the polls, two years before the event, would be worth the paper it was written on.

IV

HENRY JAMES'S FIRST INTERVIEW

PRESTON LOCKWOOD

[*New York Times,* March 21, 1915. By permission.]

One of the compensations of the war, which we ought to take advantage of, is the chance given the general public to approach on the personal side some of the distinguished men who have not hitherto lived much in the glare of the footlights. Henry James has probably done this as little as any one; he has enjoyed for upward of forty years a reputation not confined to his own country, has published a long succession of novels, tales, and critical papers, and yet has apparently so delighted in reticence as well as in expression that he has passed his seventieth year without having responsibly 'talked' for publication or figured for it otherwise than pen in hand.

Shortly after the outbreak of the war Mr. James found himself, to his professed great surprise, Chairman of the American Volunteer Motor Ambulance Corps, now at work in France, and to-day, at the end of three months of bringing himself to the point, has granted me, as a representative of the New York *Times,* an interview. What this departure from the habit of a lifetime means to him he expressed at the outset.

'I can't put,' Mr. James said, speaking with much consideration and asking that his punctuation as well as his words should be noted, 'my devotion and sympathy for the cause of our corps more strongly than in permitting it thus to overcome my dread of the assault of the interviewer, whom I have deprecated, all these years, with all the force of my preference for saying myself and without superfluous aid, without interference in the guise of encouragement and cheer, anything I may think worth my saying. Nothing is worth my saying that I cannot help myself out with better, I hold, than even the most suggestive young gentleman with a notebook can help me. It may be fatuous of me, but, believing myself possessed of some means of expression, I feel as if I were sadly giving it away when, with the use of it urgent, I don't gratefully employ it, but appeal instead to the art of somebody else.'

It was impossible to be that 'somebody else,' or, in other words, the person privileged to talk with Mr. James, to sit in presence of his fine courtesy and earnestness, without understanding the sacrifice he was making, and making only because he had finally consented to believe that it would help the noble work of relief which a group of young Americans, mostly graduates of Harvard, Yale, and Princeton, are carrying on along their stretch of the fighting line in northern France.

Mr. James frankly desired his remarks to bear only on the merits of the American Volunteer Motor Ambulance Corps. It enjoys to-day the fullest measure of his appreciation and attention; it appeals deeply to his benevolent instincts, and he gives it sympathy and support as one who has long believed, and believes more than ever, in spite of everything, at this international crisis, in the possible development of 'closer communities and finer intimacies' between America and Great Britain, between the country of his birth and the country, as he puts it, of his 'shameless frequentation.'

There are many people who are eloquent about the war, who are authorities on the part played in it by the motor ambulance and who take an interest in the good relations of Great Britain and the United States; but there is nobody who can tell us, as Mr. James can, about style and the structure of sentences, and all that appertains to the aspect and value of words. Now and then in what here follows he speaks familiarly of these things for the first time in his life, not by any means because he jumped at the chance, but because his native kindness, whether consciously or unconsciously, seemed so ready to humor the insisting inquirer.

'It is very difficult,' he said, seeking to diminish the tension so often felt by a journalist, even at the moment of a highly appreciated occasion, 'to break into graceful license after so long a life of decorum; therefore you must excuse me if my egotism does n't run very free or my complacency find quite the right turns.'

He had received me in the offices of the corps, businesslike rooms, modern for London, low-ceiled and sparsely furnished. It was not by any means the sort of setting in which as a reader of Henry James I had expected to run to earth the author of *The Golden Bowl,* but the place is, nevertheless, to-day, in the tension of war time, one of the few approaches to a social resort outside his Chelsea home where he can be counted on. Even that delightful Old World retreat, Lamb House, Rye, now claims little of his time.

The interviewer spoke of the waterside Chelsea and Mr. James's long knowledge of it, but, sitting not overmuch at his ease and laying a friendly hand on the shoulder of his tormentor, he spoke, instead, of motor ambulances, making the point, in the interest of clearness, that the American Ambulance Corps of Neuilly, though an organization with which Richard Norton's corps is in the fullest sympathy, does not come within the scope of his remarks.

'I find myself chairman of our corps committee for no great reason that I can discover save my being the oldest American resident here interested in its work; at the same time that if I render a scrap of help by putting on record my joy even in the rather ineffectual connection so far as "doing" anything is concerned, I need n't say how welcome you are to my testimony. What I mainly seem to grasp, I should say, is that in regard to testifying at all unlimitedly by the aid of the newspapers, I have to reckon with a certain awkwardness in our position. Here comes up, you see, the question of our reconciling a rather indispensable degree of reserve as to the detail of our activity with the general American demand for publicity at any price. There are ways in which the close presence of war challenges the whole claim for publicity; and I need hardly say that this general claim has been challenged, practically, by the present horrific complexity of things at the front, as neither the Allies themselves nor watching neutrals have ever seen it challenged before. The American public is, of course, little used to not being able to hear, and hear as an absolute right, about anything that the press may suggest that

it ought to hear about; so that nothing may be said ever to happen anywhere that it does n't count on having reported to it, hot and hot, as the phrase is, several times a day. We were the first American ambulance corps in the field, and we have a record of more than four months' continuous service with one of the French armies, but the rigor of the objection to our taking the world into our intimate confidence is not only shown by our still unbroken inability to report in lively instalments, but receives also a sidelight from the fact that numerous like private corps maintained by donations on this side of the sea are working at the front without the least commemoration of their deeds — that is, without a word of journalistic notice.

'I hope that by the time these possibly too futile remarks of mine come to such light as may await them Mr. Norton's report of our general case may have been published, and nothing would give the committee greater pleasure than that some such controlled statement on our behalf, best proceeding from the scene of action itself, should occasionally appear. The ideal would, of course, be that exactly the right man, at exactly the right moment, should report exactly the right facts, in exactly the right manner, and when that happy consummation becomes possible we shall doubtless revel in funds.'

Mr. James had expressed himself with such deliberation and hesitation that I was reminded of what I had heard of all the verbal alterations made by him in novels and tales long since published; to the point, we are perhaps incorrectly told of replacing a ' she answered' by a ' she indefinitely responded.'

I should, indeed, mention that on my venturing to put to Mr. James a question or two about his theory of such changes he replied that no theory could be stated, at any rate in the off-hand manner that I seemed to invite, without childish injustice to the various considerations by which a writer is moved. These determinant reasons differ with the context and the relations of parts to parts and to the total sense in a way of which no a priori account can be given.

'I dare say I strike you,' he went on, ' as rather bewilderedly weighing my words; but I may perhaps explain my so doing very much as I the other day heard a more interesting fact explained. A distinguished English naval expert happened to say to me that the comparative non-production of airships in this country indicated, in addition to other causes, a possible limitation of the British genius in that direction, and then on my asking him why that class of craft shouldn't be within the compass of the greatest makers of sea-ships, replied, after brief reflection: "Because the airship is essentially a bad ship, and we English can't make a bad ship well enough." Can you pardon,' Mr. James asked, 'my making an application of this to the question of one's amenability or plasticity to the interview? The airship of the interview is for me a bad ship, and I can't make a bad ship well enough.'

Catching Mr. James's words as they came was not very difficult; but there was that in the manner of his speech that cannot be put on paper, the delicate difference between the word recalled and the word allowed to stand, the earnestness of the massive face and alert eye, tempered by the genial 'comment of the body,' as R. L. Stevenson has it.

Henry James does not look his seventy years. He has a finely shaped head, and a face, at once strong and serene, which the painter and the sculptor may well have liked to interpret. Indeed, in fine appreciation they have so wrought. Derwent Wood's admirable bust, purchased from last year's Royal Academy, shown by the Chantrey Fund, will be permanently placed in the Tate Gallery, and those who fortunately know Sargent's fine portrait, to be exhibited in the Sargent Room at the San Francisco Exhibition, will recall its having been slashed into last year by the militant suffragettes, though now happily restored to such effect that no trace of the outrage remains.

Mr. James has a mobile mouth, a straight nose, a forehead which has thrust back the hair from the top of his commanding head, although it is thick at the sides over the ears, and repeats in its soft gray the color of his kindly eyes. Before taking in these physical facts one receives an impression of benignity and amenity not often conveyed, even by the most distinguished. And, taking advantage of this amiability, I asked if certain words just used should be followed by a dash, and even boldly added: 'Are you not famous, Mr. James, for the use of dashes?'

'Dash my fame!' he impatiently replied. 'And remember, please, that dogmatizing about punctuation is exactly as foolish as dogmatizing about any other form of communication with the reader. All such forms depend on the kind of thing one is doing and the kind of effect one intends to produce. Dashes, it seems almost platitudinous to say, have their particular representative virtue, their quickening force, and, to put it roughly, strike both the familiar and the emphatic note, when those are the notes required, with a felicity beyond either the comma or the semicolon; though indeed a fine sense for the semicolon, like any sort of sense at all for the pluperfect tense and the subjunctive mood, on which the whole perspective in a sentence may depend, seems anything but common. Does nobody ever notice the calculated use by French writers of a short series of suggestive points in the current of their prose? I confess to a certain shame for my not employing frankly that shade of indication, a finer shade still than the dash. . . . But what on earth are we talking about?' And the Chairman of the Corps Committee pulled himself up in deprecation of his frivolity, which I recognized by acknowledging that we might indeed hear more about the work done and doing at the front by Richard Norton and his energetic and devoted co-workers. Then I plunged recklessly to draw my victim.

'May not a large part of the spirit which animates these young men be a healthy love of adventure?' I asked.

The question seemed to open up such depths that Mr. James considered a moment and began:

'I, of course, don't personally know many of our active associates, who naturally waste very little time in London. But, since you ask me, I prefer to think of them as moved, first and foremost, not by the idea of the fun or the sport they may have, or of the good thing they may make of the job for themselves, but by that of the altogether exceptional chance opened to them of acting blessedly and savingly for others, though indeed if we come to that there is no such sport in the world as so acting when anything in the nature of risk or exposure is attached. The horrors, the miseries, the monstrosities they are in presence of are so great surely as not to leave much of any other attitude over when intelligent sympathy has done its best.

'Personally I feel so strongly on everything that the war has brought into question for the Anglo-Saxon peoples that humorous detachment or any other thinness or tepidity of mind on the subject affects me as vulgar impiety, not to say as rank blasphemy; our whole race tension became for me a sublimely conscious thing from the moment Germany flung at us all her explanation of her pounce upon Belgium for massacre and ravage in the form of the most insolent, " Because I choose to, damn you all " recorded in history.

'The pretension to smashing world rule by a single people, in virtue of a monopoly of every title, every gift and every right, ought perhaps to confound us more by its grotesqueness than to alarm us by its energy; but never do cherished possessions, whether of the hand or of the spirit, become so dear to us as when overshadowed by vociferous aggression. How can one help seeing that such aggression, if hideously successful in Europe, would, with as little loss of time as possible, proceed to apply itself to the American side of the world, and how can one, therefore, not feel that the Allies are fighting to the death for the soul and the purpose and the future that are in *us,* for the defense of every ideal that has most guided our growth and that most assures our unity?

'Of course, since you ask me, my many years of exhibited attachment to the conditions of French and of English life, with whatever fond play of reflection and reaction may have been involved in it, make it inevitable that these countries should peculiarly appeal to me at the hour of their peril, their need and their heroism, and I am glad to declare that, though I had supposed I knew what that attachment was, I find I have any number of things more to learn about it. English life, wound up to the heroic pitch, is at present most immediately before me, and I can scarcely tell you what a privilege I feel it to share the inspiration and see further revealed the character of this decent and dauntless people.

'However, I am indeed as far as you may suppose from assuming that what you speak to me of as the " political " bias is the only ground on which the work of our corps for the Allies should appeal to the American public. Political, I confess, has become for me in all this a loose and question-begging term, but if we must resign ourselves to it as explaining some people's indifference, let us use a much better one for inviting their confidence. It will do beautifully well if givers and workers and helpers are moved by intelligent human pity, and they are with us abundantly enough if they feel themselves simply roused by, and respond to, the most awful exhibition of physical and moral anguish the world has ever faced, and which it is the strange fate of our actual generations to see unrolled before them. We welcome any lapse of logic that may connect inward vagueness with outward zeal, if it be the zeal of subscribers, presenters or drivers of cars, or both at once, stretcher-bearers, lifters, healers, consolers, handy Anglo-French interpreters (these extremely precious), smoothers of the way; in short, after whatever fashion. We ask of nobody any waste of moral or of theoretic energy, nor any conviction of any sort, but that the job is inspiring and the honest, educated man a match for it.

'If I seem to cast doubt on any very driving intelligence of the great issue as a source of sympathy with us, I think this is because I have been struck, whenever I have returned to my native land, by the indifference of Americans at large to the concerns and preoccupations of Europe. This indifference has again and again seemed to me quite beyond measure or description, though it may be in a degree suggested by the absence throughout the many-paged American newspaper of the least mention of a European circumstance unless some not-to-be-blinked war or revolution, or earthquake, or other cataclysm has happened to apply the lash to curiosity. The most comprehensive journalistic formula that I have found myself, under that observation, reading into the general case, is the principle that the first duty of the truly appealing sheet in a given community is to teach every individual reached by it — every man, woman and child — to count on appearing there, in their habit as they live, if they will only wait for their turn.

'However,' he continued, ' my point is simply my plea for patience with our enterprise even at the times when we can't send home sensational figures. " They also serve who only stand and wait," and the essence of our utility, as of that of any ambulance corps, is just to be there, on any and every contingency, including the blessed contingency of a temporary drop in the supply of the wounded turned out and taken on — since such comparative intermissions occur. Ask our friends, I beg you, to rid themselves of the image of our working on schedule time or on 10 guarantee of a maximum delivery; we are dependent on the humors of battle, on incalculable rushes and lapses, on violent outbreaks of energy which rage and pass and are expressly designed to bewilder. 15 It is not for the poor wounded to oblige us by making us showy, but for us to let them count on our open arms and open lap as troubled children count on those of their mother. It is now to be said, moreover, 20 that our opportunity of service threatens inordinately to grow; such things may any day begin to occur at the front as will make what we have up to now been able to do mere child's play, though some of our 25 help has been rendered when casualties were occurring at the rate, say, of 5000 in twenty minutes, which ought, on the whole, to satisfy us. In face of such enormous facts of destruction —'

Here Mr. James broke off as if these facts were, in their horror, too many and too much for him. But after another moment he explained his pause.

'One finds it in the midst of all this as 35 hard to apply one's words as to endure one's thoughts. The war has used up words; they have weakened, they have deteriorated like motor car tires; they have, like millions of other things, been 40 more overstrained and knocked about and voided of the happy semblance during the last six months than in all the long ages before, and we are now confronted with a depreciation of all our terms, or, other- 45 wise speaking, with a loss of expression through increase of limpness, that may well make us wonder what ghosts will be left to walk.'

This sounded rather desperate, yet the 50 incorrigible interviewer, conscious of the wane of his only chance, ventured to glance at the possibility of a word or two on the subject of Mr. James's present literary intentions. But the kindly hand 55 here again was raised, and the mild voice became impatient.

'Pardon my not touching on any such irrelevance. All I want is to invite the public, as unblushingly as possible, to take all the interest in us it can; which may be helped by knowing that our bankers are 5 Messrs. Brown Brothers & Co., 59 Wall Street, New York City, and that checks should be made payable to the American Volunteer Motor Ambulance Corps.'

V

Good

BARRIE AT BAY: WHICH WAS BROWN?

[*New York Times*, October 1, 1914. By permission.]

As our reporter entered Sir James Barrie's hotel room by one door, the next door softly closed. I was alone (writes our reporter). I sprang into the corridor and had just time to see him fling himself down the elevator. Then I understood what he had meant when he said on the telephone that he would be ready for me at 10.30.

I returned thoughtfully to the room, where I found myself no longer alone. Sir James Barrie's 'man' was there; a 30 stolid Londoner, name of Brown, who told me he was visiting America for the first time.

'Sir James is very sorry, but has been called away,' he assured me without mov- 35 ing a muscle. Then he added: 'But this is the pipe,' and he placed a pipe of the largest size on the table.

'The pipe he smokes?' I asked.

Brown is evidently a very truthful man, 40 for he hesitated. 'That is the interview pipe,' he explained. 'When we decided to come to America Sir James said he would have to be interviewed, and that it would be wise to bring something with us 45 for the interviewers to take notice of. So he told me to buy the biggest pipe I could find, and he practised holding it in his mouth in his cabin on the way across. He is very pleased with the way the gen- 50 tlemen of the press have taken notice of it.'

'So that is not the pipe he really smokes?' I said, perceiving I was on the verge of a grand discovery. 'I suppose 55 he actually smokes an ordinary small pipe.'

Again Brown hesitated, but again truth prevailed.

'He does not smoke any pipe,' he said,

'nor cigars, nor cigarettes; he never smokes at all; he just puts that one in his mouth to help the interviewers.'

'It has the appearance of having been smoked?' I pointed out.

'I blackened it for him,' the faithful fellow replied.

'But he has written a book in praise of My Lady Nicotine.'

'So I have heard,' Brown said guardedly. 'I think that was when he was hard up and had to write what people wanted; but he never could abide smoking himself. Years after he wrote the book he read it; he had quite forgotten it, and he was so attracted by what it said about the delights of tobacco that he tried a cigarette. But it was no good; the mere smell disgusted him.'

'Odd, that he should forget his own book,' I said.

'He forgets them all,' said Brown. 'There is this *Peter Pan* foolishness, for instance. I have heard people talking to him about that play and mentioning parts in it they liked, and he tried to edge them off the subject; they think it is his shyness, but I know it is because he has forgotten the bits they are speaking about. Before strangers call on him I have seen him reading one of his own books hurriedly, so as to be able to talk about it if that is their wish. But he gets mixed up, and thinks that the little minister was married to Wendy.'

'Almost looks as if he had n't written his own works,' I said.

'Almost,' Brown admitted uncomfortably.

I asked a leading question. 'You don't suppose,' I said, 'that any one writes them for him? Such things have been. You don't write them for him by any chance, just as you blackened the pipe, you know?'

Brown assured me stolidly that he did not. Suddenly, whether to get away from a troublesome subject I cannot say, he vouchsafed me a startling piece of information. 'The German Kaiser was on our boat coming across,' he said.

'Sure?' I asked, wetting my pencil.

He told me he had Sir James's word for it. There was on board, it seems, a very small, shrunken gentleman with a pronounced waist and tiny, turned-up mustache, who strutted along the deck trying to look fierce and got in the other passengers' way to their annoyance until Sir James discovered that he was the Kaiser Reduced to Life Size. After that Sir James liked to sit with him and talk to him.

Sir James is a great admirer of the Kaiser, though he has not, like Mr. Carnegie, had the pleasure of meeting him in society. When he read in the papers on arriving here that the Kaiser had wept over the destruction of Louvain, he told Brown a story. It was of a friend who had gone to an oculist to be cured of some disease in one eye. Years afterward he heard that the oculist's son had been killed in some Indian war, and he called on the oculist to commiserate with him.

'You cured my eye,' he said to him, 'and when I read of your loss I wept for you, sir; I wept for you with that eye.'

'Sir James,' Brown explained, 'is of a very sympathetic nature, and he wondered which eye it was that the Kaiser wept with.'

I asked Brown what his own views were about the war, and before replying he pulled a paper from his pocket and scanned it. 'We are strictly neutral,' he then replied.

'Is that what is written on the paper?' I asked. He admitted that Sir James had written out for him the correct replies to possible questions. 'Why was he neutral?' I asked, and he again found the reply on the piece of paper: 'Because it is the President's wish.'

So anxious, I discovered, is Sir James to follow the President's bidding that he has enjoined Brown to be neutral on all other subjects besides the war; to express no preference on matters of food, for instance, and always to eat oysters and clams alternately, so that there can be no ill-feeling. Also to walk in the middle of the streets lest he should seem to be favoring either sidewalk, and to be very cautious about admitting that one building in New York is higher than another. I assured him that the Woolworth Building was the highest, but he replied politely, 'that he was sure the President would prefer him to remain neutral.' I naturally asked if Sir James had given him any further instructions as to proper behavior in America, and it seems that he had done so. They amount, I gather, to this, that Americans have a sense of humor which they employ, when they can, to the visitor's undoing.

'When we reach New York,' Sir James seems to have told Brown in effect, 'we shall be met by reporters who will pretend that America is eager to be instructed by us as to the causes and progress of the war; then, if we are fools enough to think that America cannot make up its mind for itself, we shall fall into the trap and preach to them, and all the time they are taking down our observations they will be saying to themselves, "Pompous asses."

'It is a sort of game between us and the reporters. Our aim is to make them think we are bigger than we are, and theirs is to make us smaller than we are; and any chance we have of succeeding is to hold our tongues, while they will probably succeed if they make us jabber. Above all, oh, Brown, if you write to the papers giving your views of why we are at war — and if you don't you will be the only person who hasn't — don't be lured into slinging vulgar abuse at our opponents, lest America takes you for another university professor.'

There is, I learned, only one person in America about whom it is impossible, even in Sir James's opinion, to preserve a neutral attitude. This is the German Ambassador, whose splendid work for England day by day and in every paper and to all reporters cannot, Sir James thinks, be too cordially recognized. Brown has been told to look upon the German Ambassador as England's greatest asset in America just now, and to hope heartily that he will be long spared to carry on his admirable work.

Lastly, it was pleasant to find that Brown has not a spark of sympathy with those who say that, because Germany has destroyed art treasures in Belgium and France the Allies should retaliate with similar rudeness if they reach Berlin. He holds that if for any reason best known to themselves (such as the wish for a sunnier location) the Hohenzollerns should by and by vacate their present residence, a nice villa should be provided for them, and that all the ancestral statues in the Sieges-Allee should be conveyed to it intact, and perhaps put up in the back garden. There the Junkers could drop in of an evening, on the way home from their offices, and chat pleasantly of old times. Brown thinks they should be allowed to retain all their iron crosses, and even given some more, with which, after

smart use of their pocket combs, they would cut no end of a dash among the nursemaids.

As for the pipe, I was informed that it had now done its work, and I could take it away as a keepsake. I took it, but wondered afterward at Brown's thinking he had the right to give it me.

A disquieting feeling has since come over me that perhaps it was Sir James I had been interviewing all the time, and Brown who had escaped down the elevator.

VI *Interesting*

JOSEPH PULITZER: REMINISCENCES OF A SECRETARY

ALLEYNE IRELAND

[Reprinted by courtesy of the *Metropolitan*.]

Before I had time to examine my surroundings Mr. Pulitzer entered the room on the arm of the majordomo. My first, swift impression was of a man very tall and thin, with a noble head, a roughly pointed reddish beard streaked with gray, jet black hair, swept back from the forehead and lightly touched here and there with silvery white. One eye was dull and half-closed, the other was of a deep, brilliant blue, which, so far from suggesting blindness, created the instant effect of a searching, eaglelike glance. The outstretched hand was large, strong, nervous, full of character, ending in well-shaped and immaculately kept nails.

A high-pitched voice, clear, penetrating, and vibrant, gave out the strange challenge: 'Well, here you see before you the miserable wreck who is to be your host; you must make the best you can of him. Give me your arm in to dinner.'

I may complete here a description of Mr. Pulitzer's appearance, founded upon months of close personal association with him. The head was splendidly modeled, the forehead high, the brows prominent and arched; the ears were large, the nose was long and hooked; the mouth, almost concealed by the mustache, was firm and thin-lipped; the length of the face was much emphasized by the flowing beard and by the way in which the hair was brushed back from the forehead. The skin was of a clear, healthy pink, like a young girl's; but in moments of intense excitement the color would deepen to a dark, ruddy flush, and after a succession of sleepless nights, or under the strain of continued worry, it would turn a dull, lifeless gray.

I have never seen a face which varied so much in expression. Not only was there a marked difference at all times between one side and the other, due partly to the contrast between the two eyes and partly to a loss of flexibility in the muscles of the right side, but almost from moment to moment the general appearance of the face moved between a lively, genial animation, a cruel and wolflike scowl, and a heavy and hopeless dejection. No face was capable of showing greater tenderness; none could assume a more forbidding expression of anger and contempt.

The well-known Sargent portrait is a remarkable revelation of the complex nature of its subject. It discloses the deep affection, the keen intelligence, the wide sympathy, the tireless energy, the delicate sensitiveness, the tearing impatience, the cold tyranny, and the flaming scorn by which his character was so erratically dominated. It is a noble and pathetic monument to the suffering which had been imposed for a quarter of a century upon the intense and arbitrary spirit of this extraordinary man.

PULITZER THE IMMIGRANT

The account which I am to give of Mr. Pulitzer's daily life during the months immediately preceding his death would be unintelligible to all but the very few who knew him in recent years if it were not prefaced by a brief biographical note.

Joseph Pulitzer was born in the village of Mako, near Buda Pesth, in Hungary, on April 10, 1847. His father was a Jew, his mother a Christian. At the age of sixteen he emigrated to the United States. He landed without friends, without money, unable to speak a word of English. He enlisted immediately in the First New York (Lincoln) Cavalry Regiment, a regiment chiefly composed of Germans and in which German was the prevailing tongue.

Within a year the Civil War ended, and Pulitzer found himself, in common with hundreds of thousands of others, out of employment at a time when employment was most difficult to secure. At this time he was so poor that he was turned away from French's Hotel in New York for the lack of fifty cents with which to pay for his bed. Twenty years later he bought French's Hotel, pulled it down, and erected in its place the Pulitzer Building, at that time one of the largest business buildings in New York, where he housed the *World*.

What lay between these two events may be summed up in a few words. At the close of the Civil War Mr. Pulitzer went to St. Louis, and in 1868, after being in various occupations, he became a reporter on the *Westliche Post*. In less than ten years he was editor and part proprietor. His amazing energy, his passionate interest in politics, his rare gift of terse and forcible expression, and his striking personality carried him over or through all obstacles.

After he had purchased the St. Louis *Dispatch,* amalgamated it with the *Post,* and made the *Post-Dispatch* a profitable business enterprise and a power to be reckoned with in national and state politics, he felt the need of a wider field in which to manœuver the forces of his character and his intellect.

He came to New York in 1883 and purchased the *World* from Jay Gould. At that time the *World* had a circulation of less than twelve thousand copies a day, and was practically bankrupt. From this time forward Mr. Pulitzer concentrated his every faculty on building up the paper. He was scoffed at, ridiculed, and abused by the most powerful editors of the old school. They were to learn, not without bitterness and wounds, that opposition was the one fuel of all others which best fed the triple flame of his courage, his tenacity, and his resourcefulness.

Four years of unremitting toil produced two results. The *World* reached a circulation of 200,000 copies a day and took its place in the front rank of the American press as a journal of force and ability, and Joseph Pulitzer left New York, a complete nervous wreck, to face in solitude the knowledge that he would never read print again and that within a few years he would be totally blind.

Joseph Pulitzer as I knew him, twenty-four years after he had been driven from active life by the sudden and final collapse of his health, was a man who could be judged by no common standards. His feelings, his temper, his point of view had been warped by years of suffering. His health and his comfort were at the mercy of a thousand contingencies.

Had his spirit been broken by his trials, had his intellectual power weakened under the load of his affliction, had his burning interest in affairs cooled to a point where he could have been content to turn his back upon life's conflict, he might have found some happiness, or at least some measure of repose akin to that with which age consoles us for the loss of youth. But his greatest misfortune was that all the active forces of his personality survived to the last in their full vigor, inflicting upon him the curse of an impatience which nothing could appease, of a discontent which knew no amelioration.

*   *   *   *   *   *

This somewhat cynical outburst [as to the accuracy of the New York papers] brought down upon me an overwhelming torrent of protest from Mr. Pulitzer.

'My God!' he cried. 'I would not have believed it possible that any one could show such a complete ignorance of American character, of the high sense of duty which in the main animates American journalism, of the foundations of integrity on which almost every successful paper in the United States has been founded. You do not know what it costs me to try and keep the *World* up to a high standard of accuracy — the money, the time, the thought, the praise, the blame, the constant watchfulness. I do not say that the *World* never makes a mistake in its news columns. I wish I could say it.

'What I say is that there are not half a dozen papers in the United States which tamper with the news, which publish what they know to be false. But if I thought that I had done no better than that I would be ashamed to own a paper. It is not enough to refrain from publishing fake news, it is not enough to take ordinary care to avoid the mistakes which arise from the ignorance, the carelessness, the stupidity of one or more of the many men who handle the news before it gets into print; you have got to do much more than that; you have got to make every one connected with the paper — your editors, your reporters, your correspondents, your rewrite men, your proofreaders — believe that accuracy is to a newspaper what virtue is to a woman.

'When you go to New York ask any of the men in the dome to show you my in-structions to them, my letters written from day to day, my cables; and you will see that accuracy, accuracy, accuracy, is the first, the most urgent, the most constant demand I have made on them.

'I do not say that the *World* is the only paper which takes extraordinary pains to be accurate; on the contrary, I think that almost every paper in America tries to be accurate. I will go further than that. There is not a paper of any importance published in French, German, or English, whether it is printed in Europe or in America, which I have not studied for weeks or months, and some of them I have read steadily for a quarter of a century; and I tell you this, Mr. Ireland, after years of experience, after having comparisons made by the hundred, from time to time, of different versions of the same event, that the press of America as a whole has a higher standard of accuracy than the European press as a whole. I will go further than that. I will say that, line for line, the American newspapers actually *attain* a higher standard of news accuracy than the European newspapers; and I will go further than that and say that although there are in Europe a few newspapers, and they are chiefly English, which are as accurate as the best newspapers in America, there are *no* newspapers in America which are so habitually, so criminally stuffed with fake news as the worst of the European papers.'

Mr. Pulitzer paused and asked me if there was a glass of water on the table — we were seated in his library — and after I had handed it to him, and he had drained it nearly to the bottom at one gulp, he resumed his lecture. I give it in considerable detail, because it was the longest speech he ever addressed to me, because he subsequently made me write it out from memory and then read it to him, and because it was one of the few occasions during my intercourse with him on which I was persuaded beyond a doubt that he spoke with perfect frankness, without allowing his words to be influenced by any outside considerations.

J. P.'S NEWSPAPER CREED

'As a matter of fact,' he continued, 'the criticisms you hear about the American press are founded on a dislike for our headlines and for the prominence we give to crime, to corruption in office, and to sensational topics generally; the charge of inaccuracy is just thrown in to make it look worse. I do not believe that one person in a thousand who attacks the American press for being inaccurate has ever taken the trouble to investigate the facts.

'Now about this matter of sensationalism: a newspaper should be scrupulously accurate; it should be clean; it should avoid everything salacious or suggestive, everything that could offend good taste or lower the moral tone of its readers; but within these limits it is the duty of a newspaper to print the news. When I speak of good taste and of good moral tone I do not mean the kind of good taste which is offended by every reference to the unpleasant things of life; I do not mean the kind of morality which refuses to recognize the existence of immorality — that type of moral hypocrite has done more to check the moral progress of humanity than all the immoral people put together. What I mean is the kind of good taste which demands that frankness should be linked with decency; the kind of moral tone which is braced and not relaxed when it is brought face to face with vice.

'Some people try and make you believe that a newspaper should not devote its space to long and dramatic accounts of murders, railroad wrecks, fires, lynchings, political corruption, embezzlements, frauds, graft, divorces, what you will. I tell you they are wrong, and I believe that if they thought the thing out they would see that they are wrong.

'We are a democracy, and there is only one way to get a democracy on its feet in the matter of its individual, its social, its municipal, its state, its national conduct, and that is by keeping the public informed about what is going on. There is not a crime, there is not a dodge, there is not a trick, there is not a swindle, there is not a vice, which does not live by secrecy. Get these things out in the open, describe them, attack them, ridicule them in the press, and sooner or later public opinion will sweep them away.

'Publicity may not be the only thing that is needed, but it is the one thing without which all other agencies will fail. If a newspaper is to be of real service to the public, it must have a big circulation, first because its news and its comment must reach the largest possible number of people, second, because circulation means advertising, and advertising means money, and money means independence. If I caught any man on the *World* suppressing news because one of our advertisers objected to having it printed I would dismiss him immediately; I wouldn't care who he was.

'What a newspaper needs in its news, in its headlines, and on its editorial page is terseness, humor, descriptive power, satire, originality, good literary style, clever condensation, and accuracy, accuracy, accuracy.'

Mr. Pulitzer made this confession of faith with the warmth generated by an unshakable faith. He spoke, as he always spoke when he was excited, with vigor, emphasis, and ample gesture. When he came to an end and asked for another glass of water I found nothing to say. It would have been as impertinent of me to agree with him as to differ from him.

After all, I had to remember that he had taken over the *World* when its circulation was less than 15,000 copies a day; that he had been for thirty years and still was its dominating spirit and the final authority on every matter concerning its policy, its style, and its contents; that he had seen its morning circulation go up to well over 350,000 copies a day; that at times he had taken his stand boldly against popular clamor, as when he kept up for months a bitter attack against the American action in the Venezuelan boundary dispute, and at times had incurred the hostility of powerful moneyed interests, as when he forced the Cleveland administration to sell to the public on competitive bids a bond issue which it had arranged to sell privately, at considerably below market value, to a great banking house.

Before leaving the subject of newspapers I may describe the method by which Mr. Pulitzer kept in touch with the news and put himself in the position to maintain a critical supervision over the *World*.

An elaborate organization was employed for this purpose. I will explain it as it worked when we were on the yacht, but the system was maintained at all times, whether we were cruising or were at Cap Martin, at Bar Harbor, at Wiesbaden, or elsewhere, merely a few minor details being changed to meet local conditions.

In the Pulitzer Building, Park Row, New York, there were collected each day several copies of each of the morning papers, including the *World,* and some of the evening papers. These were mailed daily to Mr. Pulitzer according to cabled instructions as to our whereabouts. In addition to this a gentleman connected with the *World,* who had long experience of Mr. Pulitzer's requirements, cut from all the New York papers, and from a number of other papers from every part of the United States, every article that he considered Mr. Pulitzer ought to see, whether because of its subject, its tenor, or its style. These clippings were mailed by the hundred on almost every fast steamer sailing for Europe. In order that there might be the greatest economy of time in reading them, the essential matter in each clipping was marked.

READING THE 'WORLD' TO J. P.

So far as the *World* was concerned, a copy of each issue was sent, with the names of the writers written across each editorial, big news story or special article.

As we went from port to port we got the principal French, German, Austrian, and Italian papers, and the *World* bureau in London kept us supplied with the English dailies and weeklies.

Whenever we picked up a batch of American papers, each of the secretaries got a set and immediately began to read it. My own method of reading was adopted after much advice from Mr. Pulitzer and after consultation with the more experienced members of the staff, and I do not suppose it differed materially from that followed by the others.

I read the *World* first, going over the 'big' stories carefully and with enough concentration to give me a very fair idea of the facts. Then I read the articles in the other papers covering the same ground, noting any important differences in the various accounts. This task resolved itself in practice into mastering in considerable detail about half a dozen articles — a political situation, a murder, a railroad wreck, a fire, a strike, an important address by a college president, for example — and getting a clear impression of the treatment of each item in each paper.

With this done, and with a few notes scribbled on a card to help my memory, I turned to the editorial pages, reading each editorial with the closest attention and making more notes.

The final reading of the news served to give me from ten to twenty small topics of what Mr. Pulitzer called 'human interest,' to be used as subjects of conversation as occasion demanded. As a rule I cut these items out of the paper and put them in the left-hand pocket of my coat, for when we walked together J. P. always took my right arm, and my left hand was, therefore, free to dip into my reservoir of cuttings whenever conversation flagged and I needed a new subject.

The cuttings covered every imaginable topic — small cases in the magistrates' courts, eccentric entertainments at Newport, the deaths of centenarians, dinners to visiting authors in New York, accounts of performing animals, infant prodigies, new inventions, additions to the Metropolitan Museum, announcements of new plays, anecdotes about prominent men and women, instances of foolish extravagance among the rich, and so on.

* * * * * *

On rare occasions he talked of his early days, telling us in a charmingly simple and unaffected manner of the tragic and humorous episodes with which his youth had been crowded. Of the former I recall a striking description of a period during which he filled two positions in St. Louis, one involving eight hours' work during the day, the other eight hours during the night. Four of the remaining eight were devoted to studying English.

His first connection with journalism arose out of an experience which he related with a wealth of detail which showed how deeply it had been burned into his memory.

When he first arrived in St. Louis he soon found himself at the end of his resources, and was faced with the absolute impossibility of securing work in that city. In company with forty other men he applied at the office of a general agent who had advertised for hands to go down the Mississippi and take up well-paid posts on a Louisiana sugar plantation. The agent demanded a fee of five dollars from each applicant, and by pooling their resources the members of this wretched band managed to meet the charge. The same night they were taken on board a steamer which immediately started down river. At three o'clock in the morning they were landed on the river bank about forty miles below St. Louis, at a spot where there was neither house, road, nor clearing. Before the marooned party had time to realize its plight the steamer had disappeared.

A council of war was held, and it was decided that they should tramp back to St. Louis and put a summary termination to the agent's career by storming his office and murdering him. Whether or not this reckless program would have been carried out it is impossible to say, for when, three days later, the ragged army arrived in the city, worn out with fatigue and half-dead from hunger, the agent was found to have decamped.

A reporter happened to pick up the story, and by mere chance met Pulitzer and induced him to write out in German the tale of his experiences. This account created such an impression on the mind of the editor through whose hands it passed that Pulitzer was offered, and accepted with the greatest misgivings, as he solemnly assured us, a position as reporter on the *Westliche Post*.

The event proved that there had been no grounds for J. P.'s modest doubts. After he had been some time on the paper things went so badly that two reporters had to be got rid of. The editor kept Pulitzer on the staff, because he felt that if any one was destined to force him out of the editorial chair it was not a young, uneducated foreigner, who could hardly mumble half a dozen words of English. The editor was mistaken. Within a few years J. P. not only supplanted him, but became half proprietor of the paper.

* * * * * *

It was not only in regard to mental accomplishments, however, that J. P. pursued his plan of educating everybody around him. He insisted, among other things, that I should learn to ride, not because there was any lack of people who could ride with him, but because by means of application I could add a new item to the list of things I could do. After a dozen lessons from a groom I progressed so far that, having acquired the ability to stay more or less in the saddle while the horse trotted, Mr. Pulitzer frequently took me riding with him.

We always rode three abreast, a groom on J. P.'s right and myself on his left, and conversation had to be kept up the whole time. This presented no peculiar difficulties when the horses were walking, but when they trotted I found it no easy task

to keep my seat, to preserve the precise distance from J. P. which saved me from touching his stirrup and yet allowed me to speak without raising my voice, and to leave enough of my mind unoccupied to remember my material and to present it without betraying the discomfort of my position.

During these rides, and especially when we were walking our horses along a quiet, shady stretch of road, J. P. sometimes became reminiscent. On one of these occasions he told me the story of how he lost his sight. As I wrote it down as soon as we got back to the house, I can tell it almost in his own words.

We had been discussing the possibility of his writing an autobiography, and he said, throwing his head back and smiling reflectively:

'Well, I sometimes wish it could be done. It would make an interesting book; but I do not think I shall ever do it. My God! I work from morning to night as it is. When would I get the time?'

Then, suddenly changing his mood: 'It won't do any harm for you to make a few notes now and then, and some day, perhaps, we might go through them and see if there is anything worth preserving. Has any one ever told you how I lost my sight? No? Well, it was in November, 1887. The *World* had been conducting a vigorous campaign against municipal corruption — a campaign which ended in the arrest of a financier who had bought the votes of aldermen in order to get a street railroad franchise.'

At this point he paused. His jaws set, and his expression became stern, almost fierce, as he added: 'The man died in jail of a broken heart, and I — and I —' He took a deep breath and continued as though he were reciting an experience which he had heard related of some stranger.

'I was, of course, violently attacked, and it was a period of terrible strain for me. What with anxiety and overwork I began to suffer from insomnia, and that soon produced a bad condition of my nerves. One morning I went down to the *World* and called for the editorials which were ready for me to go over. I always read every line of editorial copy. When I picked up the sheets I was astonished to find that I could hardly see the writing, let alone read it. I thought it was probably due to indigestion or to some other temporary cause and said nothing about it. The next morning on my way downtown I called in at an oculist's. He examined my eyes and then ordered me to go home and remain in bed in a darkened room for six weeks. At the end of that time he examined me again, told me that I had ruptured a blood vessel in one of my eyes, and ordered me to stop work entirely and to take six months' rest in California.

'That was the beginning of the end. Whatever my trouble had been at first, it developed into separation of the retina in both eyes. From the day on which I first consulted the oculist up to the present time, about twenty-four years, I have only been three times in the *World* building. Most people think I 'm dead, or living in Europe in complete retirement. Now go on and give me the morning's news. I 've had practically nothing, so you can just run over it briefly, item by item.'

* * * * * *

On October 25, 1911, we put in to the harbor of Charleston, S. C. There was the usual business of receiving mail, newspapers, and so on, for J. P., after five days at sea, was eager to pick up the thread of current happenings.

On the following day Mr. Lathan, editor of the Charleston *Courier,* lunched on the yacht. He and Mr. Pulitzer had an animated discussion about the possibilities of a Democratic victory in 1912. I had never seen J. P. in a more genial mood or in higher spirits.

Whether it was due to the excitement of receiving a visitor whose conversation was so stimulating I do not know, but on Friday, October 27, J. P. was feeling so much out of sorts that he did not appear on deck. On Saturday he remained below only because Brocklebank, who always kept the closest watch over his health, persuaded him to have a good rest before resuming the ordinary routine. J. P. was anxious to take up some business matters with Henderson, but Brocklebank induced him to give up the idea.

At three o'clock in the morning of Sunday, October 29, Brocklebank came to my cabin and, without making any explanation, said:

'Mr. Pulitzer wishes you to come and read to him.'

I put on a dressing-gown, gathered up half a dozen books, and in five minutes I was sitting by Mr. Pulitzer's bedside. He was evidently suffering a good deal of pain, for he turned from side to side and once or twice got out of bed and sat in an easy chair.

I tried several books, but finally settled down to read Macaulay's essay on Hallam. I read steadily until about five o'clock, and J. P. listened attentively, interrupting me from time to time with a direction to go back and read over a passage.

About half-past five he began to suffer severely, and he sent for the yacht's doctor, who did what was possible for him. At a few minutes after six J. P. said: 'Now, Mr. Ireland, you 'd better go and get some sleep; we will finish that this afternoon. Good-by, I 'm much obliged to you. Ask Mr. Schmidt to come to me. Go, now, and have a good rest, and forget all about me.'

I slept till noon. When I came on deck I found that everything was going on much as usual. One of the secretaries was with J. P.; the others were at work over the day's papers.

At lunch we spoke of J. P. One man said that he seemed a little worse than usual; another that he had seen him much worse a score of times.

Suddenly the massive door at the forward end of the saloon opened. I turned in my seat and saw the towering figure of the head butler framed in the doorway. I faced his impassive glance and received the full shock of his calm but incredible announcement: 'Mr. Pulitzer is dead.'

VII

WILLIAM ROCKHILL NELSON

[*Editor and Publisher and Journalist,* April 17, 1915. By permisson.]

'William Rockhill Nelson was a Titan among the newspapermen of America. In the largest sense he was mindful of the responsibility of his position. He knew that the fathers of the republic had taken large chances in granting freedom to the press; that they were not ignorant of the menace of a licentious journalism; but, though they might have agreed fully with Franklin that strict justice required that the freedom of the club should go with liberty of the editor, after all, the merit of unrestrained discussion was undeniable in a self-governing people and therefore they gave to men of his craft, unique privilege. All this, not only claimed his attention, but mastered his whole course of conduct.

'His contempt for the editorial pander was limitless. He gave no heed to popular clamor, if it represented a temporary emotion opposed to his conviction of enduring good. He was quite willing to find himself in a minority, or, indeed, to subject himself to widespread criticism, if he felt himself in the right. He had no care for the comfort of living at peace with his neighbors, if it meant that he could not live at peace with himself. He was a dauntless soldier for the public welfare.

'As one who knew him intimately for more than a quarter of a century, who enjoyed his confidence, listened to his hopes and fears and was stimulated by his unwavering devotion to duty, when, all the while, there was neither bluster nor parade in anything he did, but only a set jaw, a quiet defiance of rascality, and a persistent contest against corroding conservatism, I regard his passing as a supreme public calamity. For, there is none quite like him left in the newspaper field of today.' — *Melville E. Stone, General Manager of the Associated Press.*

William Rockhill Nelson, editor and owner of the Kansas City (Mo.) *Star,* one of the foremost journalists of the Middle West, died at his home in that city on the morning of April 13, of uremic poisoning. He had been ill since last December. His death caused profound sorrow throughout the city, State, and nation. President Wilson on being informed of Colonel Nelson's death immediately sent to Mrs. Nelson the following telegram:

'May I not express my deep sympathy with you in the loss of your husband. The whole country will mourn the loss of a great editor and citizen.'

During his illness Colonel Nelson gathered the members of his staff at his bedside each week for consultation. At the last meeting he discussed the fight for honest elections and told his men to keep it up no matter what happened.

MR. NELSON'S CAREER

It was not by chance that William R. Nelson selected Kansas City as the place in which he would found a newspaper. He was forty years old when he did that.

He had accumulated a fortune of $200,-000 in the building and contracting business in Indiana and had lost it, saving nothing from the wreck but a half interest in the Fort Wayne *Sentinel.* For two years after his fortune was swept away he edited that paper and then he saw that his future work was to be journalism. But he wanted a wider field, and, although he had only a few thousand dollars from the sale of his half interest in the *Sentinel,* he began casting about for a new location. He scrutinized the whole wide western field with an estimating and prophetic eye and decided upon Kansas City, which was then a muddy pioneer town without a pavement on one of its streets and with only a few plank sidewalks.

The two old and established newspapers, the *Times* and the *Journal,* were morning papers. They sold for five cents a copy. Mr. Nelson started an evening paper in a little upstairs room and sold it for two cents on the streets and delivered it to subscribers for ten cents a week.

PAPERS SOLD FOR A NICKEL

There were few pennies in this city then. The nickel was almost the smallest coin in use. People were in the habit of paying five cents for a newspaper and they were hard to break of that habit. They would hand the newsboy a nickel and walk on. Mr. Nelson gave orders that every newsboy must insist on giving change. To make that easy he imported from the mint a keg of pennies for his newsboys. He wanted to impress upon the people that for the old price of one newspaper they could get two of his and have a penny left over.

The circulation of the new paper grew but the more it increased the more money he lost, because the advertising was not coming to it yet, and he was hard pushed to make both ends meet. The paper had a circulation of 3000 within a week. It soon grew to 10,000. The capacity of his new press was pushed to its utmost. It was a hard struggle for four years. Then he was able to buy a new perfecting press and his future was assured.

The part the *Star* has played in Kansas City is the history of Kansas City. That Kansas City has become great, that it has become known the country over as a place of opportunity and achievement, that its squalid ugliness has been transformed into transcendent beauty — all this it owes more to the courage, the loyalty, the enterprise and constant endeavor of the *Star* than it does to any other agency, and it owes the *Star* to Mr. Nelson. We do not recall an instance in the history of the cities of the Republic where any single community stands as much indebted for its upbuilding to the civic patriotism of one man as Kansas City does to Mr. Nelson.

Beginning with its very first issue, the *Star* was active in asserting its citizenship and endeavoring to promote the welfare of the community. Its first campaign was for traversable streets. To city streets alone the *Star* has devoted more space, more actual area of argument, protest, information and appeal than to any other subject.

In its first year the *Star* began its long, long struggle for public parks, which finally triumphed so splendidly. It demanded better city water, and got it. It was always demanding better things for its townsmen. It fought for dollar gas, and got it. It began a fight against the lottery sharks that infested this town in the early days, and ran them out of the city. It exposed and attacked the home coöperative companies that were defrauding the poor and put them out of business; it went after the 10 per cent. a month loan sharks and eliminated them; it fought the fortune-telling frauds and the quack doctors. In all of those fights against those particular evils it was a pioneer. It was the first newspaper in this country to bar medical quacks from its advertising columns and to attack them in its news columns. It was the first daily newspaper to refuse beer and whisky advertisements in any of its editions.

Its campaign for the betterment of living conditions, and for things that meant the advancement of the city have been too numerous to mention. Mr. Nelson sometimes attributed his success in newspaper work to the fact that he did not get into it until he was forty years old. By this he meant that he was not hampered by traditions, but brought to the work the fresh viewpoint of the outsider.

At the time the *Star* was established the conventional newspaper was in a rut. Pulitzer had not yet gone to New York to stir up the dry bones there. Newspapers were chiefly the chroniclers of routine news. Mr. Nelson attacked the problem under the stimulus of poverty of resources which prevented him from attempting to compete with established newspapers in furnishing telegraphic correspondence.

'I had to find a substitute for news,' he said. 'I discovered it in reprint. It occurred to me that people wanted first to be entertained. The world was full of interesting books and magazine articles that were at our disposal. I felt that Plato and Carlyle and Emerson might be just as good correspondents as the fellows who are sending the other papers reports of dog fights in San Francisco.'

So, while the *Star* was accumulating resources to build up its news service — for nothing short of the best in news would satisfy Mr. Nelson — it developed its department of interesting material reprinted or adapted from books and magazines. This department has been extended to a degree that is unique in American journalism.

Matter that the conventional newspaper regards as 'filler,' to be stuck in when news failed, Mr. Nelson considered as highly important.

'The men are pretty apt to find something of interest to them in the news on the dullest day,' he would say. 'But women aren't interested in politics or sports. We are going to furnish them good reading, no matter how dull they may find the news.'

As the news came, Mr. Nelson devoted himself to building up the news departments. He was impatient of the traditional ways of handling material.

'Don't get the professional point of view,' he would warn his news men. 'A Washington correspondent is apt to get to thinking he is a statesman. He imagines the folks back home are interested in the details of congressional affairs. They are a whole lot more interested in a fuss between the wives of two cabinet members, or in some new development in farming that a congressman from Kansas can tell them about.'

He had no patience with perfunctory work of any sort, or with adherence to precedents. If news worth while was in sight he would throw all the resources of the paper into getting it. But if he felt that something else than news was of most public interest, then that was the thing that concerned him.

'I don't enjoy traveling in the well-trodden path,' he would say. 'The *Star* should pioneer.'

If a poem of Rudyard Kipling, or a story by Sam Blythe was the most interesting thing that had come into the office that day, his instructions were to 'play it up' on the first page.

STUCK TO HIS OWN METHODS

He had the greatest scorn for the suggestion that some other newspaper handled material in another way. 'What the other fellow does does n't interest me,' he would say. 'Newspapers that are edited with a view to attracting attention from other newspapers are failures. We are running the *Star* for our readers, not for other newspapers.'

The advent of yellow journalism never disturbed him, and he made no concessions to it in the way of big headlines, or comic supplements. His was one of the few newspapers in America that failed to be influenced by the new movement. He believed the movement was vulgar and bad. Over and over he declared he would quit the business before he would get out a shoddy, vulgar paper.

One night a few years ago there was a meeting of managing editors and publishers of a group of the most important newspapers in the United States. He gave them a dinner at his home. They asked him for a little talk as they sat at the table after the dessert.

'Well, gentlemen,' he said, 'I have one comment to make about American newspapers. The great bulk of them are allowing Mr. Hearst to edit them. They are copying his papers. Maybe Mr. Hearst had to do what he did to attract attention. But so long as I have anything to say about it, Mr. Hearst is n't going to edit the Kansas City *Star*.'

GAVE GOOD MEASURE

It was a sacred principle with him to give his readers more for their money than they could possibly buy anywhere else on earth. The question with him never was what he could make out of the *Star,* but how much he could afford to give his readers.

The *Star* was established, as I have said, as an afternoon newspaper at ten cents a week. When he felt that he could afford to increase the service he added the Sunday morning paper at no increase in price. A few years later he bought the Kansas City *Times* and made it the morning edition of the *Star,* still without increasing the price.

The last innovation was one of the great pioneering achievements of American journalism. Thirteen papers a week, delivered everywhere, for ten cents; but the outcome justified Mr. Nelson's confidence.

The same attitude was apparent in the founding of the Weekly Kansas City *Star*. It was founded, not to make money, but to make a contribution to American farm life.

'I took pencil and paper,' Mr. Nelson said, 'and figured that we could afford to print a four-page farm weekly for twenty-five cents a year. Nobody else had ever done it. But I felt it was possible, that we were in a position to do it, and that we ought to do it.'

ADOPTED READABLE TYPE

Mr. Nelson's ideals of giving the reader the most possible for his money showed in all the details of his management. He felt, for example, that the size of type used in newspapers was trying on the eyes. So he discarded it and had the *Star* set in larger type. With the larger, brevier type, he used first a style of type face that he felt was exceedingly artistic. After two or three years he decided that it was not quite as legible as a blacker type, so he threw the handsome type away and ordered the other.

For a long time he would not use illustrations in the *Star* because he felt a newspaper could not do them well, and he never was for doing anything he could not do well. But finally he decided on the use of line drawings. Other newspapers gradually adopted the mechanical form of reproduction of photographs known as half tones. This process was vastly cheaper than the one the *Star* was using, but Mr. Nelson would not consider it, for two reasons: In the first place the half tone is likely to smear and blur in the rapid printing, and in the second place a mechanical reproduction never interested him.

THE 'STAR' HIS PASSION

A young artist once brought him a painstaking copy of a photograph he had made. Mr. Nelson spoke kindly to the young man and then said:

'The great fault with your work is something that you consider a virtue. You have simply copied the photograph. You have n't put any life or spirit into it.'

The *Star* was a passion with him. Nothing hurt him so much as to see it do things in a commonplace way. Nothing delighted him so much as a piece of work that showed distinction in treatment.

Three years ago he wrote his associates from his summer home in Magnolia, Massachusetts:

'I'm afraid I am wearying you by writing so much about details of the paper. But the *Star* is my life.'

All his life Mr. Nelson was a builder. He built scores of houses, and he once remarked that he supposed that every year for fifty years he must have built at least two miles of rock road.

'Building houses,' he once said, 'is the greatest fun in the world.' He was his own architect, although in the more important buildings he relied on professional architects to work out the proportions and the details.

Things that were simple, substantial and well proportioned especially appealed to him. He could not endure anything shoddy.

THE 'STAR'S' NEW HOME

He got his inspiration for the present *Star* building from the McLean home in Washington. Taking an early morning walk with a member of the staff he stopped and looked over the tapestry brick home, in the style of the Italian renaissance.

'That's what we want for our new building,' he said.

He entrusted the designing of the building to an architect who worked out an adaptation of the McLean home under Mr. Nelson's supervision.

OAK HALL HIS RESIDENCE

Mr. Nelson's home, Oak Hall, stands within grounds some thirty acres in extent, in the center of the best residence section of Kansas City. He designed and supervised its construction.

He had a great stock farm in this county with a real farm house, a low rambling one-story building surrounded with a white picket fence. His summer home was at Magnolia Beach, Massachusetts.

VIII

NORMAN HAPGOOD

PHILIP LITTELL

[*New Republic,* December 12, 1914. By permission of author and publisher.]

Logic, an elementary course given twenty-eight years ago by Professor Royce, that was the setting in which I first saw Norman Hapgood. Of course we were n't acquainted then, having been in the same class at Harvard for only two years. The shape of his head was striking, but not so striking as his expression. In a flock of students who looked dutifully attentive or bored or conscientiously acute, Hapgood's expression was egregious. He looked amused. You would have guessed he found the detection of fallacy about the most amusing game he had ever played, and you would have been right. In those days he liked logic quite as well as baseball. None of his contemporaries could split the hair with nicer hand. As a nice yet humorously ruthless detective of fallacy he gained his earliest reputation at Harvard.

Five or six years later I had my second good look at him. Although the law was not his first choice, he was one of the best two or three men in his class at the Harvard Law School, and had emerged in a Chicago law office. I don't know how his mind lived its life by day. His real mental life began after dinner, when he and his friends would start an evening-long talk about Maletesta, or when he would stretch himself on a sofa, in his boarding-house bedroom, and read French for hours on end — Madame du Deffand, Mérimée, Stendhal. At this epoch he used to write in the *Yellow Book,* among other things about ennui, of which he has all his life had no first-hand knowledge. These essays, with the slightly later articles on Balfour, Rosebery, and John Morley which appeared in the *Contemporary Review,* were more 'written' than anything he has done in the last ten years. There was a time when it irritated him to be told that they were also written better. Even now, though the subject does n't interest him, you can make him a little tired by asking why he no longer writes as he wrote then. In this period his interest began its significant shift from books to men, from past to present, from the splittable hair to the big brush.

To his next, his early New York period, belong those solid, acute, documented lives of Lincoln and Washington which scarcely read like the improvisations they really were. They tell you more about Lincoln and Washington than about the evolution of Norman Hapgood. For documents upon Hapgood as he then was you had better consult the dramatic criticism he contributed to the old *Commercial Advertiser,* now the *Globe.* He had almost all the qualifications of a dramatic critic except taste. There was a healthy pugnacity in his articles. Plays and acting and management and the theatrical trust gave him things to say which he cared prodigiously to get said. He made his readers care, made them realize the importance of taking sides, of taking the right side. Among managers he discriminated the sheep from the goats. He belabored the goats until some of them tried to butt him off his job. Then he came back at them harder than ever, without ever losing his temper. His manner of writing could not help changing. Once you might have supposed his aim was to make subtleties clear to the subtle. Now he began to write as if he wanted the deaf to hear. By taking sides, and by wishing other people to take sides, he was learning to talk at a mark, his audience. At the end of this period he was ready for the rest of his life work. Henceforth he would address his contemporaries through a megaphone.

His association with *Collier's* started from an accident. F. P. Dunne, who was writing the *Collier* editorials, happened to be going away for a week or so, and asked Hapgood to fill in. The owners of the paper liked his work so well that later, when Dunne wanted to resign, they cabled an offer of his place to Hapgood, who was then sunning himself on the Italian Riviera, writing a few meditative essays that he has never been willing to print.

Since that spring morning in 1903 when he sat down to his desk at *Collier's,* he has renounced meditation. For the last ten years his thinking has been rapid and controversial. Believing that too much of our editorial writing has been done by men who do nothing except sit at desks, and who read nothing except

print, Hapgood has gone everywhere, met everybody, served on committees, made speeches, copiously conferred. His subjects are what every one is talking about or what every one is on the point of talking about. It is in talk and in the news of the day that he gets the topics which serve him best. His mind seizes these topics and does things to them. It digs into them until it strikes a layer of helpful truth, which must not lie too far below the surface to be exposed to average eyes. Unconsciously he has almost ceased to believe that a truth can be important if four or five hundred words cannot make it clear to the average. According to Walter Pater, the first requisite of a good prose style is a complicated subject matter to grapple with. The first requisite of a good journalistic style is a subject matter which Norman Hapgood can make clear to you before you get off your suburban train.

The second requisite is punch, which is most accurately known by counting those who feel it. A few steps toward knowledge of it may nevertheless be taken along other ways. Punch is something which Arthur Brisbane has, and Sam Adams and Dean Swift, and which Walter Bagehot and Max Beerbohm have n't. So far I can follow Hapgood, at a respectful distance, not understanding very well, getting a little muddled. Beyond this point I am lost, though I cling to the guiding doctrine that there can be no punch without emotion, that light without heat does n't interest our readers, that dry light makes dry reading.

Adherents of this creed, confined to matter which punch and repetition can make clear and interesting to an audience of several hundred thousand, are further restricted by the fear of getting in wrong, of occupying positions that cannot be defended. It is one of Hapgood's superiorities to most journalists that he has felt these restrictions less than they, that he has been free to choose so many things to fight for and to fight against. His courage has often put him in exposed positions, which he has defended so stoutly, and from which he has made such destructive sorties, that his readers have come over to his side. Armed with the goods, which he certainly had on Secretary Ballinger and President Taft, Hapgood literally did not care how many enemies he made. His moral ardor led him even into boring many readers not so morally ardent, but he lost neither head nor heart nor patience. He gained his end. His successful campaign was a sky-high warning to men who wanted their friends to grab our national resources. He put an inferior Secretary of the Interior out of business. It was a solid piece of work that Hapgood did for conservation in *Collier's*. And he did it, such are the pleasant oddities of journalism, without ever mastering, as a scholar masters all the diseases of Greek verbs, all the ins and outs of the Glavis-Ballinger-Pinchot row.

Both as an editorial writer and as a maker of speeches he is most damaging when he retorts. In his answers to opponents the old dialectician refines the worshiper of punch. When he is talking to a friend this old dialectician is still very much alive. And in talk his interest is almost as dirigible as of old. At the end of a long summer afternoon, walking home from a ball game, he is quite ready to choose, from the men and women of all epochs, the dozen who would be most agreeable together at dinner. He has time enough for all your interests, time enough to destroy, with friendly hand, a few of your fallacies.

He does this without impatience, as if you and he were playing a game. These pools of leisure, in the hurrying stream of his life, are less frequent than they used to be, but they are just as quiet. To find him in leisurely mood you must find him almost alone, or with children about, for as soon as his company has grown to four or five adults his mood becomes a little journalistic, a little impatiently controversial, a little contemptuous of the taste which rejects popular idols and of the mind which dozes over the very newest thought. As the size of his company increases, so his desire for victory in talk increases, and his wish to explore other men's minds grows less.

No, it is when you are alone with him that this successful journalist is most attractive and least journalistic. His gentleness and his humor appear, he loses his desire to impose his will, his judgment, his taste. And in talk you are secure against anything resembling his printed enormities — his disquisitions on breakfast or Shakespeare, his obituary paragraphs beginning 'Whistler is dead' or 'McKim is dead,' and reading like plaster casts of an emotion. His queer preferences in verse, for example, which irritate one in print, because they there sound as if he thought them important, are in talk only the quaint idiosyncrasies which give him feature.

In Hapgood's talk even President Wilson seems like a man of this world. His loyalty to the President is ubiquitous and combative as it is in print, but it doesn't make me dislike that image of him, half saint and half trustee and all great man, which forms itself in my mind as I read *Harper's Weekly*. When Hapgood is talking instead of writing, he doesn't impose trusting the President upon me as a disagreeable duty.

IX
THE BUILDER OF THE CANAL
FARNHAM BISHOP

[*World's Work*, August, 1912. By permission of author and publisher.]

'I explain it in one word: Colonel Goethals!' So replied Madam —— to Mr. Charles Francis Adams, when that most venerable and skeptical of American historians asked her to explain, as one born to the Isthmus, the difference between the Panama of ten years ago and that of today. And though at first inclined to regard the lady's ready reply, 'conveyed quite as much through the movements of the hands as by the mouth,' as a dining-room epigram rather than as a careful statement of historic fact, Mr. Adams became more and more impressed with its literal exactness, as he made his own painstaking investigations in the Canal Zone. Taking it for his text, in a paper read before the Massachusetts Historical Society, Mr. Adams declared:

I think Madam —— was right. Her female instinct guided her straight to the central fact. It is so in Panama. The individuality and character of Colonel Goethals today permeate, and permeate visibly, the entire Zone; unconsciously on his part, unconsciously on the part of others, his influence is pervasive. Nor, in expressing this opinion of Colonel Goethals, do I for a moment wish to depreciate, much less to ignore, the zeal and fidelity shown by the heads of departments in the present Canal organization. Gorgas, Hodges, Gaillard, Devol, Rousseau, Bishop, one and all, so far as my brief stay afforded me opportunities of reaching an opinion, were stamped by the same die. Of some, of course, I saw but little; others I did not meet at all; but indications of the influence of Goethals were, I thought, perceptible everywhere. Quiet, reserved, unassuming, known to every one engaged on the work, but noticed, as he quietly moved around, by no one, he gave the impression of conscious because innate but unobtrusive force. He was a natural diplomat as well as an educated engineer; and, whether dealing with labor conditions or Latin-American officials and races, the Panama situation of today stands in quite as much need of a skilful diplomat as of a trained engineer.

If such be the case, then the local demand for diplomacy must be great indeed. But though the Chief Engineer were to combine the wiles of Machiavelli with the virtues of Mr. Bryce, it would seem as if he had more than enough engineering on hand to keep him from exercising them. He has to dig a deep artificial cañon nine miles long; and build a dozen huge locks, each containing more solid concrete than there is stone in the great Pyramid of Cheops. In these locks must be erected forty-seven pairs of steel gates, each as tall and as broad as a six-story office building; and to move the elaborate machinery that will open and close these gates and tow ships through the locks, the Chagres River has been turned into the concrete-lined spillway of the Gatun Dam, where it will drive, with all the force of its once-dreaded floods, the turbines of the electric power-plant. The United States Government has increased the width of the locks, originally 95 feet, to 110, and their length from 950 to 1000 feet; has added half as much again to the 200-foot channel through the Cut, and has ordered $14,000,000 worth of fortifications —all to be done without delay or an increase of force. Instead of throwing up his hands in despair at these huge additions to his task, Colonel Goethals welcomed them as needed improvements. And when some one asked him whether these things and the 18,000,000 cubic yards of earth and rock brought into the Cut by slides would delay the opening of the Canal until after January 1, 1915, the Colonel replied:

'Some day in September, 1913, I expect to go over to Colon and take the Panama Railroad steamer that happens to be at the dock there and put her through the Canal. If we get all the way across, I'll give it out to the newspapers; and if we don't, I'll keep quiet about it.'

This failed to satisfy one visitor, who, after entering the Chairman's modest office with great pomp and circumstance, delivered the following oration in a voice that was distinctly heard at Bas Obispo, in spite of the noon blasting in the Cut:

'Colonel Goethals, my office in Washington is, as you probably know, the center of the diplomatic life of the capital. All the diplomats come there almost daily, and they constantly say to me, "You know the Canal will never be finished; the slides and-ah, this and that will prevent it from ever being used." Now, Colonel, what would you advise me to say to them?'

With a twinkle in his eye, and the ready smile they know so well on the Isthmus, the Colonel replied instantly,

'I wouldn't say anything.'

NIPPING A 'SPICKETY' REVOLUTION

Colonel Goethals has much diplomatic work constantly thrust upon him. Panama City is the capital of a free and independent republic and our Government maintains there a legation of the first class. The native officials and politicians, however, persist in taking their troubles to the chairman of the Isthmian Canal Commission, who is also the Governor of the Canal Zone, instead of to the American minister. This is a presidential year in Panama as well as in the United States, and early in the spring the representatives of each party came running to Colonel Goethals to warn him that the wicked men on the other side were trying to stir up riot and revolution. The Colonel smiled on them paternally.

'Well, if there should be any disturbance, you know we have a regiment here.'

'Oh, no, no, no, Señor Gobernador! It will not come to that!'

Colonel Goethals and the commander of that regiment were presently made the members of a committee, under the chairmanship of the American minister, to supervise the registration and voting. 'Before the Americans came,' the head of the Liberals assured me, 'it was not the man who had the most votes who was elected. It was the man who had the most rifles and machetes.' Refereeing a presidential campaign and teaching Central Americans to vote with ballots instead of banana-knives are among the interesting minor duties of the Chief Engineer.

A far more serious affair than any number of Spickety revolutions was the threatened strike of the American railroad men in 1911. Every shovelful of dirt that comes out of the Cut is hauled, on the average, ten miles by rail before it is finally disposed of. An elaborate network of tracks (the skilful arrangement of which is a monument to the practical knowledge of railroading possessed by Colonel Goethals's predecessor, Mr. John F. Stevens), hundreds of locomotives, and thousands of cars are required that the dirt may be carried away as fast as the big steam-shovels can dig it. Then there is the Panama Railroad, with its heavy passenger and commercial freight traffic, which must not be interrupted, though the line is being changed from a double track running through the rapidly filling bed of Gatun Lake to the new permanent single track on higher ground. Finally there are the labor trains, that are kept as busy carrying the men back and forth from their work to their quarters as the traction system of a small city. Without railroads, work on the canal would be confined to dredging at the two entrances.

One dark night in August, 1910, an engineer whom we may call Jones heard two torpedoes explode under his locomotive but, instead of stopping, kept on and crashed into the rear of a freight train, killing the conductor. Jones was found guilty of involuntary manslaughter by the Supreme Court of the Canal Zone and was sentenced to one year in the penitentiary. At a somewhat excited mass-meeting of engineers and trainmen, it was resolved that unless Jones was immediately released they would resign and return to the United States, where they could 'enjoy the protection of the Constitution, a jury trial, tranquility, and the pursuit of happiness.'

Colonel Goethals was then on his way back from a visit to Washington, and the acting chairman persuaded the men to postpone action until he reached the Isthmus. He arrived on a Thursday and, unless Jones was released by six o'clock Friday afternoon, the men were to walk out Saturday morning. About half-past seven Friday evening, a member of the union called the Colonel up on the telephone and asked for his decision. He got it.

'Call up the penitentiary and they'll tell you my decision. Jones is still there; and every man that fails to report at seven to-morrow morning goes out of the service.'

There was no walk-out Saturday morning. At a ball game the next week, the man who had telephoned came up to bat and a voice from the bleachers yelled:

'Hello, Bill! You here? Thought you and the rest were goin' up north to live under the Con-sti-too-tion!'

Bill struck out.

LIKED BY EVERYBODY

Do the free-born American citizens in the Canal Zone actually 'enjoy' this stern military despotism more than 'the protection of the Constitution, a jury trial, tranquility, and the pursuit of happiness'? They certainly behaved as if they did on a certain occasion when a very distinguished visitor came to the Isthmus and the Colonel stepped forward, as chairman of the mass-meeting that had been called in the visitor's honor, to introduce him. A large majority of the five or six thousand American employees had crowded into the old machine-shop that had been cleared and decorated for the meeting and, at the sight of that familiar white figure standing at the edge of the platform, they exploded like a stampeded National Convention. It was fully five minutes before the cheering stopped and the Colonel was able to introduce the speaker of the evening. The very distinguished visitor arose and was received with a little polite hand-clapping.

Colonel Goethals is a fighter and he will fight a trust as readily as he will fight a labor union. Whole cargoes of tainted meat have been shipped back by the Commissary, because the Beef Trust's goods were not up to sample. Thousands of square yards of screening were condemned and left unpaid for, as soon as it was discovered that the Copper Trust had put in so much iron that they were rapidly falling to pieces with rust. Colonel Goethals is determined that no contractors shall become rich by supplying the Panama Canal with rotten food and shoddy material, as so many did in the days of the De Lesseps Company.

'THE SQUAREST BOSS'

'He's the squarest boss I ever worked for,' said a gray-headed member of the Brotherhood of Locomotive Engineers, as we sat on the platform at Culebra station and listened to the hymns the Jamaican Negroes were shouting in the red and black tin chapel across the tracks. 'And I've worked for 'em all, from Jim Hill to a bunch of Spicketies in Guatemala. I've been at it twenty-five years, and I've never seen better railroading than they've got right here on the Isthmus.'

The man in the cab speaks that way of the President of the Panama Railroad; the Republic of Panama is glad to be nursed by the Governor of the Canal Zone; and Congressmen have almost ceased asking the Chairman of the Isthmian Canal Commission unimportant questions in an important manner, because, as one M. C. plaintively declared, the Colonel, though invariably courteous, 'always makes us feel like a lot of darned fools.'

The most absolute despot in the world, he can command the removal of a mountain from the landscape, or of a man from his dominions, or of a salt-cellar from that man's table. As an engineer, he could earn a millionaire's income whenever he chose to go into private employ. As a judge, he is spoken of with Solomon and Daniel and Haroun al Raschid. He has received honorary degrees from Harvard and Yale and Columbia and he has been invited to lunch by the Emperor of Germany (where, instead of kissing the hand of the Empress, he innocently shook it). Distinguished foreign visitors have assured him that in their countries such work as his would be rewarded by a title of nobility and high rank in the army. Even the praise-grudging American admits that 'about the only thing you can say against that man Goethals is that he is handing down a mighty tough name for posterity to pronounce.' Success and fame and power are his; and yet, when discussing the remote possibility of a revolutionary outbreak in Panama City, he sighed wistfully and said, 'The 10th Infantry would be sent in to put it down — and I couldn't march in at the head of them.'

For no amount of success as an engineer and administrator can quite compensate this true West Pointer for the loss of his own chosen trade of war. Though he has under his command an army of forty thousand men, with all the efficiency of the German army and none of its stiffness, and a love for their leader like that of the Old Guard for the Little Corporal, still he cannot help envying the youngest 'shavetail' who ever led a half-company in pursuit of a gang of Moro outlaws. For he has never seen active service. Entering West Point in 1876 on the appointment of the then famous 'Sunset' Cox, Colonel Goethals has spent all the thirty-two years since his graduation in building irrigation works in the West and coast-fortifications in the East, as instructor in engineering at the Military Academy, as Chief Engineer of the First Army Corps during the war with Spain, and as Chairman and Chief Engineer of the Isthmian Canal Commission. Surely this has been better service for a man of his brain-power than endlessly shouting, 'Squads right! Squads left!' on a dusty parade ground, or doing dare-devil police work in Mindanao. He is changing the whole map of the world: a change that promises to be far more permanent and profound than any brought about by a mere conqueror. And yet Colonel Goethals cannot help an almost boyish feeling of discontent because, while his classmates and a whole generation of younger men, to say nothing of untrained civilians like Wood and Funston and Roosevelt, have had their chances to lead charges and win hard-fought actions, he has been a mere peace-soldier,

Who never set a squadron in the field,
Nor the division of a battle knew.

A SOLDIER WITHOUT A UNIFORM

He has not worn his uniform since he came to Panama in 1907 (and when he does take it out of moth-balls at the end of the job he will not have to let out the sword-belt by a single hole). They waste very little time on the Isthmus changing uniforms and turning out the guard. All the military smartness you will find there, outside the camps of the Marines and the 10th Infantry, is the exclusive property of the Zone Police. To see one of those big bronzed soldier-policemen on mounted patrol is to wish that Frederic Remington could have lived to have painted him. The trooper's right hand flies up to salute a white-haired man in baggy duck trousers, a black alpaca coat, and an ugly little straw hat — and you realize that the latter is the more soldierly figure of the two. In spite of civilian clothes and more than thirty years' absence from drill, Colonel Goethals is no shapeless desk-chair warrior, but a man to inspire the words of Bret Harte's priest:

Now, by the firm grip of the hand on the bridle,
  By the straight line from the heel to the shoulder
By the curt speech — nay, nay, no offense, son,
  You are a soldier.

The only misleading thing about that quotation is the first line, for, though the Colonel keeps an exceedingly firm ' hand on the bridle ' of the whole canal organization, no one ever sees him in a McClellan saddle. His trusty steed is a swift and comfortable motor-car mounted on flanged wheels and looking more like a taxicab gone railroading than anything else in the world. It is painted the regulation bilious yellow of Panama Railroad passenger coaches, and you can scare a shirker out of a wet-season's growth by yelling, ' Here comes the Yellow Peril! ' But as likely as not the ' Yellow Peril ' (also known as the ' Brain Wagon ') is running empty, because the Colonel has dropped off to take a short-cut to a steam shovel or a bunch of compressed-air drills, or a new drainage ditch, or something else that has interested him. Presently he will come along perched on top of a loaded dirt-train (' dirt ' means anything from mud to 10-ton lumps of trap) ; or walking at a good, swinging pace over rough construction tracks and slippery fragments of splintered rock. A morning stroll with Colonel Goethals in the Culebra Cut is fully equal to a walk with Colonel Roosevelt in Rock Creek Park.

There are ninety-nine busy steam shovels on the Isthmus and one idle one, and the Colonel would rejoice more over putting that one to work than over the ninety-and-nine that are safe in the fold. That idle steam shovel is standing back of Sosa Hill, near Balboa, at the Pacific entrance of the Canal, ready to dig the great dry dock that is to be built there — when Congress gives the word. The rising waters of Gatun Lake are fast backing up to the machine shops at Gorgona, which cannot be removed to their permanent site near the dry-dock until Congress gets through playing presidential year politics. The construction force is rapidly breaking up, but the operating force cannot be organized; and hundreds of trained men, as eager to stay with their chief as he is sorry to lose them, have had to go north.

In the meantime, a few concrete wharves are being built at Balboa; and, at the other end of the Canal, the beautiful avenue of palms that used to fringe the water-front of Cristobal is being left far inland, as an elaborate system of docks is being pushed out into Limon Bay. Eight powerful electric cranes have been ordered to handle freight at Balboa, where hundreds of acres of land have been made by filling in swamps and tidal flats with earth and rock from the Cut. When this land is finally covered with docks and warehouses, it should bring in a very pretty rental to the United States Government, which owns every inch of it. Here at Balboa, Colonel Goethals plans to concentrate all the equipment of the present Commissary and Quartermaster's Departments: a cold-storage plant that can freeze a thousand carcasses of beef or a thousand gallons of ice-cream; a bakery equipped with automatic bread, pie, and cake machines; a completely-stocked general store; and a laundry that could receive an in-coming ship's linen and deliver it to her by the Panama Railroad before she reached the other end of the Canal. The Government would then, with its dry-docks and machine-shops, with its own coal-bunkers and lighters, and with the handy tanks and pipe-line of the Union Oil Company of California, be able to supply any ship that passed through the Canal with anything from a seabiscuit to a new propeller shaft. And some day this peaceful, profitable trade might save us more than could be counted in time or dollars, when a fleet of transports came through with empty bunkers, or a battered dreadnought limped into Balboa shipyards, to be sent back to the fighting line.

Colonel Goethals is thinking of all those things — but most of all of that idle steamshovel behind Sosa Hill.

The operating force (about 2500 men

with their wives and families) will live at Balboa in a model town to be built entirely of reinforced cement. Here also will be barracks for a battalion of marines, who may be needed to keep drunken stevedores and sailors from breaking up the toy police force of Panama City. The main body of the garrison which the War Department wishes to keep permanently on the Isthmus, two brigades of infantry, a regiment of cavalry, and a battalion of field artillery, besides enough coast artillerymen to man the heavy fortifications on either side, will be quartered at a place just across the Canal from the present town of Culebra. Ten years from now, the empty concrete shell of the unfinished Catholic church may serve to point out to the tourist the site of Old Culebra, as the gaunt stone tower of San Jerome does that of Old Panama. Colonel Goethals says:

'All our present towns are mere temporary construction camps, and practically all the houses in them will be falling to pieces by the time the Canal is finished. As for settling an American colony in the Canal Zone, there will be very little farming land left outside of what must be covered by the lake or taken for military purposes; and the best of that is already held by native and Chinese market-gardeners, with whom our people could not hope to compete. Americans wishing to buy farms in Panama will find more room and better land in the Province of Chiriqui. The Canal Zone should be made a military reservation, like Sandy Hook. Our primary purpose in building the Canal was not commercial but military: to make sure that no battleship of ours would ever have to sail round South America, as the *Oregon* did, in time of war.'

Colonel Goethals naturally prefers the sort of tolls that would bring the greatest volume of business to the Canal, that would enable it to pay the largest direct revenue to the Government. He favors a toll slightly lower than that of Suez, and absolutely uniform, regardless of flag or owner, except to American ships plying between our coast ports, if that trade is kept closed to foreign vessels. His idea of the way to keep down freight rates is beautifully simple, but imagine the angry protests that would go up from every American railroad and shipowner if it were put into effect:

'The determining factor in all rates is the tramp ship. Any attempt to raise rates unduly could easily be upset by the Government's chartering a number of tramps and running them as public freighters between the ports affected until the rates came down. This would be more economical than the proposed plan of turning the existing Panama Railroad Steamship Line into a permanent Government-owned line between Atlantic and Pacific ports. Such a line would probably not pay, and should not be made a charge on the Canal.'

When I asked his opinion of the scheme to use the Panama Railroad and Canal equipment, after it is no longer needed on the Isthmus, for building Government railroads in Alaska, Colonel Goethals replied:

'Its advisability must be determined by two things: the cost of transfer and the character of the roads to be built. If what are contemplated are comparatively short, isolated lines running from the coast to the coal-fields, then our 5-foot gauge equipment would probably do well enough. But if the Government is going in for railroad building there on a large scale, there would be no economy in anything but new and standard gage equipment. As for transferring the organization from Panama to Alaska, there will be none left to transfer.'

The place to see Colonel Goethals at his best is from a certain chair in his private office at Culebra, between eight and eleven on Sunday morning. Here, at a flat-topped desk and with a tin of cigarettes before him, the Colonel sits in most informal state, and every man or woman who has a grievance can come and state it to the Man at the Top. From his decisions there is no appeal, except to the President of the United States. M. Jusserand, the French Ambassador, after witnessing one of these Sunday morning interviews, compared it to St. Louis's court of justice beneath the oak at Vincennes.

In quick succession the cases pass through. A Colon banker wants the privilege of handling ships' drafts for Canal tolls, and is referred to the Treasury Department. An engineer's wife wants a 'Type 17' house in Corozal, because the baby cannot stand a flat. Couldn't the Colonel see the district quartermaster about it, before they go up on leave, Tuesday? The Colonel promises. If the

Spanish War Veterans get free transportation on the special train, Memorial Day, are the Kangaroos, who are employees, to be crowded out by the 10th Infantry, who are not? Let a committee of all the fraternal orders appear next Sunday to talk it over. When a man has been brought down from the States as a locomotive hostler, but has got a run the day he hit the Isthmus, why has n't he drawn an engineer's pay for the first month? He shall get it, if the records of the Division Office bear him out. A man's brother has been terribly injured by the relocation of the Panama Railroad, but has been told that he cannot sue for damages, because that work is being done by the Isthmian Canal Commission, which is the United States Government. The Colonel will report favorably on it if their Congressman will introduce a special bill — the only remedy. The best nurse in Colon Hospital has resigned after a tiff with the head nurse, and the doctors want her back. Can the Colonel get her to apologize for the sake of discipline? He 'll try.

No matter how sudden the change of subject, the Colonel always seems to know the rules of a man's division, or shop, or union, by heart. He never has to look them up in a pamphlet; though the touch of a button will bring it, together with the written record of any man in the service. And almost invariably he winds up the interview with a good, hearty laugh, in which the visitor joins. Even the little gray-haired woman who begged for protection from a drunken husband, 'He knows he must n't hurt me, Colonel, since you wrote him that letter, but he 's got into a fuss with another woman now,' ceased sobbing and went out almost smiling when the Colonel said, 'I 'll speak to him.'

For that office is famous also for interviews of another sort, that do not end in laughter. One stalwart Westerner, who distinguished himself at San Juan Hill but neglected his work on the Isthmus, collapsed into a chair when he reached the outer office and after five minutes said tremulously, 'I guess my knees will hold me up now.' A man who had been caught in an intrigue with another man's wife was told curtly to take his annual leave at once and resign as soon as it expired. When he furiously demanded an explanation, Colonel Goethals said simply,

'Mrs. —— was sent up on the ship before you.'

The man took his hat and left without a word.

The last visitor of the morning is Big Bill Morrison, the Socialist blacksmith from Gorgona, and he comes, not with a kick, but with an invitation. The boys in the shops are going to give a banquet, to celebrate the breaking-up of the old camp, and they want the Colonel to be there.

'Can I get such a breakfast next morning as I had at Mrs. Morrison's in 1907? That was the best I ever had on the Isthmus.'

'Sure!'

'Then I 'll come.' He passes over the cigarettes and the two sit down as amicably as if there were not a shoulder-strap or a red flag in the world.

'Colonel, did you see much of Socialism when you were in Germany?'

'The Kaiser told me he was going to stamp it all out.'

'Bismarck tried that, you know.'

'Now look here, Morrison, you must n't say we have Socialism down here. Introduce the franchise, and we 'd go to pieces. It 's a despotism; and that 's the best form of government.'

'It is,' agrees the big Socialist, with a laugh; 'if you 've got a good despot.'

The last visitor is gone and Colonel Goethals tilts wearily back in his desk-chair. The cigarette-box is empty; for the last three hours he has been nervously lighting cigarettes and throwing them away half-smoked. There are very many wrinkles in his face and the white curls are growing thin about his temples, but his smile is still patient and unwearied. Looking over his spectacles at the interviewer in the corner, the Colonel says,

'Do you know, sometimes this gets to be a blamed old grind?'

X

MAUDE ADAMS

FREDERIC DEAN

[*Good Housekeeping Magazine*, May, 1913. By permission.]

The dominant motif of Maude Adams' life is minding her own business. She 's an actress, and holds to the old-fashioned notion that her place is behind the foot-lights, and not on Fifth Avenue; that she appears to better advantage in the breeches of *Peter Pan* than in smart Parisian frocks; and she prefers a romp with her big St. Bernard, Meta, down at Sandygarth Farm, to the most select social function.

So far, she has rigidly adhered to the mode of living she set for herself when she first began to hide behind her art and foreswore all temptations to be dragged into prominence save upon her mimic stage.

Miss Adams is never seen on the street, in the park, or in the shops. Her name is never mentioned among 'those present' at matinées, professional women's league bazaars, actors' fund benefits or the many other gatherings to which stage folk flock. Since she was graduated from John Drew's company, she has never attended one of his premiers, and she never enters a theater other than the one in which she is at the time playing.

Yes; once last season she went to the New Amsterdam. Mr. Frohman had seen *The Pink Lady* and was sure the principal comedy character would please her. Miss Adams promptly bought a seat in the gallery and enjoyed the play with the other gods — who, unluckily for them, had no inkling of her identity.

A color scheme of dull gray or black is almost invariably adhered to by Miss Adams when on the street. Over her head she sometimes throws a shawl, but prefers a little round cap, and her entire get-up is distinctly severe. Her style in dress has hardly altered since 1900; she knows absolutely nothing of the prevailing modes; and the sheath gown and pannier skirt are unknown quantities in the algebra of her wardrobe; and, as for jewelry, if she possesses any, she seldom, if ever, wears it.

The one woman from whom Miss Adams accepts invitations is Mrs. Thomas Hastings, the architect's wife. Mrs. Hastings is the president of the Ladies' Four-in-hand Driving Club and was the first to teach Miss Adams to drive and encourage her in riding — a delight to which she still clings. In Mrs. Hastings' home, Miss Adams often dines, stipulating, however, that none but the immediate family are to be present. And here her social activities end.

She cares as little for equal suffrage as she does for dinner gowns, and she could n't tell the names of the box-holders at the Metropolitan Opera House if her hope of heaven depended upon its correct recital.

But with every detail of her art she is on delightfully intimate terms, and, curiously enough, it is the mechanism of the stage — the intricacies of the stage carpenter and scenic artist — that interest her most and upon which is peculiarly well informed. Gordon Craig is no more of an enthusiast upon the subject of stage-lighting than is she. Miss Adams once sent to Vienna for a color effect that was used in one play at one performance. This open-air presentation of Schiller's play was a fair example of Miss Adams' industry and endurance. When she first inspected the stadium, two weeks before the performance, she discovered that the architect had provided no means of lighting the amphitheater and had made no arrangements for water. She immediately installed her own electric plant and tapped the nearby water mains with smaller pipes for her temporary theater. Then she began rehearsals, working sixteen hours a day, coaching the supernumeraries, teaching the soldiers how to ride their mounts, giving orders to the electricians, and instructing the herders in charge of the sheep used in the spectacle.

At midnight on the eve of the performance, she was still directing the preliminaries of the morrow's exhibition. Chaos reigned. That a performance would be attempted within twenty-four hours and concluded without a serious mishap, was incredible; those who saw that first performance remember one that was almost flawless. And *Joan,* who had apparently given no heed to her own lines or stage business, was the calmest figure in the pageant.

An incident happened in connection with the performance before the Yale students that is worth repeating here. Miss Adams is diffident to a degree. When she was a very young lady, she suffered so keenly from embarrassment that she has made it one of the tenets of her creed to put at ease similarly afflicted young persons at any cost. The president of the Yale University Dramatic Club was invited to call upon Miss Adams to arrange preliminary details of the play selected. As he was ushered into the reception room, he stumbled over furniture, blushed purple, and with a whispered 'How are you?' sank into a seat. Miss Adams smiled in spite of herself, but promptly answered, 'I hope that I am half as well as you look'; and before long the two were chatting like old friends.

Miss Adams is preëminently a kind woman. Every one associated with her receives the same cheerful greeting and no one in trouble need ask for her aid; it is theirs before the request can be formulated. There used to be an old door-keeper, at the stage entrance of the Empire Theater, who was as well known to the passers-in and out as is Mayor Gaynor to the newspaper boys who frequent New York's City Hall. One day he was taken sick and his place was filled by another. Miss Adams learned that the old chap had lost his position and made a hurried search for him, tracing him, at last, to an East Side tenement. It was long after midnight when she found him. He was very ill and was being taken care of by his faithful wife as best she could. Doctors and nurses were immediately summoned and every possible comfort provided; and the next morning, and the next, and the next came Lady Bountiful — and every day, until the sufferer died, a month later.

For sixteen years, Robert Eberle was in Charles Frohman's employ as business manager. He was a man who has spent his life in theatricals; he was a favorite in the Frohman household and was given one of the first positions at the beginning of each season. Last year he was sent out as acting manager of the *Passers-By* company. Late in the season, he was taken ill and left in a hospital in South Bend, Indiana. Miss Adams was playing in the West at the time, and hearing of Mr. Eberle's illness — though several hundred miles from the hospital — left her company on Saturday night, went to South Bend, spent Sunday at the sick man's bedside, and, leaving orders for the best of medical treatment, returned to her work just in time to dress for her part on Monday night. A considerable share of Miss Adams' income is pledged to private charity. Somewhere among her papers there is a list of pensioners which only her eyes have seen. No one has learned more about these recipients of her bounty than

that they are old, destitute players and acquaintances of her childhood.

The members of Miss Adams' companies are genuinely fond of her, and, once a new production is safely launched, she is the meekest member of the organization, and is never above accepting advice and suggestions from the others; the source of the suggestion is seemingly of no consequence to her, if only it have value. The man who hauls the baggage into the theater may with safety offer counsel; the call-boy runs no risk in commenting adversely on the dramatic effect of a certain scene; and should the second violin suggest to Miss Adams that her dress in the last act did not harmonize with the color scheme of the back-drop, she would thank him and cheerfully take the matter under serious advisement.

Business pertaining to her productions is transacted in Miss Adams' own office, in the Empire Theater building in New York. No name is on the door, and but a few of the daily passers-by suspect the identity of the occupant of this particular suite. Here she selects the members of her company, gives orders to scenic artists and costumers and attends to the thousand and one details that go to make up the daily routine of preparation.

Until recently Miss Adams occupied a house in the city. She still holds title to the property, but it is down on Sandygarth Farm, Ronkonkoma, Long Island, that she really lives — until the hot weather drives her up to her bungalow in the Catskills. Sandygarth may with perfect propriety be called an estate. It measures well up in the hundreds of acres — some cultivated and some not; some wooded and some threaded with tiny streams. Sandygarth Farm is the real theater of Miss Adams' day dreams. A kennel of St. Bernards and English sheep dogs is personally looked after by the mistress of the place, whose constant companion is the rough-coated Meta.

The most interesting room in the house is the library, simply furnished with English and old Dutch solidity. Around the walls stand bookcases, shoulder high. The decorations are mainly souvenirs of Miss Adams' jaunts in Europe and northern Africa. In one corner is a Damascus blade, polished with its own history; on a shelf opposite the entrance, squats a grinning Egyptian idol; worked on the wall, is an illuminated detail of medieval fresco from a Florentine chapel; above the books, running around the room, is a series of etchings, showing points of interest in a tour recently taken by the hostess through Egypt and the East. In the music-room is a self-playing piano with music rolls of Puccini and Debussy as well as those of Wagner and Beethoven. Miss Adams plays both the piano and the harp and strums occasionally on the guitar. She goes to concerts when she can — choosing a classical program; in art she prefers the sober stand-bys to ultra modern, bizarre color effects.

Whenever Miss Adams goes abroad — whether to Chicago or to Cairo — she is attended by her secretary, the faithful Miss Boynton, who has been in her service long — so long that she has become a true companion, a companion who is consulted upon every momentous question of costume or farm produce; who is present at the trial of every stage effect and is the companion of every country drive; a true helpmeet in the small things of life as well as in the large.

From this glimpse of Maude Adams, the woman, it is plain that she has clipped away the non-essentials; that she clearly distinguishes between the fictitious and the real; that, lover of nature that she is, she is enabled to bring a freshness and spontaneity to her stage concepts, endow them richly and fully with the sunshine and the perfume of her meadows and her hills; that, as a lover of mankind, her ambitions cannot be small, nor her triumphs petty; that, by pursuing the true things in life, her art cannot but be intelligent in its aims and well-rounded in its results; and, that, by brushing away trivialities and centering upon the things of true importance she has adapted and especially prepared herself for the work of stage portraiture — for it is in stage portraiture that Maude Adams the actress excels.

In the long list of characters she has paraded upon her platform of mimicry, from *Lady Babbie* to *Peter Pan*, as the *Duke* in *L'Aiglon*, as *Joan of Arc* and *Rosalind;* in *Quality Street* and *What Every Woman Knows;* even before her starring days, as *Jessie* in *The Bauble Shop* and *Suzanne Blondet* in *The Masked Ball* — to say nothing of the still earlier successes of *Nell* in *The Lost Paradise* and *Dora* in *Men and Women* — it is always the character represented that stands out with cameo clarity; each one is an individual portrait, painted with distinction, understanding, effect; each canvas is touched with her own personality, as if she were unwilling to leave it without the familiar ' M. A.' in the lower right-hand corner.

It is the fashion to speak of Bernhardt as 'divinely inspired,' of Duse as 'magnetic,' of Nazimova as 'intense,' and of others to similar purpose — each after her kind; and, no doubt, the fashion is right. Every actress who has visited America, from Ristori to Billie Burke, has had her individual mannerisms, and, by whatever name they are called, either tricks of speech, or of dress, or of movement, these mannerisms constitute the individuality of her who possesses — or is possessed by — them. By their mannerisms, then, shall ye know them.

Miss Adams possesses a personality that is startlingly sensible and sincere, but it is her capacity for portraiture, the gift of receiving and assimilating and *representing* individual character, the craftsman's sense of material and the craftsman's delight in the use of it — *plus* the mannerisms of the Woman — that give her portraits a rank with those of Thackeray and Raeburn; with Maeterlinck's *Melisande* and the *Carmen* of Bresler-Gianoli; with the best of Cissy Loftus' mimicries of yesterday and the truest Scot in Harry Lauder's repertoire of today. Paradoxically, her exclusiveness has made her the best known actress on the American stage. True, we of the street know nothing of Maude Adams' mode of living; what she has for dinner, what she reads, or whether she prefers dumb-bells or punching-bag. But, we do know that she eats well, reads the best books and exercises with some potent body-builder — else her voice would be less musical, the interpretations of her lines would be less illuminating, her characters less convincing as living personages.

From that eventful night at the Salt Lake City Theater, when, nine months old, Maude Adams was borne bawling to the center of the stage as the chief personage in *The Lost Child*, up to her recent reappearance as *Peter Pan;* when, as a child of seven she played in J. K. Emmet's *Fritz;* and, later, when the girl of nineteen surprised friend and critic in *The Masked Ball;* when she stormed the citadel of stardom as *Lady Babbie* and since, in whatever character she has been seen, it has been the player and not the play that has left the impression. And, by her very absence from the public thoroughfare, she has made her entrance upon the stage of more consequence, possessed it with an element of mystery that has lent additional enchantment to her portrayals.

Richard Wagner weaved the patterns of his most compelling harmonies while tramping the hills with his faithful four-footed friend as his only companion; Maude Adams perfects and polishes her *Maggie Wylies* and *Phœbe Throssells,* her *Peters* and her *Chanticlers,* wandering through the woods and over the fields of Ronkonkoma with her shaggy-haired Meta by her side, reincarnating her puppets into persons, persons that live and live fully and richly; persons of wit and fun, of fine humanity and enchanting grace; persons whose perfected presentment upon the Empire stage are the results of greater things dreamed and done in secret down at Sandygarth Farm.

Fast is a relative term.

Do not praise ephemeral things. They will change.

Praising people for virtues which they do not have helps them to attain these virtues.

Everybody's business is nobody's business.

D. EXPOSITORY AND EDITORIAL ARTICLES

The previous sections have dealt mainly with persons and things; expository and editorial articles present, or should present, ideas. The editorial writer must first 'catch his hare,' no matter how much skill he may display in the cooking. The best articles of this type are the outcome of strong feeling or profound conviction, for the layman's notion of the hired swashbucklers of the press is, in the main, simply a popular delusion. Dr. Charles R. Miller, for many years editor-in-chief of the New York *Times*, said in answer to questions put to him by the Senate Committee on the Ship Purchase Bill on March 15, 1915: 'The men who write these opinions believe them. Nobody in the *Times* office is ever asked to write what he does not believe.' This is true of every large and well-conducted newspaper office, in which the editorial council is a long-established institution, and a decision on an important public issue is carefully discussed so that the resulting article is the product of more brains than one.

'Every newspaper that enjoys continuity of existence and management' (again to quote Dr. Miller's evidence) 'has a certain body of principles. They are called the policy of the paper. Those are the principles and beliefs that guide its expression of opinion. . . . The managers and editorial writers are the persons responsible for the expression of opinion. They are men. They have neither haloes nor horns. They form their opinions just as other men form their opinions, by observation and reflection and information. When it comes to a specific public measure they express in their own opinions, which they write, the opinions of the paper. The opinions and policy of one paper differ from those of another. Some are for high tariff, and some are for low tariff. Some papers are radical, and some are conservative. But each paper has a body of principles that guides its utterances.'

The man who writes over his own signature enjoys greater freedom, because he carries less responsibility, his opinion being merely a personal one; but he too is under the necessity of clear and original thinking before he can write anything worth while. After that, his task, if not easy, is at least half done. The articles selected for this section show an extraordinary variety of subject and treatment, but they are all alike in this — that the writer has something to say and knows how to say it. Such consummate masters of the art of expression as Mr. Arthur Brisbane and Mr. Clutton Brock — to take one American and one English example — have very definite ideas to present as well as admirable phrases to convey their meaning. Mr. Woodrow Wilson's article on the ideal university is as remarkable for its orderly arrangement and skilful statement as are the historic despatches he has composed since as President of the United States in a momentous crisis of the national life. The ambitious student will do well to ponder these great examples and strive to catch something of the qualities that give them distinction — intellectual insight, emotional sympathy, a firm grasp on great principles, and the power of using words to set forth precisely and forcefully the thesis the writer has in mind or the cause he has at heart.

I

THE EDITORIAL WRITER'S OPPORTUNITY

[ARTHUR BRISBANE]

[*New York Evening Journal*, November 12, 1912. By permission.]

We have been asked to express an opinion as to 'the opportunity' of the editorial writer, for the benefit of young men studying journalism under Dr. Talcott Williams, at Columbia University. Here is an outline of what might be said, among other things, on this subject:

5 Writing for a newspaper is merely talking wholesale. Instead of talking to one man, or a hundred at one time, we talk through newspapers to five millions or more.

10 The editorial writer's opportunity is the opportunity to say something.

It is the greatest and most generally

153

neglected opportunity in the world. Young men who intend to write editorials might learn by heart Boileau's lines:

'Ma pensée au grand jour partout s'offre et
  s'expose,
'Et mon vers, bien ou mal, dit toujours
  quelque chose.'

Particularly the last line, which means:

'My verse, good or bad, always says something.'

The editorial writer's opportunity is the chance to say something. Many writers neglect that opportunity.

The newspaper is many things in our life. It is the principal literature of the American people, and, therefore, 'good or bad,' it is highly important to the country.

Among other things, the newspaper's editorial column takes the place of the public square at Athens, where one man could talk to all the citizens.

The writer of the editorials is the talker in the public square of today. He can, if he chooses, do as much for this age as the Greek with the voice, instead of the pen or typewriter or phonograph, did in his age.

The best description of newspaper work, and a very early expression also of foolish misunderstanding of newspaper work, may be found in one short quotation from Schopenhauer's essay, 'Some Forms of Literature':

The newspaper is the second-hand in the clock of history; and it is not only made of baser metal than those which point to the minute and the hour, but it seldom goes right — if it's wrong, the clock is wrong.

The so-called leading article is the chorus to the drama of passing events.

Exaggeration of every kind is as essential to journalism as it is to the dramatic art, for the object of journalism is to make events go as far as possible. Tnus it is that all journalists are, in the very nature of their calling, alarmists; and this is their way of giving interest to what they write. Herein they are like little dogs — if anything stirs they immediately set up a shrill bark.

Therefore, let us carefully regulate the attention to be paid to this trumpet of danger, so that it may not disturb our digestion. Let us recognize that a newspaper is at best but a magnifying glass, and very often merely a shadow on the wall.

The newspaper, it is true, is the 'second-hand' on the face of the clock of history. It must exaggerate each second's importance, otherwise the seconds could not be counted.

It exaggerates, in comparison with the slow moving hour-hand. But it does not exaggerate, considering the needs of the individual reader.

For if the newspaper is the second-hand 'in the clock of history,' the individual is the second-hand in the clock of humanity. The nation is the minute-hand, and the race is the hour-hand.

The journalistic second-hand in its rapid, exaggerated talking keeps pace with that human second-hand, the individual, in his enforced concentration on the little things that happen in his little life.

An editorial can do four important things:
Teach,
Attack,
Defend,
Praise.
Teaching is the most important and the most difficult.

Attacking is the easiest and the most unpleasant, although sometimes necessary.

The defending of good causes, of the weak against the strong, of the new idea against ridicule, is important and usually neglected by editorial writers.

Praise also is neglected, except in a partizan sense without meaning.

The newspaper is not as Schopenhauer says, 'a shadow on the wall,' although many a newspaper is a mere shadow of what a newspaper should be.

A newspaper is a mirror reflecting the public, a mirror more or less defective, but still a mirror. The papers of the different nations reflect the nations more or less accurately. And the paper that the individual holds in his hand reflects that individual more or less accurately.

Some mirrors and some newspapers are preserved as interesting old relics, although they have ceased to reflect anything.

And some newspapers startle the unaccustomed public with the accuracy of the reflection shown, and the public takes time to get used to it.

The newspaper does about what the public does; it is the public, not the newspaper, that sets the pace.

If you have every newspaper in the United States giving first place to the result of a contest between eighteen men playing baseball and accomplishing nothing useful in a 'championship series,' you may be sure that the public is concentrated on that game.

If you have newspapers devoting space to the secret, pre-arranged murder of a gambler by other gamblers instigated by a police officer, you may know that the public's mind is concentrated on that crime and not on the proceedings of some scientific convention.

The opportunity for the editorial writer is the greatest opportunity that exists. For men have developed as men only since language gave to the individual the power to transfer his thought complete to the brain of another.

The power to transfer your thought and make it effective is the greatest power, excepting the exceptional power to discover new scientific truth.

It is possible for the editorial writer now to talk to at least five millions every day. That actually happens.

With our newspaper machinery as it exists it will be possible to talk to the entire reading public every day. No power can be greater than that. The editorial writer's power is the power of suggestion and the power of repetition — very great forces.

The opportunity of the editorial writer is wasted usually. It is true that nearly always the so-called 'leading article' or editorial 'is the chorus of the drama of passing events.' But that is not always true and it will be true less and less as the newspapers and newspaper readers realize their duty and opportunity.

The newspapers are like the churches. There are eminently respectable preachers that say nothing and less numerous preachers that say something.

In the days of slavery the Episcopal Church in New Jersey rejected a picture offered as a frontispiece for a prayer book, because it showed kneeling at the feet of Christ, with the widow and the orphan, a black slave in chains. The good religious gentlemen said that such a picture might be misconstrued as an attack on slavery and stir up hard feeling. Those good gentlemen were 'the conservative press' of their church.

At about the same time Henry Ward Beecher, in his church in Brooklyn, put up a runaway slave girl in the pulpit and sold her at public auction, the proceeds to be devoted to the work of freeing the slaves.

He was the 'yellow journalist' of the church.

He was more successful than the respectable clergymen, because he deserved to be more successful!

First have something to say. Then say it so that people will see it, read it, understand it, and believe it.

Those are the four things; the reader must see, he must read, he must understand, he must believe.

If you want to write an editorial defending Moses against the attack of Rabbi Hirsch, who denounces some of Moses's teachings, you can put almost any kind of a heading on your editorial.

If you head it 'Analysis of the Diatetic Teachings of the Ancients,' 90 per cent. of those that 'see' the heading won't read.

You can write the same editorial, head it, 'Be Kind to Poor Moses, He Had No Icebox,' and 90 per cent. of those that see will read.

logical analysis

II

MY IDEAL OF THE TRUE UNIVERSITY

WOODROW WILSON

[*Delineator*, November, 1909. By permission of author and publisher.]

The word 'university' means, in our modern usage, so many different things that almost every time one employs it it seems necessary to define it. Nowhere has it so many meanings as in America, where institutions of all kinds display it in the titles they bestow upon themselves. School, college, and university are readily enough distinguishable, in fact, by those who take the pains to look into the scope and methods of their teachings; but they are quite indistinguishable, oftentimes, in name. They are as likely as not all to bear the same title.

But practice is always the best definer; and practice is slowly working out for us in America a sufficiently definite idea of what a university is. It is not the same idea that has been worked out in England or Germany or France. American universities will probably, when worked out to the logical fulfilment of their natural development, show a type distinct from all others. They will be distinctive of what America has thought out and done in the field of higher education. Those which are already far advanced in their development even now exhibit an individual and characteristic organization.

The American university as we now see it consists of many parts. At its heart stands the college, the school of general training. Above and around the college stand the graduate and technical schools, in which special studies are prosecuted and preparation is given for particular professions and occupations. Technical and professional schools are not a necessary part of a university, but they are generally benefited by close association with a university; and the university itself is unmistakably benefited and quickened by the transmission of its energy into them and the reaction of their standards and objects upon it. As a rule the larger universities of the countries have law schools, divinity schools and medical schools under their care and direction; and training for these, the 'learned,' professions has long been considered a natural part of their work. Schools of mechanical, electrical and civil engineering have of late years become as numerous and as necessary as the schools which prepare for the older professions, and they have naturally in most cases grown up in connection with universities because their processes are the processes of science, and the modern university is, among other things, a school of pure science, with laboratories and teachers indispensable to the engineer. But the spirit of technical schools has not always been the spirit of learning. They have often been intensely and very frankly utilitarian, and pure science has looked at them askance. They are proper parts of a university only when pure science is of the essence of their teaching, the spirit of pure science the spirit of all their studies. It is only of recent years we have seen thoughtful engineers coming to recognize this fact, preach this change of spirit; it is only of recent years, therefore, that technical schools have begun to be thoroughly and truly assimilated into the university organization.

There is an ideal of everything American, and the ideal at the heart of the American university is intellectual training, the awakening of the whole man, the thorough introduction of the student to the life of America and of the modern world, the completion of the task undertaken by the grammar and high schools 5 of equipping him for the full duties of citizenship. It is with that idea that I have said that the college stands at the heart of the American university. The college stands for liberal training. Its 10 object is discipline and enlightenment. The average thoughtful American does not want his son narrowed in all his gifts and thinking to a particular occupation. He wishes him to be made free of the 15 world in which men think about and understand many things, and to know and to handle himself in it. He desires a training for him that will give him a considerable degree of elasticity and adapt- 20 ability, and fit him to turn in any direction he chooses.

For men do not live in ruts in America. They do not always or of necessity follow the callings their fathers followed 25 before them. They are ready to move this way or that as interest or occasion suggests. Versatility, adaptability, a wide range of powers, a quick and easy variation of careers, men excelling in 30 businesses for which they never had any special preparation — these are among the most characteristic marks of American life, its elasticity and variety, the rapid shifting of parts, the serviceability 35 of the same men for many different things, and the quick intelligence of men of many different kinds in the common undertakings of politics and in public affairs of all kinds. If the American col- 40 lege were to become a vocational school, preparing only for particular callings, it would be thoroughly un-American. It would be serving special, not general, needs, and seeking to create a country of 45 specialized men without versatility or general capacity.

The college of the ideal American university, therefore, is a place intended for general intellectual discipline and enlight- 50 enment; and not for intellectual discipline and enlightenment only, but also for moral and spiritual discipline and enlightenment. America is great, not by reason of her skill, but by reason of her spirit — her 55 spirit of general serviceableness and intelligence. That is the reason why it is necessary to keep her colleges under constant examination and criticism. If we do not, they may forget their own true function, which is to supply America and the professions with enlightened men.

I have described the university as a place with a college at its heart, but with graduate schools and professional schools standing about and around the college. The difficulty about thus associating teaching of different kinds, is that the spirit of the graduate and professional schools should not be the same spirit as that of the college, and that there are certain dangers of infection to which the college and schools of advanced and professional study are both alike exposed by the association. Look, first, at the danger to the college. It is in danger of getting the point of view of the graduate and professional schools, the point of view of those who prosecute study very intensively along special lines. Their object, if they be thorough, is technical scholarship. That should not be the object of the college. Its studies, as America has conceived the college (and I am sure she has conceived it rightly), are not prosecuted with a view to scholarship. Scholarship can not be had at the age of twenty-one, at the age at which youngsters graduate from college. They may by that time have been made to see the way, the arduous way, to scholarship and to desire to travel it; but they can not have traveled it. It is a long road. A lifetime is consumed before one reaches the quiet inn at the end of it. The object of the college is a much simpler one, and yet no less great. It is to give intellectual discipline and impart the spirit of learning.

We have misconceived and misused the college as an instrument of American life when we have organized and used it as a place of special preparation for particular tasks and callings. It is for liberal training, for general discipline, for that preliminary general enlightenment which every man should have who enters modern life with any intelligent hope or purpose of leadership and achievement. By a liberal training I do not mean one which vainly seeks to introduce undergraduates to every subject of modern learning. That would, of course, be impossible. There are too many of them. At best the pupil can, within the four years at the disposal of the college, be introduced to them only by sample. He can be, and should be, given a thorough grounding in mathematics, in his own language and in some language not his own, in one of the fundamental physical and natural sciences, in the general conceptions of philosophy, in the outlines of history, and in the elements of correct political thinking; and it is very desirable that he should go beneath the surface in some one of these subjects, study it with more than ordinary attention and thoroughness, and find in it, if he can, some independence of judgment and inquiry. Students in a modern college can not all follow the same road, and it is not desirable that they should do so. Besides the thorough drill in a few fundamental subjects which they should all have, they should be encouraged to make the special, individual choices of particular fields of study which will give them an opportunity to develop special gifts and aptitudes and which will call out their powers of initiative and enable them to discover themselves. The college should be a place of various studies, alive with a great many different interests.

The common discipline should come from very hard work, from the inexorable requirements that every student should perform every task set him, whether general or special, whether of his own choice or exacted by the general scheme of study prescribed for all, with care and thoroughness. The spirit of work should pervade the place — honest, diligent, painstaking work. Otherwise it would certainly be no proper place of preparation for the strenuous, exacting life of America in our day. Its 'liberalizing' influences should be got from its life even more than from its studies. Special studies become liberal when those who are pursuing them associate constantly and familiarly with those who are pursuing other studies — studies of many kinds, pursued from many points of view. The real enlightenments of life come not from tasks or from books so much as from free intercourse with other persons who, in spite of you, inform and stimulate you, and make you realize how big and various the world is, how many things there are in it to think about, and how necessary it is to think about the subjects you are specially interested in in their right relations to many, many others, if you would think of them correctly and get to the bottom of what you are trying to do.

The ideal college, therefore, should be a community, a place of close, natural, intimate association, not only of the young men who are its pupils and novices in various lines of study, but also of young men with older men, with maturer men, with veterans and professionals in the great undertaking of learning, of teachers with pupils, outside the classroom as well as inside of it. No one is successfully educated within the walls of any particular classroom or laboratory or museum; and no amount of association, however close and familiar and delightful, between mere beginners can ever produce the sort of enlightenment which the lad gets when he first begins to catch the infection of learning. The trouble with most of our colleges nowadays is that the faculty of the college live one life and the undergraduates quite a different one. They are not members of the same community; they constitute two communities. The life of the undergraduate is not touched with the personal influence of the teacher: life among the teachers is not touched by the personal impressions which should come from frequent and intimate contact with undergraduates. The teacher does not often enough know what the undergraduate is thinking about or what models he is forming his life upon, and the undergraduate does not know how human a fellow the teacher is, how delightfully he can talk, outside the classroom, of the subjects he is most interested in, how many interesting things both his life and his studies illustrate and make attractive. This separation need not exist, and, in the college of the ideal university, would not exist.

It is perfectly possible to organize the life of our colleges in such a way that students and teachers alike will take part in it; in such a way that a perfectly natural daily intercourse will be established between them; and it is only by such an organization that they can be given real vitality as places of serious training, be made communities in which youngsters will come fully to realize how interesting intellectual work is, how vital, how important, how closely associated with all modern achievement — only by such an organization that study can be made to seem part of life itself. Lectures often seem very formal and empty things; recitations generally prove very dull and unrewarding. It is in conversation and natural intercourse with scholars chiefly that you find how lively knowledge is, how it ties into everything that is interesting and important, how intimate a part it is of everything that is 'practical' and connected with the world. Men are not always made thoughtful by books; but they are generally made thoughtful by association with men who think.

The present and most pressing problem of our university authorities is to bring about this vital association for the benefit of the novices of the university world, the undergraduates. Classroom methods are thorough enough; competent scholars already lecture and set tasks and superintend their performance; but the life of the average undergraduate outside the classroom and other stated appointments with his instructors is not very much affected by his studies; is almost entirely dissociated from intellectual interests.

It is too freely and exclusively given over to athletics and amusements. Athletics are in themselves wholesome, and are necessary to every normal youth. They give him vigor and should give him the spirit of the sportsman — should keep him out of many things of a very demoralizing sort which he would be inclined to do if he did not spend his energy out-of-doors and in the gymnasium. Amusement, too, is necessary. All work and no play makes Jack not only a dull boy, but a very unserviceable boy, with no spirit, no capacity to vary his occupations or to make the most of himself.

But athletics and amusement ought never to become absorbing occupations, even with youngsters. They should be diversions merely, by which the strain of work is relieved, the powers refreshed and given spontaneous play. The only way in which they can be given proper subordination is to associate them with things not only more important, but quite as natural and interesting. Knowledge, study, intellectual effort, will seem to undergraduates more important than athletics and amusement and just as natural only when older men, themselves vital and interesting and companionable, are thrown into close daily association with them. The spirit of learning can be conveyed only by contagion, by personal contact. The association of studies and persons is the proper prescription.

Turn from the college, which lies at the heart of the university, to the graduate and professional schools which lie about the college and are built upon it, and you are discussing an entirely different matter, looking for different principles and methods. Their right relationship to the college, moreover, is a very difficult question to determine. Both the college and the high school are trying to do two things at once — two things not entirely consistent with each other. The majority of pupils in the high school — the very large majority — do not intend to carry their studies any further. They must get all the schooling they are going to get before they leave the high school. They must be given the best training, the completest awakening within the field of knowledge that the school can give them, for that is to be their final preparation for life. A small minority, however, must be prepared to enter college. Majority and minority must be handled, in some circumstances in different ways, and it is very hard indeed to arrange the courses of study in a way that will be suitable for both. The high school is clearly justified in shaping its policy and its methods to the needs, first of all, of the majority. Exceptional arrangements must be made, if possible, for the minority.

Similarly, in the college the great majority of the undergraduates mean to go at once from their courses there into some active practical pursuit; do not mean to go on to more advanced university studies. A minority, on the other hand — a larger minority than in the schools — do intend to go further, will enter the graduate schools to become teachers and investigators, or the technical and professional schools for some calling for which a special training is necessary. The difficulty of the college is to arrange courses and adopt methods which will serve both these classes. It does so, generally, by offering a much larger choice of studies than it is possible or desirable to offer. But the majority must determine its chief characteristics and adaptations. Its chief object must be general preparation, general training, an all-round awakening.

It is evident, therefore, that the college, while it should be the foundation of the professional schools, not only stands below

them, as their support and feeder, but also alongside of them; would be necessary if they did not exist; furnishes the only introduction our young men desire or need to the wider fields of action and experience which lie beyond it. It is, first of all and chiefly, a general fitting school for life. Its social organization and influence are almost as important as its classrooms. It is not a subordinate school, but the chief, the central school of the university. For the professional schools it is, at the same time, an indispensable foundation. That profession is clearly impoverished which does not draw to its special studies men bred to understand life and the broader relations of their profession in some thorough school of general training. In these higher schools the atmosphere is changed; another set of objects lies before the student; his mind has already begun to center upon tasks which fill the rest of his life. He can not, there, seek the things that will connect him with the more general fields of learning and experience.

What is called the graduate school in our universities is not, strictly, a professional school. As a matter of fact most of its pupils will be found to be looking forward to the profession of teaching; but graduate schools of the higher type do not keep that profession in mind. Their object is to train scholars whether in the field of literature, or science, or philosophy, or in the apparently more practical field of politics. They carry the college process a stage farther and seek to induct their students into the precise, exacting methods of scholarship. They not only carry the college process farther, they also alter it. Their students are thrown more upon their own resources in their studies, are expected to enter on researches of their own, strike out into independent lines of inquiry, stand upon their own feet in every investigation, come out of their novitiate and gain a certain degree of mastery in their chosen field, their professors being little more than their guides and critics. They are not taught how to teach; there is no professional tone in the life of the school. They are taught how to learn, thoroughly and independently, and to make scholars of themselves.

Schools of medicine, law and theology, on the other hand, while also, when upon a proper plane, schools of scholarship, are professional schools, and have in all their instruction the professional point of view. Their object is not only to introduce their students to the mastery of certain subjects, as the graduate school does, but also to prepare them for the 'practice' of a particular profession. They devote a great deal of attention to practical method — to the ways in which the knowledge acquired is to be used in dealing with diseases, with disputes between men over their legal rights, and with the needs and interests of men who should be helped with spiritual guidance. They are frankly and of necessity professional. The spirit of the doctor's or of the lawyer's office, of the pulpit and of the pastor's study, pervades them. They school their men for particular tasks, complicated and different, and seek to guide them by many practical maxims.

Similarly, the technical schools are professional schools, their objects practical, definite, utilitarian. Their students must not only know science and have their feet solidly upon the footing of exact knowledge, but must acquire a very thorough mastery of methods, a definite skill and practice, readiness and precision in a score of mechanical processes which make them a sort of master-workmen. The practical air of the shop pervades such schools, as the practical air of the office pervades the law school. They are intent upon business, and conscious all the time that they must make ready for it.

In the professional schools of an ideal university nothing of this practical spirit would be abated, for such schools are, one and all, intensely and immediately practical in their objects and must have practice always in mind if they would be truly serviceable; but there would always lie back of their work, by close association with the studies of the university in pure science and in all the great subjects which underlie law and theology, the impulse and the informing spirit of disinterested inquiry, of study which has no utilitarian object, but seeks only the truth. The spirit of graduate study, and of undergraduate, too, would be carried over into all professional work, and engineers, doctors, ministers, lawyers, would all alike be made, first of all citizens of the modern intellectual and social world — first of all, university men, with a broad outlook on the various knowledge of the world, and then experts in a great practical profession, which they would understand all the better because they had first been grounded in science and in the other great bodies of knowledge which are the foundations of all practice. That is the service the university owes the professional schools associated with it. The parts should be vitally united from end to end.

The professional schools, in their turn, do the university this distinct and very great service, that they keep it in conscious association with the practical world, its necessities and its problems. Through them it better understands what knowledge, what kind of men, what scholarship, what morals, what action, will best serve the age for whose enlightenment and assistance it exists. Our universities should be 'ideal' chiefly in this — that they serve the intellectual needs of the age, not in one thing, not in any one way only, but all around the circle, with a various and universal adaptation to their age and generation. America can never dispense with the enlightenment of general study, and should wish to have as many of her young men as possible subjected to its influences. She should demand that her professional schools be grounded in such studies in order that her professional men may see something more than individual interest in what they do. It is best, therefore, that professional schools should be closely associated with universities, a part of their vital organization, intimate parts of their system of study. That very association and inclusion should make them more thorough in their particular practical tasks. They should be the better schools of technical training. The ideal university is rounded out by them, and their roots are enriched by her fertile soil of catholic knowledge and inquiry. The ideal university would consist of all these parts, associated in this spirit, maintained always in this relationship.

German University — To make a scholar
French   "   —   "   " " " gentleman
American   "   —   "   " both

III

FRANCE

[A. CLUTTON BROCK]

[*Times* (London, England) *Literary Supplement*, October 2, 1914. Reproduced by permission of the *Times*, of the author, and of Messrs. Methuen and Co., who have republished this article with others by Mr. Clutton-Brock in book form under the title *Thoughts on the War*.]

Among all the sorrows of this war there is one joy for us in it: that it has made us brothers with the French as no two nations have ever been brothers before. There has come to us, after ages of conflict, a kind of millennium of friendship; and in that we feel there is a hope for the world that outweighs all our fears, even at the height of the world-wide calamity. There were days and days, during the swift German advance, when we feared that the French armies were no match for the German, that Germany would be conquered on the seas and from her eastern frontier, that after the war France would remain a Power only through the support of her Allies. For that fear we must now ask forgiveness; but at least we can plead in excuse that it was unselfish and free from all national vanity. If, in spite of ultimate victory, France had lost her high place among the nations, we should have felt that the victory itself was an irreparable loss for the world. And now we may speak frankly of that fear because, however unfounded it was, it reveals the nature of the friendship between France and England.

That is also revealed in the praise which the French have given to our army. There is no people that can praise as they can; for they enjoy praising others as much as some nations enjoy praising themselves, and they lose all the reserve of egotism in the pleasure of praising well. But in this case they have praised so generously because there was a great kindliness behind their praise, because they, like us, feel that this war means a new brotherhood stronger than all the hatreds it may provoke, a brotherhood not only of war but of the peace that is to come after it. That welcome of English soldiers in the villages of France, with food and wine and flowers, is only a foretaste of what is to be in both countries in a happier time. It is what we have desired in the past of silly wrangles and misunderstandings, and now we know that our desire is fulfilled.

For behind all those misunderstandings, and in spite of the differences of character between us, there was always an understanding which showed itself in the courtesies of Fontenoy and a hundred other battles. When Sir Philip Sidney spoke of France as that sweet enemy, he made a phrase for the English feeling of centuries past and centuries to be. We quarreled bitterly and long; but it was like a man and woman who know that some day their love will be confessed and are angry with each other for the quarrels that delay the confession. We called each other ridiculous, and knew that we were talking nonsense; indeed, as in all quarrels without real hatred, we made charges against each other that were the opposite of the truth. We said that the French were frivolous; and they said that we were gloomy. Now they see the gaiety of our soldiers and we see the deep seriousness of all France at this crisis of her fate. She, of all the nations at war, is fighting with the least help from illusion, with the least sense of glory and romance. To her the German invasion is like a pestilence; to defeat it is merely a necessity of her existence; and in defeating it she is showing the courage of doctors and nurses, that courage which is furthest removed from animal instinct and most secure from panic reaction. There is no sign in France now of the passionate hopes of the revolutionary wars; 1870 is between them and her; she has learnt, like no other nation in Europe, the great lesson of defeat, which is not to mix material dreams with spiritual; she has passed beyond illusions, yet her spirit is as high as if it were drunk with all the illusions of Germany.

And that is why we admire her as we have never admired a nation before. We ourselves are an old and experienced people, who have, we hope, outlived gaudy and dangerous dreams; but we have not been tested like the French, and we do not know whether we or any other nation could endure the test they have endured. It is not merely that they have survived and kept their strength. It is that they have a kind of strength new to nations, such as we see in beautiful women who have endured great sorrows and outlived all the triumphs and passions of their youth, who smile where once they laughed; and yet they are more beautiful than ever, and seem to live with a purpose that is not only their own, but belongs to the whole of life. So now we feel that France is fighting not merely for her own honor and her own beautiful country, still less for a triumph over an arrogant rival, but for what she means to all the world; and that now she means far more than ever in the past.

This quarrel, as even the Germans confess, was not made by her. She saw it gathering, and she was as quiet as if she hoped to escape war by submission. The chance of revenge was offered as it had never been offered in forty years; yet she did not stir to grasp it. Her enemy gave every provocation, yet she stayed as still as if she were spiritless; and all the while she was the proudest nation on the earth, so proud that she did not need to threaten or boast. Then came the first failure, and she took it as if she had expected nothing better. She had to make war in a manner wholly contrary to her nature and genius, and she made it as if patience, not fire, were the main strength of her soul. Yet behind the new patience the old fire persisted; and the *furia francese* is only waiting for its chance. The Germans believe that they have determined all the conditions of modern war, and, indeed, of all modern competition between the nations, to suit their own national character. It is their age, they think, an age in which the qualities of the old peoples, England and France, are obsolete. They make war after their own pattern, and we have only to suffer it as long as we can. But France has learnt what she needs from Germany so that she may fight the German idea as well as the German armies; and when the German armies were checked before Paris there was an equal check to the German idea. Then the world, which was holding its breath, knew that the old nations, the old faith and mind and conscience of Europe, were still standing fast and that science had not utterly betrayed them all to the new barbarism. Twice before, at Tours and in the Catalaunian fields, there has been such a fight upon the soil of France and now for the third time it is the heavy fate and the glory of France to be the guardian nation. That is not an accident, for France is still the chief treasury of all that these conscious barbarians would destroy. They know that while she stands unbroken there is a spirit in her that will make their Kultur seem unlovely to all the world. They know that in her, as in Athens long ago, thought remains passionate and disinterested and free. Their thought is German and exercised for German ends, like their army; but hers can forget France in the universe, and for that reason her armies and ours will fight for it as if the universe were at stake. Many forms has that thought taken, passing through disguises and errors, mocking at itself, mocking at the holiest things; and yet there has always been the holiness of freedom in it. The French blasphemer has never blasphemed against the idea of truth even when he mistook falsehood for it. In the Terror he said there was no God, because he believed there was none, but he never said that France was God so that he might encourage her to conquer the world. Voltaire was an imp of destruction perhaps, but with what a divine lightning of laughter would he have struck the Teutonic Antichrist, and how the everlasting soul of France would have risen in him if he could have seen her most sacred church, the visible sign of her faith and her genius, ruined by the German guns. Was there ever a stupidity so worthy of his scorn as this attempt to bombard the spirit? For, though the temple is ruined, the faith remains; and, whatever war the Germans may make upon the glory of the past, it is the glory of the future that France fights for. Whatever wounds she suffers now she is suffering for all mankind; and now, more than ever before in her history, are those words become true which one poet who loved her gave to her in the Litany of Nations crying to the earth: —

I am she that was thy sign and standard-
        bearer,
            Thy voice and cry;
She that washed thee with her blood and left
        thee fairer,
            The same am I.
Are not these the hands that raised thee
        fallen and fed thee,
            These hands defiled?
Am not I thy tongue that spake, thine eye
        that led thee,
            Not I thy child?

IV

TO THE RESCUE, AMERICA!

JOHN GALSWORTHY

[By permission of the Commission for Relief in Belgium, which distributed this appeal for publication in American newspapers on December 24, 1915.]

A nation hungry. Seven millions on the edge of famine in winter. The world has seen some black sights in its time; has it ever seen a blacker than this spectacle of Belgium starving?

America, you are a great country. America, without flattery you are the humane country. Save this little nation; this little, brave, starving nation.

A London slum-child prayed: 'O, Lord, if ye ever felt yer 'd like to 'elp a feller, now 's yer chance, O Lord.' Now is your chance, America. We in England have done something; we will do as much as we can; but the scythe of sacrifice sweeps in all our fields. Funds are many; the war long and desperate. No more foodstuffs may be sent forth from this country, or from Holland.

But from somewhere foodstuffs must be sent, for the Belgians are starving. You in America are already doing much; you have given sympathy, and time, and money. But the dimensions of this catastrophe are terrible. Eight hundred thousand to a million pounds a month — by expert estimate — are wanted to keep starvation from these seven million people. Let me quote from official sources some evidence of the appalling situation:

ORPHANS, ORPHANS; GRAVES, GRAVES

From the report of Theodore Waters, secretary of the Christian Herald:

'I do not want this to be a history of the trip through Belgium, but only to recall some impressions of the people's need. Women of refinement herded with women of the street, both dressing and undressing in sight of all the men; a woman with nine children mothering her fatherless brood in the same room — these sights were bad enough. But I drove through ruined villages all the way from Antwerp to Brussels and I could liken it to nothing but going to a funeral through a long cemetery. Indeed, the country was one huge burying ground. Always between the ruined houses we could see graves. Graves, graves, graves. In some would be stuck a bayonet with a Belgian soldier's cap upon it. Above others rough white crosses rudely inscribed, "To the memory of a Belgian soldier." On one grave was a child's shoe; poor little mark of its parents' grief. Graves, graves. Orphans, orphans. A country devastated; its trees felled in rows to make way for bullets; its crops long gone to seed, standing up leanly; dead things in rows like markers in a miniature cemetery.'

From Malines:

'In the name of His Excellency Cardinal Mercier, I beg leave to ask you for strong assistance. . . . In the city of Malines alone 12,000 mouths have to be fed every day. The children come to the German soldiers and tear the bread from their hands. . . . There is hardly a single laborer who can find any work to gain his daily bread. Everything is lacking — we are in want of potatoes, peas, beans, grain, flour, wheat and bacon.'

From the Burgomaster of Wetteren:

'Wetteren is inhabited by over 17,000 people. . . . About 11,000 workmen and numerous families of militiamen are without resources.'

From the Mayor of Hamme:

'For some time our (town) committee has had daily to distribute soup, bread, potatoes and milk for more than 5000 men. Flour is hardly to be obtained. . . . The stock of meat and corn in Hamme will not last till the end of this month.'

From the American Consul at Antwerp:

'I have been called upon by the Mayor of St. Nicholas, imploring me to hasten, if possible, such assistance as the American people could and would render, as they had over 20,000 people without bread and without work in their little town, and no means of providing them. . . . In the coal district near Charleroi a number of poor people, maddened with hunger, attacked a German military train laden with provisions.'

From Captain J. F. Lucey, representative at Rotterdam of the Commission for Relief in Belgium:

'The total amount of supply so far available is entirely insufficient to meet the immediate and urgent needs of the people. . . . Reports and requests for assistance are pouring in. . . . The districts of Liège, Namur, Dinant, are entirely out of grain, flour, salt, peas and beans. A deputation has arrived from Terhaegen and states that for three weeks they have had only potatoes to eat.'

From members of the Town Council at Namur and Liège:

'We are now threatened by famine. . . . We have suffered enough; at least let this misfortune be spared us. . . . To sum up the situation, an industrial population of high efficiency is entirely out of work and cannot earn its food. It has no reserves any more in food or savings, and a rescue is immediately and urgently needed. . . . You may rest assured that in spite of circumstances our population is full of courage and worthy of all the sympathy that the Americans and other nations can show.'

From the account of an American eye witness, Mr. Jarvis Bell, who went through from London to Brussels with the first shipload of food: 'If you could only see the gruesome surroundings in which they are struggling for existence. . . . Give each Belgian peasant $1000 and ten acres of land and then he could do little to keep himself alive. He has, in many districts, no home in which to sleep, no seed to sow with, no implements to work with, no transport with which to reach a market, and no heart to struggle against the impossible. No war ever produced such complete and tragic paralysis as we saw in many parts of Belgium. . . . We met few Belgian men; 80 per cent. of the people in these country districts are women and children; we saw them eating green vegetables, beets and apples; they have little else. There were thousands of children, all afraid to laugh.'

From the account of another American eye witness, Mr. Millard Shaler, who went from London to Brussels on behalf of the Commission for Relief in Belgium: 'Between Antwerp and Malines the destruction of habitation in every town and hamlet was practically universal. Families were living in partially burned buildings, or in improvised structures. The suffering is intense, and food supplies do not exist.'

From the letter of an Englishwoman living in Brussels: 'There is a terrible amount of poverty, sadness and distress here; people without any resources, and thankful even to any one who will give them a meal. . . . Altogether it is the saddest place you can imagine. Shops closed, every one out of work and nothing but beggars and distress on all sides. Coal is not to be had for love or money.'

THE AMOUNT OF FOOD NEEDED

The amount of food required to deal with all this terrible distress is thus summarized in a declaration signed on November 2d, 1914, by the Spanish and American Ministers in Brussels:

'We declare that the statement of M. Francqui (Director of the Société Générale de Belgique), based on a careful estimate made by authorities entirely familiar with their own country and its present material needs, is that the minimum monthly requirements of the Belgian population are 60,000 tons of grain, 15,000 tons of maize and 3000 tons of rice and peas. This estimate is accurate and wholly reasonable, is made by conservative and practical men of affairs, and may be accepted as an expression of the needs of the population.'

To meet these requirements the Commission for Relief in Belgium, whose chief offices are 3, London Wall Buildings, London, have now completed their organization in the United States 'on a basis adequate for the emergency of sending into Belgium about one million pounds' worth of food every month.'

Sufficient funds have been secured to enable the commission to supply vessels to take cargoes of relief donated in any part of the world, free of all cost, to Rotterdam, and to distribute the food in Belgium. Offices have been opened at 71 Broadway, New York, under the charge of prominent American business men who, like the other members of the Commission, are practically giving all their time to this work of philanthropy.

WHAT THE GERMANS DO

Finally, the following document records the official permit from Baron von der Goltz, the German Governor of Belgium, to the American Minister in Brussels: 'I welcome with lively satisfaction the undertaking of the Comité de Secours et d'Alimentation, and do not hesitate formally and distinctly to give assurance that foodstuffs of all kinds imported by the committee under Your Excellency's patronage, for the use of the civil populace in Belgium, shall be kept exclusively for the use of the Belgian populace; that these foodstuffs shall hereafter be exempt from requisition by the military authorities, and finally that they shall remain entirely at the disposition of the committee.' The machinery of distribution is thus complete.

THE BLACKEST CASE IN HISTORY

Such is the record.

If there be in all history so black, so pitiful a case, I do not know it. A nation's life torn up — not by the roots as yet, for faith and fortitude remain — but mown off level with the ground. Belgium is deflowered, and done to living death; Belgium is starving.

If the hands of pity be not extended swiftly, the shame of this must forever haunt the dreams of all mankind. If Belgium be left to starve, how shall the world ever again sleep quiet in its bed?

America, you are great and generous. You stand for humanity as no country has ever yet stood. You alone, of all the nations fortunate enough to be outside the ring of this mad war, have wealth and strength for a task like this. You alone can keep the flame of hope alive, the pulse of life beating in this starving nation.

The world looks to you, America; looks to you to do justice to your own great heart. You have already lifted this burden of good deeds from the ground; shoulder it as you alone know how, with that fine, fierce energy of yours. See this work of rescue through — and all the world shall bless you.

WILL AMERICA RAISE A MONUMENT OF PITY?

No words have eloquence to voice the misery and peril of that little country. Words are an insult. There is, there can be no American, of what origin soever, who has not suffered, thinking of Belgium — thinking of that charred land. Restoration will come. But to restore, needs must that the nation shall not have died first of sheer cold and hunger.

Famine is a very simple thing. First will go the old men and women; then the children — cold and hungry children — young birds with gaping beaks. And the strong last. Yes, famine is a very simple thing, with its stark and icy clutch.

Eight hundred thousand to a million pounds a month are needed to keep that clutch from the throat of Belgium.

Give, America, give! Raise the greatest monument to Pity ever built. Let it be a star in the sky of all your future that you rescued from this miserable fate the old, the little ones, the strong, of a whole nation whose only sin was that it stood firm to serve mankind. Let it be a golden memory that you succored and uplifted them, keep the breath in their bodies and in their souls faith living; faith that humanity, the sweet humanity which alone can warm and sanctify our lives, is not a spent and driven ghost, but still flesh and blood, and a comrade in the dark.

If you ever felt you'd like to help a fellow, now's your chance, America.

V

UNEMPLOYMENT: A PROBLEM AND A PROGRAM

FREDERIC C. HOWE

[*Century Magazine*, April, 1915. By permission.]

What can be done to relieve the problem of unemployment and its attendant waste is a question that is agitating officials and voluntary agencies in nearly every city in the United States. Every winter sees a seasonal rise in the number of unemployed, and every year an increase in the apparent unemployable. Breadlines gather upon the streets; private charity is wholly inadequate to meet the situation; while up to the present time municipal authorities have ignored the problem as not one for official action. Out of these conditions I. W. W. agitations have arisen in many cities, with forcible assaults upon churches and other institutions. In the winter of 1914 the Excise Commissioner of New York said that there were between 60,000 and 100,000 homeless men and women in that city who found shelter on winter nights either in the rear rooms of saloons or in lodging-houses where liquor is sold. Here thousands of men were found sleeping on the floor or in chairs; and when the agents of the commission closed the saloons, the men were driven to the streets. Only a few of our cities have provided municipal lodging-

The Saloon is the poor man's club
charity is some

houses, and in most cases the self-respecting worker refuses to patronize them because he is immediately classed with the vagrant and the tramp. None of our cities has consciously organized public work in order to care for those thrown out of employment by seasonal conditions or hard times; and in most instances authorities have refused to consider unemployment as a problem of public concern.

On the other hand, labor organizations are voicing a demand for work rather than for charity; they are insisting that a man has a right to use his hands and his brain for his own maintenance rather than be left dependent upon soup kitchens or other philanthropic agencies. There is a growing feeling among social agencies that not only as a matter of justice, but as a means of community protection as well, unemployment is a social problem, and that something must be done by the community itself to meet it.

Is there any escape from this *impasse?* Is our economic philosophy to be 'Every man for himself, and the devil take the hindmost'? Is it true that a man has a 'right' to work, or a 'right' to public maintenance if work is not provided? Is there justice in the claim that the worker has a 'right' to be cared for by other means than that offered by the accidental benevolence of other persons more fortunate than himself? Or has the man out of employment no 'rights' at all? Is he of necessity a vicarious sacrifice to modern industry?

The decision as to the right and justice of the worker's claims will determine the policy we ultimately adopt. We shall either leave the worker to his own resources, shall turn him over to organized charity, or accept unemployment as a social burden to be carried in some manner by society, as a community burden like education, police, and health protection.

There is a historical explanation of the attitude we have heretofore assumed toward this subject — an explanation born of the *laissez-faire* philosophy of America, and the very general equality of opportunity which has prevailed up to very recent times. And because of these conditions we have viewed worklessness and poverty as casual or accidental. It was isolated and personal. The assumption was that any one who wanted work could find it, and that a workless man was such

from choice. The laws of our States reflect this point of view. They specifically declared a man out of employment to be a vagrant, subject to arrest and imprisonment for his worklessness. In the city of New York a man who applies for lodging at the municipal lodging-house oftener than seven times in a month is subject to arrest and imprisonment in the workhouse.

The law and the public opinion behind the law have not kept pace with the changed industrial conditions, with the passing of domestic industry and the coming of the machine, with the great aggregations of capital which employ tens of thousands of men, and the closing of the mills of which leaves them without other opportunity for employment. In addition the great West, which for centuries drew the restless and discontented to its bosom, is now inclosed, and as a consequence increasing population has been thrown back upon the cities. The surplus population surrounds the mill and the factory; it has gone to the mines, where it stands ready to take the jobs of those inside, and by virtue of its hunger depresses the wage-scale of those already employed. In every city there is always a residuum of workless men driven by hunger and fear, and increased to portentous proportions during periods of industrial depression such as recently have periodically afflicted the country.

It is this change in the structure of society and the passing of the opportunity of an earlier age that have made unemployment a social rather than an individual problem. Labor is helpless under present-day conditions. It no longer owns the tools with which it works. And labor protests that organized charity is an inadequate recognition of the situation. It says that it is an arrogant assumption for one class to determine the personal worthiness or unworthiness of another class, when the worthiness or unworthiness of that class is the result of industrial conditions which the worker cannot control. Furthermore, labor is beginning to assert: 'We are here; we came into the world through no choice of our own; we have given the best of our years to society, and society has not even given us a living wage in return. And we protest that society has no right to use us in good times and to slough us off in bad times, or to turn us over to self-organized charitable societies supported by another class, which assumes the right to determine upon such inconclusive evidence as its agents find whether we shall receive aid or be permitted to starve.'

Labor says further: 'Capital keeps its machines in repair during bad times, it pays interest on its borrowed capital, it insures and maintains its factories, and bears the burden of depreciation and decay whether times are good or bad. (Labor is merely a part of the industrial organism, and industry or society should care for the human cogs in the industrial machine just as it cares for its inanimate investments.) This being true, society has no right to shift the cost and misery of unemployment to the shoulders of the weak and defenseless, who are least able to bear it and who, under existing conditions, have no power to make work, to acquire modern tools, or in any other way to control the industry which they serve.'

This is the new note in the problem of unemployment. It is heard in the conferences of social workers, and is beginning to find expression in official action as well.

Strangely enough, most of the countries of Europe have already accepted in part or in whole these new claims of labor; and to an increasing extent either society or industry has undertaken to shift the costs of unemployment to the community itself. Nowhere is the function of charitable relief intrusted to private agencies, and in most of the countries it is, and for generations has been, recognized as a necessary public function. And many of the countries have gone much further and evolved a comprehensive unemployment and social program. As long ago as 1884, Bismarck proclaimed that man has a 'right to work,' which was only another form of expressing the right to live. In a speech in the Reichstag he said, ' Give the working-man a right to work as long as he has health, assure him care when he is sick, assure him maintenance when he is old.' At another time he said, ' Yes, I acknowledge unconditionally the right to work, and I will stand up for it as long as I am in this place.' Continuing, he said of the workless man that ' The healthy workman desirous of work is entitled to say to the state, " Give me work." '

In a similar vein Bismarck protested against the assumption that society had a right to ignore the claims of its weaker members. He said: ' I do not think that doctrines like those of *laissez faire, laissez aller,* " pure Manchesterdom in politics," " He who is not strong enough to stand must be knocked down and trodden to the ground," " To him that hath shall be given, and from him that hath not shall be taken away even that which he hath "— that doctrines like these should be applied in the state, and especially in a monarchial, paternally governed state. On the other hand, I believe that those who profess horror at the intervention of the state for the protection of the weak lay themselves open to the suspicion that they are desirous of using their strength for the benefit of a portion, for the oppression of the rest, and that they will be chagrined as soon as this design is disturbed by any action of the government.'

These statements were made thirty years ago. During the intervening years Germany has worked out a thoroughgoing program for the protection of the working-classes — a program that has since become the model of all Europe. It has been copied by Denmark, Switzerland, and Great Britain, and to a considerable extent in Latin countries as well. It is a policy that educates the child and cares for its health; that inspects mills, mines, factories, and conditions of employment; that protects the worker from accident and disease; and through insurance shifts to the employers, the employees, and the state the cost of accident, sickness, old age, and invalidity. In some Continental cities, and now in Great Britain and Denmark, the hazards of non-employment are borne by the community through social insurance, just as are the other hazards of the working-classes. The state itself has become the guardian of the poor, just as was the church in medieval times. Public protection has been substituted for private aid. Instead of charity, there is a beginning of justice. Human labor is recognized as part of a vast industrial organism, to be protected and preserved as an asset of the highest value to the state.

To begin with, there is a labor exchange in every city of importance in Germany. There were 323 such exchanges in 1911, through which over 1,000,000 positions were filled. These employment agencies have largely supplanted private agencies. They are supported partly by public, partly by private, funds. Every local agency is connected with a central agency, which acts as a clearing-house for the entire state, and through periodic reports from all over the country it places the jobless man in connection with the manless job. During the summer months seasonal employment is found upon the farms.

Gründlichkeit characterizes the German Empire, and the labor exchanges are thorough. They study each individual applicant, and fit him to the job for which he is suited. In this way the agencies command the respect of the employer as well as of the employee. And the buildings in which the exchanges are housed are in keeping with the seriousness with which the problem is treated. The exchanges are not located in the basement of a dilapidated building, as is common in this country. They are not treated as a catch basin for the spoilsman. Rather, the employees are highly trained, socially minded men, deeply interested in the problem. The labor exchange of Berlin, the largest in the empire, occupies a handsome four-story building on Gormann-strasse, which opens upon two streets. It contains every provision for the service which it renders. There are public baths in the basement. In another part is a medical dispensary, where the men are inspected by physicians detailed for the purpose. Food is supplied at a low cost, while cobblers and tailors repair the shoes and the clothes of the waiting workmen for an insignificant charge. In the main hall, which accommodates from twelve hundred to fifteen hundred persons, men sit at their ease, with a glass of beer before them, or play at games of checkers, dominoes, or cards. The whole institution suggests a working-men's club. It is informal, comfortable, and inviting. And the surprising thing about the men in these exchanges is their cleanliness, dignity, and freedom from that haunting fear common among the workless men upon the streets of America. Everything possible is done to maintain the worker in a condition of efficiency and to protect his self-respect from impairment.

In the Berlin exchange there are separate registers for the skilled and unskilled workers, and another exchange for women. At one end of the great hall is a clearing-office, with complete card-indexes, where the names of the men and the opportunities of employment are enrolled and classified. When a request comes for an employee, men are called forward in the order of their registration, and are advised of the opportunity, the wages, and the conditions of employment. Married men are given the preference over unmarried ones. No fees are required in most of the German exchanges, although in Berlin a registration fee of five cents is charged.

The number of positions filled through these exchanges has increased with great rapidity. Of the 323 exchanges in the empire, 267 agencies reported 731,848 positions filled in 1909, 877,000 positions filled in 1910, and 1,000,005 in 1911.

The employment agency does not create work where no work exists. It is not a complete solution of the unemployment problem, it cannot cope with the effects of severe industrial depressions; but it does put the jobless man in the manless job with the minimum loss of time to the employer and the employee. It performs a sifting process by which the right man gets into the right place. It prevents exploitation by private employment agencies, which are often impelled by the commissions they receive to send to an employer men unfitted for the particular job. In addition — and this is most important — the agencies preserve the health, cleanliness, and character of the worker; they improve his efficiency; and in normal times materially reduce the extent of non-employment.

But the labor exchange is only one of many contributions made by Germany to the solution of this problem. Cities make elaborate provision for the temporary care of the wandering or homeless worker. Germany seems to recognize that it is to the advantage of industry that men should be willing to go from place to place, to adjust themselves to the nation's need; that this is an advantage to the state; and that a man should not be arrested as a vagrant when in search of a job. And to meet this situation municipal lodging-houses, or *Herbergen,* are maintained by over five hundred communities. These lodge over 2,000,000 persons a year in 20,000 beds, of whom the majority pay for their lodging either in money or in work. These municipal lodging-houses are dignified, clean, and carry no suggestion of charity. Like the labor exchange, they are part of the machinery of the state for the adjustment of men to their proper jobs. They are a recognition, too, of the uncertainty of industry and the inability of the individual man to control his place of employment.

In order to secure admission to the *Herbergen,* the worker must produce a passport showing where he has been at work. For twelve cents he receives lodging and breakfast, or he can work four hours for them. The work is of a simple sort, such as chopping wood.

These lodging-houses are usually conducted in the same building with, or closely adjacent to, the labor exchanges. They usually contain branches of the municipal savings-banks, in which the laborer can place his funds. In some cities a regular registry of houses, apartments, and rooms is maintained with full descriptive matter, so that the workman can find a place of residence with the least possible delay. Through this house registry he quickly finds in proximity to his work a domicile suited to his purse.

Through these various agencies trampdom has virtually disappeared in Germany. This is particularly true of the south, in the industrial districts along the Rhine.

Many cities supplement these agencies by providing distress or emergency work during the winter months or in times of depression. Public improvements are projected, streets are built, parks are laid out, contracts for paving and sewering are set in motion, so as to provide employment when most needed. And in order to check men from coming to the city to secure this relief, the contracts provide that only resident citizens shall be employed. Few, if any, cities have recognized the declaration of Bismarck that a man has a 'right to work.' Distress work is rather an official appreciation of the terrible waste involved in unemployment — the waste to society and the waste to the worker as well. For unemployment sacrifices not only the individual man, but frequently destroys the family, and throws the mother and children upon the community for relief. Considerations of economy as well as ultimate industrial efficiency unite with humanity in these provisions for the care of the unemployed.

Supplementing these other agencies are labor colonies open to those who have lost their grip through drink or other causes. There are upward of forty of these colonies in the empire. They are not penal colonies, to which men are sent, but are purely voluntary. Men come and go as they will. Over 10,000 persons make use of these colonies every year. The work is exclusively agricultural, and for the most part attracts the unskilled worker. The colonies are located on cheap land, which is brought under cultivation by the labor of the men, who produce potatoes, vegetables, and similar products for their own consumption. A large per cent. of the men who come to the colonies have been in jail, but strangely enough, there is virtually no insubordination and no difficulty in preserving discipline.

These are some of the means employed to prevent waste, to keep the producing power of the nation up to its highest state of efficiency, and to protect the worker.

Of even greater service are the laws for social insurance, through which the worker is protected from accident, sickness, invalidity, and old age. These, too, are part of Bismarck's program. Insurance against sickness is provided for all industrial employees, as is insurance against accident. Even agriculture and household service are covered. Virtually all employees whose salaries exceed $500 a year are protected by these means against the vicissitudes of industry. The employer is bound to provide insurance against accident when he opens his factory, and he pays its entire cost. The sickness insurance, on the other hand, is paid for by the employees, the employer, and the state, the contribution of the employee being deducted by the employer when the wages are paid. Old-age insurance is also provided, part of the fund being contributed by the state, but the bulk of it by the employers and employees in equal parts. The benefits from these funds are paid without litigation. They are looked upon as a matter of right rather than of charity.

Colossal sums are collected every year from these sources. The total income in 1909 amounted to $214,856,000, of which the employers contributed $98,312,000 and the employees $81,414,000. The disbursements for the year amounted to $167,592,-000. In addition to this, free medical services, the attendance of nurses, and hospital treatment are provided. To this extent is the maintenance of the disqualified worker assumed by the state, and to an even greater extent than the amount of money involved are the efficiency, wellbeing, and moral quality of the empire subserved.

This is by no means a complete enumeration of the protective measures which European countries have adopted to shift the costs of industry from the individual to the community. Denmark and Great Britain have evolved a public insurance against unemployment, so that the costs of hard times and seasonal unemployment are shifted from the individual to the group, or from the individual to society itself. This is the most advanced legislative step taken by any country. It involves an official recognition of the fact that the old individualism of an earlier day has passed away, and that the individual alone should not be required to suffer from social conditions which have passed beyond his power to control. America remains almost the only advanced nation that continues to ignore the fact that conditions of an earlier age have long since passed away. Social thought still treats the worker as a free man, able to turn his hand to employment if he wills, when in reality the land has been closed against him, the tools of employment are in other hands, and the industrial system is wholly beyond his control. We have not yet begun to organize, to provide means for clearance in industry such as the banks have maintained for a generation, we have not recognized the necessity for housing the itinerant worker, nor have we accepted the social obligation to shift to society the costs of sickness, accident, invalidity, and old age, all incidents of modern industry and all a proper charge against society itself.

VI

THE PROBLEM OF LIVING THINGS

JOHN BURROUGHS

[*Independent*, October 2, 1913. By permission.]

All living bodies, when life leaves them, go back to the earth from whence they came. What was it in the first instance that gathered their elements from the earth and built them up into such wonderful mechanisms? If we say it was nature, do we mean by nature a physical force or an immaterial principle? Did the earth itself bring forth a man, or did something breathe upon the inert clay, and it became a living spirit?

Such inquiries bring us at once face to face with the question of the nature and origin of life—a question which is the source of a good deal of mental activity in our time, both among scientific men and philosophers.

As life is a physical phenomenon, appearing in a concrete physical world, it is, to that extent, within the domain of physical science, and appeals to the scientific mind. Physical science is at home only in the experimental, the verifiable. Its domain ends where that of philosophy begins. It cannot go behind visible phenomena and ask 'Why?' or 'Whither?' This is the province of philosophy. It is incompetent to discuss the question of the origin of life from no life, or of something from nothing, because here its method of verification cannot be applied. Science is held by the biogenetic law—life only from antecedent life. Until it can bring about the reaction called life in its laboratories, it is tethered by this law. In order to make a start at all, it is compelled to assume the potentiality of life in matter itself, as most recent bio-physicists do, and to regard its advent into this world as a natural and not a miraculous event— as natural as the birth of a baby, inscrutable as are the mysteries that lie back of it.

So far as life involves a psychic principle or force, it is beyond the scope of positive science, and falls within the domain of philosophy.

THE ORIGIN OF LIFE

The question of how life arose in a universe of dead matter is just as baffling a question to the ordinary mind, as how the universe itself arose. If we assume that the germs of life drifted to us from other spheres, propelled by the rays of the sun, or some other celestial agency, as certain modern scientific philosophers have assumed, we have only removed the mystery farther away from us. If we assume that it came by spontaneous generation, as Haeckel and others assume, then we are only cutting a knot which we cannot untie. The god of spontaneous generation is as miraculous as any other god. We cannot break the causal sequence with a miracle. If something came from nothing, then there is not only the end of the problem, but also the end of our boasted science.

Science is at home in discussing all the material manifestations of life — the parts played by colloids and ferments, by fluids and gases, and all the organic compounds, and by mechanical and chemical principles; it may analyze and tabulate all life processes, and show the living body as a most wonderful and complex piece of mechanism, but before the question of the origin of life itself it stands dumb, and, when speaking through such a man as Tyndall, it also stands humble and reverent. After Tyndall had, to his own satisfaction, reduced all like phenomena to mechanical attraction and repulsion, he stood with uncovered head before what he called the ' mystery and miracle of vitality.' The mystery and miracle lie in the fact that in the organic world the same elements combine with results so different from those of the inorganic world. Something seems to have inspired them with a new purpose. In the inorganic world, the primary elements go their ceaseless round from compound to compound, from solid to fluid or gaseous, and back again, forming the world of inert matter as we know it, but in the organic world the same elements form thousands of new combinations unknown to them before, and thus give rise to the myriad forms of life that inhabit the earth.

The much debated question of the nature and origin of life has lately found an interesting exponent in Prof. Benjamin Moore, of the University of Liverpool. His volume on the subject in the 'Home University Library' is very readable, and, in many respects, convincing. At least, so far as it is the word of exact science on the subject it is convincing; so far as it is speculative, or philosophical, it is or is not convincing, according to the type of mind of the reader. Professor Moore is not a bald mechanist or materialist like Professor Loeb, or Ernest Haeckel, nor is he an idealist or spiritualist, like Henri Bergson or Sir Oliver Lodge. He may be called a scientific vitalist. He keeps close to lines of scientific research as these lines lead him through the maze of the primordial elements of matter, from electron to atom, from atom to molecule, from molecule to colloids, and so up to the border of the living world. His analysis of the processes of molecular physics as they appear in the organism, leads him to recognize and to name a new force, or a new manifestation of force, which he hesitates to call vital, because of the associations of this term with a pre-scientific age, but which he calls ' biotic energy.'

THE ENERGY OF LIFE

Biotic energy is peculiar to living bodies, and ' there are precisely the same criteria for its existence,' says Professor Moore, ' as for the existence of any one of the inorganic energy types, viz., a set of discrete phenomena; and its nature is as mysterious to us as the cause of any one of these inorganic forms about which also we know so little.

' It is biotic energy which guides the development of the ovum, which regulates the exchanges of the cell, and causes such phenomena as nerve impulse, muscular contraction, and gland secretion, and it is a form of energy which arises in colloidal structures, just as magnetism appears in iron, or radio-activity in uranium or radium, and in its manifestations it undergoes exchanges with other forms of energy, in the same manner as these do among one another.'

Like Professor Henderson, of Harvard, whose volume on *The Fitness of the Environment* has lately appeared, Professor Moore concedes to the vitalists about all they claim — namely, that there is some form of force or manifestation of energy peculiar to living bodies, and one that cannot be adequately described in terms of physics and chemistry. Professor Moore says this biotic energy ' arises in colloidal structures,' and so far as bio-chemistry can make out, arises *spontaneously* and gives rise to that marvelous bit of mechanism, the cell. In the cell appears ' a form of energy unknown outside life processes which leads the mazy dance of life from point to point, each new development furnishing a starting point for the next one.' It not only leads the dance along our own line of descent from our remote ancestors — it leads the dance along the long road of evolution from the first unicellular form in the dim paleozoic seas to the complex and highly specialized forms of our own day.

The secret of this life force, or biotic energy, according to Professor Moore, is in the keeping of matter itself. The steps or stages from the depths of matter by which life arose, lead up from that imaginary something, the electron to the inorganic colloids, or to the crystallo-colloids, which are the threshold of life, each stage showing some new transformation of energy. There must be an all-potent energy transformation before we can get chemical energy out of physical energy, and then biotic energy out of chemical energy. This transformation of inorganic energy into life energy cannot be traced or repeated in the laboratory, yet science believes the secret will sometime be in its hands. It is here that the materialistic philosophers, such as Professors Moore and Loeb, differ from the spiritualistic philosophers, such as Bergson, Sir Oliver Lodge, Professor Thompson, and others.

MORE THAN MECHANISM

Professor Moore has no sympathy with those narrow mechanistic views that see in the life processes 'no problems save those of chemistry and physics.' 'Each link in the living chain may be physico-chemical, but the chain as a whole, and its purpose, is something else.' He draws an analogy from the production of music in which purely physical factors are concerned; the laws of harmonics account for all; but back of all is something that is not mechanical and chemical — there is the mind of the composer, and the performers, and the auditors, and something that takes cognizance of the whole effect. A complete human philosophy cannot be built upon physical science alone. He thinks the evolution of life from inert matter is of the same type as the evolution of one form of matter from another, or the evolution of one form of energy from another — a mystery, to be sure, but little more startling in the one case than in the other. 'The fundamental mystery lies in the existence of those entities, or things which we call matter and energy,' out of the play and interaction of which all life phenomena have arisen. Organic evolution is a series of energy exchanges and transformations from lower to higher, but science is powerless to go behind the phenomena presented and name or verify the underlying mystery. Only philosophy can do this. And Professor Moore turns philosopher when he says there is beauty and design in it all, 'and an eternal purpose which is ever progressing.'

BERGSON'S CREATIVE EVOLUTION

Bergson sets forth his views of evolution in terms of literature and philosophy. Professor Moore embodies similar views in his volume, set forth in terms of molecular science. Both make evolution a creative and a continuous process. Bergson lays the emphasis upon the cosmic spirit interacting with matter. Professor Moore lays the emphasis upon the indwelling potencies of matter itself (probably the same spirit conceived of in different terms). Professor Moore philosophizes as truly as does Bergson when he says 'there must exist a whole world of living creatures which the microscope has never shown us, leading up to the bacteria and the protozoa. The brink of life lies not at the production of protozoa and bacteria, which are highly developed inhabitants of our world, but away down among the colloids, and the beginning of life was not a fortuitous event occurring millions of years ago and never again repeated, but one which in its primordial stages keeps on repeating itself all the time in our generation. So that if all intelligent creatures were by some holocaust destroyed, up out of the depths in process of millions of years, intelligent beings would once more emerge.' This passage shows what a speculative leap or a flight the scientific mind is at times compelled to take when it ventures beyond the bounds of positive methods. It is good philosophy, I hope, but we cannot call it science. Thrilled with cosmic emotion, Walt Whitman made a similar daring assertion:

There is no stoppage, and never can be stop-
    page,
If I, you, and the worlds, and all beneath or
    upon their surfaces, were this moment
    reduced back to a pallid float, it would
    not avail in the long run,
We should surely bring up again where we
    now stand,
And surely go as much farther, and then far-
    ther and farther.

Evolution is creative, whether it works in matter as Bergson describes, or whether its path lies up through electrons and atoms and molecules, as Professor Moore describes. There is something that creates and makes matter plastic to its will. Whether we call matter 'the living garment of God,' as Goethe did, or a reservoir of creative energy, as Tyndall and his school did, and as Professor Moore still does, we are paying homage to a power that is super-material. Life came to our earth, says Professor Moore, through a 'well regulated orderly development,' and it 'comes to every mother earth of the universe in the maturity of her creation when the conditions arrive within suitable limits.' That no intelligent beings appeared upon the earth for millions upon millions of years, that for whole geologic ages there was no creature upon the earth with more brains than a snail possesses, shows the almost infinitely slow progress of development, and that there has been no arbitrary or high-handed exercise of creative power. The universe is not run on principles of modern business efficiency, and man is at the head of living forms, not by the fiat of some omnipotent power, some superman, but as the result of the operation of forces that balk at no delay, or waste, or failure, and that are dependent upon the infinitely slow ripening and amelioration of both cosmic and terrestrial conditions.

THE TRANSITION TO LIFE

We do not get rid of God by any such dictum, but we get rid of the anthropomorphic views which we have so long been wont to read into the processes of nature. We dehumanize the universe, but we do not render it the less grand and mysterious. Professor Le Dantec says, 'Life is only a surface accident in the history of the thermic evolution of the globe,' and Professor Moore points out to us how life came to a cooling planet as soon as the temperature became low enough for certain chemical combinations to appear. There must first be oxides and saline compounds, there must be carbonates of calcium and magnesium, and the like. As the temperature falls, more and more complex compounds, such as life requires, appear; till, in due time, carbon dioxide and water are at hand, and life can make a start. At the white heat of some of the fixed stars, the primary chemical elements are not yet evolved; but more and more elements appear, and more and more complex compounds are formed as the cooling process progresses.

'This note cannot be too strongly sounded that as matter is allowed capacity for assuming complex forms, those complex forms appear. As soon as oxides can be there, oxides appear; when temperature admits of carbonates, then carbonates are forthwith formed. These are experiments which any chemist can today repeat in a crucible. And on a cooling planet, as soon as temperature will admit the presence of life, then life appears, as the evidence of geology shows us.' When we speak of the beginning of life, it is not clear just what we mean. The unit of all organized bodies is the cell, but the cell is itself an organized body, and must have organic matter to feed upon. Hence the cell is only a more complex form of more primitive living matter. As we go down the scale toward the inorganic, can we find the point where the living and the non-living meet and become one? 'Life had to surge a long way up from the depths before a green plant cell came into being.' When the green plant cell was found, life was fairly launched. This plant cell, in the form of chlorophyll, by the aid of water and the trace of carbon dioxide in the air, began to store up the solar energy in fruit and grain and woody tissue, and thus furnish power to run all forms of life machinery.

The materialists or naturalists are right in urging that we live in a much more wonderful universe than we have ever imagined, and that in matter itself sleep potencies and possibilities not dreamt of in our philosophy. The world of complex though invisible activities which science reveals all about us, the solar and stellar energies raining upon us from above, the terrestrial energies and influences playing through us from below, the transformations and transmutations taking place on every hand, the terrible alertness and potency of the world of inert matter as revealed by a flash of lightning, the mysteries of chemical affinity, of magnetism, of radio-activity, all point to deep beneath deep in matter itself. It is little wonder that men who dwell habitually upon these things and are saturated with the spirit and traditions of laboratory investigation, should believe that in some way matter itself holds the mystery of the origin of life. On the other hand, a different type of mind, the mere imaginative, artistic and religious type, recoils from the materialistic view.

The sun is the source of all terrestrial energy, but the different forms that energy takes — in the plant, in the animal, in the brain of man — this type of mind is bound to ask questions about that. Gravity pulls matter down; life lifts it up; chemical forces pull it to pieces; vital forces draw it together and organize it; the winds and the waters dissolve and scatter it; vegetation recaptures it and integrates and gives it new qualities. At every turn, minds like that of Sir Oliver Lodge are compelled to think of life as a principle or force doing something with matter. The physico-chemical forces will not do in the hands of man what they do in the hands of Nature. Such minds, therefore, feel justified in thinking that something which we call 'the hands of Nature,' plays a part — some principle or force which the hands of men do not hold.

VII

BEQUEATHED ENERGY

[*Nation* (London, England), February 13, 1915. By permission.]

If there is one pitfall more than another against which the young Darwinian is warned by his teachers, it is that of supposing for one moment that an acquired character can be inherited. However lustily the blacksmith may swing his hammer, till his own muscles swell like loaves, his son will not thereby be more than normally developed. And so, when a race of pigeons produces, generation after generation, more and more expert tumblers, the diligence applied by a particular bird to the art does not give an extra advance to his progeny. It is only a symptom of the progress of the tumbling habit, long ago determined by the departure in that direction of a germ cell. Conversely, the first dodo that neglected its flying-exercise did not thereby condemn its chicks to a weakness of wing likely to go further if it was not checked. It was the environment that had affected the germ cell of the first lazy dodo. We are allowed to believe, perhaps, that ever

so many generations of special exercise or idleness added together would produce an heritable quality — as though a thousand times nothing would make something 5 — but we must not think that somatic modifications acquired by one generation can be handed to the next.

A somewhat destructive interpretation reconciles most of us to this hard prohibi-10 tion. Almost the only malcontent is Professor Henslow, who, in the realm of botany, refuses to give up the right of a parent to bequeath something of its individual experience. And now, from 15 America, comes a new protagonist who, for all he says of them, may never have heard of Weismann, Mendel, or even Darwin, but who puts in a claim for somatic inheritance, and backs it with substantial 20 credentials. Mr. Caspar L. Redfield's book is called *Dynamic Evolution* (Putnam). His message is that the breeder for specific quality, whether in a trotter, a milker, or a setter, must be careful to 25 have sires and dams at their highest dynamic development. The surplus energy that is theirs will then pass to their progeny, and give them a better start in life than the parent had. The significance of 30 his claim does not yet appear. Some of the surplus energy of the sire comes from growth, and is racial. By all means, says every school, breed only from mature parents. That is elementary wisdom. But 35 Mr. Redfield asserts that the energy that comes from work also can be inherited. Does that matter? Have we denied that the energetic blacksmith will not have an energetic son? But, says Mr. Redfield, 40 you cannot have energy without location and direction, and in whatever organ work has put the energy, in that organ will it be inherited. He could scarcely go nearer to saying that the blacksmith's 45 son will inherit unusual biceps.

Excessive use would soon thin out the word 'energy' into an empty name. It seems apt enough, however, to explain the quality that distinguishes the Amer-50 ican trotter. A hundred years ago, there was not a horse in the world that could trot a mile in three minutes. Now, the record has shrunk to two minutes. 'Whence came this increase in amount of 55 available energy?' asks Mr. Redfield. 'You can't get something out of nothing.' The usual reply to the question is that when trotting came into fashion, enormous numbers of the trotting strain were produced, and by continual selection among these great numbers, swifter and swifter animals were found. The 3.10 trotter was the best of, say, a hundred of its contemporaries, the 2.30 trotter the best of a thousand, and the 2.10 trotter the best of twenty thousand. By multiplying the numbers, we have given greater scope to the tendency to vary.

Mr. Redfield seems to have a better reply than that. The method of the breeders of trotting horses has been, from one cause and another, perfectly free from the fallacy of inherited acquired characters. One horse is trained and raced, and another of the same family kept for reproducing. So long as the right blood is obtained, owners prefer to send their mares, not to the champion himself, even if he be available, but to a brother or uncle or nephew. But line after line has falsified the hopes of its backers, and time after time the champion trotter of its day has sprung from a neglected pedigree. Whenever that has happened, it has been possible to point at one or both of the factors of superior dynamic development in the immediate ancestors of the new champion. Those two factors are time and work. A horse may acquire his energy speedily on the racetrack, or in the course of more years of a normal, healthy life. Thus, of the fifty-eight sires of stallions able to do the mile in two minutes and ten seconds, forty-five with records averaged nearly ten years of age, and thirteen without records averaged nearly fourteen years of age.

The reader will see that, in spite of what we have said, champions do become the sires of champions, and that in considerable numbers. That is just the point. There are twenty or thirty thousand registered trotters, and it is estimated that only 5 per cent. of these are bred from parents with records. There are only a hundred and eighty capable of trotting a mile in two minutes and ten seconds or under, and of these, 67 per cent. were by sires with records. In one of his tables, Mr. Redfield compares the respective progeny of full brothers. It can, perhaps, be understood that a non-record horse will sire more foals than his record brother. Those that reach the class of performers are compared, with the result that eighty-eight horses with records sired

thirty-three performers apiece, and ninety-six full brothers of the same horses without records sired ten performers apiece. Not content with that, he examines the history of those non-record sires, and finds that some of them were trained though not raced, and that these had a better average of performer progeny than the others. In other words, he shows by individual cases, and from large masses of fact, that a horse that has been practised for speed is more likely to have speedy offspring than another horse of the selfsame blood that has not been practised. The energy it has acquired by work is handed on, and endows the foal in the organs that acquired it in the parent.

In a recent book, Professor Arthur Thompson especially warned us against believing that the setter could bequeath the skill it had itself acquired. The setter is one of Mr. Redfield's object lessons. Laverack began with a 'stray pair he purchased from a neighbor,' and in forty years had 'the best setters in the world.' He simply bred in and in, working one pair of dogs in the field till they were old, then breeding another pair from them.

The results were so astonishing that experts would not believe that his methods were correctly stated, the age at which his dogs bred (six, seven, or eight years) being as great a stumbling-block as the fact that he never took in new blood. Descendants of these dogs, crossed with those of Llewellin, founded the American strain about 1870, and an examination of the pedigrees of the six champion American setters of to-day proves that their lines of descent are 'through the dogs which were trained and ran for prizes in field trials,' and the average time between the generations is over six years. Younger sires than that, however good they were, have been eliminated as ancestors, except one which was trained for field trials 'at a very early age.'

That is, in part, the case presented by this searcher of pedigrees. It may be that its hostility to the doctrine of somatic unteachableness is modified by the statement that this dynamic inheritance mainly follows the same line as does secondary sexual character. Thus, the energy of the dam does not go as available energy to her son, but reappears in the daughters of the next generation. In its simplest terms, it means that the young but thoroughly adult father gives to his son no more than the racial inheritance and possibilities that he himself received. In a few years' time he is another being, and therefore another father. Circumstances have led to the greater exercise of some set of muscles, some function of the brain, or to responsiveness of the nerves to some certain stimulus. These exercises have induced an accretion of energy somewhere, and something passes in the same direction to the son. Perhaps this is a very volatile part of one's inheritance. If not closely followed up, perhaps it soon vanishes. In a state of nature, whatever one receives is usually made the most of. It may be that a woodpecker that has dealt with particularly hard trees cannot hand on his acquired skill. But it may be that he can hand on the increase of dynamic power stored in his neck muscles, and that may make an unusual woodpecker of his son.

VIII

TYPHUS, WAR'S DREAD ALLY, BEATEN

VAN BUREN THORNE, M.D.

[*New York Times,* April 18, 1915. By permission.]

The announcement of the discovery of a protective vaccine against typhus fever, the dreadful scourge that dogs the heels of war, following closely upon the confirmation of the germ origin of the disease by repeated demonstrations of a distinct causative agent visible under the microscope, is but another instance of the accuracy of modern laboratory methods and the continual progress of medical science.

The concrete view of these achievements is that they could not have occurred at a more opportune moment in the history of the world. The stricken countries of Europe, already devastated by the wrath of man, are cowering beneath the brooding shadow of disease; and science, represented by the best and bravest of its exponents, is rushing from the four quarters of the earth the cumulative resources of a thousand laboratories to wage a war with Death.

The marvel of these two laboratory achievements is that they are the products of the labor of one so young. Dr. Harry Plotz of the Pathological Laboratory of Mount Sinai Hospital in this city is not yet twenty-five years old. He looks younger. It was strange, indeed, to listen to a youth unravel intricate problems of bacteriology in the presence of a gathering of distinguished pathologists at the Academy of Medicine on Wednesday evening last.

The discovery of the protective vaccine against typhus was made public at the same meeting at which the young bacteriologist told of the experimental labors of himself and his co-workers in isolating the bacillus of typhus fever.

While there has been no opportunity to demonstrate the efficiency of the vaccine in the presence of the disease itself, Dr. Plotz and his co-workers recommend its employment. And, in this connection, a high compliment already has been paid to the young discoverer: Dr. Hans Zinsser, the eminent professor of bacteriology of Columbia University, had himself inoculated with the protective vaccine before sailing on April 3 on his perilous mission as a member of the American Red Cross Sanitary Commission to cope with the epidemics of typhus in Serbia and Austria-Hungary.

The devotion of an entire evening by the New York Pathological Society (of which Professor Zinsser, by the way, is president) to the consideration of typhus fever, and particularly as to its origin, with Dr. Plotz as the central figure, cannot be regarded in any other light than as a distinct triumph for the Mount Sinai bacteriologist.

The first announcement of his discovery of the causative agent of typhus appeared in the New York *Times* on May 12, 1914. It was stated in the article that he would make public his discovery on the following day in a paper he was to read before the Association of American Physicians at Atlantic City. It was further made known in the *Times* that Dr. Plotz had determined as the result of the isolation of the germ that it was also the causative factor of the acute infectious ailment known as Brill's disease, which Dr. Nathan E. Brill of this city had classed as a distinctive malady. Dr. Plotz maintained that Brill's disease was in reality typhus fever of a mild type.

Dr. Plotz was present at the Atlantic

City meeting, but his paper was not incorporated in the program. Neither was he called upon to address the gathering. No public reference was made by any physician present to typhus fever or its origin. When the writer of this article, who was present at the meeting, inquired of one of the officers of the association whether or not Dr. Plotz was to be invited to read his paper, the officer replied in the most emphatic manner:

'No such subject as the discovery of the typhus germ is to be discussed here.'

Privately, the writer was informed by various physicians present that the young bacteriologist, just a year out of college, was not to read his paper for the simple reason that the news of his discovery had first been announced in a lay journal, namely, the New York *Times*.

It is fitting to emphasize here, however, the fact that Dr. Plotz did not furnish the news of his discovery to the *Times*, nor was he aware that this newspaper was in possession of the news until he saw it in print.

The meeting at the academy on Wednesday evening was the first public occasion, therefore, on which Dr. Plotz had an opportunity to discuss his work in the presence of a body of physicians best calculated to appraise its value. He was acclaimed by them as a scientific investigator of the first order.

Following his failure to be called upon at Atlantic City, Dr. Plotz prepared a brief preliminary paper, written in technical terms, in which he announced the isolation of an organism which occurred in typhus fever patients and which he believed to be the causative factor of the disease. He also obtained the same organism from patients suffering from Brill's disease. This paper appeared in the issue of the *Journal of the American Medical Association,* published on May 16, 1914.

The young scientist's paper of Wednesday proved to be an elaboration of his preliminary report, and contained a wealth of highly technical detail embodying the precise methods of isolating and cultivating pathogenic bacteria.

After identifying the typhus germ as the agent of Brill's disease, he discarded the term 'Brill's disease,' referring to it thereafter as endemic typhus as distinguished (and distinguishable by its milder clinical course) from the virulent and dreaded malady known as 'European epidemic typhus,' which already is said to have claimed 65,000 victims in Serbia, among them two heroic American physicians, and threatens to overrun the warring nations on the Continent, as well as their neutral neighbors.

If Dr. Plotz's findings relative to the identity of European epidemic typhus and Brill's disease are correct, and this is now vouched for by high authority, then we have typhus fever right here in New York, and have had sporadic cases for years. But the hygienic excellence of the systems of sanitation devised by the local health officers have ever prevented it from becoming a menace to the community. And it is now some twenty-six or twenty-eight years since a case of European typhus has had an opportunity to spread contagion in this city, thanks to the watchfulness of the health officers of the port of New York.

It is true, however, that this ominous infection does sometimes reach our outposts at quarantine, as Dr. Plotz related in his paper, for it was this very circumstance that enabled him to start an investigation into the origin of the disease. He learned of the presence of typhus patients removed from ships to the isolation hospitals in the lower bay from Dr. Joseph O'Connell, health officer of the port, who permitted him to obtain blood specimens from these patients.

Dr. Plotz had formed an opinion as to the probable cause of typhus before submitting the blood of typhus patients to laboratory tests. This opinion was based on various theoretical considerations and on previous investigations. He considered it advisable to begin his search by looking for a so-called anaerobic organism as the causative agent of the acute infectious disease of unknown origin known as Brill's disease, and which owed its differentiation from other fevers, especially short-term typhoid fevers, to the keen clinical insight of Dr. Brill. An anaerobic organism is one which thrives best or thrives only when deprived of oxygen or air.

He used the anaerobic methods in examining the blood of six cases of Brill's disease, and isolated the same kind of bacillus from five of the six. He ascribes his failure in the sixth instance to the fact that the blood was not taken from the patient until after the crisis of the disease had passed. Subsequent investigation disclosed the fact that the bacillus is present in the blood when the fever is at its height, but disappears after the crisis.

Other investigators have isolated various micro-organisms from cases of typhus and Brill's disease, but none of them resembled that obtained by Dr. Plotz nor were they constantly present. The Plotz bacillus is constant both in its presence and appearance.

It is also true that in recent years other investigators have declared that Brill's disease is probably a mild or modified typhus. Some two or three years ago a discussion was carried on between two or three medical officers of the United States Government and Dr. Brill relative to the nature of the disease, the Federal physicians maintaining that it was typhus fever.

In accordance with the same belief and after having isolated the bacillus from the cases of Brill's disease, Dr. Plotz took specimens of blood from half a dozen patients suffering from European epidemic typhus in the hospitals at quarantine, the patients having been removed from transatlantic vessels, and subjected the blood to bacteriological tests in the Mount Sinai laboratories. His co-workers were Dr. George Baehr, like himself a graduate of the College of Physicians and Surgeons of Columbia University, and Dr. Peter K. Olitzky, a graduate of the Medical College of Cornell University.

From all of the typhus cases Dr. Plotz was able to recover a micro-organism apparently identical with that isolated from the cases of Brill's disease.

In order to check up or verify this discovery, the blood of 198 control cases (that is, cases in which typhus fever or Brill's disease were not present, but in which other diseases such as influenza were diagnosed) was treated and examined in exactly the same manner, but the bacillus was not found in any specimen.

The evidence indicated that the virus was present in the blood during the febrile period of the disease, that it was non-filterable and hence most likely of microscopic size, and that it was of bacterial rather than of protozoal origin.

Subjected to microscopical examination, the agent was seen to be a small bacillus; pleomorphic, or occurring in more than one form, varying from nine-tenths to 1.93 microns in length, the breadth being from one-fifth to three-fifths of the length.

When first isolated, Dr. Plotz says in his paper, the organism grows only anaerobically, or without air or oxygen, but after a time it can be grown aerobically, or in the presence of air.

During the febrile period of the disease, the organism was yielded from the blood in 100 per cent. of typhus fever cases. The blood of thirty-seven patients suffering from the endemic type, heretofore known as Brill's disease, the cultures of which were examined at various times, yielded the bacillus in 53 per cent. of cases.

From a pure culture of the bacillus, inoculations were made into the peritoneal cavities of two guinea pigs. The incubation period of the infection proved to be from twenty-four to forty-eight hours, for within that period there was a rise of temperature, which remained high for four or five days, and which dropped rapidly by crisis.

This clinical picture corresponded exactly with the result obtained in guinea pigs inoculated with the blood of typhus fever patients, with the single exception that the incubation period is shorter.

It was proved also that serum from a convalescing typhus fever patient had bactericidal action against the organism obtained from both Brill's disease and European epidemic typhus.

This paragraph ended Dr. Plotz's preliminary report:

'In a later communication it is proposed to consider the cultural characteristics of the organism, its agglutination reactions, the further results of animal experiments, and cross-immunity tests. At the same time the results of studies forming a basis for a possible vaccine prophylaxis and comparative studies of other organisms described by various authors as being found in typhus fever will be reported.'

This promised elaboration was given in detail on Wednesday evening, and the vaccine prophylaxis hinted at in the earlier communication resulted in the journey of Professor Zinsser and his fellow-scientists to the stricken fields of Europe after inoculation with an agent which it is hoped will prove effective against the acquisition of the infection.

Those who sailed with Professor Zinsser on the expedition, financed by the Red Cross and the Rockefeller Foundation, are Dr. Thomas W. Jackson of Philadelphia, Dr. Andrew W. Sellarde, Dr. George C. Shattuck, and Dr. Francis B. Grinnell of the Harvard Medical School; Dr. F. W. Caldwell, Hobart D. Brink, W. S. Standifer, and Luis de la Pena.

The two latter were members of the staff of General William C. Gorgas in the sanitary campaign in the Panama Canal Zone. Dr. Nicolle, the French expert on typhus, has been invited to coöperate with the commission.

The members of the expedition will meet in Saloniki, and proceed to the districts of Austria-Hungary which are stricken with epidemics of typhus, cholera, and other contagious diseases.

When the Rockefeller expedition was projected Dr. Richard P. Strong, Professor of Tropical Diseases at the Harvard Medical School, was appointed leader. He is already in Europe. More recently, however, announcement has been made that General Gorgas, Surgeon General of the United States Army, the world's foremost sanitarian, is to proceed to Serbia to assume charge of the commission.

Prior to the announcement of the proposal to have General Gorgas take charge of the work, he stated that he believed the commission would win the fight against disease in Serbia. He characterized the expedition as the most efficient ever organized in the history of modern sanitation.

Dr. Samuel Taylor Darling, the bacteriologist who was associated with General Gorgas in the Canal Zone, arrived here from Colon on Tuesday. It is reported that he will accompany his former chief to Serbia. He went to South Africa in 1913 with General Gorgas when the latter was invited to go there by the Rand mine owners to see what could be done to lessen the mortality among miners.

Now, as to the disease typhus fever itself. The fact has been established that the infection is communicated from one to another by a carrier, namely, the body louse. Hence it is that the disease becomes epidemic in places where large numbers are crowded together under insanitary conditions. It is the invariable sequel of prolonged warfare where large numbers are wounded.

The disease has broken out under various conditions other than warfare as an epidemic — for example, in prisons, on shipboard, and in hospitals. Hence it has been called prison or jail fever, hospital fever, and ship's fever. It has also been known as spotted fever.

Clinically, typhus is marked by a high temperature, great mental and physical depression, and skin eruptions. It lasts for about two weeks. There are no specific lesions, except enlargement of the spleen. It seems to be disappearing in those centers where municipal hygiene is making steady advances.

Dr. Plotz received a real ovation at the conclusion of his paper on Wednesday evening from the 250 or more physicians assembled. He ended by announcing that Dr. William H. Welch, the distinguished head of the medical department of Johns Hopkins University, had christened the newly discovered germ of typhus. It is called bacillus typhii exanthematici.

Among those present were some of the world's foremost medical investigators, and following the reading of two papers bearing on Dr. Plotz's discoveries by his co-workers, Dr. Olitzky and Dr. Baehr, he was the recipient of public congratulations from them. The first one called upon to express his opinion of the work was Dr. Hideyo Noguchi, a famous laboratory worker, attached to the staff of the Rockefeller Institute for Medical Research.

'I believe it must now appear to any person,' said Dr. Noguchi, 'that the organism has been isolated. I congratulate the three physicians on solving the problem of the cause of one of the most mysterious diseases of which we know anything.'

Dr. William Hallock Park, noted as a bacteriologist, and head of the bacteriological department of the board of health of this city, said:

'Dr. Plotz had the mind and the will to do this work, and he has carried it to a successful conclusion.'

Dr. Nathan E. Brill, the discoverer of Brill's disease, ungrudgingly admitted that at last it had been demonstrated beyond question that Brill's disease and typhus are identical, differing only in degree of severity.

'This discovery is a particular gratification to me,' said he warmly. 'This is the first work which has established the absolute identity of the two types of the disease.

'I long ago admitted that they were related, but I contended that this had not been established by the work of Anderson and Goldberger. I admitted the relationship, but denied the identity — which is now established beyond dispute. I doubt, however, the statement that the louse is the only means of communicating the disease from one to another.'

'I congratulate these gentlemen,' said Dr. Samuel J. Meltzer of the Rockefeller Institute, famous in many fields of medical research, 'not only on the way in which they carried on their investigations, but on the manner in which they have presented them to us.'

'Mention has been made of the fact that a vaccine has been made,' said Dr. F. S. Mandelbaum of the Mount Sinai Hospital staff. 'Some of the members of the commission on the way to fight typhus in Serbia, and others who intend to go, have already been inoculated with the vaccine — of course, without any guarantee of its efficacy. They came to us and asked to be inoculated.'

Dr. E. Libman, also of the Mount Sinai staff, interjected a touch of the romance of science into his remarks.

'This discovery was no chance observation,' he said. 'Plotz was worried about Brill's disease when a student. He took the position at Mount Sinai after graduation on purpose to find out the cause of Brill's disease. He found the organism the first time he tried for it.'

Dr. Plotz, whose discoveries may mitigate the menace of typhus, was born in Paterson, New Jersey, in 1890. He attended the schools in Newark, and for a time was a pupil at the Boys' High School in Brooklyn. Later he entered Columbia University and took a combination course which gave him his academic degree from Columbia College and his medical degree from the College of Physicians and Surgeons. He was graduated in 1913, at the head of his class. Upon his graduation he took a competitive examination for pathological interne at Mount Sinai Hospital, and was first among 200 contestants.

IX

JOHN DEWEY'S PHILOSOPHY

RANDOLPH S. BOURNE

[*New Republic,* March 13, 1915. By permission of author and publisher.]

Nothing is more symbolic of Professor Dewey's democratic attitude towards life than the disintegrated array of his published writings. Where the neatly uniform works of William James are to be found in every public library, you must hunt long and far for the best things of the man who, since the other's death, is the most significant thinker in America. Pamphlets and reports of obscure educational societies; school journals, university monographs and philosophical journals, limited to the pedant few; these are the burial-places of much of this intensely alive, futuristic philosophy. For the best educational essays one had to look until very recently to a little compilation made by an unknown London house. The 'Educational Creed,' in style and conciseness and spirit the most admirably popular of all his writings, is, I think, still lost in an out-of-print cheap bulletin in some innocuous series for elementary teachers. 'School and Society,' with some of the wisest words ever set to paper, frightens one away with its infantile cover and its university chaperonage. Only some heterogeneous essays, brilliant but not holding the exact kernel of his thought, and his 'How We Think,' in which is shown that scientific method is simply a sublimely well-ordered copy of our own best and most fruitful habits of thought, have been launched in forms that would reach a wide public. No man, I think, with such universally important things to say on almost every social and intellectual activity of the day, was ever published in forms more ingeniously contrived to thwart the interest of the prospective public.

Professor Dewey's thought is inaccessible because he has always carried his simplicity of manner, his dread of show or self-advertisement, almost to the point of extravagance. In all his psychology there is no place for the psychology of prestige. His democracy seems almost to take that extreme form of refusing to bring one's self or one's ideas to the attention of others. On the college campus or in the lecture-room he seems positively to efface himself. The uncertainty of his silver-gray hair and drooping mustache, of his voice, of his clothes, suggests that he has almost studied the technique of protective coloration. It will do you no good to hear him lecture. His sentences, flowing and exact and lucid when read, you will find strung in long festoons of obscurity between pauses for the awaited right word. The whole business of impressing yourself on other people, of getting yourself over to the people who want to and ought to have you, has simply never come into his ultra-democratic mind.

This incapacity of imagining his own distinction has put him in the paradoxical situation of a revolutionist with an innate contempt for propaganda. His philosophy of 'instrumentalism' has an edge on it that would slash up the habits of thought, the customs and institutions in which our society has been living for centuries. He allies himself personally with every democratic movement, yet will not preach. As we discover in the essay on Maeterlinck, where he shows himself poet as well as philosopher, his tolerant democracy loves all human values, and finds nothing so intolerable as artificial inequality. He hates nothing so much as the preacher who tells others how bad they are and what they must do to reform. Yet his philosophy is a great sermon, challenging in every line, in spite of his discreet style, our mechanical habits of thought, our mechanical habits of education, our mechanical morality. A prophet dressed in the clothes of a professor of logic, he seems almost to feel shame that he has seen the implications of democracy more clearly than anybody else in the great would-be democratic society about him, and so been forced into the unwelcome task of teaching it.

Orthodox philosophical thinking has usually gone along on the comfortable assumption that words always have the same meaning, and that they stand for real things, that logic is the science of thinking correctly, that reason is eternal, that if you can only get your ideas consistent you have then a true picture of what you are trying to interpret. We have taken for granted the old view, which goes back to Aristotle's logic, that

our mental life was a receiving and combining and storing of certain dead inert sensations and ideas of which words were the true symbols.

Professor Dewey's fundamental thesis has been that thinking is not like this. The mind is not a looking-glass, reflecting the world for its private contemplation, nor a logic-machine for building up truth, but a tool by which we adjust ourselves to the situations in which life puts us. Reason is not a divinely appointed guide to eternal truth, but a practical instrument by which we solve problems. Words are not invariable symbols for invariable things, but clues to meanings. We think in meanings, not in words, and a meaning is simply a sign-post pointing towards our doing something or feeling something or both. The words are the handles by which we take hold of these meanings which our intercourse with people and things presents to us. Our life is a constant reaction to a world which is constantly stimulating us. We are in situations where we must do something, and it is for the purpose of guiding this doing from the point of view of what has happened or what is likely to happen, that we think. We are not bundles of thoughts and feelings so much as bundles of attitudes or tendencies. We act usually before we 'perceive'; the perception is only important as it enables us to act again. We remember what we use, and we learn what we occupy ourselves with. Our minds are simply the tools with which we forge out our life.

If we are to live worthily and happily, it is not necessary that we should 'be' anything or 'know' anything, so much as that we should be able to meet the situation in which developing life places us, and express our capacities in our activity. Our social problem as well as our personal problem is to understand what we are doing. This is almost the whole law and the prophets. In the ideal home we should have learned as children, through social converse and the household occupations and solution of the problems which our curiosity and our work brought us, how to adjust ourselves to the demands of life. But the home can no longer effect this and the school must step in. But the school is only really educative if it is helping the child to understand the social situations in which he finds and is to find himself, and to regulate his impulses so that he can control these situations. (The ideal school would be an embryonic community life, where the child would sense the occupations and interests of the larger society into which he is to enter and so have his curiosity and practical skill awakened to meet and conquer them.)

In its larger social implications, Professor Dewey's philosophy challenges the whole machinery of our world of right and wrong, law and order, property and religion, the old techniques by which society is still being managed and regulated. Our institutions have been made as scales and measures to which we bring our actions, rigid standards by whose codes we are judged, frameworks to whose lines we strive to mould ourselves. All the revolutionary strivings of the past have been away from these institutional authorities towards greater freedom. But in spite of all the freedom we have won, society was probably never more deeply unhappy than it is today. For freedom is not happiness; it is merely the first negative step towards happiness. Happiness is control, and society, now intensely self-conscious of its imperfections, is still very helpless towards controlling its destiny. (Life, Professor Dewey says, is a modification of the present with reference to the conditions of the future, a conflict between the habits engendered in the past and the new aims and purposes, clearly envisaged, to be worked for.)

It is in showing the unity of all the democratic strivings, the social movement, the new educational ideals, the freer ethics, the popular revolt in politics, of all the aspects of the modern restless, forward-looking personal and social life, and the applicability to all of them of scientific method, with its hypotheses and bold experimentation, that Professor Dewey has been the first thinker to put the moral and social goal a notch ahead. His philosophy has the great advantage of making nonsensical most of the writing and thinking that has been done in the old terms. See how much of this can be truthfully called anything else than a 'juggling with the symbols of learning.' See how much of the energy of the moulders of opinion in politics, industry, education, religion, morality, goes to the squaring up of the activity of individuals and groups with certain principles which, however much they may once have been solutions of genuine problems and interpretations of genuine situations, are now mere caked and frozen barricades to activity and understanding.

Professor Dewey has given us a whole new language of meanings. After reading him, you can see nothing again in the old terms. And when I see college presidents and publicists who have cultivated the arts of prestige, expressing their views on every question of the day in the old caked and frozen language, thinking along the old lazy channels, I feel a savage indignation that Professor Dewey should not be out in the arena of the concrete, himself interpreting current life. I am conscious of his horror of having his ideas petrified into a system. He knows that it will do no good to have his philosophy intellectually believed unless it is also thought and lived. And he knows the uncanny propensity of stupid men to turn even the most dynamic ideas into dogmas. He has seen that in his school world. Meanwhile his influence goes on increasing to an extent of which he is almost innocently unconscious.

X

WHAT SHOULD BE A MAN'S OBJECT IN LIFE?

[ARTHUR BRISBANE]

[*New York Evening Journal.* Reprinted in *Ed. itorials from the Hearst Newspapers,* 1906. By permission.]

Sermons in stones are familiar, but few take the trouble to dig them out. Certainly none looks for sermons in a one-cent evening newspaper.

At the same time, will you kindly think over and answer the question that heads this column?

Here we are, marooned for a few days on a flying ball of earth. We don't know how we got here. We don't know where we are going. We are full of beautiful and satisfying *faith.* But we don't *know.*

Into this Universe, and *why* not knowing,
Nor *whence,* like Water, willy-nilly flowing;
   And out of it as Wind along the Waste,
I know not *whither,* willy-nilly blowing.

That's the way Omar, the old tent-maker, puts it.

We drift from dinner to the theater, thence to bed, thence to breakfast, thence to work, and so on. Or, if in hard luck, we struggle and wail, 'cursing our day,' or more frequently cursing society.

We rarely stop to think what it is all about, or what we are here for.

We know the pig's object in life. It has been beautifully and permanently outlined in Carlyle's 'pig catechism.' The pig's life object is to get fat and keep fat — to get his full share of swill and as much more as he can manage to secure. And his life object is worthy. By sticking at it he develops fat hams inside his bristles, and *we* know, though he does not, that the production of fat hams is his destiny.

But our human destiny is *not* to produce fat hams. Why do so many of us live earnestly on the pig basis? Why do we struggle savagely for money to buy our kind of swill — luxury, food, etc.— and cease all struggling when that money is obtained?

Is fear of poverty and dependence the only emotion that should move us?

Are we here merely to *stay* here and *eat* here?

A great German scientist, very learned and about as imaginative as a wart hog, declares that the human face is merely an extension and elaboration of the alimentary canal — that the beauty of expression, the marvelous qualities of a noble human face, are merely indirect results of the alimentary canal's strivings to satisfy its wants.

That is a hideous conception, is it not? But it is no more unworthy than the average human life, and the average existence has much to justify the German's speculations.

What *shall* we strive for? *Money?*

Get a thousand millions. Your day will come, and in due course the graveyard rat will gnaw as calmly at your bump of acquisitiveness as at the mean coat of the pauper.

Then, shall we strive for *power?*

The names of the first great kings of the world are forgotten, and the names of all those whose power we envy will drift

to forgetfulness soon. What does the most powerful man in the world amount to standing at the brink of Niagara, with his solar plexus trembling? What is his power compared with the force of the wind or the energy of one small wave sweeping along the shore?

The power which man can build up within himself, for himself, is nothing. Only the dull reasoning of gratified egotism can make it seem worth while.

Then what *is* worth while? Let us look at some of the men who have come and gone, and whose lives inspire us. Take a few at random:

Columbus, Michelangelo, Wilberforce, Shakespeare, Galileo, Fulton, Watt, Hargreaves — these will do.

Let us ask ourselves this question: 'Was there any *one thing* that distinguished *all* their lives, that united all these men, active in fields so different?'

Yes. Every man among them, and every man whose life history is worth the telling, did something for the *good of other men.*

Hargreaves, the weaver, invented the spinning-jenny, and his invention clothes and employs hundreds of millions.

Galileo perfected the telescope, spread out before man's intellect the grandeur of the universe. Wilberforce helped to awaken man's conscience. He freed millions of slaves. Columbus gave a home to great nations. We thrive today because of his noble courage. Michelangelo and Shakespeare stirred human genius to new efforts, and fed the human mind — a task more worthy than the feeding of the human stomach. We ride in Fulton's steamboats, and Watt's engine pulls us along.

Men who are truly great have *done good* to their fellow-man. And the greatest Soul ever born on earth came to urge but one thing upon humanity, '*Love one another.*'

Get money if you can. Get power if you can. Then, if you want to be more than the ten thousand million unknown mingled in the dust beneath you, see what good you can do with your money and your power.

If you are one of the many millions who have not and can't get money or power, see what good you can do without either.

You can help carry a load for an old man. You can encourage and help a poor devil trying to reform. You can set a good example to children. You can stick to the men with whom you work, fighting honestly for their welfare.

Time was when the ablest man would rather kill ten men than feed a thousand children. That time has gone. We do not care much about feeding the children, but we care less about killing the men. To that extent we have improved already.

The day will come when we shall prefer helping our neighbor to robbing him — legally — of a million dollars.

Do what good you can *now*, while it is unusual, and have the satisfaction of being a pioneer and an eccentric.

XI

THE ANTARCTIC DISASTER

[*Times* (London, England), February 11, 1913. By permission.]

Never since the loss of Sir John Franklin and his whole expedition sixty-six years ago has such a disaster befallen British Polar explorers as that which it is our sad duty to record today. For a time after the arrival of the news yesterday afternoon, people hoped against hope, wondering whether the information which reached New Zealand had not been misunderstood, since Arctic and Antarctic news at first is largely impregnated with rumor. Unhappily the confirmation which has since come in is such as leaves no ground for hope. A despatch of Commander Evans puts the terrible facts beyond doubt. He states, very simply and directly, that Captain Scott reached the South Pole on January 18, 1912 — which it will be remembered was about a month after Captain Amundsen had reached it — and that on his return towards his base he and his four companions were overwhelmed in a blizzard, and all perished. The first to fall was Seaman Edgar Evans, who died from concussion of the brain — how caused none can say at present — on February 17; then, on March 17, Captain Oates died of exposure; and some twelve days later, on or about March 29, the remaining three, Dr. Wilson, Lieutenant Bowers, and Captain Scott himself, died of want and exposure. They were eleven

miles from a place which the company had named One Ton Depot, and 155 miles from the base of the expedition. It is possible for us in this temperate clime to realize something of the horror, the terror, the irresistible vehemence of an Antarctic blizzard if we recall the description which we gave on November 19 last from the pen of Dr. Simpson, who was for a time lent by the Indian Government to be chief physicist of the expedition. He tells of a gale which blew continuously for six days 'at over gale strength '— more than thirty-eight miles an hour, rising at different times to fifty-two, to sixty-six, and once to eighty miles an hour; the temperature marking between thirty-one and thirty-five degrees below zero. We shall never know what degree of violence was attained by the blizzard which was fatal to Captain Scott, but it may be assumed that it was as bad as this, or worse; and the grim word 'want' used by Commander Evans implies that supplies had run out, and that the unhappy men were in no condition to resist the appalling storm.

Thus ends a great and truly heroic adventure, undertaken quite voluntarily by these officers and their followers, with the object of settling some unsolved problems of geography, natural history, and other sciences. In judging Captain Scott and his friends, let us put out of our minds all the gossip which from time to time has been circulated about 'a race' between him and his friendly rival, the Danish Captain Amundsen. That this explorer should have diverted his course from the North to the South Pole was an accident, and so was the almost simultaneous arrival of the Danish vessel and of the *Terra Nova* in those Southern waters. As was long since pointed out in these columns by one of Captain Scott's companions, Mr. Herbert Ponting, he never raced and never headed 'a mere dash to the Pole.' He went steadily forward with his scientific exploration, and if he had not had the misfortune to lose nine of his nineteen invaluable ponies, he might very probably have arrived first, and, what is of much more importance, might not have found it necessary to send that memorable despatch, when the *Terra Nova* first came to fetch him away, 'I am staying in the Antarctic another year in order to continue and complete my work.' But this was not to be. The small disaster happened and it was the prelude to the greater — to that shocking catastrophe which the English race and the whole scientific world are lamenting today. We will not at this moment raise the question whether the scientific results of these arduous Polar expeditions are, or are henceforth likely to be, adequate to the cost — to the cost of valuable lives which may always have to be paid. It is more consonant with the universal feeling of the moment simply to add our tribute to the courage, the perseverance in the face of enormous difficulties, which every member of the expedition has shown since the beginning, two and a half years ago. Their country will ever pay honor to Captain Scott, who, after a fine career as a naval officer, devoted himself with single-minded heroism to the realization of a great ideal; to Dr. Wilson, surgeon, zoölogist, and artist; to Captain Oates, of the Inniskillings; to Lieutenant Bowers, of the Indian Navy; and to Seaman Edgar Evans. For their friends we feel the keenest sympathy, and especially for Captain Scott's young wife, the distinguished sculptress, now on the high sea in the hope — how vain! — of meeting her husband in New Zealand. To her, and to all who admired Captain Scott, we can but recall the famous lines of Tennyson on Franklin, so exactly applicable if we change one single word:

'Not here! The white South has thy bones; *with*
    and thou
Heroic sailor-soul,
Art passing on thine happier voyage now
Toward no earthly pole!'

XII

THE SINKING OF THE LUSITANIA

[*World* (New York), May 8, 1915. By permission.]

The circumstances and the consequences of the destruction of the *Lusitania* by a German submarine call for all the self-restraint and self-possession that the American people can command.

Morally, the sinking of the *Lusitania* was no worse than the sinking of the *Falaba*.

In each case a passenger ship carrying neutrals and non-combatants was destroyed by a German submarine, and hundreds of helpless men, women and children left to survive or drown, as luck decreed. The destruction of the *Lusitania* makes a more dramatic appeal to the human imagination than did the destruction of the *Falaba,* but both were crimes against civilization in equal degree.

How many American lives have been snuffed out in the loss of the *Lusitania* we do not yet know. But it is no fault of the German Government that anybody escaped from either ship. It is no fault of the German Government that every American on board the *Lusitania* is not lying at the bottom of the sea.

The German authorities claim in extenuation that fair warning was given to Americans by the German Embassy in Washington that the *Lusitania* was to be torpedoed. Murder does not become innocent and innocuous because the victim has been warned in advance that the blow would be struck if he persisted in the exercise of his lawful rights.

It may be said in respect to this warning that nobody believed the Germans could or would carry out their threat. People thought better of them than they thought of themselves. And why they should have carried out the threat, abetted by the complaisant indifference of the British Government, is still a mystery.

What military advantage was gained by such a procedure comparable to the moral revulsion against Germany that it is certain to produce? Wars are not won by drowning neutrals or non-combatants. We venture to say that no single act of this conflict has so outraged American opinion or so riddled German prestige in this country as the destruction of the *Lusitania*. The Germans have sunk the largest British ship in active mercantile service. They have destroyed a small quantity of munitions of war. They have evidently killed a large number of Americans and non-combatants. In the long run they might better have lost a battle. The military gains are trifling. The moral losses are incalculable.

The whole German submarine policy in its campaign, not against British ships of war but against merchantmen on the high seas, is a revival of piracy — piracy organized, systematized and nationalized. It is piracy against neutrals as well as against enemies. One day it is a British passenger ship that is torpedoed. Another

day it is an American merchant ship flying the American flag which is destroyed
without a word of warning. And still another day it is a defenseless Swedish or a
Norwegian or a Dutch ship that is blown
from the face of the waters by a German
torpedo.

Modern history affords no other such
example of a great nation running amuck
and calling it military necessity.

During the last century the United
States has had more years of warfare than
Germany. The life of this nation has
hung in the balance too. But we never
found it necessary to make war upon neutrals, or upon non-combatants, or upon
women and children. We never found it
necessary to ignore or flout all the established rules of civilized warfare. We
never found it necessary to outrage the
moral sentiment of mankind or to defy
the public opinion of civilization.

What Germany expects to gain by her
policy is something we cannot guess.
What advantage will it be to her to be left
without a friend or a well-wisher in the
world? The war cannot last forever.
Peace will eventually come, if only through
exhaustion. What will be the attitude of
the other nations toward Germany when
the conflict is finished? How many decades must pass before Germany can live
down the criminal record that she is writing for herself in the annals of history?

It has often happened that men in their
desperation have become outlaws. But
we recall no other instance in which a
great nation has deliberately elected to become an outlaw. That is the tragedy of
the insensate policy that the German Government is pursuing, and eventually the
German people will pay a staggering price
for their Government's folly — a price
that cannot be measured even in treasure
or blood.

XIII

GERMAN FEELING TOWARD
AMERICA

[*Springfield Daily Republican*, May 17, 1915.
By permission.]

In a time of strained relations even traditional friendships between countries are
subjected to severe tension, and a standing
grudge or even a habit of contemptuous
dislike is a misfortune. How does the
case stand between the people of the
United States and the people of Germany?
So far as our side is concerned the popular
feeling has at all times been one of entire friendliness, mixed with a great deal
of admiration in recent years for German
efficiency and a sense of rivalry in which
there was no jealousy or disquietude.

With much of Germany's culture, the
American of the practical sort was unfamiliar. German music was taken for
granted and its recognized excellence and
pervasiveness commanded the respect of
the American who frankly admitted it to
be over his head. German literature has
made no great impression outside of a
very small circle in which its greatness
has been fully recognized. But the material setting of the new German kultur,
the model cities, the theaters and concert
halls, the striking novelties in architecture,
the beautiful parks and suburbs, the
whole imposing display of new wealth scientifically expended, has impressed not
only the multitude of travelers, but the
great reading public, to which the progress
of Germany and its lessons for the United
States have long been a staple for illustrated articles. Still more could Americans appreciate the wonderful development of Germany in a specialty of our
own like machinery. America long ago
formed a genuine respect for the Germans
as people who 'do things,' and America's
own confidence in its boundless resources
is too complete for the slightest envy over
this truly remarkable development.

Such has been the ordinary and therefore the significant American attitude toward Germany, the attitude of the business
man, the 'man in the street,' the 'plain
American' in varying degrees of plainness.
As for academic circles and the larger
circles which are concerned with education and kindred matters, the influence of
Germany has of course been immense,
and for a generation paramount. To
thousands of educated Americans, as to
Lord Haldane, Germany has been their
'spiritual home.' German ideas have affected American education from the kin-
dergarten to the university, and our intellectual workers, like our machinists,
have paid homage to German thoroughness and German genius.

What is the reverse of the picture?
That an eager and friendly interest in

America as the land of new hopes and new possibilities was long traditional in Germany is well known. That the mass of the German people, leaving out of account the present and let us hope passing friction, entertain a kindly feeling toward America and Americans there is reason to believe from the testimony of many observers who have known the country well. But it must regretfully be said that more has been done in Germany than in this country to mar this friendliness of spirit.

For many years systematic disparagement of American ways and ideals has characterized a large part of the German press. Many papers have conducted a special department devoted to ridiculous and silly news or anecdotes intended to show the crudity and backwardness of the United States. There are influential quarters in which this country is frankly disliked, and for the propagation of such views Germany has machinery the possibilities of which the outside world has lately had cause to realize. The outburst of feeling during the Spanish War, which Americans then visiting in Germany have cause to remember, was not wholly a spontaneous outpouring of sympathy for Spain.

It must be remembered that bureaucratic Germany has no special reason to love a republic; for its detestation of French democracy and English liberal institutions one need only turn to the life of Bismarck. Nor is the intellectual interest of America in Germany fully reciprocated; from the German point of view we have almost no scholarship worthy of the name, and very little culture. When practical studies were forcing themselves into the German school system fifteen years ago they were denounced as 'American' education; the conception of the United States as a land of sordid money grubbers is not uncommon in Europe, but it has been more carefully cultivated in Germany than elsewhere. In the present heat of feeling we should not forget the real and valuable service of Professor Muensterburg in writing in German for Germans a book setting forth American ideals and idealism.

Americans are reproached, and with some justice, for their ignorance of foreign affairs and foreign peoples, an ignorance which the past year has done much to dispel. Yet there is reason to think that in its appraisal of the true character of the German people, including even the dogged energy and the dour stubbornness shown in this war, the American people have had a truer and fuller conception than the German people have had of us. Even in the most bitter and in some cases unjustified protests against Germany's part in the war there has been an underlying recognition of the great qualities of the German people, and a feeling that not they but the system should be held responsible. In the present crisis it would greatly ease matters if the Germans equally appreciated America. Do they? It would be a relief to think so. If there are doubts they come from a sense of the long and systematic disparagement of America and Americans in the German press. If Professor Muensterburg's friendly account of us had been given equal publicity, Germany could not fail to comprehend that America is not merely the land of the almighty dollar, and that the idealism of Woodrow Wilson represents a real and important side of the national character. On the plane of 'humanity first,' Germans and Americans should be able to stand together.

XIV

A SOLDIER AND A BULLET

[*Life*, May 13, 1915. By permission.]

A German-born American letter-writer to the *Evening Post* says that he has heard from his mother that his brother, killed in France in February, 'died with an American bullet in his heart.' He complains, not of his brother's death, but about the American bullet. 'I have another brother,' he says, 'fighting for his country's cause, a father of three little ones waiting for his return; is he, too, going to be killed by a United-States-made bullet?'

It is quite possible. The Germans came self-invited into France, and it is not for them to be critical about the details of the hospitalities offered them. It strained French resources to receive and entertain so many visitors. The French had to get supplies where they could, and it was quite a scramble to get enough. They bought bullets, no doubt, in the open market, and if they got some American bullets, why not?

Let us hope there will always be American bullets available for countries fighting against invasion and subjection by their powerful neighbors.

The reason why the good German letter-writer's brother is dead is that he was a German invader fighting in France. His errand was so to crush France that she could never again get in Germany's way. No doubt it was not his fault that he was on that errand, but it was the German mind that sent him that is guilty of his death, not the American bullet that killed him.

XV

WAR BABIES

[*Chicago Tribune*, April 30, 1915. By permission.]

War, in itself an elemental expression of human emotions, has caused a reversion to hetairism which the philosophical find easy to understand but which society is perplexed to make room for in an ordered state of morals. The consequences of the reversion are babies without names. The nations at war need the babies and want them and realize that neither the mother who has borne the child nor the child itself can be permitted to suffer what in ordinary times would be the punishment imposed for irregularity.

Europe has not returned generally to a state of promiscuous concubinage, but the disposition to 'breed before you die' has followed some stronger urge than that of ecclesiastical exhortation and has embraced more opportunities than were offered by the specially simplified marriage procedure arranged for those about to go into battle.

The Church of England has been criticized for adapting itself to a situation which threatened to withdraw the youth of the country from matrimonial possibilities and consequently to have a depressing effect upon the vital statistics of the nation. It was accused of provoking a disregard of moral restraints and of causing a lapse into promiscuity by throwing aside delicacy and coming out plump with the declaration that England was going to lose men and would need babies.

It is fairer to say that the church was working as energetically as it could to regularize relations which the authorities knew were being formed irregularly as the result of the tremendous upheaval in human conditions. Considerations which were important in ordinary times disappeared in extraordinary times.

The philosophical may say that it was nature responding to a sudden and savage attack upon her most essential process. She made a readjustment in anticipation of interference with her orderly methods. She quickened the will to live and put it in the form of the will to breed. Of that impulse even the philosophical would concede that the unmarried fathers and mothers would be unconscious. Their consciousness would be restricted within simpler emotional bounds, but that would not eliminate the possibility of the greater plan. Nature was not thrown off her balance, but made readjustments and with the consequences public policy, morals, charity, church, and nation are now concerned.

Hitherto Great Britain has regarded such a subject as one far below the line. It was to be denied of experience, put out of thought and kept out of conversation and counsel. Even now the English will not even approximate Magyar candor or the policy of Maria Theresa and her regiments of hussars, but reticence has been broken down. Facts are facts and it is impossible and impolitic to pass on the other side of the highway with averted eyes.

The unmarried mother has done a service to the state. The fact that she has outweighs the fact that she did not intend to, and the state is concerned to see that her position is regularized, that she and her child are protected from shame and disgrace that would have been the punishment in ordinary times, and that they are given protection and made what they ought to be, valuable to the state.

If nature readjusted herself to meet a danger, society will have to readjust itself to accept the consequences, and then, with the normal restored, both may proceed in approved and sanctioned ways.

XVI

WHY AMERICA DOES N'T MAKE DYES

[A. B. MACDONALD]

[*Kansas City Star*, April 27, 1915. By permission.]

The European War brought to this whole country the revelation that we were getting nearly all our dyes from Germany. For the last thirty years the dye industry in this country has been protected by a 30 per cent. tariff, and yet there is made in this country only 15 per cent. of the ten million dollars' worth of dyes used here, and we made only seventeen of the 912 dyes used. The rest of our dyes come from Germany.

Then the public began asking: 'Why don't we make our own dyes and save all this money?'

'They are made by a very complex chemical process, out of coal tar,' was the answer.

'Coal tar? Why, the United States produces 125 million gallons of coal tar annually. Why don't we use it in making our own dyes?'

That question has been going the rounds of the newspapers for months, and some have answered it one way, and some another, but one of the best answers has just been made by Arthur D. Little of Boston, a chemist, and one of the greatest experts in dyestuffs in this country.

He points out that the coal-tar color and explosives industry, as developed in Germany, is the most highly organized of any industry in the world. Starting with fewer than a dozen crude raw materials derived from coal tar, it builds up by chemical processes, requiring elaborate and expensive plants and the most rigid scientific control of operating conditions, twelve hundred products. The whole system of production depends for its commercial efficiency upon the close correlation and interdependence of these many products. The industry is self-contained. It makes its own crudes and converts its own wastes into raw material for new processes. The adjustment of the economic balance is so close that even a slight change in the value of some one product may disarrange whole processes and affect disastrously many products.

There are twenty-two factories in the business in Germany and the industry is bound together by trade agreements and coöperative arrangements. Germany ships dyes to thirty-three countries. China takes four times as much German indigo as the United States consumes.

This great industry has been forty-five years in building up in Germany, and in finding its world markets. It would require, probably, nearly as long for this country to duplicate it, and a tremendous investment and loss before the success was realized, if it ever should be realized.

'The plain underlying reason why we have been unable during thirty years of tariff protection to develop a coal-tar color industry, while during the same period the Germans have magnificently succeeded, is to be found in the failure of our manufacturers and capitalists to realize the creative power and earning capacity of industrial research,' says Mr. Little. 'This power and this capacity have been recognized by Germany, and on them as corner stones her industries are based.'

And then he goes on to ask why we should try to duplicate the German dye-plants which are already capable of meeting the demands of the whole world as soon as peace is restored. That would only plunge us into a commercial warfare against the most strongly intrenched industrial position in the world.

Rather, he suggests, we should leave the dye business to the Germans, and consider some of the other things we might do with the vast expenditure of effort, money and research that would be necessary to rival the Germans in that line.

We waste 150 million tons of wood a year, a billion feet of natural gas a day, millions of tons of flax, wheat and oat straw at every harvest. Coke ovens flame for miles in Pennsylvania and Colorado, wasting precious ammonia. Untouched peat deposits fringe our entire Atlantic seaboard. The whole South is a reservoir of industrial wealth, untapped in any proper sense.

One-tenth of the research, energy and skill which would be required to rival the German dye industry, if applied to the lumber industry of the South would result in the creation of a whole series of great interlocking industries, each more profitable than lumbering.

'The South would be in a position to dominate the paper market of the world,' he says. 'It would transport denatured alcohol by pipe line and tank steamer, make thousands of tons a day of carbohydrate cattle feeds, reorganize and develop along new lines and to far better purpose its languishing naval stores industry, and find new opportunity on every hand. To do these things in one industry, and many things as good in other industries, requires only a little faith, sustained, courageous effort, and the appreciation by American financiers of the earning power of research.'

XVII

A BULLDOG, NOT A PUG

[*Charleston News and Courier*, May 19, 1915.]

Secretary Daniels's speech in New York at the banquet given in honor of the officers of the Atlantic fleet is for several reasons a notable utterance. In a sense, it may be said to have given the country the best assurance which it has yet had that the administration is not in the camp of those who scoff at the idea that preparedness is a safeguard against war. The country has never been able to determine to what extent Mr. Bryan's pacifist and disarmament ideas held sway at Washington, and it has been feared that they exerted an influence so strong as to be dangerous. Certainly Mr. Daniels's speech is reassuring on this score. When he says that the country is entering upon an era in which the navy is going to be expanded and strengthened 'in order that by our very strength we may be able to demand the right to live at peace with all the world,' one is justified in assuming that the Wilson administration has not been infected with the Bryan nonsense which holds that preparedness is productive of war instead of being a safeguard —though of course not an infallible one —against war.

That Mr. Daniels should at this time be at pains to proclaim the present high efficiency of the navy may also be significant. Just now it is especially important that certain people across the water should be under no delusions about the physical ability of this nation to take care of itself. We are more likely to be permitted to tread the path of peace that we would fain follow, if it be well known and thoroughly understood that to attack us is dangerous. If the impression is created that we are no better able to defend ourselves and our rights than China — an impression which, there is reason to fear, already prevails — we are apt to be shown scant respect; and it was eminently desirable that something should be said or done to offset the recent utterances of the National Security League, which, however well intended and however sincere they might have been, were certainly most inopportune. This is no time to tell the American people and the world in general, as the National Security League has been telling them, that the United States navy is practically worthless.

It is nothing of the kind. Mr. Daniels could not make out such a good case for the navy if he did not have truth on his side. That the navy is not all it ought to be is well known and is admitted by nobody more frankly than by Mr. Daniels. It needs more ships, it needs faster ships, it needs more men, it needs more auxiliaries; but though it is far from being what it ought to be, it is a very respectable navy nevertheless and it would give a very good account of itself if it were called upon to stand the test of battle. Mr. Daniels does not claim perfection for the navy, does not deny the existence of certain serious weaknesses; but nothing could be more effective, as far as it goes, than his categorical answer to the specific allegations of the National Security League and his concise setting forth of the facts which show that the navy, though not as large as it should be, is in good trim for the performance of any service that may be required of it.

It is very well that these facts should be set forth just at this time. The householder who has a fairly large and thoroughly capable bulldog gains nothing by assuring possible trespassers that the bulldog is really nothing but a pug and, besides, has no teeth.

XVIII

THE END OF AN ODYSSEY

[Manchester Guardian (England), April 26, 1915.]

The news from Berlin of the arrival in Arabia of the remnants of the *Emden's* crew is the finishing touch to an adventure well in keeping with the general history of the famous German commerce raider. When the *Emden* was caught by the *Sydney* off Cocos Island on November 9 she put out to meet the *Sydney* without taking on board again the landing party which had been put ashore to wreck the cable station.

By the time the *Emden* had formally surrendered and several rescues had been made of isolated members of her crew who had taken to the water, night was falling, and it was too late for the *Sydney* to get into communication with the cable station.

When she did so on the next day her captain learned that the *Emden's* landing party of forty men and three officers had made vigorous use of the delay. They had seized and provisioned a seventy-ton schooner, the *Ayesha,* and escaped in her the previous evening with four Maxims and a modest but useful amount of ammunition for them.

There was material here for a fine adventure after the heart of a sea-faring novelist, and it has been pretty well fulfilled in fact. The cable operators vowed that it would be a short one, asserting that the *Ayesha* was leaking when she was seized and would take her captors to the bottom with her before they got very far.

But she did not sink — perhaps the resourceful crew repaired her on their voyage — and in three weeks she was laying in stores at Padang, a straight 830 miles away, on the coast of Sumatra. This was on November 28, and since then, from the details given in the Berlin message, the *Ayesha* has made her way in four months across at least 4100 miles of the Indian Ocean, reaching the Arabian coast at the bottom of the Red Sea on March 27.

Presumably the intention of her crew was then to march inland to the nearest center of their allies, the Turkish army. But their adventures were by no means over, for on their way they were attacked by the Arabs of the Yemen, who have no great love for Turkish rule. The Arabs clung to the party for three days, and left their mark on it in the shape of several casualities.

The wounded, says the Berlin message, are now in hospital at Jeddah, which presumably means that the rest have got into touch with some sort of Turkish forces; and so we come definitely to the 'last of the *Emden,*' as an individual fighting unit.

XIX

SWARMING OF THE JAPANESE HIVE

[Los Angeles Times, May 7, 1915.]

Japan has nearly six tenths as great a population as the United States, with an area only one twenty-fourth as large. It has twenty two times as great a population as the State of California, with an area not quite as large, and it has four times the population of Mexico, with an area less than one fifth of that country.

The population of Japan is 370 to the square mile — about four times that of China — while that of the United States is 85, Mexico 18 and of California 15 to the square mile.

Great Britain solved the problem of a congested population by a system of colonization beyond seas. There are eight British colonies in Asia, twelve in Africa, seventeen in America and nine in Australia. France has colonies in Algeria, Senegal, Tunis, Cayenne, Cambodia, Cochin China, Tonquin, New Caledonia, Tahiti, Sahara and Madagascar, and Germany has her colonies of Eastern and Western Africa. The Netherlands have Borneo, Celebes, Java, New Guinea, Sumatra, Surinam and the Moluccas. Portugal has a larger population in Africa than in Europe. Italy has Eritrea, Tripoli and the Somali coast. With European nations colonization is a convenience, with Japan it is an immediate and vital necessity. Her people are not welcome in any Latin-American country except possibly Mexico. There is a large tract of country in northern China not so thickly settled but that it could accommodate more people, but if Japan gets a foothold there she will have to fight for it.

On the whole the most available outlet for Japan seems to be in West Mexico. That portion of our sister republic is more sparsely populated than any other part and freer from the ravages of banditti because there is not much of anything portable to steal. Japanese are welcome there and, if they go there, not to establish a Japanese colony or to retain their allegiance to Japan, but to become Mexican citizens in accordance with Mexican laws, such action would not be an infraction of the Monroe Doctrine. We could n't prevent it even if we wanted to, and it is by no means certain that we would want to.

XX

INSURANCE FOR EVERYBODY

[*Saturday Evening Post,* May 1, 1915. By permission.]

Within three or four years group insurance of lives has become an important factor in the business of life insurance, many companies now engaging in it. Say a plant employs a thousand men. The company will insure all of them under one blanket policy, without any individual application or medical examination. Generally the amount payable at death is one year's wage or salary, whatever that may have been; and the premium paid by the employer runs from 1 to 1½ per cent.

No physical examinations are necessary, because the mere fact that the men are at work is sufficient proof that, as a rule, they are in good bodily condition; and by insuring a thousand employed men in a lump the company gets the average risk, which is all it needs. It could afford to insure the whole adult population of a city *en bloc,* because then also it would get the average risk, on which its premium charges are based; in fact, experience indicates that group insurance risks run above the average. The insurance applies, of course, only to men on the pay roll. If a man's employment ceases his insurance automatically ceases with it. Presumably if he becomes decrepit his employment will cease or his wages will decline; so the company at his death will be required to pay less than if he had been vigorous.

The striking thing is the demonstrated practicability of insuring every employed man. It would be entirely feasible, that is, for a city, a state or a nation to insure every employed man within its borders in an amount equal to his yearly earnings, and at a premium of about 1 per cent. of the total yearly pay roll.

An objection raised to group insurance is that it causes men to rely on that expedient instead of taking out individual insurance, and if they are thrown out of work their insurance ceases. But it is answered that the group scheme, by demonstrating the advantages of insurance to many men who might otherwise ignore it, has just the opposite effect.

We hope the latter argument is true, for every man with dependents and without a fortune ought to insure his life.

XXI

THE FEEBLE-MINDED

[*Indianapolis News,* April 30, 1915. By permission.]

In the last issue of the Indiana Bulletin of Charities and Corrections papers read before the Indiana Academy of Science are printed. These constitute a valuable addition to the purpose of the Bulletin. They concern themselves chiefly with discussion, from various points of view, of feeble-mindedness and the problem it presents to the state in the care that must inevitably be exercised over those so conditioned, and as to what shall be done to restrict the ravages of the affliction. In the nature of a brief résumé of the practical sides of the problem is the paper read by Dr. Bliss, superintendent of the state school for feeble-minded youth at Ft. Wayne. Incidentally, he recounted the history of the subject, which began in 1800, when a French physician tried unsuccessfully to educate a 'wild boy' found in the woods. The first successful attempt was made in our own country at Hartford, Connecticut, in 1836. Several feeble-minded children were there trained to some degree. A dozen years later Massachusetts started the first state school. Other States followed, and Indiana came into line in 1879.

These schools were all started with the idea that mental defect was curable. But it is now known that it is not. It is a condition, not a disease. Feeble-mindedness is a defective brain and can never be cured, but may be relieved. There are between 5000 and 6000 such persons in our State needing institutional care, and only about one fourth are getting it. The remainder are at large producing their kind, and if we are to protect the future generations of our people from this growing burden something must be done.

What to do, Dr. Bliss says, is a perplexing question. The best thing, he thinks, for some years at least, is segregation, to be applied not to those already in institutions, but to those at large. He approves the commission recommended by Amos Butler for investigation and report to the next legislature. He recommends also a farm of 2000 acres for boys and men, and a smaller one for women, where suitable occupations can be provided. Better marriage laws also would be a great help. All this would be followed by registration of diseases that produce feeble-mindedness. But, for the present, the farm is the thing and the doctor urges that the State should realize the momentousness of the problem that it faces and undertake measures to prevent the reproduction of defectives and so set out on the way of getting the better of a condition that now is allowed to go on developing. Certainly, there is here a condition that should be met. The State can not ignore it and its thorough investigation as Secretary Butler recommended would be a long step in the right direction both as to state economy and humanity.

XXII

STONEHENGE IN THE MARKET

[*Manchester Guardian,* England, May 29, 1915.]

Between now and September next, when the Amesbury Abbey estate is to be sold, there is plenty of time for the nation to make up its mind to rescue from private ownership the oldest and most debated of its national monuments, and, even though we are at war, to secure, if necessary by public subscription, the money needed for its rescue. On the rolling chalk of 'the Great Plain' of Mr. Hardy's novels, skirted by two of those white ribbons over which the military transport wagons will have gone crunching so very noisily in the blazing sunshine of the past week — in more normal Whit-weeks they would, as like as not, have been the wagons of the East Lancashire Territorials — stands Stonehenge, and Stonehenge is part of the Amesbury Abbey estate. Perhaps 'rescue' is a rather invidious term to apply to its purchase on behalf of the nation; for if the great monument had to be in private hands it could hardly have been in better ones than those of the late Sir Edmund Antrobus. If he did startle the stranger who sought it out for the first time by the spectacle of a wire fence, a turnstile and a policeman, those unromantic adjuncts were provided with the best intentions and with the sanction of three eminent antiquarian associations. (Though apparently necessary to the safety of the stones, they were not happy additions. They took from one forever a little of the strange, hopeless beauty which Mr. Hardy had lent to the uninclosed Stonehenge in the closing chapters of *Tess of the D'Urbervilles;* they went ill with the taut, doomed happiness which Tess snatched from her reconciliation with Angel Clare, an awed idyll which ended below the great stones when the dawn showed the hunters, who 'walked as if trained,' closing round the sleeping girl from the shadows of the trilithons.) But for such a relic national ownership is better than the most considerate private hands. The great numbers of our New Army who must have made pilgrimage to the famous stones during the past nine months will have done something to increase public interest in their fate. One hopes that before the sun rises on Midsummer Day in line with the avenue' some steps will have been taken with regard to its purchase.

E.   HUMOROUS AND OCCASIONAL ARTICLES

Humorous writing is much more the result of natural disposition and of point of view than of specific training and rule. The fact, however, that every newspaper devotes space ranging in extent from a corner to a column to writing that is occasional and humorous in character, and that there are numerous weekly periodicals devoted solely to this form of writing, is sufficient evidence of a popularity as widespread as it has been perennial. Some American writers of national repute, such as Mark Twain, Bret Harte, and O. Henry, began their literary careers with obscure newspaper contributions of a humorous character. The daily paper or the monthly magazine of the majority of American colleges affords the student who has any ability or desire for humorous writing abundant opportunity to try his hand and to develop his skill.

A rough distinction between Humor and Wit is perhaps desirable, though these two phases of the Comic may often be found together in the same piece of writing. Humor is largely a matter of point of view; it is an outlook on life largely determined by temperament. Wit is manifested by a fine facility for apt speech, by the unexpected, quick-turned and appropriate remark, by the sparkling, keen-cut saying. The former calls for broad emotional sympathy; the latter, for quick intellectual perception.

The writer-in-training will have to be on constant guard against an insidious temptation to cheapness, coarseness, and exaggeration. Crude vulgarity of conception and tiresome repetition of superficial mannerisms he will have continually to strive against. Genuine humor is not a literary trick, nor is it a matter that can be reduced to a formula or recipe. It implies freshness and sincerity in point of view, and should demand real and conscious literary skill in expression, so long as this effort does not deaden that spontaneity which is one of the greatest charms of humor.

For obvious reasons examples of the ubiquitous 'joke' or humorous paragraph and the interesting but disjointed 'column' are omitted from this section. The examples here included range from the somewhat lengthy treatment of a serious subject with a light and humorous touch, as in 'The Devil and the Deep Sea' or 'System versus Slippers,' to the comparatively brief paragraph about so trivial a subject as 'Hairpins' or 'The Improved Baby.' The occasional article, often humorous in character, is suggested, like the informal essay which in many respects it resembles, by some topic of passing interest, or by some sporadic idea capable of brief development. It is interesting, informal, light, and provocative of thought by suggestion rather than by explicit didactic method.

I

THE DEVIL AND THE DEEP SEA

STEPHEN B. LEACOCK

[*University Magazine*, December, 1910. By permission of author and publisher.]

The Devil is passing out of fashion. After a long and honorable career he has fallen into an ungrateful oblivion. His existence has become shadowy, his outline attenuated, and his personality displeasing to a complacent generation. So he stands now leaning on the handle of his three-pronged oyster fork and looking into the ashes of his smothered fire. Theology will have none of him. Genial clergy of ample girth, stuffed with the buttered 5 toast of a rectory tea, are preaching him out of existence. The fires of his material hell are replaced by the steam heat of moral torture. This even the most sensitive of sinners faces with equanimity. So 10 the Devil's old dwelling is dismantled and stands by the roadside with a sign-board bearing the legend, 'Museum of Moral Torment, These Premises to Let.' In front of it, in place of the dancing imp 15 of earlier ages, is a poor, make-believe thing, a jack-o'-lantern on a stick, with a turnip head and candle eyes, labeled 'Demon of Moral Repentance, Guaranteed Worse than Actual Fire.' The poor thing grins in its very harmlessness.

Now that the Devil is passing away, an unappreciative generation fails to realize the high social function that he once performed. There he stood for ages a simple and workable basis of human morality; an admirable first-hand reason for being good, which needed no ulterior explanation. The rude peasant of the Middle Ages, the illiterate artisan of the shop, and the long-haired hind of the fields, had no need to speculate upon the problem of existence and the tangled skein of moral enquiry. The Devil took all that off their hands. He had either to 'be good' or else he 'got the fork,' just as in our time the unsuccessful comedian of amateur night in the vaudeville houses 'gets the hook.' Humanity, with the Devil to prod it from behind, moved steadily upwards on the path of moral development. Then having attained a certain elevation, it turned upon its tracks, denied that there had been any Devil, rubbed itself for a moment by way of investigation, said that there had been no prodding, and then fell to wandering about on the hilltops without any fixed idea of goal or direction.

In other words, with the disappearance of the Devil there still remains unsolved the problem of conduct, and behind it the riddle of the universe. How are we getting along without the Devil? How are we managing to be good without the fork? What is happening to our conception of goodness itself?

To begin with, let me disclaim any intention of writing of morality from the point of view of the technical, or professional, moral philosopher. Such a person would settle the whole question by a few references to pragmatism, transcendentalism, and esoteric synthesis — leaving his auditors angry but unable to retaliate. This attitude, I am happy to say, I am quite unable to adopt. I do not know what pragmatism is, and I do not care. I know the word transcendental only in connection with advertisements for 'gents' furnishings.' If Kant, or Schopenhauer, or Anheuser Busch have already settled these questions, I cannot help it.

In any case, it is my opinion that now-a-days we are overridden in the specialties, each in his own department of learning, with his tags, and label, and his pigeon-hole category of proper names, precluding all discussion by ordinary people. No man may speak fittingly of the soul without spending at least six weeks in a theological college; morality is the province of the moral philosopher who is prepared to pelt the intruder back over the fence with a shower of German commentaries. Ignorance, in its wooden shoes, shuffles around the portico of the temple of learning, stumbling among the litter of terminology. The broad field of human wisdom has been cut into a multitude of little professorial rabbit warrens. In each of these a specialist burrows deep, scratching out a shower of terminology, head down in an unlovely attitude which places an interlocutor at a grotesque conversational disadvantage.

May I digress a minute to show what I mean by the inconvenience of modern learning? This happened at a summer broading house where I spent a portion of the season of rest, in company with a certain number of ordinary, ignorant people like myself. We got on well together. In the evenings on the veranda we talked of nature and of its beauties, of the stars and why they were so far away — we didn't know their names, thank God — and such like simple topics of conversation.

Sometimes under the influence of a double-shotted sentimentalism sprung from huckleberry pie and doughnuts, we even spoke of the larger issues of life, and exchanged opinions on immortality. We used no technical terms. We knew none. The talk was harmless and happy. Then there came among us a faded man in a coat that had been black before it turned green, who was a Ph.D. of Oberlin College. The first night he sat on the veranda, somebody said how beautiful the sunset was. Then the man from Oberlin spoke up and said: 'Yes, one could almost fancy it a pre-Raphaelite conception with the same chiaroscuro in the atmosphere.' There was a pause. That ended all nature study for almost an hour. Later in the evening, some one who had been reading a novel said in simple language that he was sick of having the hero always come out on top. 'Ah,' said the man from Oberlin, 'but does n't that precisely correspond with Nitch's idea' (he meant, I suppose, Nietzsche, but he pronounced it to rime with 'bitch') 'of the dominance of man over fate?' Mr. Hezekiah Smith who kept the resort looked round admiringly and said, 'Ain't he a *terr?*' He certainly was. While the man from Oberlin stayed with us, elevating conversation was at an end, and a self-conscious ignorance hung upon the veranda like a fog.

However, let us get back to the Devil. Let us notice in the first place that because we have kicked out the Devil as an absurd and ridiculous superstition, unworthy of a scientific age, we have by no means eliminated the supernatural and the super-rational from the current thought of our time. I suppose there never was an age more riddled with superstition, more credulous, more drunkenly addicted to thaumaturgy than the present. The Devil in his palmiest days was nothing to it. In despite of our vaunted material commonsense, there is a perfect craving abroad for belief in something beyond the compass of the believable.

It shows itself in every age and class. Simpering Seventeen gets its fortune told on a weighing machine, and shudders with luxurious horror at the prospective villainy of the Dark Man who is to cross her life. Senile Seventy gravely sits on a wooden bench at a wonder-working meeting, waiting for a gentleman in a 'Tuxedo' jacket to call up the soul of Napoleon Bonaparte, and ask its opinion of Mr. Taft. Here you have a small tenement, let us say, on South Clark Street, Chicago. What is it? It is the home of Nadir the Nameless, the great Hindoo astrologer. Who are in the front room? Clients waiting for a revelation of the future. Where is Nadir? He is behind a heavily draped curtain, worked with Indian serpents. By the waiting clients Nadir is understood to be in consultation with the twin fates, Isis and Osiris. In reality Nadir is frying potatoes. Presently he will come out from behind the curtain and announce that Osiris has spoken (that is, the potatoes are now finished and on the back of the stove) and that he is prepared to reveal hidden treasure at forty cents a revelation. Marvelous, is it not, this Hindoo astrology business? And any one can be a Nadir the Nameless, who cares to stain his face blue with thimbleberry juice, wrap a red turban round his forehead, and cut the rate of revelation to thirty-five cents. Such is the credulity of the age which has repudiated the Devil as too difficult of belief.

We have, it is true, moved far away from the Devil; but are we after all so much better off? Or do we, in respect of the future, contain within ourselves the promise of better things? I suppose that most of us would have the general idea that there never was an age which displayed so high a standard of morality, or at least of ordinary human decency, as our own. We look back with a shudder to the blood-stained history of our ancestors; the fires of Smithfield with the poor martyr writhing about his post, frenzied and hysterical in the flames; the underground cell where the poor remnant of humanity turned its haggard face to the torch of the entering gaoler; the madhouse itself with its gibbering occupants converted into a show for the idle fools of London. We may well look back on it all and say that, at least, we are better than we were. The history of our little human race would make but sorry reading were not its every page imprinted with the fact that human ingenuity has invented no torment too great for human fortitude to bear.

In general decency — sympathy — we have undoubtedly progressed. Our courts of law have forgotten the use of the thumbkins and boot; we do not press a criminal under 'weights greater than he can bear' in order to induce him to plead; nor flog to ribbands the bleeding back of the malefactor dragged at the cart's tail through the thoroughfares of a crowded city. Our public, objectionable though it is, as it fights its way to its ball games, breathes peanuts and peppermint upon the offended atmosphere, and shrieks aloud its chronic and collective hysteria, is at all events better than the leering oafs of the Elizabethan century, who put hard-boiled eggs in their pockets and sat around upon the grass waiting for the 'burning' to begin.

But when we have admitted that we are better than we were as far as the *facts* of our moral conduct go, we may well ask as to the principles upon which our conduct is based. In past ages there was the authoritative moral code as a guide — thou shalt and thou shalt not — and behind it the pains, and the penalties, and the three-pronged oyster fork. Under that influence, humanity, or a large part of it, slowly and painfully acquired the moral habit. At present it goes on, as far as its actions are concerned, with the momentum of the old beliefs.

But when we turn from the actions on the surface to the ideas underneath, we find in our time a strange confusion of beliefs out of which is presently to be made the New Morality. Let us look at some of the varied ideas manifested in the cross sections of the moral tendencies of our time.

Here we have first of all the creed and cult of self-development. It arrogates to itself the title of New Thought, but contains in reality nothing but the Old Selfishness. According to this particular outlook the goal of morality is found in fully developing one's self. Be large, says the votary of this creed, be high, be broad. He gives a shilling to a starving man, not that the man may be fed but that he himself may be a shilling-giver. He cultivates sympathy with the destitute for the sake of being sympathetic. The whole of his virtue and his creed of conduct runs to a cheap and easy egomania in which his blind passion for himself causes him to use external people and things as mere reactions upon his own personality. The immoral little toad swells itself to the bursting point in its desire to be a moral ox.

In its more ecstatic form, this creed expresses itself in a sort of general feeling of 'uplift,' or the desire for internal moral expansion. The votary is haunted by the idea of his own elevation. He wants to get into touch with nature, to swim in the Greater Being, 'to tune himself,' harmonize himself, and generally to perform on himself as on a sort of moral accordion. He gets himself somehow mixed up with natural objects, with the sadness of autumn, falls with the leaves and drips with the dew. Were it not for the complacent self-sufficiency which he induces, his refined morality might easily verge into simple idiocy. Yet, odd though it may seem, this creed of self-development struts about with its head high as one of the chief moral factors which have replaced the authoritative dogma of the older time.

The vague and hysterical desire to 'uplift' one's self merely for exaltation's sake is about as effective an engine of moral progress as the effort to lift one's self in the air by a terrific hitching up of the breeches.

The same creed has its physical side.

It parades the Body, with a capital B, as also a thing that must be developed; and this, not for any ulterior thing that may be effected by it but presumably as an end in itself. The Monk or the Good Man of the older day despised the body as a thing that must learn to know its betters. He spiked it down with a hair shirt to teach it the virtue of submission. He was of course very wrong and very objectionable. But one doubts if he was much worse than his modern successor who joys consciously in the operation of his pores and his glands, and the correct rhythmical contraction of his abdominal muscles, as if he constituted simply a sort of superior sewerage system.

I once knew a man called Juggins who exemplified this point of view. He used to ride a bicycle every day to train his muscles and to clear his brain. He looked at all the scenery that he passed to develop his taste for scenery. He gave to the poor to develop his sympathy with poverty. He read the Bible regularly in order to cultivate the faculty of reading the Bible, and visited picture galleries with painful assiduity in order to give himself a feeling for art. He passed through life with a strained and haunted expression waiting for clarity of intellect, greatness of soul, and a passion for art to descend upon him like a flock of doves. He is now dead. He died presumably in order to cultivate the sense of being a corpse.

No doubt, in the general scheme or purpose of things the cult of self-development and the botheration about the Body may, through the actions which it induces, be working for a good end. It plays a part, no doubt, in whatever is to be the general evolution of morality.

And there, in that very word evolution, we are brought face to face with another of the wide-spread creeds of our day, which seek to replace the older. This one is not so much a guide to conduct as a theory, and a particularly cheap and easy one, of a general meaning and movement of morality. The person of this persuasion is willing to explain everything in terms of its having been once something else and being about to pass into something further still. Evolution, as the natural scientists know it, is a plain and straightforward matter, not so much a theory as a view of a succession of facts taken in organic relation. It assumes no purposes whatever. It is not — if I may be allowed a professor's luxury of using a word which will not be understood — in any degree teleological.

The social philosopher who adopts the evolutionary theory of morals is generally one who is quite in the dark as to the true conception of evolution itself. He understands from Darwin, Huxley, and other great writers whom he has not read, that the animals have been fashioned into their present shape by a long process of twisting, contortion, and selection, at once laborious and deserving. The giraffe lengthened its neck by conscientious stretching; the frog webbed its feet by perpetual swimming; and the bird broke out in feathers by unremitting flying. ' Nature ' by weeding out the short giraffe, the inadequate frog, and the top-heavy bird encouraged by selection the ones most ' fit to survive.' Hence the origin of species, the differentiation of organs — hence, in fact, everything.

Here, too, when the theory is taken over and mis-translated from pure science to the humanities, is found the explanation of all our social and moral growth. Each of our religious customs is like the giraffe's neck. A manifestation such as the growth of Christianity is regarded as if humanity broke out into a new social organism, in the same way as the ascending amœba breaks out into a stomach. With this view of human relations, nothing in the past is said to be either good or bad. Everything is a movement. Cannibalism is a sort of apprenticeship in meat-eating. The institution of slavery is seen as an evolutionary stage towards free citizenship, and ' Uncle Tom's ' overseer is no longer a nigger-driver but a social force tending towards the survival of the Booker Washington type of negro.

With his brain saturated with the chloroform of this social dogma, the moral philosopher ceases to be able to condemn anything at all, measures all things with a centimeter scale of his little doctrine, and finds them all of the same length. Whereupon he presently desists from thought altogether, calls everything bad or good an evolution, and falls asleep with his hands folded upon his stomach murmuring ' survival of the fittest.'

Anybody who will look at the thing candidly, will see that the evolutionary explanation of morals is meaningless, and presupposes the existence of the very thing it ought to prove. It starts from a misconception of the biological doctrine. Biology has nothing to say as to what ought to survive and what ought not to survive, it merely speaks of what does survive. The burdock easily kills the violet, and the Canadian skunk lingers where the humming-bird has died. In biology the test of fitness to survive is the fact of survival itself — nothing else. To apply this doctrine to the moral field brings out grotesque results. The successful burglar ought to be presented by society with a nickle-plated ' jimmy,' and the starving cripple left to die in the ditch. Everything — any phase of movement or religion — which succeeds, is right. Anything which does not is wrong. Everything which is, is right; everything which was, is right; everything which will be, is right. All we have to do is to sit still and watch it come. This is moral evolution.

On such a basis, we might expect to find, as the general outcome of the new moral code now in the making, the simple worship of success. This is exactly what is happening. The morality which the Devil with his oyster fork was commissioned to inculcate was essentially altruistic. Things were to be done for other people. The new ideas, if you combine them in a sort of moral amalgam — to develop one's self, to evolve, to measure things by their success — weigh on the other side of the scale. So it comes about that the scale begins to turn and the new morality shows signs of exalting the old-fashioned Badness in place of the discredited Goodness. Hence we find saturating our contemporary literature the new worship of the Strong Man, the easy pardon of the Unscrupulous, the Apotheosis of the Jungle, and the Deification of the Detective. Force, brute force, is what we now turn to as the moral ideal, and Mastery and Success as the sole tests of excellence. The nation cuddles its multi-millionaires, cinematographs itself silly with the pictures of its prize fighters, and even casts an eye of slantwise admiration through the bars of its penitentiaries. Beside these things the simple Good Man of the older dispensation, with his worn alpaca coat and his obvious inefficiency, is nowhere.

Truly, if we go far enough with it, the Devil may come to his own again, and more than his own, not merely as Head

Stoker but as what is called an End in Himself.

I knew a little man called Bliggs. He worked in a railroad office, a simple, dusty, little man, harmless at home and out of it till he read of Napoleon and heard of the thing called a Superman. Then somebody told him of Nitch, and he read as much Nitch as he could understand. The thing went to his head. Morals were no longer for him. He used to go home from the office and be a Superman by the hour, curse if his dinner was late, and strut the length of his little home with a silly irritation which he mistook for moral enfranchisement. Presently he took to being a Superman in business hours, and the railroad dismissed him. They know nothing of Nitch in such crude places. It has often seemed to me that Bliggs typified much of the present moral movement.

Our poor Devil then is gone. We cannot have him back for the whistling. For generations, as yet unlearned in social philosophy, he played a useful part — a dual part in a way, for it was his function to illustrate at once the pleasures and the penalties of life. Merriment in the scheme of things was his, and for those drawn too far in pleasure and merriment, retribution and the oyster fork.

I can see him before me now, his long, eager face and deep-set, brown eyes, pathetic with the failure of ages — carrying with him his pack of cards, his amber flask, and his little fiddle. Let but the door of the cottage stand open upon a winter night, and the Devil would blow in, offering his flask and fiddle, or rattling his box of dice.

So with his twin incentives of pain and pleasure he coaxed and prodded humanity on its path, till it reached the point where it repudiated him, called itself a Superman, and headed straight for the cliff over which is the deep sea. *Quo vadimus?*

II

MARK TWAIN AS OUR EMISSARY

GEORGE ADE

[*Century Magazine*, December, 1910. By permission.]

Mark Twain had a large following of admirers who came to regard themselves as his personal friends. Many of them he never met. Most of them never saw him. All of them felt a certain relationship and were flattered by it. Men and women in all parts of our outspread domain, the men especially, cherished a private affection for him. They called him by his first name, which is the surest proof of abiding fondness. Andrew Jackson was known as ' Andy '; Abraham Lincoln was simply ' Abe ' to every soldier boy; and, as a later instance, we have ' Teddy.' Some men settle down to a kinship with the shirt-sleeve contingent, even when they seem indifferent to the favor of the plain multitude.

Mark Twain never practised any of the wiles of the politician in order to be cheered at railway stations and have Chautauquas send for him. He did not seem over-anxious to meet the reporters, and he had a fine contempt for most of the orthodox traditions cherished by the people who loved him. Probably no other American could have lived abroad for so many years without being editorially branded as an expatriate. In some sections of our country it is safer to be an accomplice in homicide, or a stand-patter in politics, than it is to be an ' expatriate.' When Mr. Clemens chose to take up his residence in Vienna he incurred none of the criticism visited upon Mr. William Waldorf Astor. Every one hoped he would have a good time and learn the German language. Then when the word came back that he made his loafing headquarters in a place up an alley known as a *stube,* or a *rathskeller,* or something like that, all the women of the literary clubs, who kept his picture on the high pedestal with the candles burning in front of it, decided that *stube* meant ' shrine.' You may be sure that if they can find the place they will sink a bronze memorial tablet immediately above the main faucet.

Of course, the early books, such as *Innocents Abroad, Roughing It,* and *The Gilded Age* gave him an enormous vogue in every remote community visited by book-agents. The fact that people enjoyed reading these cheering volumes and preserved them in the bookcase and moved out some of the classics by E. P. Roe and Mrs. Southworth in order to make room for *Tom Sawyer* and *Huckleberry Finn,* does not fully account for the evident and accepted popularity of Mark Twain.

Other men wrote books that went into the bookcase but what one of them ever earned the special privilege of being hailed by his first name?

When a man has done his work for many years more or less under the supervising eye of the public, the public learns a good many facts about him that are in no way associated with his set and regular duties as a servant of the public. Out of the thousand-and-one newspaper mentions and private bits of gossip and whispered words of inside information, even the busy man in the street comes to put an estimate on the real human qualities of each personage, and sometimes these estimates are surprisingly accurate, just as they are often sadly out of focus.

Joseph Jefferson had a place in the public esteem quite apart from that demanded by his skill as an actor. Players and readers of newspapers came to know in time that he was a kind and cheery old gentleman of blameless life, charitable in his estimates of professional associates, a modest devotee of the fine arts, an outdoor sportsman with the enthusiasm of a boy, and the chosen associate of a good many eminent citizens. When they spoke of 'Joe' Jefferson in warmth and kindness, it was not because he played *Rip Van Winkle* so beautifully, but because the light of his private goodness had filtered through the mystery surrounding every popular actor. William H. Crane is another veteran of the stage who holds the regard of the public. It knows him as a comedian, and also it knows him as the kind of man we should like to invite up to our house to meet the 'folks.' The sororities throb with a feeling of sisterhood for Miss Maude Adams because the girls feel sure that she is gracious and charming and altogether 'nice.'

Mark Twain would have stood very well with the assorted grades making up what is generally known as the 'great public' even if he had done his work in a box and passed it out through a knothole. Any one who knew our homely neighbors as he knew them and could tell about them in loving candor, so that we laughed at them and warmed up to them at the same time, simply had to be 'all right.' Being prejudiced in his favor, we knew that if he wanted to wear his hair in a mop and adopt white clothing and talk with a drawl, no one would dare to suggest that he was affecting the picturesque. He was big enough to be different. Any special privilege was his without the asking. Having earned 100 per cent. of our homage he didn't have to strain for new effects.

His devotion to the members of his family and the heroic performance in connection with the debts of the publishing house undoubtedly helped to strengthen the general regard for him. Also, the older generation, having heard him lecture, could say that they had 'met' him. Every one who sat within the soothing presence of the drawl, waiting to be chirked up on every second sentence with a half-concealed stroke of drollery, was for all time a witness to the inimitable charm of the man and the story-teller.

The knowledge of his unaffected democracy became general. No doubt the housewives loved him for his outspoken devotion to home-cooking. Has any one told in public the anecdote of his tribute to an humble item in the bill of fare? It was at a dinner party in Washington. Senator Hearst was giving the dinner, and Mark Twain was the guest of honor. Here were two transplanted Westerners who knew more about roughing it than ever appeared in a book. As the high-priced food was being served to them, they talked longingly of the old-fashioned cookery of Missouri. The Senator wondered if there was any real corned beef and cabbage left in the world. Mark Twain spoke up in praise of the many old-time dishes, reaching his climax when he declared that, in his opinion, 'Bacon would improve the flavor of an angel!'

Furthermore is it not possible that much of the tremendous liking for Mark Twain grew out of his success in establishing our credit abroad? Any American who can invade Europe and command respectful attention is entitled to triumphal arches when he arrives home. Our dread and fear of foreign criticism are still most acute. Mrs. Trollope and Captain Marryat lacerated our feelings long ago. Dickens came over to have our choicest wild flowers strewn in his pathway and then went home to scourge us until we shrieked with pain. Kipling had fun with us, and for years after that we trembled at his approach. George Bernard Shaw peppers away at long range and the *London Spectator* grows peevish every time it looks out of the window and sees a drove of Cook tourists madly spending their money.

It is a terrible shock to the simple inlander, who has fed upon Congressional oratory and provincial editorials, when he discovers that in certain European capitals the name 'American' is almost a term of reproach. The first-time-over citizen from Spudville or Alfalfa Center indicates his protest by wearing a flag on his coat and inviting those who sit in darkness to come over and see what kind of trams are run on the Burlington. The lady, whose voice comes from a point directly between the eyes, seeks to correct all erroneous impressions by going to the table d'hôte with fewer clothes and more jewels than any one had reason to expect. These two are not as frequently to be seen as they were twenty years ago but they are still gleefully held up by our critics as being 'typical.'

Probably they are outnumbered nowadays by the apologetic kind — those who approach the English accent with trembling determination and who, after ordering in French, put a finger on the printed line so that the waiter may be in on the secret.

There are Americans who live abroad and speak of their native land in shameful whispers. Another kind is an explainer. He becomes fretful and involved in the attempt to make it clear to some Englishman with a cold and fish-like eye that, as a matter of fact, the lynchings are scattered over a large territory, and Tammany has nothing whatever to do with the United States Senate, and the millionaire does not crawl into the presence of his wife and daughters, and Morgan never can be king, and citizens of St. Louis are not in danger of being hooked by moose. After he gets through the Englishman says 'Really?' and the painful incident is closed.

Every man is handicapped and hobbled when he gets out of his own bailiwick. The American is at a special disadvantage in Europe. If he cannot adapt himself to strange customs and social regulations, he thinks that he will be set down as an ignoramus. If he tries to nullify or override them he may be regarded as a boor or a barbarian. Once in a while an American, finding himself beset by unfamiliar conditions, follows the simple policy of not trying to assimilate new rules or oppose them, and merely goes ahead in his own way, conducting himself as a human being possessed of the usual number of faculties. This odd performance may be counted upon to excite wonder and admiration. Benjamin Franklin tried it out long ago and became the sensation of Europe. General Grant and Colonel Roosevelt got along comfortably in all sorts of foreign complications merely by refusing to put on disguises and to be play-actors. But Mark Twain was probably the best of our emissaries. He never waved the starry banner and at the same time he never went around begging forgiveness. He knew the faults of his home people and he understood intimately and with a family knowledge all of their good qualities and groping intentions and half-formed plans for big things in the future; but apparently he did not think it necessary to justify all of his private beliefs to men who lived five thousand miles away from Hannibal, Missouri. He had been in all parts of the world and had made a calm and unbiased estimate of the relative values of men and institutions. Probably he came to know that all had been cut from one piece and then trimmed variously. He carried with him the same placid habits of life that sufficed him in Connecticut and because he was what he pretended to be, the hypercritical foreigners doted upon him and the Americans at home, glad to flatter themselves, said, 'Why, certainly, he's one of us.'

III

SYSTEM VERSUS SLIPPERS

[GEORGE BURWELL DUTTON]

[*Unpopular Review*, April, 1915. By permission of author and publisher.]

'The doctrine of efficiency is a modern offshoot of the doctrine of total depravity,' drawled my neighbor.

I looked incredulous. I knew that was the way he wanted me to look. But I did n't have any difficulty in conforming to his desires.

'Ye-es,' he continued, 'it all goes back to the doctrine of total depravity. Man is born to sin, as — as the sparks fly upward,' he concluded triumphantly.

'Trouble, not sin, is, I think, the Biblical phrasing,' I interposed mildly.

'All amounts to the same thing. Man is born to trouble. Trouble is the result of sin. If there were no sin there would be no trouble. Ergo, man is born to sin, — and so forth.'

He stopped to puff at his pipe.

'But the doctrine of efficiency?— How—'

'I was coming to that. What does the doctrine of efficiency mean? Only this: Just naturally you do a thing the wrong way. You have to struggle, to discipline yourself, to overcome your natural tendencies, in order to do a thing the right way: that is, with the smallest expenditure of energy. You are naturally perverse, wasteful — which is, economically speaking, sinful. You are born in economic sin, and you live in economic sin, till 'long comes the doctrine of efficiency and teaches you system, and so plucks you, a brand from the burning. It corrects your wasteful ways, it teaches you how to conserve your energies, it makes you live an economically righteous life. The doctrine of efficiency is based upon an economic statement of the doctrine of total depravity. The theological doctrine says, all men are by nature sinners; the economic says, all men are by nature inefficient — that is, are economic sinners. Even sin is economic in this age. All men by nature do their tasks wastefully, unsystematically; but they may be saved by adopting the methods of efficiency. There: that's modern theology for you.'

And he knocked the ashes out of his pipe and went home.

I am not certain about my neighbor's view of the doctrine of efficiency. He may be right, and then again he may not. But this I do know, that the preachers of the doctrine of efficiency are many — and efficient. Plan and system are extended to all things. One cannot take up a magazine without being confronted by reproachful directions for increasing one's efficiency. *Busy-bodies' Magazine* tells you of the tremendous waste of time involved in the present methods of peanut-roasting. *Dunce's Monthly* proclaims loudly the benefits to humanity that will infallibly result from adopting more efficient methods of operating a hurdy-gurdy. Diagrams and pictures stare at us from every page. We learn the waste of energy and the number of useless motions involved in the ordinary way of getting on a street-car. We find out how to carve a turkey with the fewest possible slashes. Now, all this may be desirable and necessary. We may be so 'rushed for time,' to use the expressive colloquialism, that every energy must be conserved. Nevertheless, I object; I am economically depraved. I long for the looser ways of my forebears. System chafes me. It is unyielding. Like a dress shirt, it holds me clamped. I prefer a dressing-gown and slippers — blessed symbols of mild unrestraint. Perhaps I ought not to feel this way. Perhaps I ought not to object to learning the proper method of filling my fountain-pen — that is a task, the sooner over, the better. Perhaps I ought not to object to learning the least exhausting way of buttoning my collar — though every right-minded man prizes the privilege of indignation at a recalcitrant button — and what button is recalcitrant once the appropriate system is mastered? But, be all this as it may, I do protest seriously against having to learn the most efficient way of filling my pipe!

I was not always of this mind. Like other misguided mortals of limited vision, I was disposed to welcome the new doctrines. I read with avidity the proper method of shoveling snow. I rejoiced at finding out just what and how few motions it was necessary to go through to connect a water-pipe. I was filled with indignation when I observed how wasteful of his energy was my plumber — and I paying for it! The prodigality of the man who carried in my coal filled me with despair.

Nay, more, I made some small effort to apply the doctrine of efficiency to my own pursuits. I am a humble teacher of English in a small New England college. I have many themes to correct. I had contented myself with taking up a pen and indicating errors and corrections with red ink —'squirting the red ink,' my students vulgarly called it. But this was not systematic; it was not efficient; it was too natural. So I became self-conscious in my work. I studied it. I analyzed it. Soon I found that there were certain criticisms and directions that I wrote and rewrote many times daily. So I purchased rubber stamps. Then I found that I wasted much valuable time in laying hold of the right rubber stamp; so I purchased little hooks, and hung the rubber stamps in a row, and assigned a definite hook to each stamp, and memorized the positions of the stamps on the hooks, and looked upon my work, and thought it good. This involved the expenditure of much time and energy, but I was introducing system, I was becoming efficient.

Turning my attention to other details, I found that I wasted much time — often in two minutes — in looking for papers. So I had the college carpenter construct a case of pigeon-holes and place it beside my desk. I devoted an afternoon to labeling the pigeon-holes and filing my papers. Then I spent fifteen minutes a day — by this time I had a clock in my little office and timed my every action — fifteen minutes a day in filing new letters and documents — sometimes it was only thirteen minutes, roughly speaking. But I did not begrudge this time, for it meant that I was taking another step toward efficiency.

What need to relate in detail all of the other measures that I took for the efficient administration of my duties? I installed files for all of the themes. I moved my books from my home into my little office, lining the walls with shelves — where they were not already lined with pigeon-holes. I had a swinging shelf constructed for my typewriter, and attached it to my desk. I bought a machine for sharpening pencils. I introduced the latest approved pattern of a card-index file. There was a place for everything, and everything in its place — though it took most of my time to put it there. But I was introducing efficiency into my work; system and order are the first laws of efficiency; and I spared no labor in putting them into effect.

Recently, however, a slave of efficiency visited me, and I have received a rude awakening. I have discovered that I am not really efficient.

My friend is a man with surprised hair and peering eyes. He has the appearance of seeing everything — and he does. He came with me to my recitation room one morning, and looked around in seeming idleness while I was busy planning the seating list for the new term. Then he began to talk. His comments irritated me, I must admit. I am rather proud of my recitation room. Past worthies on the wall blink in the electric light, and scenes significant in literary history confront the wandering eyes of the restless present.

However, my friend received no imaginative stimulus. He was blind to all that. But Spenser's ruff and Johnson's wig — these called forth his scorn. How could a man work, handicapped by such frills? I mildly pointed out that the gentlemen concerned did accomplish something of importance, but he ignored me. He went up to an old print of 'The Fortune Playhouse,' of which I am decidedly fond. In the foreground two men are loading a cart with kegs. Did my friend admire the ancient architecture of the building? Did he appreciate the quaint garb of the men? Did it all serve to make the past more intimate, to bring it a little nearer? Not at all. His indignation was aroused. The cart was parallel with the walk. Why wasn't it backed up to the walk? Think of how much effort was wasted in rolling those kegs around in the street to the end of the cart! He could not see the theater for the cart!

I was somewhat impatient at his attitude. But after all, could he be blamed? He thought in terms of efficiency, because efficiency was his business. Others could admire quaintness, others could dream themselves into the past, but he was an apostle with a flaming mission: to see and to correct all waste of energy. And indeed I had that which he could appreciate. I ushered him into my little office. There it was, in immaculate order. The fresh April sunshine gleamed from the polished handles of the rows of rubber stamps. The pigeon-holes gaped, ready to devour their prey in orderly fashion. Variegated inks and pencils lay on the desk ready for use at a moment's notice. It all looked so business-like! To be sure, for a moment I recalled uneasily my neighbor's remark, 'You can't always tell from a cat's looks how far it will jump.' But this 'cat' did have such an impressive appearance. I felt sure it could jump far — and efficiently. Everything had an air of preparedness, like that of a fire-engine in an engine-house. I expanded in anticipation of praise.

My friend snorted. 'Huh! What old fossils you teachers are! You wouldn't last a day in an efficiency shop!' Then he showed me why. The row of stamps was not properly placed; I had to turn around to reach some of them. My theme files were so shallow that the projecting themes drooped and obscured the labels.

My clock was behind me, and I had to crane my neck to see it. My desk was not in the best light. I was dumbfounded.

He continued relentlessly. My pigeon-holes were placed too high. They were indeed beside my desk, but I had to rise to reach them. That meant a loss, on an average, of two and three-fifths seconds. There were sixteen pigeon-holes. Perhaps I had to use each an average of three times in the course of a day's work. My friend is what he would term 'a handy man' with figures. He reckoned for a few moments.— That meant a loss of *one hundred and twenty-five seconds a day!*

'Think of it!' he cried. 'One hundred and twenty-five seconds! In less than one-tenth of the time you waste here a man could run a hundred yards, and —'

'But I don't want to run a hundred yards,' I interposed, somewhat resentfully, 'and if I did, *I* couldn't run it in that time.'

'Never mind.' He brushed aside my objections, and continued his calculations. There are six days in a working week — I refuse to work Sundays, although some teachers have to — and thirty-six working weeks in a year — and how many years one might use in the reckoning, who can tell? Why, by properly placing those pigeon-holes, I might save enough time to take a trip to Europe, according to this efficiency agent.— Of course, I have n't money enough, and if I had, how to combine these scattered moments into a unified whole would offer another problem — but that is all beside the question. The moments were there, in potential emptiness. One does n't refuse a cup because one lacks the wine to fill it.

'Let me see you at work,' commanded he of the peering eyes. Meekly I sat down at my desk. Where were my themes? Oh, yes, they were up there on a shelf, across the room. Abjectly I arose. My friend looked at me reproachfully. I reached up for the themes. *Why* had n't that shelf been placed lower? How many tenths of a second had I lost by that upward reach? I shivered, and clumsily knocked down a book. I had to stoop to pick it up. More time lost! I took up the themes again, savagely. The rubber band was old. It broke under the unwonted strain of my fervor. There was a flutter of white papers. Blunderingly I bent forward to gather them up.

Why was n't the floor built higher? Stupid piece of inefficient planning.— Why was I so high above it? Why was n't I built more efficiently?

Red-faced and scant-breathed I arose and threw the themes on my desk. My friend had considerately turned his back; but even that was eloquent.

'Oh, hang the themes!' I burst out. 'And — and — let 's go for a walk!'

That episode was bad enough, but it was n't the worst. My friend stayed with me several days, and they were stirring days for me. Ostensibly he had come for a rest — nerves all frayed — wanted to vegetate for a while — thought he 'd come to a quiet place. Now our college community is quiet, in all conscience. They tell the story of one man who once cut some figure in the world of affairs, who was prevailed upon to accept a professorship and live among us, that he announced that he was going to 'give up active life and "retire" to teach at —— College.' I think that was a somewhat undeserved slur on our faculty. I know I have to work, and I know my colleagues do. We don't feel that we have retired from active life. Still, I must admit that there is n't quite the same tension prevalent in what a visiting President of the United States tritely termed 'these academic shades,' as there is, say, in the Stock Exchange, or in Congress at the culmination of a tariff debate. Consequently I had hoped that my friend would be soothed, and would relax and yield himself to passive enjoyment. He did n't have to correct themes. Why should n't he enjoy himself? But he could n't. That terrible doctrine of efficiency was with him all the time, and gave him — and us — no rest. System, system — the word was constantly on his lips — and, what was worse, in his heart.

He carried it into all his pleasures — and mine. I like to play cards. That is, I like to use a game of cards as an excuse for idle revery or gossip. I play a leisurely game, a comfortable sort of a game, a slouching, be-slippered, relaxing game, restful beyond words. If I happen to forget that my partner played a jack of clubs three tricks previous, and consequently neglect to take the proper measures, I don't mind, and I don't want others to care. But my friend would have none of this. He had complicated 'leads' and elaborate systems. He played feverishly and snapped at me constantly for my neglect-fulness. Cards were real, cards were earnest, and there was no idle dreaming permitted. I gasped a sigh of relief when a game was ended. He played, as he worked, relentlessly.

One day we went on a tramp in the hills. I am not systematic on a tramp. I don't like to plan my route in advance; I prefer to follow the unexpected allure-ment of shady by-paths, the invitation of an unknown winding road, the beckoning of unexplored fields. To be sure, I usually get lost, and frequently get bedraggled by some unforeseen stream or slough; but I like to get lost; it has such inviting possi-bilities. Not so my friend. He de-manded maps, a definite objective point, a clear itinerary, and no side-trips. I yielded, but with rebellion smoldering in my heart.

Now I suppose I shall lay myself open to the reproaches of a multitude of very worthy persons when I confess that my dislike of system and rigidity is not con-fined to my choice of routes. Far from it. I abhor system in appreciation. I can enjoy the contour of a hill without know-ing its geological formation. The soft glow of green in the April landscape brings me pleasure which would be con-taminated by conscientious attempts to re-call the scientific explanation of the func-tion of chlorophyl in bud and blade. I love to watch the great clouds drifting lazily through a blue sea of air; but I don't care to master the nomenclature of meteorology. Nay, worst of all in these days of widespread 'bird-lore,' I can enjoy the dark flash of a bluebird's flight, but am only irked by classified lists of names and descriptions; and I am infuriated by the attitude of those who make of every walk a contest to see how many new varieties of birds may be identified and classified — as if the great Kingdom of Out-of-Doors were a mere museum of specimens and curiosities, to be grouped and labeled by every observer! Out upon those misguided creatures who mistake nomenclature for knowledge and classifi-cation for understanding; who strut through a starry evening, proud because they can clap Arcturus on the back and call him familiarly by name.

These earthly godfathers of heaven's lights,
That give a name to every fixed star,

Have no more profit of their shining nights
Than those that walk and wot not what they are.
Too much to know is to know nought but fame;
And every godfather can give a name.

Of course I do not scorn the labors of my scientific colleagues; their work, which goes far deeper than names, is necessary and beneficial. I merely sympathize with them because to them so much of the uni-verse is a symbol of labor. And I fail to see the necessity of making it a symbol of labor for myself, when I may rather see in it a garden of beauty and a place of contemplation and rest. In all this I suppose I am an ignoramus blindly stum-bling through unsuspected riches of wis-dom. I suppose I am a sinner turning my back upon the road of repentance. But I am perverse. I abominate those busy-bodies who would filch from us our few remaining careless hours and would rob them of the wayward prodigality that is their charm. For my part, I refuse to card-catalog my pleasures.

Needless to say, my friend was disgusted with me. He was as innocent of classified knowledge of the countryside as I, but he felt that he was excusable. He had spent his life in the city, and there he had ob-served with care the phenomena that had fallen under his gaze. I had not made similar good use of my opportunities. If I admired the delicate tracery of a silhouetted tree, he wanted to know its name and use. If I paused to hear the music of a tumbling brook, he wanted to estimate its volume and bemoaned the waste of power. To the spiritual signifi-cance, the soothing influence, of rural sights and sounds, he was insensible. At my lack of systematized knowledge he was disgusted. That walk was not a success.

Well, my friend has left me. I can't say I'm sorry. I like him, of course — but at a distance. A great peace has fallen upon me. I can correct my themes in my office without nervously counting my every motion. I can relax once more, cast aside the rigid garb of systematic ac-tivity, and once more don smoking-jacket and slippers, down-at-the-heel preferably. I can sit down in the evening and listen to the gobbling croak of a frog without being reproached for my inability to clas-sify it accurately in the animal kingdom. My next-door neighbor is a great comfort to me. He 'came over' last night, and while we sat before the open fire that robbed the sharp evening air of its chill, we discussed the whole matter comfortably.

'System in recreation!' he exclaimed disgustedly when we had talked a while. 'To play by plan! Why, your friend would destroy all the spontaneity of life, its fine, careless rapture.'

'Do you recall what Dr. Johnson said of such a man?' I queried. '"Sir, he is an enthusiast by rule." I despise enthusiasts by rule.'

'But of course that is n't all there was to your experience,' my neighbor remarked presently. 'Your visitor, after all, was more concerned with work than play. And in work, method and system have their place.'

'More place than they deserve,' I grumbled. 'Enthusiasts by rule infest all our activities. Systematization has become over-systematized. Too often we can't see the product for the machinery. We are victims to a pseudo-efficiency that merely clogs and retards achievement; that defeats its own ends.'

'On the other hand,' replied my friend mildly, 'I suppose that system, rightly used, does save time. I suppose that genuine efficiency does permit of greater production. However, its advocates don't consider all sides of the question. In some pursuits increase of production would be a calamity. Shall our factories, by increased efficiency, be enabled to produce more phonographs? Heaven forbid! Their efficiency is already terrible.'

'And there are many occupations,' I broke in, 'in which the time saved to the workman by system would be useless, because it comes in titbits. It can't be massed. And it must be massed, to be most effective. Suppose,' I added petulantly, 'that I *could* go to Europe in the time I might save by correcting themes efficiently; I can't go to Europe for ten minutes a day. And I 've got to use my ten minutes on the day I save them. They can't be stored up each day, till a respectable quantity accumulates.'

'No, of course. Yet, my friend, one might pick holes in your argument. The minutes may not be valueless, even though they can't be spent in Europe.'

'Oh, there are some good things about efficiency,' I hastened to interpose. 'I presume I might add the ten minutes to my daily game of golf.'

'Still, you object?'

'I object to excess of efficiency. Ultimately, the time saved by introducing more system into work is to be used in recreation. Why not strain less at our work, and make recreation of it?'

My friend nodded thoughtfully.

'At any rate,' I continued, 'if I want to do my allotted task in leisurely fashion, occasionally lingering over it to enjoy the fine flavor of achievement, I claim the right to do so. I take the time from my golf, but after six hours of work I go to my golf with steadier nerves than the man who has worked five hours at high tension. Your five-hour man with his superficial efficiency is victim of an obsession: speed. He spends himself in his work in order that he may gain time for — a sanatorium. He loses sight of his goal. To change a little the somewhat antiquated refrain, he does n't care where he 's going; he is satisfied if he is speeding on his way.'

I stopped, a bit out of breath with my earnestness. My friend was silently staring into the heart of the leisurely fire. After a moment he turned to me quizzically.

'Is this to be a defense of dilettanteism?'

'Not at all,' I exclaimed with some heat. Then I smiled at my own fervor. 'Dilettantes are beneath defense. But my plea is for moderation; for a truer sense of values. I protest against a misplaced emphasis upon output, a feverish demand for results, at no matter what expenditure of nervous energy. I protest, too, against a systematization that would reduce individuals to automatons; a mechanical efficiency that stereotypes the workman and standardizes his product. To offer freer play to personality may well be worth the sacrifice of a little efficiency.'

IV

THE HUMANIZED PROFESSOR

[*New York Times*, September 22, 1914.
By permission.]

[The letters of Professors Eucken, Haeckel, and Ostwald, referred to in this editorial, will be found in the following section, F. VII and F. VIII.]

One benefit the war has conferred upon the ordinary citizen is to diminish his terror of professors. Their utterances have startled the ordinary citizen, but they have reassured him and given him a better opinion of himself. He has discovered that, after all, there is nothing supernatural about a professor; that the professor is a man like himself, with like passions, and even — this he has discovered with a great secret joy — of like foolishness. When great professors like Eucken and Haeckel demonstrate that they can be just as furious, bigoted, and illogical as the ordinary citizen, the ordinary citizen should feel saddened, but instead he feels elated. The heavens seem nearer to him when a demigod loses his temper.

There is nothing intemperate about the remarks of Professor Ostwald, published yesterday, but they enlarge this joy of the ordinary citizen. They bring professors closer to him, make him less afraid. When Jupiter gives voice to the opinions of Bottom, Jupiter becomes human, democratic, likable. When we find this professor sketching the outcome of the war and depicting, in an off-hand way, the annexation of Canada to the United States as a result of it, he does not terrify us any more. Anybody in Celtic Park could have evolved that prophecy without even a degree of A.B., let alone a professorship.

We can love our professors, but we cannot feel afraid of them when one of them says that 'the violation of Belgian neutrality was an act of military necessity, since it is now proved that Belgian neutrality was to be violated by France and England.' No, nor when he gives us to understand that the Napoleonic wars, the wars of Frederick the Great, and the struggle between Austria and Italy, were all caused by 'the English policy of world dominion.' His vision of Russia resolving itself into a number of independent nations and his announcement that 'the principle of the absolute sovereignty of the individual nations' must be destroyed, complete a picture gratifying to the self-esteem of the humble, unlearned, ordinary citizen.

Welcome, gods and demigods, to your seats among the human race. The only reason we did n't invite you before was because we were afraid you would n't come. Check your halos at the door. Be seated, gentlemen; and make yourselves at home.

V

THE OLDEST LIVING GRADUATE

[*Sun*, New York, January 30, 1901. Reprinted in *Casual Essays of the Sun*, 1905. By permission.]

The King has no solitary preëminence in never dying. He shares his mortal immortality with another potentate and great public character, the Oldest Graduate. There is always an Oldest Graduate; and always there are heirs waiting for the succession. Mr. Benjamin D. Silliman, distinguished and fortunate in so many other regards, was also for some time the Oldest Living Graduate of Yale; and now that honor belongs to Judge Cutler of '29, who lives in Waterbury, where they make the watches. May these be wound up for many a day before he yields his crown to the heir apparent. At ninety-three the Oldest Living Graduate is or should be but a boy. After waiting seventy odd years for his title, he will be in no hurry to give it up. He should enjoy it to the full, be merciful in his reminiscences, and look with an indulgent pity on the lads of ninety and ninety-one who want his job.

For, flower unloved of Amaryllis though it be, this honor is greatly prized. The survivor in this Tontine has beaten all his contemporaries at college. He can say to Time, as Beranger said:

'Old Postilion, hold up, hold up;
Let us drink a stirrup cup.'

It is too much for this glory to go to a man otherwise famous, as Mr. Silliman was or as Horace Binney was. The latter, an illustrious lawyer whose fame is perhaps as dim now as that of most great lawyers who have not held high political office, was graduated at Harvard in 1797, if we remember well, and he was the oldest living Harvard man for some time before he was cut off in '95. An Oldest Living Graduate who has no other fame than that is to be preferred. Such was Joseph Head of Harvard, of 1804. He lived in some little town. With his bent form, his Van Winkle beard, his long staff, he looked what he was as he marched among the younger generations in the yard on Commencement Day, 'the oldest living grad-oo-ate,' as he pronounced it after the fashion of his rural youth. Good old Joseph Head, if that was his name! One thinks with kindness of him, and all his predecessors; and of his successors in the procession.

In every college from A to Z something of affection attaches to the college elder and leader of the line. Of ordinary distinction the graduate may grow tired, be it his or that of a classmate. Of the class of 1825 at Bowdoin, of 1829 at Harvard, of 1853 at Yale, it has been possible to hear too much. At Brunswick, in 1875, Mr. Blaine happily expressed the weariness which the constant celebration of the celebrated brings. 'I am glad to hear,' he said, 'that those members of the class of 1825 who are illustrious on earth are happy in heaven.'

The graduate whose ambition it is to become the Oldest Living Graduate scorns all loud and easier fames. In seclusion and with perfect modesty of spirit, he sets before himself early the high goal. He accepts philosophically all detriments which Fate and Fortune send. 'I am no longer young,' he says to himself, 'but why should I wish to be? Everybody who stays in the game must get old, and how few can become the Oldest Living Graduate! I am not handsome, witty, eloquent, or even popular. I don't have to be, in my business, which is that of living to be the O. L. G. My classmate, Hooker Haynes, has made most of the money there is in the world. My classmate, Brattle Holyoke, has married most of the rest. I don't need money in my business. Byles is a bishop, Dwight is a senator. Bill Trumbull is a trust. I have n't any office. I don't direct anything. I have little property and less hair. But I think I can outlive every man in my class and I mean to do it. Let them last into the nineties if they can. I'll take an even hundred, and one to carry, if necessary.'

The young chaps just out of college may not know this harmless ambition at first. They are too young — confound 'em! We remember hearing George Bancroft, sixty years after his graduation, imparting the fact to a freshman. The freshman gaped and gasped in wonder. How was it possible for a man to have been graduated sixty years ago? If Nebuchadnezzar had come into the room and tried to sell a book on vegetarianism, that freshman could not have been more surprised. But youth's the stuff will not endure. It does n't take the truly wise graduate long to find the most reasonable object of desire. He nourishes the gentle vision in his heart. He sees himself a well-preserved ancient of ninety-eight, with a face like a Baldwin apple and still tolerable legs. His gold-headed cane is less a staff than a part of his make-up; 't is a representative of the monumental pomp of age. He wears, for effect, a tall hat of the fashion of fifty years before. He prides himself on the cut of his frock coat. His surviving hair is soft and white. A perfect gentleman of the old school. 'Young gentlemen,' says the Oldest Living Graduate, 'I ascribe my remarkable health and long life to the fact that for seventy-five years I have never smoked nor drank. Boys,' he says to a few striplings of ninety odd assembled around the punch bowl, 'I attribute my good health and looks to the fact that for eighty years I have taken a nip of good stuff regularly every day. But I never overdid it as you do.'

We once knew an Oldest Living Graduate who would walk on the railroad track, although he was nearly a hundred and deaf as a post. This is encouraging for beginners, as it seems to show that the O. L. G. is born, not made by training. Only a very few years ago there happened to live in the same town the Oldest Living Graduate and the next-to-the-oldest living graduate. They were great cronies and as lively as crickets. But each watched the distressingly robust health of the other with some alarm. 'William is looking a leetle peaked,' John would say; 'I'm afraid he won't live through the winter.' 'John's failin',' William would say; 'he ought n't be out in the cold so much at his age.' And both lived in health to the very edge of the hundred. The man who will devote himself with a single mind to becoming the Oldest Living Graduate deserves to be happy.

VI

SLEEPING OUTDOORS

FREDERICK LEWIS ALLEN

[*Century Magazine*, November, 1913. By permission.]

The most overrated summer sport in the world is outdoor sleeping.

I speak on this subject with some feeling, as, in August last, I tested it on a week-end visit with my friend Jones at his little mosquito ranch in the White Mountains. I can now understand why sleeping under a roof, in a real bed, is insufferable to a man who has been camping all summer: what he misses is the keen excitement, the constant entertainment, the suspense, of a night in the woods. As soon as he lies down in a real bed he becomes so utterly bored that he promptly falls asleep, only to wake up in the morning and find that he has missed the whole night.

The moment I arrived at Jones's camp on Saturday afternoon I realized that he was the victim of the outdoor-sleeping fad. He was so under its spell that he immediately took me out to show me my cot. It was a frail, anemic, canvas thing that screamed and creaked protests whenever it was moved or sat upon. It stood on a roofless sleeping-porch. Over it was the branch of a tender tree and over that was the open sky.

'Here,' said Jones, expansively, 'is where you're to sleep. This region is the most wonderful place for sleeping in all the world. I get actually to look forward to the nights; I tumble in eagerly at ten o'clock, and don't know another thing till morning.'

'You never know very much,' I meditated inwardly, picking a yellow caterpillar off my cot. 'How about blankets and things?' It took a vast amount of imagination to think of blankets, for the thermometer showed several degrees of fever.

'Oh, I'll give you all you want, and lots of mosquito-netting, too,' Jones said. 'You can make your bed just as you like; that's half the fun of the thing.'

'Ah, yes.'

Way down in my heart I had a foreboding that it would be rather *more* than half the fun. 'Wonderful!' I simulated. 'I haven't slept outdoors for years.' [1]

'Good!' said Jones.

Through the long evening I kept a stout heart and a cheery face; I even joked callously about the coming night, just as men sometimes joke about death and insanity and the dentist. I ate a heavy dinner, for breakfast looked very, very far away. Then I played three-handed auction with Jones and his wife. I was as merry as

[1] Strictly true, though I had spent several nights outdoors.

ever. No one should say that I had blanched with fear. At nine-forty, Jones yawned.

'Why, it's nearly ten,' said Mrs. Jones. 'I had no idea it was so late.'

'I was just going to suggest turning in,' Jones observed. 'I'll get your blankets and netting, if you like.'

I rose, and with a steady voice bade my hostess good night. The time had come.

Jones got the things, and we went out on the sleeping-porch, where he dumped them on my cot. The temperature had gone down a degree or two, but the air was still a long way from cool. The winds were still slumbering. A mosquito was meditatively volplaning about.

'Is there anything else you want?' said Jones as he left me in what, in reasonable circumstances, would have been my bedroom, but was now merely the world at large.

'Nothing,' I said, with fortitude. 'Good night.'

I went into the house and ten minutes later I emerged, attired in a neat, but gaudy, pair of pajamas. A lamp lighted my labors. The game was on; the mosquitoes and I were alone.

I shall withhold the tedious details of bed-making. Suffice it to say that I followed the golden rule of the art: don't let the feet escape; sacrifice everything else. If a single toe projects, the blankets will be up and about your neck before you know it. Then I folded a spare blanket into a pillow. Next came the *magnum opus* — hanging the mosquito-netting.

Here I confronted several alternatives. First, there is the Romanesque style, in which one hangs the netting on a hoop and then projects the face precisely under the hoop, keeping it there all night. This style is somewhat like sleeping with an inverted waste-basket on the face, and is based on the fallacious notion that insects bite only the head. Now I could show you — but never mind.

Then there is the Renaissance style. You suspend the netting gracefully by one or two points from a branch or some such supposed fixture, and let it depend in elegant festoons to the floor, securing the corners by lamps, vases, pitchers, or shoes. This method adequately answers the question, 'What shall we do with the wedding present Aunt Alice gave us?'

There is also the Perpendicular Gothic

style — four posts erected at the corners of the cot, with netting draped over them. This, I decided, required too much construction, and I swung back to the Renaissance. Securing some string, after a short, dark, and eventful journey in the house, I hitched the string to the netting, tied it to a branch, made a beautiful pyramidal tent, and squirmed inside with all the delicate deliberation of a jackstraw-player. At last I was on the creaking cot, and my tent still stood!

The laws of physics tell us that breezes pass through netting. This merely goes to show that physics has a big future. I had distinctly felt a slight zephyr outside; but now, as I balanced on my shoulder-blades on a Spartan blanket, I thought that the heat had become even more breathless; I felt that I was being suffocated.

Isn't there some wild animal that builds itself a house and then crawls in to die?

But I was not going to give up; I forced myself to draw a long sigh of relief, and said to myself: 'Oh, what wonderful air! How I shall sleep!' Yes, how?

I humped about a few times — creaking as I have never creaked before — till I thought I was more comfortable, pulled up a blanket cautiously, kicked it off warmly, rolled back into my original position, moved down six inches, so that my head just reached the pillow, thought about mosquitoes awhile, moved up four inches, thought about pillows, and then suddenly, with a great start, realized that I wasn't asleep. The fact stood out in my brain in huge, staring capitals: YOU ARE WIDE AWAKE; YOU ARE NOT EVEN SLEEPY. It was clear that my nerves needed soothing if I was to get any sleep at all.

People recommend many ways of soothing the nerves, but at times they are all disappointing. I thought of sheep jumping over a fence until all the sheep in my head had gone lame. I counted up to three hundred and seventy-four, which must be pretty nearly the world's record, but I noted no good results. At the end of an hour I was wider awake than ever and considerably more uncomfortable.

About this time I began discovering laws of physics.

I. When a man lies on his side on a cot, his weight is evenly distributed between his ear and his hip-bone.

II. For every dead mosquito in the hand there are two live ones in the bush that will be along presently.

III. The use of netting rests on the theory that it offers an obstruction to mosquitoes. This was first proved false in 1066, but people still —

Well, to tell the truth, that's as far as I got. I inadvertently fell asleep in the middle of law number three. Physics is the loser. I blame only myself.

At dawn, which in summer occurs shortly after bedtime and lasts for several hours, I was awakened by the birds, which were making a dreadful din above me in the trees. I found that four mosquitoes were perched on the netting about fourteen inches from my face — great, hungry fellows, regular eagles. They stared at me till I could have hidden myself for embarrassment. Presently a friend of theirs, bloated with drink, sailed down and sat beside them, singing a triumphant blood-lust song in a harsh, drunken tenor. He was plainly a degenerate going the pace that kills.

They say that if you look a wild animal in the eye he will turn away uneasily. I tried this on Macbeth, the new arrival — I called him Macbeth because he murdered sleep — but he was unabashed. I even spoke to him sternly, told him to go home and take his friends away with him, asked him what sort of place this was for a chap with a family; I appealed to his better self. Macbeth's only reply was to crawl insolently through a tear in the netting and come straight at me. His song of triumph rose in sharp crescendo till he struck my nose; then it ceased. I was just reaching to kill him, even at the risk of disfiguring myself for life, when suddenly and without warning the netting gave way completely and fell about my ears. Can you imagine a worse predicament than to be pinned under so much wreckage with a mosquito that you personally dislike?

Well, I climbed out, rearranged my tent (while Macbeth's friends got at my ankles), sneaked in under the edge again, lay down once more, and looked about warily for Macbeth. He was nowhere to be seen. I suspected some treachery, and on the off chance slapped the back of my neck quickly and with tremendous force, but with no corpse to show for it.

From that moment to this I have never seen Macbeth. It is all very sad. I almost wish now that I had n't been so harsh with him.

After I had given him up for lost, I took count of the insect life about me, and discovered a delightful game, called Insides versus Outsides. At 4 A.M. the score stood as follows: Insides, three mosquitoes, one spider; Outsides, one ant, one daddy-long-legs, two mosquitoes. A vigorous campaign then began, the Insides trying to get out, and the Outsides trying to get in.

At 4:30 A.M., owing largely to my efforts, the aspect of things was somewhat changed, the score standing: Insides, one mosquito; Outsides, one wasp, six mosquitoes, two unclassified. (Mind you, I 'm no etymologist; I don't pretend to know these eight-legged, hairy lads by name.)

The list of dead and injured was simply appalling.

After awhile I tired of this game, but the mosquitoes were all for keeping it up indefinitely. Only when a breeze sprang up did they begin to reel home in twos and threes to sleep off their jag. Then, once again, I shut my eyes in the hope that sleep would knit the 'ravell'd sleave of care.' It seemed, however, that the elements were all against knitting. The sun at that moment came up through the trees and shone straight into my eyes.

This worried me not so much on my own account as on Jones's; I hated the thought of his coming out with his wife at breakfast-time and finding me dead of a sunstroke on his porch.

Then I remembered that people don't die of sunstroke. They only fainted and lost their minds.

Shortly after this I must have fainted, for I woke up to find I had been unconscious for at least two hours!

The last thing I remembered, before the coma set in, was killing a spider on my stomach at five forty-five.

It was now eight o'clock. The sun had moved round and I could hear the kitchen-pump going, and see the housemaid, indoors, hiding matches, and sweeping the dust under the rugs.

I felt sleepy, but otherwise moderately well.[1]

Presently Jones came out in his bath-robe, and asked me how I had slept. I told him that that was just what I 'd been wondering myself, and he wanted to know whether the mosquitoes had been thick.

I said no, not too thick to get through the netting, and we both laughed and joked about the night as though it were the funniest thing in the world.

That 's the way in such crises, when the terrible strain is over.

I avoided another night's excitement by telegraphing myself to come home at once on the most urgent business.

Mr. and Mrs. Jones were awfully cordial, and laid emphasis on the fact that in the future my cot would always be waiting for me on the porch. I explained that my business would be very exacting for a few years, and I doubted if I would ever be able to get away again.

I still cling to the old-fashioned idea that night is the time for sleeping, and not for hunting and recreation.

VII

THE SERVANTLESS COTTAGE

[RALPH BERGENGREN]

[*Atlantic Monthly*, June, 1914. By permission of author and publisher.]

Stairs are done for. Observe the growing popularity of bungalows. Observe the multiplication of apartment houses. Listen to the words of the man who has lately built, and written about, what he calls a servantless cottage:

'Climbing is ofttimes all too strenuous for a happy housewife, so there must be no stairs.'

For a few more decades, miserable women, unhappy housewives, and, by inference, undesirable mothers, will continue to drag out painful existences in houses of more than one story.

'No stairs! No stairs!' the young wife cried,
And clapped her hands to see
A house as like a little flat
As any house could be!

And observe also the end of the servant-problem. For in the servantless cottage, says the satisfied designer, 'milady need fear no drudgery. A very few hours will suffice for housekeeping and cookery. Work becomes a pleasure and a maid becomes undesirable.'

---

[1] Law of physics: sunstrokes are not *necessarily* fatal.

Well, well! there are solutions and solutions of this servant-problem, and of the always interesting question of how other people ought to live. The question being somewhat personal to myself, I have examined a good many of these solutions without finding that any of them solved it to my personal satisfaction.

There is, of course, much to be said for the servantless cottage, although to solve a problem by giving it up is no very startling triumph of domestic mathematics. The experience of innumerable couples with kitchenettes proves that life is possible under this solution, but the frank admission of discontent among these experimenters indicates that it leaves much to be desired. My own domesticity is of the kitchenette kind in winter, but expands in summer to a modest establishment in the country with real stairs and a real cook in a real kitchen. I can see therefore — so at least I believe — not only the possibilities of the servantless cottage, its economy of effort in the details of housework, and its excellent adaptability to a small family unaccustomed to any other standard of living, but also its complete, unwitting abnegation of some of the finer things in human existence.

Now, if this man, in describing his servantless cottage, had contented himself with a plain and simple statement of its advantages, I dare say I should have read his description in the most friendly spirit imaginable; and certainly with no desire to criticize his results. It was that silly remark about milady that aroused opposition. We live in a republic and we are most of us reasonably self-respecting men and women, not a milady among us, unless she happens to be making a visit — in which case, one place she is not visiting is a servantless cottage. And so, in a word, the servantless cottage ceases to be an honest, more or less successful effort to provide a home in which the housewife can most conveniently do her own work, and becomes a neat little example of snobbish absurdity. Work becomes a pleasure to the happy housewife for whom climbing a flight of stairs is ofttimes all too strenuous — so keen and persistent a pleasure that domestic service becomes 'undesirable!' Is anybody really expected to believe it? Or is domestic service itself a phase of domesticity that can be so cheerfully eliminated? Has the servant — and,

bless you! the word has often enough been a term of honor — no really fine and enduring place in the scheme of gracious and cultivated domestic management?

For many generations, stairs and service have been inseparable from the amenities of domestic living. One has only to imagine these two essentials suddenly eliminated from literature to experience a pained sensation at the care-free way in which the man of the servantless cottage gets rid of them. And one has only to look about the world as it stands at present, servant-problem and all, to realize that it is the value of good domestic service which actually creates and keeps alive the problem itself. For even if the happy housewife enjoys every single item of housekeeping and cookery, there are times when her personal attention to them is obviously undesirable.

Imagine our servantless cottage as an example. Milady sings at her work. The portable vacuum cleaner — milord keeps up with all the latest improvements — gratefully eats up its daily dust. The fireless cooker prepares the meals 'with a perfection and deliciousness unrealized in the old days.' *A bas* mother and the way she used to cook! But in serving these meals of a hitherto unrealized perfection and deliciousness, milord and milady must needs chase each other between kitchen and dining-room. The guest at dinner, if he is luckily accustomed to picnics, carries his own plate and washes it afterward. I have myself entertained many a guest in this fashion, and he has carried his own plate, and, being that kind of a guest or I would n't have invited him, he has cheerfully helped wash the dishes, wearing a borrowed apron. But it would be absurd to claim that this performance, indefinitely repeated, is an improvement upon an orderly, efficiently served dinner-party. Conversation at dinner is more desirable than a foot-race between the courses; nor do I believe that life under such conditions can possibly 'become so alluring that one day the great majority of us will choose it first of all.'

Concerning stairs: I perhaps have more feeling for them than most; but I am quite sure that I speak at least for a large minority. It is the flatness of the flat, its very condensed and restricted coziness, its very lack of upstairs and downstairs, which prevents it from ever attaining completely the atmosphere of a home. The feet which cross the floor above my head are those of another family; the sounds which reach me from below are the noises of strangers; the life horizontal of the flat serves its convenient use but only emphasizes the independence and self-respect of the life vertical, master of the floor above, master likewise of the basement. I feel more human, less like some ingeniously constructed doll, when I can take my candle in hand and go upstairs to sleep. I want no bungalow. There is something fine in going to sleep even one flight nearer the stars — and away from the dining-room.

And observe further, if you please: this servantless cottage necessarily has no attic. Has the man no feeling whatever for the joys of his possible grandchildren? Or is the stairless, servantless cottage — 'truly the little house is the house of the future'— meant also to be childless? An examination of the plan shows a so-called bedroom marked 'guest or children,' which indicates that the happy housewife must exercise her own judgment. There are accommodations for one guest or two children, but it seems fairly evident that guest and children exclude each other. Milord and milady must decide between hospitality and race-suicide, or two children and no week-end visitor. Some will choose guest; some will choose children. Personally I hope they will all choose children, for, even without an attic, there is plenty of playground. 'People with tiny incomes' must always be careful not to purchase too small a lot; and so we find that the servantless cottage has paths, and a lawn, and flowers, and shrubbery, and a sun-dial, and an American elm, and a 'toad-stool canopy' between the poplars and the white birches, and an ivy-covered 'cache' to store the trunks in. I am glad there is going to be such a domestic convenience as a sun-dial; and perhaps, when there is a guest, the trunks can be taken out on the lawn and the children put to bed in the 'cache.'

But I guess that, after all, stairs will survive, and attics, and the servant-problem. Innumerable families are already living in servantless houses, with stairs, and it does n't even occur to them that they are solving any problem whatsoever. Innumerable housewives are about as happy under these conditions as most of us get to be under any conditions. The servant-problem itself is not the young and tender problem that many of us imagine. An examination of old newspapers will show anybody who is sufficiently patient and curious that a hundred years ago there was much indignant wonder that young women, visibly suited for domestic service, preferred to be seamstresses! What is more modern is the grave enthusiasm with which so many persons are trying to decide how the rest of us shall live with the maximum amount of comfort and culture for the minimum expenditure. And one interesting similarity between many of these suggestions is their passive opposition to another important group of critics.

'Have large families or perish as a nation!' shriek our advisers on one hand. 'Have small families or perish as individuals!' proclaim our advisers on the other.

For this servantless cottage is typical of a good many other housing suggestions in which the essential element is the small family; and even the possibility that the children may live to grow up seems to have been left out of consideration. Milord and milady, I imagine, have chosen children instead of a guest. These children (a boy and girl, as I like to picture them) grow up; marry; settle in their own servantless cottages, and have two children apiece. There are now a grandfather and a grandmother, a son and a daughter, a son-in-law and a daughter-in-law, and four grandchildren. In each servantless cottage there is that one bedroom marked 'guest or children.' Granting all the possibilities of the ivy-covered 'cache,'— and now the trunks will simply *have* to be taken out and stood on the lawn even if the snow does fall on them — milord and milady, come Christmas or other anniversary, can entertain a visit from two grandchildren and their father and mother. And by utilizing the 'cache' a son or daughter can receive a short visit from the aged parents, not too long, of course, or it would ruin the trunks. As for any of the hearty, old-fashioned, up-and-down-stairs hospitality — I may be an old fogey myself, but the servantless cottage shocks me.

'Our bedroom resembles a cozy stateroom on board ship.' Oh! la-la-la-la-la! Why does n't somebody solve the problem of domestic living by suggesting that we all live in house-boats?

VIII

ON KEEPING A BAROMETER

[*Independent,* October 19, 1914. By permission.]

The Irishman 'keeps a pig.' The old maid 'keeps a cat.' It is much more fun to keep a barometer. That is to say, it is more fun if you are interested in the weather. And you are. If you will not admit it, you are either an untrustworthy witness or a *lusus naturæ,* a jest of nature.

Weather is one of the three great universal experiences of mankind. All men are born, all men die, all men are 'weathered.' The rain falls alike upon the just and the unjust, or would if it were not that the unjust have the umbrellas of the just. In winter we all shiver, in summer we all sweat. And all the time we all talk about the weather. There is no other perfectly common topic of conversation; because there is no other perfectly common experience. Men talk to their fellows about the weather not because they cannot think of anything else to talk about, but because it is the one thing about which they know that their fellows have thoughts ready for exchange.

Since you will talk about the weather, you should keep a barometer. It is better than a pig, in that it produces nothing that you can sell, and you may therefore know that your motives in keeping it are unsullied by greed. It is better than a cat in that it drinks no milk, yowls no yowls, sheds no hair. It is better than a dog in that — but no, we cannot admit it. Nothing is better than a dog.

Keeping a barometer is a peaceful occupation. It hangs silent on the wall, demanding nothing, asserting nothing, merely recording an impalpable fact — the pressure of the air.

But keeping a barometer is an exciting occupation. When you come down to breakfast to find its needle hovering through a narrow arc away up in the fair region above the thirty mark, a gentle thrill runs through you at the thought that the wonderful weather we have been having is to continue. When the needle executes a two-inch swoop in a few hours, as it did one day last winter, you tingle with the expectation of the 'big wind' that is surely coming, and hurry down to stoke up the furnace. And when the storm is still roaring and the cheerful little needle begins to climb, you know with a rebound of the spirit that the worst is over. An exciting occupation in its own quiet way.

An absorbing occupation no less. The last thing at night when you have locked up, put out the cat, set the screen before the embers in the fireplace, and are all ready for the ascent to bed, you turn to the faithful disc on the wall and set the index finger fair over the needle. So when morning comes and you stop on the way to the front porch for the morning paper to see what the elements have prepared over night for you, the discrepancy between finger and needle tells the tale. An absorbing occupation indeed.

IX

HAIRPINS

[*Sun,* New York, May 19, 1902. Reprinted in *Casual Essays of the Sun,* 1905. By permission.]

The comprehensive merits of the hairpin are known to all observant men. Its special value in surgery is asserted by a writer in *American Medicine.* It seems that a surgeon can do almost anything with a hairpin. He can wire bones with it, probe and close wounds, pin bandages, compress blood vessels, use it 'to remove foreign bodies from any natural passage,' and as a curette for scraping away soft material. And no doubt the women doctors can do a great deal more with that most gifted and versatile of human implements. Anthropologists have never done justice to the hairpin. It keeps civilization together. In the hands of girls entirely great it is much mightier than the sword or, for that matter, the plow. What is the plow but a development of the forked stick, and what is the forked stick but a modification of the hairpin? If there was any necessity, a woman could scratch the ground successfully now. In fact, there is no work or play in which something may not be accomplished by means of it.

Dullards will tell you that women are n't so inventive as men, don't take out so many patents. They don't have to. With the hairpin all that is doable can be done. With a hairpin a woman can pick a lock, pull a cork, peel an apple, draw out a nail, beat an egg, see if a joint of meat is done, do up a baby, sharpen a pencil, dig out a sliver, fasten a door, hang up a plate or a picture, open a can, take up a carpet, repair a baby carriage, clean a lamp chimney, put up a curtain, rake a grate fire, cut a pie, make a fork, a fish-hook, an awl, a gimlet, or a chisel, a paper-cutter, a clothespin, regulate a range, tinker a sewing machine, stop a leak in the roof, turn over a flapjack, caulk a hole in a pair of trousers, stir batter, whip cream, reduce the pressure in the gas meter, keep bills and receipts on file, spread butter, cut patterns, tighten windows, clean a watch, untie a knot, varnish floors, do practical plumbing, reduce the asthma of tobacco pipes, pry shirt studs into buttonholes too small for them, fix a horse's harness, re-store damaged mechanical toys, wrestle with refractory beer stoppers, improvise suspenders, shovel bonbons, inspect gas burners, saw cake, jab tramps, produce ar-tificial buttons, hooks and eyes, sew, knit, and darn, button gloves and shoes, put up awnings, doctor an automobile. In short, she can do what she wants to; she needs no other instrument.

If a woman went into the Robinson Crusoe line she would build a hut and make her a coat of the skin of a goat by means of the hairpin. She will revolutionize surgery with it in time. Meanwhile the male chirurgeons are doing the best they can; but it is not to be believed that they have mastered the full mystery of the hairpin.

X

THE IMPROVED BABY

[*Sun*, New York, September 2, 1903. Reprinted in *Casual Essays of the Sun*, 1905. By permission.]

The chief experts in child study and infant psychology are men. The amount of valuable advice and directions given to mothers by good, motherly men is surpris-ing. Whenever there is a Congress of Mothers, Dr. Granville Stanley Hall and Dr. Hamilton Wright Mabie are sure to unload stores of mother lore upon their listeners. Such is the unfailing wisdom of men. The infants of today must be old before their time. Much is expected of babes to whose welfare so many great masculine minds are contributing.

Dr. H. C. Carpenter lectured at a meet-ing of Philadelphia mothers the other day. He told them 'How to Take Care of the Baby,' and he showed that usually the baby is far from well taken care of. Mothers are not serious enough:

'"Don't play with the baby." Nothing could be more injurious to the infant's nervous system than to excite it with the customary entertainments with which fond mothers and admiring friends bore the helpless victim. It is a common error to imagine that because the child responds with a wonderlook, a laugh, or even a shriek of apparent delight, that it is being amused. Quite the contrary — it is not only being plagued, but is sustaining, in nine cases out of ten, an irreparable in-jury.'

Why are there not more Shakespeares, Bacons, Mabies, and Carpenters? Be-cause most babies are irreparably injured. Baby's intellectuals are not properly and systematically developed. He may seem to be enjoying himself when he coos and crows and shrieks with apparent delight, but he is not. He is pained. In isolation and aloofness he is trying to study his sur-roundings and the psychology of his nurse and relations. They will not let him think. They interfere with the growth of his mental processes. They turn him away from his lofty cogitations by their impertinent and trivial endearments. They warp his nature from its solemn bent. They kill his mind. Let him grow and meditate. He has the floor. Give him the opportunity to develop himself.

'Don't talk baby talk,' says Dr. Carpen-ter. Certainly not. Why should a baby understand broken, any better than whole, English? Why will mothers use that strange nursery Chinook, 'Did um shakum dady,' and so on? The man's vocabulary is shrunken on account of this habit. His bump of language is flattened. Long words for Little Ones; that's the talk. 'John Henry, my valued progeny, I shall discourse to you for a few moments on the subject of the Conservation of Energy.' 'Marthy Ann, let me dissuade you from your fruitless conation to ingurgitate your rattle. The impenetrability of matter is one of the earliest subjects which should engage your attention.'

'One should avoid telling young chil-dren such exciting stories as "Jack the Giant Killer."' Explain, if you choose, that it is absurd to suppose that Jack or anybody else would kill giants. Giants get large salaries. They are too valuable to kill. Don't tell stories of any kind. Read the *Gazetteer* to Baby. It will calm his nervous system and give him much statistical and geographical information.

XI

THE PORTER'S TIP

[*Chicago Tribune,* May 9, 1915. By permission.]

Probably the two bits which the spendthrift American traveler, having luxuriated under blankets of a peculiar rigidity, the composition of which is known only to the Pullman company, and having dressed without fracturing his skull, bestows upon the porter who tendered such creature comforts as may exist in a sleeping car, hits at some important props in our economic welfare.

Chairman Walsh and the committee on industrial relations evidently suspect that an evil hides behind this quarter which the average traveler deposits with the person who dusted him thus effectively. It may be making the Pullman company rich by making possible an avoidance of paying proper wages. It may be destroying the self-respect of the porter, but we doubt it, experience never having discovered one who did not look as if he had all the self-respect of a person with a bank account. We suspect that the first sleeping car porter who got the first two bits from a traveler nearly fell over in astonishment and was unable to express himself adequately. We suspect that the whole system was originated by the travelers themselves and that they will continue to hand out two bits in the morning regardless of what changes are made in the wage scale.

Naturally we want the money to go to the porters and not to the Pullman company, and for that reason we might insist that the company pay wages that would be adequate if there were no gratuities or would refund the latter to the passenger in the form of lower rates.

But we also suspect that the habit of tipping the porter is something not to be explained by any orthodox economic theory; that it inheres in the grandiloquence of the average traveler who wishes to consider himself a person important enough, in the peculiarly important circumstances of his travel, to hand out two bits to an obliging gentleman of color and that he would resent any legislative fussiness which deprived him of this expression of his own generosity and solvency. As to the colored person who takes the tip, we suspect that his self-respect is proof against this subtle suggestion. Anyway he earns the fee and it makes gracious the person who gives it.

There are very few remnants of the feudal system. Why destroy the one convenient method by which a person of modest income and small authority can, for a moment, attain and realize the subtleties of the grand estate? Purchasable at two bits the sensation is cheap. Many a man has spent a $20 bill and had his egotism flattered less.

XII

THE STRAW BREAKFAST

[*Courier-Journal* (Louisville), May 2, 1915. By permission.]

From Germany comes news that a learned man, a German professor of chemistry, has asserted that he can make a first-rate food of common wheat straw.

Wheat straw, or oats straw or rye straw, in addition to being useful for sucking cider or lemonade from a receptacle, bedding horses, exercising the leg muscles of hens when grain is concealed in it, fooling lean kine and making hats, is a fertilizer of sorts. It has in it potash, or some other chemical constituent of good soil. It possibly is quite as valuable as a given quantity of shavings ironed out into batter cake formation and then made into marcel waves to tempt the coy appetites of those to whom conformation by honest ham and eggs causes a shudder of horror at breakfast time.

The German savant proposes to make a concentrated food from straw. It is to be a lozenge or cube something like those which you drop into hot water and make a sort of sterilized dishwater which is called by a French name for soup. After eating it, no doubt, a bale of straw swells up in the inner being, and a fountain of strength wells up simultaneously in the same place. Each digit itches for the throat of the enemy, or longs, in the case of a civilian, to take a day's work by the scruff of the neck and cast it into the limbo of things that were. Full of potash and hope, the straw eater is a match for any man. And he can get outside of his concentrated bale of straw in less time than it takes a couple of roan steers to munch down one bale under the lee of a straw stack when driven by winter hunger.

The Herr Professor has, no doubt, hit upon an important discovery. The time may come when it will be said that making bricks without straw is a simple matter compared with making Prussian grenadiers without it. But, unfortunately for America, there is already in the market, for soda fountain and circus lemonade booth use, an artificial straw made of paper treated with paraffin. When Americans begin to fill up on the concentrated straw lozenges, Richmond Pearson Hobson and a brace of retired admirals will be sure to go about foretelling a German invasion, and assuring us that every mother's son of us is wadded and packed with paper straw, while the Germans, who have been eating the regular kind, are adequately prepared to strew American giblets all over the United States map, or the Japanese, bred for battle on genuine rice straw, can swim the Pacific and arrive in California with sufficient remaining strength to hammer the anti-alienism out of everybody west of the Rocky Mountains.

XIII

WHAT TO TELL AN EDITOR

[*Punch*, January 14, 1914. By special permission of the proprietors.]

In view of the *Daily Mail's* praiseworthy efforts to instruct applicants for situations in the correct phrasing of letters to prospective employers, we propose to supply a similar long-felt want, and give a little advice as to the kind of letter it is desirable to enclose with contributions to periodicals.

Begin your letter in a friendly vein, hoping the editor and his people are pretty well. Remember also that editors like to know something of the characters and histories of their contributors. So let your communication include a résumé of your personal and literary career. Don't fall into the error of making your letter too concise.

The following suggestions may serve to indicate some of the lines of thought you might follow:

(1) State where you sent your first manuscript.

(2) What you thought of it, and of the editor who returned it.

(3) Your height and chest measurement (an editor likes to be on the safe side).

(4) State who persuaded you to take up literature, and give height and chest measurement of same.

(5) Give a short but optimistic description of your contribution, not to exceed in length the contribution itself.

(6) State whether literary genius is rife in your family or has been rife at any time since 1066.

(7) Give a list of journals to which you have already sent the enclosed contribution, and state your reasons for supposing that the editors were misguided. Hint that perhaps, after all, their lack of enterprise was fortunate for the present recipient.

(8) Mention your hobbies and the different appointments you have held since the age of twelve, with names and addresses of employers. Also give your reasons for remaining as long as you did in each situation.

(9) State how long you have been a subscriber to the journal you are electing to honor, and whether you think it's worth the money. Point out any little improvements you consider desirable in its compilation, and mention other periodicals as perfect examples. Preface these remarks with some such phrase as this: 'Pray don't think I want to teach you your business, but —'

(10) Give full list (names and addresses) of friends who have promised to buy the paper if your contribution appears.

(11) Give a brief outline, in faultless English, of your religious, political and police court convictions, your views on Mr. Lloyd-George, and any ideas you may have about the Law of Copyright.

Finally, enclose a stamped and addressed envelope for the return of your article.

F. CONTROVERSIAL ARTICLES AND LETTERS

This section, like the preceding one, is really a branch of exposition. Many editorial articles are obviously controversial, though the tendency is for them to become less so except in occasional accesses of party strife. The difference between the purely expository article and the expository-controversial seems to lie in this — that while the writer of the former has a single eye to the reader, the writer of the latter has in view also sometimes 'a shadowy third,' sometimes a declared opponent. The controversial writer's constant endeavor is to pierce the joints of his opponent's armor,— less metaphorically, to point out the weaknesses of the opposing case or the fallacies involved in its arguments or assumptions. The controversialist naturally sets forth his own case too as strongly and cogently as he can, but he must have in mind, not merely the immediate effect upon his reader, but the possible openings he may leave for the adversary's counter-attack; he breathes the atmosphere of battle.

The articles in this section divide themselves into three groups: the first (I to III) centers round what is somewhat vaguely called socialism; the second (IV and V) treats two phases of what is no less vaguely called the woman question; and the third (including all the rest), deals with various issues arising in connection with the Great War. Whatever, in each case, may be the reader's sympathies, he should not fail to note the skill with which each writer states his own view, and scores at the expense of his imagined or realized antagonist. It is possible to admire and enjoy the brilliant sword-play of a controversial writer without sympathizing with the cause for which he fights. Indeed, it is only after observing the shrewd devices of the tried champions of debate that the young aspirant to the honors of the lists can venture into them without certainty of discomfiture. The first thing, undoubtedly, is to have a good cause to fight for, or at least one that commends itself to the writer's inmost conviction; but he must also know how to defend his cause according to the art of war.

Inequality between millionaire and pauper.

I

THE CASE FOR EQUALITY

GEORGE BERNARD SHAW

[*Metropolitan*, December, 1913. Reprinted by courtesy of the publishers.]

When I speak of The Case for Equality I mean human equality; and that, of course, can only mean one thing: it means equality of income. It means that if one person is to have half a crown, the other is to have two and sixpence. It means that precisely. You, Mr. Chairman, have spoken of equality of opportunity. The difficulty about that is that it is entirely and completely and eternally impossible. How are you going to give everybody in this room equal opportunities with me of writing plays? The thing is, I say, a ghastly mockery. In one sense it might be said:

'Well, any of us are welcome to try our hands at play-writing.' I might say that and smile. But I am quite safe in saying that to the majority of you it is just exactly like saying to a beggar: 'Well, my friend, Mr. Barnato made a large fortune; you have the same opportunities as Mr. Barnato; go and make that fortune,' at which Mr. Barnato would smile; but it is of no use at all to the beggar. The fact is that you cannot equalize anything about human beings except their incomes. If in dealing with the subject you would only begin by facing that fact, it would save you a very great deal of trouble in the form of useless speculation. I have chosen this subject for to-night because it is an extremely practical and important political subject. You have been for a long time using the power of Parliament to redistribute income in this country more or less. The very moment the Income Tax

218

was introduced by Sir Robert Peel, somewhere in the 'forties — 1842, I think — from that moment you were beginning to effect a redistribution of income. If you just glance over the subsequent succession of Chancellors of the Exchequer, you will find them all redistributing income unconsciously, until you come to Sir William Harcourt with his death duties, Mr. Asquith with his discrimination between earned and unearned income, and Mr. Lloyd-George with his Supertax, all doing it consciously. The object of supertaxation, and the object of the threatened land taxation, is to effect a further redistribution of income in this country. There is another point which has not been quite so closely observed as that. The working classes have been using their power, at first indirectly, and of late years directly through the Labor Party in Parliament, to effect a redistribution. This used to be a redistribution in kind. Instead of getting money, the working classes got municipal dwellings; they got education; they got sanitation; they got the clearing away of slum areas; and this mass of municipal work was largely paid for by rating richer people than themselves, and by grants-in-aid, which came from the Income Tax, from which the working classes were exempt themselves. Thus they were deliberately transferring wealth from one class to another by Parliamentary power. They were redistributing part of the national income, and diverting it in their own direction. This went on for many years; but a few years ago they took an entirely new departure. Instead of saying, 'We will get more schools out of you; we will get more houses out of you; we will get more plumber's work out of you,' they suddenly took the step which was sooner or later inevitable, and said: 'We will have some money out of you. We will have some money straight out of your pockets into our pockets to do what we like with.' There was an apparent precedent for this in Poor Law outdoor relief, or the giving of public money to poor persons on the ground that they are poor. But when you passed Old Age Pensions, then, for the first time, you had money paid down without regard to the differences between one person and another. It was not given exclusively to the people who were poor, except that there was a certain limit of income, which was really rather a concession

to the snobbery of the people who did not like to take it than a real essential difference of principle. The fact remains that a few years ago the Chancellor of the Exchequer began to put his hand into the national pocket, and to give every person aged seventy of the working class, without reference to his ability or sex, if he claimed it and had not a certain income at the time he claimed it, the sum of 5s. a week. The recipients of that 5s. a week included among them every possible variety of character. They all have exactly the sum of 5s. a week, no more and no less. Here is a process which has begun, and a process which we all know is going to go on. We know that that 5s. a week will not remain at 5s. a week. We know that it will be presently 10s. a week. (Dissent.) I should have thought that everybody here present would know that in New Zealand at the present time it is 10s. a week; and that the Labor Party know it; and that it is 10s. a week at an earlier age than the age of seventy. If any man present is simple enough to believe that it is going to stay at 5s. a week, I ask him to retire to the smoking-room downstairs, because he is congenitally (I must say it, though I say it without malice) incapable of understanding any address that I possibly can give. I take it now you are all convinced that it will not stay at 5s. a week; and I hope there will be no hesitation about this also; that the Supertax is not going to remain at what it is at present. I think you must all admit, though some of you may deplore it, that the Supertax is going to go up, which means a further redistribution of income in this country.

Having put the matter on a thoroughly practical basis, I now want to ask you whether you have made up your mind what is going to be the final result of this process; because if you are not like the mere opportunists who are outside the Political and Economic Circle and in the smoking-room downstairs — if you really are serious in your pretensions as members of this Circle, you must either have made up your minds already on that point, or you must be in the process of making up your minds; you must be asking yourselves what is the final level to be? I am here to-night to say that I have quite made up my mind as to the only possible solution of the question. I am going to show you that my solution, which is the solution of an equal distribution, is one which has over-whelming practical arguments in its favor.

Perhaps the strongest argument to peo-ple who are not very fond of abstract thought, is that equality of income is the only plan that has ever been successful, the only plan that has ever been possible. It is the plan that has always prevailed; and it is prevalent at the present time to a greater extent than any other rule of dis-tribution. The moment you begin to try and think of any other, you are met with such difficulties and such absurdities that, however reluctant you may be to come to the solution of equality, you are finally driven to it by the elimination of every other solution, except, of course, the solu-tion of the mere brute scramble that we have at the present time. If you take our Civil Service and our Military Service, you find that equal pay is the rule. If you take our trades, you find in every class of society a certain conception of what con-stitutes a becoming livelihood in that class of society; and everybody in it aims at and claims an income representing that standard. Nobody seriously asks to have more than the other persons of his class. Every soldier of the same rank gets prac-tically the same pay; every policeman of the same rank gets the same pay; every colonel gets the same pay; every general gets the same pay; and every judge gets £5000 a year. You do not find Mr. Justice Darling getting up and saying: 'I really think that because I have put a little hu-mor into the proceedings, I ought to have an extra allowance.' Nor do you find that the judges who put a little extra stupidity and cruelty into the proceedings, ever sug-gest that their salaries should be reduced on that ground; nor do the people who ad-mire and uphold their cruelty and stupidity propose that they should get any more.

Now suppose you do not agree, suppose you think there should be some other standard applied to men, I ask you not to waste time arguing about it in the abstract, but bring it down to a concrete case at once. Let me take a very obvious case. I am an exceedingly clever man. There can be absolutely no question at all in my case that in some ways I am above the average of mankind in talent. You laugh; but I presume you are not laughing at the fact, but only because I do not bore you with the usual modest cough, and pretend to consider myself stupid. Very well.

Take myself as an absolute, unquestionable case. Now pick out somebody not quite so clever. How much am I to have, and how much is he to have? I notice a blank expression on your countenances. You are utterly unable to answer the question. In order to do so, you would have to com-pare us in some quantitative way. You would have to treat human capacity as a measurable thing; but you know perfectly well it is not a measurable thing. Taking some person whom we will call X, an av-erage man, you may think I am fifty times as clever as X; and you may think that I, perhaps, ought to have fifty times as big an income. But if anybody asks you: 'Where did you get that numerator of fifty from, and what does your denomina-tor represent?' you will be compelled to give it up. You cannot settle it. The thing is impossible. You cannot do it. Every attempt you make in that way re-duces itself to absurdity in your hands; and that silly dream of the nineteenth cen-tury which began with: 'The career open to the talents,' the idea that every man could get his value; all that is the vainest Utopian dream; and the most ridiculous, the most impracticable idea that ever came into the head of men. The reason it has been talked about so much, is that the peo-ple who were talking about it had no seri-ous intention of ever bringing it into prac-tice and never pleaded it in practice except as an excuse for giving somebody less than themselves. It would have been far more sensible to go at the question in the old mystic, religious way; when you would have immediately seen that all human souls are of infinite value, and all infinities equal.

It is now plain that if you are going to have any inequalities of income, they must be arbitrary inequalities. You must say flatly that certain persons are to have more than others, giving no reason for it. I am quite sure again, from the expression of your faces, that you have not any rea-sons. Well, I will give you one. As you know, obedience and subordination are necessary in society. You cannot have a civilized society unless tolerably large bodies of men are willing to obey other men, even by executing orders that they do not themselves understand. That is the real foundation of our traditional feudal inequality. In order to make a common man obey some other man, you had to take some means of making that other man an uncommon man; and the simplest way was to set him apart from common men by giving him more money, by putting him in a different sort of dress, by making him live in a different sort of house, by setting up a convention that under no circumstances could his son marry the daughter of the common man, or the common man's son marry his daughter. In short, you resorted to idolatry to secure subordination in society; for the man so set apart became literally an idol. I do not deny that idolatry served its turn; but I suggest to you that modern democracy and modern conditions are exploding it. The very idols themselves have made the fatal mistake of allowing the invention of photography and the half-tone process to destroy the glamour on which the whole social structure is based. So long as you have a peer or millionaire who is known only by name and by reputation, people may believe him to be a great man, quite unlike themselves; but the moment you put his portrait into the papers, it is all up: the show is given away. The time has gone by for the old privacy, the old mystery, the old seclusion; that is how our idols are beginning to get found out in all directions. The whole movement of Liberalism in the history of the world — I do not mean the Liberalism of Parliament, or the Liberalism even of this Club, which, as you know, has very little to do with Liberalism at all — the history of Liberalism in the world, when you understand it thoroughly, has been the history of Iconoclasm. In America they will not allow their ambassadors to put on the uniform that European ambassadors wear; and they will not allow their judges to assume the ridiculous costume our judges put on to persuade people that a judge is not a man, but Justice incarnate; and they do not allow their President to put a crown on his head, in order to produce illusions as to its interior. I think you will admit that nowadays, in spite of the costumes of our judges, and in spite of our crowns, there is very little of such illusion left. As a matter of fact, the popularity of our last two monarchs has been due, I think you will agree with me, not at all to a belief in them as extraordinary and supernatural persons, but to the precisely contrary belief in them as rather good fellows much like ourselves. I am glad you agree

with me; because that disposes of the last and only argument in favor of inequality of income: absolutely the last and only one.

Now I come to the objections to inequality, which have been too little considered in this country. I am going to show you that there is an overwhelming political objection to it. I will then show you that there is a still more overwhelming economic objection to it; and I will finish by showing you that there is a biological objection to it which, in my opinion, outweighs all the others. Let us begin with the political objection. As long as you have inequality of income, you may have Franchise Acts, and you may have votes for men, and votes for women, and you may have votes for babies if you like, but there will be no such thing as real democracy in this country. There will be class government of the very worst description. There will be class government based on plutocracy, as there is at the present time; and there will be no possible real representation of the people in Parliament. It does not matter how high the characters of the members may stand. I will take two gentlemen who are at the head of Parliamentary life at the present time. Take Mr. Asquith on the one hand, and Mr. Balfour on the other. How can Mr. Balfour or Mr. Asquith represent men with £300 a year; much less men with £50 or £60 a year? How can they pursue in Parliament the interests of men with only a very small fragment of their income? I say, furthermore, that even if they wanted to do it, they would not be let do it. I say they are subject to public opinion. I say that public opinion is manufactured at the present time by newspapers; and I say that the newspapers are absolutely in the hands of the plutocracy. The extent to which they are in the hands of the plutocracy I could illustrate in fifty ways; but you cannot be so destitute of intelligence — I have no right to assume that you are lacking in intelligence at all — as not to feel this every day of your life. If you do not feel it, there is nothing that I could say which would convince you of it; but the extent to which our newspapers are under the personal control of the plutocracy, I may illustrate by a harmless little incident.

A little while ago I had the pleasure of holding a public debate in Queen's Hall with Mr. Hilaire Belloc. It was reported at some length in all the newspapers of London. It was considered an event of sufficient public importance to occupy from one to three columns — the three columns were in a highly conservative paper in London. All over the country the newspapers had reports. But there were two papers that made absolutely no mention of the debate. One of them was the *Times* and the other was the *Daily Mail*. It has remained a profound mystery why those papers took absolutely no notice of a debate of which they were informed, and at which they were represented by their reporters. The only conjecture that was made on the subject was based on the fact that one of the speakers, by an unfortunate slip, mentioned Lord Northcliffe not as Lord Northcliffe but as Mr. Harmsworth. Now, gentlemen, I am not so absurd as to suppose that Lord Northcliffe went down to the offices of these two papers of his, and said: ' This blasphemer has called me " Mr. Harmsworth," as if I were not Lord Northcliffe; never mention him in my papers again.' I do not believe anything of the kind; but I am perfectly prepared to believe that the gentlemen in his employment may have been so under the influence of Lord Northcliffe's position, and may have been themselves so unjustly mistrustful of Lord Northcliffe's breadth of mind, that they may have thought it safer on the whole not to mention the debate, in which they would have had to report that deplorable slip; and so got out of the difficulty by not mentioning it at all. Any of you who are in public life must know that the moment you take part in any anti-plutocratic movement you are boycotted by the newspapers. Nothing is reported and worked up in the newspapers except the interests of the plutocracy. Those papers form public opinion. Public opinion cannot be formed in any other way. The consequence is that you have no genuinely popular government in this country. I will give you just one other instance which comes back to my memory: it is also a personal one. I once went to a meeting on the temperance question. That meeting was addressed by me; and it was addressed by a bishop. Under ordinary circumstances, when a meeting is addressed by me and addressed by a bishop, the bishop is very fully reported; and I am somewhat briefly reported. On this occasion, it happened that I said some-

thing, being a lifelong teetotaler, and the meeting talking a great deal of nonsense about the publicans, in defense of the publican. The bishop did not speak in defense of the publican. He spoke in the conventional manner against the liquor trade. The consequence was that in the *Times* next day my speech was reported at full length; and the only thing that was mentioned about the bishop was that ' the Bishop of Kensington then addressed the meeting.' When Bishop Gore, who was then Bishop of Birmingham, delivered a most eloquent protest in London against the assumption that political science, any more than religion, was on the side of industrial sweating he fared worse than the Bishop of Kensington: for he was not mentioned at all except by one morning paper, which shortly afterward changed its editor.

Gentlemen, leaving the question of the press, you know that every one of you wants to get into Parliament. I have never yet met a member of the National Liberal Club who did not intend to get into Parliament at some time, except those who, like our Chairman, are there already. Well, most of you will get no further than taking part in other men's election meetings. You will hardly ever have an opportunity of speaking on behalf of a man who really represents your opinions. Nine times out of ten, for the sake of what you call the Liberal Party, you will be speaking on behalf of a rich man. You will be answering for his magnificent Liberal principles; you will be explaining his views on the Welsh Church, and on Home Rule, and on Free Trade. And the gentleman on whose behalf you are speaking, and who will be returned if your oratory is successful, will be sitting there on the platform wondering what on earth you are talking about, but perfectly prepared to foot the bill, to pay the expenses, to bribe the constituency on the chance of getting into Parliament. Doubtless, when he gets into Parliament, he will go into whatever lobby the Liberal whip tells him is the proper lobby to go into. That is what you get in the shape of democracy; and that is all you ever will get as long as you have inequality of income.

Now I come to the economic objection; and you will all now please put on your best expressions, being all of you political economists. Now, gentlemen, I am really a political economist. I have studied the thing. I understand Ricardo's law of rent and Jevons's law of value. I can also tell you what in its essence sound economy means for any nation. It means, gentlemen, just what sound economy means for any individual; and that is <u>that whatever powers the individual has of purchasing or producing, shall be exercised in the order of his most vital needs.</u> Let me illustrate. Suppose you find a man starving in the streets. You are sympathetic: you give that man sixpence. Suppose that man, instead of buying some bread and eating it, buys a bottle of scent to perfume his handkerchief with, and then dies of starvation, but with the satisfaction of having his handkerchief perfumed! You will admit that that man is an unsound economist, will you not? You will even declare that he is a lunatic? Well, allow me to tell you, gentlemen, that is exactly what this country is doing at the present time. It is spending very large sums on perfuming its handkerchief while it is starving, and while it is rotting. How are you going to remedy that? As long as you have inequality of income, that mad state of things is compulsory. If one man has not enough money to feed his children properly, and another man has so much that after feeding and clothing and lodging himself and his family as luxuriously as possible he has still a large surplus fund, you will find that the richer man will take his surplus purchasing power into the market, and by that purchasing power set the labor of the country, which ought to be devoted to producing more food for people who have not enough food, to the production of 80 horse-power motor-cars, and yachts and jewels, and boxes at the opera, and to the construction of such towns as Nice and Monte Carlo. The thing is inevitable. Production is determined by purchasing power and always will be. If you were to attempt to do away with money and with purchasing power, then you would have, in order to satisfy your nation, to ascertain what every man particularly wants and likes; and as that would be impossible, you would have to give every man exactly the same thing, with the consequence that the man who wanted a race-horse as a luxury would get a gramophone, and the man who wanted a gramophone would get a race-horse. In order to enable men to determine production according to their own tastes, you must give a man his income in the shape of purchasing power. By that purchasing power he determines production; and if you allow the purchasing power of one class to fall below the level of the vital necessities of subsistence, and at the same time allow the purchasing power of another class to rise considerably above it into the region of luxuries, then you find inevitably that those people with that superfluity determine production to the output of luxuries, while at the same time the necessities that are wanted at the other end cannot be sold, and are therefore not produced. I have put it as shortly as possible; but that is the economic argument in favor of equality of income. All the arguments which have been brought forward against it, and all the more personal considerations in favor of inequality, seem to me, as an economist, to be practically swept away by the overwhelming weight of that economic objection.

I now come to the biological reasons for equality. I do not know, gentlemen, what may be the outcome of your experience in progressive political work, but I must confess to you here that I, having devoted more than thirty years, the most active part of my life, to political questions in their most serious aspect — not to the ridiculous game, not half as interesting as golf, which you call party politics and with which you debauch your intellects and waste your time, but to the genuine problems of the condition of the country and the condition of the people: in short, to the life of the country — I must confess to you that all my experience and all my thought on the subject have left me with very grave doubts as to whether mankind, as it exists at present, is capable of solving the political and economic problems which are presented to the human race by its own multitudinous numbers. If you take a few persons like ourselves, and put them into a new colony, in a climate which is not too rough, to make little pioneer villages like the pioneer villages in the days before Capitalism overwhelmed America, in that village you may get a reasonable and decent kind of life; a rough life, but a natural life; not in any very high sense a civilized life, and certainly not a cultured life; but a tolerably human kind of life. But the moment you attempt to go beyond the village stage, the moment you attempt to create the complicated political, social and industrial organization required by our great modern empires and cities, the human constituents of these communities are hopelessly beaten by the problems created by that organization, and by their own numbers. Our House of Commons, to do it justice, does not even pretend to know what it is legislating about. Read its speeches on the subject, and you will find that it practically gives up the problem. It goes on in a hand-to-mouth fashion trying to remedy grievances, making five or six new messes every time it clears up an old one. You see measure after measure brought out, accompanied by extensions of the franchise; but all the time we are going more deeply into the mire, and increasing the evils I have been fighting all my life. Although people are constantly assuming that these evils are being got rid of, I assure you that they are not being got rid of at all; and the reason of that, it seems to me, is that we are not capable of getting rid of them. We are a stupid people; and we are a bad looking people. We are ugly; we have narrow minds; and we have bad manners. A great deal of that is due to the effect of being brought up in a society of inequality. I know perfectly well what happened to myself. I can remember one of my earliest experiences in life was my father finding me playing with a certain little boy in the street, and telling me I was not to play with that little boy, giving me to understand that he was a very inferior and objectionable kind of little boy. I had not found him so. I asked my father 'Why?' He said: 'His father keeps a shop.' I said to my father: 'Well, but you keep a mill.' Therefore my father pointed out to me that he sold things wholesale, and that this little boy's father sold things retail; and that, consequently, there was between me and that boy a gulf which could never be respectably bridged; and that it was part of my duty and part of my honor to regard that boy as an inferior, which I did ever after, in so far as I could safely do so, having regard to the fact that the boy was a more vigorous and larger boy than myself. I was also taught, being an Irish Protestant boy, what Protestant children are habitually taught in Ireland: that the great bulk of my fellow countrymen, being Roman Catholics, were condemned to eternal damnation. Perhaps you can see that this was blasphemy; but in my opinion the doctrine that the wholesaler should excommunicate the retailer was a much more dangerous blasphemy. At all events, when you are brought up, as you inevitably are in a society like ours, with that sort of blasphemy being continually dinned into your ears; when you are taught to be unsocial at every point, and brought up to be unsocial, then any little chance that your natural endowments at your birth may have left you of being able to grapple with the enormous problems of our modern civilization — problems that demand from you the largest scope of mind, the most unhesitating magnanimity, the most sacred recognition of your spiritual and human equality with every person in the nation — is utterly destroyed. That is why I doubt whether these problems can be solved by us, brought up in that way. To solve them, you need a new sort of human being.

And now we have come to what we call Eugenics. Ever since the time of Plato — and I dare say the subject was practically as old in Plato's time as it is now — sensible men have always said: 'Why cannot we breed men with the same care that we breed horses?' (Hear, hear.) Several gentlemen say 'Hear, hear.' Have they ever tried it? You must always test yourselves, when you have these ideas, by asking yourselves how would you begin. Suppose we could go as a deputation to Parliament, and were allowed to address Parliament at the bar of the House, and impressed them with the importance of this problem to such an extent that they passed an Act and sent it through the Lords and got the Royal Assent, indemnifying us and giving us power practically, we here, to make an attempt at breeding; to pick out a mother and father and try to produce a better sort of human being; we should not know where to begin. You see it is all very well when you come to breed a horse, because when you want to breed a horse you know the sort of horse you want. If you want a race-horse, all you care about is that the horse should be a very fast horse. If you want a draught horse, you know that all you want is a powerful horse. You do not bother about the horse's soul; you do not bother very much about its temper; you do not care whether it is a good horse in the pulpit sense of the word. You want a horse that will go round a race-course in a shorter time than any other horse. Or you want a horse that will carry a hundredweight more than any other horse you can get hold of. It is quite simple, because you know the sort of horse you want. But do you know the sort of man you want? You do not. You have not the slightest idea. You do not even know how to begin. You say: 'Well, after all we do not want an epileptic. We do not want an alcoholic.' (It is a barbarous word, but drunken people are now called alcoholics.) But for all you know to the contrary, the Superman may be a self-controlled epileptic, fed exclusively on proof spirit, and consuming perhaps ten gallons a day. You laugh; but the thing is entirely possible. You do not know what a healthy man is. All your doctors are not able to tell you. All they can tell you is that if you bring them a healthy man, they will very soon have him in bed. Still less do you know, gentlemen, what is a good man. Take a vote as to whether I am a good man or not. Some people will tell you that my goodness is almost beyond that of any other living person. They will even tell you that I am the only hope of religion in this country. You will not have to go very far to find persons who are of exactly the contrary opinion. I tell you that you really do not know. I think the very first thing you have to do is to face the fact that you do not know, and that in the nature of things you never can know. Your capacity does not run to it. You have no clue, as far as your own judgment is concerned; and, therefore, you are thrown back on the clue that Nature gives you.

Let me propose to you an experiment which I am always proposing to large audiences in this country. I ask you tomorrow in the afternoon, if it is a fine afternoon, to walk down Park Lane or Bond or Oxford Street, or any well-frequented thoroughfare, and to look carefully at all the women you see coming along and to take a note of how many of those women you would care to be married to. If we are to judge by the utterances of some of our Moral Reform Societies, the members when they walk down Oxford Street, are so wildly and irresistibly attracted by every woman they meet, old or young, that nothing but the severest and most stringent laws restrain them from instant rapine. I cannot imagine how any man gets himself into such a deplorable condition of mind as to believe that this is true of himself, much less of any other human being. There may be some men of low type, who are nearly indiscriminate in their appetites; but I am perfectly certain, with regard to the great majority of men, that they may very often walk down Oxford Street without meeting one single woman to whom they could tolerate the idea of being married; and they will in any case be fortunate (because I like the sensation when it comes to me) if, on the most crowded day and in the finest weather, they meet two women for whom they feel that curious physiological attraction which we all recognize as the sex attraction. That attraction means something. If that attraction meant something destructive and ruinous to the human race, the human race would have been wiped out of existence long ago. It is what you call the Voice of Nature. You fall in love, as the saying is. You see a woman whom you have never spoken to, about whom you know absolutely nothing at all; you do not know her character, and you do not know her aims; but you look at her and fall in love with her. If you were a free person in a free society, you would feel very strongly in love with her; but nowadays you seldom feel more than that timid little — what shall I call it? — sort of sinking feeling, which is about as much as, in our present society, is left of any of our natural emotions. But you do feel some attraction. My contention is that this attraction is the only clue you have to the breeding of the human race, and I do not believe you will ever have any improvement in the human race until you greatly widen the area of possible sexual selection; until you make it as wide as the numbers of the community make it. Just consider what occurs at the present time. I walk down Oxford Street, let me say, as a young man. I see a woman who takes my fancy. I fall in love with her. It would seem very sensible, in an intelligent community, that I should take off my hat and say to this lady: 'Will you excuse me; but you attract me very strongly, and if you are not already engaged, would you mind taking my name and address and considering whether you would care to marry me?' Now I have no such chance at present.

Probably when I meet that woman, she is either a charwoman and I cannot marry her, or else she is a duchess and she will not marry me. I have purposely taken the charwoman and the duchess; but we cut matters much finer than that. We cut our little class distinctions, all founded upon inequality of income, so narrow and so small that I have time and again spoken to English audiences of all classes throughout the Kingdom, and I have said to every man and woman in the audience: 'You know perfectly well that when it came to your turn to be married, you had not, as a young man or a young woman, the choice practically of all the unmarried young people of your own age in our forty million population to choose from. You had at the outside a choice of two or three; and you did not like any of them very particularly as compared to the one you might have chosen, if you had had a larger choice.' That is a fact which you gentlemen with your knowledge of life cannot deny. The result is that you have, instead of a natural evolutionary sexual selection, a class selection which is really a money selection. Is it to be wondered at that you have an inferior and miserable breed under such circumstances? I believe that this goes home more to the people than any other argument I can bring forward. I have impressed audiences with that argument who were entirely unable to grasp the economic argument in the way you are able to grasp it, and who were indifferent to the political arguments. I say, therefore, that if all the other arguments did not exist, the fact that equality of income would have the effect of making the entire community intermarriageable from one end to the other, and would practically give a young man and young woman his or her own choice right through the population — I say that that argument only, with the results which would be likely to accrue in the improvement of the race, would carry the day.

I am sorry there are no ladies present here. There ought to have been, to have full justice done to the last argument. But the final argument which prevails with me is that it is half-past nine. I hope I have given you enough to talk about for some little time. I hope you understand that equality means equality of income. In justification of equality of income, I have given you a political argu-

ment, I have given you an economic argument, I have given you a biological argument; and now make what you can of it.

* * * * * * *

II

THE CASE FOR INEQUALITY

LINCOLN STEFFENS

[*Metropolitan*, February, 1914. Reprinted by courtesy of the publishers.]

The only difficulty I find in answering Mr. Shaw when he is wrong is that I don't want to. It is sport to hear his purposeful fallacies running over the innocent sins of his generation, and mine. It's a cruel sport, but it's sport. And who would be a spoil-sport? Not I; not if the Superman would limit his hunting to his own country, where the libel laws make muckraking an intellectual game and British complacency requires that it be played by artists. But over here, in our country, muckraking is serious business. We are running down the truth that shall make us free. Mr. Shaw, addressing the Liberal Club of England on 'The Case for Equality,' is a gentleman shooting over his own preserves; the same man with the same case in the *Metropolitan Magazine* is a poacher. He is fair game for any of us; big game, but fair. I protest that Mr. Shaw should either stay at home, where the greater the truth is the greater the libel, or get down here with us to the hard but honest labor of raking up and marketing said truth. And why should he not deal in that precious commodity?

The truth divine is funnier than any man-made joke.

His joke on the Liberal Club shows that. The truth about the case for equality is more entertaining than Mr. Shaw's argument for it.

'When I speak of the Case of Equality,' he begins, 'I mean human equality.'

Now the joke in this thesis, the humorous truth divine about human equality is that we don't want it. By 'we' I mean not merely the editorial I; not myself alone; I mean Mr. Shaw also; and not only him and me, but Nature and human nature. And I certainly would include under that impersonal pronoun all those who agree with him and me when I shall have made over for him the Superman's case for the Superman.

For my contention is that Mr. Shaw's case for human equality is an argument for human inequality; he doesn't know just how to get it, but that is what he means and wants.

'I say,' as he says — I say that we are striving, not for human equality, but for the opposite: human inequality. Not democracy; aristocracy is what we are after; or, to be more precise, aristocracies. Again I define 'we' as Nature, human nature and Shaw, and, with all the force Mr. Shaw puts into a doubtful statement, I say that we democrats work and argue for democracy as a means to aristocracy; the free, natural development of human inequality. We do, and we must. Nature compels us to.

Nature is working toward the development of variations in all species.

Human nature is a part of Nature. Man is a species. So man is being worked toward variations in his species. Human variations appear as human inequalities and the process we call evolution tends to develop them into greater and greater inequalities. Hence my conclusion:

It is human inequality, not human equality, that Nature makes for and makes our human nature work for.

No matter what men say, it is distinction and differences they want. But Mr. Shaw says it, sometimes; he says it in the bewildering course of his case for 'equality, meaning human equality.'

'I must confess,' he confesses, 'that all my experience and thought have left me with very grave doubts as to whether mankind as it exists at present is capable of solving the political and economic problems presented by its own multitudinous numbers. . . . To solve them you need a new sort of human being.'

This sigh for a new sort of human being is merely a literary expression of Nature's brutal demand for the further variation of the human species; for more inequality, or for the more unequal development of existing inequalities. That is an amusing, confusing thing to cry for in a plea for human equality; and I think the statement is upside down. We don't want the Superman to solve our political and economic problems. We want to solve our political and economic problems

to get our Superman. But of this later. What I want to fix now is the point upon which Mr. Shaw and I and Nature agree:

We all want human inequality.

And that's why Mr. Shaw wants economic equality: because he wants human inequality. That isn't what he says; not all the time. As we have just seen, he sometimes puts it the other way. Most of the time, however, he has it right; most of his case is an argument for the solution of our economic problem in order to the development of the race.

And, 'of course' (as he says), this is the only way we can proceed. We can't create new sorts of human beings; we have to grow them; we have to evolve our superman out of mankind as it exists at present.

If Mr. Shaw (or anybody else) can't see that, I shall have to extend to him the invitation he gave to the 'congenitally incapable' members of the Liberal Club — 'to retire to the smoking-room downstairs.'

But Mr. Shaw does see that, sometimes he says it; and I think he means it all the time. It would be quibbling, therefore, to hold him to his exact words when we can, by an effort, get at his thought. Let's do that:

'When I speak of the case for equality,' he says, 'I mean human equality; and that, of course, can mean only one thing; it means equality of income.' And, as if to clinch my case, he adds: 'The fact is you cannot equalize anything about human beings except their incomes.'

So I will correct his thesis for him, and make him say what he says part of the time and means all of the time:

'When I speak of the case for equality, I mean human inequality; and that can mean but one thing: it means economic equality.'

My statement of his case is better because, first, it sounds more like Shaw than his own; second, it is nearer the truth; third, it illustrates what I said about the truth being funnier even than a Shaw jest, and there's a fourth reason which should have a paragraph by itself:

By reversing thus his main proposition, Mr. Shaw's argument becomes suddenly good; not precisely, but pretty good.

His case for equality (meaning human inequality) now faces the fundamental problem of the race: to develop the breeds of men. And it gives Mr. Shaw's solution: economic equality. 'Equality of income' is his phrase, and he goes on to show that he means equal pay. 'It means,' he says, 'that if one person is to have half a crown, the other is to have two-and-sixpence. It means that precisely.'

That's right. If we are to have human inequality, we must have economic equality. Not precisely; no; Mr. Shaw is precisely too precise there. But he is approximately right. He sees that the reason we have no aristocracies now is because we have only plutocracies. His happiest illustration is given under the unhappy head of 'Biological Reasons for Equality.' He agrees with me that we cannot make his 'new sort of human being'; he goes beyond me to say that we cannot even breed him as we do animals. The breeder of horses, he argues, knows the sort of horse he wants. But, says Mr. Shaw, 'you do not know the sort of man you want. . . . You have no clue, as far as your own judgment is concerned, and therefore you are driven back on the clue Nature gives.'

This clue to natural selection is the sex attraction. 'My contention,' he says, 'is that this attraction is the only clue you have to the breeding of the human race.' And he shows that the money standards of our plutocratic organization of society interfere with this natural instinct in all classes of society. 'You have,' he concludes, 'instead of a natural evolutionary sexual selection, a class selection which is really a money selection.'

One might quarrel with some of this. A pretty good case could be made for the improvement of some breeds of men under existing conditions. And I, for one, know some sorts of human beings I want; musicians, for example; artists generally, and Bernard Shaws; and I think the day may come when we shall know how to continue some such transmissible human inequalities. But I accept the main argument, that we cannot improve the stock fast or far so long as we breed as we do so generally now for money, position or other privilege. That is as absurd as breeding horses, not for speed or strength, but for the amount of money their owners possess.

And I quote sympathetically the close of his argument: 'Equality of income would have the effect of making the entire community intermarriageable from one end to the other and would practically give a young man or woman his or her choice right through the population with results likely to accrue in the improvement of the race.'

That's right, too. Equality of income might do the trick. But isn't it impossible? And unnecessary?

Mr. Shaw says every other kind of human equality is impossible. Scientists say no precise equality occurs in Nature; not even among crystals; and, as for incomes, the inhuman inequality between thrift and joyousness would spoil that arrangement, unless economic opportunities were equalized. He says most human beings get 'equal pay' now; and he refers to the wages of labor, and the army, navy and civil lists. And he observes the leveling process of redistribution in pension legislation, in income and all super-taxation. There is no denying these facts; the tendency of political and social reform is toward the redistribution of wealth by force through confiscation. But all this makes, not for equality of incomes; not precisely; it makes only toward approximate equality. And in the wrong way; and here is where I take issue with Mr. Shaw on his whole case, whether he is for human equality, as he says, or for human inequality, as he also says. Our evils are due, not to private wealth, but to excessive wealth and power in the hands of individuals. Equally bad, both must be prevented. Mr. Shaw would not prevent either. He proposes to redistribute accumulated wealth by some power greater than the state puts into the hands of statesmen now. This is implied in 'precisely equal incomes,' which only a highly organized governmental machine could establish. And even if that were done, it wouldn't stay done unless we had economic equality. And why attempt the impossible?

We can prevent excessive individual wealth by socializing the sources of unearned money. These are either natural resources or leaks through which social value flows into private pockets. In a word, we should abolish privileges; and, for the rest, let Labor democratize industry. These two courses would not increase centralized power; they would give us what Mr. Shaw wants: economic democracy; by giving us what he despises: equal opportunities — not to get rich, but to develop each his own gifts or inequalities freely. No man could get rich if he had access to no value except that which he produced, and I think that few would want to.

Men's activities and desires are determined, not only economic conditions, but by resultant social ideals, and long before economic equality was reached; with the passing of the sources and example of distinguishing riches, we would be free; free from the fear of poverty and power; free to form some other ideal than money. The aristocratic few seek distinction or satisfaction now in service or skilful work. Some such ideal would soon spread through a free society, and free the sex instinct to further by natural selection, human, instead of economic, inequalities.

III

SOCIALISM

THEODORE ROOSEVELT

[*Outlook*, March 20 and 27, 1909. By permission of author and publishers.]

I — WHERE WE CANNOT WORK WITH SOCIALISTS

It is always difficult to discuss a question when it proves impossible to define the terms in which that question is to be discussed. Therefore there is not much to be gained by a discussion of Socialism *versus* Individualism in the abstract. Neither absolute Individualism nor absolute Socialism would be compatible with civilization at all; and among the arguments of the extremists of either side the only unanswerable ones are those which show the absurdity of the position of the other. Not so much as the first step towards real civilization can be taken until there arises some development of the right of private property; that is, until men pass out of the stage of savage socialism in which the violent and the thriftless forcibly constitute themselves co-heirs with the industrious and the intelligent in what the labor of the latter produces. But it is equally true that every step toward civilization is marked by a check on individualism. The ages that have passed have

fettered the individualism which found expression in physical violence, and we are now endeavoring to put shackles on that kind of individualism which finds expression in craft and greed. There is growth in all such matters. The individualism of the Tweed Ring type would have seemed both commonplace and meritorious to the Merovingian Franks, where it was not entirely beyond their comprehension; and so in future ages, if the world progresses as we hope and believe it will progress, the standards of conduct which permit individuals to make money out of pestilential tenements or by the manipulation of stocks, or to refuse to share with their employees the dreadful burdens laid upon the latter by the inevitable physical risks in a given business, will seem as amazing to our descendants as we now find the standards of a society which regarded Clovis and his immediate successors as preëminently fit for leadership.

With those self-styled Socialists to whom 'Socialism' is merely a vaguely conceived catchword, and who use it to express their discontent with existing wrongs and their purpose to correct them, there is not much need of discussion. So far as they make any proposals which are not foolish, and which tend towards betterment, we can act with them. But the real, logical, advanced Socialists, who teach their faith as both a creed and a party platform, may deceive to their ruin decent and well-meaning but short-sighted men; and there is need of plain speaking in order accurately to show the trend of their teaching.

The immorality and absurdity of the doctrines of Socialism as propounded by these advanced advocates are quite as great as those of the advocates, if such there be, of an unlimited individualism. As an academic matter there is more need of refutation of the creed of absolute Socialism than of the creed of absolute individualism; for it happens that at the present time a greater number of visionaries, both sinister and merely dreamy, believe in the former than in the latter. One difficulty in arguing with professed Socialists of the extreme, or indeed of the opportunist, type, however, is that those of them who are sincere almost invariably suffer from great looseness of thought; for if they did not keep their faith nebulous, it would at once become abhorrent in the eyes of any upright and sensible man. The doctrinaire Socialists, the extremists, the men who represent the doctrine in its most advanced form, are, and must necessarily be, not only convinced opponents of private property, but also bitterly hostile to religion and morality; in short, they must be opposed to all those principles through which, and through which alone, even an imperfect civilization can be built up by slow advances through the ages.

Indeed, these thoroughgoing Socialists occupy, in relation to all morality, and especially to domestic morality, a position so revolting — and I choose my words carefully — that it is difficult even to discuss it in a reputable paper. In America the leaders even of this type have usually been cautious about stating frankly that they proposed to substitute free love for married and family life as we have it, although many of them do in a roundabout way uphold this position. In places on the continent of Europe, however, they are more straightforward, their attitude being that of one of extreme French Socialist writers, M. Gabriel Deville, who announces that the Socialists intend to do away with both prostitution and marriage, which he regards as equally wicked — his method of doing away with prostitution being to make unchastity universal. Professor Carl Pearson, a leading English Socialist, states their position exactly:

' The sex relation of the future will not be regarded as a union for the birth of children, but as the closest form of friendship between man and woman. It will be accompanied by no child bearing or rearing, or by this in a much more limited number than at present. With the sex relationship, so long as it does not result in children, we hold that the State in the future will in no wise interfere, but when it does result in children, then the State will have a right to interfere.' He then goes on to point out that in order to save the woman from ' economic dependence ' upon the father of her children, the children will be raised at the expense of the State; the usual plan being to have huge buildings like foundling asylums.

Mr. Pearson is a scientific man who, in his own realm, is as worthy of serious heed as Mr. Flinders Petrie, whom I mention later, is in his realm; and the above quotation states in naked form just what logical scientific Socialism would really come to. Aside from its thoroughly repulsive quality, it ought not to be necessary to point out that the condition of affairs aimed at would in actual practice bring about the destruction of the race within, at most, a couple of generations; and such destruction is heartily to be desired for any race of such infamous character as to tolerate such a system. Moreover, the ultra-Socialists of our own country have shown by their attitude towards one of their leaders, Mr. Herron, that, so far as law and public sentiment will permit, they are now ready to try to realize the ideals set forth by Messrs. Deville and Pearson. As for Mr. Herron, I commend to those who desire to verify what I have said, the article in the Boston *Congregationalist* of June 15, 1901; and to those, by the way, who have not the time to hunt up all the original authorities, I would commend a book called *Socialism; the Nation of Fatherless Children,* a book dedicated to the American Federation of Labor. The chapters on Free Love, Homeless Children, and Two Socialist Leaders are especially worth reading by any one who is for the moment confused by the statements of certain Socialist leaders to the effect that advanced Socialism does not contemplate an attack upon marriage and the family.

These same Socialist leaders, with a curious effrontery, at times deny that the exponents of ' scientific Socialism ' assume a position as regards industry which in condensed form may be stated as, that each man is to do what work he can, or, in other words, chooses, and in return is to take out from the common fund whatever he needs; or, what amounts to the same thing, that each man shall have equal remuneration with every other man, no matter what work is done. If they will turn to a little book recently written in England called *The Case Against Socialism,* they will find by looking at, say, pages 229 and 300, or indeed almost at random through the book, quotations from recognized Socialist leaders taking exactly this position; indeed, it is the position generally taken — though it is often opposed or qualified, for Socialist leaders usually think confusedly, and often occupy inconsistent positions. Mrs. Besant, for instance, putting it pithily, says that we must come to the ' equal remuneration of all workers'; and one of her colleagues, that 'the whole of our creed is that industry shall be carried on, not for the profit of those engaged in it, whether masters or men, but for the benefit of the community. ... It is not for the miners, bootmakers, or shop assistants as such that we Socialists claim the profits of industry, but for the citizen.' In our own country, in *Socialism Made Plain,* a book officially circulated by the Milwaukee division of the Socialist party, the statement is explicit: 'Under the labor time-check medium of exchange proposed by Socialists, any laborer could exchange the wealth he produced in any given number of hours for the wealth produced by any other laborer in the same number of hours.' It is unnecessary to point out that the pleasing idea of these writers could be realized only if the State undertook the duty of taskmaster, for otherwise it is not conceivable that anybody whose work would be worth anything would work at all under such conditions. Under this type of Socialism, therefore, or communism, the government would have to be the most drastic possible despotism; a despotism so drastic that its realization would only be an ideal. Of course in practice such a system could not work at all; and incidentally the mere attempt to realize it would necessarily be accompanied by a corruption so gross that the blackest spot of corruption in any existing form of city government would seem bright by comparison.

In other words, on the social and domestic side doctrinaire Socialism would replace the family and home life by a glorified State free-lunch counter and State foundling asylum, deliberately enthroning self-indulgence as the ideal, with, on its darker side, the absolute abandonment of all morality as between man and woman; while in place of what Socialists are pleased to call 'wage slavery' there would be created a system which would necessitate either the prompt dying out of the community through sheer starvation, or an iron despotism over all workers, compared to which any slave system of the past would seem beneficent, because less utterly hopeless.

'Advanced' Socialist leaders are fond of declaiming against patriotism, or announcing their movement as international, and of claiming to treat all men alike; but on this point, as on all others, their system would not stand for one moment the test of actual experiment. If the leaders of the Socialist party in America should to-day endeavor to force their followers to admit all negroes and Chinamen to a real equality, their party would promptly disband, and, rather than submit to such putting into effect of their avowed purpose, would, as a literal fact, follow any capitalistic organization as an alternative.

It is not an accident that makes thoroughgoing and radical Socialists adopt the principles of free love as a necessary sequence to insisting that no man shall have the right to what he earns. When Socialism of this really advanced and logical type is tried as it was in France in 1792, and again under the Commune in 1871, it is inevitable that the movement, ushered in with every kind of high-sounding phrase, should rapidly spread so as to include, not merely the forcible acquisition of the property of others, but every conceivable form of monetary corruption, immorality, licentiousness, and murderous violence. In theory, distinctions can be drawn between this kind of Socialism and anarchy and nihilism; but in practice, as in 1871, the apostles of all three act together; and if the doctrines of any of them could be applied universally, all the troubles of society would indeed cease, because society itself would cease. The poor and the helpless, especially women and children, would be the first to die out, and the few survivors would go back to the condition of skin-clad savages, so that the whole painful and laborious work of social development would have to begin over again. Of course, long before such an event really happened the Socialistic régime would have been overturned, and in the reaction men would welcome any kind of one-man tyranny that was compatible with the existence of civilization.

So much for the academic side of unadulterated, or, as its advocates style it, 'advanced scientific' Socialism. Its representatives in this country who have practically striven to act up to their extreme doctrines, and have achieved leadership in any one of the branches of the Socialist party, especially the parlor Socialists, and the like, be they lay or clerical, deserve scant consideration at the hands of honest and clean-living men and women. What their movement leads to may be gathered from the fact that in the last presidential election they nominated and voted for a man who earns his livelihood as the editor of a paper which not merely practises every form of malignant and brutal slander, but condones and encourages every form of brutal wrongdoing, so long as either the slander or the violence is supposed to be at the expense of a man who owns something, wholly without regard to whether that man is himself a scoundrel, or a wise, kind, and helpful member of the community. As for the so-called Christian Socialists who associate themselves with this movement, they either are or ought to be aware of the pornographic literature, the pornographic propaganda, which make up one side of the movement; a pornographic side which is entirely proper in a movement that in this country accepts as one of its heads a man whose domestic immorality has been so open and flagrant as to merit the epithet of shameless. That criminal nonsense should be listened to eagerly by some men bowed down by the cruel condition of much of modern toil is not strange; but that men who pretend to speak with culture of mind and authority to teach, men who are or have been preachers of the Gospel or professors in universities, should affiliate themselves with the preachers of criminal nonsense is a sign of either grave mental or moral shortcoming.

I wish it to be remembered that I speak from the standpoint of, and on behalf of, the wage-worker and the tiller of the soil. These are the two men whose welfare I have ever before me, and for their sakes I would do anything, except anything that is wrong; and it is because I believe that teaching them doctrine like that which I have stigmatized represents the most cruel wrong in the long run, both to wageworker and to earth-tiller, that I reprobate and denounce such conduct.

We need have but scant patience with those who assert that modern conditions are all that they should be, or that they cannot be improved. The wildest or most vicious of Socialistic writers could preach no more foolish doctrine than that contained in such ardent defenses of uncontrolled capitalism and individualism as Mr. Flinders Petrie's *Janus,* a book which is absurd, but which, because of this very fact, is not mischievous, for it can arouse no other emotion than the very earnest

desire that this particular archeological shoemaker should stick to his early-Egyption last. There are dreadful woes in modern life, dreadful suffering among some of those who toil, brutal wrong-doing among some of those who make colossal fortunes by exploiting the toilers. It is the duty of every honest and upright man, of every man who holds within his breast the capacity for righteous indignation, to recognize these wrongs, and to strive with all his might to bring about a better condition of things. But he will never bring about this better condition by misstating facts and advocating remedies which are not merely false, but fatal.

Take, for instance, the doctrine of the extreme Socialists, that all wealth is produced by manual workers, that the entire product of labor should be handed over every day to the laborer, that wealth is criminal in itself. Of course wealth is no more criminal than labor. Human society could not exist without both; and if all wealth were abolished this week, the majority of laborers would starve next week. As for the statement that all wealth is produced by manual workers, in order to appreciate its folly it is merely necessary for any man to look at what is happening right around him, in the next street, or the next village. Here in the city where the *Outlook* is edited, on Broadway between Ninth and Tenth Streets, is a huge dry goods store. The business was originally started, and the block of which I am speaking was built for the purpose, by an able New York merchant. It prospered. He and those who invested under him made a good deal of money. Their employees did well. Then he died, and certain other people took possession of it and tried to run the business. The manual labor was the same, the good-will was the same, the physical conditions were the same; but the guiding intelligence at the top had changed. The business was run at a loss. It would surely have had to shut, and all the employees, clerks, laborers, everybody turned adrift, to infinite suffering, if it had not again changed hands and another business man of capacity taken charge. The business was the same as before, the physical conditions were the same, the good-will the same, the manual labor the same, but the guiding intelligence had changed, and now everything once more prospered, and prospered as had never been the case before. With such an instance before our very eyes, with such proof of what every business proves, namely, the vast importance of the part played by the guiding intelligence in business, as in war, in invention, in art, in science, in every imaginable pursuit, it is really difficult to show patience when asked to discuss such a proposition as that all wealth is produced solely by the work of manual workers, and that the entire product should be handed over to them. Of course, if any such theory were really acted upon, there would soon be no product to be handed over to the manual laborers, and they would die of starvation. A great industry could no more be managed by a mass-meeting of manual laborers than a battle could be won in such fashion, than a painters' union could paint a Rembrandt, or a typographical union write one of Shakespeare's plays.

The fact is that this kind of Socialism represents an effort to enthrone privilege in its crudest form. Much of what we are fighting against in modern civilization is privilege. We fight against privilege when it takes the form of a franchise to a street railway company to enjoy the use of the streets of a great city without paying an adequate return; when it takes the form of a great business combination which grows rich by rebates which are denied to other shippers; when it takes the form of a stock-gambling operation which results in the watering of railway securities so that certain inside men get an enormous profit out of a swindle on the public. All these represent various forms of illegal, or, if not illegal, then anti-social, privilege. But there can be no greater abuse, nor greater example of corrupt and destructive privilege, than that advocated by those who say that each man should put into a common store what he can and take out what he needs. This is merely another way of saying that the thriftless and the vicious, who could or would put in but little, should be entitled to take out the earnings of the intelligent, the foresighted, and the industrious. Such a proposition is morally base. To choose to live by theft or by charity means in each case degradation, a rapid lowering of self-respect and self-reliance. The worst wrongs that capitalism can commit upon labor would sink into insignificance when compared with the hideous wrong done by those who would degrade labor by sapping the foundations of self-respect and self-reliance. The Roman mob, living on the bread given them by the State and clamoring for excitement and amusement to be purveyed by the State, represent for all time the very nadir to which a free and self-respecting population of workers can sink if they grow habitually to rely upon others, and especially upon the State, either to furnish them charity, or to permit them to plunder, as a means of livelihood.

In short, it is simply common sense to recognize that there is the widest inequality of service, and that therefore there must be an equally wide inequality of reward, if our society is to rest upon the basis of justice and wisdom. Service is the true test by which a man's worth should be judged. We are against privilege in any form: privilege to the capitalist who exploits the poor man, and privilege to the shiftless or vicious poor man who would rob his thrifty brother of what he has earned. Certain exceedingly valuable forms of service are rendered wholly without capital. On the other hand, there are exceedingly valuable forms of service which can be rendered only by means of great accumulations of capital, and not to recognize this fact would be to deprive our whole people of one of the great agencies for their betterment. The test of a man's worth to the community is the service he renders to it, and we cannot afford to make this test by material considerations alone. One of the main vices of the Socialism which was propounded by Proudhon, Lassalle, and Marx, and which is preached by their disciples and imitators, is that it is blind to everything except the merely material side of life. It is not only indifferent, but at bottom hostile, to the intellectual, the religious, the domestic and moral life; it is a form of communism with no moral foundation, but essentially based on the immediate annihilation of personal ownership of capital, and, in the near future, the annihilation of the family, and ultimately the annihilation of civilization.

II — WHERE WE CAN WORK WITH SOCIALISTS

It is true that the doctrines of communistic Socialism, if consistently followed, mean the ultimate annihilation of civilization. Yet the converse is also true. Ruin faces us if we decline steadily to try to reshape our whole civilization in accordance with the law of service and if we permit ourselves to be misled by any empirical or academic consideration into refusing to exert the common power of the community where only collective action can do what individualism has left undone, or can remedy the wrongs done by an unrestricted and ill-regulated individualism. There is any amount of evil in our social and industrial conditions of to-day, and unless we recognize this fact and try resolutely to do what we can to remedy the evil, we run great risk of seeing men in their misery turn to the false teachers whose doctrines would indeed lead them to greater misery, but who do at least recognize the fact that they are now miserable. At the present time there are scores of laws in the interest of labor — laws putting a stop to child labor, decreasing the hours of labor where they are excessive, putting a stop to unsanitary crowding and living, securing employers' liability, doing away with unhealthy conditions in various trades, and the like — which should be passed by the National and the various State Legislatures; and those who wish to do effective work against Socialism would do well to turn their energies into securing the enactment of these laws.

Moreover, we should always remember that Socialism is both a wide and a loose term, and that the self-styled Socialists are of many and utterly different types. If we should study only the professed apostles of radical Socialism, of what these men themselves like to call ' scientific Socialism,' or if we should study only what active leaders of Socialism in this country have usually done, or read only the papers in which they have usually expressed themselves, we would gain an utterly wrong impression of very many men who call themselves Socialists. There are many peculiarly high-minded men and women who like to speak of themselves as Socialists, whose attitude, conscious or unconscious, is really merely an indignant recognition of the evil of present conditions and an ardent wish to remedy it, and whose Socialism is really only an advanced form of liberalism. Many of these men and women in actual fact take a large part in the advancement of moral ideas, and in practice wholly repudiate the purely ma-

terialistic, and therefore sordid, doctrines of those Socialists whose creed really is in sharp antagonism to every principle of public and domestic morality, who war on private property with a bitterness but little greater than that with which they war against the institutions of the home and the family, and against every form of religion, Catholic or Protestant. The Socialists of this moral type may in practice be very good citizens indeed, with whom we can at many points coöperate. They are often joined temporarily with what are called the ' opportunist Socialists '— those who may advocate an impossible and highly undesirable Utopia as a matter of abstract faith, but who in practice try to secure the adoption only of some given principle which will do away with some phase of existing wrong. With these two groups of Socialists it is often possible for all far-sighted men to join heartily in the effort to secure a given reform or do away with a given abuse. Probably, in practice, wherever and whenever Socialists of these two types are able to form themselves into a party, they will disappoint both their own expectations and the fears of others by acting very much like other parties, like other aggregations of men; and it will be safe to adopt whatever they advance that is wise, and to reject whatever they advance that is foolish, just as we have to do as regards countless other groups who on one issue or set of issues come together to strive for a change in the political or social conditions of the world we live in. The important thing is generally the next step. We ought not to take it unless we are sure that it is advisable; but we should not hesitate to take it when once we are sure; and we can safely join with others who also wish to take it, without bothering our heads overmuch as to any somewhat fantastic theories they may have concerning, say, the two hundredth step, which is not yet in sight.

There are many schemes proposed which their enemies, and a few of their friends, are pleased to call Socialistic, or which are indorsed and favored by men who call themselves Socialists, but which are entitled each to be considered on its merits with regard only to the practical advantage which each would confer. Every public man, every reformer, is bound to refuse to dismiss these schemes with the shallow statement that they are ' Socialistic'; for such an attitude is one of mere mischievous dogmatism. There are communities in which our system of state education is still resisted and condemned as Socialism; and we have seen within the past two years in this country men who were themselves directors in National banks, which were supervised by the government, object to such supervision of railways by the government on the ground that it was 'Socialistic.' An employers' liability law is no more Socialistic than a fire department; the regulation of railway rates is by no means as Socialistic as the digging and enlarging of the Erie Canal at the expense of the State. A proper compensation law would merely distribute over the entire industry the shock of accident or disease, instead of limiting it to the unfortunate individual on whom, through no fault of his, it happened to fall. As communities become more thickly settled and their lives more complex, it grows ever more and more necessary for some of the work formerly performed by individuals, each for himself, to be performed by the community for the community as a whole. Isolated farms need no complicated system of sewerage; but this does not mean that public control of sewerage in a great city should be resisted on the ground that it tends toward Socialism. Let each proposition be treated on its own merits, soberly and cautiously, but without any of that rigidity of mind which fears all reform. If, for instance, the question arises as to the establishment of day nurseries for the children of mothers who work in factories, the obvious thing to do is to approach it with an open mind, listen to the arguments for and against, and, if necessary, try the experiment in actual practice. If it is alleged that small groups of farmers have prospered by doing much of their work in common, and by a kind of mutual insurance and supervision, why of course we should look into the matter with an open mind, and try to find out, not what we want the facts to be, but what the facts really are.

We cannot afford to subscribe to the doctrine, equally hard and foolish, that the welfare of the children in the tenement-house district is no concern of the community as a whole. If the child of the thronged city cannot live in decent surroundings, have teaching, have room to play, have good water and clean air, then not only will he suffer, but in the next generation the whole community will to a greater or less degree share his suffering.

In striving to better our industrial life we must ever keep in mind that, while we cannot afford to neglect its material side, we can even less afford to disregard its moral and intellectual side. Each of us is bound to remember that he is in very truth his brother's keeper, and that his duty is, with judgment and common sense, to try to help the brother. To the base and greedy attitude of mind which adopts as its motto, 'What is thine is mine,' we oppose the doctrine of service, the doctrine that insists that each of us, in no hysterical manner, but with common sense and good judgment, and without neglect of his or her own interests, shall yet act on the saying, 'What is mine I will in good measure make thine also.'

Socialism strives to remedy what is evil alike in domestic and in economic life, and its tendency is to insist that the economic remedy is all-sufficient in every case. We should all join in the effort to do away with the evil; but we should refuse to have anything to do with remedies which are either absurd or mischievous, for such, of course, would merely aggravate the present suffering. The first thing to recognize is that, while economic reform is often vital, it is never all-sufficient. The moral reform, the change of character — in which law can sometimes play a large, but never the largest, part — is the most necessary of all. In dealing with the marriage relation the Socialist attitude is one of unmixed evil. Assuredly woman should be guarded and honored in every way, her rights jealously upheld, and any wrong done her should be regarded and punished with severe judgment; but we must keep in mind the obvious fact that equality of consideration does not mean identity of function. Our effort should be to raise the level of self-respect, self-control, sense of duty in both sexes, and not to push both down to an evil equality of moral turpitude by doing away with the self-restraint and sense of obligation which have been slowly built up through the ages. We must bring them to a moral level by raising the lower standard, not by depressing the high. It is idle to prattle against the 'economic dependence' of woman upon man. In the ideal household — an ideal which I believe, though very far from being universally realized, is yet now more generally realized than ever before — there is really complete economic interdependence, as well as the high spiritual and moral interdependence which is more nearly attained in happy wedlock, in a permanent partnership of love and duty, than in any other relation of life which the world has yet seen. Rights should be forfeited by neither partner; and duties should be shirked by neither partner. The duty of the woman to be the child-bearer and home-keeper is just as obvious, simple, and healthful as the duty of the man to be the breadwinner and, if necessary, the soldier. Whenever either the man or the woman loses the power or the will to perform these obvious duties, the loss is irreparable, and, whatever may be the gain in ease, amiable softness, self-indulgent pleasure, or even artistic and material achievement, the whole civilization is rotten and must fall.

So with our industrial system. In many respects the wage system can be bettered; but screaming about 'wage slavery' is largely absurd; at this moment, for instance, I am a 'wage slave' of *The Outlook*. Under certain conditions and in certain cases the coöperative system can to a greater or less degree be substituted with advantage for, or, more often, can be used to supplement, the wage system; but only on condition of recognizing the widely different needs occasioned by different conditions, which needs are so diverse that they must sometimes be met in totally different ways.

We should do everything that can be done, by law or otherwise, to keep the avenues of occupation, of employment, of work, of interest, so open that there shall be, so far as it is humanly possible to achieve it, a measurable equality of opportunity, an equality of opportunity for each man to show the stuff that is in him. When it comes to reward, let each man, within the limits set by a sound and farsighted morality, get what, by his energy, intelligence, thrift, courage, he is able to get, with the opportunity open. We must set our faces against privilege; just as much against the kind of privilege which would let the shiftless and lazy laborer take what his brother has earned as against the privilege which allows the huge capitalist to take toll to which he is not entitled. We stand for equality of opportunity, but not for equality of reward un-

less there is also equality of service. If the service is equal, let the reward be equal; but let the reward depend on the service; and, mankind being composed as it is, there will be inequality of service for a long time to come, no matter how great the equality of opportunity may be; and just so long as there is inequality of service it is eminently desirable that there should be inequality of reward.

We recognize, and are bound to war against, the evils of to-day. The remedies are partly economic and partly spiritual, partly to be obtained by laws, and in greater part to be obtained by individual and associated effort; for character is the vital matter, and character cannot be created by law. These remedies include a religious and moral teaching which shall increase the spirit of human brotherhood; an educational system which shall train men for every form of useful service — and which shall train us to prize common sense no less than morality; such a division of the profits of industry as shall tend to encourage intelligent and thrifty tool-users to become tool-owners; and a government so strong, just, wise, and democratic that, neither lagging too far behind nor pushing heedlessly in advance, it may do its full share in promoting these ends.

IV.

THE JUSTICE AND DESIRABILITY OF WOMAN SUFFRAGE

[*Independent*, April 5, 1915. By permission.]

The men of three eastern States — Massachusetts, New York and New Jersey — will have an opportunity this fall to put themselves on record for or against woman suffrage. In each State a constitutional amendment extending the suffrage to women is to be submitted to the voters at the polls. What will the men of Massachusetts, New York and New Jersey do with the opportunity? Will they follow the enlightened example of the men of Wyoming, Colorado, Idaho, Utah, Washington, California, Arizona, Kansas, Oregon, Alaska, Illinois, Montana and Nevada? Or will they choose to keep their States a while longer groping in the mists of reaction?

Women should vote for four good and sufficient reasons — and for one other reason greater than all four. And the four reasons are these:

It will be good for the women.

It will be good for the men.

It will be good for the family.

It will be good for the State.

In the first place, then, it will be good for women to vote — not, it should be noted, to have the right to vote, but *to vote,* for the suffrage is not only a privilege but an unescapable obligation — because it will broaden their mental and moral horizon. It will give them something new to think about; and there is no better, one might almost say no other, road to intellectual development than thinking. It will give them new responsibilities — responsibilities to their neighbors, to the community, to the State. There is no better road to moral development than the assumption and the bearing of responsibility.

In the second place, to have women vote will be good for men. It will put them on their mettle, for it would go hard with masculine pride to find the 'weaker sex' beating them at their own traditional task. It will make the men think too. For there is no greater incentive to clear thinking than, first, the necessity of explaining a matter to an inquiring mind and, second, the need of defending one's own position in argument. It will sharpen men's moral responsibility. For women have a way of going straight to the heart of things; and it might be a new and stimulating experience for a man to have to explain to his wife, or his mother or his daughter — as fellow voters — just why he was voting on the side of a corrupt boss or in favor of the liquor traffic or against the suppression of child labor.

In the third place, the voting of women will be good for the family. It will create a new bond of union among its members. Husband and wife with a common duty to the State will find themselves drawn closer together. The mother who goes to the polls with her son, the father who accompanies his daughter to the performance of their common civic task will find a new pleasure in their parenthood and a new outlook upon its possibilities. The son who grows up to find his mother a voter, informed on public affairs and intelligent to discuss them, will have a new appreciation of his mother's companionship, a broadened respect for womanhood.

In the fourth place, woman suffrage will be good for the State. The comment has been keenly made that the State, like the family, needs not only a father but a mother. Women, by the very nature of their being, and of their normal existence, are experts on certain vital subjects. And the State needs expert knowledge quite as much as it needs good intentions and sound principles. Municipal housekeeping could not but gain in efficiency from the participation in its affairs of those in the community whose peculiar business housekeeping is. Women will bring to the activities of government a new point of view, valuable because it is a sound point of view and no less valuable because it is a different point of view. On such subjects of the highest importance to the well-being of the State as education, working conditions for women, the purity of food, child labor, the liquor traffic, the social evil, and war, women have that to contribute in the way of special knowledge and special sympathy which the State can ill afford to be without.

Women have different qualities of mind from men. Men are, in theory at least and often in practice, reasoning beings. Women are creatures of intuition. Men plod to a conclusion; women leap to it. It is sometimes startling to observe how woman's intuition surpasses man's reason in soundness of result. But to whichever quality be awarded the palm for usefulness, there is no question that the two taken together are greatly more valuable than either alone.

But to come to the last and greatest reason of all. Partial suffrage — the suffrage of men alone — is a denial of democracy. Democracy will never be full and complete until every individual in the community has an equal right to determine how the affairs of the community shall be managed. Democracy — the rule of the people — is no democracy while half of the people are excluded from the ruling. The United States is a nation 'conceived in liberty, and dedicated to the proposition that all men are created equal.' There is no liberty while women are free only to be governed and not to govern. There is no equality which does not include political equality — and political equality for all persons regardless of sex.

V.

THE BUSINESS OF BEING A WOMAN.

IDA M. TARBELL

[*American Magazine*, March, 1912. Republished as Chapter III of *The Business of Being a Woman* (Macmillan Company), New York, 1913. By permission of author and publishers.]

Respect for the Creator of this world is basic among all civilized people. The longer one lives the more thoroughly one realizes the soundness of this respect. The earth and its works *are* good. Most human conceptions are barred by strange inconsistencies. The man who praises the works of the Creator as all wise not infrequently treats His arrangement for carrying on the race as if it were unfit to be spoken of in polite society. Nowhere does the modern God-fearing man come nearer to sacrilege than in his attitude toward the divine plan for renewing life.

A strange mixture of sincerity and hypocrisy, self-flagellation and lust, aspiration and superstition, has gone into the making of this attitude. With the development of it we have nothing to do here. What does concern us is the effect of this profanity on the Business of Being a Woman.

ON THE MOST IMPORTANT SUBJECT — UNINFORMED

The central fact of the woman's life — Nature's reason for her — is the child, his bearing and rearing. There is no escape from the divine order that her life must be built around this constraint, duty, or privilege, as she may please to consider it. But from the beginning to the end of life she is never permitted to treat it naturally and frankly. As a child accepting all that opens to her as a matter of course, she is steeered away from it as if it were something evil. Her first essays at evasion and spying often come to her in connection with facts which are sacred and beautiful and which she is perfectly willing to accept as such if they were treated intelligently and reverently. If she could be kept from all knowledge of the procession of new life except as Nature reveals it to her there would be reason in her treatment. But this is impossible. From babyhood she breathes the atmosphere of unnatural prejudices and misconceptions which envelop the fact.

Throughout her girlhood the atmosphere grows thicker. She finally faces the most perilous and beautiful of experiences with little more than the ideas which have come to her from the confidences of evil-minded servants, inquisitive and imaginative playmates, or the gossip she overhears in her mother's society. Every other matter of her life, serious and commonplace, has received careful attention, but here she has been obliged to feel her way and, worst of abominations, to feel it with an inner fear that she ought not to know or seek to know.

If there were no other reason for the modern woman's revolt against marriage, the usual attitude toward its central facts would be sufficient. The idea that celibacy for woman is 'the aristocracy of the future' is soundly based if the Business of Being a Woman rests on a mystery so questionable that it cannot be frankly and truthfully explained by a girl's mother at the moment her interest and curiosity seek satisfaction. That she gets on as well as she does, results, of course, from the essential soundness of the girl's nature, the armor of modesty, right instinct, and reverence, with which she is endowed.

UNCONSCIOUS OF THE SUPREME IMPORTANCE OF HER MATE

The direct result of ignorance or of distorted ideas of this tremendous matter of carrying on human life is that it leaves the girl unconscious of the supreme importance of her mate. So heedlessly and ignorantly is our mating done to-day that the huge machinery of church and state and the tremendous power of public opinion combined have been insufficient to preserve to the institution of marriage anything like the stability it once had, or that it is desirable that it should have, if its full possibilities are to be realized. The immorality and inhumanity of compelling the obviously mismated to live together, grow on society. Divorce and separation are more and more tolerated. Yet little is done to prevent the hasty and ill-considered mating which is at the source of the trouble.

Rarely has a girl a sound and informed sense to guide her in accepting her companion. The corollary of this bad proposition is that she has no sufficient idea of the seriousness of her undertaking. She starts out as if on a life-long joyous holiday, primarily devised for her personal happiness. And what is happiness in her mind? Certainly it is not a good to be conquered — a state of mind wrested from life by tackling and mastering its varied experiences, the *end,* not the beginning of a great journey. Too often it is that of the modern Uneasy Woman — the attainment of something *outside* of herself. She visualizes it, as possessions, as ease, a 'good time,' opportunities for self-culture, the exclusive devotion of the mate to her. Rarely does she understand that happiness in her undertaking depends upon the wisdom and sense with which she conquers a succession of hard places — calling for readjustment of her ideas and sacrifice of her desires. All this she must discover for herself. She is like a voyager who starts out on a great sea with no other chart than a sailor's yarns, no other compass than curiosity.

A YOUNG BRIDE'S AXIOMS

The budget of axioms she brings to her guidance she has picked up helter-skelter. They are the crumbs gathered from the table of the Uneasy Woman, or worse, of the pharisaical and satisfied woman, from good and bad books, from newspaper exploitations of divorce and scandal, from sly gossip with girls whose budget of marital wisdom is as higgledy-piggledy as her own.

And a pathetically trivial budget it is: 'He must *tell* her everything.' 'He must always pick up what she drops.' 'He must dress for dinner.' 'He must remember her birthday.' That is, she begins her adventure with a set of hard-and-fast rules — and nothing in this life causes more mischief than the effort to force upon another one's own rules!

That marriage gives the finest opportunity that life affords for practising not rules but principles, she has never been taught. Flexibility, adaptation, fair-mindedness, the habit of supplementing the weakness of the one by the strength of the other, all the fine things upon which the beauty, durability, and growth of human relations depend — these are what decide the future of her marriage. These she misses while she insists on her rules; and ruin is often the end. Study the causes

back of divorces and separations, the brutal criminal causes aside, and one finds that usually they begin in trivial things — an irritating habit or an offensive opinion persisted in on the one side and not endured philosophically on the other; a petty selfishness indulged on the one side and not accepted humorously on the other — that is, the marriage is made or unmade by small, not great things.

HOME A REAL ECONOMIC PARTNERSHIP

It is a lack of any serious consideration of the nature of the undertaking she is going into which permits her at the start to accept a false notion of her economic position. She consents that she is being 'supported'; she consents to accept what is given her; she even consents to ask for money. Men and society at large take her at her own valuation. Loose thinking by those who seek to influence public opinion has aggravated the trouble. They start with the idea that she is a parasite — does not pay her way. 'Men hunt, fish, keep the cattle or raise corn,' says a popular writer, 'for women to eat the game, the fish, the meat and the corn.' The inference is that the men alone render useful service. But neither man nor woman eats of these things until the woman has prepared them. The theory that the man who raises corn does a more important piece of work than the woman who makes it into bread is absurd.

The practice of handing over the pay envelope at the end of the week to the woman, so common among laboring people, is a recognition of her equal economic function. It is a recognition that the venture of the two is common and that its success depends as much on the care and intelligence with which she spends the money as it does on the energy and steadiness with which he earns it. Whenever one or the other fails trouble begins. The failure to understand this business side of the marriage relation almost inevitably produces humiliation and irritation. So serious has the strain become because of this false start that various devices have been suggested to repair it — Mr. Wells' 'Paid Motherhood' is one; weekly wages as for a servant is another. Both notions encourage the primary mistake that the woman has not an equal economic place with the man in the marriage.

"Schools for Mothers"
"The Woman & The Family Morale"   *"The Uneasy American Woman"*
"Feeding The Brute"   *" Chief End of Woman*

IS HOUSEHOLD ECONOMY NARROWING?

Marriage is a business as well as a senti-mental partnership. But a business part-nership brings grave practical responsibili-ties, and this, under our present system, the girl is rarely trained to face. She be-comes a partner in an undertaking where her function is spending. The probability is she does not know a credit from a debit, has to learn to make out a check correctly, and has no conscience about the funda-mental matter of living within the allow-ance which can be set aside for the family expenses. When this is true of her she at once puts herself into the rank of an in-competent — she becomes an economic de-pendent. She has laid the foundation for becoming an Uneasy Woman.

It is common enough to hear women ar-guing that this close grappling with house-hold economy is narrowing, not worthy of them. Why keeping track of the cost of eggs and butter and calculating how much your income will allow you to buy is any more narrowing than keeping track of the cost and quality of cotton or wool or iron and calculating how much a mill requires, it is hard to see. It is the same kind of a problem. Moreover, it has the added in-terest of being always an independent *personal* problem. Most men work under the deadening effect of impersonal rou-tine. They do that which others have planned and for results in which they have no share.

WOMAN'S DUTY AS A CONSUMER

But the woman argues that her task has no relation to the State. Her failure to see that relation costs this country heavily. Her concern is with retail prices. If she does her work intelligently she knows the why of every fluctuation of price in stand-ards. She also knows whether she is re-ceiving the proper quality and quantity; and yet so poorly have women discharged these obligations that dealers for years have been able to manipulate prices prac-tically to please themselves, and as for quality and quantity we have the scandal of American woolen goods, of food adul-teration, of false weights and measures. No one of these things could have come about in this country if woman had taken her business as a consumer with anything like the seriousness with which man takes his as a producer.

Her ignorance in handling the products of industry has helped the monopolistically inclined trust enormously. I can remem-ber the day when the Beef Trust invaded a certain Middle Western town. The war on the old-time butchers of the village was open. 'Buy of us,' was the order, 'or we'll fill the storage house so full that the legs of the steers will hang out of the windows and we'll give away the meat." The women of the town had a prosperous club which might have resisted the tyranny which the members all deplored, but the club was busy that winter with a study of the Greek drama! They deplored the tyranny, but they bought the cut-rate meat — the old butchers fought to a finish and the housekeepers are now paying higher prices for poorer meat and railing at the impotency of man in breaking up the Beef Trust!

If two years ago when the question of a higher duty on hosiery was before Con-gress any woman or club of women had come forward with carefully tabulated ex-periments, showing exactly the changes which have gone on of late years in the shape, color, and wearing quality of the 15-, 25-, and 50-cent stockings, the stock-ings of the poor, she would have rendered a genuine economic service. The women held mass-meetings and prepared petitions, instead, using on the one side the informa-tion the shopkeepers furnished, on the other that which the stocking manufactur-ers furnished. Agitation based upon any-thing but personal knowledge is not a pub-lic service. It may be easily a grave public danger. The facts needed for fix-ing the hosiery duty the women should have furnished, for they buy the stockings.

UP TO THE WOMAN

If the Uneasy American Woman were really fulfilling her economic functions to-day she would never allow a short pound of butter, a yard of adulterated woolen goods, to come into her home. She would never buy a ready-made garment which did not bear the label of the Consumer's League. She would recognize that she is a guardian of quality, honesty, and human-ity in industry.

A persistent misconception of the nature and the possibilities of this practical side of the Business of Being a Woman runs through all present-day discussions of the changes in household economy. The woman no longer has a chance to pay her way, we are told, because it is really cheaper to buy bread than to bake it, to buy jam than to put it up. Of course, this is a part of the vicious notion that a woman only makes an economic return by the manual labor she does. The Uneasy Woman takes up the point and complains that she has nothing to do. But this release from certain kinds of labor once necessary merely puts upon her the obligation to apply the ingenuity and imagination necessary to make her business meet the changes of an ever-changing world. Because the conditions under which a household must be run now are not what they were fifty years ago is no proof that the woman no longer has here an important field of labor. There is more to the practical side of her business than preparing food for the family! It means, for one thing, the directing of its wants. The success of a household lies largely in its power of selection. Today selection has given away to accumulation. The family becomes too often an incorporated company for getting things — with frightful results. The woman holds the only strong strategic position from which to war on this tendency as well as on the habits of wastefulness, which are making our national life increasingly hard and ugly. She is so positioned that she can cultivate and enforce simplicity and thrift, the two habits which make most for elegance and for satisfaction in the material things of life.

Whenever a woman does master this economic side of her business in a manner worthy of its importance she establishes the most effective school for teaching thrift, quality, management, selection — all the factors in the economic problem. Such scientific household management is the rarest kind of a training school.

HOME AS AN EDUCATIONAL CENTER

Every home is perforce a good or bad educational center. It does its work in spite of every effort to shrink or supplement it. No teacher can entirely undo what it does, be that good or bad. The natural joyous opening of a child's mind depends on its first intimate relations. These are, as a rule, with the mother. It is the mother who 'takes an interest,' who oftenest decides whether the new mind shall open frankly and fearlessly. How she does her work depends less upon her

ability to answer questions than her effort not to discourage them; less upon her ability to lead authoritatively into great fields than her efforts to push the child ahead into those which attract him. To be responsive to his interests is the woman's greatest contribution to the child's development.

I remember a call once made on me by two little girls when our time was spent in an excited discussion of the parts of speech. They were living facts to them, as real as if their discovery had been printed that morning for the first time in the newspaper. I was interested to find who it was that had been able to keep their minds so naturally alive. I found that it came from the family habit of treating with respect whatever each child turned up. Nothing was slurred over as if it had no relation to life — not even the parts of speech! They were not asked or forced to load themselves up with baggage in which they soon discovered their parents had no interest. Everything was treated as if it had a permanent place in the scheme to which they were being introduced. It is only in some such relation that the natural bent of most children can flower, that they can come early to themselves. Where this warming, nourishing intimacy is wanting, where the child is turned over to schools to be put through the mass drill which numbers make imperative — it is impossible for the most intelligent teacher to do a great deal to help the child to his own. What the Uneasy Woman forgets is that no two children born were ever alike, and no two children who grow to manhood and womanhood will ever live the same life. The effort to make one child like another, to make him what his parents want, not what he is born to be, is one of the most cruel and wasteful in society. It is the woman's business to prevent this.

NOT TOO SMALL, BUT TOO GREAT A JOB

The Uneasy Woman tells you that this close attention to the child is too confining, too narrowing. 'I will pity Mrs. Jones for the hugeness of her task,' says Chesterton; 'I will never pity her for its smallness.' A woman never lived who did all she might have done to open the mind of her child for its great adventure. It is an exhaustless task. The woman who sees it knows she has need of all the education the college can give, all the experience and culture she can gather. She knows that the fuller her individual life, the broader her interests, the better for the child. She should be a person in his eyes. The real service of the 'higher education,' the freedom to take a part in whatever interests or stimulates her — lies in the fact that it fits her intellectually to be a companion worthy of a child. She should know that unless she does this thing for him he goes forth with his mind still in swaddling clothes, with the chances that it will not be released until relentless life tears off the bands.

The progress of society depends upon getting out of men and women an increasing amount of the powers with which they are born and which bad surroundings at the start blunt or stupefy. This is what all systems of educations try to do, but the result of all systems of education depends upon the material that comes to the educator. Opening the mind of the child, that is the delicate task the State asks of the mother, and the quality of the future State depends upon the way she discharges this part of her business.

MAKING DEMOCRATS

I think it is historically correct to say that the reason of the sudden and revolutionary change in the education of American women, which began with the nineteenth century and continued through it, was the realization that if we were to make real democrats, we must begin with the child, and if we began with the child we must begin with the mother!

Everybody saw that unless the child learned by example and precept the great principle of liberty, equality, and fraternity, he was going to remain what by nature we all are, imperious, demanding, and self-seeking. The whole scheme must fail if his education failed. It is not too much to say that the success of the Declaration of Independence and the Constitution depended, in the minds of certain early Democrats, upon the woman. The doctrines of these great instruments would be worked out according to the way she played her part. Her serious responsibility came in the fact that her work was one that nobody could take off her hands. This responsibility required a preparation entirely different from that which had been hers. She must be given education

and liberty. The woman saw this, and the story of her efforts to secure both, that she might meet the requirements, is one of the noblest in history. There was no doubt then as to the value of the tasks, no question as to their being worthy national obligations. It was a question of fitting herself for them.

HER FREEDOM DEFEATING HER

But what has happened? In the process of preparing herself to discharge more adequately her task as a woman in a republic, her respect for the task has been weakened. In this process, which we call emancipation, she has in a sense lost sight of the purpose of emancipation. Interested in acquiring new tools, she has come to believe the tools more important than the thing for which she was to use them. She has found out that with education and freedom, pursuits of all sorts are open to her, and by following these pursuits she can preserve her personal liberty, avoid the grave responsibility, the almost inevitable sorrows and anxieties which belong to family life. She can choose her friends and change them. She can travel, and gratify her tastes, satisfy her personal ambitions. The snare has been too great, the beauty and joy of free individual life have dulled the sober sense of national obligation. The result is that she is frequently failing to discharge satisfactorily some of the most imperative demands the nation makes upon her.

Take as an illustration the moral training of the child. The most essential obligation in a Woman's Business is establishing her household on a sound moral basis. If a child is anchored to basic principles it is because his home is built on them. If he understands integrity as a man, it is usually because a woman has done her work well. If she has not done it well it is probable that he will be a disturbance and a menace when he is turned over to society. To send defective steel to a gunmaker is no more fatal to making safe guns than turning out boys who are shifty and tricky is to making an effective, honest community.

Appalled by the seriousness of the task, or lured from it by the joys of liberty and education, the woman has too generally shifted it to other shoulders — shoulders which are waiting to help her work out the problem, but which can never be a substitute. She has turned over the child to the teacher, secular and religious, and fancied that he might be made a man of integrity by an elaborate system of teaching in a mass. Has this shifting of responsibility no relation to the general lowering of our commercial and political morality?

EMANCIPATION AND POLITICAL CORRUPTION

For years we have been bombarded with evidence of an appalling indifference to the moral quality of our commercial and political transactions. It is not too much to say that the revelations of corruption in our American cities, the use of town councils, State legislatures and even of the Federal Government in the interests of private business, have discredited the democratic system throughout the world. It has given more material for those of other lands who despise democracy to sneer at us than anything that has yet happened in this land. And *this has come about under the régime of the emancipated woman.* Is she in no way responsible for it? If she had kept the early ideals of the woman's part in democracy as clearly before her eyes as she has kept some of her personal wants and needs, could there have been so disastrous a condition? Would she be the Uneasy Woman she is if she had kept faith with the ideals that forced her emancipation? — if she had not substituted for them dreams of personal ambition, happiness, and freedom!

The failure to fulfil your function in the scheme under which you live always produces unrest. Content of mind is usually in proportion to the service one renders in an undertaking he believes worth while. If our Uneasy Woman could grasp the full meaning of her place in this democracy, a place so essential that democracy must be overthrown unless she rises to it — a part which man is not equipped to play and which he ought not to be asked to play, would she not cease to apologize for herself — cease to look with envy on man's occupations? Would she not rise to her part and we not have at last the 'new woman' of whom we have talked so long?

SUFFRAGE NEEDED?

Learning business careers, political and industrial activities — none of these things is more than incidental in the national task of woman. Her great task is to prepare the citizen. The tools for this are in her hands. It calls for education, and the nation has provided it. It calls for freedom of movement and expression, and she has them. It calls for ability to organize, to discuss problems, to work for whatever changes are essential. She is developing this ability. It may be that it calls for the vote; I do not myself see this, but it is certain that she will have the vote as soon as not a majority — but an approximate half — not of men — but of women feel the need of it.

What she has partially at least lost sight of is that education, freedom, organization, agitation, the suffrage are but tools to an end; what she now needs is to formulate that end so nobly and clearly that the most ignorant women may understand it. The failure to do this is leading her deeper and deeper into fruitless unrest. It is breeding, too, a crop of problems which stagger the thoughtful by their difficulty and their elusiveness, and among these problems none is more serious or more delicate than that of the Homeless Daughter. It is she whom we will consider in the next paper in this series.

Make Out Budget Plan

VI

AN OPEN LETTER ON THE WAR SITUATION

SIR CLAUD SCHUSTER

[*New York Times*, April 18, 1915. By permission.]

March 11, 1915.

To Albert J. Beveridge, Esq.

Dear Senator: I found our conversation yesterday afternoon so interesting that I became really anxious that you should have before you the point of view which I believe to be typical of the English middle class, so that at the risk of wearying you I venture to set down in this letter some of the points which I could not state in conversation as clearly as I could have wished.

In the first place, I should like you to think of the state of mind in which we all were in the middle of last July — and when I say all, I mean that this state of mind was common more or less to all classes, from the highest to the lowest. We were all very much concerned with our own affairs. We had great domestic and political difficulties. There was much industrial unrest, and the Irish situation was such that those in the inner circles of politics were greatly troubled, though I do not think that the ordinary Englishman thought it possible that what he looked upon as an ordinary political row could develop into a real conflict. But we had been in industrial and political trouble often enough before, and few of us, if any, gave these matters much thought when once we had finished reading our morning newspapers. Our thoughts were mainly with our own businesses, as an Englishman's thoughts generally are.

We were in a period of abounding prosperity. During the period from 1903 to 1913 the yearly value of our imports had increased from 542 millions to 768 millions, and our exports from 360 millions to 634 millions. During the three years 1910, 1911, and 1912 the British shipping entered and cleared in the foreign trade at ports in the United Kingdom increased from about 80 million tons to about 88½ million tons, and the amount of foreign shipping in the same period so entered and cleared from 54 millions to nearly 64 millions. These figures of the total exports include foreign and colonial transshipments as well as United Kingdom products. The exports of articles wholly or mainly manufactured in the United Kingdom had increased in about the same period from 234 millions to 385 millions. We were, in fact, largely absorbed in our own prosperity.

JEALOUSY ABOUT FOREIGN MARKETS

There was, of course, as there often is between nations, a certain amount of jealousy between ourselves and Germany as to foreign markets, and probably that jealousy was more strongly accentuated among the merchants in the foreign ports than among those at home. In the greatest of our staple trades, that of the spinning of cotton and manufacturing of cotton goods, we were completely confident of our power to hold our great markets. We based that confidence partly on the course of trade, which had flowed for some years in ever-increased volume, and partly on the experience which taught us that the Lancashire climate and the long-held skill and inherited aptitude of the Lancashire cotton operative would enable us in the future, as it has done in the past, to hold our own against any competitor.

It is true that to many observers it seemed that the cotton trade was about to enter upon a period of depression. It is notorious that this trade is subject to periods of great inflation and great depression, which follow one upon the other with such uniformity that they can almost be predicted for some years in advance. In this case prosperity had probably induced a period of overtrading. Then came the Balkan War, which cut off a large section of the Continental market, and the probability of an unusually heavy cotton crop in the Southern States rendered it probable that the price of raw cotton would fall abnormally, just at a time when merchants and manufacturers were overstocked.

NO ENGLISHMAN WANTED WAR

But it did not cross the mind of any single human being of any class or shade of political belief that a cure could be found for any of such evils as there might be in the economic or political situation of this country by making war, and, least of all, so far as the economic questions were concerned, by making war on Germany. Including transshipped goods, in 1913 Germany took from us £80,000,000 worth of goods and sent us £60,000,000. In 1912 she took from us £17,500,000 worth of cotton yarn and woolen goods.

It is a common saying here that whenever a British shell goes off it kills a customer. We had as much as we could do with the capital at our command, and none of us were insane enough to think that we should get a better return on what was left if we made war upon a country where millions of British money was outstanding at the moment.

It is perhaps not a very noble attitude for a country to be entirely absorbed in business, though I must admit that I, for one, look upon an increase in the country's wealth as the surest agent in promoting the material comfort and, as I think also, the moral and other interests of the weekly wage earner. But be that as it may, that was the condition in which we were in late July, and we were looking forward rather eagerly to our usual August holiday after what had been a strenuous year. Most people, I expect, had taken their rooms or hotel accommodation at seaside places on the English coast — places which have since been wrecked by German shells. Into this state of material comfort there crashed, as unexpectedly as those shells themselves, first, the crisis of the last week of July, and then the hell which, as we say, Germany has seen fit to let loose on earth.

When we were awakened to realize that there really was a European crisis our first state was one of muddled astonishment. We had made provision in the past for the protection of our coasts and trade routes and colonies through the means of a fleet. We had watched, some of us more anxiously than others, the building up of a fleet on the other side of the North Sea, the reasons for whose existence seemed to us impossible to explain. We know it now.

We had equipped an army, very efficient for matters within its scope, but wholly unfit, so far as numbers were concerned, for a conflict on a European scale. We had not spent a penny upon the fortification of our coasts, except upon the actual defenses of such places as Portsmouth and Plymouth and Sheerness, which serve as bases for the fleet.

And our preparations had been so limited because we have never believed that any European power would wantonly provoke a great war. The inhabitants of the great Continental States saw more clearly than we did, because on the frontiers of all of them great forces had moved up and down for years and great fortresses served as an object lesson. Some even of them, however — Belgium, for instance — had no real sense of impending danger.

In these circumstances we learned of the murder of the Austrian Archduke. English people have a dislike of conspiracy and secret assassination, just as Americans have, and a very considerable wave of sympathy went out to the Austrians in what we regarded as their trouble. People who knew anything of the history of the Balkan States were, however, not very greatly surprised. I think every one who was well informed, but not the great mass of the people, feared that some European complication might arise.

Then followed a long period of apparent calm. No doubt the Foreign Offices had enough information to make them uneasy, but this uneasiness was not communicated to the outside world. Then came the Austrian note to Serbia, and it was immediately apparent to those who could adjust their vision (it took most of us a few days to do so) that a very dangerous crisis had arisen.

ENGLAND MIGHT HAVE BEEN DIVIDED

It is unnecessary, since you are fully acquainted with the diplomatic history of the ten days immediately preceding the war, to set it out here in detail. I am only trying to tell you how it looked to us then, and to assure you that deep as was our slowly growing conviction that Germany had predetermined to commit this crime, our certainty that we were right to arrive at that conclusion grows larger still with every fresh scrap of evidence.

We saw immediately that such a note as this could not have been delivered, and that Sir Edward Grey's desperate efforts to obtain some peaceful solution could not have been constantly repulsed by the Germans, were it not that they had decided to make war on Russia. If war was to be made on Russia, war with France must follow. We were not bound to France by any treaty of alliance; and if the war had been confined to one between Germany and Austria on the one hand and France and Russia on the other, it is probable that a wide divergence of opinion would have manifested itself here.

There were some of us who thought that such a war, deeply as it might stir our sympathies and much as it might affect our material interests, still was no more a direct concern of ourselves than the majority of the inhabitants of the United States think it to be of theirs. Others thought, and still think, that the suppression of France would be so intolerable a crime against civilization and liberty that it would be better for this country to stand against it even to the shedding of blood — even at any risk to herself or any damage to her material interest. This party thought that this crime was heightened tenfold when it was committed deliberately, and that these results would be still more deplorable in that they must enthrone as the supreme dictator in Europe and the world the power which had deliberately plotted it and carried it out.

BELGIUM UNITED ALL ENGLAND

There were, therefore, doubts and waverings here as to our proper course of action. All these doubts and waverings were set at rest by the invasion of Belgium, and, from the moment when it became clear that Germany intended to take that course, no one in this country doubted the necessity for and the justice of the war, except a few people to whose voices no one listens because they are known always to be raised in support of a paradox or to deny the incontestable. Add to all this the manner in which the war has been conducted on the other side: the devastation of Belgium; the strewing of mines loose in the North Sea; the sinking of merchant ships and emigrant ships and the attempts to sink hospital ships; the outrages and burnings in northern France; the bombardment of English open places and the murder of English women and children; the cruel treatment of our prisoners, even the wounded (evidence of which accumulates day by day).

Do you think that if these things had happened to the United States her citizens would not have been angry, and can you suppose that we are otherwise than very angry, with that kind of surly, taciturn English rage which is not so picturesque as the French fury, nor so plain to see as the German hate, but is, at least, as durable and destructive?

You asked me why, if we were not seeking war with Germany, and if we did not hope to destroy her trade by force of arms, Germany should have wished a war herself. It is almost impossible, at this stage of our knowledge, to estimate what motives or what motiveless impulses may have actuated her. Some people think that her long preparation and her final rush to arms were as much the creatures of instinct as the mysterious unrest in a hive of bees which culminates in the act of swarming. Others see in her acts evidence of a collective insanity seizing upon the whole nation. These theories have something fantastic in them, but they probably contain also some germs of truth.

History alone, informed by a knowledge which we cannot possess of the true character of the chief actors, and of the actual events in the palace at Potsdam, the imperial yacht, and at the meeting place of the Kaiser and the Archduke Franz Ferdinand some little time before the murder of the latter, may be able to pronounce exactly what forces on the German side produced the catastrophe. It seems to us, in our limited knowledge, that the following motives and currents, crossing and reacting on one another, were the main causes which impelled Germany to war:

1. The personal and professional ambitions of the leaders of the army and navy, who, you will remember, exercise upon the government of the country a direct influence.

2. The personal position of the Emperor. The French believe that he, for some little time, has watched with anxiety and jealousy the growing popularity of the Crown Prince with the military party, and has feared to be supplanted, if not on his throne, at least in the hearts of his people.

3. A national sense that the country and its inhabitants were not received by the world at a sufficiently high valuation. The Germans, both as a people and as individuals, are intensely conscious of their national achievements and greatness. Up to 1870 their thought had bidden fair to conquer the world. 1870 made them conscious of great material strength such as they had before hardly realized. Yet they found that people still looked to France or to England. The advance of French methods of thought, French historians, and French artists, and their influence on other countries, has been strongly marked during the last few years; and the Germans felt that they were, in a Europe which reckoned by centuries, a young people whose strength was undervalued. This feeling manifested itself in personal acts, wherever you met Germans over the Continent, in an uneasy self-assertion. You must remember that Germany and Germans had grown rich rather suddenly, and had the defects which are sometimes associated with that process.

NO ECONOMIC ADVANTAGE FROM WAR

4. Trade interests, or what are believed to be trade interests, no doubt influenced them greatly. In my view, Great Britain has no economic advantage to gain from the present struggle. Germany is in different case, and it is easy to see why Germans should believe that such a war would bring them commercial prosperity. For one thing, they hold an economic theory which is different from ours, and they believe, as we do not believe, that one state can grow rich through the impoverishment of another.

Secondly, they make war on a system different from ours. Both in 1870 and in this war, but far more in this war than in 1870, they have exacted large monetary contributions from the territory which they occupy. This was more or less the theory of the Middle Ages, and it is obvious that if one feudal baron took the lands of another, and the gold plate which he had in his coffers, he was richer at the end of the struggle than at the beginning. It is not so obvious that one State is really better off by such conduct, still less so that the inhabitants of that State are individually enriched by it.

But the theory looks tempting, and if one is not deterred by scruples of morality, no doubt one takes some satisfaction from the spoils of Antwerp, Brussels, and Liège, the appropriation of the coal mines of northern France, and the wholesale plunder of the factories of Lille. But the more deeply seated economic cause lies in the methods of German finance.

The huge ' go-downs ' which you saw in China are financed probably by the big German banking houses at heavy interest. There has been no form of commercial expansion which has not found financial support on a lavish scale in Germany. Hence comes the necessity for continually expanding markets, for quick and large returns, and overinflation and overtrading based on insufficient capital lent out on insufficient security.

STORM CENTER OF WORLD FINANCE

The German money market, therefore, has for a long time been one of the storm centers of the finance of the world. There is reason to suppose that, with the depression consequent upon the Balkan wars, a crisis was approaching, and that some desperate stroke was necessary to avoid collapse. Hence it is supposed that the big German financiers and commercial men were in a mind more easily disposed to welcome war than in more normal times.

5. Undoubtedly the agrarian classes felt their power to be shaken. They had lately had to submit to heavy taxation on capital to provide the means of defense. It is very probable that they were persuaded to endure this burden by promises that this was the last time — that in the glory of a successful war the dreams of the Socialists would be forgotten (as has indeed proved to be the case), and that, the domi-

nation of the world once secured, their domination over Germany would be rooted more firmly than ever.

6. No doubt there intervened also some feeling of fear. German statesmen, ever since there began to be any thought of a united Germany, have always looked uneasily toward the East. Russia was recovering slowly, but too fast, from the disaster of the Japanese War. She has now access to the great savings bank of the world — the pocket of the French peasant. The landowner of East Prussia naturally fears the Cossack. It may well have been that the moment seemed to have come to make an end of the Russian peril.

7. For such an effort the time seemed propitious. Indeed, it may have seemed as if it was now or never. The Balkan wars seemed to have shut the door to the Near East. They did more than that. It was not likely that the young, strong, and victorious Serbian Kingdom would acquiesce for long in the possession by Austria of Bosnia and Herzegovina. In the Near East, and especially in the Valleys of the Euphrates and Tigris, lay the next task of Germany, as her desires prefigured it. Here was the chance to open the door, and at the same time to separate France from Russia or to destroy them both.

It was no doubt hoped that France, and certainly England, would be but little interested in a squabble arising in the Balkan Peninsula. France, therefore, might perhaps not stand by her ally, and in that case the Dual Alliance was broken forever and the Germanic group remained supreme in Europe. If France stood by her ally, at least England might be depended upon, with her well-known internal difficulties, her soft desire for peace, and her lack of immediate interest in a Balkan quarrel, to stand aside. If the Allies stood together, then there would be war, but war could not come at a better time for Germany, just when the widening of the Kiel Canal was completed and Russia had not finished the reorganization of her armies or begun the construction of the strategic railways in Poland which were to be financed out of the French loan. If the Allies did not stand together, the diplomatic triumph was immense.

If these were the predisposing causes, conscious or subconscious, there is one circumstance yet to be mentioned which finally determined the matter. For many years Germany has rattled the saber or shaken the mailed fist and expected that the nations of Europe would cower and give way. At the time of Agadir she put on her shining armor and showed her sword and clenched her fist, and nobody minded. She began to be afraid that the world at large was ceasing to be afraid of her.

This time, when she had given a free hand to her ally and assumed her usual panoply of war, she could not put it off again without looking ridiculous, and if she had looked ridiculous her diplomatists and her military powers would have looked ridiculous to themselves and to the German people. Hence when the threats to Serbia had once been uttered they could not be withdrawn.

GERMAN VICTORY MENACE TO PEACE

These seem to us to have been the moving causes of Germany's aggression. Add to them the careless teaching of professors and military historians that war is a god-like thing and that the Germans are the greatest people upon earth, and you have a result which is enough to account for the present situation.

I fear that all this is very tiresome. Most of it you knew before, but I am most anxious that you should not have any doubt about the determination of this country. My own fear is, not that we shall flag in the struggle but that we may, from time to time, get out of hand. It may be that we shall be beaten. If so, we shall at least have done our best, and we shall go down in what we regard as the worthiest cause in which a nation can fall. We believe that if we go down the cause of liberty throughout the world will suffer. Assuredly the result will not be a period of peace; nor will Germany's domination endure forever.

You have seen the military preparations and the state of the powers engaged in war in the western theatre, and can judge better than I can of the chances of success. But I do not think, so far as I can form an opinion, that we shall be beaten. It is true that Germany occupies almost all Belgium and some of the richest areas of northern France; that her spirit is unbroken, and that her people have not contemplated the possibility of defeat.

Yet the comparative military strengths of the contending powers are vastly different from what they were in the early days of the war, and all that difference is on our side. We began the war with an army whose numbers were to be considered as little more than a make-weight in the struggle. By the middle of this year we shall have as many troops in the field as France herself.

FRENCH TROOPS CALLED BEST OF ALL

France began with her eastern fortresses admitted to be in no state of defense, with admitted deficiencies in the higher command, and with troops who, though they still possessed the unquenchable ardor of the historical French infantry, were difficult to hold in the field. The French troops were described to me the other day by a competent observer as the best troops in the field on either side.

Germany began with an overpowering preponderance in heavy artillery and an enormous store of ammunition. We have already redressed the first of these inequalities, and on the second, while Germany is shut off from help from overseas, every country in the world is furnishing us with munitions of war, and every resource possessed by this country herself is at our service. Our fleet was to be worn down by a war of attrition until the Germans possessed an equality of numbers, and was then to be destroyed in a fleet action. The war of attrition has gone the other way. And we hear no more of it. So far as we know, besides one cruiser playing hide-and-seek in the Pacific, the only German ships of war which venture out of harbor are a few submarines, and we do not know how many return home to recount their exploits.

We have every confidence in the strength and loyalty of those Continental nations which are embattled on our side. We think that both the fleet and the army have proved themselves worthy. But beyond all this we have ' great allies '— and a determination that ' government of the people, by the people, and for the people shall not perish from the earth.'

Yours very truly,

CLAUD SCHUSTER.

VII

A GERMAN DECLARATION

RUDOLF EUCKEN AND ERNST HAECKEL

[*New York Times*, September 10, 1914.
By permission.]

The whole German world of letters is today filled with deep indignation and strong moral indignation at the present behavior of England. Both of us, for many years bound to England by numerous scientific and personal ties, believe ourselves prepared to give open expression to this inward revulsion. In close coöperation with like-minded English investigators we have zealously exerted ourselves to bring the two great peoples closer together in spirit and to promote a mutual understanding. A fruitful reciprocal interchange of English and German culture seemed to us worth while, indeed necessary, for the spiritual advance of mankind, which today confronts such great problems. Gratefully we recall in this connection the friendly reception which our efforts received in England. So great and noble were the traits of English character which revealed themselves to us that we were permitted to hope that in their sure growth they would come to be superior to the pitfalls and seamy sides of this character. And now they have proved inferior, inferior to the old evil of a brutal national egoism which recognizes no rights on the part of others, which, unconcerned about morality or unmorality, pursues only its own advantage.

History furnishes in abundance examples of such an unscrupulous egoism; we need recall here only the destruction of the Danish fleet (1807) and the theft of the Dutch colonies in the Napoleonic wars. But what is taking place today is the worst of all; it will be forever pointed at in the annals of world history as England's indelible shame. England fights on behalf of a Slavic, half-Asiatic power against Germanism; she fights on the side not only of barbarism but also of moral injustice, for it is indeed not forgotten that Russia began the war because she would permit no radical reparation for a shameful murder. It is England whose fault has extended the present war into a world war, and has thereby endangered our joint culture.

And all this for what reason? Because she was jealous of Germany's greatness, because she wanted to hinder at any price a further growth of this greatness. For there cannot be the least doubt on this point that England was determined in advance to cast as many obstacles as possible in the way of Germany's existence in this struggle of the giants, and to hinder her as much as possible in the full development of her powers. She (England) was watching only for a favorable opportunity when she could break out suddenly against Germany, and she therefore promptly seized on the invasion of Belgium, so necessary to Germany, in order that she might cover with a small cloak of decency her brutal national egoism. Or is there in the whole wide world any one so simple as to believe that England would have declared war on France also if the latter had invaded Belgium? In that event she would have wept hypocritical tears over the unavoidable violation of international law; but as for the rest she would have laughed in her sleeve with great satisfaction. This hypocritical Pharisaism is the most repugnant feature of the whole matter; it deserves nothing but contempt.

The history of the world shows that such sentiments lead the nations not upward but downward. For the present, however, we trust firmly in our just cause, in the superior strength and the unyielding victorious spirit of the German people. Yet we must at the same time lament deeply that that boundless egoism has disturbed for an immeasurable period of time the spiritual coöperation of the two peoples which promised so much good for the development of mankind. But they wished it, so there — on England alone falls the monstrous guilt and the historical responsibility.

VIII

A GERMAN VIEW OF THE FUTURE

WILHELM OSTWALD

[*New York Times*, September 21, 1914.
By permission.]

[Professor Ostwald sent the following letter to Edwin D. Mead, Director of the World Peace Foundation, in London, with a request that it might be published in America.]

1. The war is the result of a deliberate onslaught upon Germany and Austria by

the powers of the Triple Entente, Russia, France, and England. Its object is on the part of Russia an extension of Russian supremacy over the Balkans, on the side of France revenge, and on the side of England annihilation of the German navy and German commerce. In England, especially, it has been for several centuries a constant policy to destroy upon favoring occasion every navy of every other country which threatened to become equal to the English navy.

2. Germany has proved its love of peace for forty-four years under the most trying circumstances. While all other States have expanded themselves by conquest, Russia in Manchuria, England in the Transvaal, France in Morocco, Italy in Tripoli, Austria in Bosnia, Japan in Korea, Germany alone has contented itself with the borders fixed in 1871. It is purely a war of defense which is now forced upon us.

3. In the face of these attacks Germany has until now (the end of August) proved its military superiority, which rests upon the fact that the entire German military force is scientifically organized and honestly administered.

4. The violation of Belgian neutrality was an act of military necessity, since it is now proved that Belgian neutrality was to be violated by France and England. A proof of this is the accumulation of English munitions at Maubeuge, aside from many other facts.

5. According to the course of the war up to the present time, European peace seems to me nearer than ever before. We pacificists must only understand that unhappily the time was not yet sufficiently developed to establish peace by the peaceful way. If Germany, as everything now seems to make probable, is victorious in the struggle not only with Russia and France, but attains the further end of destroying the source from which for two or three centuries all European strifes have been nourished and intensified, namely, the English policy of world dominion, then will Germany, fortified on one side by its military superiority, on the other side by the eminently peaceful sentiment of the greatest part of its people, and especially of the German Emperor, dictate peace to the rest of Europe, I hope especially that the future treaty of peace will in the first place provide effectually that a European war such as the present can never again break out.

6. I hope, moreover, that the Russian people, after the conquest of their armies, will free themselves from czarism through an internal movement by which the present political Russia will be resolved into its natural units, namely, Great Russia, the Caucasus, Little Russia, Poland, Siberia, and Finland, to which probably the Baltic provinces would join themselves. These, I trust, would unite themselves with Finland and Sweden, and perhaps with Norway and Denmark, into a Baltic federation, which in close connection with Germany would insure European peace, and especially form a bulwark against any disposition to war which might remain in Great Britain.

7. For the other side of the earth I predict a similar development under the leadership of the United States. I assume that the English dominion will suffer a downfall similar to that which I have predicted for Russia, and that under these circumstances Canada would join the United States, the expanded republic assuming a certain leadership with reference to the South American republics.

8. The principle of the absolute sovereignty of the individual nations, which in the present European tumult has proved itself so inadequate and baneful, must be given up and replaced by a system conforming to the world's actual conditions and especially to those political and economic relations which determine industrial and cultural progress and the common welfare.

IX

THE LAST SPRING OF THE OLD LION

GEORGE BERNARD SHAW

[New Statesman, London, England, December 12, 1914. By permission.]

What is the English press coming to when it can find nothing in the French *Yellow Book* but the single morsel of garbage that disgraces it? In the heat and scare of the first outbreak of war there was some excuse for swallowing that general order of the Kaiser in which, finding the German language too inexpressive, he exhorted his army to take no notice of the French and Russian millions but concentrate their wrath on General French's 'contemptible little army.' Yet that journalistic effort was plausible compared to the 'official and secret report from a trustworthy source' which M. Etienne sent to M. Jonnart on April 2, 1913. M. Jonnart's reception of it is not chronicled. I make haste to announce that I am not taken in and that nothing more on that subject is to be feared by readers of this article.

From an authentic part of this *Yellow Book* there emerges a picture so stirring that it is amazing to me that no Englishman has yet rescued it from its wrappings of official correspondence, for in it you see the old British lion, the lion of Waterloo, the lion of Blenheim, the lion of Trafalgar, making his last and most terrible and triumphant spring. You see him with his old craft and his old courage and strength unimpaired, with his old amazing luck, his old singleness of aim, his old deep-lying and subtle instinct that does better without great men in a pinch than his enemies do with them.

For centuries now the Lion has held to his one idea that none shall be greater than England on the land, and none as great on the sea. To him it has been nothing whether a rival to England was better or worse than England. When Waterloo was won, Byron said 'I'm damned sorry,' and humanitarians and libertarians looked aghast at the reëstablishment of the Inquisition and the restoration of an effete and mischievous dynasty by English arms on the ruins of liberty, equality, and fraternity. Little recked the Lion of that. England's rival was in the dust; England was mistress of the seas; England's General (what matter that he was an Irishman?) was master of Europe, with its kings whispering in his presence like frightened schoolboys. England right or wrong, England complete with her own native corruptions and oppressions no less than her own native greatness and glory, had risen all English from the conflict and held the balance of power in her hand.

For a hundred years after that no Englishman knew what it was to turn pale at the possibility of invasion. For more than two generations of Englishmen the Lion lay and basked and smelled no foe that the pat of his paw could not dispose of. Then a rival arose again. Battles more terrible than Waterloo were fought against the same foe, but it was not England that won them. The Lion rose and began to watch. The old instinct stirred in him. He heard the distant song, 'Deutschland, Deutschland, über Alles,' and something in him said 'Never that while I live.'

The rival built a warship, built another warship and yet another, openly challenged the sovereignty of the sea. That was the end. From that moment it was only a question of when to spring, for a lion with that one idea at heart, with that necessity deep in his very bowels, must be crafty; he must win at all hazards, no matter how long he crouches before the right moment comes.

You see it coming in the *Yellow Book*. Germany with Austria and Russia with France stalk each other, finger on trigger, France avoiding the fight, Russia gradually arming herself and training herself for it, Austria speculating on it all, even Austria afraid of the Lion's rival, Germany. France (always manœuvering for peace, being outnumbered) at last finds that Germany, defiant of her and of Russia, contemptuously sure that she can crush the one with her right hand and the other with her left, yet fears the Lion and well knows that if he comes to the aid of France and Russia, the odds will be too terrible even for the victors of Sedan. France sounds the Lion on the subject. The Lion, grim and cautious, does not object to his naval and military commanders talking to the commanders of France and discussing what might happen and how, in that case, things might be arranged. France suddenly bullies Germany — tells her to clear out of Morocco and clear out sharp. Germany looks at the Lion and sees him with quivering tail about to spring. The odds are too great. With mortification tearing her heart, Germany clears out, successfully bullied for the first time since the rise of her star.

The Lion is balked. Another few years of waiting and the British taxpayer may tire of keeping ahead of that growing fleet. The old instinct whispers, 'Now, now, before the rival is too strong.' Voices begin to cry that in the London streets, but there are new forces that the Lion must take account of. If the rival will not fight, it is not easy to attack him, and Germany will not fight unless the Lion can be detached from France and Russia, yet is sick with the humiliation of that bullying, and knows that nothing but the riding down of the bullies can restore her prestige and heal her wounded pride. But she must swallow her spleen, for at every threat France points to the Lion and saves the peace France alone really desires. Every time Germany is humiliated the Lion is balked. Austria's Balkan speculation is postponed, and Russia does not quite know whether she is balked or respited.

The Lion broods and broods, and deep in his subconsciousness there stirs the knowledge that Germany will never fight unless — unless — unless — the Lion does not quite know what, does not want to know what, but disinterested observers complete the sentence thus: Unless Germany can be persuaded that the Lion is taking a fancy to Germany and is becoming a bit of a pacifist and will not fight.

Then the luck that has so seldom failed the Lion sent Prince Lichnowsky as German Ambassador to London. There was nothing wrong in being very friendly to the Prince, a charming man with a very charming wife; there was our Sir Edward Grey, also a charming man, always ready to talk peace quite sincerely at tea parties with all Europe if necessary. The Lion knew in his heart that Grey knew nothing of the ways of lions, and would not approve of them if he did, for Grey had ideas instead of the one idea, and Prince Lichnowsky knew so much less of the ways of lions than Grey that he actually thought Grey was the Lion. The Lion said: 'This is not my doing. England's destiny has provided Grey, and provided Lichnowsky; England's star is still in the zenith.' Lichnowsky thought Grey every day a greater statesman and a more charming man, and became every day more persuaded that the lion's heart had changed and that he was becoming friendly, and Grey thought Lichnowsky, perhaps, rather a fool, but was none the less nice to him.

Then there was Asquith, the lucid lawyer, the man who could neither remember the past nor foresee the future, yet was always a Yorkshireman with ancient English depths behind his mirrorlike lucidity, in which something of lion craft could lodge without troubling the surface of the mirror. Asquith suddenly found working in himself an unaccountable but wholly irresistible impulse to hide and deny those arrangements with the French commanders which had frightened Germany. He said to Grey: 'You must go to the French and say that we are not bound to anything.' Grey, the amiable lover of peace, was delighted. He went, and the French, with imperturbable politeness, made a note of it, and then Asquith and Grey, with good conscience, found themselves busily persuading the world that the Lion was not bound to help France and Russia when the great day of Armageddon came. They persuaded the nation, they persuaded the House of Commons, they persuaded their own Cabinet, and at last — at last — they persuaded Germany. And the Lion crouched. Almost before he was ready the devil's own luck struck down the Archduke by the hand of an assassin, and Austria saw Servia in her grasp at last. She flew at Servia, Russia flew at Austria, Germany flew at France, and the Lion, with a mighty roar, sprang at last, and in a flash had his teeth and claws in the rival of England and will now not let her go for all the pacifists or Socialists in the world until he is either killed or back on his Waterloo pedestal again.

That, gentlemen of England, is the epic of the *Yellow Book,* that was the roar that your tradesmen pretended not to hear because it frightened them into assuring the Germans that it was only the bleat of a pack of peaceful sheep attacked by a wicked wolf. Much you will care for their babble about old treaties and their assurances that you are incapable of anything so wicked as the hurrah with which your share in the lion heart responds to his roar and their piteous stories, like the old stories of Boney eating babies, and their frantic lies and shameful abuse of the enemy whom you know you must now hold sacred from every weapon meaner than your steel.

As for me, I understand it. I vibrate to it; I perceive the might and mystery of it and all sorts of chords in me sound the demand that the Lion's last fight shall be the best fight of all and Germany the last foe overcome. But I am a Socialist and know well that the Lion's day is gone by and that the bravest lion gets shot in the long run. I foresee that his victory will not, like the old victories, lead to a century of security. I know that it will create a situation more dangerous than the situation of six months ago, and that only by each western nation giving up every dream of supremacy can that situation be mastered. A lion within frontiers is after all a lion in a cage, and the future has no use for caged lions fighting to defend their own chains. In future we must fight, not alone for England, but for the welfare of the world. But for all that the Lion is a noble old beast and his past is a splendid past and his breed more valiant than ever — too valiant, nowadays, indeed, to be merely Englishmen *contra mundum*. I take off my hat to him as he makes his last charge and shall not cease to wave it because of the squealing of the terrified chickens.

X

BERNARD SHAW AND THE WAR

GEORGE W. KIRCHWEY

[*Nation*, London, England, February 13, 1915. By permission.]

The mental devastation caused by the war which is exacting such a toll of the world's civilization is scarcely less deplorable than the ruin which it has brought on our accumulated store of life and industry, of goodwill and morality. The dislocation of mind which has made the utterances of grave German professors and men of science come to our ears as the ravings of madmen has its counterpart in the outpourings of certain English men of letters. But surely the Lucifer of this divine tragedy is G. Bernard Shaw. Even that crystal-clear mind, insanely sane, with its almost miraculous freedom from cant (except, of course, its own) has fallen from its high estate. No more can we look to it for light and leading through this tangled web of chance and design, of doubt and apprehension, in which the diplomatic and ruling persons of Europe have enmeshed us. Never have we needed more that penetrating intelligence, the drastic word with which he was wont to purge our souls. The familiar spirit of perverseness which has so often given the needed 'bite' to his criticism of life appears for the moment to have taken complete possession of him. How else can we explain that deliberate justification of bad faith between nations which he has recently published to the world?

It may, perhaps, be admitted that public opinion was in need of the medicine administered in his more elaborate paper, which he whimsically entitled 'Common Sense about the War.' That Great Britain had, through her engagements with her partners in the Triple Entente, virtually bound herself to go to war in the event that France became involved; that she must have entered into the conflict, Belgium or no Belgium; that her solicitude over the fate of small nations was in exact ratio to her interest in the fate of those nations — these were all things which it was well that the public should bear in mind. That the morality of nations is of more importance than their success in war, and that the first condition of morality is to rid oneself of cant, hypocrisy, and self-delusion — these are principles with which Shaw has made us familiar, and which many of us accept as fully and unqualifiedly as he does. If to do this for one's people means extending aid and comfort to the enemy, so much the worse for a people so bemused, so much more imperative the need of speaking out. In this view the thin plausibilities which disfigured the paper, the gratuitous imputation of motives, the tricky identification of Mr. Asquith and Sir Edward Grey with Prussian Junkerism, are easily forgiven. They are, at the worst, evidence that Shaw's perverse spirit does not know (for such is the nature of perverse spirits) when to keep in the background.

The same may be said of the whimsical letter to President Wilson, requesting him to ask the belligerents to withdraw from the soil of Belgium and fight out their quarrel on their own soil. It is their fight, not Belgium's. Only people absurd enough to regard a president of the United States as a sort of divine person — like a pope or a kaiser — could regard this letter as an impertinence. It was only the most dramatic, and therefore the most effective, way of calling the attention of the world to two vitally important but neglected facts — that nations that go to war have no right to involve pacific nations in the dreadful consequences of their enmity, and that a great neutral power like the United States lies under a duty to prevent such an outrage, or, at least, to make its disapproval known and felt.

Thus far we can loyally follow the master — and forgive him. But the next article, the 'British Lion' paper, gives us pause. In what menagerie of chimeras did he discover such a beast? Never, surely, was there limned a more fantastic picture of the British mind and purpose than the Shavian conception of the British Lion, couching watchfully on his white cliffs, slowly moving his tail to and fro as he looks for the appearance of any power great enough to dispute with him the supremacy of the world, and then springing on his rival and bringing him to earth. Poor, inept, unready, muddling old lion! Like his near relation, the American Eagle, never suspecting what is to happen until it has happened, never looking beyond the claws of his outstretched paws, finding himself, he knows not how, burdened with an empire by the grace of a hundred accidents, now trying to shake off the burden, now dumbly accepting, or even, in an inspired hour, glorying in it, but never knowing what to do with it, never quite sure whether it is in truth an empire or merely a grandiose but uneasy dream. One can only guess at the motive which inspired this bold piece of Nature-faking. Was it mere waggery or was it satire? Doubtless the latter; for Shaw has not left us under any illusions as to his real opinion of the British beast — a sham lion strutting across the stage with the stride of Lloyd-George and roaring with the voice of Winston Churchill; an Androcles' lion, that needs only to be confronted with the real lion of Shaw's imagination to be laughed off the stage. And if he is not laughed off, if the audience really identifies the two, and in Shaw's lion sees only a faithful picture of the familiar, official beast; if, in other words, the satirist has spent his barbed shaft in vain, the game is still worth the candle; for the other Shaw, the perverse spirit, has his innings. Has he not once again made the British lion an ass?

But when we come to the matter of Belgian neutrality, our mood of bewilderment flares up in a flame of indignation. Shaw's definition of neutrality, and the fine-spun argument which he draws from it, belong in the Wonderland of Alice and the Red Queen, not in a world of realities. Neutrality does not mean the self-effacement of a nation, either in 'the conventional legal sense' nor in any other intelligible sense. It means only that a people which, in the midst of war's alarms, chooses to live in peace, shall be let alone, shall not be made a pawn in the desperate game of the outlaw nations that choose to live by war.

Apparently Mr. Shaw commits himself unreservedly to the view that if England, to punish Servia for such a crime as she is alleged to have committed against Austria, decided to go to war with that unhappy country, she would be justified in regarding as an enemy any neutral country through which she desired to pass in order to reach her victim. 'We should have to treat the declaration of neutrality as a declaration of war on us, and fight our way through — *durchhauen*, in fact,' are his words. This doctrine that a nation which lies in the way of a belligerent may rightfully be forced to choose between hari-kari and war was a favorite principle of the Europe of Frederick the Great, and is still practised by those who believe that the earth and the fullness thereof belong to the fighting nations. But the world has moved since those piping times of war, even if Mr. Shaw has not, and the notion that neutral peoples have rights which belligerents are bound to respect, and especially that a nation has a right to be let alone, to hold herself aloof from the predatory strife of her bandit neighbors, and pursue, if she will, the inglorious ways of peace — however this may inconvenience or annoy them, however much they may want to get at one another's throats across her territory — has in these days attained the proportions of a full-sized principle of public right. Here in America we believe in it so fiercely that we have, in some sort, neutralized the whole of the Western Hemisphere.

If Germany should conclude to use the historic route up our Hudson Valley for the purpose of invading Canada, or if Great Britain should reach a similar conclusion in order to check a German invasion by way of the St. Lawrence, I am afraid we should not listen with patience to the plea of military necessity as a justification for dragging us into the war between them against our will. We should probably make use of Voltaire's reply to the scoundrelly courtier who made a similar plea, 'But one must live!' by retorting, 'We do not see the necessity.' And it is quite likely that we should, with such force as we could command, proceed to put that conviction into effect.

As to the treaty of which Mr. Asquith makes so much and Mr. Shaw so little, that, of course, is no concern of Belgium's. As has been pointed out, her right to be unravished rests upon no 'scrap of paper' whatsoever, but upon recognized principles of public right, to which no treaties or conventions could add a feather's weight. The quarrel over the treaty is between the great Powers · which neutralized Belgium — that is, imposed a compulsory neutrality upon her, bound her to perpetual peace — and pledged their good faith to keep her territory inviolate in the event of war between themselves; not, be it observed, for her sake nor in the interest of the public peace of Europe, but for their own selfish ends. The question, then, is, Have France and Great Britain the right to charge Germany with bad faith in disregarding their treaty? Mr. Shaw says 'No!' Treaties, like engagements between individuals, are binding only under the conditions existing at the time they are made — *rebus sic stantibus* — and Germany's military necessity constituted a new condition which absolved her from the obligation which the treaty of 1839 had imposed on her. An 'obvious barrister's point,' Mr. Shaw; and the 'business' about Mr. Balfour's influenza and his pledge to Sir Almroth Wright and the burning of his house 'equally obvious barrister's claptrap.' Here we have a case where the ordinary law of the land — of Germany as well as of England and France — better represents the common morality, and where the common morality better represents the interests of civilization than does the doctrine to which the perversity of Shaw has led him to give the sanction of his backing. It is the common teaching of experience that all obligations are not of equal validity, and that a changed condition of affairs which will absolve the promiser in one case will be wholly ineffectual to relieve him in another and different case. A violent headache may be a perfectly valid excuse for not keeping a dinner engagement, but would hardly avail a soldier in the firing-line who should plead it as a reason for keeping out of the battle.

To assert seriously that the solemn engagement of a nation not to use the territory of a neutral State as a base of operations against another nation (for that is what the Belgian treaty comes to) is invalidated by the circumstance that the nation so bound finds a war on her hands which makes it highly inconvenient for her to keep her pledge, is to reduce the *rebus sic stantibus* doctrine to an absurdity; especially when it is considered that it was to meet just this situation — to cut off the very advantage which Germany now claims as her indefeasible right — that the treaty was made. To such straits of sophistry are the defenders of Germany's high-handed violation of public right reduced.

In his reply to Shaw's 'Common Sense about the War,' Mr. Arnold Bennett had the boldness to suggest that Mr. Shaw, before republishing that paper, 'reconsider his position and rewrite.' We do not join in this request. The perversities which stung Mr. Bennett and other friends and admirers of Shaw to reply — not very effectively — to that scathing satire on our *haute politique* are perhaps an inseparable part of it. We would not risk spoiling the indictment by recasting it. But as to this matter of the Belgian Treaty, it is certainly to be hoped that Mr. Shaw will set himself right with the world. He is too fine and penetrating an influence for good to stand forth as the apologist of private or public bad faith.

XI

THE WAR AND THE WAY OUT

G. LOWES DICKINSON

[*Atlantic Monthly*, April, 1915. By permission.]

I

In a previous essay, published in the *Atlantic Monthly* for December last, I showed at length how this war, like all European wars, was caused by the working of a false theory of the State on the minds and passions of rulers, statesmen, journalists, and other leaders of opinion. In the pages that follow it is my object to discuss in some detail the kind of settlement which will be needed at the peace, if such wars are not to recur again and again. But since men's ideas as to the kind of peace that is desirable are affected by their conception of the causes of the war, I must begin by protesting against the view, industriously disseminated by the English, and, no doubt, by the French and Russian press, that the only cause of the war was the wickedness of Germany. For this view clearly is much too simple and superficial; and it leads to a wrong conception of the remedy. Let us then briefly examine it.

'Germany,' we say, 'made the war.' Germany? But what is Germany? The German people? The peasants? The factory laborers? The millions of Social Democrats? They made the war? Is it likely? Ten days before the war broke out they, like the people everywhere, were working, resting, eating, sleeping, dreaming of nothing less than of war. War came upon them like a thunderclap. The German people are as peaceable as every other. Their soldiers complain of it. We are fond of quoting General Bernhardi, but we never quote the passage in which he explains why he wrote his book. He wrote it, he tells us, to counteract 'the aspirations for peace which seem to dominate our age and threaten to poison the soul of the German people.' Now that the war has come, the German people are fighting; but they are fighting, as they believe, to protect their hearths and homes against the wanton aggression of Russia, France, and, above all, England. Like all the other peoples, they are fighting what they believe to be a defensive war. That is the tragic irony of it. Whoever made the war, it was not any of the peoples.

'Then, it was the German government.' Yes, or else it was the Russian, or else it was both. In any case, it was a very few men. The peace of Europe was in the hands of some score of individuals. They could make war, and the hundreds of millions who were to fight and to suffer could not stop it. That is the really extraordinary fact. That is what is worth dwelling on. How could it happen? Why are the nations passive clay in the hands of their governments?

First, because they do not know one another. They speak different languages, live different kinds of lives, have different manners and customs. They do not hate one another, but neither do they understand or trust one another. They do not feel that they belong together. Left to themselves, they would never, it is true, want to fight one another. They do not even think of one another; they are occupied with their own lives. But, since they do not know foreigners as they know one another, they can easily be made to believe that foreigners are their enemies. They do not think of them as real individual men and women. They think of them as a great solid mass, and attribute to this mass any qualities suggestion may put into their heads. So, at the moment, the ordinary Englishman believes that 'the Germans' are treacherous, brutal, bloodthirsty, cruel, while the Germans believe that 'the English' are cowardly, hypocritical, and degenerate. They believe these things because they are told to believe them, by the people who want to make bad blood. And they believe them the more readily because they are at war.

The fact, then, that to every nation every other is 'foreign,' makes the peoples of Europe the prey of those who want to make wars. We see in Germany who these people have been. They have been professors, like Treitschke, militarists like Bernhardi, journalists like Harden. And in England, they have been a Maxse, a Northcliffe, a Cramb. The same kind of people are and have been at work in all countries for the same end. For years past they have been setting the Germans at the English and the English at the Germans. The German literature against England we have drawn from its obscurity since the war began. But what about the English literature against Germany? Here is a specimen from one of our most prominent and intellectual journals:

'If Germany were extinguished to-morrow, the day after to-morrow there is not an Englishman in the world who would not be the richer. Nations have fought for years over a city or a right of succession; must they not fight for two hundred and fifty million pounds of yearly commerce?'[1]

Policy, playing on ignorance — that is the origin of wars. But why the policy? What is it aiming at? That, too, we must make clear.

We accuse Germany of making an unprovoked attack upon France and Russia, and we are indignant. But we forget that, if Germany so acted, she was acting in accordance with the principles and practice dominant throughout Europe for cen-

[1] This passage is referred to in Prince von Bülow's book, *Imperial Germany* (p. 99, English translation), as illustrating English feeling against Germany.— THE AUTHOR.

turies past. Our English national hero, Lord Roberts, warned us that she would act just so. But he added that she would be quite right and that we ought to do the same. When the Germans began to build their fleet there were plenty of Englishmen who urged us to pick a quarrel with her at once and destroy her before she grew too strong. There is nothing peculiarly monstrous or unique about the conduct we impute to Germany. It is the conduct fostered by the European system which England, too, supports. That system is one of armed states always expecting to be attacked, and therefore always ready to anticipate attack. We are engaged merely in one act of a long and tragic drama. Let us look for a moment at the whole set of facts from which this war proceeded.

In 1870 there was war between Germany and France — a war of mutual jealousy and fear, with no good cause behind it and no good end before. In that war Germany was victorious. She took from France two of her provinces and left her burning for revenge. Germany had made a permanent enemy on the west. On her east lay Russia. Between Russia and Germany there was no cause of quarrel. They had coöperated to crush Napoleon, and since then had commonly acted in sympathy. There was no talk, during all those years, of Russian barbarism, or of the inevitable conflict between Teuton and Slav. That idea was the effect, not the cause, of the hostility between the two nations. The cause was the alliance of Germany with Austria in her quarrel with Russia. Russia and Austria were contending for the mastery of the Balkan peninsula. Greed of territory and power was the ultimate source of their dispute — supported, on the part of Russia, by the sentiment of race. And this quarrel in the east was presently knit up with the quarrel in the west. To strengthen herself against Germany, France allied herself with Russia. Henceforth a war in the east would make a war in the west. Italy had already joined Germany and Austria.

But England was not yet involved. What brought her in was the building of the German fleet. We regarded it as a menace. Perhaps it was. At any rate we thought so. And to secure ourselves we joined hands with France and Russia. The Triple Entente faced the Triple Alliance in arms. The materials for the explosion were there. It was merely a question who should first drop the match. Our discussions as to who that was are not as important as we think. This year, we believe it was Germany. But if it had not been Germany this year, it might have been Russia next. And some other year it might have been France or England. The war came out of the European system, the system of states armed against one another, and dominated by mutual suspicion and fear. While that system continues, war will continue. If we want to stop war, we must alter that.

II

At the origin, then, of this war, there was no good cause at all. It was one of the many wars for power and position. Englishmen, it is true, have been strongly moved by the invasion of Belgium, and I throw no doubt on the genuineness of their feeling. But it was not the invasion of Belgium that made the war, although that was a contributory cause of the English intervention. The origin of the war was ambition and fear. But the origin is not the same as the purpose. The purpose is what we choose to make it. What then is our purpose, now we are at war? This question has been little discussed, and there is little willingness in Europe to discuss it, while the issue of the war hangs in the balance. But it is already clear that it will divide the nation. We are united in pursuing the war. We shall not be united in ending it.

On one point, no doubt, the peoples of the allied nations are agreed. The Germans must evacuate Belgium and indemnify her, so far as it can be done, for the martyrdom inflicted on her by one of the greatest crimes of history. That, at least, if the Allies win. But what more? There are two ways of answering that question, and much of future history will depend on which is adopted.

The one answer accepts frankly the traditional system. It assumes that the states of Europe must always be enemies and always settle their differences by war. That being so, the only end it can conceive for any war is the weakening of the vanquished and the aggrandizement of the victors. It is thus that all former wars have been ended, and thus that they have always prepared new wars. The view I am considering accepts this consequence.

It means to 'crush Germany' in order to strengthen England. Quite openly it sneers at the profession that this is 'a war to end war,' the profession that the best of our youths carry in their hearts to battle. Quite openly it justifies the militarism against which we have announced to the world that we are fighting. It approves militarism. All that it disapproves is the militarism of Germany. It wants to make us too a military power, prepared by compulsory military service for that 'next war' which it proposes to make 'inevitable' by the peace. This view, already frankly expressed by the *Morning Post,* will, no doubt, when the moment is thought to have come, be urged also by the *Times* and its group of associated newspapers. It will be supported by educated people, and will appeal to the passions of the uneducated, and will probably be urged by some members of the government. Let us then consider it.

We are to 'crush Germany'; or, as a progressive newspaper phrases it, we are to drive her, 'at no matter what cost to ourselves in lives and money, into unconditional surrender.'[1] That is, we are to carry on the war (if we can) far beyond the point at which the Germans have abandoned Belgium; beyond the point, even, at which they have abandoned Alsace-Lorraine and Posen. The Allies, as it is sometimes explained, are to 'dictate terms at Berlin,' whatever terms and however reasonable may be offered before they get there. A war which is destroying men as they have never been destroyed before, from which at the best the nations will emerge permanently degraded in their stock, poorer in physique, duller in intelligence, weaker in will than they went in, this war is to be protracted until the whole manhood of Europe is decimated, in order — in order to what? Let us ask in detail.

In order, we are told, that the Germans may 'feel they are beaten.' And then? They will be good in future? They will admit they were wrong? They will lick the hand that chastised them? Who believes it? The more completely they are beaten, the more obstinately they will be set on recovery. When France was beaten to the dust in 1870, did she repent for having provoked the war? On the contrary, she gathered up her forces for revenge. And Germany will do the same.

[1] *New Statesman.* December 19, 1914.

'But we shall prevent her!' How? By partitioning her? By disarming her? By changing the form of her government? All those things were tried by Napoleon, and none of them can achieve their purpose. A nation does not consist in its territory, or its armaments, or its government. It consists in the tradition, the character, and the spirit of its people. While Germany wants to be one, while she wants to be strong, while she wants to be monarchic, nobody and nothing can prevent her. A nation has never been crushed by anything short of annihilation. Look at Ireland! Look at Italy! Look at the Balkan States! You may weaken Germany, yes; you may cripple her for a time, as she, if she were victorious, could weaken or cripple us. What of it? She will rise from humiliation more determined than ever to assert herself. We can no more crush her than she can crush us. It is certain, then, that if we can succeed in 'crushing' Germany, and if we do nothing else, we are preparing war for the future, not peace.

It may be easier for us to realize this point if we remember that there are Germans, too, who expect and desire to get peace out of this war, and that they too hope to do it by 'crushing' their enemies. Thus, for example, the *Frankfürter Zeitung* writes:

'One cannot count upon any other way of carrying out the idea of peace except by "force." By that, of course, we do not refer to the evil generally connected with the word, but to something which has been expressed in various ways during the last few months: we wish to have as the result of this war a state in which the countries which have now attacked us shall for all time be unable to repeat their attack. Germany, peaceful, as its allies, has with them been entrusted with the historical mission of dictating a permanent peace to Europe. We are fighting primarily for existence, but still more for this — that there may be rest in Europe from vain, ambitious madmen and brigands, and that they may be shown, like all others, the fit and natural sphere to which they belong. They must be deprived once and for all of the desire to attack us; till then, not a word of peace! Then, and then only, can the law of peace, protected by forces which are strong and just, be established.'

This is the German version of the same

idea that is sometimes put forward on behalf of the Allies. Peace, say we, by crushing Germany, since she is the only disturber of the peace. Peace, say the Germans, by crushing the Allies, since they are the only disturbers of the peace. But how does this view of the Germans look to us? Does it look like peace? Do we imagine ourselves lying down forever, beaten, humbled, and repentant, under the contemptuous protection of an armed Germany? Just as we feel about the German idea, so, we may be sure, do they feel about ours. That route does not and cannot lead to peace. Nothing can, except a radical change in the ideas and policy of the nations of Europe, and an expression of that change in a definite political organization.

III

Those, then, who really desire a settlement that will secure peace in the future, must abandon the idea of 'crushing' Germany. Let us turn, now, to the other view of our purpose in this war.

We are fighting, say our best spirits, for freedom, and against domination. What do these terms mean? By domination we mean the imposition of rule, by force, upon unwilling subjects. In the relation of man to man the simplest form of domination is slavery. In that of state to state its form is empire.[1] It is one of the great contending powers in the tragedy of history. It is real; and also it has been championed as an ideal. Macchiavelli is its philosopher, Carlyle its prophet, Treitschke its historian. Rome stood for it in the ancient world, Spain in America, England in Ireland. And Germany stands for it now in Belgium. By freedom, on the other hand, we mean the power and right of individuals and of nations to live their own lives and unfold their own capacities. This does not imply that they should do simply what they like, but that the restrictions they admit should be self-chosen and self-approved, with a view to the equal freedom of others. The formula is so familiar as to be tedious. But its meaning is infinite and profound. We have hardly yet begun to spell its first letters. It inspires the whole movement of democracy and all the wars of liberation. It is

[1] I use this term in the sense of a system in which one state or nation imposes its power by force on other states or nations.— THE AUTHOR.

the other great protagonist of history; and of the history of the last century it is the very nerve. For that reason, it cannot be truly claimed as the principle of this or that nation. It has been contending in them all at death grips with its enemy. The angels of light and darkness do not preside over different nations. They contend in each for victory.

Nevertheless there is truth in the idea that modern Germany stands for domination, and modern France and England for freedom. The unification of Germany in an empire obscured, if it did not ruin, the German spirit of liberty. The governing and articulate classes became arrogant and aggressive. The mass of the people became passively acquiescent. They were content to formulate freedom instead of struggling for it. They became the harmless pedants of democracy. Meanwhile the government pursued the ordinary course of empire. Wherever they ruled over people of alien race and ideals, they set themselves by force to convert them into their own likeness. In Poland, in Alsace-Lorraine, in Schleswig, they imposed on the unwilling natives their language, their education, and their 'culture.' In Poland they have been endeavoring for years to expropriate the Poles and substitute a German population. 'No consideration for the Polish people,' writes Prince von Bülow, 'must hinder us from doing all we can to maintain and strengthen the German nationality in the former Polish domains.' And he adds with unconscious irony, 'In our policy with regard to the schools we are really fighting for Polish nationality, which *we wish to incorporate in German intellectual life.*'

This is the traditional policy of empire. The English pursued this policy in Ireland with even greater vigor and ruthlessness throughout the eighteenth century. And it is, perhaps, only the happy accident that we are an island power that has prevented us from being, to this day, the champions of domination. But history has helped us, and we have learned from history. It is a chance, but a very significant chance, that made the outbreak of this war coincide with our final abandonment of the policy of coercion in Ireland. The British system now, so far as men of white race are concerned, is one not of empire but of free communities. And the spirit that has brought about this change will proceed, if we escape reaction, to inspire our policy in the great dependencies of men of alien race. Abroad, as at home, the English have been learning the lesson of freedom. And there is good hope, if we are true to our tradition, that our victory may contribute to the extension of freedom in Europe. In France, too, the long fight between antagonistic ideals has been inclining toward freedom. She too will join with us, we may believe, to confirm the liberty for which, throughout a century, she has been shedding her blood in civil strife.

While, then, it is unhistorical and unjust to pretend that Germany, as such, stands for domination, and the western powers for freedom, yet we may say with truth that a victory of the western powers, so far as their influence can reach, should make for freedom, while a victory of Germany will make for domination. That is the ideal cause, rising above our mere need of self-defense, that may inspire us in our efforts for victory. But if it be that which we carry in our hearts — and the young among us, I believe, do carry it — how must we endeavor, when the time comes for peace, to translate it into acts?

Mr. Asquith has given us the formula in words which I have quoted once in the *Atlantic*, but shall repeat again — for they cannot be too often repeated. Never, perhaps, has a responsible statesman had the courage and the wisdom to look so far and so generously ahead.

'I should like, if I might for a moment, beyond this inquiry into causes and motives, to ask your attention and that of my fellow countrymen to the end which in this war we ought to keep in view. Forty-four years ago, at the time of the war of 1870, Mr. Gladstone used these words. He said, "The greatest triumph of our time will be the enthronement of the idea of public right as the governing idea of European politics." Nearly fifty years have passed. Little progress, it seems, has yet been made toward that good and beneficent change, but it seems to me to be now, at this moment, as good a definition as we can have of our European policy. The idea of public right — what does it mean when translated into concrete terms? It means first and foremost the clearing of the ground by the definite repudiation of militarism as the governing factor in the relation of states, and of the future mould-

ing of the European world. It means next that room must be found and kept for the independent existence and the free development of the smaller nationalities — each with a corporate consciousness of its own.

'Belgium, Holland, and Switzerland, the Scandinavian countries, Greece, and the Balkan States — they must be recognized as having exactly as good a title as their more powerful neighbors — more powerful in strength as in wealth — exactly as good a title to a place in the sun. And it means, finally, or it ought to mean, perhaps by a slow and gradual process, the substitution for force, for the clash of competing ambitions, for groupings and alliances and a precarious equipoise, the substitution for all these things of a real European partnership, based on the recognition of equal right and established and enforced by a common will. A year ago that would have sounded like a Utopian idea. It is probably one that may not or will not be realized either today or tomorrow. If and when this war is decided in favor of the Allies, it will at once come within the range, and before long within the grasp, of European statesmanship.'

Let us comment a little on this noble utterance and show how the ideas it voices hang all together. Those ideas are nationality, law, and peace. Let us remind ourselves of their meaning and connection.

Nationality is a Janus, facing both ways. So far as it stands for the right of a people to govern itself, it stands for freedom. So far as it stands for the ambition to govern other people, or to destroy them, or to shape them into an alien world, it stands for domination. Throughout history it has stood for both. Athens had no sooner beaten back the Persian attempt at domination, that she set out, herself, to dominate the Greek world. Rome won freedom at home to destroy it abroad. Free Holland, free England, set forth to conquer a world. Italy, liberated, falls upon Tripoli. The Balkan nations unite to expel the domination of the Turk, and divide to impose domination on one another. Finally, the German nationality is no sooner established in security than it threatens that of every other people. Nationality, then, is respectable only when it is on its defense. When it is waging wars of liberation it is sacred. When it is waging wars of domination it is accursed. It is therefore an ideal only when it is associated with law and peace. And it is only in that association that the Allies can desire to foster and secure it. They should seek on the one hand to deliver the nations that are suffering oppression, and on the other to prevent them in future from becoming oppressors themselves.

To achieve this the new rectification of frontiers will not suffice. Nothing can achieve it but toleration carried through with faith and courage in every state. Poland may be freed from Russian and German and Austrian domination; but that, of itself, will not free Polish Jews from domination by Poles. The Serbs may be freed from Hungary, but that, of itself, will not free the Turks or Greeks or Bulgars who may still be included in a greater Servia. It is impossible to make territorial boundaries correspond accurately with nationality. A change of heart is therefore as necessary as a change of frontiers and allegiance. Still, since changes of frontiers will and shall be made, the Allies, if they stand for the ideal of freedom, must see that such changes are made with a view only to the desires and the well-being of the peoples to be transferred, and not with a view to the aggrandizement of the victors. Every German colony that the English or French may take for the sake of their own power, will be a proof that they have abandoned the ideal of freedom. The English, through their Prime Minister, have said that they seek no territory. Let them prove it to the world, or stand self-convicted of hypocrisy.

The settlement of Europe, in such a way as to deliver nationalities from oppression, so far as that can be done by political arrangements, and so far as territory comes up for readjustment, will itself make for the other great purposes of the war, the substitution of law for force, and therefore, and in consequence, the maintenance of peace. The only wars between civilized nations that are justifiable are wars of defense. But there can be no defense without offense. Let the nations, having acquired the right to govern themselves, do so in peace without aggressive ambition. That must be the rule for the new Europe. But it too implies a change of heart. It implies the abandonment of the base and crude ambition that hitherto has dominated states, and the substitution of a noble ideal of free and progressive personality.

States hitherto have measured their worth in terms of population, territory, and power. That estimate leads them inevitably to war. For while they are governed by it they must always desire to expand at the cost of one another. Every war in Europe since the wars of religion may be traced to this cause. And even the wars so-called of religion were largely wars for power. The wars of nationality in the nineteenth century were reactions against this false ideal. Yet the nations that reacted have not discovered or pursued a truer one. There can be no peace, not even genuine desire for peace, until men realize that the greatness of a people depends upon the quality of life of the individual citizens. A city like Athens or Florence is worth all the empires that have ever been. A state of a few thousands among whom should be found a Socrates, a Michelangelo, a Goethe, outweighs beyond all calculation one whose gross insignificant millions shall be dragooned by the drill sergeant and sophisticated by the university professor.

The nobility of a people lies not in its capacity for war, but in its capacity for peace. It is indeed only because the nations are incapable of the one that they plunge so readily into the other. If they had the power of living they would neither endure to kill, nor desire to die. The task of war is to destroy life; the task of peace is to create it; to organize labor so that it shall not incapacitate men for leisure; to establish justice as a foundation for personality; to unfold in men the capacity for noble joy and profound sorrow; to liberate them for the passion of love, the perception of beauty, the contemplation of truth. Of all these things war is the enemy. All men of profound experience have known this — not the teachers of religion only, but the prophets of secular life. Virgil, Dante, Goethe, Shelley, preach peace no less than Jesus Christ or Francis of Assisi or George Fox. For peace is not a negative ideal; it is the condition of all positive ones. In war man seeks escape from life in blind intoxication. In peace he discovers and fulfils life by impassioned reason. It is because our peace is so bad that we fall into war. But every war makes our peace worse. If men had given to the creation of life a tithe of the

devotion they have offered again and again
to its destruction, they would have made
of this world so glorious a place that they
would not need to take refuge from it in
the shambles. It is our false ideals that 5
make for war. And it is the feebleness of
our intelligence and the pettiness of our
passions that permit such ideals to master
us. We seek collective power because we
are incapable of individual greatness. We 10
seek extension of territory because we
cannot utilize the territory we have. We
seek to be many because none of us is able
to be properly one. Once more we are
witnessing whither that course must lead 15
us. Once more we are witnessing the vast
and vile futility of war. Once more we
shall recover reeling from the horrible intoxication in which we have taken refuge,
to look with dismay on our bloody hands, 20
and the bloody work they have achieved.
Once more we shall have a chance of
learning the lesson. Shall we learn it?
I cannot tell.

But I hope. I hope because of the
young. And to them I now turn. To
you, young men, it has been given by a
tragic fate to see with your eyes and hear
with your ears what war really is. Old 30
men made it, but you must wage it — with
what courage, with what generosity, with
what sacrifice, I well know. If you return
from this ordeal, remember what it has
been. Do not listen to the shouts of vic- 35
tory; do not snuff the incense of applause.
But keep your inner vision fixed on the
facts you have faced. You have seen bat-
tleships, bayonets, and guns, and you know
them for what they are, forms of evil 40
thought. Think other thoughts, love other
loves, youth of England and of the world!
You have been through hell and purga-
tory. Climb now the rocky stair that
leads to the sacred mount. The guide of 45
tradition leaves you here. Guide now
yourselves and us! Believe in the future,
for none but you can. Believe in what is
called the impossible, for it waits the help
of your hands to show itself to be the in- 50
evitable. Of it and of all our hopes, the
old, the disillusioned, the gross, the practitioners of the world are the foes. Be
you the friends! Take up the thought and
give it shape in act! You can and you 55
alone. It is for that you have suffered.
It is for that you have gained vision.
And in your ears for your inspiration

rings the great sentence of the poet —

Libero, dritto, sano e lo tuo arbitrio,
E fallo fôra non fare a suo senno,
Per ch'io te sopra te corono e mitrio.[1]

XII

ORGANIZATIONS FOR PEACE

THEODORE ROOSEVELT

[*Chicago Herald*, April 16, 1915. By permisson.]

My Dear Mrs. Rublee:

I assume from your letter that you have
not read my recent little book called *America and the World War,* and that you wish
my judgment about joining the peace organization of which you write. I em- 20
phatically advise you not to join such an
organization. The platform of principles
inclosed in your letter seems to me both
silly and base.

This does not mean that all those signing and championing it are silly and base.
It is unfortunately true that the very worst
movements in human history have sometimes had very high-minded men and
women enlisted in their support. Accord- 30
ing to my views, the effort to break up this
Union, in order to perpetuate slavery,
would have meant most dreadful woe to
mankind, if successful; yet my own kins-
folk on my mother's side all took part in 35
it; and I do not believe there ever was a
movement which enlisted more ardent support from big-hearted men and women or
which was served with greater fervor and
disinterestedness.

Fifty years ago the Copperheads of the
North held exactly the views about peace
which are set forth in the platform you
inclosed and to a man they voted against
Abraham Lincoln. They did all they could 45
to break up the Union and to insure the
triumph of slavery, because they put peace
as the highest of all good; just exactly as
it is put by the people who have constructed the paper you sent me. Some of 50
the finest and most honorable men I have
known in my life were former Copperheads. One of the men of whom I am
fondest at this present day was once a Copperhead.

Nevertheless, I should stigmatize the

[1] 'Free, right, and sane is thy will, and it will
be base not to act at its bidding. Wherefore I
crown and miter thee lord over thyself.'

Copperhead movement of fifty years ago exactly as I stigmatize the movement preached by the individuals whose paper you inclose to me. Moreover, a very large proportion of the peace at any price or copperhead sympathizers were undoubtedly physical cowards; and equally undoubtedly a very large proportion of ultra-pacificists of today who uphold such views as those outlined in the paper you inclosed, in championing peace without regard to righteousness are really most influenced by physical cowardice. They fear death or pain or discomfort beyond anything else and like to hide their fear behind high-sounding words.

I speak with scientific accuracy when I speak of this movement as both base and silly. It is silly because it is absolutely futile. It proposes to go on with just the same kind of futile agitation which, by the experience of a century and, above all, by the experience of the last thirty years, has proved wholly useless and on the whole slightly mischievous. Not one particle of good will be obtained by any such action as that outlined in that paper you sent.

But this is not all. It is base as well as futile. There is nothing more repulsive than to see people agitating for general righteousness in the abstract when they dare not stand up against wickedness in the concrete. On the whole there is nothing that does so much damage to a church as to have a minister who thunders continually against wrong in the abstract, or against wrong committed by the Pharisees a couple of thousand years ago, but who cannot be persuaded to stand up against present-day wrong in the concrete; and the professional pacificist leaders in the United States are in exactly this position.

I assume, of course, that you are for peace in reality and not merely for the name of peace, and that you are for peace based on justice and right and not for peace that consecrates successful wrong; for peace that consecrates wrong may be actually worse than any war. Well, the paper you inclose is in effect exactly as much an indorsement of the 'peace' once obtained in Warsaw by trampling liberty and humanity under foot as of the 'peace' obtained at the same time in the United States by restoring the Union and freeing the slave. Any movement that fails emphatically to discriminate between the two kinds of peace and the two kinds of war

is an evil and not a good movement. Any movement that speaks against war in terms that would apply as much to such a war as that waged by Lincoln as to the war waged to destroy free people is a thoroughly base and evil thing.

Above all it is base and evil to clamor for peace in the abstract, when silence is kept about concrete and hideous wrongs done to humanity at this very moment. Belgium has been trampled into bloody mire. Frightful wrongs have been committed upon the men, women and children of Belgium. The Belgians have fought valiantly against their oppressors. Yet this paper you inclose does not contain one protest against the commission of such wrongs as have been committed on Belgium, and does denounce war in such fashion as to include in the condemnation the Belgians just as much as the oppressors of Belgium.

There is nothing easier. There is nothing on the whole less worth while entering into than vague and hysterical denunciations of wrong in the abstract, or vague and hysterical demands for right in the abstract, coupled with the unworthy and timid refusal even to allude to frightful wrongs that are at the very moment being committed in the concrete.

Congresses that pass resolutions against war and in favor of peace in the abstract do not do one particle of good, because their resolutions are utterly meaningless, and must be utterly meaningless unless they are reduced to concrete cases. We have before us that concrete case.

Let the people who advocate the platform and principles you inclosed hold a meeting specifically to denounce the invasion of Belgium by Germany and to demand that in the interests of peace, the United States do what it can to put a stop to those wrongs.

Let them denounce Messrs. Wilson and Bryan for trying to force through the ship purchase bill, which was in the interest of the power that wronged Belgium and in spite of the fact that their action might tend to bring us into war with the powers that have sought to defend Belgium.

Let them do something that shows that they mean what they say and that they are really striving for righteousness.

Until they do this let every wise and upright man and woman refuse to have anything more to do with a movement which is certainly both foolish and noxious, which is accompanied by a peculiarly ignoble abandonment of national duty and which, if successful, would do only harm and the mere attempt to accomplish which rightly exposes our people to measureless contempt.

Sincerely yours,

THEODORE ROOSEVELT.

Mrs. Juliet Barret Rublee,
Washington, D. C.

XIII

SERBIAN ATROCITIES

GEORGE MACAULAY TREVELYAN

[*New York Times,* May 22, 1915. By permission.]

In the letter by Professor Yandell Henderson, in the *Times* of today's date, he says:

As for atrocities, Belgium, Serbia, East Prussia, and Poland have probably been no more thoroughly desolated than Georgia after Sherman's march to the sea. Away from ordinary social restraints men always do such things. It is rare for a militia company here to have a field day, or a college class to hold a reunion, without a certain percentage making beasts of themselves.

As a stranger in this land I am not in a position to contradict Professor Henderson about your present-day militia companies and college students, though from what I have seen of your people, particularly at the universities where I have principally been, I read his statement with some surprise. But as regards Sherman's march to the sea, I am prepared, as a historian, to deny that Sherman's troops either burned women and children alive or gouged peoples' eyes out or murdered civilians wholesale, as the Austro-Hungarian troops did in Serbia in the middle days of August last. If college students and militiamen do these things today, or such things as are reported by the Bryce Commission on Belgium, I can only say that they are very studiously kept out of your papers. But Sherman's troops at least did not do them. They 'desolated' the land, no doubt, though whether they desolated it as completely as the part of Serbia through which I rode last January I am not sure. But they did not commit 'atrocities' on persons. The two things are in a different category and Professor Henderson confuses the issue by putting them into the same sentence as if they were one and the same thing. Here are a few specimens of what the Austro-Hungarian troops did:

1915, Aug. 18.— Prnivoor Village (near Losnitza:), Simana Mijatovitch, age 25; her daughter Doniza, age 3, and her son Milan, age 1, shut up in house and burned alive. Zivana Samowrovitch, age 27; Yveta Samowrovitch, age 3 years, and boy, not yet baptized, age 3 days, shut up in house and burned alive. Nedeljiza Village: Aniza Jesditch, age 35, eyes gouged out and killed; Micosava Vasilijevitch, age 21, violated, cut open, and murdered.

Multiply these things by several hundred and you get two August days' work of the Austro-Hungarian army last year. These facts do not remind me, any more than the facts related in the Bryce report remind me, either of Sherman's soldiers or of your college students and militiamen. I am sorry I cannot at this time stay to make a more profound study of American institutions and social customs, but I am compelled to return to-morrow to England, with much gratitude for the kindness I have received over here, which has perhaps blinded me to the dark spots in your national character perceived by Professor Henderson. As I am departing, I inclose to you the report on the atrocities in Serbia, based on the first-hand evidence of Dr. Arius Van Tienhoven of The Hague, Holland, and Jules Schmidt, Swiss engineer. And I further refer you to the article by Dr. Reiss of Lausanne University, in the *Revue de Paris,* April 1, 1915. The evidence is particularly full, because the Austrians were driven out of the scenes of these atrocities a day or two after they had committed them and the dead bodies and charred remains of the women and children were photographed. I have seen scores of these photographs, and read and heard masses of first-hand evidence on the subject, when I visited the scene of these atrocities in January.

G. LITERARY CRITICISM

Literary criticism makes use of some of the same mental processes that the writer of the expository article or the editorial brings to bear upon his material: in both cases there is the same striving to place certain facts clearly before the reader, and the same effort to express an unbiased and illuminating judgment upon these facts.

Literary criticism covers a wide range, from the humble endeavor of the journalistic man of all work to tell what a book is about, to Anatole France's 'adventures of a soul among masterpieces.' There is no kind of work for which the literary tyro is more inclined, and none for which, as a rule, he is less fitted, for good reviewing involves a degree of the critical faculty with which the inexperienced are seldom endowed.

Roughly speaking, there are two kinds of literary criticism found in periodicals. The book note or notice gives a short statement of the contents of a volume and seeks to characterize it in only the briefest and most general way. Such a notice is usually unsigned, and as its purpose is less serious than that of the larger reviews of the next class, its literary art is not so conspicuous. The book review proper is a more elaborate consideration of a volume, its relation to its subject in general, and to the other works of its author. Book reviews of this latter sort are often noteworthy for their keen insight, their sound critical judgment, and their trained literary style; they are written and signed by authorities on the subject with which the book deals, and in many cases they become permanent contributions to critical literature.

Among the illustrations here printed such notices as those of the *Salamander* will serve as examples of the briefer kind of notice, and the review of J. P. Mahaffy's *What Have the Greeks Done for Modern Civilization?* is a good representative of the more elaborate, carefully constructed, and well expressed treatment of more serious or extensive subjects. Examples of the shorter notice will be found in numbers XII–XV, and of the longer in numbers I–IV.

A combination of these two methods is employed in the composite review which groups together several books of the same kind, or on the same subject, or by the same author. In such cases, a brief notice is usually given to each book separately and an attempt is made to compare them or to indicate their relations to the general subject with which they deal or to the previous work of their authors. Specimens of this kind will be found in numbers V–XI.

I

THE GREEK GIFT TO CIVILIZATION

SAMUEL LEE WOLFF

[*Nation*, New York, April 7, 1910. By permission.]

I

The Greeks meant one thing to men of the early Renaissance, another thing to Pope and Addison, another thing to Germans of the nineteenth century. Every generation has taken its Greek in its own way. And the present generation, heir of all the ages, is taking its Greek in nearly every way — except one. It is *not* taking its Greek for granted. An expositor of Hellenism today is almost obliged to be-

come an apologist. He must 'show us.' Even as seasoned a Grecian as Professor Mahaffy,[1] who surely is entitled, if any one is, to be at his ease in Hellas, does not resist this compulsion. The quiet and still air of his delightful studies is stirred with argument, about Greek in the college curriculum, about the neglect of Aristotelian logic by American youth, about, on the one hand, Greek *versus* 'Science,' and, on the other hand, the truly 'scientific' temper of Greek thought. Throughout he seems to feel that the Greeks need to be vindicated; and their vindication, throughout, is that they are 'modern.'

This seems to mean that they are free

[1] *What Have the Greeks Done for Modern Civilization?* The Lowell Lectures of 1908–09. By John Pentland Mahaffy, C.V.O., D.C.L. (Oxon.), etc., of Trinity College, Dublin. New York: G. P. Putnam's Sons.

from mysticism and obscurantism, those sins of the Middle Ages; and Professor Mahaffy is the more inclined to praise Greek clear-sightedness in virtue of his own long-standing feud with medievalism. There is a fine old-fashioned flavor, as of some clergyman in Thomas Love Peacock — a Ffolliott, a Portpipe, an Opimian — in the valiant no-Popery flings of our author against the church and against the theological prepossessions of medieval science and philosophy. The modern contentiousness about Greek here receives a temperamental reinforcement.

All good things being Greek, and all bad things non-Greek, the Middle Ages were non-Greek; and the Renaissance, which put an end to them, was Greek. Such seems to be the latent reasoning at the bottom of Professor Mahaffy's view — and we admit it to be the popular view — that by means of a resurgence of Greek art, literature, and philosophy, the Renaissance superseded the Middle Ages, and that the Renaissance was in spirit and accomplishment truly Greek, truly classical. The naïve assumption of the humanists that they had emerged from a 'thick Gothic night,' Professor Mahaffy would modify by substituting 'Latin' for 'Gothic'; and, having thus given a bad name to the Scholastic Philosophy, to Romanesque and Gothic architecture, to the 'Dies Iræ' and to the chansons de geste, he would contentedly hang them all. Now, he believes, upon the thick Latin night up rose Greek, and up rose the sun: the classical Renaissance and the 'modern spirit' were a twin birth of the revival of Greek studies (pp. 18–19). This view seems to us erroneous; and, as the conceptions underlying it determine Professor Mahaffy's treatment of his subject, we shall examine it at some length. Waiving all questions of chronology, disregarding therefore all medieval anticipations of the Renaissance or of the 'modern spirit,' granting that the light did not dawn till Greek began to reappear, and then dawned decisively, we believe it would not be difficult to show that the Renaissance itself was not essentially Hellenic.

II

The literature of the Renaissance, both in and out of Italy, is four-fifths of it Latinistic — Virgilian, Ciceronian, Senecan, occasionally Horatian, very heavily Ovidian. It springs not immediately, often not mediately, from Homer, Demosthenes, Pindar, Æschylus, Sophocles, or even Euripides. The other fifth, which does draw nourishment from Greek literature, draws it from the Greek literature not of the golden but of the silver and the pinchbeck ages. Boccaccio, Professor Mahaffy points out (p. 95n), is indebted to Greek prose fiction; but what he does not point out is that Boccaccio's debt runs mostly to very late Byzantine romances now lost. Lyly draws from Plutarch on Education. Sannazaro breaks from the Virgilian pastoral tradition to return to Theocritus. Tasso's Aminta, as is well known, gets what is probably its most famous passage from the late prose romance of Achilles Tatius. As is not so well known, the Jerusalem Delivered, too, professedly a restoration of the classical — that is, the Virgilian — epic, in reprobation of the composite romance-epic of Pulci, Boiardo, and Ariosto, is itself full of the conceits of late Greek rhetoric. The Pastor Fido is based upon a story in Pausanias. It seems well within the truth to say that where Renaissance literature is Greek at all, it is almost certain to be in the Alexandrianized, Romanized, Byzantinized, and Orientalized vein that we call Greek only because we have no better name for it.

The art and the philosophy of the Renaissance, like its literature, do not draw from pure Hellenic fountains. Botticelli, Raphael, and Titian are not inspired by Greek statuary of the best period, very little of which had been unearthed; Greek painting was probably unknown to them, and, at any rate, Greek painting, as far as it has survived at all, is of the Campanian, the Alexandrian style — distinctly postclassical. The putti of the Renaissance may, indeed, it is thought, be traced to the 'Egyptian plague of Loves'— those Cupids, which, whether attendant upon the amorous adventures of the gods, or nesting in trees, or wreathing garlands, or exposed in cages for sale, 'flutter through the Pompeian pictures.' And where the great painters of the Renaissance thought of themselves as illustrators of 'literary' themes (we are just rediscovering how decidedly they did so think of themselves — to the confusion of 'Art for Art's sake'), they looked for their themes not in Homer, or the tragedians, or the myths of Plato, but in Ovid, or Apuleius, or Philostratus, or Lucian. Raphael's frescoes in the Farnesina got their Olympians not from Hesiod but from Apuleius. Botticelli's 'Calunnia,' as Professor Mahaffy mentions elsewhere, is derived from Lucian's description of the Διαβολή of Apelles. Mantegna, Titian, Raphael, Giulio Romano, and others deliberately retranslated into color and visual form the verbal descriptions by Philostratus of paintings in a supposed picture-gallery.

As for the Platonism of the Renaissance, that too was composite, with its leaning toward pseudo-Dionysian hierarchies and toward elaborate theories of love. It was the Platonism of Plotinus, rather, after the school of Alexandria; for, in spite of Ficino's translation, the Platonism of Athens was to them unknown — or, when known, too purely Attic to be assimilated. There was, indeed, an echo of pre-Socratic Greek thought in the animistic philosophies of southern Italy; but these Professor Mahaffy does not mention, despite their influence upon Bacon by way of Telesio and Campanella.

In general, Renaissance taste is distinctly unclassical. It runs to digression and irrelevancy; to inserted descriptions and episodes; to huge verbosity. It revels in the 'word-paintings' (ἐκφράσεις) which were a specialty of the late sophists and rhetoricians; it never tires of their speechmaking. It favors whole bookfuls of orations invented as patterns of the kind of thing that might be said upon a given occasion by persons imaginary, mythological, or historical. These ἠθοποιεῖαι and μελέται bulk large in the Anthology, and reappear in collections like 'Silvayn's Orator'— to mention, perhaps, the most familiar name among many. The prose of the Renaissance, again, like late Greek prose, tends, without resistance, to the most exaggerated conceits and antitheses, each country in Europe developing its own particular brands of bad taste — Euphuism, Gongorism, Marinism, and the rest — upon a common basis of Ciceronian and late Greek rhetoric. In imitation, too, of the *tours de force* of degenerate Greek and Roman rhetoricians, the versifiers of the Renaissance often chose the most trivial themes, and embellished them with all the graces of *double entendre*. To match the antique disquisitions Of Long Hair, and In Praise of Baldness, we have the *capi-*

toli of Berni and his school on Figs, Beans, Sausages, Bakers' Ovens, Hard-Boiled Eggs, Chestnuts, Paint-Brushes, Bells, Needles, Going Without Hats, and Lying Late Abed. It is a far cry from this sort of thing to Homer or to the Periclean age. Indeed, if by Greek we mean 'classic,' the Renaissance was not Greek. Not until the late eighteenth century, after the way had been cleared by those 'pedants,' German and other, to whom this work alludes so slightingly, was the true Renaissance of classic Greek accomplished; only then may the modern world be said to have entered fully upon its Greek heritage. What the Renaissance of the fourteenth and fifteenth centuries achieved was rather a Pan-Latinistic revival, which attended especially to the process of recasting and enriching the vernacular tongues, mostly by means of Latin or post-classical Greek models, into vehicles of a modern *Eloquentia* that might rival the antique. Its degenerate models, together with its own taste in choosing them, made it not pure, reposeful, imaginative, but composite, unquiet, fantastic, rhetorical, loquacious — all that is suggested when we say 'Alexandrian.'

III

One cannot help feeling that Professor Mahaffy's taste in these matters has been 'subdued to what it works in' by his extensive studies of post-classical Greek. This bias appears in the estimate of Aristotle's 'Poetics' and the dicta about Wordsworth, Tennyson, and others. The 'Poetics' is treated as if it were merely a collection of judgments upon individual works in Greek literature: if these judgments are erroneous, the work is a failure, of course. It is not perceived, apparently, that the 'Poetics' is an exposition of basic principles, the principles of poetry and of art in general; and that, in its justification of poetry as an imaginative embodiment of the *universal* (a view which Plato, for all his poetry, completely missed), and in its promulgation of the law of unity, it laid sure foundations for the criticism of all time, and established an unassailable canon of classic or ideal art. All this apart from the historical importance of the 'Poetics' misunderstood — apart from the pseudo-classic of the sixteenth, seventeenth, and eighteenth centuries, apart from the controversies about 'imitation,' *catharsis,* and the 'three uni-

ties.' Of this really fundamental book
Professor Mahaffy says (p. 62): 'I know
of no poorer and more jejune exposition
of a great subject'; and on the next page
he cavalierly dismisses it upon the plea of
lack of time. The same want of appreciation of the universal in Hellenism is responsible for some of the opinions here expressed upon the Greek in modern English poetry. Of the 'galaxy that illumined
the early nineteenth century,' Wordsworth
is considered to be 'the least Greek' (pp.
56–7); and this because of his failure to
distinguish prose diction from poetical, and
because of the inordinate length of the
'Excursion.' Keats, however, had caught
the Greek spirit, though at second or third
hand (p. 46); in Shelley, 'we have that
perfect combination of romantic imagination with Greek culture' which makes him
the greatest of this group (p. 56); and
Tennyson is 'the most classical of our
modern lyric poets' (p. 59).

Read in view of the critic's Alexandrian
bias and of the quotations which illustrate
his criticism, these dicta become plain.
Keats is Greek in being a master of isolated sensuous images, chaste or volup-
tuous — not in virtue of his delicacy in
selection or his passion for beauty; certainly not in virtue of that architectonic
which he never possessed. Shelley's
'clouds and sunsets' and spirits and
flower-bells and pavilions — the imagery
of romanticism — are at the service of his
revolt and of his love of Greece and liberty. What matter that Shelley hardly
touched human experience, hardly touched
the general life of man? The case is still
clearer when we come to Wordsworth and
Tennyson. Of Wordsworth's purity and
wisdom — of his *universality,* and of his
'plain and noble' style — of all that makes
him a true classic, a true Greek despite his
recurrent prosiness — there is not a word;
though, of course, the specific Platonism in
Wordsworth's wonderful Ode (misquoted
at p. 243) is recognized. But what of
'Laodameia'? —

. . . For the gods approve
The depth, and not the tumult, of the soul.

What of 'Dion'? —

So were the hopeless troubles, that involved
The soul of Dion, instantly dissolved.

. . . .

Him, only him, the shield of Jove defends,
Whose means are fair and spotless as his
ends.

Or — to take Wordsworth not on classical
ground, and in a vein not sententious —
what can be more Greek than those au-
tochthonous figures of the Leech-Gatherer,
and of Michael at the unfinished sheep-
fold? —

. . . 'T is believed by all
That many and many a day he thither went,
And never lifted up a single stone;

or this about Michael's wife:

Whose heart was in her house: two wheels
she had
Of antique form, this large for spinning
wool,
That small for flax; and if one wheel had
rest,
It was because the other was at work.

— lines of which Homer would not need
to be ashamed. One might as well say
that Millet's 'Sower' is not Greek, or that
Lincoln's speech at Gettysburg is not
Greek — Greek as Simonides! Finally
the Hellenism of Tennyson is here supposed to be shown by the 'Lotos Eaters'
and the Theocritean 'Come down, O
maid,' and that well-nigh intolerable piece
of oxymoron and antithesis,

His honor rooted in dishonor stood,
And faith unfaithful kept him falsely true.

So much of Tennyson's work is Greek
in a very pure sense that it seems a pity
to try to prove him Hellenic by what at
best can prove him only Alexandrian.

IV

While professing to deal with Hellenism
in the modern world, the present volume
gives much space to an examination of its
remote origins, under the various aspects
of race, poetry, prose, philosophy, and the
like. To us this seems irrelevant; what
we ought to be concerned with here is issues, not origins. We have already ad-
verted, perhaps more than enough, to the
treatment of the Greek decadence as if
that were the essentially Greek. Both
ways attention is too much drawn from
the center to the ends, and not fixed, as in
so short a work it ought to be fixed, upon
that definite period during which the
Greeks were most themselves. We want
a focus; and we have here a penumbra.

Are we demanding too narrow a canon of Hellenism? We think not; for it is only a strict sense of what the Greeks stood for that gives weight and value to assertions about their influence. That which they really contributed to modern civilization is obfuscated by inquiries into their origins, hardly less than by the inclusion of their decadence upon the same footing with their prime.

But one begins to realize after a while that the author is scarcely appreciative of the characteristic *universality* of the Greeks; that what appeals to him is rather their rhetoric than their idealism, rather their fancy than their imagination, rather their cleverness than their genius. He himself steadfastly declines to generalize — and who could more safely generalize than he? — about the nature of the Greek gift to civilization. He refuses to grasp *this* universal. Surely he sees it; he presents abundant material for the induction; why will he not, for the real illumination of his readers, tell them what he sees? He will make no synthesis. He resides in detail, detail which, as has been seen, too often concerns irrelevant beginnings or degenerate endings; and he yields now and again to the temptation to digress and to argue, like any Alexandrian of them all. In a word, this book about the Greeks is not written in the spirit of the Greeks.

Some merits it undoubtedly possesses. Its dedication, its close, are noble in feeling. Its chapter on politics is vital with modern instances: the abdication of power by an aristocracy, exemplified by Ireland; the conflict of centralizing with decentralizing forces in a federation, exemplified by the United States. And as Professor Mahaffy's venerable experience justifies him in coming to us to admonish and to warn, he speaks, in the same chapter, words of weight upon the failure of intellectual refinement to guard against political decadence, and upon the decay of the middle classes through limitation of the size of the family as a result of heightened cost of living — troubles which threatened Athens no less than they threaten us today. Here Professor Mahaffy might say with Whistler: 'I am not arguing; I am telling you.' In passages of such 'timely' purport, intensified as they often are by the author's personal feelings and experience, this book is at its best. Compared with the works of other writers in the same field, it seems to us inferior, say, to Professor Butcher's *Some Aspects of the Greek Genius* and *Harvard Lectures on Greek Subjects,* and to Mr. Lowes Dickinson's *The Greek View of Life;* the first two full of safe generalizations amply supported by specific facts, the last, by its admirable coherence and exquisite employment of transition recalling the prose of Plato himself. Yet, despite these, and despite Professor Sandys's *History of Classical Scholarship,* the true history of the Greek element in modern civilization — of its varying acceptance by different peoples and ages, of its varying combinations with national spirit and with *Zeitgeist,* and of the varying outcome — remains still to be written: *valde desideranda.*

May we, without attempting any part of such a history, be permitted to suggest the generalization that this book withholds?

V

The Greeks, more than all other peoples before or since, believed in the power of mind, and practised their belief. Applying mind to the raw material of sensation, they turned experience into wisdom, fact into truth, the Many into the One, chaos into law, the particular and provincial into the ideal and the universal. But they were not content to rest in this supersensible region: they reëmbodied their ideals in noble sensuous and intellectual forms, which they chose from amid a welter of forms possible but ignoble or insignificant, and which therefore have appealed to mankind *semper, ubique.* So that, whether in the subtle curves of a building, or in the proportions of a statue, or in the shape of a vase, or in the notes of the musical scale, or in finding how the human mind, out of an infinite number of ways in which it can work, actually does work towards truth; whether in art, or letters, or logic, or science, or a hundred other departments of human activity, we still perceive that they have performed for mankind, once for all, the labor of *selection.* It is impossible to overestimate this accomplishment in the racial economy, just as it is impossible to overestimate the specific nobility and loftiness of the ideal heritage they have left to the race.

Those who follow the Greek ways, and, without limiting themselves to old experience, fearlessly, and with confidence in the power of mind, push into the new data of modern life along the path that has proved possible — these are the pioneers; these are subduing chaos and bringing it province by province under the rule of spirit. Those who, refusing to profit by the Greek economy, try old failures again in ignorance or from choice, throw away their heritage. It is only by accident that they may happen upon some worthy thing. Their aberration, generally speaking, takes either or both of two forms, according as they fail to value one or another phase of the Greek accomplishment. Either they deny the validity of the results achieved by selection, and still fancy that 'the world is all before them where to choose'; or they deny the right of mind to work selectively at all upon the data of experience, insist that all things are of equal value except as weeded out by *natural* selection, and enslave themselves to the crude fact. The first error is the error of modern art, the second that of modern politics — at least, so far as both have been evolved under democratic institutions. The art of democracy is supposed to demand that no forms be rejected as ignoble. The politics of democracy, theoretically allowing free play to the conflicting wills of individuals, each striving for the ends indicated by his 'enlightened self-interest,' fails to provide for right leadership, for a chosen *mind* to control the welter, and so falls into the gripe of wrong leadership. For a mind of some sort is sure to gain control, soon or late. Modern science has escaped the second error, by selecting from the method of Bacon that part which is Greek in spirit. The Baconian induction, just in so far as it enslaved itself to fact, and disallowed hypothesis, and denied the rights of mind — just in so far as it was un-Greek — was a failure; and just in so far as it 'married mind with matter'— to use Bacon's own similitude — was, and is, a success. We are not to be, says Bacon again, like the ant, which gathers and stores up her hoard untransformed by aught that she does; nor yet like the spider, which spins her subtle thread all from within; but rather like the bee, which both gathers from without and transforms from within that which she gathers. Only thus shall we get 'sweetness and light.'

The Hellenist still believes that, things being given, ideas shall prevail. And so, instead of *fighting* things out, or letting the stress of competing forces among things work out its wasteful end, as Nature does, at dreadful expense of pain, at dire expense of spirit and of life, he endeavors to *think* things out. He may, by international arbitration, substitute the sanction of ideas for the sanction of arms. Or, upon a broad basis of facts, he may build a luminous hypothesis or rise to a law. He may be designing a subway or a city, and planning it so that the work will not have to be done over after the lapse of years. He may raise wages or share his profits not under the compulsion of a strike, but again under the compulsion of an idea — his own idea of equitable distribution. In many ways his mind, dealing with fact, will draw wisdom out of life; in many ways he will reëmbody that wisdom in chosen forms of beauty, and with whatever materials life gives him will make of himself a poet, and of life an art. We leave the subject with a question for those of an inquiring mind: Is our 'modern' way of life favorable to tempers of this kind? Do *we* believe in the supremacy of spirit? And would it have been a merit in the Greeks had they been like us?

II

ULYSSES GRANT [1]

[*Times* (London, England), Literary Supplement, January 2, 1915. By permission.]

Biographies to which the epithet 'true' is affixed are apt to be a little suspect. Usually they are either collections of unsavory gossip, or, like those ill-omened little books which call themselves 'The Truth about' this or that well-known country, the perverted expositions of faddists. Let us say at once that General King's new life of Grant is quite free from such follies. It is a careful and enthusiastic biography of one soldier by another, a study of character rather than of military achievement, and nothing could be better than the spirit in which it is written. The writer dwells lovingly on the details of Grant's career, such as his West Point days, and fills his pages with the names of soldiers whom he desires to rescue from oblivion. He has the most whole-hearted

[1] *The True Ulysses S. Grant*. By Charles King. (Philadelphia and London: Lippincott.)

admiration for his hero, and can yet be perfectly just to his rivals and opponents. The manner is old-fashioned, the kind of thing we associate with American biographies of fifty years ago. General King is very fond of the biographer's anticipation—'Little did he think that so many years hence he would be such and such,' etc.; and he uses the word 'gifted' so constantly that it becomes comic. '"Before night," said one of their gifted leaders, "we'll water our horses in the Tennessee or hell."' One would have thought that Oliver Wendell Holmes had killed this epithet. He becomes terribly self-conscious, and rather foolish in his description of Grant's visit to Europe and his intercourse with Royalties. But the author has the saving virtues of spirit, candor, and generosity, and we could have wished for more of his honest rhetoric.

Few great soldiers have had a stranger career than Grant, for at forty he was unknown, and at forty-five the first citizen of his country. Born near Lincoln in the Middle West, he had soldier stock in his ancestry; but he drifted into the army by accident, and had no military ambition. He did not want to go to West Point, and at the end of his course there he asked nothing more than to be a professor of mathematics. He distinguished himself in the Mexican War and earned a captain's brevet, but his unfortunate experience in California drove him into civil life. He tried farming and failed, then took to a humble kind of store-keeping, at which he made a bare living. His family and acquaintances thought little of the short, bent, dusty, and silent man who seemed the stark opposite of 'gifted' or 'magnetic' or 'silver-tongued,' or any of the things which won favor in the Middle West. Then came the Civil War and his chance. He was made colonel of the 21st Illinois, and immediately proved himself a professional soldier among voluble amateurs. He showed a power of command over the roughest materials, and presently, to his immense surprise, for he was the most modest of men, was given a brigade.

From that hour he never looked back. His victory at Fort Donelson heartened the North after the fiascos of McClellan and Buell, and he did much to retrieve the disaster of Shiloh. He had to fight against endless misrepresentation and the unplumbed incapacity of the Civil Government, but his stout heart and his military talent brought him triumphantly to the victory of Vicksburg, which made certain the ultimate triumph of the North. After that the sides of the quadrilateral began to close in upon the doomed Confederacy. Vicksburg was planned in defiance of the advice of his most trusted friends, like Sherman, and it was probably his greatest personal achievement in the field. He was now a major-general and commander-in-chief in the West, and Sheridan's winning of Missionary Ridge convinced Washington that the West must now furnish the Northern generalissimo. Early in 1864 the office of lieutenant-general was revived for Grant, and he found himself matched against the famous army of Virginia. The North held the winning cards, and all that was needed was the man who could play the game out and would not be disturbed by newspaper and political clamor. Grant proved himself such a man, and the desperate campaign in the Wilderness, the most bloody ever known in civilized war, was probably the right strategy. Sherman's march to the sea, Sheridan's brilliant cavalry work in the Valley, and Thomas's great victory at Nashville paved the way for the success of Grant's frontal attack. He made mistakes, for he tried to remove Thomas from his command on the very eve of Nashville, but on the whole he made few, and he had in Sherman not only the most loyal of friends but the ablest of colleagues. So in time came that April day at Appomattox, when the stately gentleman, the greatest of modern soldiers, surrendered to a weary, shabby, dusty little man, who represented the Union and the North.

Grant's subsequent career brought no stain to his military record. Had Lincoln lived he would have found the statesman he desired, and as it was he behaved like an honorable soldier, and did much to frustrate the politicians who would have disregarded the terms of surrender. He succeeded the deplorable Andrew Johnson as President of the United States, and held the office for two terms. He tried for a third term, like Mr. Roosevelt, but failed. He carried the manner of the camp to the White House, and was occasionally betrayed into blunders by his innocence of the devious ways of politicians. Yet he did good work as Chief Magistrate, and has the Treaty of Washington and the settlement of the Alabama question to his credit. In his last years he engaged in business, for which he was by no means suited, and suffered a financial *débâcle*. He died at the age of sixty-three, having enjoyed, after a youth of poverty and failure, such personal prominence as can only come to a soldier-citizen in a Republic.

General King, with pardonable enthusiasm, calls Grant the greatest of American soldiers. That is not the general opinion of those competent to judge. If we limit the list of the great commanders of the world to half a dozen, Lee's name would be in it; if we increase it to thirty, Grant's would not be there. He was not as great as Washington; he had not the genius of Stonewall Jackson, and was probably not as good as Thomas, the ablest and least appreciated of the Northern commanders. He did a great work, but he had all the weight of men and money behind him, and it cannot be said that in the doing of it he showed military talent of the highest order. The strategy of the 'quadrilateral' was obvious as soon as the fall of Vicksburg cleared the Mississippi. Grant was a 'slogger' who took and gave terrific punishment with a firm heart, and won by weight. But if he was not in the front rank of soldiers he was in the front rank of men. His character, at which the prudish North looked askance, was his greatest asset, and this General King most rightly emphasizes. Sherman's uncanonical words get very near the truth.

Wilson, I'm a damned sight smarter man than Grant; I know a great deal more about war, military history, strategy, and grand tactics than he does; I know more about organization, supply, and administration, and about everything else than he does; but I'll tell you where he beats me and where he beats the world. He don't care a damn for what the enemy does out of his sight, but it scares me like hell.

'Ulysses does n't scare worth a damn,' was the verdict of a Wisconsin volunteer who saw him writing despatches amid bursting shells. But physical courage was the least of his endowments. He had infinite patience, and could stand up before a storm of abuse and ignorant criticism, which is difficult in a democratic country with no military caste and a volunteer army. His taste for liquor, manfully striven against, was wildly exaggerated by jealous rumor, and few commanders have

had to fight in such an atmosphere of suspicion. The core of granite in the man carried him through, and he was able to 'break' ruthlessly old comrades who proved incompetent, and, himself the most soft-hearted of men, to disregard the national outcry at the terrible carnage of the Wilderness battles. To the world he appeared cold-blooded and brutal, and only the staff knew the truth, when they found him sobbing in his tent after Cold Harbor. In victory he was modest and magnanimous, and, though he had not the personal glamour of Lee, the uncouth Westerner was, no less than the courtly Virginian, a great gentleman.

III

MR. BRYAN'S SPEECHES

P[HILIP] L[ITTELL]

[*New Republic*, December 5, 1914. By permission of author and publisher.]

Every man, people say, gets the interviewer he deserves. It is not true. Few notables have any such luck. In my whole life I 've read the perfect interview just once. This was in January, 1895, not long after the first performance of *An Ideal Husband*, when the London *Sketch* published Gilbert Burgess's interview with Oscar Wilde. Mr. Burgess was a man who knew the difference between questions and questions. He asked the right ones:

'What are the exact relations between literature and the drama?'
'Exquisitely accidental. That is why I think them so necessary.'
'And the exact relation between the actor and the dramatist?'
Mr. Wilde looked at me with a serious expression which changed almost immediately into a smile, as he replied, 'Usually a little strained.'
'But surely you regard the actor as a creative artist?'
'Yes,' replied Mr. Wilde with a touch of pathos in his voice, 'terribly creative — terribly creative!'

The interview is republished in the volume called *Decorative Art in America* (Brentano's, 1906), and is still as fresh as ever, after twenty years. I turned back to it the other day, after reading here and there in two small blue volumes published in 1909, *Speeches of William Jennings Bryan, Revised and Arranged by Himself,* and wondering whether Mr. Bryan would ever fall into the ideal interviewer's hands. You, for example, could not interview Mr. Bryan properly, nor could I. We should feel both supercilious and intimidated. The man for the job is somebody who could mediate fearlessly between the remote Bryan period and the present time. Does such a man exist? By accident I have hit upon the right party — Hector Malone. Of Hector his creator has written, in the stage directions to *Man and Superman,* that 'the engaging freshness of his personality and the dumbfounding staleness of his culture make it extremely difficult to decide whether he is worth knowing; for whilst his company is undeniably pleasant and enlivening, there is intellectually nothing new to be got out of him.' You already perceive a certain affinity between Hector Malone and Mr. Bryan. Now for their unlikeness: when Hector 'finds people chattering harmlessly about Anatole France and Nietzsche, he devastates them with Matthew Arnold, the Autocrat of the Breakfast Table, and even Macaulay.'

It is an affair of proportion. As Nietzsche and Anatole France are to Macaulay, Matthew Arnold and the Autocrat, so, in the scale of modernity, are these authors to those with whom Mr. Bryan does his devastating. Mr. Bryan's culture would seem about as dumbfounderingly stale to Hector Malone as Hector's does to a generation fed on Anatole and Nietzsche. Hector is too modern and sophisticated to quote Gray's *Elegy, The Deserted Village,* Tom Moore and William Cullen Bryant. He knows that people don't do such things. But Mr. Bryan does them, and adds other incredibilities. Like Tennyson's brook, Demosthenes has said, Rollin tells us, Muelbach relates an incident, as Plutarch would say — here they are, and more of the same, in these two blue volumes. Looking backward, Mr. Bryan quotes 'breathes there a man with soul so dead' and 'truth crushed to earth.' Looking forward, he says that after Alexander and Napoleon 'are forgotten, and their achievements disappear in the cycle's sweep of years, children will still lisp the name of Jefferson.'

The earliest of these speeches and lectures is dated 1881 and the latest 1909.

In reality all of them have the same age. They all taste of '*das Ewig-gestrige, das Flache.*' In 1904 Mr. Bryan gives 'the reasons which lead me to believe that Christ has fully earned the right to be called The Prince of Peace,' and meditates thus upon eggs: 'The egg is the most universal of foods and its use dates from the beginning, but what is more mysterious than an egg? . . . We eat eggs, but we cannot explain an egg.' From its context in a lecture on 'Man,' delivered at the Nebraska State University in 1905, and also at Illinois College, I take this: 'Ask the mother who holds in her arms her boy, what her ideal is concerning him and she will tell you that she desires that his heart may be so pure that it could be laid upon a pillow and not leave a stain; that his ambition may be so holy that it could be whispered in an angel's ear. . . .'

If there is already too much superciliousness in the world such passages do harm. They do good if there is not superciliousness enough. In either case they do good in their context. They and their context have helped thousands upon thousands of Chautauquan early risers to be cheerful and industrious and unselfish and kind. These speeches reveal an incomparable mental unpreparedness to deal with their grave subjects, with the resurrection of the body, the atonement, miracles, inventions, evolution, faith, the soul, the secret of life. With an easy, happy flow the make-believe thought comes out in sincere and shallow sentences, which make one respect Mr. Bryan's good intentions, and admire his sweetness and good will. Thousands of good men and women have grown better on this thin food. Blessed are those who mean well, for they shall be spared the labor of thought.

It sounds patronizing, my attitude, and it is. Although you and I can no more write significantly of life or death than Mr. Bryan can, yet we have a superficial sophistication, we have acquired a suspicion that twaddle exists and may be distinguished from its opposite. Therefore do we smile complacently, in our offensive way, when Mr. Bryan sets forth 'the reasons which lead me to believe that Christ has fully earned the right to be called The Prince of Peace.' Little as we patronized him in 1896, how can we help patronizing Mr. Bryan now when we find him patronizing Christ?

Chronic good will, courage, a capacity for sudden formidableness, an early perception of important discontents, sympathy with the unprivileged average — in this mixture, I suppose, we must seek the explanation of his hold upon his followers. His size and importance were measured at the Baltimore convention in 1912, and again in the following spring, when President Wilson, afraid to leave him outside and hostile, turned him into a third-rate secretary of state and a useful backer of presidential legislation. One likes to imagine him sitting in the state department, mellowed by his popularity, set free from old jealousies, showing an unexpected capacity for team play, frock-coatedly glad-handing and kind-wording a hundred callers a day, always glib and sunny and sincere. Is he a shade more acquisitive than you 'd think to find such a very popular hero? Perhaps. Is he, for a man with exactly his reputation, a little too smooth, too unrugged, too deficient in homely humor? Why not? In every reputation, however explicable, there is a residuum of mystery. 'What,' as Mr. Bryan himself says, 'is more mysterious than an egg?'

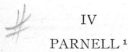

IV

PARNELL [1]

F[RANCIS] H[ACKETT]

[*New Republic*, December 5, 1914. By permission of author and publisher.]

Married in her twentieth year or thereabouts to a cornet in a sporting regiment, Katherine O'Shea had lived thirteen years with Willie O'Shea and borne him three children before she met Charles Stewart Parnell. Her relations with O'Shea had long been unsatisfactory. Handsome, gay, sarcastic, self-assured, O'Shea was a spoiled and rather dictatorial specimen of the petty aristocracy. Already bankrupt through mismanagement of his racing stable, he spent a great deal of his time away from Mrs. O'Shea engaged in patching up his fortunes, being absent as long as eighteen months at a time on mining ventures in Spain. When they were to-

gether O'Shea was rather jarring and possessive, easily made jealous, insisting on visits, visitors and entertainments his wife disliked, with which he alternated periods of undependability and neglect. His wife's impulsiveness and mettle he did not understand, and before the entry of Parnell into their lives 'the wearing friction caused by our totally dissimilar temperaments began to make us feel that close companionship was impossible, and we mutually agreed that he should have rooms in London, visiting Eltham to see myself and the children at week-ends.'

Mrs. O'Shea's father was an English clergyman, Sir John Page Wood. She was the youngest of a family of thirteen. Brought up in a household where men like Trollope, the older Cunninghame Graham, John Morley came to visit, she spent a great deal of her life with an august aunt at a Georgian lodge in Eltham, to whom George Meredith used to come almost every week for a stipulated two hours of 'the classics and their discussion.' Mrs. O'Shea knew George Meredith well, and I dare say he, behind his badinage and 'effectiveness,' knew that flashing spirit rather better.

In 1880 Willie O'Shea was urged to stand for an Irish constituency. 'I wrote back strongly encouraging him,' says Mrs. Parnell, 'for I knew it would give him occupation he liked and keep us apart — and therefore good friends. Up to this time Willie had not met Mr. Parnell.'

At this time Parnell was thirty-four years of age. The actual leader of the Irish Parliamentary Party, he had already broken away from the 'fine reasonableness' of Isaac Butt at which 'the English parties smiled and patted the Irish indulgently on the head,' and he had initiated his policy 'of uncompromising hostility to all British parties and of unceasing opposition to all their measures until the grievances of Ireland were redressed.'

Because he disliked all social intercourse with Saxons, Mrs. O'Shea's attempts to secure Parnell for her dinners were repeatedly unsuccessful, but, a determined lady, she eventually decided to deliver her invitation in person at the House. 'He came out, a tall, gaunt figure, thin and deadly pale. He looked straight at me smiling, and his curiously burning eyes looked into mine with a wondering intentness that threw into my brain the

1 *Charles Stewart Parnell, His Love Story and Political Life.* By Katherine O'Shea (Mrs. Charles Stewart Parnell). New York: George H. Doran Company.

sudden thought: "This man is wonderful — and different."' Mrs. O'Shea planned a theater party for his distraction, and 'he and I seemed naturally to fall into our places in the dark corner of the box. I had a feeling of complete sympathy and companionship with him, as though I had always known this strange, unusual man with the thin face and pinched nostrils, who sat by my side staring with curious intent gaze at the stage, and telling me in a low monotone of his American tour and of his broken health . . . and his eyes smiled into mine as he broke off his theme and began to tell me of how he had met once more in America a lady to whom he had been practically engaged some years before.'

A few months later, when Mrs. O'Shea was in great distress over the death of Lucy Goldsmith, her lifelong friend and nurse, the tenor of Parnell's notes from Dublin revealed the truth. 'I cannot keep myself away from you any longer, so shall leave to-night for London.' They did not meet, but Mrs. O'Shea pictures the subsequent weeks. 'And my aunt would doze in her chair while I dropped the book I had been reading to her and drifted into unknown harmonies and color of life . . . and I was conscious of sudden gusts of unrest and revolt against these leisured, peaceful days where the chiming of the great clock in the hall was the only indication of the flight of time.'

'In the autumn of 1880 Mr. Parnell came to stay with us at Eltham.' There he fell ill, brought near to death's door by 'his exertions on behalf of the famine-stricken peasants of Ireland,' and Mrs. O'Shea nursed him back till he was nearly strong. Hovering over him as he slept, 'pulling the light rug better over him,' she recalls his murmur: 'Steer carefully out of the harbor — there are breakers ahead.'

Next year Captain O'Shea came to Eltham without invitation, found Parnell's portmanteau there, sent it to London and left declaring he would challenge Parnell to a duel. The challenge was accepted but 'Willie then thought he had been too hasty.' Parnell's real emotions seem to have centered on his portmanteau. 'My dear Mrs. O'Shea,' he wrote, 'will you kindly ask Captain O'Shea where he left my luggage? I inquired at both parcel office, cloak room, and this hotel, and

they were not to be found.' But the incident cemented the fate of O'Shea. 'From the date of this bitter quarrel Parnell and I were one, without further scruple, without fear, and without remorse.'

In 1881 Parnell was arrested for his Land League activities, and was in Kilmainham at the will of Gladstone until the following May. It was a period of unremitting agony for Mrs. O'Shea, and for him on her account. In February, 1882, she bore Parnell a daughter whom he saw for the first and last time for a day in April. 'My little one's paternity was utterly unsuspected by the O'Sheas.'

From that time till 1890, the year of the divorce case, Parnell and Mrs. O'Shea lived their double life. A 'volcano capped with snow,' Parnell endured secrecy and deception, and she with him, for the sake of the Home Rule bill. When the crash came Mrs. O'Shea was afraid, but his mind was clear. 'Put away all fear and regret for my public life. I have given, and will give, Ireland what is in me to give. That I have vowed to her, but my private life shall never belong to any country, but one woman. There will be a howl, but it will be the howling of hypocrites; not altogether, for some of these Irish fools are genuine in their belief that forms and creeds can govern life and men; perhaps they are right so far as they can experience life. But I am not as they, for they are among the world's children. I am a man, and I have told these children what they want, and they clamor for it. If they will let me, I will get it for them. But if they turn from me, my Queen, it matters not at all in the end. . . . You have stood to me for comfort and strength and my very life. I have never been able to feel in the least sorry for having come into your life. It had to be, and the bad times I have caused you and the stones that have been flung and that will be flung at you are all no matter, because to us there is no one else in all the world that matters at all — when you get to the bottom of things.'

Between O'Shea and Mrs. O'Shea there were friendly relations till the end of 1886. She induced Parnell to work for his parliamentary candidacy in 1886, and while O'Shea was willing to use Parnell to further his own necessities (he seems to have been a tool of Joseph Chamberlain) he hated and railed against the imperturbable Parnell. All during their intimacy, Mrs. O'Shea acted as an intermediary between Parnell and Gladstone in negotiations which she vividly recounts. Whenever Gladstone sought Parnell in an emergency he sent for him to Mrs. O'Shea's house. The pious surprise of Gladstone when the crash came was characteristic hypocrisy.

Mrs. O'Shea was married to Parnell in June, 1891. Worn out by his campaign against his own former adherents, now under the dictation of Gladstone and the priests, Parnell succumbed in October. He died October sixth, less than four months after his marriage, in his forty-seventh year.

Now a woman of nearly seventy, Mrs. Parnell has been induced to reveal her intimate life for the sake of Captain O'Shea's child, her eldest son. That young man, whose psychology is not worth discussing, is 'jealous for his father's honor,' and it is ostensibly to prove that Captain O'Shea was not a willing beneficiary of her relations with Parnell that these two volumes were written. The real motive, however, is the deep human motive of self-vindication. Mrs. Parnell loved one of the great men of his generation. She loved him purely, passionately, consumedly. Possessing the great treasure of his love in return, she has been unwilling to die without rebutting all the slander, all the contumely, all the belittlement and reproach and vilification that were the price she paid for seeming to have cheated Ireland of her uncrowned king. Writing these two volumes 'without scruple, without fear, and without remorse,' she has brought to her aid all the resources of imagination, keen intelligence, and vivid memory, and she has produced a work of consummate significance and touching humanness. Defiant of convention, she has given full reality for her reader to the extraordinarily powerful and fascinating personality to whom she dedicated her life. Exposing for this purpose much that is painfully private and sacredly naïve, dwelling on facts that belong, if anything belongs, to that inner life to which Parnell asserted his right so implacably, she has, at this great cost, succeeded in asserting the quality of their personal relation. It was true love, if ever love was true, and it honored human nature. If Captain O'Shea was 'deceived,' it was the fruit of

his own mean inadequacy, determined as he was to keep Mrs. O'Shea in bond, to enforce a legal advantage that flattered his vanity at the expense of everything generous, noble and free. He struggled, as small people always struggle, to keep the springs of life from finding their level, but they were too strong for him. After many years' effort to reconcile herself to insuperable limitations, Mrs. Parnell found an adequate, a complete, an immeasurable appeal to every power and sympathy she possessed. She answered that appeal heroically, failing to conform with the written law in order to conform with what may curtly be called the unwritten law of her own and Parnell's being.

When these volumes were published in London, they were dismissed in twenty lines by the *British Weekly* as an outrage against decency, a 'glorification of adultery . . . the foulest treachery and vice.' It is quite in keeping with the Gladstone tradition and, indeed, with English righteousness in general, that this work, which the *British Weekly* 'would fain consign to oblivion,' is now offered to us in this country by the agents of the *British Weekly* in America.

V

GEORGE MEREDITH

OLIVER ELTON

[This is a recast of an article in the London *Tribune* of January 17, 1906, published in book form along with other essays in *Modern Studies* (Edward Arnold), London, 1907. By permission of author and publisher.]

I

'Who really cares for what I say? The English people know nothing about me. There has always been something antipathetic between them and me. With book after book it was always the same outcry of censure and disapproval. The first time or two I minded it, then I determined to disregard what the people said altogether, and since then I have written only to please myself. But even if you could tell the world all I think, no one would listen.'

Mr. Meredith, who is reported thus to have spoken some years ago, has notwithstanding won the only kind of fame for *critical criticism*

which he can be supposed to care. Not only has he received the Order of Merit, the last official *imprimatur* set by English society upon brains that are pronounced to be eminent and also harmless; he has the honor paid him by all his fellow craftsmen, and by thousands of other persons. In such a case the good of fame is greater to those who proffer it than to the possibly weary winner of the fame. Mr. Meredith is now a kind of Field-Marshal of English letters. He is the man who has done most, and seen most service. To the general joy he is amongst us and still upon the watch. His first verses were printed in the year (1851) after Wordsworth's *Prelude*. His poetry is still being commented, proclaimed, and defended, it is alive and singing in our ears. *The Odes in Contribution to the Song of French History* were collected in 1898. Last year (1906) saw his jubilee as a novelist; for in 1856 appeared the *Shaving of Shagpat*, which disclosed the costly treasure-house of his fancy and the overrunning springs of his wit. *The Ordeal of Richard Feverel* came out in 1859, the same year as *Adam Bede* and *The Origin of Species; Lord Ormont and His Aminta,* in 1894. Some thirteen novels, besides short tales, criticisms, and poems, are the fruit of those forty years. Mr. Meredith wrought unweariably through the later day of Dickens and Thackeray, through the day of George Eliot and the jaunty revulsion against her, and now through the day of Mr. Hardy and Mr. Henry James. He was neglected or patronized by many of the critics in the sixties and the early seventies, and perhaps the habit of feeling induced by this treatment may linger in the words quoted above. The bigger reading public, the masses of the English community overseas, no doubt are still recalcitrant. Mr. Meredith has never struck home to them, as Dickens struck home to them with his splendid humanity, his uncertain art and moderate education, and his true wealth of genial and farcical type. Some, too, of those devoted to Thackeray's vast and populous canvas, to his occasional classic sureness and constant elegance of speech (amidst much that is merely journalistic fiction), and to his half-dozen scenes of vehement human drama, may have shivered at the refreshing east wind and shrunk from the mountain sickness that the reader of Meredith must face. To read him is like climbing, and calls for training and eyesight; but there is always a view at the top, there are the sunrise and the upper air. Nor is such a tax always paid him willingly by the better-trained, serious public of escaped and enlightened puritans, the dwindled public of George Eliot. Nor has he much in common with the novelists, English and other, of a later day.

For he, like Goethe, 'bids you hope,' while *Tess of the D'Urbervilles* and *The Wings of the Dove* do not. The movement of later fiction is towards pessimism, and its best makers, Guy de Maupassant, Gorky, D'Annunzio, agree in their want of hopefulness if in nothing else. They have been catching up and expressing in fiction ideas that found a nobler expression, philosophical or lyrical, nearly a century ago, in Schopenhauer and Leopardi. The same discouragement lay at the base of Tolstoy's thought, before he found his peculiar salvation, and it still tinges his fiction when he forgets his creed and remembers that he is an artist. The history of this pessimistic movement in fiction is still unwritten, and the movement itself is unexhausted.

But the groundwork of Mr. Meredith, with his forward look, his belief in love and courage, is different. It is stoical rather than pessimistic; and in that he resembles Zola, whose method — laborious, serried, humorless — is the opposite of his. Mr. Meredith grew up on the high hopes fed by the revolutions of the mid-century, and the most heroic figure in his books is Mazzini, the 'Chief' in *Vittoria*. He has a moral and spiritual afflatus of the nobler order, peculiarly and traditionally English, in that line of the great English prophets which comes down from Langland and Sir Thomas More to Carlyle. His creed does not depend, visibly, on formal doctrine for its force, but neither does it rest on any preoccupying enmity towards doctrine. His inspiration plays in various moods — strenuous, ethereal, ironical — rarely serene, over his vision of 'certain nobler races, now dimly imagined'; and casts a new interpreting light, above all, on the rarer forms of love and patriotism and friendship. Yet there are none of the airs of the prophet, for the media preferred by Mr. Meredith in his prose are wit and aphorism, situation and portraiture, and to these the lyrical and didactic elements are subordinate.

II

Mr. Meredith has run a course of his own, and has owed little to any man of his own craft. It may be guessed, indeed, that the author of *Harry Richmond* had before him in *Copperfield* the example of a new, humorous, natural, and beautiful form of autobiographic fiction. And Thomas Love Peacock, to whom Mr. Meredith's first book was inscribed, may have lent a happy turn to his generous and repeated and witty praise of wine, and have supplied some hint for those country-house gatherings of humorists and fantasts of which a specimen is found so late as 1890 in *One of Our Conquerors*. In such a gathering the inmates and visitors are endowed with a surprising point, wit, and agility of soul in their tongue-combats. But Peacock's humorists all come from London, or from the void, for the week-end, and go back on the Monday. These are minor debts, and Mr. Meredith stands apart from all the recognized groups of schools of English novelists. For his true and chosen background is the real, feudal, Tory, country world of old Victorian England, with its ineradicable shades of caste-feeling, its surface gallantry, its reluctance to think, its vigor of physique and its excellent manners. It is not likely that such a world, which is still alive and long will be, should trouble much about its own countenance as reflected in the 'steel glass' of the novelist. His favorite characters are the bravest and fairest that such a society can breed, or at least cannot prevent from being bred, in its midst; and his frequent subject is the struggle of these favorites to rise above the spiritual and mental level of their world. Many of his personages are real gentry, rooted in their estates, persons of the upper untitled or the lower titled classes, or else in some defined social relationship to these — great dames, young soldiers, eldest sons of the land, naval commanders, scholars of the strenuous or the portly type, parsons of good estimation, usually ponderous, and the babbling society mob. In natural connection with these are the tenants, oaken old yeomen or farmers, Fleming or Blaize, often the fathers of fair daughters, who rise by natural selection, like Lucy Feverel; or gentlemen proved such by trial of circumstance, like Evan Harrington, the tailor's son. There are, further, the retainers, butlers, intelligent handmaids, sporting coves, and prize-fighters like that admirable light-weight Skepsey, the servant of Natalie Radnor. There are the ladies of clouded fame, who serve the unauthorized amusements of gentlemen, and who are somewhat unreal, though tragically-conceived, characters. Mr. Meredith, by choosing within this province an immeasurably higher range of interest and passion than the accurate patient Trollope, has added a new stratum of semi-barbarian territory to English fiction.

It may be called the Empire-making stratum, and the profound feeling for the work and future of our race that throbs through Mr. Meredith's writings provides him with an outlet into a freer air. He is, I have said, a liberal idealist, whose hopes are rooted in the tenacious, the Norman, the constructive aspirations of the Englishman. And his faith is strengthened by his outlook upon the European stir for freedom, which carries him beyond the political creed of the class he portrays. A rare reconciliation of ideals, that may perhaps hereafter be noted as prophetic! In *Vittoria* he finds a subject that is free from any of the limitations imposed by irony. Music and freedom, the freedom of Italy and its signal, the singing of the heroine in *La Scala,* are its animating powers. The compass of his gifts, both as an epical narrator and a painter of noble character, are best seen in the pair of stories that take us from the humors of the English lawn to the struggle of Italian liberation. In *Emilia in England,* otherwise *Sandra Belloni,* and in *Emilia in Italy,* otherwise *Vittoria* (all three being names for one woman), he has described, as no English writer ever yet, a true artist-soul, with a patriot soul behind it of equal stature. The companion-book is Mr. Swinburne's *Songs before Sunrise,* for the spirit of Mazzini breathes in both. And in other stories Mr. Meredith has found an air freer than that of England. There are bright and keen glimpses of France in *Beauchamp's Career* and in the gracious Renée de Rouaillout. The study of Lassalle and Helène de Racowitza, made from the authorities, in *The Tragic Comedians,* does not fully reach the high-strung purpose of the writer, in spite of the elemental or tidal energy of Alvan-Lassalle. But Alvan is a relief after the manly, self-restrained, pattern Englishmen commonly invented by Mr. Meredith in order to find some one worthy of his heroines.

III

He seems to have 'reversed the order of Paradise,' and to have created his women first, and so to have had less clay at disposal for fashioning their mates. Renée, Emilia, Carinthia, Lucy, with their musical names — in their talk, and his talk about them, his style is at its purest and clearest, and the colors of the portraits are unfading. Women are nearer to nature than men, and the power to paint them can only come straight from the breast of nature — from experience lived through and transmuted into artistic form. Indeed, the business of 'reading the female heart' has not often been practised in English prose without a dispiriting effect. The tradition of unreality is old and obstinate. It runs far back into the Renaissance romance, like Sidney's *Arcadia* — where, indeed, there is one tragic feminine figure, the queen Gynecia; and to the long-winded books in French and English consumed by our seventeenth-century ancestresses. But those old romances were apt to be made either by courtly, artificial men or by spinsters without any profitable experience of humanity. One of these spinsters, Samuel Richardson, succeeded once, despite his fussy morals and clammy rhetoric. The laborious knife of George Eliot sometimes bites deep. But a man, if only he is great enough and can rise above the natural barrier ('La haine entre les deux sexes,' says Joubert, 'ne s'éteint guère'), is the best and kindest painter of women and of their ailments of the soul, and the best describer of them. Or so the event seems to have proved. This is not a reflection upon women; for, after all, it is better to belong to the class that is pictured than to the class that paints pictures.

Balzac and Mr. Meredith, diverse in almost all ways, have both left behind them a portrait gallery of actual and living women. Balzac excels with older, harder, and stranger natures. The Englishman, more of a poet at the heart, prefers to celebrate youth and beauty that are victorious after long inward and out-

ward trial. But he has, more than once, his Hermiones as well as his Perditas, figures of the 'sanctissima coniux,' September faces, thrown into contrast with those fresher ones without loss of charm. The friendship of Diana of the Crossways and her 'Tony' is an instance. *One of Our Conquerors* essays the hardest and nicest problem in Mr. Meredith's later books, as *Rhoda Fleming* does among the earlier. It is a demonstration of the mystery of pain in the hearts of a mother and a daughter. The mother dreads the disclosure, which the daughter has to face, of their socially unauthorized position. The girl is illegitimate, owing to a foolish marriage made by her father long ago. Words are found for her discovery of the circumstance; for this is required the delicacy of the great masters. The mother dies, the girl becomes a magnificent spirit, a sworn defender of the unfortunate among her own sex, and her own happiness is at last assured, a handsome and chivalrous hero being provided for her with some surface failings that make him possible.

But for such work Mr. Meredith has had to invent his own dialect. He sets himself, continually, to realize motives that have their life only in the antechambers of consciousness, and sensations that fade in the effort to give them words. Here he forswears whim and witty fancy; in the best passages, all is attention and grave precision. The bending of English prose to this finer purpose is one of Mr. Meredith's substantial glories. Undiscovered forces of vanity, of self-protection that is sure of its danger but not of its reasons, of self-regard and self-distrust, find their calculus. He is taxed with obscurity, but he is as lucid a writer, in this province, as the nature of the subject permits. He moves as safely in the dark as Dostoieffsky, the great specialist; and though, unlike him, he is sometimes hampered by the satiric aim, and is less content to let the nakedness of our nature plead for itself, he is also free from the wildness and mirage and crazy touch that prove refracting elements in *Crime and Punishment* or *The Idiot*. In the scientific dissection of motive, filament by filament, Mr. Henry James ranks beside him, and in the power to realize deep-plotting, ambiguous natures, may be his superior, just as his hold on beauty of style is more certain and steady. But the characters of Mr. Meredith are fuller than any other novelist's of strong, natural vitality; they fight, and swim, and wander in scented forests, and wipe the sweat from their brows, and intercept mad dogs, and make love in their youth beneath the wild cherry-blossom, and give their lives to save some 'little mudlarking waif,' like Beauchamp; and his words accordingly ring and rush as the blood runs faster. Out of this kind of strength comes the power that lies behind the finer, tenderer passages that interpret obscure matters of the heart. The intellect remains the master while threading the mazes of unuttered painful feeling. In the episode already mentioned, Natalie, the nominal wife, who is caught in the birdlime of false social position, asks a friend for the counsel which yet she fears to receive.

'She bowed to her chastisement. One motive in her consultation with him came of the knowledge of his capacity to inflict it and honesty in the act, and a thirst she had to hear the truth loud-tongued from him: together with a feeling that he was excessive and satiric, not to be read by the letter of his words: and in consequence, she could bear the lash from him, and tell her soul that he overdid it, and have an unjustly-treated self to cherish. But in very truth she was a woman who loved to hear the truth; *she was formed to love the truth her position reduced her to violate;* she esteemed the hearing of it as medical to her; she selected for counselor him who would apply it: so far she went on the straight way: and the desire for a sustaining deception from the mouth of a trustworthy man set her hanging on his utterances with an anxious hope of the reverse of what was to come and what she herself apprehended; such as checked her pulses and iced her feet and fingers.'

Mr. Meredith's analysis, in serious romance, is nearly always *moral* analysis; it is concerned with complex refinements of the profounder pieties and veracities. He is always testing human nature with his finger, like a glass, to see if it rings clear and right. Or rather, to read him, before the heart is hardened, is like going to the dentist, who does not spare to touch the nerve. This is another reason for his incomplete popularity; but, inasmuch as his science is genuine, it is also a reason

for his name enduring. In his dramatic, ironic way, he is one of the masters of the spiritual life: — not the life of the lonely mystic or thinker (for such persons do not figure in his books as they do in Balzac's) but the life of men and women in contact, snared by instinct or egoism, but capable of emerging with made souls, marked and scarred but ready to begin afresh. Historically, this kind of special power leaves him somewhat solitary amongst English novelists.

IV

There is, however, no monotony of tragic note. Mr. Meredith's chosen weapon is comedy, and his discourse *On the Idea of Comedy,* given in 1877 at the middle of his career, throws a backward and forward light upon his artistic practice. It is a classic piece of criticism, written by a fellow of Hazlitt, with the advantages that the craftsman, like Dryden in the *Discourse of Satire,* is speaking of his own craft; and that, like Dryden, he has ample reading and scholarship as well as the memory of his own creative processes. As we read, we feel that since Goldsmith the higher comic spirit, as distinct from that of farce or irony, has fled from the stage to the novel. Mr. Meredith is not popular, because he is full of the comic spirit as he conceives it. It is not the high and bare cynicism of Congreve, the emperor of phrasing. It is distinguished from farcical humor by its different treatment of the victim.

'If you laugh all around him, tumble him, roll him about, deal him a smack and drop a tear on him, own his likeness to you and yours to your neighbor, spare him as little as you shun, pity him as much as you expose, it is the spirit of Humor that is moving you.'

But even this is not the whole of the comic spirit. Lessing had said that 'Comedy is laughter, not derision'; and derision with a moral purpose is still further off from comedy than farce. Even irony is only part of its essence.

'If instead of falling foul of the ridiculous person with a satiric rod, to make him writhe and shriek aloud, you prefer to sting him under a semi-caress, by which he shall in his anguish be rendered doubtful whether indeed anything has hurt him, you are an engine of Irony.'

In the view of Mr. Meredith the comic

spirit, as distinct from inferior or allied forms of humor, cannot flourish except in a disinfected society where manners are highly trained. Like most honest readers, he finds the Restoration and Revolution comedy, which records quite another society, generally dead and tiresome, presupposing as it does an audience not a little inhuman. The flowering of the comic spirit is bound up, he insists, with the due position and honorable estate of women. Where they are the cheap butts, rather than the arbiters and voices of the comic spirit, there is no hope for it.

'Now, comedy is the fountain of good sense, not the less perfectly sound on account of the sparkle; and comedy lifts women to a station offering them free play for their wit, as they usually show it, when they have it, on the side of good sense. The higher the comedy, the more prominent the part they enjoy in it. . . . Célimène is undisputed mistress of the attribute (of common sense) in the *Misanthrope,* wiser as a woman than Alceste as a man. In Congreve's *Way of the World* Millamant overshadows Mirabel, the sprightliest male figure of English comedy.'

It may be replied that Alceste, with his passion for Célimène conflicting with his passion for sincerity, is the higher of the two; but in respect of pure wit he is doubtless the smaller. It may also be added that Mr. Meredith's women are not often witty, or that when they are their wit is strained. But good sense, barbed with disconcerting smiles, they have in supreme measure. We can best understand Mr. Meredith's idea of the comic spirit from the malady which it is intended to show up and, if possible, to cure. That is 'sentimentalism'; and by the term is understood, not the simple movements of the heart in simple persons, with their untrained expression, but the impulses of vanity or selfish craving, masquerading as those of the heart and uttering phrases too big for the occasion or false to it. Sentimentalism implies the absence both of clear reason, and also of the one other thing, besides religion and country, that the comic spirit respects, simple and healthy passion. *Evan Harrington* and *The Egoist* are built upon this conception of a vanity which is the target of thoughtful glancing ridicule, and which is at last exposed, if not cured, by the daylight of reason — and banished, if at all, by the warmth of authentic love. *Evan Harrington* is a second *Book of Snobs,* the air being some hundred feet higher of social elevation, and the scene being laid amidst the classes where the sense of rank and caste, at the era depicted in the book, is Chinese in its strictness. It is the lightest and blithest of Mr. Meredith's English tales, and in it his tragic force is sleeping, while his heroic force is at play. *The Egoist,* with its more intricate and mature subject, is now long established in all our affections, and answers best to the author's own 'idea' of the comic spirit. Here he writes intoxicated with his own wit, in the way that is so rare in Englishmen. He is like some irresistible executant, unafraid of the most discordant or fantastic witch-dance of words, and yet striking continually into impeccable expression. The same relish is felt in all his later books, but never for so long.

v

Though no one speaks less from a chair or pulpit, Mr. Meredith stands to be judged as a teacher and prophet. He is not content to be an observer. Comedy and morality are in history old and lawfully wedded lovers. If we cannot have the perfectly free poetical life of Arden, then give us that *L'Ecole des Femmes* or *The Egoist.* In *The Amazing Marriage,* in *One of Our Conquerors,* and everywhere, the pleasure of the educator is apparent. The characters are plunged into trial, they are beaten and tempered and annealed, partly by ridicule, partly by their own passion; and this is done in the name of Nature, to see how they will stand the shock. Mr. Meredith's ethic is best applied in his prose and best expounded in his verse, though his verse comes, far less often than his prose, to rightness of form. He has his own divinity, pagan by name. Where other writers appeal to God or to Humanity, he speaks, somewhat insistently, of the Earth; and the Earth is not the malign stepmother of pessimistic theory, but a stern genial mother, if at times something of a governess. In Mr. G. M. Trevelyan's clear exposition of *The Poetry and Philosophy of George Meredith,* there is heard a welcome note of caution:

'Some may think that the value of the lessons he would enforce is not much enhanced by the alleged sanction of Earth. They may think that it is really much the same as the more usual formula of the sanction of Heaven, and that it has equally much or equally little weight.'

Earth, however, is less a 'sanction' than an emotional symbol of Nature, and its incessant recurrence does more harm to Mr. Meredith's art than to his thinking. Earth lends us our bodies, our fund of power, and our capital of instinct, which may be turned to uses fruitful or sterile. Our life is the adjustment and realization of the forces that Earth has given us. It is love, rightly understood, that tasks and rewards our power of directing those forces. Such love helps us, in its better forms, to the vision of those 'nobler races,' for out of love they must be begotten. The creed is not unlike Carlyle's in its courage, but it is more possible, less savage, and less solitary. There is to be no tampering with the intellect by soothing illusions; 'we must do,' as George Eliot said, 'without opium.' The volume called *A Reading of Earth,* and the poem therein called *A Faith On Trial,* give us Mr. Meredith's religion. Whatever the power or complexion of the enemy, whether it be ignorance, or languor, or bereavement, or self-deception, he is always in the attitude of the challenger; like Ivanhoe, who rode up the lists, and in token of mortal combat touched the shield with the sharp end of his spear, despite the well-meant hints of 'some of the lower classes.'

VI

Soon or late has to be faced the hindrance of Mr. Meredith's verbal strangeness, which is still supposed to warrant or explain his slow acceptance by the public. The robust older critics, who were still flourishing when he began to write fifty years ago made much, it is said, of this hindrance. But they did not try to understand. Their idea was to decree rewards and punishments to an artist — so many stripes of the cat on the shoulders balanced by so many of good conduct on the sleeve. The author, if not a criminal, who had to come up for punishment, was a kind of ticket-of-leave man who must report himself under suspicion. And if the sentence was capital, the executioner wore a mask of blue or buff, according to the complexion of the journal that sheltered his anonymity. It was the kind of

criticism that trained its readers to lose the instinct for literary power, and it is now nearly dead. No doubt there was, at first sight, colorable matter for reproach. In every book by Mr. Meredith, from *The Shaving of Shagpat* to *The Amazing Marriage,* the outline of the figures and even of the events is more or less veiled under a sparkling mist or spray of commentary, an emanation of bewildering light.

Self-suppression does not enter into such a method, as it does into that of Flaubert, and there is as much choric interlude as drama. There is a heady, subtle element, which beguiles and dislodges the reader, and dazes him with myriads of epigrams. The epigrams of Mr. Meredith might be fairly divided into those which leave a headache behind them and those that do not. So great a rapidity of comment does not make for proportion and composition. But take the story, and strip it, at whatever momentary sacrifice, of all but the actual narrative and dialogue, keeping also the passages that expressly describe motive and sensation, but leaving out the chorus of aphorisms, and the test will be nobly met. We can then go back again and put in as much of the rainbow as we will.

The difficulty of style is felt most keenly in Mr. Meredith's poetry. There, in its most restless form, is the swift intellect, working for the writer's cherished ethical or spiritual ideas, and working through a torrent of images, sometimes turbid, and sometimes abstrusely delicate, but huddling on one another as fast as in the dying speech of Romeo. As Lamb said of Shakespeare, ' before one idea has burst its shell, another is hatched and clamorous for disclosure.' But the poetry also often suffers (the prose less, because prose will bear more of such vagrancy than poetry, and yet remain true to the law of its art) because the intellect, so far from being content to let the sensuous matter clear itself and rely on itself, as Keats in his finest passages is content to do, is always interposing and enlisting that material in the service of the ' criticism of life.' Many are the verses where the issue is doubtful, or rather not doubtful; where the night-long wrestle with words is continued from sheer courage rather than in the hope of possibility of victory. Many, again, for instance in *Modern*

Love, are those where the result is impeccable and the sense of strain is lost. More seldom are the imagery and the music all-sufficient to one another, in a kind of Goethe-like repose, as here:

The pine-tree drops its dead;
They are quiet, as under the sea.
Overhead, overhead,
Rushes life in a race,
As the clouds the clouds chase:
    And we go,
    And we drop like the fruits of the tree,
    Even we,
    Even so.

But commonly, in Mr. Meredith's verses, imagination is at war with and outraces its own power of expression, and thus is too frequently defeated, though its triumphs are not rare, and would, if selected and arrayed together, form a 'golden treasury' large enough. But, as with some older poets like George Chapman, words, lines, and passages, which are informed with lofty and gracious ideas, are so variably cast that the innermost soul of poetry must alternately repudiate and welcome them.

In the novels the proportion is different; the pages that go quite amiss and do violence to the writer's own ideals of form are relatively fewer. The diction of Mr. Meredith in his prose is, for long spaces, pure, chosen, and simple. The oddness is produced by slight dislocations of historic English, an unusual order of words, a curious disposal of particles and abstract nouns, which in cumulation give a superficial effect of freakishness. As so often with Latin or Italian, the decipherer finds himself gazing at a sentence made up of common words without getting to their sense. The subject may be commended to some young Germanized American for a golden or leaden dissertation. There is, indeed, no reason why a classic author should not be treated by the usual methods of scholarship, if they are applied with tact, as Mr. Trevelyan applies them. This is only a sign of respect, which we offer to Chapman or to Donne. But it may be well to have the transpicuous page of Fielding open before us, that we may keep our heads while we study the heir of his noble art.

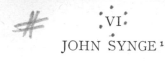

VI

JOHN SYNGE [1]

STUART P. SHERMAN

[*Evening Post,* New York, January 11, 1913. By permission.]

John Synge was so skilful in eluding biographers that he was dead before it was generally known in this country that he had existed. Within the last year or two he has become one of the most conspicuous figures in the literary world. Yet current discussion has proceeded for the most part in ignorance of the facts of his life and has confined itself mainly to one or two of the plays. Even among the better informed there still remain the widest differences of opinion regarding his character, his relation to the so-called Irish Renaissance, and his appropriate niche in the temple of fame. And in consequence of various non-literary forces, the division has been rather partizan than critical. It is darkly hinted in one quarter that he owes everything to the French decadents. On the other hand, Mr. Yeats would have us believe that his work came straight from the heart of Erin. On the one hand it is argued that he is only a clever craftsman. But Mr. Howe holds that he stands by his absolute achievement only a little lower than Shakespeare. 'If he had lived,' says Mr. Howe, 'he could not but have added to the number of his plays; and yet in the six plays he has left us, what that is essential in life has he failed to include?' This is the question one asks of the supreme geniuses; this is the question one asks of Shakespeare.

With the collected works of Synge now before us and with eager advocates and jealous disparagers on each side of us, it may be worth while to inquire in an entirely dispassionate way what manner of man this was.

[1] *The Works of John M. Synge.* Boston: J. W. Luce & Co. 4 vols.
The Cutting of an Agate. By William Butler Yeats. New York: The Macmillan Co. In this are gathered up Mr. Yeats's principal articles on Synge; also articles on Lady Gregory, John Shaw-Taylor, Spenser, and miscellaneous thoughts on poetry and drama.
J. M. Synge; A Critical Study. By P. P. Howe. New York: Mitchell Kennerley.

I

Synge was for a considerable portion of his life practically as well as theoretically a tramp. We know that he was born at Rathfarnham, near Dublin, in 1871, and that he passed through Trinity College. Then the door is almost closed upon his occupations till 1898-9, when he was called from abroad to take part in the new movement in Ireland. Yet we are permitted to catch one significant glimpse of a poverty-stricken, silent, rather morose young man in ill health, who has left his native land and is apparently seeking to escape from his memories in aimless wanderings among alien people and alien modes of thought. His first wayfaring was in Germany, where Heine was perhaps the will-o'-the-wisp to his feet, but all roads lead the literary vagabond ultimately to Paris, and when he had made his pilgrimages, he brought up in the Latin Quarter. 'Before I met him,' says Mr. Yeats, 'he had wandered over much of Europe, listening to stories in the Black Forest, making friends with servants and with poor people, and this from an esthetic interest, for he had gathered no statistics, had no money to give, and *cared nothing for the wrongs* of the poor, being content to pay for the pleasure of eye and ear with a tune upon the fiddle.'

Synge's transformation from a tramp into an Irishman of letters his sponsors represent to us as a kind of modern miracle. But they can preserve this air of mystery only by insisting that the return to Ireland meant an abrupt break and a fresh beginning rather than the natural evolution of his career — only, in short, by maintaining that what is clearly illuminating is wholly irrelevant. Now about 1895 Synge installed himself in solitary lodgings in Paris and undertook to prepare himself to be a 'critic of French literature from the French point of view.' At this point our authorities diverge, and Mr. Yeats executes a bit of skilful and characteristic legerdemain. He lifts the curtain in the garret of the Latin Quarter some four years later and discovers the author of two or three poor poems studying the works of Racine. George Moore, on the other hand, says explicitly that Synge was writing indifferent impressionistic criticisms of Lemaître and Anatole France. There is no necessary conflict between these two reports, but there is a noticeable difference of emphasis. Between Synge and Racine I should never attempt to establish any affinity. But between Anatole France and Synge? — that is quite another matter. For the discreet discoverer of the new poet admits that he found Synge 'full of that kind of morbidity that has its root in too much brooding over methods of expression, and ways of looking upon life which come, not out of life, but out of literature.' Was that Mr. Yeats's covert way of confessing that Synge was steeped in Anatole France? This, at any rate, can be established: Synge's point of view in comedy is identical with that of Anatole France. Despite the Frenchman's vastly greater range of culture, the two men are absolutely at one in their aloof, pyrrhonic irony and their homeless laughter — the laughter of men who have wandered all the highways of the world and have found no abiding city.

Mr. Yeats, who is crammed with convictions and constitutionally incapable of understanding this desperate and smiting skepticism — no one, I think, asserts that Synge acquired his humor from the Dublin singers — Mr. Yeats gives a puzzled account of Synge's ideas which unintentionally confirms our conjecture. Synge had, he tells us, 'no obvious ideal'; he seemed 'unfitted to think a political thought'; he looked on Catholic and Protestant alike with amused indifference; all which comes down to us from education, and all the earnest contentions of the day excited his irony; 'so far as casual eye could see,' he had 'little personal will.' This description of moral and volitional prostration would be applied with hardly an alteration to Anatole France. And it should help put to rest the legend of the joyous Synge, bounding over the hills with the glad, wild life of the unspoiled barbarian. There are passages in the *Aran Islands,* to be sure, which reveal high nervous excitement induced by conflict with the elements. But there are also clear indications of chronic weariness and low vitality. In the grim humor of his little narrative, *Under Ether,* there is something more than a manly resolution in the face of death; there is in it the nonchalance of one who has long made death his familiar.

II

Synge's verse is what we should expect of a rather despondent young Bohemian, unsure of himself, and seeking among other poets food and forms for his melancholy. I wish to tarry for a moment upon his small collection of poems and translations, partly because, though little known, it is intrinsically interesting, and partly because it reveals so clearly on a small scale the nature of his literary talent. The poems are due to the influence of various masters — to Burns, Wordsworth, Swinburne, and, notably, to that fascinating outlaw, Maistre François Villon. In about one-third of them he sings of death, and in nearly all of them there is a distinguishable echo of some earlier singer.

In the poem, 'To the Oaks of Glencree,' to take a single example, we notice how Maistre Villon helps him shape and round out the first pure impulse of lyric exultation:

My arms are round you, and I lean
Against you, while the lark
Sings over us, and golden lights and green
Shadows are on your bark.
There'll come a season when you'll stretch
Black boards to cover me;
Then in Mount Jerome I will lie, poor
    wretch,
With worms eternally.

The startling and paradoxical fact about this collection is that the original poems constantly remind us of some one else; the translations alone seem unmistakably Synge's. The original poems have the merits of skilful literary imitation. They might have been written, however, by Stevenson or Lang or by Mr. Edmund Gosse, or by half a dozen other cultivators of old French verse. But neither Mr. Gosse nor Lang nor Stevenson could have written a line of the poem that follows:

Are you bearing in mind that time when there was a fine look out of your eyes, and yourself, pleased and thoughtful, were going up the boundaries that are set to childhood? That time the quiet rooms, and the lanes about the house, would be noisy with your songs that were never tired out; the time you'd be sitting down with some work that is right for women, and well pleased with the hazy coming times you were looking out at in your own mind.

May was sweet that year, and it was pleasantly you'd pass that day.
Then I'd leave my pleasant studies, and the paper I had smudged with ink where I would be spending the better part of the day, and cock my ears from the sill of my father's house, till I'd hear the sound of your voice, or of your loom when your hands moved quickly. It's then I would set store of the quiet sky and the lanes and little places, and the sea was far away in one place and the high hills in another.
There is no tongue will tell till the judgment what I feel in myself those times.

Here are all the peculiar marks of Synge himself — the irresistibly quaint idiom, the drifting rhythm, the loose sentence structure, thought thrown out after thought, as it were, without premeditation, and blossoming from phrase to phrase, the window opened upon a mist of vague and limitless emotion, the poignant and adorable Celtic wistfulness: while, as a matter of fact, these lines are a tolerably close translation of the first half of Leopardi's 'Silva.' We are here in the presence of a pure miracle of that style which is Synge's special creation, and which distinguishes him not merely from Leopardi, but also from all his Anglo-Irish contemporaries. With all its apparent spontaneity, his style is as patiently and cunningly wrought out as the style of Walter Pater — wrought of a scrupulously select vocabulary, idiom, and images, with an exacting ear controlling the cadence and shepherding the roving and dreamy phrases. With the aid of this perfected instrument he is able to appropriate and seal as his own poems from authors as diverse as Petrarch and Walter von der Vogelweide, Leopardi and Villon. This fact, taken together with his dependence on the original poems, tends to justify a search beneath the surface of his other work for alien forces secretly shaping his emotions and determining his forms.

III

The orthodox method of 'explaining' Synge is to ignore the poems and translations and point to the volume on the Aran Islands. This is the record, we are told, of Synge's literary salvation; here lies the key to the dramas. In other words, we are asked to believe that Mr. Yeats's theory of poetry has been demonstrated. A stranded Irishman living gloomily in Paris without ideal and almost without ideas is sent to a little group of lonely islands to the southwest of Galway, inhabited by stolid fisher-folk in a very backward state of culture. He spends part of every year there — we pass over the fact that the other part is spent in Paris — wearing the rawhide shoes of the natives, warming his blood with their fires and their poteen, living in their kitchens, hearing their legends, and sharing in their noble primitive customs till the folk passion streams through him and makes him a genius. If any one is skeptical, we point to the fact that something like the 'germ' of two or three of Synge's plays is actually present here in the form of jottings on folk story and belief. Now, this is a delightfully simple recipe for making a genius. If this were the whole truth, one might agree without reservation with one of the reviewers who declares that the *Aran Islands* is of 'vast importance as throwing light on this curious development,' and who adds that it 'is like no other book we have ever read.'

When I first read the *Aran Islands,* I thought of that much-experienced vagabond and subtle exploiter of exotic and primitive cultures, Pierre Loti; and I have learned recently with some satisfaction, from a foot-note in Mr. Howe's book, that 'Synge thought Pierre Loti "the best living writer of prose."' And when I found Synge comparing conditions in the Aran Islands to a disadvantage with what he had seen in his rambles in Brittany, I thought of Anatole le Braz and all his charming studies of the songs and superstitions and customs and characters of that other Celtic people. And then there drifted into my remembrance the pensive face of another wanderer and exile, half-Irish and half-Greek, known in the Orient as Koizumi Yakumo, and in the Western world as Lafcadio Hearn. As I turned once more the pages of his book on Japan and ran through the *Life and Letters,* glancing at his Eastern costume and at the almond eyes of his sons, I reflected that he, at any rate, had possessed the courage to realize the dreams of his favorite author, Théophile Gautier, and the Oriental reveries of Victor Hugo. Finally, I opened the book of Chateaubriand, great father of them all, and read: 'When he arrived among the Natchez, René had been obliged, in order to conform to the customs of the Indians, to take a wife, but he did not live with her. A melancholy disposition drew him to the depths of the forest; there he passed whole days alone, and seemed a savage among the savages.'

The attitude, the point of view — that is the question about this Irishman and his book on the Aran Islands. Que diable allait-il faire dans cette galère? Now, it is an essential error to imagine that when Synge passed from the Latin Quarter to the Aran Islands he was returning to his own people. He never desired to return to his own people. He went to this group of islands, and then to the most remote and backward of them, because he wished to escape into a perfectly strange and virgin environment.

The peculiar charm of the *Aran Islands* and other books of its class consists not in the identification of the narrator with the life of the people whom he describes, but rather in accentuating the contrast between the sophisticated son of the cities and the simple barbarian. It is the esthetic charm of looking upon illusions through the eyes of the disillusioned. In the earlier examples of this *genre* the sense of the sundering gulf is emphasized by bringing the weary heir of all the ages into sentimental relations with a 'noble' female savage — an unspoiled daughter of the wilderness. But the sentiment now smacks of the romanticism of the old school. In the various books in which Pierre Loti pictures his exotic amours, you may trace the declension of the lovely and beloved barbarian into a mere transitory symbol of the 'soul' of the land in which she is found. In the *Mariage de Loti,* for example, there is still a breath of strange passion for the poor Samoan girl, yet the lover comments as follows: 'In truth, we were children of two natures, widely sundered and diverse, and the union of our souls could be only transitory, incomplete, and troubled.' But in that most heartlessly beautiful book in contemporary literature, *Madame Chrysanthème,* the breath of passion has given way to sheer nervous disgust. With the little yellow poupée, Loti has nothing in common, not even an emotion. As he takes pains to point out in the dedication to the Duchesse de Richelieu, though Madame Chrysanthème seems to have the longest rôle, it is certain that the three principal personages are: 'Moi, le Japon et l'Effet que ce pays m'a produit,' 'Myself, Japan, and the Effect which that country produces in me '— the bitter perfume which a crushed chrysanthemum of Nagasaki exhales for the nostrils of a disillusioned Academician.

Essentially Synge was seeking the same thing — the perfume which the Aran Islands could yield to a disillusioned Irish-Parisian. He, too, has transferred the sentiment, which was formerly attached to the fair savage, to the land itself. Despite his apparent solicitude for realistic detail, it is the subjective soul of the islands that he is striving to capture. His book, like Loti's, is pieced together of short impressionistic sketches which are related to one another only through the mood of the author. 'It is only in the intonation of a few sentences,' he writes, 'or some fragment of melody that I catch the real spirit of the island, for in general the men sit together and talk of the tides and fish, and of the price of kelp in Connemara.' The traditional lovely savage has here suffered a further declension into a peasant girl in her teens towards whom only a friendly attachment exists. Yet this girl, like her famous predecessors, becomes the symbol of what he has come to seek: 'At one moment she is a simple peasant, at another she seems to be looking out at the world with a sense of prehistoric disillusion and to sum up in the expression of her gray-blue eyes the whole external despondency of the clouds and sea.' And after he has talked to her of the 'men who live alone in Paris,' he notes that 'below the sympathy we feel there is still a chasm between us.' I do not wish to push this parallelism farther than it goes. In the Aran Islands the Moi, as well as the maiden, is subdued almost beyond comparison. But both men, like all the children of Chateaubriand, avail themselves of picturesque exotic scenes as a kind of sounding chamber to enlarge and reverberate the lyric cry of their own weariness in civilized life and their loneliness out of it.

IV

Synge's dramas are all sad, tragedies and comedies alike, because they are all based upon a radical and hopeless disillusion. In them the native lyrical impulse, which in the poems we found checked by the cynicism of Villon, and which in the Aran Islands expanded under the influence of Loti, is again checked and controlled by the irony of Anatole France. This is no doubt a bald and over-emphatic way of putting the case, but it may serve to indicate the general modes in which foreign forces determined his talent. Synge has been praised by many critics on the ground that he has reconciled poetry with life. In the sense that he has broken through the old 'poetic diction' and invented a new poetic dialect with a fresh savor of earth in it, this is doubtless true. But in a profounder sense it is nearer the truth to say that he has widened the rift that was between them. For the drift of all his work is to emphasize the eternal hostility between a harsh and repugnant world of facts controlled by law, and the inviting realm of a lawless imagination. In one of the longest of his plays, The Well of the Saints, this idea becomes perfectly explicit. Two blind beggars who have long pleased themselves with thinking of each other's beauty are, through a miracle, restored to sight. But the vision of 'things as they are' is so hideous that they fall into a violent hatred of each other. And they are both so thankful when they go blind again that they reject with scorn the holy man's offer to repeat the miracle. This is perhaps the most elaborate expression of an idea in all Synge's works, and one is not surprised to learn that four years before The Well of the Saints there was performed and printed in Paris a 'Chinese' play by M. George Clemenceau, called the Voile du Bonheur, which contains identically the same idea, and which, as Mr. Howe concedes, it is 'perfectly probable' that Synge knew.

For us The Well of the Saints is significant only as illustrating with especial clearness that profound sense of disillusion which underlies all Synge's eccentric comedies, and constitutes, as I have said, his point of contact with Anatole France. The most France-like comedy that he ever conceived was never written, but the scenario is reported to us by Mr. Yeats. 'Two women, a Protestant and a Catholic, take refuge in a cave, and there quarrel about religion, abusing the Pope or Henry VIII, but in low voices, for the one fears to be ravished by the soldiers, the other by the rebels. At last one woman goes out because she would sooner any fate than such wicked company.' Now it is just this homeless elfishness of his mirth that distinguishes Synge from Jonson and Molière and Congreve, with whose names his has been so fearlessly coupled. In all the classical comedy of the world one is made aware of the seat whence the laughing spirit sallies forth to scourge the vices or sport with the follies and affectations of men. When the play is over, something has been accomplished towards the clarification of one's feelings and ideas; after the comic catharsis, illusions dissolve and give way to a fresh vision of what is true and permanent and reasonable. Synge's comedies end in a kind of ironical bewilderment. His, indeed, is outlaw comedy with gipsy laughter coming from somewhere in the shrubbery by the roadside, pealing out against church and state, and man and wife, and all the ordinances of civil life.

It is not that many of the *dramatis personæ* are vagrants, but that the dramatist himself is in secret heart a vagrant, and his inmost vision of felicity is a purposeless vagabondage. What are the passages in these plays that all the critics delight to quote, and that the playgoer carries home from the theater — fragments of them — singing in his memory? They are the passages in which some queen or beggar, touched with lyric ecstasy, expresses a longing to go roaming down the open road or into the wilderness. You will find this gipsy call in every one of Synge's dramas except *The Riders to the Sea.* Even to that piece built of the heroic stuff of the bards, *Deirdre of the Sorrows,* he gives the same turn: here it is a wondrously fair woman scorning a share in sovereignty and the high king of Ulster to go salmon-spearing and vagabonding with the sons of Naisi. To this man in whose vision of joy we are invited to participate, life presents itself in its comic aspects as a juxtaposition and irreconcilable opposition of hideous realities and hopeless dreams, dreams like the glens of Neifin in the dews of night, realities like Old Mahon in the potato field — 'He was a dirty man, God forgive him.'

What, then, shall we say of his tragedy? Those who are sealed of the tribe of Synge speak high praise of *The Riders to the Sea,* that picture of the drear old woman who has lost all her sons. As Mr. Edward O'Brien declares in the preface printed in the collective edition, this drama is set in the atmosphere of universal action; it holds the 'timeless peace' that passeth all understanding. This were vision, indeed. It is a noble phrase, this 'timeless peace.' It connotes in my imagination the serene enduring forever of victorious heroes and saints who have passed out of tribulation. It is not, at any rate, an empty euphemism for annihilation, but a state in which those of the living dwell who, like the Stoic emperor, have caught a vision of the central beauty and abiding harmony in all the works of God. It is the mood in which all high tragedy leaves us; the still elation into which we rise when blind Œdipus answers the call of the god; the 'calm of mind, all passion spent' with which we are dismissed by that superb last chorus in 'Samson Agonistes,' beginning,

All is best, though oft we doubt
What the unsearchable dispose
Of Highest Wisdom brings about.

Such, they tell us, is the atmosphere of *Riders to the Sea.* It is like *Lear,* it is like Greek tragedy; it is not, as they hasten with somewhat suspicious eagerness to say — it is not like Maeterlinck's *Home* or *The Intruder.* Synge certainly does differ from Maeterlinck in two striking respects. While the Belgian 'mystic' deprives his persons of personality and locality and confers a kind of demonic personality upon death, the naturalistic Irishman steeps his lines in personality and the reek of the gray sky and the smell of the sea, and he represents death, in spite of the premonitions of Maurya, as only the old dark way of nature. But so far as what the Germans call the 'inner form' is concerned, Synge gives us simply an Irish transposition of Maeterlinck. Strictly speaking, *Riders to the Sea* is not a tragedy at all, because it is not a drama. It might with more propriety be called a tragic idyl — a sombre picture, impressive enough in its kind, with the fearful whispering of the young girls, whose necks have not yet bowed beneath the ancient burden, and the gray broken old mother, who looks before and after and has passed through all illusions, sitting there patiently, passively, receiving the tidings of disaster. Protagonist in the proper sense of the word there is none; no act of the will turning against destiny as a token of human participation in that divine energy into which death resumes us all. It is this turning of the will that makes just the difference between what is drama and what is not; and between the mood with which Samson in Gaza affects us when he says, 'And I shall shortly be with them that rest,' and the mood with which Maurya affects us when she says, 'No man at all can be living forever, and we must be satisfied.' It is the difference between Milton looking into the timeless peace and Synge looking into the noisome grave. We heard him before crying aloud under the golden lights of the oaks of Glencree that in the end black boards would cover him and he should lie with worms eternally. Just that is the tragic vision and significance of *The Riders to the Sea*.

 VII

GEORGE BERNARD SHAW

HARLEQUIN OR PATRIOT?

JOHN PALMER

[*Century Magazine*, March, 1915. By permission.]

The first fallacy is that Bernard Shaw is an immensely public person; that he is a sort of twentieth-century Grand Monarch who, if manners allowed, would dine like Louis XIV in the presence of the people and receive the press in his dressing-gown. Now, it is true that Bernard Shaw has been photographed by Alvin Langdon Coburn without a stitch; that at one period of his career he almost lived upon a public platform; that he invariably tells us the private history of each of his books and plays; that, partly from a sense of fun, and partly from a determination that what he has seriously to say shall be heard, he talks and writes a good deal about himself; and that he has allowed Mr. Archibald Henderson to compile a sort of concordance to his personality.

Nevertheless, it is not true that Bernard Shaw is an immensely public person. Or perhaps I should put it this way: Bernard Shaw whom the public knows is not an authenic revelation of the extremely private gentleman who lives in Adelphi Terrace. The Bernard Shaw whom the public knows might more accurately be described as a screen. What the public knows about Bernard Shaw is either trivial or misleading. Thus the public knows that Bernard Shaw can read diamond type with his left eye at a distance of twenty-eight inches; that he can hear a note the pitch of which does not exceed 30,000 vibrations per second; that, when he sits down upon a chair, the distance between the crown of his head and the seat is 3 feet 1.8 inches. These things are trivial. Or the public knows that Bernard Shaw is a very striking and provocative writer of plays, that he is also a socialist and a vegetarian; and these things are misleading.

That is why any satisfactory account of Bernard Shaw rendered to those who have allowed themselves to be deceived by common fame must necessarily take the form of a schedule of popular fallacies. Such a schedule will at any rate be found more useful, and certainly less hackneyed, than a personal 'interview' and description of one who has been more often photographed and handled in the picturesque and familiar way of the expert pressman than the most popular member of the British Cabinet. Perhaps, therefore, I may regard myself as excused from accurately sketching the wicket-gate which leads to Bernard Shaw's private dwelling, or from telling the story of his velvet coat, or from recording the number of times he has been met upon the top of an omnibus (where he used virtually to live), or betraying what he writes to young people in confidence about the nose of a celebrated author.

Intimate revelations of this kind do not take the public far. They do not seriously disturb the inaccessible privacy which Bernard Shaw has always contrived to maintain. The truth is that the authentic author of *Man and Superman* has never really been interviewed; has never really 'plucked me ope his doublet and offered them his throat to cut' to visitors who are likely to be hiding a kodak under their coat or to be surreptitiously fingering a note-book. Bernard Shaw of the interviews and the funny stories is public enough; but this Bernard Shaw is almost entirely a legend. Before this legend gets as firm a hold upon New York as it has upon London, it may be well to number some of the more striking fallacies of which it is composed. There is only one serious drawback to this method of approach, and this drawback vanishes almost as soon as it is explained. Exploding popular fallacies is disagreeable work, and it usually gives to the sentences of the author engaged upon it an air of quarreling violently with his readers and with his subject.

Such is not the intention or mood of this present article. I have an immense enthusiasm and liking for Bernard Shaw and for the greater part of most of what Bernard Shaw has written. I claim, indeed, to admire Bernard Shaw for sounder and weightier reasons than have yet occurred to Bernard Shaw himself. These reasons will be presented later in a postscript of appreciation. When the worst fallacies regarding Bernard Shaw have been briefly described and contradicted (it would require a large volume to describe and contradict them in detail), I shall be in a better position to assert, briefly again, wherein Bernard Shaw's genius truly consists; exactly how serious he is; and, more particularly, why he has just written a pamphlet about the war, and why he ought not to have done so. Meantime I hope that readers of this article will agree to digest the fallacies and to wait for the postscript; also to believe that my habitually indignant manner is simply the result of writing regularly about the British theater.

The first fallacy is already declared; namely, that Bernard Shaw is a public person. The second fallacy is that Bernard Shaw is an easy and profitable subject to write about. He is not. It is true that Bernard Shaw's interviews with the press are the best interviews, and that he invariably galvanizes the dullest of his appreciators into liveliness. Pronounce the name of Bernard Shaw in almost any company, and immediately every one perks up with an epigram or a paradox or an anecdote. Bernard Shaw, like *Falstaff*, is not only witty himself; he is the occasion that wit is in other men.

Nevertheless, Bernard Shaw is not a good subject. It is not encouraging to embark upon an enterprise with the sure knowledge that the thing has been done before and better done. Bernard Shaw is not a good subject because he has already been exhausted. There is not more than one expert upon Bernard Shaw. Every one professionally required to write about Bernard Shaw sets out under an unfortunate sense that the ground has already been covered; that the job has already been done brilliantly, thoroughly, and finally.

The best essays on the work of Bernard Shaw, the most impartial, authoritative, and penetrating, are by Bernard Shaw himself. The best stories about Bernard Shaw, whether they are the cruel, illuminating anecdotes which delight the envious, or the flashes of resource and honesty which are cherished by his friends and admirers, are once again by Bernard Shaw himself. Should you set out to extol or to advertise Bernard Shaw, you know that this has already been done with incomparable energy and talent, and that it has been done by one who knows. Should you, on the other hand, set out to expose or pull to tatters the reputation and character of Bernard Shaw, again you know that you are the merest amateur compared with G. B. S.; know also that, if you want to do the business effectively, and leave Bernard Shaw obviously for dead on the field of controversy, you will have to call in G. B. S. to help you. It is possible to slay Bernard Shaw; but it is possible to slay him only in alliance with himself. It is a joke of the two hemispheres that Bernard Shaw better understands his merits than any one else in the world. It is a finer joke, and not so threadworn, that he better understands his limitations. Either way, whether you are celebrating his genius or asserting your position as the candid friend, you are forced to acknowledge at the last that your researches into Bernard Shaw are simply not in the same class with his own either in intimacy (which is surprising in an age when the press is often more intimate with a man than his own tooth-brush); in detachment and absence of favor (which, again, is surprising, in an age when men of letters take themselves very seriously); or in a severely just recognition of the subject's merit (more surprising still in an age when public men carefully cultivate a reputation for modesty).

SHAW NOT AN ORIGINAL THINKER

The third fallacy is that Bernard Shaw is a profoundly original thinker and a propagandist of absolutely new ideas. He has repeatedly told his readers and his friends that he is nothing of the kind.

His biographer somewhere quotes him as saying, 'I am an expert picker of men's brains, and I have been extremely fortunate in my friends.' Nor need we go to Bernard Shaw's biographer for this. Bernard Shaw has spent half his life in telling the world the exact scientific truth about himself, and of course the world has refused to believe him. It is hardly exaggeration to say that whenever Bernard Shaw tells people soberly and honestly exactly the sort of man he is, and exactly the kind of work he has done, they laugh heartily, and say that Bernard Shaw is a very funny and inventive person. Similarly, whenever he ventures into fun and fiction, his hearers insist upon taking him as seriously as they would take a prophet.

It follows that Bernard Shaw, who is a modest, conscientious, kindly, industrious, and well-read man of letters, is commonly regarded as a reckless firebrand who lives by the cart and the trumpet, is up to his neck in all that is lawless and improper, is without compassion or shame, speaks always in paradoxes, and claims to be greater than Shakespeare. Not fewer than fourteen years ago Bernard Shaw told the world that he was an elderly gentleman who had made an immense reputation by being the best of a bad lot and by plagiarizing the English classics. He really meant what he said; but the preface in which he said it is still supposed to be the *locus classicus* of his claim to supersede the author of *Macbeth*. Here, again, it is impossible to say of Bernard Shaw any true thing he has not already said of himself. He has repeatedly urged his critics and followers to reject utterly the legend of G. B. S. 'I find myself,' Bernard Shaw wrote in 1900, 'while still in middle life almost as legendary a person as the *Flying Dutchman*. Critics, like other people, see what they look for, not what is actually before them. In my plays they look for my legendary qualities, and find originality and brilliancy in my most hackneyed claptrap. Were I to republish Buckstone's *Wreck Ashore* as my latest comedy, it would be hailed as a masterpiece of perverse paradox and scintillating satire.'

Nothing in modern literary history is more remarkable than the reputation of G. B. S. for original and daring speculation; and no one, myself possibly excepted, more thoroughly appreciates the funny side of G. B. S. as philosopher than the man to whom this reputation is so persistently attached. Five years ago I came to London burdened with the classic wisdom of an ancient university. I had read some philosophy in one school and some economy in another. As a musician I had read Wagner for a venerable classic. As the merest Philistine in connoisseurship, I recognized in Rodin a great sculptor of the last generation, as firmly established in immortality as Michelangelo, and I saluted in the New English Art Club a thoroughly respectable academy of painting. As a playgoer destined to succeed Max Beerbohm, who himself in remote antiquity had succeeded G. B. S. on the *Saturday Review,* I had become weary of Ibsen, and had begun to wonder why Granville Barker seemed old enough to be my uncle. Now, I do not regard myself as being in the least in advance of my time; yet when I came to London I found that Bernard Shaw, who still preached Ibsen and Wagner, who spoke with Rodin as a contemporary, who preached a philosophy which was already introduced into examination-papers at a place not suspected of modernism, who talked economy out of university text-books which it was a scholarly and pedantic exercise to confute in the lecture-rooms of Oxford — that this thoroughly safe, orthodox, and almost medieval Bernard Shaw was being received by the literary societies and the press of London as an original and revolutionary thinker. I then began to understand why Bernard Shaw has very little respect for some of his contemporaries.

THE 'BETTER THAN SHAKESPEARE' FALLACY

This brings us to the fourth fallacy. The fourth fallacy is that Bernard Shaw has made enormous and extravagant claims for himself as a critic, philosopher, sociologist, and dramatist. Let us take a passage of Bernard Shaw's preface to the *Plays for Puritans*. It is the famous 'Better than Shakespeare' passage, the foundation of a public charge that George Bernard Shaw thinks too highly of himself. It is a conclusive proof that he does nothing of the kind. It harks back to our second fallacy:

My stories are the old stories; my characters are the familiar harlequin and columbine, clown and pantaloon (note the harlequin's leap in the third act of *Cæsar and*

Cleopatra); my stage tricks and suspenses and thrills and jests are the ones in vogue when I was a boy, by which time my grandfather was tired of them. . . . It is a dangerous thing to be hailed at once, as a few rash admirers have hailed me, as above all things original; what the world calls originality is only an unaccustomed method of tickling it. Meyerbeer seemed prodigiously original to the Parisians, when he first burst on them. Today he is only the crow who followed Beethoven's plow. I am a crow who have followed many plows. No doubt I seem prodigiously clever to those who have never hopped hungry and curious across the fields of philosophy, politics and art. Karl Marx said of Stuart Mill that his eminence was due to the flatness of the surrounding country. In these days of Board Schools, universal reading, newspapers and the inevitable ensuing demand for notabilities of all sorts, literary, military, political and fashionable, to write paragraphs about, that sort of eminence is within the reach of very moderate ability. Reputations are cheap nowadays.

Who, after that, will say that Bernard Shaw has in him a particle of author's conceit? He has never claimed more than is due to him. There is not the least evidence of vanity or self-importance in the printed work of George Bernard Shaw, there is even less in his speeches, letters (the private letters of George Bernard Shaw will be his masterpiece when, and if, they ever come to be published), conversation, or general demeanor. It is true that he has frequently and vigorously claimed not to be entirely foolish, and that sometimes he has insisted that he really does know what he is writing about. But it is also true that no critic has more persistently assured the public that there is nothing really important or new in any of the ideas and devices which so curiously amazed the first audiences of his early plays. Has he not soberly assured the American public that 'the novelties of one generation are only the resuscitated fashions of the generation before last'? And has he not proved this with instances out of *The Devil's Disciple?* Did he not prophesy that a few years would expose that play for 'the threadbare popular melodrama it technically is'? Nevertheless, though it is possible for any one read in the works of Bernard Shaw to parallel these instances of self-assessment from almost any volume, pamphlet, speech, or anecdote of his life, the belief still rules that Bernard Shaw is too highly appreciated by Bernard Shaw. The truth is that Bernard Shaw has had to expend vast stores of energy and time in reproving his friends for thinking too much of him and in snubbing the worship of his followers. He has had continually to explain to the superior socialists that he is not really a great orator; to the dramatic critics that he is not really the greatest dramatist who ever lived; to men of science that he is not the erudite physician they have imagined from *The Doctor's Dilemma* and not the expert in acoustics they have inferred from *Pygmalion;* to distracted heads of families that he is not in the least qualified to tell them how to control their marriageable daughters. Bernard Shaw has worked harder to escape the greatness which is thrust upon him than many of his contemporaries have worked to achieve wealth and a blue ribbon; and the harder he has worked, the more he has convinced the public has become that he is an incorrigibly insolent and pertinacious champion of his title to be infallible.

It is essential to get this notion of Bernard Shaw as the *miles gloriosus* corrected at the start, otherwise we shall never handle the key to his achievement. You will ask how it has arisen. It has arisen simply and inevitably from the fact that Bernard Shaw was for many years of his life a professional critic, and that he was by nature able to regard himself and his own performances with complete detachment. Naturally, when he came to write plays, and found that the said plays were incompetently criticized, he used his native gift for regarding himself impartially, and his acquired skill as a professional critic, to inform his readers exactly how good and how bad his plays really were. Hence he has acquired a reputation for vainglory, for it is a rooted idea with some people that a man who talks about himself is necessarily vainglorious.

Bernard Shaw's detached and disinterested observation of his own career and achievements is not within the power of the average man of letters. It was accordingly misunderstood. Not every one can discuss his own work as though it were the work of a stranger. The self-criticism of Bernard Shaw, read as a whole, shows an amazing literary altruism. It shows exactly how far he is from consenting to occupy the throne into which he has been thrust. Bernard Shaw, in his prefaces, is not a prophet claiming inspiration for his script; he is one of the crowd that reads and judges for itself; only he reads and judges a little more closely and severely than the rest. Bernard Shaw's modesty — his curious aloofness from his own fame — is the more attractive in that it is absolutely innocent of stage-management. There are men who have made corners in retirement — men of whom it is at once exclaimed how humble and unspoiled they are. Shrewd observers will always suspect the man of letters who is famous for his modesty; who seems to think it positively indecent that his face should be seen; who has always 'just left the theater' when there is a call to be taken; who has a reputation for inaccessibility. Bernard Shaw, of course, is entirely free of this organized and blushing humility. His very real modesty consists in his being able to assess himself correctly. He is one of the few living authors who has not been taken in by his own performances. It does not occur to him to divide the literature of the day into (a) the works of Bernard Shaw and (b) other people's works. He thinks of *Man and Superman* as he thinks of *The Silver Box*. It is a play of contemporary interest and of some merit, and he does not see why he should be barred from discussing it as an expert critic just because he happens to be the author. Bernard Shaw has certainly imposed upon many of his friends and observers. He has not imposed upon himself.

SHAW NOT A JESTER

The fifth fallacy is that Bernard Shaw is an incorrigible jester, that he is never serious, that he is ready to sacrifice his best friend and his firmest conviction for the sake of a really good joke. Now, the first thing to realize about Bernard Shaw is his overflowing gravity. He has taken more things seriously in his career than any living and notable person. He has taken music seriously, and painting and socialism and philosophy and politics and public speaking. He has taken the trouble to make up his mind upon scores of things to which the average heedless man hardly gives a second thought — things like diet, hygiene, vaccination, phonetic spelling, and vivisection. He has even taken seriously the English theater, unlike virtually every other English man of letters who has had anything to do with it. Compare for a moment the conduct of Bernard Shaw at a rehearsal of one of his own plays with the conduct, say, of Barrie. Barrie is happy so long as no one takes any notice of him. He has so immense a disdain for the minutiæ of theatrical production that he would rather write ten plays than control the rehearsal of one. Bernard Shaw, on the other hand, with the amazing industry of a really serious person, turns up with a closely written volume of notes, determining down to the minutest detail where, how, and when his company shall deliver their lines and do their necessary 'business.' It is only because Bernard Shaw is so immensely serious that he can be so tremendously casual and brilliant. He is ready for everything and everybody because he has seriously considered everything and seriously regarded everybody. A first-rate impromptu usually indicates a mind richly stored and well arranged. Bernard Shaw can extemporize on most subjects because he has seriously thought about them. The more brilliantly he sparkles upon a given theme, the more sober has been his education in its rudiments. Unfortunately, many people have come to exactly the opposite conclusion. Because Bernard Shaw has a rapid and vital way of writing, because he presents his argument at a maximum, seasons it with boisterous analogies, and frequently drives it home at the point of a hearty joke, he is suspected of sacrificing sense to sound. The dancing of his manner conceals the severe decorum of his matter. It is true that Bernard Shaw can be funny, but it is wholly false that he is in the least a flippant writer or a careless thinker. He is as serious as Praise-God Barebones and as careful as Octavius Cæsar.

HIS REPUTATION OF REASON

The sixth fallacy has to do with the all-head-and-no-heart formula. It is said of Bernard Shaw by some very excellent critics that he is an expert logician arguing *in vacuo,* that he has exalted reason as a god, that his mind is a wonderful machine which never goes wrong because its owner is not swayed by the ordinary passions, likes, prejudices, sentiments, impulses, infatuations, enthusiasms, and weaknesses of ordinary mankind. How the critics square this notion of Bernard Shaw with the kind friend and counselor who lives in Adelphi Terrace they alone can tell. It is probably this idea of Bernard Shaw which most heartily tickles him. Bernard Shaw greatly enjoys contemplating the motley crowd of his legendary selves; but none can please him more thoroughly — because none could be more outrageously fictitious — than Bernard Shaw the vivisector of his kind, the high priest of reason and common sense.

This last superstition has grown mainly out of the simple fact that G. B. S. as a critic of music, art, and the drama was actually a critic. He took his criticism as seriously as he took his socialism or his conviction that tobacco was a noxious weed. Being a serious critic, he found it necessary to tell the truth concerning the artistic achievements of many sensitive and amiable young people. Naturally, Bernard Shaw got the reputation of being a heartless brute for his candor, and a logical brute, owing to the soundness of his arguments. Then, when Bernard Shaw came to write plays, it was discovered that his young women behaved like reasonable creatures and that his young men appreciated the importance of 5 per cent. This was unusual in the soft, romantic stage creatures of the late nineties; so here was more evidence of Bernard Shaw's insensibility, of his arid and merciless rationalism, of his impenetrable indifference to all that warms the blood of common humanity.

Of course there was not the slightest real evidence of all this. If there is one idea more than another that persists all through the work of Bernard Shaw, and defines his personality, it is to be found in his perpetual repudiation of reason. Almost his whole literary career has been spent in adapting the message of Schopenhauer to his own optimism and belief in the goodness of life. Not reason and not the categories determine or create, but passion and will. Bernard Shaw has always insisted that reason is no motive power; that the true motive power is will; that the setting up of reason above will is a damnable error. Life is the satisfaction of a power in us of which we can give no rational account whatever — that is the final declaration of Bernard Shaw; and his doctrine corresponds with his temperament. Rudyard Kipling has described

the rationalists as men who 'deal with people's insides from the point of view of men who have no stomachs.' Bernard Shaw would agree. No one, in habit or opinion, lives more remotely than Bernard Shaw from the clear, hard, logical, devitalized, and sapless world of Comte and Spencer.

SHAW FAR FROM BEING AN ANARCHIST

The seventh fallacy is that Bernard Shaw is an anarchist, a disturber of the peace, a champion of the right of every man to do as he pleases and to think for himself. This idea of Bernard Shaw is so deeply rooted in the public mind, despite Bernard Shaw's serious and repeated disclaimers of its accuracy, that, if any young person in London runs away from her parents, or if any elderly gentleman abandons his wife and family, these things are not only regarded as the results of Bernard Shaw's pernicious teaching, but their perpetrators are upheld and justified by the belief that they are disciples following the lead of G. B. S. as prophet and master. These startling misconceptions have arisen from the fact that Bernard Shaw has pointed out in a popular play that children do not always agree in all points with their parents, and that he has argued in a less popular play that one or two reforms in the marriage laws of Great Britain are already overdue. Was ever a reputation won upon slenderer evidence? Why, Shakespeare told us three hundred years ago how

The hedge-sparrow fed the cuckoo so long
That it had its head bit off by its young,

and it is now on record in a British bluebook that a committee of the most respectable gentlemen of the British bar and church have agreed with Bernard Shaw that British divorce is unnecessarily expensive, inequitable, and humiliating. The practical extent of Bernard Shaw's anarchism coincides with the anarchism of our judges and our bishops. Those who dig deeper than this, with the preconceived resolution to find that Bernard Shaw is an anarchist, will only be more hopelessly misled. They will find that he preaches, as we have already discovered, the ultimate supremacy of passion and will; that he sees the gods and the laws of each generation as mere expressions of the will and passion of their generation; and that he claims for posterity the right to supersede them as soon as posterity is moved by a higher will and a finer passion. But this is not anarchism. It is so far from being anarchism that side by side with these doctrines Bernard Shaw has, in *The Sanity of Art,* written down one of the best defenses of law and order — of the convenience and necessity of policemen, churches, and all kinds of public authority — that has appeared in popular form within recent years. It is true that Bernard Shaw pleads for liberty, and points out that it is better for a man to act and think responsibly for himself than to run to the nearest constable or parish priest. But it is also true that he wants people to have no more liberty than is good for them, and that he very seriously distrusts the ability of the average man to think for himself. Bernard Shaw knows that the average man has neither the time nor the brains nor the imagination to be original in such matters as crossing the road or getting married or determining whether he ought or ought not to cut the throat of his neighbor.

Nothing could be further from the mind of Bernard Shaw than the philosophic anarchy of Godwin or John Stuart Mill. Bernard Shaw is not an anarchist either in speculation or in practice. He is as sound on the question of law and order as Mr. Asquith. He is as correct in deportment and as regular in his conduct as the Vice-Chancellor of Oxford. The most pictorial way of emphasizing the difference between a real anarchist and Bernard Shaw is to compare the handwriting of Bernard Shaw and, say, of Cunninghame Graham. Bernard Shaw writes like a sensible citizen who intends his pages to be read. It is true that he asserts his individuality as one who values what is comely by writing the most beautiful hand of any author living, just as he insists that his books shall be printed in a style that proclaims him a pupil of William Morris. But he writes mainly to be read, aware that the liberty of writing illegibly is not worth the trouble it would give to a community which practised it. The writing of Cunninghame Graham, on the other hand, requires an expert in caligraphy. It has baffled half the big printing-houses in London. It is the last, insolent assertion that every man has the right to do as he pleases regardless of the discom-

fort and loss of time he thereby inflicts upon his neighbors. It is, in one word, anarchic, a graphic illustration of the great gulf that is fixed between two public figures of the time who, nevertheless, have impartially been described by the careless as anarchists.

SHAW A PRECISIAN RATHER THAN A CARELESS MAN OF LETTERS

The eighth fallacy is that Bernard Shaw is a headlong, dashing, and opinionative writer, without technical equipment, who succeeds by an impudent trust in his unassisted genius, and brings off his best efforts by a happy fluke. This fallacy has stuck to Bernard Shaw all through his career as a critic of music, painting, the drama, as a playwright, as a pamphleteer, as a public speaker. When G. B. S., as Corno di Bassett, was writing about music for a London newspaper, the public insisted that his appointment was a joke. It was the public's own joke, and the public enjoyed it immensely. Indeed, it chuckled so heartily that G. B. S. had not the malice to undeceive it. He played with this popular legend of himself, as he has so often played with a hundred others. He was thought to be merely a rude young man who knocked the professors' heads together without the least idea of what they contained. Bernard Shaw's characteristic confutation of this public error was to reduce it to absurdity. When people handed him a score, he held it carefully upside down and studied it in that position. When he was asked to play the piano, he walked to the wrong end. Bernard Shaw's conduct as a critic of music, acting under provocation, was very natural; but it was in the result unfortunate. Popularly imagined to be an irresponsible amateur with a literary knack, Bernard Shaw, in all he has undertaken, has, if anything, erred from an excessive knowledge and interest in the expert professional and technical side of his subject. Bernard Shaw knew years ago all about the enormity of exploding undiminished chords of the ninth and thirteenth on the unsuspecting ear, just as today he thoroughly understands the appallingly scientific progressions of Scriabin. Similarly he can tell you the difference at a glance between real sunshine in an open field and the good north light of a Chelsea studio, or explain why 'values' are more difficult to capture when colors are bright than when they are looked for in a dark interior. As to the technic of the theatre — well, the subject is hardly worth discussing. Some of his later plays are nothing if they are not technical.

The fallacy that Bernard Shaw is a happy savage among critics and artists, ignorant and careless of form, unread in the necessary conventions, speaking always at random with the confidence that only a perfect ignorance can give, is particularly deplorable, because it necessarily blinds its adherents to Bernard Shaw's most serious defect both as critic and creator. Usually Bernard Shaw knows too much, rather than too little, of his subject. He is too keenly interested in its bones and its mechanism. His famous distinction between music which is decorative and music which is dramatic is quite unsound, as I would undertake to show in nothing less than a small pamphlet; but it is not the mistake of a critic ignorant of music. It is rather the mistake of a critic too keenly absorbed in the technic of music.

If the professors in the early nineties had objected to G. B. S. because he was liable to lapses into the pedantry of which they themselves were accused, they would have been nearer the mark than they were in foolishly dismissing him as an ignoramus. Similarly, as a dramatic critic, G. B. S. erred not by attaching too little value to the forms and conventions of the theatre, but by attaching too much. It is true that he did not make the absurd mistake of some of his followers, and regard Ibsen as a great dramatist on account of one or two pettifogging and questionable reforms in dramatic convention, such as the abolishing of soliloquies and asides and extra doors to the sitting-room. But he certainly attached too much importance to these things, mainly because he knew so much about them; and this critical insistence of his as a Saturday Reviewer has had its revenge in some of his own plays, where his purely technical mastery of theatrical devices, his stage-cleverness, and craftsman's virtuosity have led him into mechanical horse-play and stock positions unworthy of the author of *John Bull's Other Island* and *Major Barbara*. Bernard Shaw has continually suffered from knowing his subject too well from the angle of the expert, and he has frequently fallen into the mistakes of the expert.

Far from being the happy and careless privateer of popular belief, he is usually to be found struggling for freedom under the oppression of things stored for reference in his capacious memory. The great critic, like any ordinary, unskilled spectator, should be able to look at a work of art without prejudice in favor of any particular form or fashion. It should not matter to him a jot or influence his judgment in the slightest whether the music he hears is symphonic or metrical, whether the thirteenth is exploded as a thirteenth or prepared as a six-four chord. He should be similarly indifferent whether a dramatist talks to him in blank-verse soliloquy or in conversational duologue. Preoccupation with manner, *apart from matter* — usually implying an *a priori* prejudice in favor of one manner over another — is the mark of pedantry; and of this pedantry — always the pedantry of a man who is expert and knows too much — Bernard Shaw is not always free, though he is far too good a critic to be often at fault.

THE REAL SHAW

We have not yet exhausted the popular fallacies about Bernard Shaw, but as most of my readers will already be wondering what is left of the man who has just described Sir Edward Grey as a Junker, I will turn now from George Bernard Shaw, who is as legendary as the *Flying Dutchman,* to the very positive and substantial author of *Commonsense and the War.* I have yet to explain why Bernard Shaw, stripped of his professional masks, and rescued from the misconceptions of his admirers, remains one of the most striking public figures of our day, and must fairly be regarded as the most important apparition in the British theatre since Goldsmith and Sheridan. We have seen that Bernard Shaw is not original in what he preaches, is erudite rather than adventurous, is in no sense revolutionary or anarchical, is extremely serious, and is far from being an orgiastic and impudent rationalist for whom drifting humanity is stuff for a paradox. Bernard Shaw has not won the notice of mankind because he has thought of things which have hitherto occurred to no one else; nor has he won the notice of mankind because he has a native gift of buffoonery and a talent for the stage. The merit of Bernard

Shaw has to be sought outside his doctrine. The secret of his genius lies deeper than his fun, and has scarcely anything to do with his craft.

HIS SELF-CRUSHING CRITICISM

It ironically happens that Bernard Shaw as a critic has virtually made it impossible for those who accept his criticism to allow that Bernard Shaw as a dramatic author has any right to be really famous. We have seen that Bernard Shaw as a critic repeatedly fell into the grievous error of separating the stuff he was criticizing into manner and matter. Thus, confronted with the Elizabethan dramatists, Bernard Shaw always maintained that they had nothing to say and that they were tolerable only because they had an incomparably wonderful way of saying it. Comparing Shakespeare with Ibsen, for example, he would point out that, if you paraphrased Ibsen's *Peer Gynt,* it still remained good intellectual stuff, and that, if you paraphrased Shakespeare's ' Life's but a walking shadow,' it became the merest commonplace. Bernard Shaw thence proceeded to draw the moral that Ibsen, apart from mere favor and prettiness, was the greater and more penetrating dramatist. Fortunately for Bernard Shaw, as we shall shortly realize, this criticism of his is not only false in fact, but it is also nonsense in theory. It is false in fact, because it is quite untrue that Shakespeare paraphrased is commonplace whereas Ibsen paraphrased is an intellectual feast. It would be more to the point if Bernard Shaw had said that Shakespeare paraphrased is commonplace for all time and that Ibsen paraphrased is commonplace for only the nineteenth century. It would be still more to the point if Bernard Shaw had said that it is quite impossible to paraphrase any work of genius in so far as genius has gone to its making. It is absurd to talk of paraphrasing Shakespeare because Shakespeare is of genius all compact; and it is as true of Ibsen as of Shakespeare that, so far as he is a genius and not merely a scientific naturalist, it is absurd to separate what he says from his way of saying it. When Shakespeare has written:

. . . Out, out, brief candle !
Life's but a walking shadow, a poor player

That struts and frets his hour upon the stage
And then is heard no more : it is a tale
Told by an idiot, full of sound and fury,
Signifying nothing,

5 he has written more than the equivalent of ' life is not worth living.' If Bernard Shaw will not admit that Shakespeare in this passage is no more than an utterer of a universal platitude for pessimists, he 10 will have to agree that Ibsen is no more than an utterer of parochial platitude for the suffragette platform. Probably, however, now that Bernard Shaw has himself become a classical author, he has realized 15 that to distinguish between the ideas of a literary genius and the language in which they are expressed is as absurd as to distinguish between the subject of a painter and the way in which it is painted, or be- 20 tween the themes of a musician and the notes in which they are rendered.

At any rate, Bernard Shaw must realize how very badly he himself would fare under such a distinction. We have seen 25 that Bernard Shaw *in doctrine and idea* is in no sense original. His celebration of the state is as old as Plato. His particular sort of puritanism is as old as Cromwell. His particular brand of so- 30 cialism is as old as Owen. A paraphrase of Bernard Shaw — a reduction of Bernard Shaw to the bare bones of his subject matter — would be as intolerable as the speeches of his disciples and some of his 35 masters usually are. In a word, if Bernard Shaw is a genius, he is a genius for the same reason that Shakespeare is a genius. He is a genius not because he has anything new to say, but because he has a 40 passionate and a personal way of saying it. If I had the time to go deeper into this matter, I should like to ask whether it is really possible to get hold of a new idea as distinguished from a new way of 45 presenting an old one. But, at all events, I have already said enough to justify the assumption that, if Bernard Shaw can claim an immortality, however brief, it will not be by virtue of his original, novel, 50 and startling opinions, but by virtue of his literary presentation of them in a manner entirely his own. The equations read:

The ideas of Bernard Shaw = the commonplaces of his time.

55 The ideas of Bernard Shaw + his way of presenting them = G. B. S.

PASSION AND STYLE THE SECRETS OF SHAW'S SUCCESS

Bernard Shaw, then, has won the attention of the present generation, and he will hold the attention of posterity not because he has new theories about the world, but because, by virtue of strictly personal and inalienable qualities, he is able to give to the most 'hackneyed claptrap' (Bernard Shaw's own description) an air of novelty. Were he baldly to tell us that incomes should be equally divided, and that interest is an iniquitous and profoundly unsocial device invented by those who have too much money for the purpose of levying blackmail upon those who have not enough, we should simply remember that we had read all this years ago in an old book and turn to something rather more worth our time and attention.

But when Bernard Shaw writes *Widower's Houses* or *Socialism and Superior Brains,* it is quite another matter. Here we have original work of the first quality. The ideas are common to us all; but Bernard Shaw's presentation of these ideas thrills us with a conviction that nothing quite like it has ever come within our experience. We realize that we have never before encountered just this blend of wit and sense, this intellectual wrestle and thrust, this fervor and fun, this argumentative and syllabic virtuosity, this apparently impudent disregard of style that only the more piquantly emphasizes a perfectly individual and highly cultivated literary art. Then we begin to wonder what is the inspiration of this rapid Jehu; whence does he get his impulse to drive all these ancient ideas so furiously through the modern world. How are we to explain the passion that fills him and lifts his work to levels higher than the platform he undertakes to fill? We are sensible in Bernard Shaw's best work of a horse-power, of a spiritual energy, which is no more the product of his doctrinal prejudice against rent and interest than the energy which drove Wagner to compose the *Nibelung's Ring* was the product of his desire to justify his revolutionary principles or to improve the operatic stage scenery of his generation. We know that the inspiration of Bernard Shaw must be something deeper than a dislike of Roebuck Ramsden or a desire to abolish Mr. Sartorius. We know, in fact, that Bernard Shaw, like every man of genius, is the happy agent of a power and a passion which uses his prejudices, memories, and doctrines, in a way he is intellectually powerless to resist.

The real thrill of his work is conveyed in some sentences of his preface to *Man and Superman* — sentences used by him in quite another connection:

This is the true joy of life: the being used for a purpose recognized by yourself as a mighty one; the being thoroughly worn out before you are thrown on the scrap-heap; the being a force of nature, instead of a feverish, selfish little clod of ailments and grievances, complaining that the world will not devote itself to making you happy.

To apply this passage to the work of Bernard Shaw is again to destroy the popular conception of him as merely the acute *raisonneur,* the intellectual critic of his kind, with a wallet of revolutionary propaganda whereby his reputation lives or dies. Not his doctrine and not his deliberate pulpiteering make Bernard Shaw a vital influence in modern literature. The real secret of his influence can be explained in a sentence: Bernard Shaw has passion and he has style. Therefore, like every man of genius, he is driven to say more than he intends, and to say it in an arresting voice.

It remains to ask what is the prime irritant of this passion in Bernard Shaw. Where are we to look for the catfish which keeps his mental aquarium alive and astir? First, without preliminary, let us dart on that preface 'Why for Puritans,' which more than any other gives us the key to Bernard Shaw's work and character. Bernard Shaw writes as follows:

I have, I think, always been a Puritan in my attitude towards Art. I am as fond of fine music and handsome buildings as Milton was, or Cromwell, or Bunyan; but if I found that they were becoming the instruments of a systematic idolatry of sensuousness, I would hold it good statesmanship to blow every cathedral in the world to pieces with dynamite, organ and all, without the least heed to the screams of the art critics and cultured voluptuaries.

Bernard Shaw's primal inspiration, that is to say, is not esthetic or intellectual, but moral. We have to reckon with a moral fury where he most individually rages. The demon which seizes his pen at the critical moment, and uses him for its own enthusiastic purpose, is the demon which drove Milton to destroy Arminius. When Bernard Shaw imagines that he coolly and reasonably desires, simply as a practical socialist and in the name of common sense, to nationalize land and capital, and give to everybody as much money as he requires, he is mistaken. Like every other prophet who has succeeded in moving his generation, Bernard Shaw begins with a passion and a prejudice, and afterward manufactures and systematizes the evidence. That Bernard Shaw is a socialist is an accident of the time. The essential thing is that Bernard Shaw passionately hates all that is complacent, malevolent, callous, inequitable, oppressive, unsocial, stupid, irreligious, enervating, narrow, misinformed, unimaginative, lazy, envious, unclean, disloyal, mercenary, and extravagant. Hating all this with the positive, energetic, and proselytizing hatred of an incorrigible moralist, he has naturally seized on the biggest and most adequate stick in reach with which to beat the nineteenth-century sinner. This stick happened to be the socialist stick. If G. B. S. had lived with Grosseteste in the thirteenth century, it would have been the no-taxation-without-representation stick. If he had lived with Star Chamber in the sixteenth century, it would have been the Habeas Corpus stick. If he had lived with Rousseau in the eighteenth century, it would have been the social-contract-and-law-of-nature stick. Bernard Shaw's socialism stick is simply his weapon — the most convenient weapon to hand — with which to convict a society founded upon capitalism of the greatest possible amount of sin with the least possible opportunity of an overwhelming retort from the sinner. The important thing is not that Bernard Shaw preaches socialism, but that he uses the doctrines of socialism as Cromwell's troopers used the psalms of David or as Tolstoy used the gospels of Christ — namely, to put the unjust man and his evil ways out of court and countenance. To this end he employs also his craft as a dialectician, his gift as a stylist, his clear exposition and wit, his fun, irony, observation of men, genius for mystification and effective pose — all, indeed, that enters into the public idea of G. B. S. These things are merely auxiliary; any moment they are likely to be caught up in the service of his passionate mission —

a mission of which Bernard Shaw is often himself aware when he is most firmly under its dominion.

OUR MODERN TREATMENT OF PROPHETS

This brings us within view of Bernard Shaw's pamphlet on the war. It is natural in a preacher that the most unpardonable sin of the many he is called to denounce should be the sin of complacency; for the sin of complacency virtually amounts to the sin of refusing to hear what the preacher has to say, or, at all events, of refusing to take it seriously. Bernard Shaw has said continuously for many years that the average man is an unsocial sinner; and the average man, instead of hanging his head and mending his ways, has smiled in the face of the prophet. At one time the prophet was stoned, and at another time he was poisoned or ostracized or pelted in the pillory. But we have lately learned a more effective way of dealing with a prophet: either we turn him into a society preacher and enjoy his denunciation of what our neighbors do, or we pay him handsomely to amuse us in the theater. We have thus improved immensely on the methods of the scribe and the Pharisee; for where the scribe and the Pharisee destroyed only the bodies of their prophets, we, with an even more thorough complacency, aim also at destroying their souls — usually with some success.

But the British public has not succeeded with Bernard Shaw, who continues to be periodically stirred to frenzy by his inability to make every one realize that he or she is directly responsible for all the crimes and miseries of modern civilization. Moreover, because Bernard Shaw has lived most of his life in England, and has therefore been less seriously taken in England than elsewhere, he has concluded that the English are more complacent than any other people in the world. More and more he has come to regard it as his special mission to humble this complacency, to convict the Englishman, above all men, of sin, and of the necessity for humility and repentance. Therefore, whenever the British public becomes, in the view of Bernard Shaw, unduly exalted — whenever, in fact, it thinks it has a reason to be proud of the British name — Bernard Shaw is at once suspicious and usually incensed. Latterly he has been unable to

resist any occasion of pricking the inflation, real or imagined, of the British
spirit; and latterly, misled by habit, and
exaggerating the sins he was born to chas-
tise, Bernard Shaw has made some serious
mistakes.

SHAW A PROPHET OF HUMILITY
TO THE ENGLISH

Thus when, more than two years ago,
the whole British nation was struck with
grief at the loss of the *Titanic,* and was
reading with a reasonable pride of the
splendid behavior of her heroic crew, Bernard Shaw rose in his robe of the prophet
and told the public not to exaggerate
its vicarious gallantry. Then in August,
1914, when Great Britain was straining
every nerve to get her army to the Continent in time to save Belgium from the
worst of war, Bernard Shaw published an
article in the British press virtually to the
effect that Great Britain was not fighting
for the sanctity of treaties or the rights of
a little nation, but for British homes and
British skins. Maliciously he chose for
the publication of this assault upon British complacency the most obstinately and
hatefully complacent British newspaper at
his disposal.

Finally there came the celebrated
pamphlet *Commonsense and the War.*
This must be read as Bernard Shaw's
most audacious effort to puncture the self-
esteem of the British public. It has
caused much brain-searching among those
who have simply regarded George Bernard
Shaw as a very discreet and financially
successful mountebank; for Bernard
Shaw, in writing this pamphlet, has done
a clearly unpopular thing. Undoubtedly
he has angered and estranged many of his
admirers. Some regard the pamphlet as
an obscure attempt to discredit the allied
cause. Others regard it as an escapade
of revolting levity, inexpedient from a
patriotic point of view and essentially
wrong in its conclusions. The real point
that concerns us here is that the pamphlet
is not a new, unexpected, or isolated performance of Bernard Shaw, but a natural
sequel of all he has hitherto written.
Those who have followed Bernard Shaw
to the threshold of his pamphlet on the
war have no right at this time to be astonished or to refuse him their applause.
Commonsense and the War is simply
a topical and a later edition of *Widow-*
er's Houses. That is to say, it is a tract
in which the case against British complacency is put at a maximum by a fearless
and passionate advocate for the prosecu-
tion.

Not Bernard Shaw, but the time, has
changed. Here we strike at the root of
Bernard Shaw's mistake. Hitherto, he
was doing salutary work in his campaign
against the silent self-assurance of the
mean, sensual man. There are as many
complacent persons in Great Britain as
elsewhere, and so long as Great Britain
was at peace with her neighbors, it was
beneficial that Bernard Shaw should imagine that the British, among whom he
lived, were more guilty in this respect
than any other extant community, and
that he should lose no opportunity for
satirical, ironical, comic, or didactic re-
proof. But when Great Britain and her
allies had their back to the wall, when
there were opponents to be countered and
met, Bernard Shaw's insular mistake that
the British as a nation are any more complacent than any other nation with a past
to be proud of and a future to believe in
became a really injurious heresy. It began, indeed, to look rather like giving
away his people to the enemy. Of course
it was nothing of the kind. *Common-*
sense and the War, intelligently read,
vibrates with patriotism, and it proudly
proclaims the essential rightness of the
struggle in which Great Britain is now
engaged. But the patriotism of *Com-*
monsense and the War is less apparent
to the audiences which laugh at Bernard
Shaw in the theater and outrageously regard him as a privileged fool at the court
of King Demos, than the fact that it begins by asserting that Sir Edward Grey is
a Junker, and goes on to examine whether
we really have the right to condemn our
enemies without a preliminary inquiry
into our own consciences and affairs.

Bernard Shaw has made a mistake, but
it is a natural, not an ignoble, mistake.
It will have no permanent effect upon
those who are sensible, even in Bernard
Shaw's most special pleading, of the passionate moral sincerity which gives con-
sistency and fire to all he writes. *Com-*
monsense and the War was a blunder;
but it was also an act of disinterested
courage. It was not dictated by any wish
to stand in front of the picture or to
splash in a sea too deep for purposes of

exhibition. Bernard Shaw, in writing *Commonsense and the War* is simply the priest who insists upon sacrifice before going into battle, or believes that every good fight should be preceded by confession, absolution, and high mass.

THE PERSONAL EQUATION IN SHAW

One word more. Bernard Shaw, the prophet and the puritan, lives in his work. But the passion which gives him uniformity and purpose as a public figure has not impaired his personal humor, his tolerance for all that is sweet and commendable, his broadness of view and eagerly inquisitive outlook upon life, his candor and honesty of mind, his generous welcome of new ideas, his love of beautiful things, his ability to appreciate and sympathize even with those forces which are banded to destroy him. These are the qualities which have obscured from contemporaries the essential simplicity of his mind, and have warmly endeared him to the younger generation of authors and critics who have learned from their master how profitably they may supersede him. This younger generation, though it very frequently turns the weapons of Bernard Shaw against himself, will never forget or neglect the debt it owes to the helpful, patient, and wise counselor it has been privileged to observe and know.

VIII

TOLSTOY'S RELIGION

EDWARD A. THURBER

[*Open Court, January,* 1914. By permission of author and publisher.]

A man's creeds provide such an inadequate road-book to his religious experiences, that, like a conscientious traveler who wishes to get certain things over with, I shall begin this sketch by quoting three statements made by Tolstoy concerning his beliefs. The first occurs at the opening of the twelfth chapter of his tractate, *My Religion,* and bears the date 1884 or thereabouts, Tolstoy being at the time in his fifty-seventh year.

'I believe in Christ's teaching, and this is my faith:

'I believe that my happiness is possible on earth only when all men fulfil Christ's teaching.

'I believe that the fulfilment of this teaching is possible, easy and pleasant.

5 'I believe that even now, when this teaching is not fulfilled, if I should be the only one among all those that do not fulfil it, there is, nevertheless, nothing else for me to do for the salvation of my life from 10 the certainty of eternal loss but to fulfil this teaching, just as a man in a burning house, if he find a door of safety, must go out.

'I believe that my life according to the 15 teaching of the world has been a torment, and that a life according to Christ's teaching can alone give me in this world the happiness for which I was destined by the Father of Life.

20 'I believe that this teaching will give welfare to all humanity, will save me from inevitable destruction and will give me in this world the greatest happiness. Consequently, I cannot help fulfilling it.'

25 The second statement which I shall quote was written some seventeen years later when Tolstoy was seventy-three. It was occasioned by the act of excommunication directed against him by the Holy 30 Synod on account of a chapter in his great book, *Resurrection,* relative to mass and the eucharist.

'I believe in God, who is to me the Spirit, Love, the Principle of all things. 35 I believe that he is in me and I in him. I believe that the will of God has never been more clearly expressed than in the teaching of the man, Christ, but we may not think of Christ as God and address 40 him in prayer without committing the greatest sacrilege. I believe that the true happiness of man consists in the accomplishment of the will of God. I believe that the will of God is that every man 45 should love his neighbor and do unto him as he would be done by; herein is contained, as the Bible says, all the law and the prophets. I believe that the meaning of life for each one of us is solely to 50 increase this love within us; I believe that the increase of our power to love will bring about in this life a joy which will grow day by day, and in the other world will become a more perfect happiness. I 55 believe that the growth of love will contribute more than any other force to establish on this earth the kingdom of God, that is, will replace an order of life in which division, guile and violence are all powerful by another order in which concord, truth and brotherhood will reign. I believe that for the increase of love there is but one means — prayer. Not the public prayer in temples, which Christ expressly reproved, but the kind of prayer of which he himself gave an example, solitary prayer, which reaffirms in us a consciousness of the meaning of life and the knowledge that we depend absolutely on the will of God. I believe in life eternal. I believe that we are rewarded according to our acts here and everywhere, now and forever. I believe all this so firmly that at my age — on the borders of the grave — I ought often to make an effort to think of the death of my body as merely the birth of a new life.'

My third quotation is taken from a letter written by Tolstoy the year before he died, that is, in 1909, when he was eighty-one.

'The teaching of Jesus is to me but one of the beautiful religious teachings which we have received from Egyptian, Jewish, Hindu, Chinese, Greek, antiquity. The two great principles of Jesus: the love of God, that is, absolute perfection, and the love of one's neighbor, the love of all men without any distinction whatsoever, have been preached by all the sages of the world,— Krishna, Buddha, Lao-tze, Confucius, Socrates, Plato, Epictetus, Marcus Aurelius, and among the moderns, Rousseau, Pascal, Kant, Emerson, Channing, and many others. Religious and moral truth is everywhere and always the same. I have no predilection for Christianity. If I have been especially interested in the teachings of Jesus, it is, first, because I was born and have lived among Christian people; second, because I have found a great intellectual pleasure in disengaging the pure teaching from the surprising falsifications affixed to it by churches.'

These professions I do not intend to dwell upon except to note that Tolstoy, in his very old age, seemed inclined on occasion not to realize that his religion was after all profoundly Christian. In the crisis of it or at the time of what we might call his final conversion, he was drawing very little inspiration from Krishna, Confucius, Epictetus; the fountain of his religious experiences was the

Scriptures and their teaching, as it culminated, to him, in the character of Jesus. But ignoring his dogmas for the moment, I wish simply to present in brief outline the life and makeup of this remarkable man as a sort of background for the conclusions he came to, and also to his multifarious and powerful influence.

Of our primary, our animal passions, Tolstoy had more than his share, and also of those other more human passions, expressed most unequivocally perhaps in that sharp conflict between fact and dream in violent, tumultuous natures. He possessed the cruelty of a confirmed and eager hunter; indeed, hunting was the last pleasure of all vicious and cruel pleasures, as he called them, which he sacrificed. After giving an account of the slow death of a wolf which he had killed by hitting it with a club on the root of the nose, he adds, 'I fairly reveled as I contemplated the tortures of that dying animal.' Nor to jealousy, as well as to cruelty, was he a stranger, as many a story of his boyhood testifies. In a fit of jealousy he once pushed from a balcony a little playmate of his, a girl. She was lame for a long time afterward.

Here is an early note in his journal concerning the three demons that were tormenting him: ' 1. Gambling. Can possibly be overcome. 2. Sensuality. Very hard struggle. 3. Vanity. Most terrible of all.' Gambling was one of the routine pastimes of young men born in Tolstoy's social environment. As late as the year before his marriage, a night's high play cost him the manuscript of The Cossacks, which he sold to an editor for $500 to pay his debts of honor.

Vanity, pride, conceit and self-pity were companions of his early years. Mention of them crops out constantly in his half autobiographical books, Childhood, Boyhood, Youth. 'I imagined there could be no happiness on earth for a man with so big a nose as I had, such thick lips and little eyes.' He speaks disconsolately of 'this face without expression. These feeble, soft, characterless features remind me of peasants' features — these great hands and feet.' 'I wanted everybody to know me and love me,' he writes, 'I wished that merely on hearing my name all would be struck with admiration and thank me.' From his journal again, 'My great fault, pride. A self-love immense.

I am so ambitious that if I had to choose between glory and virtue (which I love), I am ready to believe that I should choose the former.' Turgenev spoke at one time of Tolstoy's stupid, nobleman's pride, his blustering and braggadocio. Those who have read his book, *Childhood,* will recall the tears that Tolstoy poured forth, tears of self-pity, Werther tears, expressive of the sorrows that were engulfing him; they were the tears of a self-conscious, imaginative, sentimental boy. At five years of age, he felt (he says) that life was not a game, but a long, hard travail.

If it is part of the office of genius to marshal and direct vehement passions, then Tolstoy was rich in his endowment. His quiver was full of the arrows of wrath — more akin to Milton, I should say, than to any other figure of his rank in letters I can think of — to Milton whom one has called the most emotional of our English poets. Tolstoy's path was blazed with zeal, rage, indignation — boisterous, uncontrolled, calm even, satisfying. 'I get drunk,' he says, 'with this seething madness of indignation which I love to experience, which I even excite when I feel it coming because it throws me into a sort of calm and gives me, for some moments at least, an extraordinary elasticity, the energy and fire of all physical and moral capacities.' [1] This riotous temperament was housed, as we know, in a superb body; it was employed ultimately in a great passion to serve mankind. This is why one likes to dwell upon the wrath of Tolstoy.

Tolstoy divides his life into three periods which he calls, characteristically, the period in which he lived for himself; the period in which he lived for mankind; and the period in which he lived for God. Though such a division is somewhat arbitrary, I shall adopt it, as it emphasizes rather conveniently certain crises in his life. The first period came to an end at the time of his marriage; it had lasted thirty-four years. He was brought up like a good Russian in the Greek church, and as a boy accepted frankly its ritual and its dogma. Many pious and simple-hearted people were about him, some of them relatives, some servants in the house, and others peasants of the estate. They and he were instinctively drawn to one another. He ad-

[1] From the journal of Prince Nukludov, 1857.

mired, he could not help admiring, their poverty of spirit, their loyalty, their unquestioning self-sacrifice. He used to watch old men at prayer in silent reverence. And naturally with his own frankness and sympathy and love of truth, he was just the sort of boy to win the confidence of these great-hearted people. Tolstoy owes them much both on account of their real wisdom of character and on account of the stories they used to tell him, those embodiments of joys and sorrows, actual, undefiled.

But Tolstoy's world was after all not this peasant world, but the world of the landed proprietor. As a young man at college he threw off all beliefs of the church and became an out and out nihilist, — he believed in nothing at all. This indeed was the correct attitude of the young blades of his day. It was the exaltation, one might say, and in his case a perfectly honest exaltation, of the intellect. A man must submit the beliefs of the world to the scrutiny of his reason, and if his reason says 'reject,' rejected they must be. It is a pure matter of logic, the cruel, uncompromising logic of youth.

This, I presume, was the most unhappy period of Tolstoy's life and it lasted a good many years. Here was a man who earnestly desired to make a signal contribution, to impress a glowing personality upon the life of his time, and his intellectual philosophy was negation. He looked about him and discovered that many who believed as he did — the great majority of them, he averred — were plain rascals; gain was the key to their conduct. They were greedy, sensual and quarrelsome; they sneered at piety and were themselves master hypocrites. And yet the creed or lack of creed of these nihilists was unimpeachable. Tolstoy put all this down in the journal; he weighed the problem, analyzed himself scathingly, and yet could come to no other conclusion. Here, then, was an *impasse.* There was, indeed, one way out of it; that was to kill himself. The demon of suicide kept Tolstoy pretty close company for many a day. Just why he did not put an end to his life is a little hard to explain, if he has given us absolutely just data of his experiences. Why did not St. Augustine kill himself? They are comparable characters; both were miserably unhappy. The demon of suicide appears to have been superseded at critical moments by a divinity that was shaping his ends. Perhaps, too, he exaggerated. Men like this always overstate; they also in their fury fail to account for the hidden influences that transcend their logic.

There was in his case, to be sure, an alleviation other than suicide — story writing. In the distribution of talents that goes on in this world, Tolstoy was invested with an almost uncanny creative imagination. He could put himself definitely in the place of other people. And so intense and of so wide a range were his experiences and his sympathies that this talent of his allowed him to ignore momentarily his philosophy. I shall not dwell upon his early stories. They were received with immediate applause, and placed him at once in the front rank of Russia's writers. Later, in his religious zeal, he rejected them almost entire as examples of perverted art. A vain disclaimer! They were uneven, of course; of a hundred stories not all can be supreme. Yet I am not aware that one could honestly call any one of them feeble; many are masterly — none artistically untrue; nor was Tolstoy capable of writing an impure story. His intuitions belied his reason. These stories express the sort of man Tolstoy was, and Tolstoy the man, Tolstoy as he appeared in his creative work, was, I am inclined to believe, a finer personality than Tolstoy the thinker.

I do not mean by this statement, of course, that an imaginative writer should not possess a philosophy of life. The truth lies in the opposite direction. Great poets are seers; their wisdom is the wisdom of the searching minds. The poems of Homer epitomize Greek wisdom of the heroic age; Don Quixote, the plays of Molière and of Shakespeare stand for definite views of life, unexpressed, to be sure, in the language of philosophy, but still there, and there, I assume, consciously. A poet should not be deprived of his humanity. This view was realized most clearly, I imagine, by the Greeks in their attitude toward their great dramatists. The Greeks expected from their dramatists distinct and tangible interpretations, and they were not disappointed. Æschylus, Sophocles, Euripides, Aristophanes analyzed for them the principles of moral and religious conduct.

With such a conception of art no one could have been in greater sympathy than Tolstoy, and nowhere did he practise it on a greater scale than in the two great novels of his maturity, *War and Peace,* and *Anna Karenina.* The former of these novels comes as near being a cosmos as any single work of the nineteenth century. It soon forced itself into translation, and was received the civilized world over with astonishment. That one man could know so much of life! And yet this book bears evidence of a troubled, discordant mind. That may not be a misfortune in a great work of art; it is, however, likely to be. For those later pages of dialogue in *Paradise Lost* justifying the ways of God to man are no more surely an artistic blemish than are the chapters of preaching in Tolstoy's great novel. The lessons in a work of art follow a far different lead from the lessons in a sermon. In the former case you gather them as you may, you are somewhat loath to restate them; an appeal to the imagination can never be logically restated. But a sermon *is* statement; the preacher is at pains to tell you precisely in terms of reason what he means. These two methods will not combine. That Tolstoy should have been a preacher is, I think, to our great advantage, but he might have spared us his philosophical discussions in his novels.

This distinction of mind is thrown into relief by a couple of sentences taken from his correspondence. 'At this moment,' he writes, 'I am yoking myself anew to that tiresome and vulgar *Anna Karenina,* with the sole desire of getting rid of it with all possible speed.' Tolstoy was not bored merely with *Anna Karenina;* he was weary of art. The life of this modern St. Augustine had been a prolonged agony of religious doubt; the salvation of his soul, his personal responsibility, was its chief concern. How he ultimately came to see the light, he has told us in *My Confession.* From that tractate, begun in 1879, I shall quote a few passages to mark the stages of his progress from his first period of denial to his final period of faith.

'I began,' he says, 'to draw nearer to the believers among the poor, the simple, and the ignorant; the pilgrims, the monks, the peasants. The doctrines of these men of the people like those of the pretended believers of my own class, were Christian.

Here also much that was superstitious was mingled with the truths of Christianity, but with this difference, that the superstition of the believers of our class was entirely unnecessary to them, and never influenced their lives beyond serving as a kind of Epicurean distraction; while the superstition of the believing laboring class was so interwoven with their lives that it was impossible to conceive them without it — it was a necessary condition of their living at all. The whole life of the believers of our class was in flat contradiction with their faith, and the whole life of the believers of the people was a confirmation of the meaning of life which their faith gave them.'

And so he began to study the lives and the doctrines of the 'people.' He returned, as it were, to the past, to his childhood and youth. 'I united myself,' he says, 'to my ancestors — to those I loved, my father, mother, and grandparents. I joined the millions of the people whom I respect. Moreover there was nothing bad in all this, for bad with me meant the indulgence of the lusts of the flesh. When I got up early to attend divine service, I knew that I was doing well, if it were only because I tamed my intellectual pride for the sake of a closer union with my ancestors and contemporaries, and, in order to seek for a meaning in life, sacrificed my bodily comfort.'

It was the same with preparing for the communion, the daily reading of prayers, with genuflections, and the observance of all the fasts. 'However insignificant the sacrifices were,' he says, 'they were made in a good cause.' He prepared for the communion, fasted, and observed regular hours for prayer both at home and at church.

Such is the picture of Tolstoy, a communicant of the orthodox church — as we shall see, a somewhat uncertain figure.

'I shall never forget,' he goes on, 'the painful feeling I experienced when I took communion for the first time after many years. . . . It was such happiness for me to humble myself with a quiet heart before the confessor, a simple and mild priest, and, repenting of my sins, to lay bare all the mire of my soul; it was such happiness to be united in spirit with the meek fathers of the church who composed these prayers; such happiness to be one with all who have believed and who do be-

lieve, that I could not feel my explanation was artificial' . . . 'But,' he adds, 'when I drew near to the "holy gates" and the priest called on me to repeat that I believed that what I was about to swallow was the real body and blood, it cut me to the heart; it was a false note, though small; it was no unconsidered word; it was the cruel demand of one who had evidently never known what faith was.'

In this condition Tolstoy lived for three years; it was while he was writing *Anna Karenina*. The ideals of his own class, represented by the chief characters in that book, had become odious to him, he was turning for religious guidance to the people. They only were on the right track; they only had grasped the teachings of Jesus. Yet a searcher must make distinctions. 'The people,' he affirms, 'as a whole had a knowledge of truth; this was incontestable, for otherwise they could not live. Moreover, this knowledge of truth was open to me; I was already living by it, and felt all its force; but in that same knowledge there was also error. Of that again I could not doubt. All, however, that formerly repelled me now presented itself in a vivid light. Although I saw that there was less of what had repelled me as false among the people than among the representatives of the church, I also saw that in the belief of the people what was false was mingled with what was true.'

Tolstoy is now passing into his third period — as he puts it, the period in which he lived for God. The immediate occasion of his break with the church was the Turko-Russian war of 1877. 'At this time,' he says, 'Russia was engaged in war; and in the name of Christian love, Russians were engaged in slaying their brethren. Not to think of this was impossible. But at the same time in the churches men were praying for the success of our arms, and the teachers of religion were accepting these murders as acts which were the consequence of faith. Not only murder in actual warfare was approved, but, during the troubles which ensued, I saw members of the church, her teachers, monks and ascetics, approving of the murder of erring and helpless youths. I looked round on all that was done by men who professed to be Christians, and I was horrified.'

The Tolstoy who now emerges, Tolstoy

at the age of fifty, is the man we know best. 'Leon is always working,' his wife writes. 'Alas! he is writing some sort of religious treatises. He lies and reflects until his head splits, and all to prove that the church is not in accord with the teaching of the Gospels. I doubt if his efforts interest a dozen people in Russia. But there is nothing to do for it. I only hope that it will be over with quickly, and pass away like a disease.' To him she wrote: 'That you should waste such extraordinary intellectual force in chopping wood, heating the samovar and in cobbling shoes, saddens me.' And later: 'Well, I take comfort in the Russian proverb, "Let the child have his way, provided he doesn't cry."'

This is expert testimony; yet the views of Mme. Tolstoy concerning her husband do not coincide fully, I imagine, with our own. A prophet, to be sure, is likely to be troublesome about the house. And Tolstoy, we must know, was what William James calls a twice-born man. His mother gave birth to him in 1828; but one birth is never enough for a saint. The Isaiahs and the Pascals and the Bunyans always have to be born again; otherwise, like most of us, they die. No Greek that I know of, and no Roman, was ever born more than once; they were, as Carlyle says, the best of them, terribly at ease in Zion. But the Hebrews and the Christians, the prophets and the saints among them, were never satisfied — are never satisfied — with but one birth. Tolstoy had several of them, and the latest was always prone to be a little more painful than the one before. Such profusion is undomestic. Let us now turn to one or two other considerations.

If you recall the statements I quoted at the beginning of this sketch, you noted one spirited denial, the denial of the divinity of Christ. Tolstoy was excommunicated from one church and could have joined no other, Catholic or Evangelical; nor could he have become an active member of the Y. M. C. A. All connections of such a nature would have entailed an intellectual compromise as abhorrent to him as it was impossible. To Tolstoy's imperious, Russian mind, creeds could not be 'restated,' and yet he was as far removed from a mere moralist as was a medieval saint. His religion was a religion of faith, it rested not at all on 'good works.' The first article in the creed of a man of religion is to get himself right with his God. This becomes his passion and until that matter is settled, the world about him counts for nothing. The words, 'benevolence,' 'philanthropy,' 'horse-sense,' while the struggle is on, bring no comfort to such a man. They appear rather as mere babblings, a cheap way out of it. Tolstoy is not at home with the moralists; his place is among that rarer, more positive company of men of religion, whose good works are simply an inevitable offshoot of their faith. Thus, in spite of the denial I have mentioned, Tolstoy ranks with the great religious leaders.

A question naturally arises, Can a man be at once both a prophet and an artist? And the answer is, I take it, Yes, religion and art may lie down together like the tiger and the lamb, but the lamb must always lie inside the tiger. Tolstoy remained a great artist, but during his later life his art always served his religion. In his book, *What is Art?* published in 1898, Tolstoy being at the time seventy years of age, he denies to art the quality of beauty, a quality which the Greeks insisted upon. To his mind the artistic activity is simply the evoking in oneself feelings one has once experienced and then having evoked them, consciously handing them on, by means of certain external signs, so that others may be infected by these feelings and also experience them. His definition proper goes no further than this; but the definition is not the most significant part of that book. Distinctions between good and bad art do not interest Tolstoy, although he uses those words constantly; his distinctions, as a man of religion, are between art 'worth while' and art perverted. Art worth while, he affirms, should in the first place express those primary emotions — love, hatred, jealousy, fear — in such terms that all people, the peasant as well as the philosopher, may understand them. Ibsen's *The Master Builder* is intelligible only to a class; it is therefore an example of perverted art. The Odyssey is an example of art worth while. In the second place, great art, supreme art, should have as its fundamental theme the Christian gospel of brotherly love. That is art most worth while. *Adam Bede, The Christmas Carol,* the works of Dostoievsky, the story of

Joseph and his brethren, are a few examples of art on the theme of brotherly love.

Those who have familiarized themselves with the sequence of Tolstoy's imaginative writing have noticed the effect of these theories upon it. His art undergoes a renewal. No longer are his stories mere transcripts of life; in fact, most of them, his assertions to the contrary notwithstanding, were never quite that. But now they serve much more consciously his religious ideals. Among them appear what might be called parables, *Two Old Men, The Death of Ivan Iliitch, Master and Man* — with this distinction: The characters in Tolstoy's finest parables, unlike those in the parables we are most familiar with, are never types; they are always individualized. The stories wear their rue of sermonizing with a difference. I seem to see the lamb of art lying down most trustfully very near but yet outside the tiger of religion. *Resurrection,* the great novel of his old age, is a Pilgrim's Progress through a *real* world. Perhaps the main characters are not so sharply defined as in *Anna Karenina;* Tolstoy did not know them quite so well. He is an old man now, and the turmoil and contradictions of youth have in part escaped him. But the critic approaches *Resurrection* softly, for it stands among the fairest and most authentic 'poems of human compassion.'

Tolstoy's character takes on much of the complexity of the modern age, yet so sharp are its main features that it seems at times almost simple. It was a brutal act, perhaps, for him to thrust his diary into the hands of his betrothed, knowing that she would read it in tears; the act may have been brutal; to him it was a gage to sheer honesty. On the evening of his return from a visit to the slums of Moscow, he began to argue with a friend, but with such warmth and so angrily that his wife rushed in from an adjoining room to ask what had happened. 'It appeared,'[2] he says, 'that I had, without being aware of it, shouted out in an agonized voice, gesticulating wildly, "We should not go on living in this way! We must not live so! We have no right!"' He was rebuked for his unnecessary excitement, was told that he could not talk quietly upon any question, that he was irritable, and it was pointed out to him that

[2] From *What Shall We Do?*

the existence of such misery as he had witnessed should in no way be a reason for embittering the life of the home circle. Simple-minded Tolstoy! 'I felt,' he adds naïvely, 'that this was perfectly just, and held my tongue; but in the depth of my soul I knew that I was right, and I could not quiet my conscience.' It was this unquiet conscience that sent him off finally to die alone.

In the morning papers of December 8, 1912, there appeared among the headlines the announcement of the printing of Tolstoy's diary. The appended article gave a few extracts, evidently from a preface. From this, in closing, I shall quote briefly, allowing Tolstoy the ultimate word. 'After all,' he wrote, 'let my diaries remain as they are. It may be seen from them that in spite of the misery of my youth, God did not abandon me and that as I grew older I learned, however little, to understand and to love Him.' 'I have had moments,' he continues, 'when I have sometimes been so impure and so subject to personal passions that the light of this truth has been obscured by my own obscurity; but in spite of all, I have served at times as the intermediary for His truth, and those have been the happiest moments of my life.' What a change here from that head-long Tolstoy who one day came from the Caucasus to ally himself with the devotees of art! And what a contrast, too, between the fine renunciation of these words and the arrogance of that other confessor of a century before — Rousseau! 'May God will that, passing through me, these truths have not been sullied, and may mankind find in them its pasture. It is only in that that my writings have importance.' Finally, 'If the people of the world wish to ready my writing, let them dwell on those passages where I know the Divine power has spoken through me, and let them profit from them throughout their lives.'

IX

RUSSIAN NOVELISTS AND ENGLISH

[*Nation,* New York, February 25, 1915.
By permission.]

When the uttermost causes of the present war are recorded some day in the great Blue Book of history, a fair measure of responsibility will fall upon Dostoievsky, Tolstoy, and their successors. Such a Blue Book will print copious extracts from the Russian novelists and copious extracts from the younger English novelists, and will show how the Anglo-Russian *entente* which made the present conflict possible had been encouraged, or at least accompanied, by a remarkable *rapprochement* between Russian fiction and the newest British schools. The influence of Dostoievsky, as the most typical representative of the Slav soul, upon the ideals and method of writers like Compton Mackenzie, W. B. Maxwell, J. D. Beresford, Gilbert Cannan, and half a dozen others, is unmistakable. It is an influence acknowledged. Imitation of the Russians is revealed not only in the way these younger men have gone in for the novel of psychology, or in their discovery of the 'lower classes,' or in their exploiting of the lower emotions, or in their extreme frankness. It is shown in a close modeling of character upon character, and almost of phrase upon phrase. One might take Mr. Gilbert Cannan's latest story, *Young Earnest* (Appleton), and point out people, situations, turns of expression, which are straight from Dostoievsky, though modified — and not infrequently misapplied — in accordance with the English temperament and the writer's special equipment. Dostoievsky's *Crime and Punishment* has been for some time a sort of Bible to the circle of younger writers in England.

Unfortunately, there is evidence that the younger English novelists, in subjecting themselves to the influence of the Russians, have followed not only the masters but the third-rate men. Even the Russians can do fairly poor work at times. As an example there is the famous *Sanine,* by Michael Artzibasheff, which appeared in Russia half a dozen years ago, and is now put forth in an English translation (B. W. Huebsch), with an introduction by Mr. Gilbert Cannan. The writer of the introduction admits that the book is an uncomfortable one. What he seems to overlook is that *Sanine* is uncomfortable in an utterly different way from *Crime and Punishment*. The Russian novel has always been sincere, outspoken, and faithful to the complexities of life. *Sanine* is fearfully outspoken, and is probably sincere, but it is not a novel of life, but a novel with a purpose. It inculcates the ideal of the man who stands beyond good and evil with almost exclusive emphasis on the dogma that the aim of life is in the satisfaction of physical desire. *Sanine* has been explained as marking the reaction from the shattered hopes and ideals of the Russian revolution. Since altruism, self-sacrifice, had been proved a failure in the thousands of Russian youth who had gone to the gallows in vain, there must be a sharp swing towards egoism, self-indulgence in a very specific sense. In this sharp reaction from pole to pole the book is typically Russian. It is not typical in the lifelessness of its principal characters. For all his playing the Superman, Sanine is an abstraction and a good deal of a bore. He is utterly removed from the flesh and blood that crowd the pages of Tolstoy, Dostoievsky, and Turgenieff.

Plainly, the writers of the English novel who would master the secret of the great Russians must study their 'Bible' more carefully; though even then it is evident that they will assimilate the new teaching under the limitations of racial temperament and social tradition. The one lesson they should and may acquire is that the great Russians never worked by formula, even when they worked for a purpose. It is true that Turgenieff's novels have a social meaning in the sense that his successive stories chronicle the emergence of new types from changing social conditions. Only Turgenieff's characters are never 'types,' but intensely living men and women. It is true that Tolstoy in *Anna Karenina* is already the moralist, but his ethical purpose is quite submerged in the epic of life, the preacher is drowned in the artist. And so in Dostoievsky, that gospel of redemption through suffering, which comes nearest to being a formula, is always exemplified in men and women of an almost terrifying reality. It follows that the outspokenness of the Russian masters arises entirely out of an inner necessity, out of the need of depicting the truth. Their frankness may at times be excruciating, but it is never shocking. It proceeds from life and not from formula.

Whereas formula, in setting or in expression, is very prominent among the English imitators of the Russians, just as it is prominent in *Sanine* which is scarcely anything but imitation. It is prominent in the English writers who are apt to think that sincerity is that which shocks the bourgeois. Mr. Gilbert Cannan, for example, is realistic by formula and idyllic by formula. When realistic he is very, very realistic. On such occasions men and women 'hunger for the possession' of each other, and their kisses are 'bitter sweet.' When idyllic, he is very idyllic, and men and women run hand in hand down sun-kissed slopes — pure spirit, in fact. Now, the great Russians are neither sultry by rule nor idyllic by rule; but they blend spirit and body, sin and ecstasy, into that single thing called life.

X

HUGH WALPOLE AND THE NOVEL

H. W. BOYNTON

[*Evening Post*, New York, April 24, 1915. By permission.]

It was very recently that England found time to be interested in certain rising or newly risen novelists who seemed to be bringing fresh matter, or at least a fresh flavor, to English fiction. They owed much to Messrs. Wells, Bennett, and Galsworthy, and probably more to the Continental masters, French and Russian, with whose weapons the death-blow (we flatter ourselves) has at last been dealt to Respectability and Victorianism. Their workmanship is of the uniform brilliancy to which British authorship has recently been speeded up. And there is something approaching uniformity in the larger process behind their virtuosity. Henry James has called it a process of saturation: 'The process of squeezing out to the utmost the plump and more or less juicy orange of a particular acquainted state, and letting this affirmation of energy, however directed or undirected, constitute for them the "treatment" of a theme — that is what we remark them as mainly engaged in.' Applying this generalization, Mr. James observes that Arnold Bennett's saturation is that of a special provincial milieu, the Five Towns; Mr. H. C. Wells's, that of the extraordinarily intense and versatile experiences of his own

mind; Hugh Walpole (to come to our particular instance) that of Youth. 'Mr. Walpole offers us indeed a rare and interesting case,' says Mr. James. 'We see about the field none other like it; the case of a positive identity between the spirit, not to say the time of life or stage of experience, of the aspiring artist and the field itself of its vision.'

We wonder if this is the right explanation of the phenomenon. It is true that, under the age of thirty, Mr. Walpole has produced six novels tingling with the consciousness of youth. But is normal youth quite so conscious of itself? Are not your middle-aged novelists and poets the ones who really worship it? What if Mr. Walpole were simply precocious? His six novels, saturated with the worship of youth, are in much the mood that inspired *The Princess and the Butterfly*. When that play was written, Mr. Shaw, then a dramatic critic, at once nicknamed it *Turning Forty*. Its author, Mr. Pinero, had just passed the turn, and its mood, however coddled for dramatic purposes, was natural. For a boy in his twenties, on the other hand, to write a *Maradick at Forty* seems unnatural — until we perceive that by an excess of sensibility and out of the very intensity of his worship of youth, he has dramatized his dread of its loss. And he has not perceived that the mood in which middle-age regrets youth is incidental and relatively slight. Youth, after all, is not the only thing worth having.

Because he thinks it *is* the only thing, or the chief thing, Mr. Walpole's middle-aged men are represented as mainly occupied in clinging to it. The hero of his first novel, *The Wooden Horse,* is a man with a grown-up son and the heart and mind of a healthy boy. His triumph is precisely that he himself has not grown up. This is true also of Mr. Zanti, in *Fortitude.* The pathos of the protagonist of *The Gods and Mr. Perrin* is that he has lost, with youth, his chances of happiness; and so it is with Maradick.

Therefore, although the later novels of this writer show a steady advance in workmanship, and the emergence of a desire to interpret life in its larger aspects, we never quite get away from that initial preoccupation. Mr. Walpole's first book, *The Wooden Horse,* is (like most first books) so far inferior to its successors that it may safely be ignored. His 'Trojan' family are the aristocratic puppets of tradition; the types appear again in *The Duchess of Wrexe,* but greatly humanized and individualized. It is almost possible to believe in the Beaminsters — never in the Trojans. *The Wooden Horse* was written while Mr. Walpole was teaching in an English school. On the strength of its acceptance by a publisher, he made the plunge from schoolmastering to professional authorship. *The Gods and Mr. Perrin* is evidently based on his experiences as a schoolmaster. It is much shorter and, in scope, less pretentious than any of the other stories except *The Prelude to Adventure,* and this is perhaps why these books seem to me his strongest pieces of work. There is a grim intensity and economy about them which is far more impressive than the diffused enthusiasm and at times strained sensibility of the longer novels. They spring more directly from the writer's experience — or perhaps we should say they spring from experiences which the writer is better able to interpret. *The Gods and Mr. Perrin* is subtitled *A Tragi-Comedy,* and is, in fact, a well-nigh terrifying study of the mental and moral desolation of a certain type of provincial school. Moffat's is in its way as dreary as Do-the-Boys Hall, but here it is the dreariness of the masters upon which the eye is focussed. *Mr. Perrin* is simply the most hapless of a hapless group, hating their task and each other to the verge of murder and madness. That he falls short of murder and is rescued from madness is hardly more than a piece of luck. The 'unconvincing' part of the story is that in which he is represented as deliberately planning, in a spirit of heroic bravado, to turn back again to the dreadful existence which he has roused himself to fling off. *The Prelude to Adventure,* which followed *Mr. Perrin* in point of time, deals with a sort of obverse problem: it begins with a murder, and goes on to show that even such an act may not be the be-all and the end-all of character and experience for the murderer — may, indeed, be but the rising of the curtain, a 'prelude to adventure.' How it happened that our Cambridge undergraduate killed his man, that he was never legally brought to book, and that his life was not hopelessly ruined by the episode, is the subject of this strangely original and powerful tale.

Its successors, *Fortitude* and The *Duchess of Wrexe,* have won a much wider audience and more enthusiastic praise. *Fortitude* is a story upon the big scale, a 'life' novel of the type to which novelists are so generally returning from the novel of episode which supplanted it for a decade or two. There is an advantage in following a human experience from beginning to end, or at least from infancy to maturity for which the episodic method has no equivalent. Only the pursuit must be worth while, the companion of so long a journey must be something more than a weakling. The heroes of these young English novelists are too often mere bundles of desire and sensibility. They are in fact the offspring of a strange *mésalliance.* We cannot believe that there is a new race of Englishmen whom they fairly represent. If any proof were needed of their alien blood, it would be in their easy habit of bursting into floods of tears. Some day one of them will forget and kiss his comrade on both cheeks, after which the very finest of Oxford accents will not be able to conceal the mongrel that he is — Tolstoy, as it were, out of Mrs. X —— Y ——. Mr. Walpole's young men are more manly and more English than Mr. Compton Mackenzie's or Mr. Gilbert Cannan's; but they are not free from strained emotionalism. *Fortitude,* the book which made the writer known in America, is a sort of extended 'prelude to adventure.' At the end of it Peter Westcott has just learned the lesson that by losing the world a man may gain his soul. We leave him baring his bosom, a trifle theatrically (he is always self-conscious), to the storm. 'He was alone, and he was happy, happy as he had never before known happiness, in any time, before. . . . The rain lashed his face and body. His clothes hung heavily about him. He answered the storm: "Make of me a man — to be afraid of nothing . . . to be ready for everything — love, friendship, success . . . to take it as it comes . . . to care nothing if these things are not for me — make me brave! Make me brave."' So the book ends as it has begun, with a cry for courage — a cry with a touch of hysteria in it.

With *The Duchess of Wrexe,* Mr. Walpole has begun, it is clear, a new adventure of his own, an adventure towards the interpretation of society as contrasted with the individual. This story is the first of a group to be called *The Rising City,* but for some reason the writer has taken special pains to disclaim it as a trilogy. '*The Duchess of Wrexe,*' he says, ' is entirely a novel complete and independent in itself. . . . The three novels will be connected in place, in idea, and in sequence of time. Also certain of the same characters will appear in all three books. But the novels are not intended as sequels of one another, nor is *The Rising City* a Trilogy.' Mr. Walpole's people have a way of reappearing in later books, but, trilogy or not, something more than that seems to be here presaged. *The Duchess of Wrexe,* in its larger aspect, is a study of the passing of an ancient order, the British ' Autocrats,' as typified by the Beaminsters, with the old Duchess of Wrexe at their head. The Duchess dies at the moment when the relief of Mafeking lets loose the ' tigers ' of London, the mongrel democracy kept, for the most part, within strictest bounds. The moral drawn is that tigers must have some sort of freedom, and that democracy can succeed only when it has had free play — when ' Love thy neighbor as thyself ' may be looked for as the upshot. ' That 's my Individualism, my Rising City,' says the chorus-philosopher of the book; and seems to give a key to the treatment of the two novels which are to be its successors, if not in a strict sense its sequels. Mr. Walpole still has youth, and if, as Mr. James surmises, what he needs is to ' work free of this primitive predicament,' in order to do mature work, that is a matter which time will doubtless attend to.

XI

MRS. WHARTON'S WORLD

ROBERT HERRICK

[*New Republic,* February 13, 1915. By permission of author and publisher.]

The exclusive aim of literary criticism can hardly be that of drawing the mental and spiritual portrait of a creative personality, as Mr. Brownell, reaffirming the faith derived from his master Sainte-Beuve, has recently asserted. That may be a fruitful enough ideal for the professional critic reading anew the ancient monuments; but for the less exacting task of reckoning the claims of contemporary creators to our attention, there are simpler methods than an elaborate portraiture of what may very possibly prove to be lacking in salient or permanent traits. At least before undertaking any such task, criticism might well attempt to answer the question that every thoughtful contemporary must put to an imaginative effort, especially to the novel which deals with the known appearances of life: what has this hand made of my world? For it is here that the novelist touches us all most closely.

What has Mrs. Wharton done for our world — for the American scene, to use Mr. Henry James's somewhat precious phrase? The experts have told us again and again that Mrs. Wharton's touch is the deftest, the surest, of all our American manipulators in the novel form. Quite recently Mr. James has reiterated in his reverberating periods his authoritative praise of Mrs. Wharton's accomplishment. Hers is the only American name he has found occasion to mention in his latest appraisal of contemporary English fiction. The ground for according such distinction to Mrs. Wharton is plain to one acquainted with the craftsman's side of the novelist's business. Mrs. Wharton writes well — perhaps too consciously well. Technically she has formed her method on the approved tradition of French fiction, the tradition of refinements and exclusions, of subtleties and intentions, the tradition of Flaubert and Turgenieff, on which Mr. James admiringly formed himself a generation ago, rather than on the richer if less esthetically satisfying tradition of English and Russian fiction, of Fielding and Thackeray, of Tolstoy and Dostoievsky. In this approved school triumphs are more easily won, at least more enthusiastically recognized by the expert who has served his term there, than in the other looser tradition.

Technical proficiency of any sort, according to any intelligent ideal, is commendable surely, but only in measure as it achieves the purpose of all technique, which is effective creation. No true artist can be content with a triumph of manner alone. If Mrs. Wharton were forced to remain on a solitary pedestal of technical proficiency, hers would be a lonely position in this day of unacademic freedom in all creative effort, and her admirers by dwelling too insistently on her excellent manner would do her a dubious service, all the more as their praises seem to deny the validity of other and robuster ideals for the novel. It may well be, indeed, that the French tradition with all its reservations is already doomed in favor of that freer, more epic treatment of life so much deprecated by Mr. James in his comments on Tolstoy.

However all this may be judged by the few who are absorbed in the how rather than the what of the finished product, it is futile to deny that the what is always of first importance to that large mute audience of the uninitiated to which every creator must appeal in the last resort. And respecting Mrs. Wharton's content, it has been her misfortune that her publishers should have advertised so persistently and complacently her peculiar advantage in possessing an accurate knowledge of her material, for observing, that is, that small portion of American humanity intensively occupied with purely social ambitions. Mrs. Wharton, we have been told, has actually been part of what she presents as fiction, the inference being that the fiction must inevitably be the better for this fact. It is a naïve conviction that intimate experience is a condition of imaginative realization. The truth seems to be that the least influential factor is the observed fact, while the personality through which the fact must pass with its fundamental knowledge and power of realization is the controlling one. It scarcely needs the illustrious example of a Balzac, who constructed solidly an entire social system out of the meagerest of observed data, to suggest that Mrs. Wharton may actually have been hampered in her imaginative representations by a too exclusive and intimate acquaintance with her material. Certainly she has not done least — been least convincing — in those occasional excursions into the less familiar reaches of her field such as Ethan Frome.

Possibly it was an instinctive realization of this commonplace that led Mrs. Wharton in the three American novels of which I am especially thinking to choose that portion of the abundant material at her command which presumably appealed least to her own heart and soul — the shoddy part. For it is the shoddier part of rich and fashionable New York, indubitably authentic as 'society' though it be, that preponderatingly occupies the scene in The House of Mirth and The Custom of the Country — the part Mrs. Wharton has least zealously embraced, however carefully she may have studied its manifestations. The House of Mirth, offering that most significant of Mrs. Wharton's discoveries, the lamentable Lily Bart, contains less of obvious shoddy than The Custom of the Country, with its Undine Spragg and Elmer Moffatt. Indeed, so far to the extravagant verge of the social world has Mrs. Wharton moved in this latter novel that it remains fantastically unreal, with the generic unreality of the parable, betrayed even by the stage names of the heroine and of her origin, 'Apex City.' Apex City! As expert a realist as Mrs. Wharton must have been aware to what unreality of the typical she was surrendering herself with those satiric names. One feels that extremely little of this variegated chronicle of marriage and divorce, of 'Wall street deals' and vulgarian millionaires, ever really entered into Mrs. Wharton's delicate perceptions. They emerge from beneath her trained hand almost as raw as from the reportorial insignificance of the newspaper to which she so often refers the reader for corroboration. The singular characteristic of imaginative presentations is that they provide their own test of their validity, whether or not the reader has happened to have similar experiences. Crusoe's island was never doubted by boy or man. But one doubts Undine Spragg, Apex City, Elmer Moffatt and their world, although the newspapers authenticate them daily with precise detail. That something human, essential for conviction, which the newspaper paragraph must perforce omit, the novelist should provide — at any rate a novelist such as Mrs. Wharton. Otherwise why piece together the shoddy chronicle of Undine Spragg's career?

In The Fruit of the Tree Mrs. Wharton has largely ignored the loud, the shoddy, the super-fashionable. Yet the world here displayed is scarcely more of her own hearth, I suspect, than that of the two others mentioned. The reforming, sociological hero is an emanation of the serious world that customarily revolves somewhere within hail of the more hectic orbit of 'society.' But Amherst and his philanthropic yearnings over the Westmore mills has the fatal stamp of amateurishness — the unrealized — almost as plainly as the preposterous Spragg family. With all his earnest intention Amherst merely scratches the surface of the immense field of American social endeavor. His creator still thinks of these matters in the terms of 'doing good' and 'social settlements.' Fortunately *The Fruit of the Tree* holds much else that is better realized if not better worth realizing than social service; it contains the soft, shallow Bessie, the best done of Mrs. Wharton's many rich women, as well as Justine, the most daring of her young women. And the conflict between the rich wife and the idealistic husband, the reactions of Amherst and his venturous second wife, are all much more in Mrs. Wharton's real province — the analytic and psychological province where the subtleties of the subtly-minded are neatly unraveled.

What has Mrs. Wharton done toward painting in our national canvas? Granting the utility and significance of all elements in the scene, granting at least for *The House of Mirth* and *The Fruit of the Tree,* the authenticity of portrayal, nevertheless, beyond the single figure of Lily Bart, which is doubtless the most authoritative version ever rendered of the shallowly rooted and socially obsessed American girl, there is little of importance that remains. For one reason, Mrs. Wharton's stories are almost manless in any real conception of the sex, and in spite of the dominance of American women in our social world we have not yet reached the point where men are utterly negligible, where Selden or Marvell, Rosedale or Gus Trenor will answer for men. As for the woman side of the picture, Mrs. Wharton's chosen contribution has been quite exclusively in the realm of social passion, which she has correctly portrayed as the pathological absorption of American women. Even her skill and her special knowledge have not saved her from exaggerations, unrealities, and repetitions. The prevailing tone, the final taste of this American society is that of a marvelous thinness — tinniness, rather. Are we as a people when we evolve into 'society,' are our women, even, as mentally and spirit-

ually anemic as Mrs. Wharton's world betrays them? Without too easy a patriotism it may be doubted whether this clever observer has 'been fair' even to our 'most fashionable circles.' Certainly she has not cared to tone her pictures by vigorous contrasts or shaded examples. Instances of these she has offered, but with little enthusiasm; they are pallid ghosts, her 'nice' people, who by right of soul as well as of blood belong to the world she has chosen to exploit. Why has Mrs. Wharton never cared to do more for them, for the Seldens, the Marvells?

The explanation may lie in the truth of which I have already hinted, that Mrs. Wharton is not primarily a social historian, that she does not use the novel for this epic purpose, although these longer American stories suggest quite naturally such a presumption. *Ethan Frome* betrays the secret of her true power. This shortened novel, this monochrome prose tragedy so exquisitely dealt with, reveals the spiritual interest with which Mrs. Wharton is innately sympathetic — this and the suppressed drama of Bessie and Amherst, the expressed drama of Amherst and Justine. These spiritual conflicts involve no necessity of picturing a civilization; they are universal. Just because, perhaps, they are not conditioned by special environment or caste, because they lie outside the hard actualities of her personal contracts, their creator's imagination seems to have been happily released, to work more freely and convincingly in them. Ethan Frome conceivably sprang from no more intimate experience than Undine Spragg and her crew, yet his subdued and twilight tragedy of relaxed will spoke to his creator with all the fidelity of high art. This is the field of creative interest to which Mrs. Wharton has repaired more frequently in her short stories than in her novels. Her talent, a defining, analyzing, and subtlizing talent, has found little that was really congenial or suggestive in the common run of our coarsely accented national life. She has rarely caught its more significant notes or tried to peer beneath its obvious superficialities, nor has she been warmly charmed by its kaleidoscopic glitter. The larger canvas, therefore, I infer, is not her natural opportunity, competent artist that she is.

XII

THE SALAMANDER

[*Times* (London, England) *Literary Supplement*, April 2, 1915. By permission.]

The Salamander, by Owen Johnson (Martin Secker), though it has undoubted merits as a novel, must equally be described as a sociological monograph on a very extensive scale. It is an exact report of the conditions of the life led by the Salamander. What, then, is a Salamander? From a portentously serious foreword, in the best manner of the sociological treatise, we learn that the Salamander is a type of young woman that has been rapidly developing in New York, whose ' passion is to know, to leave no cranny unexplored, to see, not to experience, to flit miraculously through the flames — never to be consumed ! ' Out of the States somewhere she flings herself, unintroduced, upon New York, determined to ' see the world' like her brothers. She sticks at nothing, except the loss of her ' virtue '; and the more perilous the adventure, the more ' dangerous ' the man, the better she likes it. How does she live? Well, as she represents one side of the feminist movement, which would encourage women to share with men the work of life and be economically independent, the answer is an odd one. She gets some easy occupation — she typewrites or ' plays at art,' or ' touches the stage,' or does a little journalism — and so gets ' the little ready money she needs.' But she lives in taxis and motors, dines at a new restaurant every night, ' knows the insides of pawnshops, has secret treaties with tradesmen, and by a hundred stratagems procures herself presents which may be converted into cash.' The day of the Salamander is from eighteen to twenty-five; then she either marries, as does Doré, the heroine of this novel, or takes up some serious career, or flouts the true gospel of a Salamander by definitely stepping outside the social pale.

The Salamander is undeniably a portent, at least to the American sociologist. But it must be doubted whether even that resolute inquirer, in his thirst for knowledge, could stand any long experience of the Salamander's world. To ordinary individuals the unending whirl of buzzing telephones, joyrides, noise, kisses, orchids,

champagne, and surreptitious banknotes must become, almost at once, inexpressibly tedious. It is just that to which Mr. Johnson has devoted nearly 400 pages of close print, and it loses none of its tediousness at second hand. But to complain that the subject is immensely over-weighted is only to recognize that Mr. Johnson is following the approved method of some of our younger novelists on this side of the Atlantic. And, indeed, the reader who persists with the story, nerved by the same devotion to social science as that which animates Mr. Johnson, will often be well rewarded. For one thing, his searchlight plays relentlessly into the recesses of New York life. The method of the procured husband who can frank all escapades of his wife in her rôle of mistress is explained in perfectly candid detail; and in a lighter vein the story of how Estelle Monks became Ferdie Amsterdam, of the famous Society column of the *Free Press,* is a master-picture of American push and American slang. But there are plenty of effective scenes, *genre* pictures worked up with an immense amount of vivacious realism; the amours of men and women rigorously followed out, dissected, and discussed with much skill and insight — though the serious intensity with which they are handled would not be excessive if the fate of the United States depended upon them; and the heroine emerges from the whole a sympathetic figure whom we gladly resign at the end to a conventional matrimonial career.

XIII

THE SALAMANDER

[*Punch*, April 21, 1915. By special permission of the proprietors.]

I have just read *The Salamander* (Secker) of Mr. Owen Johnson — a name new to me and one to keep on the select list — and I feel I know just all about one side of that city of surprises, New York. The Salamander is either a native of New York or a migrant thither from a Western State. It is of the so-miscalled gentler sex, of any age from eighteen to nominal twenty-five. It plays with fire to the extent of eating it and living on it — that, roughly, is Mr. Johnson's idea. It can (as the saying is) take care of itself.

Naturalists observe that it has a long head and a little heart. Quintessentially a cold and dishonest reptile, it offers all and gives nothing in particular in exchange for anything from 'bokays' to automobiles. Beginning with male flappers, preferably the young of plutocrats, it later fastens on the plutocrats themselves or their robust enemies. Strong men, at whose nod railroad and chewing gum trusts go quaking, fight publicly over it in equivocal restaurants. Mr. Johnson's particular salamander, Doré by pseudonym, eschews the rigor of the game. She allows herself to be hard hit, and, instead of running away with the hitter, is betrayed by a maternal instinct (with which she has, properly speaking, no business) to take unto herself a young rotter with a determined spark of character glinting behind his eyes, who has for her fair sake fought himself free of the widow Cliquot and others. This, I suppose, is a concession to the molasses formula, though our author is too sincere a person to accept it, and hints in an epilogue that burnt salamanders don't dread the fire as much as would be comforting to their converted husbands to believe. This clever novel has n't the air of caricature which the subject might seem to invite. Doré herself is made plausible enough — no mean feat. Salamanderism is presented as a phase of the new feminism in U. S. A. An allied species has been reported in Chelsea by detached observers.

XIV

WIFE AND NO WIFE [1]

[*Evening Post*. New York, April 24, 1915. By permission.]

The place is Shanghai, the time the present, the persons a woman and three men, all in love with her — the situation therefore an advance upon the consecrated one, by virtue of being a quadrangle instead of a triangle. It is a very pretty complication, to begin with. Hilary, the heroine, has once (innocently) planned to become John's mistress, but has withdrawn at the last moment and married Nash. After four years of marriage she has fallen in love with young Louis. Nash is about to sail for Manila; Hilary

[1] *The Chalk Line*. By Anne Warwick. New York: John Lane Company.

plans to lose the boat and Nash, and become Louis's mistress. But John is in Shanghai and has learned their plans. He calls at Louis's bachelor establishment at the moment when Hilary has joined it. He remonstrates. Nash presently drops in also, knows what is happening, but is prepared to give the lovers a blessing, though not a divorce. Hilary asserts her right to live in the sun. Nash and John are about to go their ways, when 'Stop!' came an order like a pistol-shot — to the two men about to pass out of the door. 'No one leaves here. There is cholera in the house. You are in quarantine.' So there we are. In the end (the quarantine lasts eight days) Hilary discovers that John is the only man she has ever loved. Nash, the husband, crosses the chalk line to the cholera-quarters, and so gets himself permanently out of the way, Louis is disposed of readily, and all ends comfortably for people who take comfort in this kind of nonsense.

XV

SHOCKING REVELATIONS [1]

[*Nation*, London, England, February 13, 1915. By permission.]

Armageddon has discovered the governess. Next to the Archangelic hosts, there has been no more popular legend than that of the German governess in the household of the Prime Minister (or was it the Foreign Secretary? or the First Lord of the Admiralty?) whose bedroom, when searched, yielded diagrams of every fort in the kingdom and a bonnet-box lined with bombs. Then, shortly after the outbreak of war, came the entertaining memoirs of Miss Anne Topham, ex-governess to the Kaiser's children; and now we have the revelations of an anonymous lady, for five years English governess to a princely family in Germany.

It is instructive to compare these two memoirs. Miss Topham's, written some years before the war, was a candid and friendly account of the Imperial family, valuable because of its cordial sincerity and freedom from prejudice. The volume before us is a remarkable example of the psychological effects of war. With-

[1] *What I Found Out*. By an English Governess (Chapman & Hall.)

out for a moment suggesting that the anonymous lady is actuated by any motive other than the strictest regard for accuracy, the reader cannot but be struck by the almost uncanny precision with which these notes ring true to the tune of the moment.

The public mind, for instance, is anxiously engaged in the consideration of a Zeppelin raid. 'Anonyma's' volume opens with an account of her arrival in Germany: her princely charges, boys of five and six, are discovered at play, and so absorbing is their game that the entrance of the governess is unheeded. And what is this game? It is a *Kriegspiel* for infants, manufactured by Count Zeppelin, consisting of miniature airships supplied with sugar bombs, and a costly and elaborate model of London. As the governess comes into the room, she overhears the tutor exclaiming: 'Now, watch again the way I do it. One over Westminster Abbey —'

The same ominously apposite impression is conveyed in turn by every member of the German war party. Take General von Bernhardi: 'the most ruthless, brutal-looking man I had ever met, the very type of militarism in flesh and blood — especially blood.' With a bow so stiff that it 'seemed as though he grudged bending his thick, short neck for my benefit,' the General raps out the harsh inquiry: 'You are English?' 'She was born in Washington,' tactfully explains Herr Krupp, hurrying to the rescue of an awkward situation. 'Ach, that is better,' the General grunts. A few minutes later, however, the governess is indiscreet enough to express her admiration for England. 'That is nonsense,' observes Bernhardi savagely:

'You have only to read their newspapers to see that the English know they are degenerating fast. But the hand of Fate is on them. They are asleep, and will wake up with a rude shock only when it is too late.'

As he departs, Bernhardi observes (aside) to Krupp, 'Ah, you will have your big surprise all ready for us at the *Festakt!*'

Or turn to Von Kluck, with his 'great dome head' and his 'air of being absent-minded and thinking deeply of something far away in space,' and he will be overheard remarking mysteriously that '"they" wanted him to go to France to look at it.' A few days afterwards a box of chocolates arrives from France with the General's card enclosed. No harm surely in a box of chocolates? Why, then, does the Prince chuckle when he sees it and exclaim ecstatically, 'The old dare devil!' Anonyma is ready with the explanation:

'I have heard it said since I came back to England, by a Frenchman, that General von Kluck is supposed to have visited France incognito, to look at some quarries near Soissons, which Germans bought and secretly made ready to use as trenches a year before the war broke out.'

Thus, cunningly, by the method of innuendo and suggestion, the governess works her fateful spell. Everything utters the same note of secret menace. Out of the mouth of babes Bernhardism babbles unchecked; the very servants give away important political secrets as readily as they receive tips. All is in order, from the German governess spy story (with names and addresses complete) to the improper proposals of the Prussian Lieutenant. It would be unjust to Anonyma to quit this notice without a reference to the Kaiser. One afternoon as she is reading quietly in the garden, two gentlemen in uniform are seen approaching. The governess looks up, and is so startled by the sight of one of them that she overturns her chair. The Emperor (for it is he) gallantly replaces it, remarking as he does so, 'Ah, I see that I have upset the United Kingdom!' The two enter into an animated conversation, but the governess observes, 'an occasional odd, wandering look come into his eyes'; and that his left hand, 'although beautifully kept, is not an attractive shape, and looks somehow unhealthy.' The left hand is bad; but the motive for the Kaiser's visit puts the crowning seal on our suspicions:

'What do you suppose brought *Him* to the Schloss?' enquires an artful baroness. 'No, it was not to see the children, nor the Prince, nor Lieutenant von X——, he's seen them all — he came to see you!'

Machiavellism can go no further.

H.   DRAMATIC CRITICISM

The purpose of dramatic criticism is to do for a play or a playwright very much what literary criticism does for a book or its author. There is, however, in dramatic criticism a less general agreement of critical opinion and, owing to the changing character of modern drama, a less definitely organized body of critical theory for the guidance of individual judgment. It must also be remembered that the time limitations under which the average first night notice is produced, while they no doubt tend to preserve freshness and vividness of impression, at the same time do not allow for that slow process of maturing thought which gives to good writing the smoothness and flavor of old wine.

The student who looks forward to the writing of dramatic criticism should have a knowledge of the history of dramatic literature and an acquaintance with the best of the numerous recent books on the drama and the stage. He needs also to keep in close touch with the better newspapers of such cities as London, Paris, Berlin, Vienna, and New York, which are noteworthy for the number and character of their dramatic productions, nor should he neglect the magazines devoted to the drama, where he will find good examples of dramatic criticism and carefully written reviews of the season's productions.

Careful distinction should be made between the conscientiously written, independently formed judgment of a play and the commonplace and valueless press-agent kind of notice so common in the newspapers, a notice usually as lacking in literary skill as it is in critical discrimination. While the technique of the dramatic review has fortunately not yet become so stereotyped as that of the news-story, some of the topics which are ordinarily included may be mentioned: the name of the play, the author, the theater, the occasion (first performance, anniversary, revival, or benefit), the star or chief actors (sometimes the whole cast), a summary of the action, and some statement as to the character of the production, the quality of the acting, and the general impression made by the play. The hybrid nature of many of the recent theatrical productions makes it impossible to predict in any given case how much space should be given to any of the factors enumerated above, but it is safe for the young critic to remember that 'the play's the thing,' and that its importance should not be overshadowed by actors or scenery or audience.

In the illustrations of dramatic criticism which follow the student will find not only the brief (*Rosy Rapture*) and the more lengthy notice ('Typically American'), but also examples of the revival of the preface (Barker's *Midsummer Night's Dream*), of the critical article on a dramatic movement or school (W. B. Yeats on 'The Irish Drama'), of the appreciation of a playwright (W. P. Eaton, 'Concerning David Belasco'), and of the author's personal attitude toward his craft (Arnold Bennett, 'Writing Plays,' and B. Veiller, 'How I Wrote *Within the Law*').

I

WRITING PLAYS

ARNOLD BENNETT

[*Metropolitan,* July, 1913. Reprinted by courtesy of the publishers.]

There is an idea abroad, assiduously fostered as a rule by critics who happen to have written neither novels nor plays, that it is more difficult to write a play than a novel. I do not think so. I have written or collaborated in about twenty novels and about twenty plays, and I am convinced that it is easier to write a play than a novel. Personally, I would sooner *write* two plays than one novel — less expenditure of nervous force and mere brains would be required for two plays than for one novel. (I emphasize the word 'write' because if the whole weariness between the first conception and the first performance of a play is compared with the whole weariness between the first conception and the first publication of a novel, then the play has it. I would sooner get seventy and seven novels produced than one play. But my immediate object is to compare only writing with writing.) It seems to me that the sole persons entitled to judge of the comparative difficulty of writing plays and writing novels are those authors who have succeeded or failed equally well in both departments. And in this limited band I imagine that the differences of opinion on the point could not be marked. I would like to note, in passing, for the support of my proposition, that whereas established novelists not infrequently venture into the theatre with audacity, established dramatists are very cautious indeed about quitting the theatre. An established dramatist usually takes good care to write plays and naught else; he will not affront the risks of coming out into the open; and therein his instinct is quite properly that of self-preservation. Of many established dramatists all over the world it may be affirmed that if they were so indiscreet as to publish a novel the result would be a great shattering and a great awakening.

SEVEN FAULTLESS BROMIDES

An enormous amount of vague reverential nonsense is talked about the technique of the stage, the assumption being that in difficulty it far surpasses any other literary technique, and that until it is acquired a respectable play cannot be written. One hears also that it can only be acquired behind the scenes. A famous actor-manager once kindly gave me the benefit of his experience, and what he said was that a dramatist who wished to learn his business must live behind the scenes — and study the works of Dion Boucicault! The truth is that no technique is so crude and so simple as the technique of the stage, and that the proper place to learn it is not behind the scenes, but in the pit. Managers, being the most conservative people on earth, except compositors, will honestly try to convince the naïve dramatist that effects can only be obtained in the precise way in which effects have always been obtained, and that this and that rule must not be broken on pain of outraging the public. And indeed it is natural that managers should talk thus, seeing the low state of the drama, because in any art rules and reaction always flourish when creative energy is sick. The mandarins have ever said and will ever say that a technique which does not correspond with their own is no technique, but simple clumsiness. There are

some seven situations in the customary drama, and a play which does not contain at least one of those situations in each act will be condemned as 'undramatic' or
5 'thin,' or as being 'all talk.' It may contain half a hundred other situations, but for the mandarin a situation which is not one of the seven is not a situation. Similarly there are some dozen character
10 types in the customary drama, and all original — that is, truthful — characterization will be dismissed as a total absence of characterization because it does not reproduce any of these dozen types. Thus
15 every truly original play is bound to be indicted for bad technique. The author is bound to be told that what he has written may be marvelously clever, but that it is not a play. I remember the day — and it
20 is not long ago — when even so experienced and sincere a critic as William Archer used to argue that if the 'intellectual' drama did not succeed with the general public, it was because its technique
25 nique was not up to the level of the technique of the commercial drama! Perhaps he has changed his opinion since then. Heaven knows that the so-called 'intellectual' drama is amateurish enough, but
30 nearly all literary art is amateurish, and assuredly no intellectual drama could hope to compete in clumsiness with some of the most successful commercial plays of modern times. I tremble to think what the
35 mandarins and William Archer would say to the technique of *Hamlet,* could it by some miracle be brought forward as a new piece by a Mr. Shakespeare. They would probably recommend Mr. Shakespeare to
40 consider the ways of Sardou, Henri Bernstein and Sir Herbert Tree, and be wise. Most positively they would assert that *Hamlet* was not a play. And their pupils of the daily press would point out — what
45 surely Mr. Shakespeare ought to have perceived for himself — that the second, third, or fourth act might be cut wholesale without the slightest loss to the piece.

In the sense in which mandarins under-
50 stand the word technique, there is no technique special to the stage except that which concerns the moving of solid human bodies to and fro, and the limitations of the human senses. The dramatist must
55 not expect his audience to be able to see or hear two things at once, nor to be incapable of fatigue. And he must not expect his interpreters to stroll round or

come on or go off in a satisfactory manner unless he provides them with satisfactory reasons for strolling round, coming in, or going off. Lastly, he must not expect his interpreters to achieve physical impossibilities. The dramatist who sends a pretty woman off in street attire and seeks to bring her on again in thirty seconds fully dressed for a court ball may fail in stage technique, but he has not proved that stage technique is tremendously difficult; he has proved something quite else.

One reason why a play is easier to write than a novel is that a play is shorter than a novel. On the average one may say that it takes six plays to make the matter of a novel. Other things being equal, a short work of art presents fewer difficulties than a longer one. The contrary is held true by the majority, but then the majority, having never attempted to produce a long work of art, are unqualified to offer an opinion. It is said that the most difficult form of poetry is the sonnet. But the most difficult form of poetry is the epic. The proof that the sonnet is the most difficult form is alleged to be in the fewness of perfect sonnets. There are, however, few more perfect sonnets than perfect epics. A perfect sonnet may be a heavenly accident. But such accidents can never happen to writers of epics. Some years ago we had an enormous palaver about the 'art of the short story,' which numerous persons who had omitted to write novels pronounced to be more difficult than the novel. But the fact remains that there are scores of perfect short stories, whereas it is doubtful whether anybody but Turgenieff ever did write a perfect novel. A short form is easier to manipulate than a long form because its construction is less complicated, because the balance of its proportions can be more easily corrected by means of a rapid survey, because it is lawful and even necessary in it to leave undone many things which are very hard to do, and because the emotional strain is less prolonged. The most difficult thing in all art is to maintain the imaginative tension unslackened throughout a considerable period.

'ENTER MILLICENT'

Then, not only does a play contain less matter than a novel — it is further simplified by the fact that it contains fewer kinds of matter, and less subtle kinds of matter. There are numerous delicate and difficult affairs of craft that the dramatist need not think about at all. If he attempts to go beyond a certain very mild degree of subtlety he is merely wasting his time. What passes for subtlety on the stage would have a very obvious air in a novel, as some dramatists have unhappily discovered. Thus whole continents of danger may be shunned by the dramatist, and instead of being scorned for his cowardice he will be very rightly applauded for his artistic discretion. Fortunate predicament! Again, he need not — indeed he must not — save in a primitive and hinting manner, concern himself with 'atmosphere.' He may roughly suggest one, but if he begins on the feat of 'creating' an atmosphere (as it is called), the last suburban train will have departed before he has reached the crisis of the play. The last suburban train is the best friend of the dramatist, though the fellow seldom has the sense to see it. Further he is saved all descriptive work. See a novelist harassing himself into his grave over the description of a landscape, a room, a gesture — while the dramatist grins. The dramatist may have to imagine a landscape, a room, or a gesture; but he has not got to write it — and it is the writing which hastens death. If a dramatist and a novelist set out to portray a clever woman, they are almost equally matched, because each has to make the creature say things and do things. But if they set out to portray a charming woman, the dramatist can recline in an easy-chair and smoke while the novelist is ruining temper, digestion and eyesight, and spreading terror in his household by his moodiness and unapproachability. The electric light burns in the novelist's study at 3 A.M. — the novelist is still endeavoring to convey by means of words the extraordinary fascination that his heroine could exercise over mankind by the mere act of walking into a room; and he never has really succeeded and never will. The dramatist writes curtly, 'Enter Millicent.' All are anxious to do the dramatist's job for him. Is the play being read at home — the reader eagerly and with brilliant success puts his imagination to work and completes a charming Millicent after his own secret desires. (Whereas he would coldly decline to add one touch to Millicent were she the heroine of a novel.) Is the play being performed on the stage — an experienced, conscientious and perhaps lovely actress will strive her hardest to prove that the dramatist was right about Millicent's astounding fascination. And if she fails nobody will blame the dramatist; the dramatist will receive naught but sympathy.

THE PLAY STORY VS. THE NOVEL STORY

And there is still another region of superlative difficulty which is narrowly circumscribed for the spoiled dramatist — I mean the whole business of persuading the public that the improbable is probable. Every work of art is and must be crammed with improbabilities and artifice; and the greater portion of the artifice is employed in just this trickery of persuasion. Only, the public of the dramatist needs far less persuading than the public of the novelist. The novelist announces that Millicent accepted the hand of the wrong man, and in spite of all the novelist's corroborative and exegetical detail the insulted reader declines to credit the statement and condemns the incident as unconvincing. The dramatist decides that Millicent must accept the hand of the wrong man, and there she is on the stage in flesh and blood, veritably doing it! Not easy for even the critical beholder to maintain that Millicent could not and did not do such a silly thing when he has actually with his eyes seen her in the very act! The dramatist, as usual, having done less, is more richly rewarded by results.

Of course, it will be argued, as it has always been argued, by those who have not written novels, that it is precisely the 'doing less'— the leaving out — that constitutes the unique and fearful difficulty of dramatic art. 'The skill to leave out'— lo! the master faculty of the dramatist! But, in the first place, I do not believe that, having regard to the relative scope of the play and of the novel, the necessity for leaving out is more acute in the one than in the other. The adjective 'photographic' is as absurd applied to the novel as to the play. And, in the second place, other factors being equal, it is less exhausting, and it requires less skill, to refrain from doing than to do. To know when to refrain from doing may be hard, but positively to do is even harder. Sometimes, listening to partizans of the drama,

I have been moved to suggest that, if the art of omission is so wondrously difficult, a dramatist who practised the habit of omitting to write anything whatever ought to be hailed as the supreme craftsman.

Whether in a play or in a novel, the creative artist has to tell a story — using the word story in a very wide sense. Just as a novel is divided into chapters, and for a similar reason, a play is divided into acts. But neither chapters nor acts are necessary. Some of Balzac's chief novels have no chapter-divisions, and it has been proved that a theater audience can and will listen for two hours to 'talk,' and even recitative singing, on the stage, without a pause. Indeed audiences, under the compulsion of an artist strong and imperious enough, could, I am sure, be trained to marvelous feats of prolonged receptivity. However, chapters and acts are usual, and they involve the same constructional processes on the part of the artist. The entire play or novel must tell a complete story — that is, arouse a curiosity and reasonably satisfy it, raise a main question and then settle it. And each act or other chief division must tell a definite portion of the story, satisfy part of the curiosity, settle part of the question. And each scene or other minor division must do the same according to its scale. Everything basic that applies to the technique of the novel applies equally to the technique of the play.

DRAMA NEED NOT BE DRAMATIC

In particular I would urge that a play, any more than a novel, need not be dramatic, employing the term as it is usually employed. In so far as it suspends the listener's interest every tale, however told, may be said to be dramatic. In this sense *The Golden Bowl* is dramatic; so are *Dominique* and *Persuasion*. A play need not be more dramatic than that. Very emphatically a play need not be dramatic in the stage sense. It need never induce interest to the degree of excitement. It need have nothing that resembles what would be recognizable in the theater as a situation. It may amble on — and it will still be a play, and it may succeed in pleasing either the fastidious hundreds or the unfastidious hundreds of thousands, according to the talent of the author. Without doubt mandarins will continue for about a century yet to excommunicate certain plays from the category of plays. But nobody will be any the worse. And dramatists will go on proving that whatever else divides a play from a book 'dramatic quality' does not. Some archmandarin may launch at me one of those mandarinic epigrammatic questions which are supposed to overthrow the adversary at one dart. 'Do you seriously mean to argue, sir, that drama need not be dramatic?' I do, if the word dramatic is to be used in the mandarinic signification. I mean to state that some of the finest plays of the modern age differ from a psychological novel in nothing but the superficial form of telling. Example, Henri Becque's *La Parisienne,* than which there is no better. If I am asked to give my own definition of the adjective 'dramatic,' I would say that that story is dramatic which is told in dialogue imagined to be spoken by actors and actresses on the stage, and that any narrower definition is bound to exclude some genuine plays universally accepted as such — even by mandarins. For be it noted that the mandarin is never consistent.

My definition brings me to the sole technical difference between a play and a novel — in the play the story is told by means of dialogue. It is a difference less important than it seems, and not invariably even a sure point of distinction between the two kinds of narrative. For a novel may consist exclusively of dialogue. And plays may contain other matter than dialogue. The classic chorus is not dialogue. But nowadays we should consider the device of the chorus to be clumsy, as, nowadays, it indeed would be. We have grown very ingenious and clever at the trickery of making characters talk to the audience and explain themselves and their past history while seemingly innocent of any such intention. And here, I admit, the dramatist has to face a difficulty special to himself, which the novelist can avoid. I believe it to be the sole difficulty which is peculiar to the drama, and that it is not acute is proved by the ease with which third-rate dramatists have generally vanquished it. Mandarins are wont to assert that the dramatist is also handicapped by the necessity for rigid economy in the use of material. This is not so. Rigid economy in the use of material is equally advisable in every form of art. If it is a necessity it is a necessity which all artists

flout from time to time, and occasionally with gorgeous results, and the successful dramatist has hitherto not been less guilty of flouting it than the novelist or any other artist.

And now having shown that some alleged differences between the play and the novel are illusory, and that a certain technical difference, though possibly real, is superficial and slight, I come to the fundamental difference between them — a difference which the laity does not suspect, which is seldom insisted upon and never sufficiently, but which nobody who is well versed in the making of both plays and novels can fail to feel profoundly. The emotional strain of writing a play is not merely less prolonged than that of writing a novel — it is less severe even while it lasts, lower in degree and of a less purely creative character. And herein is the chief of all the reasons why a play is easier to write than a novel. The drama does not belong exclusively to literature, because its effect depends on something more than the composition of words. The dramatist is the sole author of the play, but he is not the sole creator of it. Without him nothing can be done, but, on the other hand, he cannot do everything himself. He begins the work of creation, which is finished either by creative interpreters on the stage or by the creative imagination of the reader in the study. It is as if he carried an immense weight to the landing at the turn of a flight of stairs, and that thence upward the lifting had to be done by other people. Consider the affair as a pyramidal structure, and the dramatist is the base — but he is not the apex. A play is a collaboration of creative faculties. The egotism of the dramatist resents this uncomfortable fact, but the fact exists. And further, the creative faculties are not only those of the author, the stage-director (producer) and the actors — the audience itself is unconsciously part of the collaboration.

Hence a dramatist who attempts to do the whole work of creation before the acting begins is an inartistic usurper of the functions of others, and will fail to proper accomplishment at the end. The dramatist must deliberately, in performing his share of the work, leave scope for a multitude of alien faculties whose operations he can neither precisely foresee nor completely control. The point is not that in the writing of a play there are various sorts of matters — as we have already seen — which the dramatist must ignore; the point is that even in the region proper to him he must not push the creative act to its final limit. He must ever remember those who are to come after him.

AUTHOR GIVES WAY TO PRODUCER

When the play is 'finished,' the processes of collaboration have yet to begin. The serious work of the dramatist is over, but the most desolating part of his toil awaits him. I do not refer to the business of arranging with a theatrical manager for the production of the play. For, though that generally partakes of the nature of tragedy, it also partakes of the nature of amusing burlesque, owing to the fact that theatrical managers are — no doubt inevitably — theatrical. Nevertheless, even the theatrical manager, while disclaiming the slightest interest in anything more vital to the stage than the box-office, is himself in some degree a collaborator, and is the first to show to the dramatist that a play is not a play till it is performed. The manager reads the play, and, to the dramatist's astonishment, reads quite a different play from that which the dramatist imagines he wrote. In particular the manager reads a play which can scarcely hope to succeed — indeed a play against whose chances of success ten thousand powerful reasons can be adduced. It is remarkable that a manager nearly always foresees failure in a manuscript, and very seldom success. The manager's profoundest instinct — self-preservation again — is to refuse a play; if he accepts, it is against the grain, against his judgment — and out of a mad spirit of adventure. Some of the most glittering successes have been rehearsed in an atmosphere of settled despair. The dramatist naturally feels an immense contempt for the opinions, artistic and otherwise, of the manager, and he is therein justified. The manager's vocation is not to write plays, nor (let us hope) to act in them, nor to direct the rehearsals of them, and even his knowledge of the vagaries of his own box-office has often proved to be pitiably delusive. The manager's true and only vocation is to refrain from producing plays. Despite all this, however, the manager has already collaborated in the play. The dramatist sees it differently now. All sorts of new considerations have been presented to him. Not a word has been altered; but it is noticeably another play. Which is merely to say that the creative work on it which still remains to be done has been more accurately envisaged. This experience could not happen to a novel, because when a novel is written it is finished.

And when the director of rehearsals, or producer, has been chosen, and this priceless and mysterious person has his first serious confabulation with the author, then at once the play begins to assume new shapes — contours undreamed of by the author till that startling moment. And even if the author has the temerity to conduct his own rehearsals, similar disconcerting phenomena will occur; for the author as a producer is a different fellow from the author as author. The producer is up against realities. He, first, renders the play concrete, gradually condenses its filmy vapors into a solid element. . . . He suggests the casting. 'What do you think of X for the old man?' asked the producer. The author is staggered. Is it conceivable that so renowned a producer can have so misread and misunderstood the play? X would be preposterous as the old man. But the producer goes on talking. And suddenly the author sees possibilities in X. But at the same time he sees a different play from what he wrote. And quite probably he sees a more glorious play. Quite probably he had not suspected how great a dramatist he is. . . . Before the first rehearsal is called, the play, still without a word altered, has gone through astounding creative transmutations; the author recognizes in it some likeness to his beloved child, but it is the likeness of a first cousin.

THE ACTORS FINISH THE WORK

At the first rehearsal, and for many rehearsals, to an extent perhaps increasing, perhaps decreasing, the dramatist is forced into an apologetic and self-conscious mood; and his mien is something between that of a criminal who has committed a horrid offense and that of a father over the crude body of a new-born child. Now in truth he deeply realizes that a play is a collaboration. In extreme cases he may be brought to see that he himself is one of the less important factors in the collaboration. The first preoccupation of the in-

terpreters is not with his play at all, but —
quite rightly — with their own careers; if
they were not honestly convinced that
their own careers were the chief genuine
excuse for the existence of the theater and
the play they would not act very well.
But more than that, they do not regard his
play as a sufficient vehicle for the furtherance of their careers. At the most favorable what they secretly think is that if they
are permitted to exercise their talents on
his play there is a chance that they may be
able to turn it into a sufficient vehicle for
the furtherance of their careers. The attitude of every actor toward his part is: 15
'My part is not much of a part as it
stands, but if my individuality is allowed
to get into free contact with it, I may
make something brilliant out of it.'
Which attitude is a proper attitude, and 20
an attitude, in my opinion, justified by the
facts of the case. The actor's phrase is
that he *creates* a part, and he is right.
He completes the labor of creation begun
by the author and continued by the pro- 25
ducer, and if liberty is not accorded to him
— if either the author or the producer attempts to do too much of the creative
work — the result cannot be satisfactory.

As the rehearsals proceed the play 30
changes from day to day. However autocratic the producer, however obstinate the
dramatist, the play will vary at each rehearsal like a large cloud in a gentle wind.
It is never the same play for two days to- 35
gether. Nor is this surprising, seeing that
every day and night a dozen, or it may be
two dozen, human beings endowed with
the creative gift are creatively working on
it. Every dramatist who is candid with 40
himself well knows that, though his play
is often worsened by his collaborators, it
is also often improved — and improved in
the most mysterious and dazzling manner — without a word being altered. Pro- 45
ducer and actors do not merely suggest
possibilities, they execute them. And the
author is confronted by artistic phenomena
for which lawfully he may not claim
credit. On the other hand, he may be 50
confronted by inartistic phenomena in respect to which lawfully he is blameless,
but which he cannot prevent; a rehearsal
is like a battle — certain persons are
theoretically in control, but in fact the 55
thing principally fights itself. And thus
the creation goes on until the dress rehearsal, when it seems to have come to a

stop. And the dramatist lying awake in
the night, reflects stoically, fatalistically:
'Well, that is the play that they have
made of *my play!*' And he may be
5 pleased or he may be disgusted. But if he
attends the first performance he cannot
fail to notice, after the first few minutes
of it, that he was quite mistaken, and that
what the actors are performing is still an-
10 other play. The audience is collaborating.

II

THE IRISH DRAMA

WILLIAM BUTLER YEATS

[*Twentieth Century Magazine,* November, 1911.
By permission.]

I will not criticize the contemporary
theater as a whole. If you were satisfied
with it you would not have formed yourselves into a Drama League. If I were
25 satisfied with it I should not have spent
so much time over our Irish players. We
all know, owing to the commercial conditions of the times, contemporary drama,
as a whole, does not take its place beside
30 the best painting, the best music, and the
best books of our times; the contemporary
theater makes a pretense of representing
reality — of showing us people no more
exciting than we are ourselves, no more
35 eloquent than we are ourselves, no more
picturesquely dressed than we are ourselves, and it is right that it should do
so. Reformers of the theater, for the
most part, accept the same idea. And
40 they, at least, do give you reality, and they
make it interesting to you, as Mr. Galsworthy does in his *Strife* and in his *Justice,* by showing the great hidden forces of
the modern world — the strife between
45 capital and labor, the contest of men
against theological institutions, against the
accepted social code, etc. There is another way to change the stage, and that
is to show there a life, whether ideal or
50 real, that is exciting and picturesque in
itself. Italy, where they have made the
verse drama once more a really popular
thing, is doing that in one way. In Sicily,
where Grasso is creating a wonderful
55 school of players, and in Ireland, it is being
done in a different way. We are putting
upon the stage a real life where men talk
picturesque and musical words, and where

men have often strange and picturesque characters; that is to say, the life of far-away villages where an old leisurely habit of life still remains.

From the first start of our intellectual movement in Ireland, our faith in success has come from our knowledge of the life of the country places, and the imaginative beauty of their speech. One discovers thoughts there not very much unlike those of Homer, not very unlike those of the Greek dramatists. Of course there is a great deal that is crude, but there are songs and stories, showing an attitude of mind that seems the very root of art.

Close to the house where I spend every summer there is the little picturesque village of Ballylee, two or three houses gathered about an old castle, a very old bridge, and beside the bridge great stones that helped the traveler when the stream was flooded, probably for centuries before the bridge was built. Seventy years ago there died in that village Mary Hynes, a beautiful peasant girl, and the poet Rafftery put her into a song. A few years ago I heard old men and women describe her beauty after all these years with wonder and excitement in their voices. 'The sun and the moon,' said one, 'never shone upon anybody so lovely.' 'I tremble all over when I think of her,' said another. Nor was the poet's praise that made her so famous unworthy praise. 'Mary Hynes, the calm and easy woman, has beauty in her mind and beauty in her body.' That's what Rafftery said of her. It is like hearing the old men on the walls of Troy speak of Helen.

In Ireland the country life has for us the further fascination that it is the only thoroughly Irish life that is left. Everywhere else English influence has made a conquest more thorough than any that the sword could make. All our patriotic movements go back to the peasant, just as similar movements have done in Norway. We try to re-create Ireland in an Irish way by mastering what he knows, and by using it to understand what the old manuscripts contain. To understand the peasant by the Saga, the Saga by the peasant — that was the Norwegian formula. If you keep this in mind it will show you that our theatre of folk art is no artificial creation of a literary clique, but an expression of the Irish mind of today. It will explain to you also how our players,

who are not peasants, but young men and women taken from various businesses in Dublin, have come to understand the peasant so well. We took them at the start from different patriotic societies, where everything encouraged them to study the country life. In 1902 a group of young men and women were playing old-fashioned farces at a coffee palace in Dublin, and when they gave up their farces and took to our plays instead, they did it in the first instance more from patriotism than anything else. Many of them belonged to the Gaelic League; some of them knew Irish, and living Irish is a peasant speech. But if politics helped us, politics injured us also. We did not realize when we began that we should have to fight and conquer conventional conceptions of Irish character. And yet we should have foreseen it.

All Irish thought has been artificial for years. In the earlier parts of the nineteenth century England had met the Irish national demand by slandering our characters. She did not wish to give us self-government and so she said we were unworthy of it. The Irish peasant, for instance, was caricatured in *Punch,* in speeches and in newspapers. He was represented as half animal, or as all but a savage. To meet this, beginning, I think, with O'Connell, who said that the Irish peasantry were the finest peasantry upon earth, Ireland created a whole literature of national glorification. We repeated to one another the real or supposed virtues of our people. We had them always ready to meet the foreign slander. This attitude of mind lasted long after the need for it had gone by. Every kind of enthusiast, political, religious, social, had endowed some section of Irishmen with the virtues he most admired, and national song and national novel — we used the word nation constantly — were expected to show Ireland in the best possible light. We were not a people curious about life, looking at it with disinterested contemplation, but a kind of army organized for offense and defense. We understood nothing but propaganda.

The first play of country life that we set upon the stage was in Irish. Our own players had not then come together and we got players from a branch of the Gaelic League. At the last moment one player refused to go upon the stage because the cottage he was to play in was too shabby to do credit to his country, and another demanded the banishing of a pack of cards that had been given to a group of young men who were to sit playing in the corner. He admitted that he spent most of his own evenings playing cards, but he did not think it right that the Irish should be represented as playing them upon the stage.

The history of imaginative thought is generally a history of violent reactions. Synge came to destroy all that unreality. I met Synge in 1897, in a students' hotel in Paris. He had learned Irish from a Gaelic professor at Trinity College, Dublin, and had spent some years wandering through Europe. Nothing interested him but the life of the poor, not because they were poor, for he was nothing of a philanthropist, an artist merely, but because there was something in their way of thinking that excited him. He was very poor himself, though of an old family, and a fine scholar. He had lived with German peasants in the Black Forest and with a chairmaker in Paris, and brought his fiddle everywhere that he would be more welcome. I got him to come back to Ireland, and there in the Arran and Blasket Islands he found a life after his own heart. There he escaped the squalor of the poor and the nobility of the rich. He had nothing of the modern humanitarian; he had no interest in economics, no interest in social forces, and he had little of the Irish politician. He was a Nationalist, but he never spoke of politics; nothing interested him but the individual man: in fact I think his own ill health and poverty had made individual destiny momentous to him. All the things that we forget in the excitements of newspapers and crowds and business, were always present to him. In one of his early poems he asks on his twenty-fifth birthday if the twenty-five years to come are to be as evil as the twenty-five gone by. But gradually he attained happiness through his art, coming to see in his individual infirmities but a sort of burning glass that gathered for his study the general lot of men. All became but a subject for artistic creation, and an occasion for the creative joy.

It was inevitable that a man like this, who seemed ignorant of the mere existence of all these Irish controversies, should outrage the feelings of the crowds. Just as he felt in his own life continual struggle between his ideal purpose and his infirmity and his poverty, so did he see in the world about him an ideal dream and a grotesque reality. He knew the country places as no Irish writer for fifty years had known them, but he selected from them strange, passionate and grotesque types, to set beside his dream. It was no malice, no love of mischief, that made him imagine instead of colleens of the old sort, and the good young men of Boucicault, blind Martin and his wife in *The Well of the Saints,* the erring wife in *The Shadow of the Glen,* the fantastic, mistaken heroworship of the people in his *Playboy of the Western World.* He took his types from reality indeed, but exaggerated them and arranged them according to his fancy, until he had created something as strange as the wandering knight and the Sancho Panza of Cervantes. I can imagine some patriotic Spaniard saying to Cervantes, 'Do you really pretend that this fat, cowardly peasant, and this crack-brained knight are typical of the peasants and the gentlemen of Spain?' I can imagine others even without any patriotic bias asking why he gave them such strange types. He, too, took from life the violent and incomplete that through its symbolism he might reveal a heroic dream. When we have filled our minds with the work of Synge, we remember, even more vividly than the strange persons he has created, blind Martin's dream of the splendid life that might be, Nora Bourke's pre-occupation with the fine men she fancied, the Playboy's poetical reveries of far-off exciting things. Dublin for a time saw but one-half his meaning and rejected him, rioting for a week after the first performance of his greatest play, rejecting him as most countries have rejected their greatest poets. But Dublin has repented sooner than most countries have repented, and today the *Playboy* is played constantly in Dublin to good houses, drawn from all political and social sections. The six days' rioting was his laurel wreath.

Lady Gregory's plays were accepted from the first, for she is attracted, not by the harsh, but the gracious elements in life. She has no sarcasm. It was sarcasm, aimed at the whole of life, that made Synge his worst enemies. There is no bitterness in her laughter, in her vision no delight in the grotesque things. Some of her plays, those that touch upon some patriotic emotion, are so well loved that men passing the Abbey Theater door and seeing some favorite name upon the bill will pay their sixpence, and having seen, say, *The Rising of the Moon,* for perhaps the fortieth time, will come out after twenty minutes of emotion and go upon their way. No new play can mean as much to them, and so they only stay for the old one. Our other dramatists, Mr. Robinson, Mr. Murray, Mr. Boyle, Mr. Irving, are less full of the folk life; probably they may be half conscious of some reaction against us older writers, because at moments they seem almost as much interested in economic problems as a Galsworthy or a Shaw; but what interests me most in their work is that by their means we are setting upon the stage the life of most classes in Ireland that have anything Irish about them. We have begun to go beyond the peasant to find themes in the workhouse parlor, the house of the strong farmer, in the seminary and the shop.

III

GRANVILLE BARKER'S PRODUCTION OF 'A MIDSUMMER NIGHT'S DREAM'

[*Times,* London, England, February 7, 1914. By permission.]

Is it Titania's 'Indian Boy' that has given Mr. Barker his notion of Orientalizing Shakespeare's fairies? Or is it Bakst? Anyhow, they look like Cambodian idols and posture like Nijinsky in *Le Dieu Bleu.* But the most startling thing about them is that they are all gold — gold hair, gold faces, gold to the tips of their toes. A golden Oberon is flouted by a golden Titania, Peas-Blossom and Cobweb and Moth and Mustard-Seed are golden children — the only children among these fairies, three in flakes of gold and the fourth in golden baggy trousers out of *Sumurûn.* The rest are 'golden lads and lassies,' who, some of them, dance old romping, obviously English, dances, while the others, the Cambodian idols, fall into stiff postures in corners. One with a scimitar stalks like a black marionette, with *His* scimitar, in *Petrouchka.* Evidently the Russian ballet, which has transformed so much in London, has transmogrified Shakespeare. The golden fairies chase one another through the woods in single file or lie prone on a low green mound, grouped round Titania, under great shafts of green mounting to the sky, against a purple background. This color-effect, the heavy mass of old gold against the purple and the green, is wonderfully beautiful. In the end the golden fairies play hide-and-seek round the columns of Theseus's palace. Gradually their numbers dwindle. At last only one, a girl, is left — the last patch of gold to fade from the sight, and to leave on the mind the strange, new impression of the play as golden, a 'golden book of spirit and sense.' Who is the magician who invented these golden fairies? Is it Mr. Barker or Mr. Norman Wilkinson? One might perhaps have had misgivings about the thing in advance, a fear of tawdriness, dreadful associations with the golden image in Kensington-gardens. But the thing turns out to have been an inspiration, something to strike us all with wonder and delight. As soon as you see the thing you know that Mendelssohn would never do. For our part, we should have welcomed Stravinsky. But Mr. Cecil Sharp has given us old English folk-music, rather dolorous, always *piano,* more quaint than tuneful. Well, somehow or other, as the Americans say, it 'goes.' It goes quite well with the gold.

A PATCH OF SCARLET

On the gold is one single patch of scarlet. This is Puck, with a baggy wig and baggy breeches, a hobgoblin. He — Puck is this time really a he — is Mr. Donald Calthrop, gyrating, sitting at Oberon's feet cross-legged, tumbling head over heels, or, like a mischievous boy, putting finger to nose behind Bottom's back. A most uncanny Puck, this scarlet patch.

As for Theseus and Hippolyta and their train, we do not know where their dresses come from. We can only make shots. Is it from the mural decorations of Minos's palace unearthed in Crete? But some of them seem Byzantine and suggest a Ravenna fresco. All, men and women alike, wear 'peg-top' trousers, tight at the ankle. But in the last scene, at the performance of *Pyramus and Thisbe,* they, so to speak, put on their evening clothes — flowing Greek robes. So clad, they recline on couches in the very front of the stage

(Mr. Barker's now familiar 'apron stage') while the performance of Quince and his fellows takes place on the palace steps in the rear. This, again, is a novel arrangement and an admirable. Quince (Mr. Whitby) is *impayable*, Bottom (Mr. Playfair) immense, Flute (Mr. Quartermaine) deliciously absurd as Thisbe. And then the 'Bergamask' dance! It never came out of Bergamo, but is right Warwickshire, the acme of the clumsy grotesque, with vigorous kickings in that part of the anatomy meant for kicks. Perhaps the best thing in the performance, however, was the behavior of the audience; Theseus's courtly lead in the applause, the whispered comments of Demetrius and Lysander, the lively interest of the courtiers. It was all alive, this scene, all at the high water mark of excitement.

As always in *A Midsummer Night,* the difficulty is with the bewitched quartet of lovers. The difficulty is that they are often in imminent danger of becoming bores. If they escape being bores, they may be said to have succeeded. We are not sure that the men did altogether escape; but the ladies, Miss McCarthy and Miss Cowie, were more lucky. Miss McCarthy hardly shows at her best in a flaxen wig, but no doubt she must needs be contrasted with Miss Cowie's *brunette*. The quarrel of the two girls gives, as always, a tremendous 'lift' to this part of the play. Miss Cowie makes a surprisingly intense vixen — an anticipation of *Carmen*.

THE GOLDEN OBERON

But it is not of these one thinks in the end. The mind goes back to the golden fairies, and one's memories of this production must always be golden memories. The golden Oberon, Mr. Dennis Neilson-Terry, is a figure of slim, noble, and Giorgionesque beauty. His movements are grace itself. His voice, with the familiar family *timbre*, is the very voice for some of the most beautiful lines Shakespeare ever wrote. This Oberon, for the first time, dominates not only the scene, but the whole play, informs it with graciousness and majesty (fairy majesty, golden majesty) and exquisite rhythmic beauty. Miss Christine Silver's Titania is a delicate, fragile pendant to the Oberon. The little golden child-fairies are delightfully childish, even in their stiff Cambodian-idol attitudes. There was a great

outburst of enthusiasm — pent up in silent absorption during the evening — at the fall of the curtain. Mr. Barker, standing amid his golden fairies, seemed to be thinking that silence, too, has been said to be golden; but he was compelled, nevertheless, to utter a word of thanks. If only he can keep it up! If only he can run through all Shakespeare in the spirit of daring artistic adventure with which he has turned the fairy-land of *A Midsummer Night* into gold.

IV

A PREFACE TO 'A MIDSUMMER NIGHT'S DREAM'

GRANVILLE BARKER

[*New York Times,* February 17, 1915. By permission of author and publisher.]

'September 29, 1662 . . . and then to the King's Theater, where we saw *Midsummer Night's Dream,* which I had never seen before, nor shall ever again, for it is the most insipid, ridiculous play that I ever saw in my life. I saw, I confess, some good dancing and some handsome women, which was all my pleasure.' How many of us nowadays would dare confide that even to a cipher diary? But Pepys, as usual, is in the fashion. Shakespeare was out-moded, and the theatre manager was already bolstering up his mere poetry with sensuality and display. We have, of course, reformed all that. Still, if I must choose between this cheerful Philistine, and the pious, awestruck commentator, who tells me that 'the germs of a whole philosophy of life are latent in the wayward love scenes of *A Midsummer Night's Dream,* I turn rather to Pepys. He has done less to keep Shakespeare from his own. If you go to a theatre to scoff you may remain to enjoy yourself; if you go to pray (once in a while) you likelier leave to patronize.

Why waste time in proving that *A Midsummer Night's Dream* is a bad play, or proving otherwise, since to its deepest damnation one must add: — Written by a man of genius for the theatre, playwright in spite of himself? Does not vitality defeat doctrine? The opening of the play may be bad. The opening speech surely is even very bad dramatic verse. There is nothing much in the character of The-seus; there's nothing at all in Hippolyta. The substance of the opening scene is out of keeping both with its own method and with the scope of the play. But before the end of it, earlier than usual even in his later days, Shakespeare has begun to get into his stride. If he couldn't yet develop character he could write poetry, and:

> . . . O happy fair,
> Your eyes are lode stars and your tongue
>   sweet air,
> More tuneable than larke to shepherd's ear
> When wheat is green and hawthorn buds
>   appear.

At the sound of that we cease to demand from Helena — for the moment, at least — any more material qualities. How he could and seemingly couldn't help but flower into verse! It was still a question, I suppose, whether he remained a poet or became a dramatist. He was, in every sense, nearer to *Venus and Adonis* than *Macbeth*. If he hadn't been a man of the people, if he hadn't had his living to earn, if he hadn't had more fun in him than the writing of lyric poetry will sat-isfy! If it was he made the English the-atre, did not the theatre make him what he is — what he might be to us?

Next come the clowns. It is neces-sary, I am ashamed to say, to remark, that Clown does not, first of all, mean a person who tries to be funny. A clown is a countryman. Now, your Cockney audience finds a countryman comic, and your Cockney writer to this day often makes him outrageously so. Shakespeare presumably knew something about coun-trymen, and he made the simple discovery and put it into practice for the first time in this play, that, set down lovingly, your clown is better fun by far than mocked at; if, indeed, apart from an actor's gri-maces, he had then been funny at all. Later on Shakespeare did this, as he did most other things, better, but he never did it so simply. If Shallow and Silence are finer, they are different; moreover, though countrymen, they are not clowns. If Dogberry is as good, he hasn't, for me, quite the charm. There are little sketches in the last plays; that delightful person, for instance, at the end of *An-tony and Cleopatra,* with his 'I wish you joy of the worm.' But from the moment Bottom, gloweringly mistrustful of poor

Snug, asks, 'Let me play the lion, too,' from that moment they have my heart, all five forever. It is a little puzzling to discover just how bad their play is meant to be. Did Quince write it? If he is guilty of 'now I am dead,' then is not the prologue a plagiarism? But a good deal of more respectable play-writing than this was plagiarism, as who knew better than Shakespeare? I suspect he was of two minds himself on the point, if any at all.

Then come the fairies. Can even gen-ius succeed in putting fairies on the stage? The pious commentators say not. This play and the sublimer parts of *King Lear* are freely quoted as impossible in the theatre. But, then, by some trick of reasoning they blame the theatre for it. I cannot follow that. If a play, writ-ten for the stage, cannot be put on the stage, the playwright, it seems to me, has failed, be he who he may. Has Shakes-peare failed, or need the producer only pray for a little genius, too? The fairies are the producer's test. Let me confess that, though mainly love of the play, yet partly, too, a hope of passing that test, has inspired the present production. Foolhardy one feels, facing it. But if a method of staging can compass the diffi-culties of *A Midsummer Night's Dream,* surely its cause is won.

Lacking genius one considers first how not to do a thing. Not to try and realize these small folk who war with rere-mice for their leathern wings; that goes with-out saying. In this play I can visualize neither a beginning nor an end to realism of either scenery or action. Nor yet to use children. To my mind neither chil-dren nor animals fit with the theater. Perfect in their natural beauty, they put our artifice to shame. In this case one is tempted, one yields a little, over Cobweb and Co. It's possible, even probable, that children served Shakespeare. But I ex-pect that the little eyases of that time were as smartly trained in speaking verse as is a crack cathedral choir now in the singing of anthems. That there might be a special beauty, an impersonal clarity, in a boy's Oberon or Titania, I can well believe. To take a nearly parallel case who would not choose to hear treble than soprano, through Bach's *Matthew Pas-sion?* This is an interesting point, and it opens up the whole question of the loss and gain to pure poetry on the stage by the coming of women players. But where are our children with the training in fine speech and movement? Stop beneath the windows of an elementary school and listen. Or worse, listen to the chatter of a smart society gathering; in the school playground at least there is lung power. It will take some generations of awakening to the value of song and dance, tune and rhythm, to reëstablish a standard of beauty in the English language.

The theater might help if it were allowed. Though, first of all, heaven knows, it needs to help itself. One may say that the tradition of verse-speaking on the English stage is almost dead. So much the better. Our latest inheritance of it, at the least, was unsound, dating not from Shakespearean times, the great age of verse, but from the 'heroic days' of Rowe and Otway; later from the translators of 'the immortal Kotzebue' and the portentous Sheridan Knowles. Comic verse found its grave (at times a charmingly bedizened grave in the rhymed burlesque of Planché and Byron. But Shakespeare was a classic and must be spoken 'classically,' and what you couldn't speak classically you had better cut. Look at the Shakespeare prompt-books of even the last few years and see how mercilessly rhymed couplets were got rid of, blots upon the dignity of the play. From this sort of thing William Poel has been our saviour, and we owe him thanks. In the teeth of ridicule, he insisted that for an actor to make himself like unto a human megaphone was to miss, for one thing, the whole merit of Elizabethan verse with its consonantal swiftness, its gradations sudden or slow into vowelled liquidity, its comic rushes and stops, with, above all, the peculiar beauty of its rhymes. We have had, of course, individual actors or speakers of taste and genius (one instances Forbes Robertson), and there might be now and then a company inspired by such scholarly ideals as Benson could give, but Poel preached a gospel.

What else was Shakespeare's chief delight in this play but the screeds of word-music to be spoken by Oberon, Titania, and Puck? At every possible and impossible moment he is at it. For Puck's description of himself there may be need, but what excuse can we make for Titania's thirty-five lines about the dreadful weather except their sheer beauty? But what better excuse? Oberon is constantly guilty. So recklessly happy in writing such verse does Shakespeare grow that even the quarrel of the four lovers is stayed by a charming speech of Helena's thirty-seven lines long. It is true that at the end of it Hermia, her author allowing her to recollect the quarrel, says she is amazed at these passionate words, but that the passage beginning, 'We, Hermia, like two artificial gods,' is meant by Shakespeare to be spoken otherwise than with a meticulous regard to its every beauty is hard to believe. And its every beauty will scarcely shine through throbbing passion. No, his heart was in these passages of verse, and so the heart of the play is in them. And the secret of the play — the refutation of all doctrinaire criticism of it — lies in the fact that though they may offend against every letter of dramatic law they fulfil the inmost spirit of it, inasmuch as they are dramatic in themselves. They are instinct with that excitement, that spontaneity, that sense of emotional overflow which is drama. They are as carefully constructed for effective speaking as a messenger's speech in a Greek drama. One passage in particular, Puck's 'My mistress with a monster is in love,' is both in idea and form, in its tension, climax, and rounding off, a true messenger's speech. Shakespeare, I say, was from the first a playwright in spite of himself. Even when he seems to sacrifice drama to poem he — instinctively or not — manages to make the poem itself more dramatic than the drama he sacrifices. And once he has found himself as a playwright, very small mercy he has on verse for its own sake. He seems to write it as the fancy takes him, badly or well, broken or whole. Is there a single rule he will not break, lest his drama should for a moment suffer? Is there a supreme passage in the later plays but is supreme more in its dramatic emotion than its sheer poetry? Take for an instance the line in *King Lear* —'Never, never, never, never, never.' Can you defend it as poetry any more than you can defend 'Oh, Sophonisba, Sophonisba, oh'? As a moment of drama what could be more poignantly beautiful?

Whence comes the tradition that a blank verse play is, merely by virtue of its verse, the top notch of achievement?

Shakespeare's best work, seen alive in the theatre, gives, I maintain, no color to it. Verse was his first love, his natural medium — the finest medium for the theatre in general of his day, I 'll admit. But how far he was, in principle and practice, from those worthy disciples who have for these centuries attempted and do indeed still attempt to drag us wearily up their strictly decasyllabic pathway to Parnassus, only a placing of their work and his side by side in the living theatre will show. It has all come, I suppose, from learned people elevating him to the study from the stage. Despise the theatre; it revenges itself. I digress.

The fairies cannot sound too beautiful. How should they look? One does one's best. But I realize that when there perhaps is no really right thing to do one is always tempted to do too much. One yields to the natural fun, of course, of making a thing look pretty in itself. They must be not too startling. But one wishes people were n't so easily startled. I won't have them dowdy. They must n't warp your imagination — stepping too boldly between Shakespeare's spirit and yours. It is a difficult problem: we (Norman Wilkinson and I — he to do and I to carp) have done our best.

One point is worth making. Oberon and Titania are romantic creations: sprung from Huon of Bordeaux, etc., say the commentators; come from the farthest steppe of India, says Shakespeare. But Puck is English folklore.

How should the fairies dance? Here I give up my part of apologist to Cecil Sharp. I only know they should have no truck with a strange technique brought from Italy in the eighteenth century. If there is an English way of dancing — and Sharp says there is — should not that be their way?

And what tunes should they sing to? English tunes. And on this point Sharp has much to say — more sometimes than I can quite follow him in. I have no doubt there is a lyric missing at the end of the play, and to set a tune to the rhythm of Oberon's spoken words seems absurd. If this most appropriate one we borrow from *Two Noble Kinsmen* is not Shakespeare's (Swinburne thought it was), I 'm sorry. I 'm sorry, anyway, if it 's vandalism, but something has to be done.

Finally I divide the play into three parts. I don't defend the division; it only happens to be a convenient one. I can't defend any division, and some day I really must ask a modern audience to sit through two hours and a half of Shakespeare without a break; the play would gain greatly. This is less absurd, that is all, than the Jonsonian five-act division of the Folio, for which, of course, there is no authority.

V

CONCERNING DAVID BELASCO

WALTER PRICHARD EATON

[*American Magazine,* January, 1913. By permission.]

If the average theatregoer were asked who is the commanding figure on the American stage today, he would probably reply without hesitation, 'David Belasco.' David Belasco, indeed, has been an important figure on our stage since 1882, when he first came from California to New York. With all his theatrical and rather tiresome tricks for obtaining publicity, he could not, of course, have achieved and maintained his eminence without solid and unusual artistic merit. But his merit is so conspicuous in one particular line, that of creating scenic and histrionic illusion, that it seems completely to have blinded many people to his shortcomings in many other important respects. Even the critics, in New York at any rate, completely lose their faculty of judgment when he mounts a new play, and mistake illusion for intellect, scenic realism for reality. Because the acted drama is composed of many elements, and because illusive scenery and naturalistic acting are only a part of perfection, and ultimately not the most important part, it is time we considered David Belasco and his work a little more dispassionately. When considering him and his work at present, we are in grave danger of forgetting altogether that literature has some claims, that dramatic realism is as much a matter of character selection and deeds as of scenery or acting, that progress in the drama is marked not only by the multiplication of electric switchboards, but by the increased power of the stage to interest people in the vital problems of the life about them. Mechanically, David Belasco's productions are in the very van of dramatic progress. Spiritually, they mostly belong back in the days of Dion Boucicault, whom Mr. Belasco once served as secretary.

It is rather important that this distinction should be made, and made clearly, and driven if possible into the public consciousness. Progress in any branch of human endeavor is difficult enough, and the theatre is peculiarly conservative. When, therefore, a leader arises who can carry the crowd with him, it is a pity to see him neglect his opportunities, and still more a pity to see the crowd, deceived by the outward show of progress, fancy they are marching on when they are only marking time. Belasco has unquestionably set a new standard of production on our stage; he has, just as unquestionably, done almost nothing to advance the standard of play-writing, to substitute reality for sentimentality, literature for trivial story-telling, poetry for pasteboard, ideas for tradition. As far as advancing the art of play-writing is concerned, apart from the art of play-producing, he has been as negligible a factor as was Joseph Jefferson. Indubitably a supreme artist in his line, that line is narrow, so narrow that, until it is widened, he cannot justly be regarded as a true leader, nor his claims either as a dramatist or an adapter of other men's dramas be taken very seriously.

In a book called *The American Dramatist,* by M. J. Moses, there is a chapter devoted to Belasco, which contains a partial list of the plays which he either wrote, adapted, or collaborated on, after he came to New York in 1882. While connected first with the Madison Square and then with the Lyceum Theatre, Mr. Belasco wrote wholly or in part, according to Mr. Moses, *La Belle Russe, The Stranglers of Paris, Hearts of Oak* (with James A. Herne), *May Blossoms, Valerie, Miss Hellyet, Pawn Ticket 210, The Moonlight Marriage, The Doll Master, A Christmas Night, Within an Inch of His Life, The Lone Pine, American Born, Not Guilty, The Haunted House, Cherry and Fair Star, Sylvia's Loves, Paul Arniff, The Curse of Cain, The Millionaire's Daughter, The Ace of Spades,* and *The Roll of the Drum.* Not one of these has

survived. With Mr. De Mille, Belasco wrote *The Charity Ball, Men and Women, The Wife,* and *Lord Chumley* (acted by E. H. Sothern). The first three were effective dramas in the prevailing manner — nothing more; the last was a character sketch. In 1893 Belasco collaborated with Franklyn Fyles on *The Girl I Left Behind Me.* In 1895 he brought out Mrs. Carter in *The Heart of Maryland.* Soon after, the same actress appeared first in *Du Barry* and then in *Zaza,* the latter a sentimentalized adaptation from the French. Since 1900, when Blanche Bates acted John Luther Long's pathetic *Madame Butterfly* under his management, he has capped one popular success with another. Merely out of David Warfield's acting of Charles Klein's sentimental play, *The Music Master,* he would have made a snug fortune. He has mounted a pseudo-Japanese play, *The Darling of the Gods;* a sentimental melodrama of the Forty-niners, *The Girl of the Golden West;* a Civil War drama, *The Warrens of Virginia;* a California play, *The Rose of the Rancho;* a French adaptation, *The Lily;* a Viennese adaptation, *The Concert;* a drama of the supernatural, for David Warfield, *The Return of Peter Grimm;* Eugene Walter's *The Easiest Way;* a play about dual personality, called *The Case of Becky;* a political play, *The Woman,* and latest of all, *The Governor's Lady.*

This is a long list, and it is by no means complete either. It represents almost no popular failures, and it represents a great deal of remarkably good theatrical entertainment, for which we should be, and are, rightly grateful. But it represents, nevertheless, almost no new dramatic literature, and it includes no classics; it marks no development of the art of play-writing; as a body, it takes almost no account of the new forces of social criticism at work in our drama and our literature; it makes almost no contributions to the American stage, apart from the individual production of each work under the Belasco guidance.

Most of these plays were not written by Mr. Belasco himself. But so potent is his individuality as a producer, and so slight is the personality and message of the author behind each one, that each seemed, when seen, to bear in every detail the Belasco stamp. There are at least two striking exceptions, Eugene Walter's acid drama of the Tenderloin, *The Easiest Way,* and Leo Dietrichstein's adaptation of Herman Bahr's satiric comedy, *The Concert.* In each of these plays the personality of the author emerged, because in each there was a definite, vital idea which was the author's own, and to express which he wrote his play. Each of these works approximates, at least, dramatic literature, and each can have, and has had, an independent existence and a pronounced influence, quite apart from the Belasco production. So too, in lesser degree, has *Madame Butterfly.*

Now, the very fact that so few of the Belasco productions speak the author's individual message, that so very few of them emerge as independent plays, is a pretty good indication that he isn't doing much as a producer to encourage authorship. He took *The Easiest Way* after Walter had made a reputation. He took *The Concert* after it had been produced all over the Continent. He has apparently dropped John Luther Long, who brought him his one touch of poetic fancy. Charles Klein, who wrote *The Music Master* and *The Auctioneer* for Warfield, produced independently his more important dramas, such as *The Lion and the Mouse,* in which he tried, at least, to touch on real American problems. Nearly all the rest of Mr. Belasco's authors are quite negligible. They exist for the public only as the Belasco wizardry of stage manipulation can give their concoctions illusion. This is the very negation of leadership in the progress of a native drama.

The true first and fundamental duty of a producer is not to reflect his own temperament and tastes, but to reflect the author's, to stage the author's message, not his own. Most of Belasco's authors, to be sure, have had no message. Can it be that he has preferred it so? Can it be that he has preferred to take a negative drama and shape it into a stage entertainment of sure popularity, compounded of old-fashioned sentimentality and new-fashioned superficial and scenic realism, rather than to work with material which he could not in conscience bend to his own purposes? That is a question Time is going to answer for Mr. Belasco, and answer not uncertainly, unless he takes care.

Let us consider for a moment his latest production, *The Governor's Lady,* written by Alice Bradley (whoever she may be). This drama, shown in New York last September with great acclaim, is perhaps one of the most marvelously mounted plays of the decade. But when a certain hypnotized New York critic declares it one of the most marvelous plays of the decade, he is talking nonsense. It is a false, sentimental, trivial play, perverted in ethics and twisted in logic, not worthy of an hour's serious consideration, apart from its superb production on Mr. Belasco's stage. And the greater the genius of production, the greater the pity that it should be wasted on such trashy material.

In *The Governor's Lady* we find an undisguised and persistent plea for our sentimental sympathy, and this sympathy is to be extended to a woman who is a bad wife. Daniel Slade, it seems, started life as a poor, rough miner, but he has made his pile, built a magnificent house in a Western city, wishes to go to the opera, entertain important people, get elected governor. His wife, however, is homely and humble, and absolutely refuses to assist him in his ambitions. She will not even try. Of course it is never safe to say that anything isn't possible where a woman is concerned, so we will pass over the point that the rough miner's wife is generally more eager to go to the opera than he is. The indubitable fact remains that Mary Slade was a bad wife, and stupidly, stubbornly, and intentionally a bad wife. As a matter of fact, instead of pitying her when Daniel desired a divorce and the companionship of a young woman who would help him in his legitimate ambitions, we rather pity Daniel. Daniel, however, is represented incongruously as still loving his wife, and the wife as still loving Daniel. The young woman is represented as loving somebody else. She accepts Daniel for his money. She puts his wife aside, not because her pigheaded selfishness has killed the subtle bond of affection in his breast, but purely for political reasons. By the time the play is in mid-flight there is scarcely a character who hasn't done something despicable. In the clear light of logic, in a Pinero satire, for instance, these people would be so unpleasant that the dear, shocked public would refuse to look upon them. But they are here so rose-watered with sentimentality that the dear public loves them all, and when the injured wife tells the young woman who is about to succeed her how much she loves Daniel, all the laundries in New York rejoice. Yet we talk about Belasco realism!

The last act of the play takes place in a replica of one of those numerous white tiled Childs' restaurants in New York. Daniel and Mary are reconciled in this spot. There is no reason why they should be reconciled here, of course. People with their incomes don't eat at Childs'; and as the whole point of Mary's character was her humble, home-loving instincts, New York was the last place she would have chosen to live in anyway. But Childs' had never been shown on the stage before. That was reason enough.

Scenically, the interior of the restaurant is reproduced with photographic fidelity; you almost gasp at the faithfulness of detail, even down to the arc-lamps outside, sputtering in the winter storm. And so we rave about realism. But is this realism which really matters? The characters in this play do not belong in Childs'. The people who lunch at Childs' are the myriad more humble toilers, clerks, stenographers, and the like, who can afford nothing more luxurious. Any true realism in the drama, if it employed Childs' as a setting, would employ such people as characters, and would let us see a little more clearly, a little more significantly, into their lives. We all know Childs' restaurants have white walls, a griddle-cake grill in the window, and a cash-register. But the problems of the workers who eat there we do not know, or know but dimly. Show us those problems, as Tolstoy would show them, or Hauptmann, or Gorky, or Galsworthy, or even Eugene Walter, and you have true realism. Mr. Belasco's realism goes no deeper than his scenery — and scenery is but the background of drama, merely a secondary aid to illusion. As a scene-painter and coach of acting Belasco is indeed a realist. In any deeper and more truly dramatic sense he is not a realist at all, and few if any of his productions have shown that he understands what this deeper realism is. He is merely the traditional sentimentalist of the playhouse.

Nor has his contribution to the art of acting in America been so great as is sometimes supposed, even though it appears to be the goal of every actor to be under his management. As far back as 1882 he taught the gospel of naturalism in acting, and in *The Governor's Lady* he is still teaching it, and teaching it with marvelous results. It is difficult to see how that drama could be acted with a greater illusion of life. We gladly give him full credit for this. But what becomes of the actors and actresses he makes? Do they go on growing? Do they enlarge their scope, their repertoire? What has Blanche Bates done any better or more important than *Madame Butterfly?* What has become of the golden promise of David Warfield? He has played just four parts in the twelve years since Belasco took him out of the Weber and Fields' Music Hall. Time is not standing still for David Warfield any more than for the rest of us. He has attempted no great part yet. His *Peter Grimm* is but a variant of his *Music Master*. The heights are still unscaled, still unattempted. What has become of his ambition to play Shylock? With his talents and ambition, with Belasco's vaunted ability to manipulate the switch-board and flood the moon on Portia's garden, with Blanche Bates's once brilliant promise and eager hopes, we might have a Shylock and a Portia and an atmospheric production of the great classic which would mark an epoch on our stage. But we do not have it. We do not even hear of it any more. We have no true romance from Belasco. We have no true realism. We just have wonderfully mounted sentimental, old-fashioned stories, doctored up, to be sure, with settings in psychotherapists' laboratories or Childs' restaurants, to give them a spurious 'scientific' or contemporary tone.

And the pity of it! Here is a man who is the one undoubted genius we have as a producer of plays, whose ability to create stage illusion is not exceeded in any country, who has an enormous public following, who is one of a very few managers who is also himself an artist, capable of designing the scenery, training the actors, devising the lights, adapting the play — who is, in short, a real 'man of the theatre.' He might, if anybody can, give us in America a Théâtre Libre or a Deutsches Theater, even as Antoine and Adolf L'Arronge and Max Reinhardt.

He might, if any one can, call out the best and newest and most earnest in the playwrights of America, giving their work such illusive production as would cause it to conquer, to win the public. He might, if any one can, make literature and the stage no longer inimical in New York, make the American drama respected and worthy of respect, and the classics, too, once more popular and enjoyable. But he has, instead, evidently chosen the Easiest Way. He has exploited his genius as a producer, above the material produced; and however much he may have done for the dress of the American drama, the drama itself has gained nothing from his talents. It is still struggling upward outside of his theatres, and unaided by his influence and prestige.

VI

HOW I WROTE 'WITHIN THE LAW'

BAYARD VEILLER

[*Metropolitan Magazine*, June, 1913. By courtesy of the publishers.]

At a dinner one evening in January, 1910, several of my friends were discussing a certain very popular, lurid crook melodrama then running in a New York theatre. I never thought much of that piece and said so. Furthermore, I maintained that that sort of thing was the easiest stuff in the world to turn out.

'Well, if you know so much,' said Mrs. Veiller, 'why don't you write one yourself and make a little money for us?'

'Oh, very well, I will,' I replied. 'What is more, I'll do it in a month.' (Chorus of jeers.)

Two days later I set to work. And I finished the job in three weeks. *Within the Law* as it is being played today is substantially the same — with the exception of the first act — as the original manuscript I turned out in that time. Of course there have been numerous changes, but they were in minor details and not in the general form.

I wrote it for money. Up to that time I had made several contributions to art. The most notable of them was a superb thing which ran for one week, *The Primrose Path*. The only person I ever found who really liked it — besides the author — was a conductor on a Seventh Avenue street car. He spoke to me one night six months after the play had ended its triumphant career. I was getting off the car with Mrs. Veiller and he stepped down to help us off and said:

'Mr. Veiller, I want to tell you I liked *The Primrose Path*, and thought it was a shame it didn't get over. It was the best show I saw this year.'

He jumped back on his car before I had time to thank him, and I never saw him again. I've been rather worried about that man.

Within the Law in its original form was an attack on the jury system. The character corresponding to Gilder, the department store proprietor, was the judge who sentenced Mary Turner to prison. Mary was pretty much as she is now, a salesgirl accused of theft. The scene of the first act was a court room. The jury had been out all night. Everybody was worn out with the long, tedious wait for the verdict. The jury filed in, sleepy, blear-eyed and cross. The proceedings were hurried as much as possible. The clerk of the court gabbled through the usual formulas. The foreman in a weary voice announced the verdict of 'guilty.'

In a word, I showed the case of a girl who was being railroaded to prison in order that the judge might get away on a hunting trip and that everybody else concerned might hurry through with their work. The judge pronounced sentence — three years — and it was to him instead of the department store proprietor that Mary Turner made the speech that now ends the first act of *Within the Law*.

I did not have to invent this. Such conditions actually exist and have existed for years. I knew the whole police and criminal courts situation backwards, thanks to my experience of several years as a reporter. I 'covered' police headquarters in New York for a long period before I took to play-writing. During that time Theodore Roosevelt was police commissioner, 'Jake' Riis was doing headquarters for the *Sun*, Lincoln Steffens for the *Evening Post*, and I for the *Evening Mail*. In no other way can a man acquire such a thorough knowledge of and insight into the realities that make our civilization hideous as by the work that falls to the lot of a police reporter.

He knows the inside of the system by which poor people are exploited for the benefit of the unscrupulous. He sees nothing but the reverse of the medal. He learns the hollowness of the pretenses by which the system is maintained.

THE IDEA OF REVENGE

The next three acts developed naturally out of this situation. It is only right to make due acknowledgment to Alexandre Dumas, for, as you have no doubt recognized, the idea of the person wrongfully convicted and imprisoned carrying out a systematic plan of vengeance is nothing but the plot of *Monte Cristo*. The main difference is that it is a girl instead of a man. Most of the managers I subsequently took the play to threw up their hands in horror at this idea. They declared we never in the world could win the sympathy of audiences for a woman who devoted all her energies to revenge. They could not see that this is one of the most elemental feelings in human nature. Some big elemental feeling must be the basis of all drama. And the instinct to say 'I'll get even with you' is one of the most universal. I made the girl set out deliberately to injure the man who had sent her to prison. The natural thing for her to consider was: 'Where can I hurt him most?' Obviously his affection for his boy was his tenderest spot. Moreover as he had irreparably ruined her life, it was logical for her to attack his. And the best way to damage it was to associate it by marriage with that of a convicted felon. So that by marrying his son she inflicted a two-fold injury on her enemy. Hence her crucial speech in the second act: 'You took away my name and gave me a number. Now I have given up that number and I've got your name!'

The original title of the piece, by the way, was *The Miracle*. This was taken from a line in the third act. The father, remonstrating with his son for clinging so obstinately to the girl in the belief that he can change her, says: 'What are you waiting for — a miracle?' Then the son replies: 'No, I'm going to make it.' The title was altered later for fear that it might conflict with a spectacular production of Max Reinhardt's by the same name.

The change in the first act from an attack on the jury system to an attack on department stores came about in this way: After the play was finished the first manager I took it to was George Tyler. He said he liked it, thought it would probably be a hit and make a great deal of money. He would not produce it, however, because he had already arranged to produce another piece which was sure-fire and bound to be the melodrama hit of the season.

'But,' he said, 'your first act has a fine idea for a play by itself. Why don't you write a new first act in its place and write another play for me on the theme contained in this first act, the attack on the jury system?'

As George Tyler is my best friend, and as I was under obligations to him which I hope I can never repay, I followed his suggestion. I set aside the court room scene so as to use it in another play. I left the heroine as she was, a salesgirl wrongfully accused of theft. And I made her plight the basis of an attack on the department store system in particular and our economic system in general. I am a Socialist. Some of the things I learned at police headquarters made me especially interested in conditions at the New York department stores. The fact is that they are just 1000 per cent. worse than anybody not in touch with them has any idea of. The fact is that our social fabric is so rotten that the entire industrial world is simply riding on the backs of women. Day by day I hear of instances at first hand that confirm these convictions beyond doubt. However, all this leads away from the subject. I am free to admit that I saw the pictorial value of these conditions and particularly for the first act of *Within the Law*. They made a first act just as suitable as the previous one that I set aside for future use. The subsequent acts followed it just as naturally as they followed the other.

To return to the original process. Knowing the police methods, it was perfectly easy to imagine the girl's history after she was let out of jail. It is the almost invariable practice of the police when they see an ex-convict to warn the employer. So naturally the first thing that would have happened to Mary Turner soon after she obtained a job would be for a detective to come into the shop and give the boss full information about her. After a few attempts to earn an honest living, being determined not to become a prostitute, she would say to herself: 'Oh, very well; if they won't let me be honest I'll get money in the same way the big, successful crooks, the politicians and the grafters get theirs,— dishonestly, but within the law.' At the same time I made her execute her scheme for revenge on Gilder.

The fourth act I stole. Almost every incident in it is a matter of public record. The third degree trick worked on Joe Garson by Inspector Burke in the play is precisely the same trick that was carried out by Inspector Byrnes, undoubtedly the best policeman who ever lived, on a crook named McGloin. Everybody down at headquarters knows about it — in fact it is related in Byrnes' book.

LIVE SUGGESTIONS

As for the trap laid for Mary Turner by the inspector, that also was comparatively easy. Police methods are invariably simple. Whenever they want to catch criminals and cannot procure evidence the policy is to entrap them into committing some crime at which they can be caught. This they do by means of a stool pigeon; hence the character of English Eddie. Originally I had the woman take part in the burglary of Gilder's home for additional revenge. It was, thanks to an excellent suggestion from Charles Klein, that I changed this. He pointed out that this would alienate the audience's sympathy which her previous wrongs had won for her. Accordingly, I had her go to Gilder's house, not to share in, but to prevent the robbery. Then occurred the problem of how to account for her finding out about the burglary scheme. One thing a playwright always has to avoid is giving audiences cause to puzzle over any point. Once they do that their attention is distracted from the action and the suspense is broken. It was Roi Megrue who suggested that I have the inspector telephone her anonymously so as to inveigle her into the trap. These changes were made after the play had opened in Chicago.

The Maxim silencer business I put in because there was a great deal in the newspapers about the invention just at the time I was writing the piece. I think every play should be, as largely as possible, a reflex of what is in the papers at the present time — not only in lesser details such as this, but in larger affairs. When the silencer was publicly tested it was said that reporters in the next room had been unable to hear the sound of the shot. So I thought: 'If reporters, why not policemen?' The introduction of the incident in the second act, when Joe Garson shows how effective the silencer is by shooting at a vase, was merely a matter of ordinary technical skill. You must let the audience see things like that for themselves: it is not sufficient to explain them.

Incidentally, a great many people who saw the play have wondered whether the vase is really shot. If guns used on the stage were actually loaded with bullets I shudder to think of the calamities that might follow. I would not trust my life to the marksmanship of the average actor. There is a very simple mechanism by which the vase is smashed at just the right moment in such a way that it seems to have been shattered by a bullet.

The revolving searchlight from the Metropolitan Tower which flashes in through the window in the third act and reveals the dead body of English Eddie to Inspector Burke was the result of mere accident. This was not in the play originally but was introduced during the Chicago run of the piece. For some time, however, I felt the need of a spot light to account for the inspector's seeing the body while the room was almost in total darkness. But I could not figure out any plausible excuse for bringing it in. One afternoon I was talking to Al Woods in his room on the sixth floor of the Sherman House in Chicago. Suddenly a bright light was reflected on the ceiling from the street. I jumped up, went to the window and saw that a wagon was passing by with a large plate of glass. This had caught the sunlight and flashed it up into the room. That gave me the idea for the third act: 'Why not a searchlight?' I remembered that there were two such in New York, one on top of the Hippodrome and the other on the Metropolitan Tower, and it just became a question of which was the more expedient to use.

It was not until after the play was written that trouble really began. I was unknown. No play of mine had ever approached a success. I peddled it all over New York. Charles Klein, who is interested in the Authors' Producing Company, thought of doing it, but came to the conclusion finally that he would need all his time to dramatize *The Ne'er-Do-Well*.

Eventually Mr. Brady agreed to produce it. The original idea was that the part of Mary Turner should be played by Grace George, who had read the play and liked it. The matter was left in abeyance for a while. When Mr. Brady was ready to produce it, he sent for me and said: 'Look here; this play won't do as it stands; it needs a good many changes. You haven't enough experience to make them. The only thing to do is to let George Broadhurst rewrite it.' Of course this meant giving Mr. Broadhurst a third of the royalties. However I was willing to make almost any concessions for the sake of having the part played by Miss George, which means a certain $9000 or $10,000 a week box office returns for almost any play. So Mr. Broadhurst — who is a very skilful dramaturge — took the play and made what changes he saw fit. They were very well done, but they entirely changed the meaning of the piece. We started rehearsals, and when Miss George read the new version she said: 'This is not the play I accepted,' and threw up her part and refused to have anything to do with it. Emily Stevens was then engaged for the part and gave an admirable performance.

The play did not do well in Chicago. Whether this was owing to the changes made in it or not I won't pretend to say. But I came back to New York feeling terribly despondent over the outlook.

Mr. Brady had produced the piece with second-hand scenery, an act from *The Boss*, an act from *The Gentleman from Mississippi*, an act from *The Dollar Mark*, then some five or six years old, being used, and its use freely was commented upon by the Chicago critics.

I saw Mr. Brady and we discussed the situation freely. I told him that I didn't think the play had a chance in its present form and he grimly agreed with me. He refused, however, to allow me to make such changes as I saw fit.

WE BUY OUT MR. BRADY

I then went to Archie Selwyn, who was, still is, and always will be, my business agent, and talked the matter over with him. We both felt that the play had a big chance if it was properly cast, and put back as it had been originally written.

During my conversation with Mr. Brady he had said, 'If you and Selwyn don't like the way I'm doing your play, why don't you buy and run it to suit yourselves?'

I repeated this to Mr. Selwyn. He gave the matter a good deal of thought and finally said to me, 'Bayard, do you think if I give the play a really first-class production and a good cast, you can put it over?'

I said that I thought that it had a big chance under the proper conditions.

I am going into these details because it has become the fashion with many makers of plays to revile the play broker, and I am extremely anxious to tell frankly what one play broker named Selwyn has done for me.

The negotiations for the sale of the play took about ten minutes. Mr. Selwyn paid Mr. Brady ten thousand dollars for the property, and assumed Mr. Brady's contract with me, which called for an unusually high royalty for a beginner: five per cent. on the first four thousand of the gross receipts and 10 per cent. on everything over that amount. Selwyn had been very pleased, as a play agent, over this contract, and he didn't seem to mind it greatly when he took it over as a manager. But we both thought it a good deal of a joke. I especially enjoyed it.

A SUCCESS UNDREAMED OF

Up to this time Mr. Selwyn had not figured to any great extent as a producing manager, but in order to protect a client, in whom he had great faith, which faith I hope eventually to justify, he risked what at that time was a great deal of money to him, and this was only the beginning.

So the matter was settled. I took the train for Chicago that afternoon with carte blanche to do what I wanted to — the happiest man you ever saw. I set to work the next day. I took out all the changes Mr. Broadhurst had made and restored the play to its original form. I pruned and revised and built up. Everybody in the world, stage doorkeepers, charwomen and mechanics had suggestions to make. There is always a host of people willing to rewrite your play for you. Occasionally I even heard a good suggestion. The rest of the play's history you know.

And to be quite frank with you, I don't think *Within the Law* is a great play. But I do admit that it's theatrically effective. And I think that is due to the fact that I went over it as carefully as I could during the weeks it ran in Chicago, tying up loose ends wherever I saw them and building the thing up: for instance, Mary's speech that now rings down the curtain at the end of the third act, after she has accused her husband of the death of English Eddie. 'Arrest him,' the inspector says. 'You can't.' 'Why not?' 'Because that man was a burglar and my husband shot him in defense of his home!' is *Mary's* final answer. Originally that speech occurred in the fourth act. And the curtain for the third act was unsatisfactory until I got the idea of transferring that speech from the fourth.

None of us thought for a minute that *Within the Law* would be the success that it is. We all looked for a moderate hit and a run possibly until the first of the year, but that we should sell out on the second night that the play was presented in New York and never have an empty seat in the house for three hundred performances was beyond our wildest dreams.

The play will make a fortune for Mr. Selwyn and his associates, and it's doing very well indeed for me, too, thank you kindly.

Has it accomplished anything else? What real good has it done? Frankly, I don't know. I hope that it has served its sociological purpose. I feel very strongly that when a maker of plays has pointed out strongly and fearlessly a social situation that needs a remedy he has done his work. The stage is not the place for the discussion of reforms; but I am quite sure that it is the surest place to make their necessity known to the greatest number of people.

The plight of underpaid working-girls has been known for years; brilliant thinkers have talked about it, great writers have written about it, but it remained for my bedraggled, tear-stained shop girl on her way to prison, with glittering steel handcuffs on her wrists, and her reiterated, 'but you won't pay them enough to live on,' to make three of the department store proprietors in New York City establish a minimum wage scale of eight dollars a week in their stores. My play has done at least that much good.

VII

'TYPICALLY AMERICAN'[1]

FRANCIS HACKETT

[*New Republic*, November 14, 1914. By permission of author and publisher.]

What foreigners think of America is a matter of slight importance. So long as foreigners begin by drinking ice-water the minute they land, they will continue to suffer dire results and form equally dire impressions. But what Americans think of themselves, and especially of things said to be 'typically American,' is a matter of considerable importance. Who will be right about America if Americans are wrong?

Mr. George M. Cohan, the gifted adapter of *The Miracle Man,* is supposed to be 'typically American.' When one contrasts the Chicago stockbroker with the Kentucky mountaineer, the buoyant daughter of Oregon with the wizened great-granddaughter of Vermont, this phrase seems slightly vague. What, after all, is 'typically American'? It is true that Mr. Cohan is as familiar as currency. One associates him with every blinking electric sign in the country, with hustlers and drummers, girls who are perfect peaches and men who are princes, bellhops and night-letters, the cannon-ball express and *The Saturday Evening Post.* All these things, pushed into the shopwindow of American life, are undoubtedly indigenous and typical. But are they really American? They come with Trade, and their homogeneity is the homogeneity of the business world. In so far as Americans are spiritually commercialized, these things are psychologically national. But where commerce stops, they stop; and the woods know them not, nor the sun on the prairie.

In its clever and definite organization, its swift manœuvers, sharp contrasts, quick changes, sprints, slides, dives, Mr. Cohan's drama affords the same excite-

[1] *The Miracle Man,* a four-act play by George M. Cohan, from the story by Frank L. Packard. Presented at the Astor Theatre, New York, October, 1914.

ment as the 'national' game. Abasing myself before all the fans in the nation, I suggest that the reason is simple. The spirit of star baseball, like the spirit of Mr. Cohan's drama, is the spirit of the business world. It is not possible, in passing, to prove that commercialism has given the game of baseball its character. I am content to venture the suggestion that it is business enterprise which is the source of these supposed Americanisms, and not Americans who are the source of business enterprise. Popular taste in games, in the theatre, in literature, even in politics, is modified by the general business preoccupation. As Mr. Cohan himself says, busy people want succinct plays and stories — 'small but complete and electric doses,' just as they want a Religion Movement with a high-speed motor. It is an inevitable development, and just because Mr. Cohan is imbued with the same spirit, and is one of its really great exponents, he rivals baseball in popularity and appeal.

What sort of drama comes from the disciple of business enterprise? Mr. Cohan compares the production of plays with that of garters or canned asparagus. His lingo is subservient to the patrons who hustle and drum. But, disregarding this rather refreshing difference in idiom, where does Mr. Cohan 'get off'? Assuming that he has a right to can asparagus, what sort of asparagus does he can?

Judging by *The Miracle Man* there is a great deal to be said for the business ideology in drama. This play is derived from a story which 'got' Mr. Cohan by the way it introduced 'crooks with a sense of humor into the novel atmosphere of religion.' Adapted from fiction, the play proves its adapter to have a superb nose for situation. It was a departure for Mr. Cohan, but just as P. D. Armour progressed from hams to soaps and perfumes, so Mr. Cohan, equally fertile and adventurous, could move from musical comedy to a drama of religion. The asparagus might be religious asparagus, but he canned it just the same.

Where *The Miracle Man* shows the benefits of its author's commercial psychology is in its astonishing clarity and intelligence. Setting out to tell a given story, it tells that story without superfluity or waste. It seeks to show how a band

of crooked New Yorkers tried to turn a remote New England Patriarch's religious miracles to their own profit, and how in doing so the crooked ones went straight. To tell such a story for a national audience, to relate it to national institutions and national ideologies, to give it the same credibility as a two-cent stamp — that was Mr. Cohan's ambition, backed by the belief that the idea was big enough to 'get across.' And get across it does, where many greater ideas have incontinently failed.

In spite of his own repudiation, Mr. Cohan is a genuine artist. The Patriarch in this play is a little conventionalized, but not a bit more than Walt Whitman or John Alexander Dowie. He is an impressive Patriarch, and Mr. Thompson intones him like a psalm. The cocaine fiend, also, is slightly conventionalized, and could hardly have fooled the inhabitants of Needley, Maine. The girl who falls in love with the cocaine fiend is, also, not sufficiently hand-made. One would prefer a little more violet and a little less shrink. But with these objections registered, there is much in which to rejoice. As the Flopper, Mr. James C. Marlowe was quite human, funny and American. The fake cripple introduced to the shrine of the Patriarch, he revealed not only Mr. Cohan's excellent sense of humor, but also his imagination and his taste. The real cripple, acted by Mr. Percy Helton, was also admirably conceived — pallid, venomous, intense. And when the dumbfounding real miracle takes place, just after the fakers had 'worked' the Patriarch for the sake of manufacturing publicity, the whole cast is manœuvered for a 'curtain' of the highest emotional effect.

But in spite of the homely touches so cleverly observed, and so well conveyed by Mr. Frank Bacon as the Yankee hotel proprietor; in spite of the spacious dignity and impressiveness of the Patriarch; in spite of the Flopper's conviction that 'Napoleon's noodle was a billiard ball' compared to the chief crook's; in spite of the shrewdness with which this gentleman makes good his boast that 'he'd have sick millionaires throwing certified checks through the windows of the Shrine'; there is, in the dénouement of *The Miracle Man*, a proportion of buncombe almost too great to be borne. At no point was the tool of the crooks, passed off as the Patriarch's long-lost grand-niece, quite in the picture as real. But as time went on, and as Miss Gail Kane kept asseverating that her heart had changed after five years' wicked life, and that she could not deceive the kind old man, one parted company from Mr. George M. Cohan. Miss Gail Kane undulates in voice and figure, but she is only verbally 'tough.' As an actress she rises, or stoops, neither to the possibilities nor probabilities of her part, so that while one is reluctantly willing to believe in sudden conversions in real life, one is quite incapable of accepting this one in *The Miracle Man.* As for the men's conversions they are dreadfully reinforced by love affairs straight from the warehouse. As for the chief crook, Mr. George Nash made him too true ever to be turned good.

In piling up sentimentality Mr. Cohan is faithful to the psychology of commercialism. But some day, being full of real artistic perception, Mr. Cohan may see the truth. On that day he will see why fresh asparagus is better than canned.

VIII

'ON TRIAL' AT THE LYRIC THEATRE

[*Times,* London, England, April 30, 1915.
By permission.]

Why does American melodrama bear export better than American farce? For one reason, because jokes are apt to be local whereas thrills never are. For another, because the American virtue of strict attention to business is all the more effective when the business is serious business.

On Trial is an American melodrama which distributes its thrills on a novel plan. Its framework is a murder-trial, and you have all the orthodox excitements of a trial scene; speeches of counsel, agitation of accused, demeanor of jury, and so forth, *plus* the amusement of noting the differences between an American criminal court and one of our own. But the court scene is only a framework. As each important piece of evidence is reached the lights are suddenly extinguished, the scene revolves, and you are shown in action and *in situ* what the witness is telling the jury. Thus the murdered man's widow in the box — we beg pardon, on the stand — says, 'At that moment my husband's telephone-bell rang,' and at that moment you are transported to the room where the bell is ringing and see all that follows. Or the accused's child tells the jury how she was sitting down to the piano — and hey presto! there she is sitting at the piano, and you get another instalment of the action subjected *oculis fidelibus.* Or the accused's wife relates how in the long, long ago she met the murdered man and was deceived by him — and, on the spot, you are shown the meeting and the deception.

Of course, this means that the story is told backwards — you start with the murder and go on to the cause of the murder, and finish up with the long, long ago — but perhaps that is as good a way of telling a melodramatic story as any other, and it is, anyhow, a novel way. Besides, you have the fun of constantly speculating about the moment at which the court scene is going to vanish into darkness and be superseded by a bit of the actual story which the court is trying to unravel. Why the murder was no vulgar crime, but what Bacon calls a kind of wild justice, it would be spoiling sport to tell. The audience is soon let into that secret, and it looks as though the interest would prematurely fade, but it is revived and kept up to the end by the ingenious introduction and detection of a subordinate criminal — who had been in court all the time, a mere insignificant and unobserved item until he was wanted for the *dénouement.*

Miss Edyth Goodall and Mr. Arthur Wontner take the principal parts. They are both excellent at this kind of work, and in a scene — not new, but always effective — wherein the truth is wrung by a relentless man out of a lying woman, they last night strung the audience to the topmost pitch of excitement. There is a clever child-actress, Odette Goimbault, Mr. Julian Royce and Mr. Bassett Roe obviously enjoyed themselves as the opposing counsel — American counsel, of course, with a manner more free-and-easy than forensic, and the house as obviously enjoyed the whole affair.

IX

'FANNY'S FIRST PLAY'

W. S. CATHER

[*McClure's Magazine*, March, 1913. By permission.]

While *Fanny's First Play* can by no means be ranked among Mr. George Bernard Shaw's best plays, it is one of the most amusing, and its unconventionality pleased the New York public. Mr. Shaw sets out to ridicule certain conventions — theatrical conventions, domestic and social conventions. Miss Fanny O'Dowda, a student of a woman's college in Cambridge and a member of a socialist society, has written a play, and her father arranges to have it produced on her birthday — produced by a professional company, with the London critics in attendance to pass judgment upon the piece. Count O'Dowda, an esthetic survival of the eighteenth century, has not read the play himself, and probably would not have understood much of it if he had. The name of the author is withheld from the company and critics, as Miss O'Dowda wishes no allowance made for her youth and sex.

On the evening when the play is to be given, the critics meet at Count O'Dowda's house and before dinner deliver themselves upon plays and play-writing in general. They insist upon knowing the authorship of the play they have come to see. 'How,' says Gunn, 'is one to know what to say about a play, if one does n't know the author?' Says Bannel: 'You would n't say the same thing about a Pinero play and one by Henry Arthur Jones.' After this introduction follows Fanny O'Dowda's play, in three acts. When Fanny's play is over, the critics come forward, and attempt to decide upon the authorship. In attempting to place the play in the right locker, the critics take up the best known English playwrights one after another, and, in their own way, define the work of Mr. Shaw and his contemporaries, tagging each playwright by some external and unimportant characteristic that has nothing to do with his real manner or method, much less with his dramatic purpose. They characterize each brand of modern play by comments which remind one of the woman who said she 'could always tell Meredith's style, because there were so many parentheses.'

The *divertissement* by the dramatic critics by no means exhausts the satiric humor of the piece, though it seems to have attracted more attention than anything else in the play, both here and in London. The complexion of Fanny's budding talents seems to have afforded Mr. Shaw a great deal of amusement; he fairly outdoes himself to be shocking in the play he makes Fanny write. He seems to relish the notion of attributing a flippant and rather 'raw' burlesque on the respectable, middle-class English home to a young girl, gently bred. This, Mr. Shaw seems to chuckle, is the sort of thing young ladies who are impelled toward literature are thinking about today.

But to Fanny's own play. Knox and Gilbey are partners, drapers, most respectable. Margaret Knox is betrothed to Bobby Gilbey — both young people had been reared in the pure atmosphere of the British tradesmen's home, and both are being carefully educated. Margaret, whose mother is a religious fanatic, has had rather more than her fair share of cant. But both young people, according to Fanny, are quite unregenerate, normal savages, absolutely untouched by the moral and social standards under which they apparently live. Margaret, to give vent to her high spirits on a boat-race night, goes alone to a public dance-hall, picks up as escort a French naval officer whom she has never seen before, and, when the police raid the place, knocks out an officer's two front teeth with a well aimed blow. She and her escort are taken to Holloway jail and locked up for two weeks.

Bobby goes out for a lark with 'Darling Dora,' a little girl who lives as she can and who has been in jail before. They go to a dance-hall, drink too much, exchange hats, and walk about the streets singing until they are sent to jail for disturbing the peace and resisting arrest. And yet these are all, as they say in New England, pleasant young people, not at all vicious or unattractive. Even 'Darling Dora,' Fanny thinks, is not in the least a degraded person. Here, says Fanny, we have the normal young of the species expressing their healthy animal spirits. That they get locked up is, of course, an accident for the young people, a structural convenience for Fanny. But neither Fanny nor Bobby nor Margaret regard two weeks in jail as a retribution — the blush is for the jail!

When Margaret finds out that she likes liberty, she is honest about it; she says she enjoyed the dance-hall and the street-fight; she conceals nothing about the po- 10 liceman's teeth, not even the teeth them-selves, which she keeps as a trophy; and she avows that she has long been in love with Bobby's butler. But living under a respectable roof, and expressing his youth under cover, has made a sad sneak out of 15 Bobby. He cuts his little Dora when he is out walking with his mother, and coaxes the butler to tell him how he can break his engagement and put all the blame of it on Margaret. And Fanny 20 does manage to put the onus of Bobby's unattractive qualities on his respectable bringing-up. He is certainly more like-able in his natural unregenerateness than when he tries to conform to what he 25 thinks respectable. One imagines that 'Darling Dora' sees the best of him, when he 'always imagines himself a kit-ten and bites her ankles coming up the stairs.'

In the last act the old gods of the Brit-ish hearthstone meet their twilight, crum-ble to dust at the thrust of Fanny's bold quill. Everybody takes down the Sunday shutters and lays bare the windows of his 35 soul: Bobby declares that he will have nobody but his Dora; Margaret proclaims her love for the butler; the butler modestly confesses that he is the son of a duke, that his older brother has just died, and 40 that he has succeeded to the title; Mar-garet's fanatical mother admits that she is not so sure about the 'inner light,' after all; and the two drapers, Knox and Gil-bey, resolve to take a highball and be less 45 respectable in the future. One can't help wondering whether Fanny would advise a similar relaxation in all British house-holds, and where, if it occurred, she thinks we would come out. Fanny has her own 50 engaging ideas to tie to; they will always keep her up to a certain pitch. But peo-ple without ideas must have something. The question is, whether Fanny might not find Knox and Gilbey less interesting, un- 55 respectable than respectable; and Mrs. Knox's hysteria might easily take a more offensive form than religious mania.

X

'ROSY RAPTURE' AT THE DUKE OF YORK'S

[*Illustrated London News*, March 27, 1915. By permission.]

Not even the brilliant talents of a Bar-rie can convert a *revue* into something else 10 than its inconsequent self, nor does the atmosphere of home and baby which he affects in his example harmonize too well with the machinery of burlesque, wild dancing, and beauty-chorus. The ma- 15 terial in which an artist works cannot but influence his art, and so, notwithstand-ing the piquancy of a combination of Sir J. M. Barrie as author and Gaby Deslys as actress, with its consequence of this 20 embodiment of gaiety being involved in scenes of domestic sentiment, we hardly get the best sort of satire or the prettiest fancy of which our English Puck is cap-able under these conditions. His travesty 25 is devoted to stage devices and stage fash-ions which are already rather *démodés*, and which soon exhaust their humorous possibilities. Skits on the problem play and the triangle of sex, on stage hus- 30 bands who hide in wardrobes, and hero-ines of melodrama who shiver in the snow, are a bit old-fashioned nowadays; and the Barrie travesties of *David Cop-perfield* and Sir Herbert Tree are no bet- 35 ter and no less superficial than average burlesques in *revues*. The best thing in *Rosy Rapture* is the little episode in which Mlle. Deslys as French peasant girl and Mr. Jack Norworth as English Tommy 40 make love with the help of a phrase-book and with Lord Kitchener's homily to sol-diers in mind, and give us also a new ver-sion of *Sally in Our Alley;* that is the daintiest of ideas — Barrie at his best. 45 No less happy is the set of moving pic-tures describing the adventures of the baby in his perambulator discovering for his actress mother 'how to be happy though at home.' There are songs and 50 dances and jokes to be sure, and a beauty-chorus which is beautiful, and 'Gaby' herself is delightfully vivacious, and Mr. Norworth has a tongue-twisting ditty, and Mr. Eric Lewis is fine fun as a butler 55 urging the chorus to fling themselves into a polka — in fact, it would be quite a good *revue* if we had not expected something so superlatively good from a Barrie *revue*.

I. MUSICAL CRITICISM

If one may vary the opening phrase of Professor Daniel Gregory Mason, editor-in-chief of *The Art of Music*, 'So many and varied are the paths of musical enjoyment and profit, so difficult and sometimes so conflicting are the types of music presented, that the timid or inexperienced writer may well pause at the threshold, afraid of wholly losing his way in such a labyrinth.' The timidity of the inexperienced critic is a wholesome fear, especially if he is not acquainted with the technique and history of the form of musical art he undertakes to discuss. It may fall to the lot of a young journalist to be sent, much against his will, to report a concert, and if this happens, he will doubtless do his best in the way of judicious, or, at least, inoffensive praise, describing, with such variety of phraseology as he can command, the pleasure derived by the audience from the efforts of the performers. Such notices can hardly be called musical criticism, which has to do not merely with the effect upon the audience, but with the merits of the compositions rendered, as well as the way in which they are interpreted. Obviously for such a responsible task, musical knowledge and artistic sympathy of a high order are necessary if the judgment of the critic is to carry weight. In addition to these qualifications he must have the power of presentation; there are many skilled musicians who would make poor critics, because they have not the power of expressing themselves in writing. The examples of the best American criticism here submitted will give the young student some idea of the character and extent of the qualifications required, and may serve to warn him that great natural capacities as well as prolonged study are necessary before the career of a musical critic can be begun with any hope of success.

I

CAMILLE SAINT-SAËNS

[*Evening Post*, New York, May 15, 1915.
By permission.]

Camille Saint-Saëns, France's foremost musician, and held by many to be the greatest living composer, landed on these shores on Thursday, in the performance of a patriotic duty. And to it, in spite of his eighty years, he is bringing, as those who saw him hurry down the gangplank of the *Rochambeau* can testify, all the keenness and nervous energy which have driven him through a vigorous career into every quarter of the globe and every realm of music, to say nothing of the other arts and sciences.

Now in the evening of his life, at the request of the French Government, he has undertaken to represent France at the Panama-Pacific Exposition. What is a more arduous undertaking, he has agreed, also at the request of his government, to be 'First Delegate to the Franco-American Commission for the Development of Political, Economic, Literary, and Artistic Relations,' and as such to deliver a series of lectures throughout this country during a visit of three months. What M. Saint-Saëns is about to do constitutes not 5 the least of his many patriotic services to France.

HIS UNUSUAL VERSATILITY

It is not easy to reconcile the appearance of the man with one's knowledge 10 of the extraordinary range of his experiences, the distinction of his artistic accomplishments, and the universal recognition he has received for half a century. He stepped ashore like any simple 15 voyager — albeit one who had business to transact and was eager to be at it. A dark suit and plain black overcoat — a trifle dingy it must be admitted — a derby 20 hat, close cropped gray hair, and square beard, strong aquiline nose, and quick, keen eyes, gave to their rather small-sized but sturdy possessor anything but the suggestion of temperament or of gen- 25 ius. A small leather bag supported by a strap over his shoulder added to his business-like appearance.

Could this be the man of whom Liszt

once said: 'I and Saint-Saëns are the only two left who know how to play the piano in Europe'? or of whom Wagner said: 'He is the greatest living French composer,' or Gounod that 'he could write at will a work in the style of Rossini, of Verdi, of Schumann, or of Wagner.' M. Saint-Saëns knew these celebrities well; they with many more of the most distinguished Europeans of the nineteenth century were his friends. And yet here was he who first won fame when he made his premier public appearance as a pianist in Paris two years before the French Revolution of '48, now trudging down a gangplank on a New York dock, without attracting any more notice than any returning traveler receives.

All of this emphasizes the sanity, the lack of ostentation, the independence, and the *savoir faire* which are M. Saint-Saën's distinguishing traits. Eccentricities, at least surface eccentricities, are no part of him. He is essentially a man of the world. His interests are worldwide, and his knowledge is in keeping. Not inaptly he has been dubbed the Admirable Crichton of the Boulevards. Beyond a doubt, even such a prototype could not surpass him for versatility. He loves all the arts only less well than music. He writes verses and occasional sonnets. His musical criticism did valiant service for music in France in a critical period. His literary publications include besides critiques, reminiscences, verse, essays, and comedies.

As for his talk, that which was heard at his 'Mondays' is famous. Ordinarily somewhat cold and self-contained, on occasions like these the composer unbent, as once for instance when to the delight of his visitors, he and Bizet acted and sang Offenbach's Homeric travesty, *La Belle Hélène*. From boyhood, he showed a keen interest and aptitude for science, which enabled him to master the formal side of music with most surprising celerity. Mathematics and astronomy were very much to his taste. And he has frequently contributed papers to scientific societies and magazines. An archeological treatise on the Greek theatre was an early excursion, and at another time, upon returning from a visit to the East, he amazed a learned society with a paper on his studies of mirages.

HONORS HEAPED UPON HIM

Oxford found him early worthy of the honorary degree of doctor of music; Cambridge showed wider recognition of his abilities by conferring upon the composer the degree of doctor of letters. In his own country honors innumerable have been heaped on him. Indeed, few men live to enjoy more acknowledgments of success than have been tendered him. Thirty-four years ago he became a member of the Institute, and he has since been made a member of the Royal Academies of Belgium, Prussia, Sweden, Greece, and Spain.

The striking thing today about Saint-Saëns is the vigor he has retained through a working life of remarkable fullness. It began when he was ten, and his fecundity has been nothing short of marvelous; more than ten pages of small print are necessary to catalogue his musical compositions, which range through every style of musical writing. In addition, he has had over half a century of continual travel, performing his own works, conducting and helping to produce others, and giving organ and piano concerts in all the capitals of Europe. His travels have taken him to Asia and Africa, and he has been in the United States before this. He has furthermore found time as at present to identify himself with national movements. He was the prime mover in the organization of a society for the promotion of French music as long ago as 1871. And he helped to establish a league against vulgar and incorrect words threatening to become part of the French language.

M. Saint-Saëns has undoubtedly been able to accomplish so much because of his early start. He was a 'wonderchild.' In many respects his infancy resembled Mozart's. Born on October 9, 1835, in Paris, he was hardly out of his nurse's arms before the world of sounds began to claim him. 'I began listening to every noise,' says his own account. 'My greatest pleasure was the symphony of the kettle on the hob. I used to listen with passionate interest to its slow and surprising crescendo and finally its song like that of an oboe. Berlioz must have listened to that same oboe, for I heard it afterward in the *Damnation of Faust* in the *Ride to Hell*.'

At two and a half years he played the piano; he played with taste and skill at five. And at ten he gave his first public concert, playing, among other things, Beethoven's *C minor Concerto* and one of Mozart's pieces, accompanied by the orchestra of the Italian Opera. He was seven when Stamaty took him as a pupil, and he had shown his ability to play parts of Mozart's *Don Juan* at sight. In 1847 Saint-Saëns entered the Conservatoire, where he studied under Benoist and Halévy, devoting himself to piano, organ, and theory to such purpose that he became a prize winner.

His first symphony was written and performed when he was seventeen with success by the Société de Sainte Cécile. He became organist of the Church of St. Merri in 1853, and organist of the Madeleine in 1858. He did some teaching also at that time, but gave most of his time to his beloved occupation of composing. His facility in that direction is the basis of many stories. There are few erasures on his manuscripts. He puts his ideas down rapidly on paper, chatting sometimes the while, and he needs no piano to assist him. He wrote his opera *Proserpine* without having an instrument in reach.

As a student of the music of other masters, he is probably without a rival. Von Bülow was so much impressed by this knowledge that he recorded his wonder at the young musician's prodigious memory, saying that even at that time nothing in a musical way was unknown to him. Berlioz was equally impressed with his talent and musical erudition. 'Camille Saint-Saëns is one of the greatest musicians of our time,' he said, and that time was 1867. One of the peculiarities of Saint-Saëns and his work — it is said to be a distinction which he alone of recent composers of consequence possessed — is his complete independence of Richard Wagner. He alone, in the opinion of most authorities, would have been what he has been if Wagner had never existed. And yet he helped France to understand Wagner. As he himself said: 'I admire the works of Richard Wagner profoundly, in spite of their eccentricities. They are superior and powerful, which suffices for me. But I have never belonged, I do not belong, and I never shall belong to the Wagnerian religion.'

M. Saint-Saën's most celebrated musical compositions are, with the date of their publications: *Les Noces de Prométhée,* 1867; *La Princesse Jaune,* 1872; *Le Timbre d'Argent,* 1877; *Samson et Delila,* 1877; *Étienne Marcel,* 1879; *Rouet d'Omphale, Danse Macabre, Jeunesse d'Hercule, Symphonies en mi, en la, et en ut, Henry VIII,* 1883; *Ascanio,* 1890; *Phryné,* 1893; *Chœurs d'Antigone,* 1893; *Javotte,* 1896; *Déjanire,* 1898; *Les Barbares,* 1901; *Parysatis,* 1902; *Hélène,* 1903; *L'Ancêtre,* 1906, and many concertos, sonatas, and quintettes.

It was on his visit here in 1906 that Saint-Saëns announced that he would quit the concert stage, after sixty years of hard work. He had, ten years before, had the satisfaction of celebrating the fiftieth anniversary of his first appearance in public by giving a concert in the identical chamber — the Salle Pleyel — in which as a boy of ten he made his début.

On that visit in 1906 the composer expressed himself as delighted with America. But he said that what interested him most was not America as it was, but what it would become some day, when a thousand elements were amalgamated in forming a product as yet unknown. Today he looks forward to observing just how far that process of amalgamation has gone. He is bitter against the foes of France, but he permits himself to talk little on the subject of the war. But he could not conceal his real feelings when he landed the other day. Some admirers who rushed to welcome him were brushed off with the protest that he would have none of them, for being German.

II

'BORIS GODOUNOFF'

KURT SCHINDLER

[*North American Review*, February, 1913. By permission.]

With *Boris Godounoff,* a drama of the Russian people, a new type of 'historical opera' has been founded; far from the stereotyped pattern of Halévy's and Meyerbeer's ambiguous and artificial creations, this is a work of the simple and compelling logic of a master playwright, in which the great emotional forces, the revolutionizing sentiments of a period are depicted through the medium of music.

There have been great musical geniuses who summed up every development that had gone before; of this type were Bach and Mozart. Then there were those volcanic temperaments, those prophetic minds who definitely formulated new ideals — Monteverde, Gluck, Beethoven, and Wagner, and among these must be included the Russian Moussorgsky, who with clear purpose steered the ship of art, as he said, 'unto new shores.' Moussorgsky was not only a wonderful composer individually, but behind him lay the unexplored musical wealth of the great Slav nation — a mine of rhythmically and melodically unusual folk-songs; of Byzantine church-chants flavoring of the mysterious early Christian period; of old bard tunes, rhapsodical and full of grandeur; of new and violent vocal inflections rooted in the dialects of a rich and varied language. While Tschaikowsky had adapted his Russian nature to the cosmopolitan surroundings in which he lived, his poor and obscure contemporary (for Moussorgsky was little known outside of Russia till long after his death) built the edifice of his art on purely racial grounds.

It was this intimate love of his own people that led Moussorgsky to base his greatest work, *Boris,* on a play by Pushkin, the poet who 'took Russia away from the artificiality of the eighteenth century and revealed the possibilities of native material in the native tongue.' And as the intense humanism of Moussorgsky's art made it a graphic reflection of his own experiences as well as of the life of his nation, a knowledge of the man in the artist is essential to an understanding of his work.

Modest Petrovitch Moussorgsky was born in Karevo, a village two hundred miles south of St. Petersburg, on the 28th of March of the year 1839, as the son of simple people belonging to the small nobility. Here he passed his childhood to his tenth year in the midst of fields and forests, the typical Russian landscape, in intimate touch with nature and the life of the peasants. His father and mother were both very musical, and his mother it was who first taught him the piano. The young Moussorgsky had a strong and vivid imagination which was nourished by the Russian fairy-tales, so highly colored and barbarically gorgeous in their picturing, which he heard from the lips of his 'Njanja,' the nurse. At an early age he used to sit down and improvise at the piano on these fairy-tales. The devotion of the boy to his mother was of the tenderest kind. In later years he used to speak of her as 'a saint,' and his impressive cradle song is inscribed to her memory. In 1849, when he was ten years old, his father sent him to St. Petersburg, where he first went to a preparatory school, later to a high school for noblemen. He kept on with his piano studies, developing a remarkable proficiency; and through an old priest, who taught him in religion, he came to know about the old Greek liturgical chants and about the music of the Roman Catholic Church, a knowledge which benefited him much in later years. He also learned German and Latin and showed marked interest for the study of history, of German philosophy and psychology. When, in 1856, he entered the Preobrajenki Regiment, he soon became very popular through his lovable character and his many accomplishments, both among his comrades and in social circles.

At this time he became acquainted with Dargomyszky, the greatest Russian composer of those days, whose fine personality and high ideals made a profound impression on the young man, and at whose house he met all the young composers of the day. Dargomyszky, mature alike in his work and years, had developed the theory in his new opera, *The Guest of the Stone,* that the musical sound should be the exact translation of the spoken word. This was, of course, very much the same idea that Richard Wagner carried out when in *Die Meistersinger* he let Eva and Magdalene, David and Hans Sachs, sing in vocal inflections conforming absolutely to the inflections of the speaking voice, a principle which, naturally, led to very different results when applied to the Russian language, so rich in sonority, so changeful in modulations. While Dargomyszky's *Guest of Stone* impresses one today as dry and theoretical, it was left to Moussorgsky, who eagerly absorbed Dargomyszky's axioms and instructions, to carry this idea of *musical naturalism* to its utmost convincing conclusions.

Moussorgsky now began to compose larger works, and in 1860 Anton Rubinstein conducted an orchestral scherzo of his in St. Petersburg. Already the year before Moussorgsky had sent his resignation to the regiment, feeling that his musical calling needed his entire and undivided devotion. No advice from his family or his friends was of any avail; the examples of Cui and Lermontoff, the poet, that were held up to prove to him that art and service in the army could be combined, failed to impress him. He said, ' I am not Lermontoff; I cannot serve two masters.' This resolution was in one respect most dangerous to Moussorgsky, because, not being blessed with wordly means, he was deprived of an assured income and soon faced grave financial troubles. These sorrows, together with the strain of his feverish zeal in music, led very soon to a nervous breakdown, and he had to be removed to the country, where his mother had remarried after the death of his father. From now on for the rest of his life Moussorgsky's health was frail, his manners feverish, restless, irregular, and his sensitiveness high strung to a degree. In the meantime he worked on a grand opera on the subject of Flaubert's *Salammbo*. This work was never finished, but a great many of its melodies have been rescued, being incorporated in *Boris Godounoff* and in the religious cantata *Joshua*. In the white heat of his enthusiasm he scorned the advice of his friends to acquire a better knowledge of musical technique, because he mistakenly confounded technique with conventionalism and because he was too full of inspiration to wait for the years of dry preparatory work, and, further, because he believed that a new path can only be found by creating a new style together with a new inspiration.

The year 1865 forms a turning-point in his composing. His mother, Julia Ivanovna, had died, and in the days of deepest emotion that sent his mind wandering back to the early days of his childhood he wrote his *Cradle Song of the Poor* and dedicated it to the memory of his mother. Here a new type of song is created; it is a picture of real life, a *genre* scene of the deepest meaning, this song of the peasant mother bent over the child, wailing and lamenting the doom to which it is predestined in the small and prescribed circuit of its life. From 1866 to 1868 Moussorgsky lives again in the country and comes once more in touch with the peasant population; and in the new light of the ideal that Dargomyszky inculcated in him, he sees a new beauty in the Russian peasant songs, in the simple and direct utterances of these village types. A little episode became of momentous interest in his life development: by chance he witnessed unseen from his window a scene where a poor little wretch, the village simpleton, makes love to the beautiful Ivanovna, the belle of the village. The touching and throbbing accents of this poor, loveless, feeble-minded creature, the direct truth that speaks out of his instinctive passion, made a profound impression on Moussorgsky.

And he tries to embody this little scene exactly as he has witnessed it in a song for which he wrote both words and music. This incident is used in *Boris Godounoff* most effectively, and because of its importance it is, perhaps, worth while to recall the fact that the Russian country people treat these unfortunate 'yourodivy,' the village simpletons, of which they have so many, with awe and superstitious reverence, believing that they have divine foresight, an idea that is to some extent borne out by science, which claims that their lack of intellect is often compensated by a keener intuition.

The witnessing of this pathetic little drama inspires him to a further resolution in his work. He will from now on not only seek to make the song an exact translation of the spoken word, but he will try to reveal through music those instinctive hidden undercurrents of emotion which lie beneath the veneer of civilization and which psychologists study in the insane and feeble-minded. He will thus, with his music, approach mysterious thresholds which among poets only Shakespeare dared to cross. The culmination of these efforts of Moussorgsky was to be the mad scene of *Boris Godounoff*. But not everything in Moussorgsky's work deals with sad and gruesome things. He shares with some of the great men of Russian literature the reverse side of the national character — a keen sense of humor and mockery. A delightful specimen of this side of his talent is a character song called *The Seminarist,* in which he shows the troubles of a young student of theology, who, under the watchful eyes of his teacher, the priest, essays a flirtation with the latter's daughter, is caught and drastically punished and now tries to repeat his Latin lesson of irregular verbs, while choked with sobs and haunted by vivid, unpleasant memories.

Even more amusing and original is another song called *The Peep Show,* a kind of musical pamphlet in which he lets the five most important music critics of St. Petersburg pass by as in a *camera obscura,* each one parodied in a good-natured way. There is Famyntsine, the classic, for whom great music ends with Mozart. There is Fifi Tolstoi, who raves about Patti and dances an ecstatic waltz to the air of 'Patti-Patti,' and there is Zaremba prostrated before the genius of Wagner. This musical pamphlet, in its humor and *bonhomie,* was an immense success. What Moussorgsky would have done had he finished the music to Gogol's comedy, *The Marriage,* we cannot tell. He completed but one act, in which he realized a verisimilitude in reproducing the types of the Russian *bourgeoisie,* faithful alike in manner of speech and of action, that strikes us today, forty-five years later, as extremely modern and really ahead of the times. But he gave up the work on this musical comedy when the idea of setting to music Pushkin's historical drama *Boris Godounoff* was proposed to him by the actor Nikolsky, whom he met at the house of his intimate friend Stassof at St. Petersburg. At Stassof's house he also met Rimsky-Korsakoff, with whom he liked to discuss music and with whom in later years he even shared an apartment.

In September, 1868, he started to work on *Boris.* The first act was already finished in November, and in the fall of 1869 the first version was completed. He orchestrated it in the subsequent winter, and the circle of musicians that first heard it received it with great enthusiasm because it seemed to carry out the ideals of the young Russian school desiring absolute veracity and minute reproduction of life. His friends, though, unanimously objected to the absence of the female element and of a love story in the opera, which he remedied by inventing the scene of the Polish Princess Marina and by giving such subordinate personages as the hostess and the little Tsarevitch (played by a woman) several arias to sing. He had the good taste, though, to keep these arias in the folk-song style, thus preserving the unity of the opera's historical character.

In February, 1873, the second act was produced on a private stage, and owing to its success the entire work was taken up at the Imperial Theatre, where the first performance took place on the 24th of January, 1874. It had an enormous success, especially with the younger generation, the progressive faction of the students. Twenty performances were given, but, much to the grief of the composer a great many scenes, because of court intrigue, were censored as revolutionary and had to be omitted. Just for a few weeks the life of the composer had seemed to reach a climax of recognition and success, but from now on one disappointment succeeded another. The only real gleam of hope that still shone into his life was a message of appreciation from Franz Liszt, who had received through mutual friends a set of children's songs called *The Child's Nursery* in which Moussorgsky had noted the little joys and troubles of child life with an accuracy and fidelity to detail hitherto unheard of. Liszt sent Moussorgsky word that he was enchanted with it and wanted to transcribe it for the piano.

During the last seven years of Moussorgsky's life he worked on another opera taken from Russian history and dealing with the conspiracy of the Khovanskis. Its Russian title is *Khovantchina.* He did not live to complete this, although some parts of it were given under the direction of Balakireff during Moussorgsky's lifetime. The work was actually finished by Rimsky-Korsakoff, who also re-orchestrated a great many parts of *Boris* to suit the exigencies of large opera-houses. The service that Rimsky-Korsakoff tried to render the memory of his comrade is of questionable value. Rimsky was not a big enough man to realize the beauty and originality of Moussorgsky's genius, and he often tried to cover and soften what seemed to him harshness, but what was really visionary audacity and the force of inspiration. His corrections, although giving higher color, often detracted from the vigor of Moussorgsky's drawing.

Over the last few years of Moussorgsky's life it is well to pass quickly. The story is too sad. Deep melancholy had settled on him, and he was so poor that in order to make a living he had to take up inferior clerical work in the various ministerial departments and was obliged to accept a position as accompanist in a singing-school.

When he returned to St. Petersburg in 1880, he was already desperately ill and addicted to the use of cognac. His friends tried to raise money for him by giving a concert of his own compositions in February, 1881, but it was too late; and a few days later he had to be taken to the military hospital, where he died on the 16th of March, 1881.

The story of *Boris Godounoff* is founded on some facts in Russian history between the years 1598–1605. It is the story of the False Dimitri, used by many dramatists, among them the German, Schiller, and the Russian, Pushkin; and it is the text of the latter author which forms the basis of Moussorgsky's libretto, but certain scenes were written by Moussorgsky himself after descriptions by the historian, Karamzine. After the death of Ivan the Terrible, Feodor, the feeble-minded brother of the Tsar, had ascended the throne; and there being only an infant son, Dimitri, Boris, the brother-in-law of Feodor, was made regent and tutor of the child. Before the opening of the opera the gruesome deed had already taken place — that is, the murder of the Tsarevitch Dimitri in the church of Ouglitch at the hidden instigation of Boris, who knows that he thus paves for himself the way to the throne. Feodor meanwhile has died, and when the curtain rises the scene is the monastery of Novo-Dvejtchi near Moscow, whereto Boris has retired, professing that he will not accept the crown. A great crowd of country people, ignorant and docile, pour into the courtyard, driven by prefects and Boïars to implore Boris to become their Tsar. This blind multitude is a mere tool in the hands of the noblemen. The next scene shows the coronation of Boris on the Kremlin, where, though surrounded by the cheers of his subjects, the new Tsar, haunted by his deed, is sad and filled with ominous forebodings. This ends the prologue of the opera.

The first scene of Act I reveals a cell in a monastery of Moscow at night. The venerable monk, Pimenn, is in the act of finishing his chronicle of the history of Russia, in which he has described the murder of the Tsarevitch Dimitri. A young novice, Gregory, who shares the cell, awakes from obsessing dreams of ambition, and Pimenn, to quiet him, tells him of the vanity of earthly power and how even those who wear the crown are not free from sorrow. While speaking of the murder of Dimitri the old monk mentions the fact that the Tsarevitch, had he lived, would have been exactly the same age as the young monk Gregory now is. Instantly an idea flares up in the mind of the fanatic novice; he persuades himself that he is God's instrument to bring just punishment upon Boris and to avenge the death of the Tsarevitch.

The second scene of the first act is at a village inn near the Lithuanian frontier, where the authorities are seeking the fugitive young monk, who is stirring up the people by proclaiming that he is the young Dimitri. They find Gregory in the company of two jolly vagabond friars, but he escapes through the window bound for the Polish frontier. The second act is in Polish Lithuania, where a great festival is being held at the Castle of Sandomir. Marina, a Polish princess, urged on by her Jesuit advisers, has received the false Dimitri hospitably, seeing in him a means to strike at the Russian throne. Dimitri, who has fallen in love with Marina, is stirred by her to his utmost ambition. She says that only when he becomes Tsar of Russia will she marry him. The next scene, in the palace of the Tsar Boris, in the nursery of the Imperial children, is an intimate picture of tender home life, offering opportunities for charming children songs and nursery ditties. Here the Tsar is seen in his human aspect as a grave and affectionate father capable of the deepest love for his children. Yet always the shadow of his crime moves beside him. He hears through the sly and cunning Boïar Chouisky, of an uprising at the frontier and of the appearance of a young man claiming to be Dimitri. Doubts arise in his soul as to whether his commands were actually carried out and if the Tsarevitch may not really still be alive. Left alone, a growing horror seizes him; the ghost of the murdered child seems to arise before his eyes — a vision he seeks in vain to repel — and with a prayer to God for forgiveness he sinks down fainting.

The next scene is the death of Boris. For reasons of operatic expediency the scene has been put at the end of the opera, a proceeding which is legitimate because the composer himself at one time had proposed the arrangement. In the great vaulted hall of the Kremlin the Duma of the Boïars is assembled to discuss the punishment of the usurper *Dimitri*. They have not caught him yet, but they are already planning what mode of death to choose. There they sit in solemn session in their sumptuous robes and furs when Boris, still in the throes of his terrible vision, appears, haggard and haunted. The old monk, Pimenn, enters, the chronicler of the first act, who, in the midst of intrigue and lying ambition, typifies Truth in this drama. He recounts to the *Tsar* a miracle of the restoring of sight to a blind peasant who made a pilgrimage to the grave of the dead Dimitri. While this proves the actual death of the Tsarevitch and the falsity of the pretender's claim, it only intensifies the mystic terror by which Boris is obsessed. He completely collapses under the clear gaze of the old monk, feeling that Pimenn reads the guilt in his soul. His attendants, seeing that his end is near, send for his little son to receive his benediction, and they then clothe Boris in the Imperial Skima, the funeral shroud of the Tsars. Boris dies.

The last scene, as Moussorgsky planned it, shows us the highway to Moscow on which on a bitter cold winter day the pretender is advancing with his troops toward the capital. A group of peasant serfs have caught an Imperial messenger and vent their rage upon him. Children are tormenting a poor feeble-minded lad, a 'yourodivy,' as they call them in Russia. The two vagabond friars of the scene in the inn again appear, seeking to rouse the people to revolt, with the result that a new storm of fury breaks out. In their frenzy they seize upon two Jesuits who are accompanying the victorious army of the false Dimitri (who is, in fact, the Jesuits' tool). While they are about to tear in pieces these monks the pretender appears riding at the head of his troops and proclaiming freedom and forgiveness to all. Equally frantic patriotism succeeds the outburst of fury, and cheering and shouting, the multitude joins the advancing army. Only the poor idiot boy remains behind, and while the snow falls more and more thickly he sits alone, sending forth his sorrowful plaint: 'Fall, fall, bitter tears, weep, O soul of the righteous! The enemy approaches, blood will flow, fire will rage. Woe on Russia! Weep, ye starving people!'

In reviewing the life-work of Moussorgsky we find a variety of novel aspects that distinguish it, as well as a wide range of themes that his work comprises; we find poignant pathos, and delightful humor, strong dramatic contrasts on one side, and again, when needed, the monotony of an incessant invariable rhythm, the refined subtle charm of the children songs, and a barbaric stirring force in the folk scenes of his operas. With an extraordinarily precise vision he draws the musical pictures of a Russian landscape in the charm of spring and summer or in the grim clutches of Russia's frosty winter, and more in particular the picture of the Russian village in all the phases of peasant life, showing the mother and the child, the beggar and the 'yourodivy,' the young lovers, and the sad housewives, the Jews, and the monks. Such interior scenes as the pompous assembly of the peasant family at a holiday celebration, or the jollities of a village inn, are drawn by him with humor and precision.

Moussorgsky always needs a pictorial vision to inspire him to music; his understanding of musical truth means absolute adherence to life, absolute nature-likeness. This is decidedly a limitation of his talent, a one-sidedness that he shares with Berlioz and with Richard Strauss. He always has in view a goal not purely musical; the idea of thematic development, as it forms an intrinsic part of symphonic composition, never appeals to him. His strict adherence to the inflections of the Russian spoken word leads him to a liberty and freedom from regular rhythms hitherto unheard of. There is no regularity of musical periods corresponding to each other, as in the classical masters, and there are continual changes of bar and tempo such as nobody had dared to write up to his time. It means boldness, indeed, on the part of Moussorgsky in the year 1868, to change the bar twenty-three times inside of one song (No. 1 of the children songs); today we have become accustomed to such proceeding through the modernists of France and Germany; yet none of these followers have done it with so much logic as Moussorgsky, who merely sought after the most correct musical notation of the speech of the people. Modern musical explorers of Russia, who, like Madam Lineff, have traveled through the peasant districts, taking down the Russian folk songs by means of the phonograph, have stated scientifically how variable and flexible the character of the Russian folk melos is. We have become accustomed to the celebrated five-four rhythm of Tschaikowsky's *Pathétique,* but by acquaintance with the work of Moussorgsky one learns another typical Russian rhythm, the seven-four, and Rimsky's fairy opera entrances with its pompous and stately eleven-four that is as old as the oldest Slavonic traditions.

A new and fertile soil of exploration Moussorgsky had before him when with his keen ears and scrutinizing eyes he watched the country people at work and in song. He had caught as well the weird melodic outline of the Russian lament or wail, the strange incantations of those bards or 'rhapsodes' that now, as centuries ago, wander through the plains of Russia singing the old ballads and folk songs or lamenting at the funeral of the dead in long-drawn-out melodious phrases that are like the falling of tears. Moussorgsky's songs are the songs of the soil. His spirit of observation, of musical experimentation, let him describe the very graphic movements and gestures of the moujik or Russian peasant in music, an achievement that helps the dramatic effectiveness of the folk scenes of his operas greatly. The idiom of the Russian folk song had so completely become his own that it is hard to say in his work where the nature product stops and where his own invention begins. Far from blaming him for relying thus upon the nation's resources, we ought to admire the truth and strength of his unconscious atavistic music heritage which allowed him to speak with the original force of the people, a spokesman of the dumb millions. Many other Russian composers have used the treasure hold of folk songs, but none like Moussorgsky without tainting and soiling them,

without adding the smallness of individual taste to the pure gold of the people's own greatest possession.

This is exactly the corner where Moussorgsky grips us with his boundless love of truth and this is why his work, although strictly national in its idiom, reaches far over the Russian boundaries in its appeal to the entire civilized world. It is a singular power of music that it can convey the very soul essence of a nation even to those who have never come in any touch with it and who do not understand its language.

In *Boris Godounoff* the 'people' are actually in the foreground of the happenings, the great masses are really the principal actor; at first dumb, oppressed, easily guided, then stirred up, threatening, finally in open revolt and jubilant war spirit. The strong veracity of these folk scenes can be likened without blasphemy to such eternal masterpieces as Shakespeare's *Coriolanus* and *Julius Cæsar.* And in all dramatic music there is nothing as near to *Macbeth* as the specter scene of *Boris.*

One important innovation is that Moussorgsky uses principally prose diction instead of verse, which makes possible the intense realism of his style, and which permits him to faithfully picture scenes of every-day life. His acts begin without elaborate orchestral preludes, and the music ends with the falling of the curtain; in fact, his self-imposed restraint keeps him from drawing one more line or inventing one more melody than is actually demanded by the situation. The idea of spinning out or developing themes symbolically, as Wagner did, is entirely excluded from his operatic credo. On the contrary, it is to the singers, the actual exponents of the dramatic message, that supremacy is given. Much attention is paid to the acting not only of the soloists, but also of the chorus, and the gestures are often indicated by the music itself.

Since Wagner's death there is no work that has so stirred the musical world through its freedom from convention, its direct truth, and its compelling sincerity; and a singular pathos is attached to the fact that *Boris* was written forty-three years ago, but only came to the knowledge of the international public since the sumptuous performances in Paris in 1908. Since then the work has been given in Italian in both Monte Carlo and Milan, and is shortly to be heard in New York. This wider recognition of Moussorgsky's genius, which only began when his ideals struck fire from the susceptible musicians of France, has meant nothing less than a reawakening of musical conscience by this naturalist in art, who declared: ' I want Truth above all! To seek and find these treasures hidden in the masses and in individuals which no hand as yet has touched, and to feed hungering humanity with them as with a wholesome food, this is the artist's problem and the joy of joys. Art is not a goal, but the means to talk to one's brethren!'

III

WORLD PREMIERE OF 'MADAME SANS-GENE'

[W. J. HENDERSON]

[*Sun*, New York, January 26, 1915.
By permission.]

' MADAME SANS-GENE '— METROPOLITAN OPERA
HOUSE

Caterina Hubscher	Geraldine Farrar
Lefebvre	Giovanni Martinelli
Napoleon	Pasquale Amato
Fouque	Andrea de Segurola
Count de Neipperg	Paul Althouse
Queen Carolina	Vera Curtis
Princess Elisa	Minnie Eggener
Despreaux	Angelo Bada
Gelsonimo	Riccardo Tegani
Leroy	Robert Leonhardt

Madame Sans-Gene, opera in four acts, the book by Renato Simoni after the comedy by Victorien Sardou and E. Moreau, the music by Umberto Giordano, was performed last night at the Metropolitan Opera House for the first time on any stage. The comedy should be remembered by local theatregoers from its interesting representations with Kathryn Kidder in the title rôle and from the production in which Mme. Rejane was the principal actor. Umberto Giordano is the composer of *Andrea Chenier,* an opera produced at the Academy of Music by the late Colonel Mapleson on November 13, 1896; *Fedora,* produced by Heinrich Conried at the Metropolitan on December 5, 1906, and *Siberia,* produced at the Manhattan Opera House by Oscar Hammerstein on February 5, 1907. Not one of

these three operas made any serious impression or effected a lasting occupation of the local stage.

Last evening's production was witnessed by a large and eager audience. The brilliancy of the stage pictures, the swift movement of Sardou's skilfully planned action, the disclosure of Geraldine Farrar's gifts in a new investiture and the new demonstration of a pleasing skill within a limited field of impersonation on the part of Mr. Amato, for which he has few opportunities, all served to hold the interest of the assembly and furnished food for much animated discussion in the entr'actes.

SUCCESS DEPENDS ON SINGERS

But there was no ground for belief that the opera had made any deeper conviction of creative power than its predecessors from the same pen. If the work obtains any vogue it will be entirely due to the achievements of the principal impersonators. And it must be kept in mind that this can confidently be said in spite of the fact that Arturo Toscanini, the foremost opera conductor. of the world, has devoted to the interpretation of the work his unique endowments and his inexhaustible energy.

Of the liberties taken with history by Sardou and Moreau in their comedy nothing need now be said. Mr. Simoni has made as good an opera book out of the play as could be expected. He has kept close to his original, and his labor has naturally been chiefly that of omission and condensation in order that the piece might be reduced to practicable proportions. If the libretto is not a great one, it can hardly be called the fault of Mr. Simoni.

It is too crowded with incident and action. An ideal opera book would seldom be able to stand performance without the music, because it would be too ' talky.' The numerous sustained lyric utterances which are the life of an opera are the death of a play. On the other hand a composer cannot work to advantage when he is encumbered with a mass of details of stage business. What he requires for his purposes is a few grand dramatic situations in which the elemental emotions are to be expressed not by doing but by speech which he is to translate into song.

The first opera makers tried to construct this type of poetic drama by carrying on their explanatory dialogue in recitative and publishing their emotional states in arias. Their purpose was defeated by the decadence of their method into a mere stereotyped formula. Later masters sought to reconstruct the form by modifying the large difference between the recitation and the air. Still later composers abolished the conventions of the recitative entirely and wrote their dialogue in a continuous melos, known technically as arioso. When they needed the larger lyric utterance they gave it, but not in any conventional pattern such as that of the eighteenth century aria.

MEMORABLE GREAT ACTS

But no great operatic masterpiece has ever been created which contains no moments of rapturous melodic song, of pure lyric utterance. Without pausing to search the archives of the mind any operagoer will think of the great third act of *Aïda*, of Otello's farewell to 'the pomp, the pride and circumstance of war,' of the dialogue of *Pelleas and Melisande* beside the fountain, of 'O sink' hernieder' and 'Mild und leise' in *Tristan*, of Wotan's farewell, of *Bruennhilde's* immolation. These things are music, great music, and an opera book to be a good one must not only make room for great music but must inspire it.

If the objection be raised that Giordano's work is comedy and we are quoting tragedies, it is necessary only to recall the frequent and beautiful instances of lyric utterance in a baker's dozen of works, among them Rossini's *Barber of Seville*, Mozart's *Marriage of Figaro*, Wolf-Ferrari's *Le Donne Curiose*, Smetana's *Bartered Bride*, Wagner's *Die Meistersinger* and Verdi's *Falstaff*. Surely Comedy with her smile and her rod of satiric castigation has done as much for music as Tragedy with her grim portents and her agonies.

The book of *Madame Sans-Gene* supplies only a few dramatic points for strong and vital music. The point at which the development of this vivacious comedy calls for the most moving emotional utterance is in the second act, when Lefebvre repeats to his wife the Emperor's suggestion of divorce. For the rest there are some delightful bits of comedy in the book and some of them clamor for that style of delicate and fanciful music with which Massenet has delighted our ears and our taste in his *Manon,* music which wears the powdered wig, the exaggerated gallantry and the pirouette of Paris of the close of the eighteenth century.

That Giordano has written his score in a workmanlike manner goes almost without saying. The routine of operatic composition is well known to Italian composers. In fact they know more about this than about anything else, and much of the lyric art which emanates from the land of the 'drama per musica' discloses its inheritance of the blood of a generation in which one who could write an effective opera finale was called a skilful contrapuntist. Giordano is a competent routinier; he knows how to put an opera score together.

His method has no new features. It is that of the contemporaneous Italian stage. His dialogue is carried on in continuous melody, with rare excursions into the modern type of recitative. His larger dramatic situations he seeks to embody in broader lyric form, but as already said he is too frequently hampered by the nature of the situations themselves.

The melodic flights which do occur disclose no lofty flight of musical invention. They are pretty and pleasing, but they lack the directness, the individuality, the incisiveness essential to the excitement of enthusiasm. Thematic representation is not employed at all in the manner of Wagner or even Puccini's *Tosca*, but the older device of fixed ideas and reminiscences is utilized rather baldly and ineffectively. The repetitions of the love melodies are of course obvious; all such repetitions are. The crashing chords of brass which herald Napoleon are mere noise without musical design.

The composer has said that his thought centralized on the Little Corporal. Although he does not appear till the third act everything portends him, foreshadows him, is prologue to him. It is always interesting and instructive to know what are the purposes of an artist; but to measure his achievements by them is frequently disappointing. In the score of Giordano Napoleon is an ante-climax. The composer unwittingly shot his bolt in the second act, and when the third brings the figure of the first Emperor the stage is still dominated by the wilful Sans-Gene.

FEW MUSICAL TRICKS

The orchestration is on the whole work-manlike. But there are some pages in which it is much overdone, and in the third act at times even the powerful tones of Mr. Amato were inaudible. Musical tricks of the time are not numerous. There are some harp sweeps along the whole tone scale. Stopped trumpets inevitably impart a nasal twang to certain passages. The bass drum wearies itself in futile struggles to indicate the tumult of a troubled historical period.

So much for a swift review of the music in its more immediate revelations. But certain problems larger than those indicated in this examination confronted Giordano. In common with every other writer of opera he had to face the difficulties of characterization. These presented themselves to him in two general phases, of which the more familiar may be discussed first. In *Madame Sans-Gene,* as in any other lyric drama, there is an imperative demand for definition of the characters of the protagonists as well as for that broader characterization which creates a style perfectly adapted to the emotional movement of the play.

Both of these requirements Giordano has met but feebly. His assertion that the musical thought of his composition revolves around Napoleon may be true, but there is no individuality in the music of the Emperor. He speaks precisely the same lyric language as the other persons of the comedy, and he speaks it with less directness than *Sans-Gene.* Nor can it be said that the general emotional scheme of the play has given the composer any larger inspiration than this historical figure which he believed to occupy his mind. The music of the whole opera is lamentably deficient in power of characterization.

We are not therefore disappointed when we consider the other phase of characterization which was placed before this musician. He was called upon to make a deeply significant contrast between his first and his second act. The accomplishment of the task would have been a veritable tour de force for even a master, and it was quite beyond the powers of Giordano.

In his first act he was asked to find a musical expression for the spirit of the revolution, a historical event portentous even in its outward and pictorial aspects, which the composer tried to seize, and still more momentous in its profounder significance which was not to be published to us merely by echoes of the *Marseillaise,* the *Carmagnole* and the *Ça ira.* In the second act the composer was invited to embody the unhealthy, overdrawn and even apprehensive ceremonials of a mushroom aristocracy striving to inspire itself with confidence by the exercise of sheer audacity. Into this had to be projected the outspoken thought and untrammeled feelings of a woman of the people rebelling against a society of pretenders. It was a formidable task indeed and it proved to be far beyond the abilities of the composer of *Fedora* and *Siberia.*

Having examined the broader requirements of the score, we may now proceed to pass in review some of its salient details as they appear in the several acts. The first act bristles with incidents. The composer has endeavored to give some musical coherence to it by entrusting the principal figuration and movement to the orchestra, which thus provides a well tinted background for animated dialogue. The first real success of the method is found in the scene between Caterina and Fouque, in which old French melody of rustic type, well suited to suggest Caterina's Alsatian origin, is worked up into an extended scherzando which is quite pleasing.

There is a light touch in the music accompanying the entrance of Lefebvre and his soldier companions, and the tenor has a respectable bit of semi-declamatory melody beginning with ' Ah, perdio fu un travaglio rude.' After that all is rapid dialogue, as was most of that which went before, together with the bustle of action, crowds rushing on and off the stage, passing the windows at the rear and battering at the door. The last crowd which passes at the rear just before the curtain falls sings the *Marseillaise,* which always was a good tune and still is. At an opportune moment, too, the composer finds a happy use for the *Carmagnole,* for its thought resounds through the action :

' Le canon vient de resonner:
Guerriers, soyez prêts de marcher.'

In like manner one hears echoes of the *Ça ira.* The composer is quite right in introducing those melodies of the period. They belong to the story, and as all good and true theatregoers know, we must have local color. Any composer who knows his business can get it from the native color shop, and it is not hard to remember that the best tune in Giordano's *Siberia* was 'Ay ouchnem,' made in Russia.

The second act opens delightfully. It is perhaps one of the curiosities of the lyric drama that three minor characters, a tailor, a dancing master and a valet, have a trio, which is almost the best bit of music in the entire score. The fact that it is woefully wanting in originality affects the matter not in the least, for unoriginal composition is often the happiest product of mediocrity. This trio has grace, charm and elegance of style and aptly expresses the mood of three servants trained under the old nobility and now waiting upon the upstart creations of the Corsican.

The scene between Caterina and the dancing master is well written, but there is nothing in the music which discloses more than the familiar technical skill of a professional composer of Italian opera. It is the work of a man who knows his business, but has nothing to demand particular consideration. In the next scene, that between Caterina and her husband, the composer has the largest opportunity of the entire book, and it is here that he most strikingly reveals the weakness of his invention.

This is the scene in which Lefebvre, returning from the Emperor, tells Caterina that his Majesty is wearied of her manners and her language and has suggested that her husband divorce her. When she asks him what he answered he says: 'What would you have said?' Then the woman pours out her soul in the words with which she would have spurned the royal suggestion and ends with: 'So would you have said, if you had a bit of heart.'

SPLENDID EMOTION

One can imagine a Verdi voicing in poignant phrases a splendid emotion like this, or a Montemezzi letting it flame through a clear medium of pure melody. Giordano has done fairly well with it, but it never rises to a thrill. It commands respectful admiration and that is all. Lefebvre quietly remarks, 'Well, that's what I said to him.' Caterina runs into

his arms, and then it is his turn with, 'Questa bocca tua perfumata e pure'— 'this, thy mouth, perfumed and pure'— and again the composer writes commendably and without inspiration. A musician scrutinizing these two lyric passages will see that their technical weakness lies in the want of organic relation in their phrases. The development of a melodic climax is thus rendered impossible, and the whole scene is without cohesion.

A little further on in this act there is a well written bit of ensemble for Caterina, Lefebvre and Neipperg, but it is marred by thick orchestration. The entrance of the court ladies gives opportunity for some more music of grace and elegance, sung by the women who surround Fouque. But this music, charming as it is, has no more distinction than that of the trio at the beginning of the act. It sounds like Bizet waking from a *Carmen* dream in a Massenet entourage. The rest of the act is action and dialogue, some of the latter heated in character, as in the defiance of the Queen of Naples by Caterina. There is little room for great music. What Giordano has made exposes its mechanism plainly and one sees the ancient wheels going around.

In the third act Caterina visits the Emperor in obedience to his command, and we see Napoleon for the first time. But, as has already been noted, the composer could find no expression for this remarkable personality save a noise of trumpets and trombones. It would be futile to attempt a description of the music of this act. Here indeed and hence to the finish 'the play's the thing.' No one has anything to sing except declamation, which is frequently shouting rather than speech.

There is one well made passage, to wit, that in which Caterina reminds Napoleon of a long past visit to his room and how he neglected her proffered love for the study of a war map. This speech, 'Che in quel tempo io pensavo,' might have given us something movingly tender in its musical expression, but Giordano contrived to miss his opportunity once again through his inability to write firmly organized melody.

From this point to the end of the opera little could be done by such a writer as this and indeed not much even by a master. Yet the observant hearer feels that a musician with ability to create an orchestral utterance would have accompanied with music of delineative force the tense action of Neipperg's stolen visit and capture, and of Napoleon's attempt to trap his Empress. In the present case one may reasonably doubt that an audience will take note of this music or even be insensibly affected by it.

MISS FARRAR'S ACTING

Of the production at the Metropolitan little can be said that is not commendatory. Miss Farrar was the chief offender against probability and against good taste, for her Caterina was too rude, too vulgar and suddenly too rid of her awkwardness. There was much cleverness in her acting and much that was astonishingly pointless. She sang the music well enough. If there were anything calling for great delicacy of treatment or for an art of deep resource there might be much more to say. But vocally Caterina is simple. In the combination of song and action which constitutes an operatic impersonation Miss Farrar made a lively impression on the audience, but just what the various members of that audience will think about it all when at home and not under the immediate influence of the young soprano's magnetic personality may be another matter. However, Miss Farrar usually makes progress in her rôles, and may in this one.

Mr. Amato achieved a genuine success with his Napoleon. His makeup was good, his rapid walk and energetic action well fitted into the moods of his scenes and his delivery of the lines was intelligent. He presented a well composed character of a type different from anything he has given us before, clearly and firmly drawn and full of interesting personality.

Mr. Martinelli sang the music of Lefebvre well and made a manly figure of him. Mr. de Segurola showed his customary histrionic skill in the comparatively small rôle of Fouque. Mr. Bada commanded the warmest possible praise for his admirable character sketch of the dancing master and Mr. Tegani must be mentioned for his neat singing of the music of Gelsonimo. Mr. Althouse was very vigorous as Neipperg, but praise can follow him no further. The scenery was of course all new and excellent, and the costuming of the opera such as Mr. Gatti-Casazza has customarily given us.

IV

GILBERT AND SULLIVAN

H. E. KREHBIEL

[*New York Tribune*, May 23, 1915. By permission.]

There have been sporadic seasons of the operettas of Gilbert and Sullivan in the theatres of New York as long as the operettas have existed; but last week was the first week in thirty years, if we are not mistaken, in which the same work occupied two stages for days together at the same time. Then, as now, it was *The Mikado* which was performed, and the operetta was brand new. It would be a pleasant reflection, could it be indulged, that the simultaneous performances at the Forty-eighth Street and Standard theatres were an indication of a return of Gilbert and Sullivan's works to the extraordinary vogue which they had a quarter of a century ago, before idiotic buffooneries and vulgar jingles had debauched public taste. It may be an extravagant hope that this might be so, but there are indications of a return to better standards than those which gradually took possession of the Broadway playhouses after the last of the Gilbert and Sullivan works had been brought forward, and a cataclysm may be impending which will submerge the now-dominant frivolity and bring back a love for comedy which shall be bright and clean and music which shall be worthy of the name. Such appreciation as *The Lilac Domino* received might be looked upon as a preliminary step toward this desirable consummation, for that clever work at least gave no offense to lovers of good music and showed how much more refinement and skill the best foreign composers have than the best of those who live in this country. Now, in his day Sir Arthur Sullivan was a much more thoroughly schooled musician than any of the men of France and Germany whose works he supplanted in the popular taste of England and America, and, no doubt, frequently regretted that fate had turned his muse into the comic path. His friends knew that he cast many a regretful look upon the scores of *The Prodigal Son, The*

Golden Legend and *Ivanhoe* when in the full flush of his victories on the operetta stage; but the most discerning critics among them must have known that in the serious vein which he would have preferred to follow he had added nothing to music with all his fine talent (or genius, if one would have it so), whereas, in the light dramatic style into which he was drawn by his partnership with Gilbert he did a distinct and even great service to his generation, his art, his people and all peoples who use the English tongue. The props which Mr. Gilbert placed under the structure of his reputation were more numerous and more varied, but he, too, was at his best in the refined whimsicality and polite satire of his operetta books. Their destruction would be a severe loss to the literature of the stage, while the wiping out of all his other dramatic writings might be contemplated with equanimity. It will be interesting for a long time to come to read the social history of the closing decades of the nineteenth century in Gilbert's skits, which, in spite of their farcical character, served the true and best purposes of comedy in their smiling chastisement of popular follies.

Looked at from one point of view it may safely be said that through their ministrations Gilbert and Sullivan placed their native England far in advance of all the nations of the world. Theirs was peculiarly the age of operetta. During the last forty years no form of theatrical entertainment has compared in popularity with musical comedy in England, Germany, France, and America. Yet it was only in England and America that, through their efforts, popular taste was turned and developed in a direction which deserved commendation by the standards at once of good art and good morals. In France the descent from the *opéra comique* of Auber, Boieldieu and Adam to the *opéra bouffe* of Offenbach was great; but it was atoned for, measurably, by the gracefulness and piquancy of Offenbach's melodic talent, and also, to some extent, by the satirical scourge which his librettists applied to the manners of the Second Empire. In Germany French *opéra bouffe* crowded out the *Singspiel* of men like Lortzing, whose talent was most ingratiating, without putting works of characteristic originality in its place. Clever as the best operettas of Suppé (a Dalma-

tian to the Italian manner born), Strauss and Millöcker were (we can only say 'are' of a few of them), it cannot be said for them that they were at all unique in their genre. They were but developments of the French type tricked out with German dance rhythms. Not so the creations of Gilbert and Sullivan. They are racy of the English soil.

SOME OBSERVATIONS ON THE NEW YORK PERFORMANCES

Every revival of one of the operettas of the fortunately mated collaborators recalls interesting memories to the minds of veteran playgoers. It is not likely that any one who was at the first performance of any operetta in the list will ever have the recollection of the incident forced from his mind. It was the happy lot of the writer to attend the first American production of all the operettas since *Iolanthe* in his capacity of music reviewer for *The Tribune*. Every one of the incidents stands out so prominently in his memory that he can recall the place without difficulty, some of the people of the company and in some cases the name of the companion who enjoyed the pleasure with him; yet the first première took place nearly thirty years ago and the last more than twenty-one. He saw *Iolanthe* in rehearsal, but the trefoil of P's — *Pinafore, Pirates* and *Patience* — antedate his New York experiences, as, of course, do *The Trial by Jury* and *The Sorcerer*. It was significant that when the time came for the successor of *Iolanthe* to appear there was less advance speculation touching the name and character of the next operetta than there had been indulged thitherto. Already in that early day there was a feeling, not entirely unmixed with fear, that the two arch funmakers had reached the climax of their powers and that though they might continue to turn out an operetta every year or two it would be vain to expect the freshness of wit and affluence of melody which characterized the three works whose names began with a P. *Iolanthe* betrayed a decline in both text and music by exposing to the crowd a good many of the formulas which the clever Englishmen employed. Though not a failure in the common sense, it fell short of the success of its predecessors. It seemed as if Mr. Gilbert had been unfortunate with his plot; that the object of his satire was not obvious enough and he spoiled its effect by mixing together fairies and noblemen in a manner that was too far-fetched even for Gilbertian extravaganza. *Princess Ida,* which had its first performance at the Savoy on January 5, 1884, reached New York five weeks later, its first performance taking place at the Fifth Avenue Theatre, then under the management of John Stetson, on February 11. The basis of its book was a comedy, or rather, a burlesque, called *The Princess,* which Gilbert had brought out fourteen years before at the Royal Olympic Theatre, in London, with incidental music borrowed from *La Perichole* and other *operas bouffes* and comic operas, even Rossini's *Barber* being put under tribute. Mr. Gilbert called his burlesque ' a respectful parody on Mr. Tennyson's exquisite poem' when he printed it in a volume of his plays in 1875, and his operetta he called ' a respectful perversion of Tennyson's 'Princess.' The people concerned in the first American performances were C. Brocolini (*King Hildebrand*), Wallace McCreery (*Hilarion*), W. S. Rising (*Cyril*), Charles J. Lang (*Florian*), J. H. Ryley (*King Gama*), Ainsley Scott (*Arac*), James Early (*Guron*), E. J. Cloney (*Scynthius*), Cora Tanner (*Princess Ida*), Florence Bemister (*Lady Psyche*), Genevieve Reynolds (*Lady Blanche*), Hattie Dolaro (*Melissa*), Eva Barrington (*Sacharissa*), Eily Coghlan (*Chloe*) and Clara Primrose (*Ada*). The company had been brought together for the production by Edward E. Rice. In his notice of the first performance, which was followed by an extended review a few days later, the *Tribune's* critic said that the verdict, so far as it could be read in the applause of the audience, was in favor of the work, for about ten of the musical numbers were demanded a second time and one a third.

The Mikado brought a sword into the camp of the New York theatrical managers, among whom rivalry for the privilege of performing the Gilbert and Sullivan operetta had grown keen. The new work had its first performance on March 14, 1885, in London. Among the American managers who wanted it, and went to London to negotiate for it, was J. C. Duff, of the Standard Theatre. Mr. D'Oyly Carte, however, had planned to organize an English company and bring the new work out at the Fifth Avenue Theatre under Mr. Stetson's management. Sullivan, who had been in the United States some six years before with his collaborator for the purpose of protecting the financial interests of the firm, came again with the same purpose in view. While the new company was preparing and the managers waiting for the dog days to pass Mr. Duff determined to make a trial whether or not an operetta of which the libretto and vocal score had been published and put on sale was protected against public performance. He enlisted a very capable company and hurriedly began preparations, with a view to a simultaneous production with that of Mr. Stetson. Both announced August 19 as the date, but at the eleventh hour Mr. Duff found that he had to postpone his opening for a week. While these managers were fighting for precedence, however, Harry Miner ran away with the prize, such as it was. At the Union Square Theatre he pitchforked a ridiculous perversion upon his stage some ten days before Mr. Stetson's date, using, as Mr. Duff proposed to use, orchestral parts made by some hack musician from the pianoforte accompaniment in the vocal score. The device was not new, nor was it confined to the managers of operetta companies. Operas of the highest type, like *Carmen,* had been thus shabbily treated before, and works of Mascagni and Puccini have had to suffer the same indignity since. The Union Square perversion, in which Roland Reed and Alice Harrison took part, killed itself without hurting the opera which was soon running at both of the other rival houses. The Fifth Avenue Theatre première took place on August 19, 1885, the Standard Theatre's on August 24. All the singers in Mr. D'Oyly Carte's company were English except Miss Geraldine Ulmar, the parts being distributed as follows: *The Mikado,* F. Frederici; *Nanki-Poo,* Courtice Pounds; *Ko-Ko,* G. Thorne; *Pooh-Bah,* Fred Billington; *Pish-Tush,* G. Bryan Browne; *Yum-Yum,* Geraldine Ulmar; *Pitti-Sing,* Kate Forster; *Peep-Bo,* Geraldine St. Maur; *Katisha,* Elsie Cameron. The best people in Mr. Duff's company were Mrs. Zelda Seguin, who had been an admired contralto in English opera for years (*Katisha*), Harry Hilliard (*Nanki-Poo*), J. H. Ryley (*Ko-Ko*), A. E. Stoddard (*Pish-Tush*), and W. H. Hamilton (*The Mikado*), Miss Vernona Jarbeau was a crude and rude *Yum-Yum*. The *Tribune's* reviewer remarked of the Standard Theatre performance that the operetta was still in process of baking, as well as making (the opening night being intolerably hot), and this was half true also of the Fifth Avenue performance, which had been unduly hurried. Meanwhile Mr. Carte had brought an action in equity in the United States Circuit Court to restrain Mr. Duff, and his performance on August 24th was allowed by the court, Mr. Duff having given an indemnity bond in the sum of $1500. On September 17th Judge Wallace decided against the application for an injunction, holding that the publication of the libretto and vocal score was a dedication of the entire composition to the public, the only right reserved by the authors being that of multiplying and selling copies of the orchestral parts which were still in manuscript. One month after the first performance the composer conducted a performance of the operetta at the Fifth Avenue Theatre, and on a curtain call made a short speech, in which he expressed the hope that the day would come 'when the legislators of this magnificent country may see fit to afford the same protection to a man who employs his brains in literature and art that they do to one who invents a new beer-tap or who accidentally gives an extra turn to a screw, doing away with the necessity of boring a hole first.'

The Mikado raised its authors to the topmost crest of popularity. When their next operetta, *Ruddigore,* was brought forward for its first American performance at the Fifth Avenue Theatre, on February 21, 1887 (it had had its London première on January 22), the *Tribune's* reviewer observed that the audience had been better advised of what to expect than any assembly ever before gathered together for such a purpose in America. 'Neither Wagner's *Parsifal,* nor Verdi's *Otello,* nor Sardou's *Theodora* caused in anticipation one tithe of the excitement created by *Ruddigore,*' was the added comment. The greater, therefore, was the disappointment. Sir Arthur had striven with more than his customary zeal and conscientiousness on the score, and, without cutting loose from any of his old formulas, had brought in new interest with the flavor of old English airs;

and such pieces as the madrigal, gavotte and country dance will be reckoned among his happiest inspirations; but Mr. Gilbert had failed, largely because he had not presented a subject for satire which had contemporaneous vitality and validity. He was wasting his ingenuity in poking fun at old-fashioned stage melodrama, and possibly at features of old English baronial life, in which we had only a literary or romantic interest. And so the opera lived out its first season and soon disappeared in the limbo of things forgotten. The audience that greeted the first performance was an exceedingly well disposed one. It crowded the playhouse in every part, of course, and as Miss Ulmar, Miss Forster, Mr. Pounds, Mr. Thorne, Mr. Billington and Mr. Frederici (all of whom had won the hearts of New Yorkers in *The Mikado*) appeared in turn they were made to feel that they had been kept in warm and kindly memories during the intervening year. Few repetitions were demanded, however, and though the finale of the first act was given twice, a deal of the applausive call sounded perfunctory.

As we look back upon the works of the happily mated collaborators and their reception by press and public we see a gradual ascent from *The Sorcerer* to *The Mikado,* with interruptions which were not grievously disappointing in *Iolanthe* and *Princess Ida.* From *The Mikado* to *Utopia, Limited,* there is a descent, with a breathing spell at *The Yeomen of the Guard.* To understand the popular attitude toward the works it must be remembered that the standard of comparison was that created by the authors themselves. No person of good literary, dramatic and musical taste thought of comparing any of the operettas with the works of their French and German competitors. Of the latter only Johann Strauss could have endured such a comparison. Public taste had been educated to a point which it has never reached since; instead, it has degenerated steadily, until it is now willing to accept the buffooneries and musical dishwater of present day 'musical comedy'— heaven save the mark! Things were different even when the post-*Mikado* operettas were received with disappointment. The records were always made by the serious critics regretfully. In the presence of Mr. Gilbert's effervescent intellectuality they could always forgive his cynicism, and in the hearing of Sir Arthur's music retain their respect for him and their appreciation of the art, even while wishing that he had a more fecund fancy and a more varied style.

So the *Tribune* reviewer is found always seeking out the good in each successive work and holding up the excellencies which had been overlooked by the public. In his criticism of *The Yeomen of the Guard* which had its first performance here at the Casino on October 17, 1888 (London a fortnight earlier), he said: 'The good qualities of both [authors] are present in a measure in the new operetta, but are scarcely obvious enough to meet the demands which they have taught us to make of each new work from their pens; and so it must regretfully be recorded that *Pinafore, Patience* and *The Mikado* have not a worthy successor in *The Yeomen of the Guard*. Least of all can the new work be consorted with *Princess Ida,* for its greatest weakness is found right where the greatest charm of the "respectful perversion" of Tennyson's poem lay — namely, in the book. In its literary quality *Princess Ida* was distinctly above any of its congeners, and its failure was best explained on the ground of a want of appreciation on the part of a public that had come to look for broad farce where it should have gone for refined comicality. *Princess Ida* seemed to point in the direction in which Messrs. Gilbert and Sullivan might have developed the unique style of operetta which is their invention. With all its paradox and logic gone mad, with all its burlesque of oldtime chivalry and the severity of its satire on so-called "woman's rights," there was in it a delicacy of treatment, an affectionate touch, so far as the central character was concerned, that brought the whole play pretty near the standard of true comedy.' The reviewer then pointed out that the satire of the new comedy seemed to be directed against love, and therefore could not meet with sympathy, or Shakespeare's fool, 'a manifestly absurd proceeding; for to the world of today the stage fool can only be a vehicle, not an object of satire. He lacks contemporaneous human interest. Besides, there is no satire in the treatment of the fool who seems to have been introduced to play exactly the same part that he does in Shakespeare.' Mercy on

us! How serious we were in those days! Who would think of cogitating such solemnities over the invertebrate vulgarities called comic operas and musical comedies now? But *The Yeomen of the Guard* had its prescribed run, and now that it has been revived by Mr. Hopper and his helpers we find a mental refreshment and an esthetic delight in its text and music, and count as naught against it all the other doings in musical theatredom.

Before the next operetta of Gilbert and Sullivan reached New York an effort was made by Rudolph Aronson to revive an interest in Offenbach's *Les Brigands* and *La Fille du Tambour Major* in English adaptations — the first an old one by Gilbert. At the other theatres short experiments were made with other European works (Czibulka's *May Queen,* originally *Der Glücksritter,* at Palmer's; Von Suppé's *Clover,* otherwise *Die Jagd nach dem Glück,* also at Palmer's, and Lecocq's *La jolie Persane,* effectually disguised as *The Oolah,* at the Broadway). A disastrous experiment was made with a vulgar and amorphous thing called *Dovetta,* for which the music had been written by a New York woman, at the Standard Theatre, but it broke down in the second week. So also *The Drum Major* had to give way to a revival of *Erminie* at the Casino. 'Can Gilbert and Sullivan find no more themes?' wailed the *Tribune.* 'Does the fault of their barrenness lie with them, or has the taste of the public degenerated so that horse-play is wanted in place of humor, farce instead of fancy, and gaudy mummery instead of music? . . . In the hands of these masters of satirical paradox we may safely leave all the elements of our social, political and artistic life. They know a satirist's privilege and will not abuse it.'

Finally the longed-for new operetta came, on January 7, 1890, at the New Park Theatre, under the management of A. M. Palmer. It was *The Gondoliers,* which had been produced in London just a month before. It had been eagerly waited for, yet it was the first of the Gilbert and Sullivan operettas which made an unqualified fiasco, chiefly because of the poor performance at the hands of the English company which D'Oyly Carte sent over with it. The incapacity of the actors was so obvious that a re-organization of the company was undertaken at once. Mr. Billington and Mr. Temple, identified with earlier productions of Mr. D'Oyly Carte, were brought from London to replace two of the inefficients, and the operetta was removed to Palmer's Theatre. How long it held the boards there we do not recall, but there was a story that John Stetson, who had backed the American season of the operetta, expressed his opinion of it in a characteristic speech, ending with: ' " Gondoliers "— huh! " Gone Dollars," I call it.' An amiable incident of its career was a performance at a special matinée given by Francis Wilson and his company, playing at the time in Philadelphia. Mr. Palmer invited them to give a performance at his theatre, which they did, as Mr. Wilson said in a curtain speech, to show the people of New York what Americans could do with the opera.

The Gondoliers was still enjoying popularity in England when Gilbert and Sullivan fell out because of a quarrel between Mr. D'Oyly Carte and one of them touching the management of the Savoy Theatre. For nearly three years the partnership between the men, financially profitable to them, artistically profitable to all English speaking peoples, remained sundered. Meanwhile both turned to other collaborators. With Alfred Cellier Gilbert wrote *The Mountebanks,* and Sullivan collaborated with Mr. Grundy in writing *Haddon Hall.* New York heard *The Mountebanks* at the Garden Theatre for the first time on January 10, 1893, but *Haddon Hall* had no production in the metropolis.

There was general rejoicing when the men, whose experiences with other partners had plainly demonstrated how necessary each was to the other, were reconciled and created *Utopia, Limited.* Over four months elapsed after the London production before the operetta had its first American performance at the Broadway Theatre, on March 26, 1894. It provided the most grievous disappointment ever given by a creation of the men. The book was labored and the score the weakest of any written by the composer. It was the last of the Gilbert and Sullivan productions; dramatist and musician both seemed to realize that they had exhausted the vein which had yielded a glorious treasure.

V

BOSTON SYMPHONY REHEARSAL

PHILIP HALE

[*Boston Herald,* October 17, 1914.]

The first Public Rehearsal of the Boston Symphony Orchestra, thirty-fourth season, Dr. Karl Muck, conductor, took place yesterday afternoon in Symphony Hall, which was completely filled. The program was as follows:

Symphony No. 3, 'Eroica'........Beethoven
Variations on a theme of Haydn....Brahms
Tone-poem, 'Don Juan'..........R. Strauss
Overture to 'Euryanthe'............Weber

The reception of Dr. Muck was extraordinary. As soon as he appeared on the stage many in the audience arose and remained standing during the minutes of enthusiastic applause. More than once Dr. Muck, ready to begin the symphony, was obliged to turn and bow in recognition. We do not remember in the course of twenty-five years a welcome like that of yesterday to any returning conductor of this orchestra. The tribute was spontaneous and magnificent. It was a tribute to the man as well as to the conductor.

It has been said that Dr. Muck was anxious to serve his native land by enlisting in her army. The wish was natural; but here in Boston he can serve her more effectively by representing an art that has long been cultivated in Germany, an art that Germany has fostered, a peaceful art that has made Germany famous throughout the world. Nor could the interpretative branch of this art find a more brilliant, a more intellectual, representative than Dr. Muck.

And as in Germany for years, the composers and virtuosos of Italy, France and Russia have been welcome, so at these concerts there will be no display of chauvinism. The greatest art knows no narrow boundaries; it is universal, not national. It matters not that Beethoven's family came from a little village near Louvain; that, born in Germany, he became an Austrian by adoption. It matters not whether Haydn were a Croatian or an Austrian; that Berlioz was a Frenchman and Rimsky-Korsakoff a Russian. If the program of yesterday bore the names of four composers whose works have honored Germany, the program next week introduces works by a Frenchman, an American, and a Finn.

The choice of Beethoven's *Eroica* symphony to open the season was a fortunate one. There is no doubt that the composer wrote this symphony in honor of Napoleon, and erased the conqueror's name on the title page when he heard that his idol had become Emperor to trample on the rights of man, to serve his own ambition. For this symphony heard at a time like the present the lines of Walt Whitman might well serve as a motto:

With music strong I come — with my cornets
    and my drums,
I play not marches for accepted victors only
    — I play great marches for conquer'd
    and slain persons.

Have you heard that it was good to gain the
    day?
I also say it is good to fall — battles are lost
    in the same spirit in which they are won.

I beat and pound for the dead;
I blow through my embouchures my loudest
    and gayest for them.

Vivas to those who have failed!
And to those whose war-vessels sank in the
    sea!
And to those themselves who sank in the
    sea!
And to all generals that lost engagements!
    and all overcome heroes!
And the numberless unknown heroes, equal
    to the greatest heroes known.

After the strangely impressive and eloquent performance, there was long-continued applause. Dr. Muck was recalled many times and Major Higginson, leaving his seat, shook hands with him in the sight of the people.

Mr. Max Kalbeck, who has written the life of Johannes Brahms in seven octavo volumes, attempts to find in each one of the variations on the St. Anthony Choral, something illustrative of the Saint's temptations in the Egyptian desert. He thus gives another instance of the attempted extraction of sunbeams from cucumbers. If Mr. Kalbeck's theory that each variation portrays or hints at a temptation is true, the bored Saint had little difficulty in resisting. Only one, the charming Grazioso, is alluring; the charm is soothing, not intoxicating; the allurement is not sensuous. However admirable the technic displayed in the composition of this work, however interesting the variations may be to the student of Brahm's architectural talent, the music, with the exception noted and with the exception of the choral as stated at the beginning, makes little appeal to the average hearer. St. Anthony, if the painters are to be believed, was more fortunate.

The reading of Strauss's *Don Juan* — would that his latest symphonic poems could be ranked with the earlier one! — was brilliantly fiery and passionate. The long episode portraying the love scene between Don Juan and the Anna of Lenau's poem — or is the heroine, Princess Isabella? for the commentators and glossarists differ here in a distressing manner — this episode, with the oboe solo played exquisitely by Mr. Longy, was wondrously beautiful in its sensuousness.

It is not necessary, however, to speak in detail of the performance of the orchestra as a whole. There are new comers. One or two of them take the place of men now engaged in active military service. It is enough to say that the orchestral performance was uncommonly spirited, elastic and emotional for the first one of a season.

VI

MISS HINKLE WITH THE BOSTON SYMPHONY

PHILIP HALE

[*Boston Herald*, December 19, 1914.]

The eighth Public Rehearsal of the Boston Symphony Orchestra, Dr. Karl Muck conductor, took place yesterday afternoon in Symphony Hall. Miss Florence Hinkle, soprano, was the soloist. The program was as follows:

A Faust Overture..................Wagner
'Voi che Sapete'...................Mozart
Five pieces for orchestra:
  Presentiments, The Past, The Changing Chord, Peripteia, The Obbligato Recitative ....Schoenberg
First time in Boston
'Ave Maria' from 'The Cross of Fire'
                      Bruch
Symphony in G (The Surprise).....Haydn

Bill Nye said, many years ago, that the music of Wagner was better than it sounded. Arnold Schoenberg says today that his own music is better than it sounds.

The pieces played yesterday are extraordinary. It is easy to say that the composer is a maniac or a poseur. Neither statement would be accurate. Those who have read his treatise on harmony know that he is a man of unusual knowledge, force, originality. Those who heard his quartette last season know that he can write music of uncommon beauty and towering imagination in a more familiar form.

It would also be easy to say that when Strauss's *Til Eulenspiegel* was first performed in Boston, the majority in the audience thought the music chaotic, incomprehensible and the composer mad. To-day, in comparison with Schoenberg's pieces, this symphonic poem is as clear as music by Haydn. Remember, too, that when Debussy's *Nocturnes* were played twice in succession at Chickering Hall they were thought to be incomprehensible.

These instances will not answer the objectors to Schoenberg. What is to be said of his five pieces? Personal impressions are interesting chiefly to the person impressed. No two persons hear music in the same way. I could make little out of the first and the fifth pieces. There are fine moments in *The Past* and *The Changing Chord;* beautiful suggestions of moods; strangely beautiful effects of color. Nor is the fourth piece wholly inexplicable. To argue for or against this music, which might be of another planet, after even several hearings, would be presumptuous and foolish. It took many Bostonians, well acquainted with orchestral and chamber compositions, a long time to familiarize themselves with the idiom of Cesar Franck, and later with that of Debussy. These composers, however, are not so fundamentally radical, anarchistic, as Schoenberg.

Thomas Hardy in that noble prose epic, the description of Egdon Heath, asks if the exclusive reign of orthodox beauty is not approaching its last quarter. 'The new vale of Tempe may be a gaunt waste in Thule; human souls may find themselves in closer and closer harmony with external things wearing a sombreness distasteful to our race when it was young. . . . The time seems near, if it has not actually arrived, when the mournful sublimity of a moor, a sea, or a mountain, will be all of nature that is absolutely consonant with the moods of the more thinking among mankind. And ultimately, to the commonest tourist spots like Iceland may become what the vineyards and myrtle gardens of South Europe are to him now, and Heidelberg and Baden be passed unheeded as he hastens from the Alps to the sand dunes of Scheveningen.'

When Schoenberg's *Five Pieces* were performed for the first time in London, and in Chicago, there were scenes of outspoken disapproval. Yesterday the behavior of the audience was highly creditable to Boston. There was smiling; there was giggling at times; there was applause. Nobody rose to remonstrate. Nothing was thrown at Dr. Muck and the orchestra. There was no perturbation of Nature to show that Schoenberg's pieces were playing: the sun did not hasten its descent; there was no earthquake shock. It was as it should have been in Boston.

Miss Florence Hinkle has a beautiful voice which she uses with rare skill. The *Canzona* of Cherubino, sensuous in its suppressed passion, should be sung by a darker voice to gain full effect. It served yesterday to display the art of Miss Hinkle in sustained and flawless song. The lyrical measures of Bruck's *Ave Maria,* conventionally suave, were sung with unexaggerated emotion, and the singer gave dramatic importance to the agitated passages that in themselves are of a perfunctory and meaningless nature. It has been said by some that Miss Hinkle is a cool, impassive singer. They probably mean by this that she is not spasmodic and hysterical. Seldom at Symphony concerts of late years has there been such a delightful display of pure vocal art as that of yesterday.

Dr. Muck gave an eloquent reading of the *Faust* overture in which there are hints at the Wagner to come. The symphony of Haydn, admirably performed, is not among his most interesting.

J. ART CRITICISM

Good art criticism is as difficult and as rare as adequate musical criticism. The ground covered by this form of writing is so extensive and the processes involved are, from the layman's point of view, so technical that it is unusual to find in any but the specially trained writer that thorough acquaintance with the materials and the methods of art without which esthetic criticism remains but the perfunctory notice of an outsider.

Though painting and sculpture are the main objects of art collections, each year brings to public attention exhibits of etchings, pastels, pencil sketches, miniatures, textiles, tapestries, jewelry, metal work, ceramics, furniture, and architectural drawings, including landscape gardening and city planning. To master the history and technical vocabulary of any one of these is no light task. The student should therefore make the most of every opportunity not merely to familiarize himself with the aims and possibilities of these various branches of art, but also actually to see how their products are planned and executed in studio and workshop before they reach the art gallery or the exhibition room.

If he is so fortunate as himself to have some skill, however slight, in one of these arts, his understanding and appreciation of all will be the clearer and more intimate. When he comes to write, however, he should remember his reader, and, especially as a beginner, shun that too prevalent artistic pose which delights in parading a newly acquired vocabulary. There is nothing esoteric or obscure about great art, and good art criticism ought to cast light and not shadow upon the object which it asks the reader to contemplate.

In the selections which follow will be found good examples of art criticism dealing with a school or a movement ('The P. R. B.' and 'Fallacies of the Futurist and New Thinking'); of the extended notice of an exhibition ('The Hudson-Fulton Exhibition,' 'The Pittsburgh Exhibition,' and 'An American Salon of Humorists'); of the short topical or occasional paragraph or note ('War in Art' and 'The American Art Collector'); and of the critical article dealing with the application of art to some wide phase of life such as the theatre or the home ('Leon Bakst's Designs' and 'The Garden as a Means of Expression').

The reader should bear in mind that the nature of the subjects with which art criticism deals and the necessary limitations of language require, in a great many cases, that the text of an article be supplemented by illustrations. These have of necessity been omitted in the reprint of articles III, IV, V, and VII, and, in fairness to the authors, attention is here called to this omission.

I

THE P. R. B.[1]

[*Times* (London, England), *Literary Supplement,* December 8, 1905. By permission.]

This book has a threefold interest — historical, artistic, and human. Mr. Holman Hunt, as every one knows, was one of the original members of the Pre-Raphaelite Brotherhood. Indeed he is at some pains to prove that he was the chief originator of the ideas and principles which that brotherhood was formed to advance, and that it was his influence which made Pre-Raphaelites of Rossetti and Mil-

[1] *Pre-Raphaelitism and the Pre-Raphaelite Brotherhood.* By W. Holman Hunt, O.M., D.C.L. Two volumes. (Macmillan.)

lais. He is, at any rate, able to tell the story of the beginning and early struggles of the most important movement in modern English painting more fully than 5 it has ever been told before. He is also able to give us a very clear and precise account of the intentions of that movement and of the state of things which it proposed to reform. Besides this he has 10 related, with some natural bitterness, but with constant humor and vivacity, the tale of his own fight with poverty and with a professional hostility so bitter that one can scarcely believe it was disinterested. 15 The brunt of this hostility was borne by Millais as well as by Mr. Holman Hunt; and, to judge from Mr. Hunt's account of a conversation he had with Millais years afterwards, Millais was still sore at the thought of it, not only with those who had abused him so recklessly, but also with certain members of the brotherhood whose weaknesses hindered the advancement of their cause. Many books have been written in which Rossetti has been made to appear the chief of the Pre-Raphaelites. Millais seems to have resented this misrepresentation as much as Mr. Hunt himself. 'You have written a very readable and plausible book about Rossetti,' he said to the author of one of these works, 'but it is altogether a romance. Why, instead of getting your information from the family, did n't you come to me or go to Holman Hunt?' It ought to be perfectly clear to every one that most of Rossetti's pictures have little in common with the great mass of the pictures that are usually called Pre-Raphaelite. Rossetti's art is weak in its grasp of facts. His object in painting was nearly always to express his emotions, and he was apt to be impatient of the only means by which in a picture emotions can be expressed. Sometimes he was able to simplify his pictures to such an extent that he was not hindered by details in the expression of his emotions, and then he produced beautiful works of art. But too often the faults of his pictures are the very emptiness and evasion which the Pre-Raphaelites held to be the prevailing vices in the art which they set out to reform. Their first object was a closer study of nature, based upon the belief, which has inspired so much of the best modern art, that all life has a significance and a nobility of its own, and that art can advance only as the artist's sense of that significance is enlarged by a larger study of life. This, of course, is the very opposite of the academic doctrine that only certain portions and aspects of life are worthy of artistic treatment, and that the experience of the masters has determined once and for all what those portions and aspects are.

It is pretty clear from Mr. Holman Hunt's account of Pre-Raphaelite ideas that the Pre-Raphaelites discovered their own principle of selection for themselves; and they believed that a right and living principle of selection could only be discovered by artists inspired by noble emotions and ideas, and determined to flinch from no difficulties of representation in their eagerness to express those emotions and ideas. This insistence upon the necessity of noble emotions and ideas was the second great article of their creed. They saw that realism means nothing and leads nowhere; that it is only the blind energy of scepticism. Science investigates life with the purpose of discovering some truth valuable to man; and art, they held, must study life with the purpose of expressing some truth valuable to man, and of expressing it in a manner suited to the understanding of contemporaries:

The course of previous generations of artists which led to excellence [says Mr. Holman Hunt in the same conversation] cannot be too studiously followed, but their treatment of subjects, perfect as they were for their time, should not be repeated. . . . The language they used was then a living one, now it is dead. . . . For us to repeat their treatment for subjects of sacred or historic import is mere affectation. . . . If I were to put a flag with a cross on it in Christ's hand, the art-galvanizing revivalists might be pleased, but unaffected people would regard the work as having no living interest for them. I have been trying for some treatment that might make them see this Christ with something of the surprise that the Maries themselves felt on meeting Him as One who has come out of the grave.

We can see in the last sentence the beginning of those ideas which afterwards led Mr. Holman Hunt to fill his sacred pictures with local color laboriously studied in Palestine. The fallacy of such ideas is easy to expose. Local color is no part of the essence of the story of Christ to our imaginations; and no amount of local color will make it real to us. Every one from childhood thinks of the great events of the Bible as having taken place in his own country and of the actors in them as his own countrymen. For us Christ plucked ears of corn in an English cornfield and His tomb was in an English garden. When, therefore, He is represented to us in strange surroundings, painted with painful accuracy, our attention is distracted from Him to those surroundings, and the picture becomes merely a conscientious study of local color, not only for us, but for the artist himself. For he, too, is working against the grain of his own imagination. It is only by a conscious effort, and by taking a journey to Palestine, that he can think of Christ as an Oriental, living and moving in a strange Oriental world; and this effort hinders the working of his imagination. Pictures such as the 'Finding of Christ in the Temple' and 'The Shadow of Death,' prove that in painting them Mr. Holman Hunt was distracted, by his determination to be correct in local color, from the emotions and ideas which he hoped to express by means of it. Compared with the 'Hireling Shepherd,' which is a picture of an English man and woman in an English pasture, these works are laborious failures. It is one of the chief excellencies of the best Pre-Raphaelite works that they are racy of the soil beyond any other modern English pictures; and none of them are more racy of the soil than the 'Hireling Shepherd.' But the 'Finding of Christ in the Temple' and 'The Shadow of Death,' and others like them, lack this excellence altogether. A painter, however hard he may try, cannot make his work racy of a foreign soil, and Mr. Holman Hunt, being one of the most English of painters, was less fitted to make the attempt than most. 'His object was,' he tells us, 'to use his powers to make more tangible Jesus Christ's history and teaching. Art,' he remarks, 'has often illustrated the theme, but it has surrounded it with many enervating fables and perverted the heroic drama with feeble interpretation.' He hoped by going to Palestine and studying the very scene in which that drama was played to purge his mind of all the conventional associations that had gathered round it. Even Ruskin 'refused to admit that any additional vitality could be gained by designing and painting in Syria with its life and manners before his eyes.' And the result has proved that Ruskin was right. Every one must respect Mr. Holman Hunt for the force of character which made him carry his principles so far; but every one must regret that he should have wasted so much of his great talents upon what is, after all, only a perversion of the principles upon which the best Pre-Raphaelite pictures were based.

But to return to these principles — the Pre-Raphaelites were very far from despising all art except that of the Primitives. Indeed, Mr. Holman Hunt speaks with surprising reverence of artists famous in his youth and almost forgotten now. He admired Raphael and most of the great painters of the past; while Mil-

lais, he tells us, was essentially conservative in his nature, and far too good a painter, in those early days, not to appreciate all kinds of excellence. It is pretty clear that the popular artists of the time were afraid of Millais's great talent and of the manner in which it shamed their own plausible evasions. There is no other way of accounting for the brutality of the attacks that were made upon him. Perhaps the most brutal of all came from Dickens, who, knowing nothing of pictures himself, was probably incited to make it by some of the popular painters who were friends of his. Speaking of Millais's beautiful 'Christ in the Carpenter's Shop,' he said:

In the foreground of that carpenter's shop is a hideous, wry-necked, blubbering, red-haired boy in a night-gown, who appears to have received a poke in the hand from the stick of another boy with whom he had been playing in an adjacent gutter, and to be holding it up for the contemplation of a kneeling woman, so horrible in her ugliness that (supposing it were possible for any human creature to exist for a moment with that dislocated throat) she would stand out from the rest of the company as a monster in the vilest *cabaret* in France or the lowest gin-shop in England.

Mr. Holman Hunt tells us how the term Pre-Raphaelite first came into being. He and Millais discussed Raphael's 'Transfiguration' with other Academy students, and condemned it 'for its grandiose disregard of the simplicity of truth, for the pompous posturing of the Apostles, and the unspiritual attitudinizing of the Savior.' It was, they said, a signal step in the decadence of Italian art. 'When we had advanced this opinion to other students, they, as a *reductio ad absurdum*, had said, "Then you are Pre-Raphaelite." Referring to this as we worked side by side, Millais and I laughingly agreed that the designation must be accepted.' The Pre-Raphaelites may seem romantic enough to us now, but they were as hostile to any kind of romanticism which hindered disinterested observation and good workmanship as to the most pedantic classicism.

The danger of the time [says Mr. Hunt] arose from the vigor of the rising taste for Gothic art rather than from the classical form of design, whose power was fast waning. . . . The fashion for feudal forms had grown altogether slavish. . . . To follow ancient precedent line for line had become a religion. To reproduce the English round and pointed styles with barbarous embellishments wherewith the rudest of ancient masons had often satisfied their patrons was the limit of modern ambition.

It cannot be repeated too emphatically that the Pre-Raphaelites sought no short cuts to excellence. They had a passion for honesty and hard work. They were filled, too, with high ideas, and, though some of these ideas may have been extravagantly applied and expressed, they came nearer to founding an original school of painting than any other set of English painters in the nineteenth century. Mr. Holman Hunt was the first of them, and throughout his long life he has never deserted their faith. He was, therefore, the man of all others best fitted to tell the story of their prime, and this book of his, though we could wish that some passages in it were less bitter, deserves to be read with attention and reverence. We hope that an index will be added to the next edition.

II

FALLACIES OF THE FUTURISTS AND NEW THINKING

G. K. CHESTERTON

[New York Morning American, March 14, 1915. By permission.]

The other day, when I opened an advanced magazine which I always read with interest, there fell out of it a large, shiny piece of paper on which there was reproduced a Work, a product of the human will — a thing done on purpose anyhow, if one could scarcely call it a design. If you ask me what it represented, you have formed no conception of the very nature of this fair thing. It is quite inadequate to say that it represents nothing. I should not be content with saying even that it does not suggest anything.

I affirm, with entire and untroubled certainty, that it is nothing: so far as is possible when some space is occupied, the thing is not there. There is something a little like a dilapidated railing at the bottom of the picture, and something a little like Chinese lettering at the top of the picture: all the rest is exactly like used-up blotting paper — which perhaps it is. I infer which is supposed to be the right way up merely by the position of the printed title, which says, 'Supplement of the New Age. A study by Picasso.'

In another place there is an explanation that Picasso is the first important artist that this planet has produced, and that the sodden blotting paper opposite represents, not indeed a Table, a Wineglass, and a Mandoline, but the 'souls' of a Table, a Wineglass, and a Mandoline.

Now, as the Frenchman said at Mugby Junction, 'Heavens! how arrives it?' How does human dignity descend to these monkey antics? How does the human brain sink back into this bestial darkness? Let us see if we can roughly trace the origin and operation of the process. There are running about England today some thousands of a certain sort of people. They are, of course, a small minority of the nation; but they are a large minority of the middle class; and if one's life moves down certain ways, the world may well seem to be full of them.

They are in revolt against something they have forgotten in favor of something else which (by their own account) they have not yet found. They are always alluding to Thought of various kinds — Free Thought and Higher Thought and Advanced Thought. As a matter of fact, they never, under any circumstances, think at all; but they do lots of other things which are much jollier than thinking: they listen to music and look at sunsets and go to tea parties, and are kind to children as far as they know how.

'Well,' you will say, 'a good and happy life. Why should they be bothered with thinking? What would become of their gimcrack cottages in the country and their corrugated iron ethical societies if they began to think? They live artistically, as do the lower animals — by a general sense of suitability to the senses and the habits. One esthete knows another esthete by the color and the smell — the color of his coat and the smell of his favorite flower. One spirit in revolt knows another spirit in revolt, just as one dandy knows another dandy — by the necktie.

The ordinary artistic Socialist throws out signals to his own kind, and naturally gravitates to his own environment. He does not in the least know what Socialism

is, and he does not need to: he does know
that he gets on with the kind of men who
call themselves Socialists. He knows the
other man's extravagances will be of his
sort, and not of another sort. He knows
a Socialist can be trusted to call another
Socialist's wife 'comrade' without taking
her on a gin-crawl. He knows that a Socialist can be trusted at tea-time to destroy the whole morality of mankind without using a word that could bring a blush
to the cheek of a young person. In short,
he knows that there are a sort of people
like himself in the world, and certain sociological conjectures (about which he
never thinks seriously at all) are among
the outward tests for detecting them.'

In saying all this you speak with your
usual noble delicacy and unerring wit.
But there is a further complication, which
I can no longer conceal from you. The
tragedy is this: that these happy, thought-
less people did once really have a Thought.
This one isolated thought has stuck in
their heads ever since. Nobody can get
it out of their heads; and nobody can get
any other thought into their heads.

It is a thought which, uncorrected by
other thoughts, is quite foolish and dangerous; but it is a connected string of concepts, intelligible and even true in itself:
it is the only one they have; and it gives
them a dickens of a time. The one only
and original connected Thought that ever
penetrated these people's heads runs as
follows: My grandfather thought wires
were necessary for telegrams: I know now
that he was wrong; therefore, whatever
I think is right my grandson will probably think wrong.

Upon that one mental process the whole
of our 'progress' is conducted; and, very
naturally, it ends in a smash — or, rather,
in a splash, by Picasso. That there is
some truth in the Thought is not to be
denied. Some things do alter; different
generations do have different standpoints;
truth should be kept reasonably flexible to
fit fashions which are often genuine human moods. But the worshipers of the
Thought think it idolatry to have any
other thoughts but that.

They insist that on every subject all
the things we understand must be wrong,
and consequently all the things that nobody could conceivably understand (like
poor old Picasso) must be right. Their
fallacy, one would suppose, was simple

enough even for the modern mind to follow; the distinction is quite obvious. If
there exist plausible reasons for supposing
that an innovation is an improvement,
then, of course, it is a valid argument to
say that many real improvements have
been denounced as innovations.

If I think a man honest, and it is answered that he has been in prison, then
it is rational for me to reply that St.
Paul or Cervantes was in prison. But
it is not rational of me to say that all the
people in prison must be like Cervantes
or St. Paul. There must be a *prima facie*
case for the new thing; otherwise it is
obvious that nothing is being asked of it
but newness. Now the number of new
things that are possible is at any given moment by its nature infinite. When we do
anything we deny ourselves a thousand
other things. When we go to Tunbridge
Wells we may be said to be avoiding a
million other places from China to Peru.

Whenever a man puts on his hat he is
refusing to put on an infinite number of
other things, from the flower-pot to the
waste-paper basket. If, therefore, you
have no other test of a new idea except
its newness, you will only be able to say:
'Well, I, at my present stage of evolution,
do not see the good of wearing a flower-
pot for a hat. But I must not offend my
great-grandson, who is so very particular,
and for all I know (since he does not exist yet), may absolutely insist on this uniform for all his ancestors.'

Perhaps you think this is an improbable example and an unlikely way of talking. Perhaps, in some rural seclusion,
you have failed to meet any people who
talk like that. Turn, then, to the subsequent issue of the advanced paper to
which I have referred, and you will find a
gentleman talking exactly like my imaginary ancestor, with his flower-pot hat.

An art critic of conspicuous intelligence
sits in front of my absurd piece of blotting paper, dazed but submissive. He
does actually say, in so many words, that
he can make neither head nor tail of it,
but that the Future will. He does, with a
really beautiful humility, prostrate himself
in the dust, not only before Picasso, but
before a totally imaginary great-grand-
child, who will profess to see some sense
in Picasso. This condition is plainly intolerable: we cannot go about thinking
that all our thoughts are wrong without

having even any notion of what thoughts are right. Shall we try to get that Thought out of these people's heads? Or shall we try to get some others in? Either will involve the most horrible mental torture.

III

THE HUDSON-FULTON EXHIBITION

FRANK FOWLER

[*Scribner's Magazine*, November, 1909. By permission.]

The occasionally recurring festivals and celebrations which mark the commemoration of some historical event or achievement possess, among other advantages, that of recalling facts of interest contemporaneous to those thus specifically signalized; and the various exhibitions, now in progress in connection with the Hudson-Fulton ceremonies seem particularly to suggest this beneficent result. The human mind loves to wander through productive periods of the past; and in this case while the fancy plays around the material significance of achievements like those of the two figures in whose honor the recent demonstrations have been made, the doors of our art collectors have incidentally been thrown open revealing veritable treasures of painting of the best period of Dutch art, that of about Hudson's time.

At just this moment in the practice of painting when subtlety of seeing is so opening a new world that the painter in his elation at the vision is sometimes neglectful of his means, it is singularly propitious to be given access to an unusual collection of what is perhaps the soundest method of painting recorded in the annals of art. As it is of the genius of rectitude in any activity that its meliorative attributes are widespread, the art connoisseur and amateur have peculiar cause for congratulation that the present occasion happens to commemorate the enterprise of the Dutch at an epoch particularly rich in the art of painting. Earlier than this the art of Holland had not the distinct national note that at this moment it reached.

The painting of few nations indeed offers so interesting a study as that of Holland, for we know of none so little derivative, so essentially characteristic of the people who produced it, so eminently direct and personal — in fact so entirely indigenous and original. Fully to appreciate and enjoy it one need not study the craft of immediate predecessors, but should rather bear in mind the political and social conditions which preceded this flowering of an art born of a large leisure purchased by a past of strenuous combat with nature at home and oppression from abroad. These obstacles, this discipline, this long abstinence from the lighter moments of existence, this repression of the spiritual side of humanity seems to have prepared the ground for a rich harvest when the time arrived in which these people could look about them in security and comfort. This land they had saved from the sea, these homes they had established through privation and hardship became objects of delight and pride; and when they sought subjects upon which to lavish their artistic skill it was these familiar things that appealed to them — the things they loved.

Holland had by this time cast off the Spanish yoke, the Italianate influence of traveled painters and of its Flemish neighbors, and had become its own independent self looking honestly in the face of nature and reporting her with an integrity that to the knowing ones is simply admirable. These interiors and the life of the home, as may be noted in the work here of de Hooch, Terborch, Metzu and others, furnished subject enough — their art ceased to be that of mere picture-making and religious imagery which until now outside influence had largely stimulated; while in the splendid school of landscape they founded may be discovered the forerunners of the Rousseaus, Troyons, Daubignys of a later day in France.

The Dutch also celebrated themselves, their personalities — they were so essentially national that guilds, corporations, charitable institutions, municipal bodies and public buildings encouraged portrait painting, and it may be to this fact that they owe the noble school of portraiture of which many fine examples may be studied here, and which adds such lustre to their art.

The richness of the holdings of Dutch pictures by a few discerning collectors in this country will be a matter of surprise to many visiting these galleries, and they will be moved to an expression of appreciation to the owners of these treasures for their public spirit in collecting them and permitting them to be shown. The extent of the collection is so unlooked for that it may be well to mention that of the seven Vermeers owned in the United States, five are here on view, while some thirty Rembrandts, and in the neighborhood of twenty Franz Hals, many of finest quality, are distributed among this profusion of lesser, but still brilliant lights of the time.

As mere demonstrations of how to paint one need look no further than to certain examples of Hals, for instance; and there are others among these who might serve as exemplars of sane and wholesome technical methods, although none, save Hals, perhaps, so obviously demonstrates the actual application of pigment — this, too, in his case, in conjunction with intelligent composition and often good, if not great color. There are others again who in perfection of seeing and doing elude definition and enter into the mysteries of the circumambient air. In these particular canvases there appears no thought of clever accomplishment, they simply exist as the world about us exists bathed in that all-enveloping atmosphere which the Dutch were first to successfully render. The consciousness of drawing, technique, methods, is lost in the unconsciousness of satisfied vision. Of the producers of these marvels of painting Rembrandt ranks supreme, but there are painters of works of smaller size who, from the standpoint of perfection rank little lower than he.

To the lover of processes alone, then, there is material in these galleries for boundless enjoyment. One may go from canvas to canvas with varying emotions, but unvarying delight. The beautiful veracity of Vermeer, the competency of Van der Helst, unerring vision of Hals, mysterious *enveloppe* of Rembrandt, suavity of Dou, Terborch, Metzu and de Hooch, dignity and impressiveness of Ruisdael, versatility of Cuyp, simplified breadth of Van Goyen, vitality of Jan Steen, and homeliness of Van Ostade are some of the qualities peculiar to a few among this host of masters.

One may discuss only a small portion of this stately whole and then with feelings of regret that much must necessarily be ignored. But as we are on the search for some representative examples where so many appear to represent adequately, can one do better than to hail with pleasure the Vermeer entitled: 'Woman Writing a Letter'! This is one of those canvases whose perfection is almost elusive, but which may be appreciatively approached by comparing it with it matters little what modern master of genre. Something of the magic of Holland's softened light seems to have filtered through the aperture by which this figure with the still-life objects on the table is illuminated, although the window is not seen. This is a Vermeer that places him near the great Rembrandt himself in its rendering of graduated light. This light plays from object to object with the inevitableness of nature, and so perfect is its management that the spectator forgets to analyze the source of its undoubted charm. When one seeks to account for this wonderful result it is found perhaps in the perfect adjustment of the figure to its surroundings. The theme is trivial enough, which only goes to prove that art can make any moment great. The melting into the background and the material itself of the ermine bordering the yellow sacque the figure wears, the quiet merging of the hand with the objects it touches are all demonstrations of a vision as fine, as subtle and as true as one can recall in the whole range of painting. This is not painting in the sense of Hals, of Van der Helst, it is an emanation of a sensitive personality using pigment as a medium. If space permitted a fuller discussion — 'The Lady with Guitar,' 'The Music Lesson,' 'Girl Playing a Guitar,' 'Young Woman at Casement,' should each and all be reviewed, for this painter is one of the rarest.

'The Music Party,' by Pieter de Hooch, is less naïve in its presentation than the above-mentioned works, more sought-for as a tableau, not so genuinely felt as he is sometimes in his earlier works where the less formal occupations of home-life engaged his brush. He is still interested, however, in varying cross-light and scrupulous in his attention to detail.

A larger method of painting and probably of seeing is to be noted in the picture by Gerard Terborch, 'Lady Pouring Out

Wine.' This group of three persons is given with a breadth more often found in life-size work than in a canvas of this dimension. All is painted with a free touch, the figures in half-tone strongly put in, the still-life of truthful observation, while the salient figure of the woman in the foreground is of a mastery quite delightful. This is not of Terborch's most usual subjects, but it reveals the large competency and painter-like quality which gave such value to his transcriptions of the interiors of the patrician class of Holland, and his glimpses of the domestic life of the Dutch merchants. He displays high accomplishment in the practice of painting in this work, which may also be remarked in 'Interior with Soldiers,' and in the portrait of a man and one of a woman to be seen here.

Had Cuyp been less varied in subject, had he pursued, for instance, out-door light exclusively, such as we see in his 'Landscape with Cattle,' one feels that he would have gone farther and have exerted a more potent influence on his school. His very versatility seems to militate against surpassing excellence in any one direction; he is spread over too large a field to strongly impress in any; but in these landscapes with living interests he is at his best, and this makes one regret that his curiosity did not here penetrate deeper, for the unmistakable sensitiveness to surface-light remarked in this picture as it plays on the hides of the cattle and touches the various substances of earth and vegetation goes to prove that here is a painter who by happy disposition and lightness of touch seemed destined to vivify the art of painting, who had something to say, something to reveal concerning the world of sight that for the time in which he worked was new and stimulating.

We will now turn to Jan Steen, who is here with, among other things, a 'Dutch Kermess' full of a rollicking vitality and tipsy mirth, and of excellent color. He certainly could give movement, and the spirit of the scene, as may be observed in his 'Dancing Couple,' 'Drunken Family,' and 'Grace Before Meat.'

Adrian van Ostade's 'The Old Fiddler' is, from our present-day ideas of such a scene, rather conventionally lighted, the foreground foliage kept somewhat arbitrarily in half-tone with the evident intention of emphasizing more effectually the central incident. The color, however, is good, and the painting solid.

Of the group of landscapists, Jacob van Ruisdael comes out with the strength that is his own. It is not difficult to detect here the fountain-head of that splendid stream of technical influence which inspired later the Fontainebleau school. One picture, entitled 'Landscape,' showing a foreground pool where float swan and water-plants and edged with well-observed sedges, at the foot of a knoll where tosses a wind-driven tree, is of a tonality that compels admiration. Other 'Landscapes' attest the solemn sentiment and dignity of this painter, who, if not brilliant in his color or facile in his touch, is profound in temper, and a master of drawing and terrestrial construction.

As already suggested, it was typical of the Dutch at this period that they devoted themselves to portrait painting as well as to landscape and genre. If nature outside and indoors appealed strongly to them, so did the men who made the state, the women who ruled the home. Portraiture pure and simple probably never reached a higher level of accomplishment than at this time through the genius of Rembrandt, Franz Hals, Van der Helst, Ravesteyn, Flinck, Santvoort, and Bol, all of whom sought this human characterization with much directness and vitality.

It will be impossible to speak fully of the masterpieces of this side of their art, to be met with in this exhibition, but a number must be signaled as among the finest examples.

Perhaps for emphasis of personal identity there never painted a man more marvelously equipped than Franz Hals. Not only is he the most dexterous, but with celerity and sureness of touch he managed to preserve the sentiment of the presence of the subject before him to an extraordinary degree; while for the address and precision with which he treats various articles of human attire, the damasked pattern of a silk, for example, obeying the laws of perspective in its design and of construction in its retreating folds, there has yet to be found so consummate a master. Trinkets, ornaments, filmy cuffs, fluted collars, books of devotion, or what not, these are observed and given with a fidelity of vision and an obedience of hand little short of miraculous. His wizard touch is no less noted in the constructive planes of the head, the hands, the superficies of the flesh of his sitters, while he preserves always a breadth of treatment which never degenerates into useless detail. He is the king of practitioners in the virtuosity of his performance, but he does not sacrifice the personality of his subject to the exhibition of his skill. We find portraits here which exemplify these observations concerning his method of painting. His 'Woman with a Rose' is an instance of this splendid *bravura* of brushwork, this swift but accurate differentiation of textures, tactful emphasis of the important, and the discriminating subservience of the secondary incidents of sight. The amplitude of stroke in broad passages and planes of the dress, the quick but decided touches that suggest the detail of ornament and pattern so justly given that they sustain their rightful surface in the constructive modeling of the gown, all this, with largeness of gesture and of pose mark this canvas as a sumptuous example of the painter. The portraits of Heer and Vrouw Bodolphe are of that intimacy of likeness which seems a documentary record of an existing type, almost ethnical in its searching definition of race. They are painted with a sobriety of statement that is in contrast to the 'Woman with a Rose' as befits the presentation of elderly persons of settled condition, and which goes to prove that Hals is possessed of a valuable artistic judgment which equals that of his technical superiority. 'Portrait of a Man Standing' is one of the broad, crisp, but fluent, examples of his dexterity.

After all is said, even he, it must be admitted, sometimes plays with his brush in a way not too edifying from the point of view of art; so that for all his excellence he is to be admired with reserve, and, at his best, hailed a master.

As if to point the lesson that superlative performance may still lack that something which is almost incommunicable but of undoubted power, surpassing in its profundity the achievements of his most accomplished fellows, Rembrandt stands in this brilliant circle of painters as the one possessed of this gift divine.

This solitary, living practically apart in an atmosphere of his own creation, appeared in his higher moments to wrest secrets from the surrounding air. Without losing the concrete quality of substance all objects existed for him in an intervening world of light where they lost certain accents of outline that guide lesser men to the conservation of the contours which developed this outline, and to which they resorted as a necessary convention for the interpretation of form. Rembrandt did not, as a rule, depend on this to give reality to the figures he painted — they seem to emerge into visibility as images of this thought, this thought potential enough to become real, and real enough to touch the profound. Neither 'The Gilder' nor the 'Portrait of an Old Woman' is of this phase of his art, superb as they are; but 'The Savant' emits this note of profundity and becomes, so to say, impalpably real. This spacious canvas is of a sentiment and significance quite other than may be felt in his portraits mentioned above. Those are of this world of conventional existence — 'The Savant' is of Rembrandt's own.

One would like to dilate on the 'Young Man Putting on His Armor,' 'Lucretia,' 'Hendrickje Stoffels,' and many more, but we may only call attention to the vivid although restrained canvas named 'The Noble Slav,' with its unctuous painting and concentrated chiaroscuro causing it to stand out by some apparent illumination peculiar to itself. This voluminous presence is seizing in corporeity, while in the painting of the chain about the shoulder and the sacrifice of needless accessories it is one of Rembrandt's most characteristic moods of vision and production. 'The Portrait of Himself' is in the sentiment of this kind of evolution of a figure in a costume of no particular date, but sitting there, staff in hand, a clothed entity of serious mien betraying the ravages of life on a stalwart frame, vital still in its decline. It is haunting in its personality telling of a life passed in seeking to embody plastically its thought. Massively pathetic, yet of a splendor of presentation which appeals to the connoisseur, announcing that he is confronted by not only a great figure of the past, but by that ever present joy — a work of art. When painting thus freely and unhampered by a commission, there is observed something in Rembrandt's treatment of the apparel of his subject that is peculiarly his own. The dress is of no particular time, nor is it quite recognizable as drapery — it clothes his thought and drapes the person painted; but one forgets these matters in experiencing a sense of satisfied vision. He is a creator in more ways than one, and at these times it is as though some brooding and elemental sentiment became invested with a form which he evolved; became indeed in his hands, as I have said, a thing of art.

Among the deductions that occur to one who has examined this exhibition with attention and a certain familiarity with the processes of painting are these: these Dutch can still hold their own, nay, we may learn much from them about frank, solid and sincere manipulation of paint — their work is done to stay, to withstand the deterioration of time, it is of honest execution so far as the medium is concerned, and in some respects mere painting cannot be better done. Where perhaps we moderns have surpassed them is in our manner of seeing, of using the eyesight, in which, with the years, we have developed an almost new sense of sight; so that a lighter, more subtle, more amusing aspect of nature seems to have been revealed to us, permitting us, through painting, to touch a now wider range of emotions through painted art. And even this advance is more appreciable in the field of landscape painting than in that of figure work and portraits.

If these two qualities, then, could be united, sanity of method and subtlety of sight, there would burst upon this age of art a splendor of achievement which might rival that of Haarlem and of Amsterdam.

IV

PITTSBURGH INTERNATIONAL EXHIBITION, 1914

W. H. de B. NELSON

[*International Studio* (John Lane Co.), June, 1914. By permission of author and publisher.]

The season of American art, limited by custom and convenience to the period extending from November to the end of May, meets with its apotheosis at Pittsburgh, after which the grim message of Shipka Pass, 'All is Still,' is applicable to the reign of art, until once more winter resumes its interrupted sway. The Eighteenth Annual Exhibition, so eagerly awaited and speculated upon by painters, critics, art lovers and collectors has shown once more the immense prestige of the Carnegie Institute and its colossal importance as America's only Salon, the supreme tribunal of art in the Western Hemisphere. Pittsburgh has no rival city; New York sinks into insignificance beside it; it is the one and only location in America where once a year are congregated in a harmonious ensemble the best examples obtainable of national and foreign art. No previous show has succeeded in presenting so many exceptionally good canvases and Director J. W. Beatty deserves the fullest recognition for his untiring zeal and discretion in presenting a display of work so convincingly representative of the best painting that is being accomplished at home and abroad. Very noticeable is the fact that the young painters have been given opportunity. There is a distinctly vital and vigorous impression imparted by the different galleries and wholesome absence in a great measure of those tedious monsters known as exhibition pictures, and of those academically painted ever-recurring theses which point to stagnation in art and induce apathy and indifference in the minds of the discerning public. The impression gained at private view and increased by subsequent visits, is an impression of fresh, spontaneous art, of the kind that reacts on the beholder, forming in imagination an intimate bond of thought between him and the artist.

Courtesy to the stranger would induce one to mention foreign performances first, even if no other reason prevailed; comparisons may be odious, but in a case where canvases from all countries meet on a common footing it is forced upon the critic to see how the painting by artists of one nation compares with that of another. At the very first encounter, and strengthened by later visits, it is clear that the English contingent represented by sixty and more artists make the strongest impression in portraiture, and in such pictures as represent what is felt and imagined rather than what is merely visualized. When it comes to downright painting of sea or mountain, snow-clad river banks, weird, majestic canyons or a city's traffic, no country can defeat the American painter in his big and bold portrayal of facts, but when it comes to subtlety of conception, to imagery, to a fantasy unseen of mortal eyes, there the British painter shows his superiority. In spite of unquestioned mastery over the medium, of an undoubted capacity for clear and truthful vision, it is to be wondered whether the soul of Peter Bell be not reflected within the souls of many American painters of high rank:

A primrose by the river's brim
A yellow primrose was to him —
And it was nothing more.

There is another explanation, and it is perhaps nearer to the truth. It may well be that the American artist does not consider subject matter of particular importance in his canvas, but is ruled by his desire to express freely and powerfully luminous skies, characteristic sketches of his own native heath or some one else's and, above all things, a solidly painted foreground, quality of paint, luminosity, well-adjudged planes of light and dark being the compelling forces. This theory is borne out by the fact that the room of honor was bestowed upon Paul Dougherty, who though still young is already in the fortunate position of having to search, like Alexander, for fresh kingdoms to conquer. No one, after touring Gallery L, could deny to him all the gifts mentioned above and many others, in his twenty-six exhibits of sea and Alps, but at the same time it must be advanced that these pictures lack that peculiar quality which is the essence of real art, and which distinguishes the nature copyist from the true genius who combines what he has seen with what he has felt. The same applies to the medal picture of E. W. Redfield and to the canvases of such men as Elmer Schofield, Gardner Symons, and many others. They are giants within their limits. They copy nature superbly and there they stop contented. Is there not the fear of traveling a lane that has no outlet?

There is an excellent Japanese word, *esoragoto* — all acknowledgment to Mr. A. J. Eddy — which has no exact equivalent in English or French, and which amounts to a canon. Every painting, to be effective, must be *esoragoto, i.e.*, an invented picture or a picture into which certain fictions are painted. Realistic transcriptions must yield to idealistic compositions, with a maximum of self. A good picture, besides being true to nature, in order to be great art, must excite curiosity and pique the intelligence. Materialism is an excellent attribute, but it should not be the sum total of a picture. The soul of the artist must look behind his pigment or his work threatens to become commonplace.

It fell to a Spaniard and an Englishman to show the strongest harbor scenes. 'Fishermen of the Cantabrique,' by Martinez-Cubells, is an imposing canvas, splendidly painted, showing a fishing smack at the pier, with the crew at work, while other boats are at anchor close by. A ray of light illumines the sluggish water in the right-hand corner, gaining tremendous force by contrast. Hayley-Lever, the Englishman, is represented by one of his characteristic paintings of St. Ives Harbor, full of light and movement, the boats in the foreground dancing on the sunlit waves. Each picture is a masterpiece.

Comparison is invited between British and American painters for the reason that no other country stands so high in the quality of work submitted. Some of the Britishers that have helped to make this year's international a red-letter event are W. Orpen, T. C. Dugdale, J. da Costa, Arnesby Brown, Anning Bell, Hayley-Lever, W. Nicholson, and Hilda Fearon. Some big men are not mentioned, for the reason that their contributions fall below standard. Much is expected of Charles Sims, but his 'Month of Mary' is a disappointing canvas — heavy in color, unrelated, and with miniature groups in the foreground, resembling in conception a shepherd's calendar. One charm only it possesses, namely, a background of delightful design and richness of tone. The Orpen self-portrait, with its *outré* background and quaint accessories, is a magnificent piece of characterization and quite outstrips other essays in portraiture, with very few exceptions.

Gaston La Touche, the Frenchman, has two pictures, but they do not represent him at his best. They appear to be hurriedly executed and contain bad color. Will Ashton received an honorable mention for his 'On the Seine.' His sky-line of buildings is typically Parisian and interesting. His barge, too, in shadow has been well handled, but he seems to miss that peculiar color which every one knowing the river appreciates and discerns.

John W. Alexander has a large and somewhat detached composition entitled 'Her Birthday,' in which three graceful and pleasant-looking young women in different well-studied poses are busy arranging flowers. The canvas contains many very beautiful passages and is full of delicate distinction.

Chicharro, whose admiration for Zuloaga is clearly mirrored in his performances, shows some Castilian peasants breaking bread, very black bread, with sun-baked fingers. They are not pleasant, these nut-brown, hard-featured peasants with their piercing black eyes and sullen demeanor. The artist lacks the fluidity and imagination of his leader. Chicharro carries realism to a point where the observer is less impressed than repelled by his brutality. This brutality is also evident in the work of George W. Bellows, who was deservedly awarded a medal for his exceedingly vital picture entitled 'Cliff Dwellers,' being an admirable rendering of the sordid east-end life of New York's slummery by the river. The picture is frank to a degree and distinctly Rabelaisian in flavor.

Portraits and still life were wisely denied the right to be too insistently in evidence. Landscapes were admitted in overwhelming proportion. W. M. Chase has a portrait and a still life. We all know and respect his fishes. The portrait is of his youngest son, dressed in Etons, full of animation and dashing out of the canvas as through an open door. The lad's bright face, dark hair and olive complexion have been finely handled, better, a great deal, than the advancing right leg, which is just a little unconvincing in the action. 'The Madonna of the Applecart' aptly describes an excellent portrait by T. C. Dugdale, entitled 'Coster-girl and Child.' It is a glowing tribute to London's east-end and to the memory of Phil May, who alone of artists depicted the real coster type. Splendid in color and composition, this picture is one of the real gems of the exhibition.

Among pictures of allegorical import must be mentioned first and foremost an exquisite decorative scheme by Anning Bell, entitled 'The South Wind,' which is reproduced on the first page of this article, and in second place 'Summer Night'

by the great German master, Franz von Stuck, both of which pictures have unfortunately been relegated to odd corners in the minor galleries. A good third place in this line of effort may be fairly accorded to the Cleveland artist, H. G. Keller, who in his 'Wisdom and Destiny' has given a delightful piece of color and composition. 'Old House in the Hills,' by W. L. Lathrop, proves how effective the simplest subject may prove in the hands of a master; painted by a man of mediocrity, no one would have given this canvas a second glance. Jonas Lie shows the lower bay blocked with ice and sentinelled by its grim line of snow-clad skyscrapers. Charles Bittinger's 'Road to the River' compels applause by the unaffected treatment of a simple subject, where powerful sunlight is effected without trickery. Caro-Delvaille presents a nude of Rubenesque proportions, entitled 'La Nature Endormie,' which conjures up visions of the Autumn Salon and previous efforts by the same artist. Good as it is, we infinitely prefer his 'The Young Maid,' which in smaller compass shows a waitress, back to the beholder, depositing a tray upon the table. Head and neck are beautifully modeled, and the flesh tones contrast well with the conventional black frock. Robert Henri's 'Thomas' will please the superficial observer, but we wonder what would be said of a pupil who dared to exhibit such bad draughtsmanship.

A. J. Mannings is a better painter of horses than of cattle, but his 'Cow and Calf' command more than respect. The best cows in the exhibition are in the foreground of Arnesby Brown's fine painting, 'In Suffolk.' They are beefy and elemental, and form no part of a set piece. Mary Cassatt is a disappointment. Her picture in pyramidal construction shows a mother bending over a boy of tender years and huge feet, who gazes into his mother's face. It is Raphaelesque without tenderness and good drawing. Though Raphael erred occasionally in draughtsmanship, even in the 'Sistine Madonna,' yet he never could have modeled such feet upon an infant.

V

AN AMERICAN SALON OF HUMORISTS

LOUIS BAURY

[*Bookman*, January, 1915. By permission of author and publisher.]

I

Just why it is that painting should be deemed the most irrevocably grave of all artistic manifestations, no one has ever explained. But such certainly appears to be the case — particularly here in America. In literature a man has every chance, if he can, to be as hilariously unbridled as Mark Twain, and still take his place, unchallenged, on the shelf with the greatest; on the stage he may be as essentially a humorist as Joseph Jefferson, and yet go down in history with a halo round his memory; even in the uncorporeal sphere of music he may be as light and bizarre and impish as fancy will permit, without in any way jeopardizing his artistic dignity; but let him attempt any such galahearted display in terms of paint, and the most staid Academician and the most perfervid Futurist bang their doors with equal vigor in his face. Which, in this day when there is more talk than ever before of the development of a really national art, seems just a trifle rash.

That ebullient spirit that, without 'mission' or 'message' or 'school,' craves only the privilege of making holiday with facts and pelting impartially with its own gay, inimitable, irreverent confetti every head that bobs up in the carnival of civilization seems too thoroughly American to be consigned always to the lighter, more ephemeral pictorial avenues. Mark Twain and O. Henry are American in a sense in which Poe and Lowell, for instance, never can be. That the spirit which caused them to multiply the gaiety of nations is really inherent in the hearts of American painters, one has to travel no further than to the rooms of the old 'Fakers' to realize.

Around the time of the Spanish War that little off-shoot of the National Academy of Design contained a group of students with conspicuous aptitudes for satirizing passing artistic foibles. Pressed, they will admit that the present form of the society is somewhat in the nature of an anti-climax; but in their day people flocked to the exhibitions where, each year, they held up to merciless ridicule the staid, decorous productions of the regular Academy shows. And there was a certain buoyant inspiration and technical felicity pervading all their merriment which raised these affairs far above the plane of mere undergraduate decorative revels.

Today, the men who once poured forth these festive creations are for the most part in the heyday of their prime. But one journeys from 'important exhibition' to 'interesting group of canvases' to 'noteworthy shows,' looking in vain for a place where the spirit of the old 'Fakers,' in matured and mellowed form, may logically disport itself, and yet remain faithful to the highest artistic conscience. It begins to look as if the only place where such things can pursue their joyous way unfettered amid all the intensity of 'modernity' is in a gallery especially devoted to their interests — just as the playgrounds for children have to be solemnly marked off by act of legislature and maintained sacrosanct by the police force.

Actually to have to offer arguments in favor of a Salon of Humorists in this country, where a sense of humor is as much a standard national institution as George Washington's truthfulness or Bunker Hill or true democracy, would seem too paradoxical. Fortunately, though, the work of the men who without the least encouragement do make occasional forays in this manner is sufficient argument of itself. There are, for example, the pictures of Boardman Robinson — among which is a pungent little wash drawing called 'The Romanticist'— never before exhibited or published — which could most appropriately open an American Salon of Humorists — and that without the slightest disrespect to romance itself.

The man depicted herein is not a painter. Quite unmistakably, he belongs to 'the literati.' But his influence upon gallery exhibitions has been extensive. For he is an 'apostle of art.' He it is who, over the tea-cups, has converted our daughters, and so gained a certain ascendancy in an age of feminism. He has interior-decorated the halls of Philistia itself — and very nearly persuaded the lot of us to sell our birthright for a pot of lilies. And now one enjoys the gratification of seeing all his suspicions about him upheld.

A raven of butterfly fragility, he rises against his nicotine-misted background, his rapturous eyes seeking the heavens — and stopping at a low-hung ceiling. Even the most literal-minded would desire no snatch of superimposed dialogue to enforce the humor of the thing. The humor is inherent in every line of the drawing, in all the subtle force and forceful subtlety of the entire handling. One senses at once the impalpability of the chin beneath those curled whiskers, the scrawniness of the stringed neck somewhere in the floss of that hair, the timidity of those too-small pale hands which are, one is sure, fidgetting under the ceremonious folds of his Inverness.

After this the ladies who peer at canvases anxiously through veils, and murmur of 'perspective'; the people who flutter catalogue pages and talk hesitatingly of 'tone' and 'value' and 'quality' and other safely elusive things, after having looked up the artist's name — these may walk with a new sprightliness now and hold up their heads. Which, after all, is a very excellent thing for 'art.' And even the most strident anarchists shouting for 'wider latitudes' should be appeased. For just as it is said that what cannot be spoken can be put to music, so, in another sense, what cannot be told can be painted. For there are people boasting of portraits, even by Sargent who, if they studied them attentively, instead of pointing them out with a casual reference to the price paid, would be more inclined to try suing the painter for libel. So let us fling open the doors and see if we really are as irrevocably grave as all this talk of art in the Sunday supplements and the public libraries would lead one to suppose.

II

In the field of American art, no place is more genuinely recognized and assured than the high one occupied by George Luks. What Arthur Davies is to the poetry of contemporary painting, Luks is to its prose. So it is particularly pleasing, on entering the American Salon of Humorists, to find a canvas of his prominently hung. One simply cannot help feeling that at last this man who has ever been as a red rag to academies and revolutionaries alike, has found a truly congenial setting. For if ever man was a humorist at heart, that man is Luks. He is in direct line of descent from Swift and Rabelais and Fielding. Humor there is in his most terribly poignant studies, in his most heartrending delineations of slum life, of stricken urchins and ignorant, experience-wise old apple women. But when humor predominates, when it is the irrepressible motive of his theme, then Luks is at his best. Then he is most unrestrainedly himself.

Look over his sketch-books where are jotted down the swift, undeniable first impressions of his journeyings among men. It is humor that radiates through every vibrant line of them. Turning the pages is like walking along a crowded thoroughfare in company with one of those jovially shrewd old eighteenth-century commentators on human foibles. No word is spoken. One simply feels a nudge in the ribs, and, looking, the essential flavor of a group, a situation, a personality is made inimitably manifest. A cabby lolling on his box, a too-young matron whispering imprudent stories into the ear of a promising débutante, a couple from 'hall-roomdom' parading at the fashionable hour on the avenue, the manner in which a young restaurant omnibus fetches *vin ordinaire* — it is such things as these that most inevitably attract Luks's attention. The painting of 'Amateur Night,' reproduced here, though perhaps not the best example of this phase of Mr. Luks's work, unquestionably possesses the authentic spirit. And it is a work for which he has special fondness.

'I felt that very deeply when I was painting it,' he said recently. 'At the time, I was doing a good deal of pot-boiling in the form of posters for those extravagant melodramas which were in such favor then; and so I was quite in the atmosphere of this sort of thing. I've attended dozens of "amateur nights," and I like those kids that get up there and make fools of themselves. They're not always such fools as they act.'

No half-tone reproduction of this painting can begin to do justice to the masterly observation and handling of the play of footlights over the figures — which, technically, is the most notable achievement of the picture. But it retains unimpaired the full force of that girl's desperately clenched hands, the modeling of that youth's legs, the significance of the taut postures of both performers. And it loses little in the understanding with which those faces are rendered.

Gazing on them, one understands pretty well how the comedienne of the team fired her adoring one with histrionic desire — and how, though remaining forever 'minor chords,' they will return again and again to 'Amateur Night.' It is this power of Luks's — evinced even in his slightest things — to make one feel the past and probable future of all his characters, as well as the intensely living present he sets before you, which makes of him an undeniable master.

Hanging near this picture of his is Glackens's 'Roller Skating.' There is no more sincere artist than Glackens in America today. Among painters he is especially esteemed for his technical abilities — and for the magnitude of the technical problems he so often undertakes to solve. In the old days, though, when Glackens concerned himself more with cartoons and illustrations, there used to be a certain rollicking buoyance pervading his work which somehow seems too frequently missing in his later and more elaborate oils. But ever and again it returns joyously and takes possession of his brush for long stretches. The 'Roller Skating' canvas is one of those in which its influence is apparent. Perhaps the murkiness of the atmosphere is rather too palpable in the original, but after one peeps through this, he is very willing to forgive it for the wealth of humor underneath. There are a score of keen, delightful points made here — of character, of anecdote, of gesture, of attitude, of incident — all set forth with that strict economy of detail and sense of *ensemble* rhythm which belongs, perhaps above all else, to a proper interpretation of crowds.

Possibly after the Salon of Humorists has become thoroughly established, Mr. Glackens will relent and give us more oils in this vein — things like those Dickensian observations he has made in crowded slum streets where really all is not poverty and stark misery, and there do exist other occupations than having the milk inspected and dodging the charity workers, who — poor things! — should not be blamed too much, because they, too, have to make a living somehow. Possibly he will go even further. Meanwhile we have this vision of 'society' disporting itself at the rink for all the world as the Sunday supplements have recorded that it disports itself — just the same 'easy informality' and 'sang froid' — and the visitor will probably spend some time in studying out and enjoying the details for himself before turning to the red chalk drawing by Everett Shinn.

Shinn, it must be understood — even though the catalogue, in its official impartiality cannot commit such confidences — is among the bright particular stars of this exhibition. Falling, as a craftsman, into the same general category as Glackens, there is, among other things, the difference that when Shinn turns illustrator he is very likely to be at his unqualified worst. But when he gets down to the 'serious work' which your average artist undertakes with a portentous frown — and maybe one eye on the predilections of the judiciary committee — then Everett Shinn becomes his most debonair, charming, airy, slightly cynical, but always diverting, entertaining, and amusing self. And it is in this guise that he appears at the Salon of Humorists.

It might be that the ultra-captious would take some exceptions to the drawing of the figure on the left of the group shown here, but certainly no one could offer any objection to the pose and spirit of it. And every one of that trio is alive — alive with a life of its own, gay, racy, undeniable. Here again a title is a mere superfluous footnote. The picture's humor is intrinsic, and so completely summed up within itself that no slightest further touch, whether of word or crayon, is necessary. And the beauty of it is, as the New England woman said of the doughnuts that were so appreciated, 'there's plenty more of the same kind where that came from.'

Unfortunately, the Salon of Humorists as yet has few sculptured pieces to offer. But it is significant that some of the most notable of those that are available represent the work of a man whose star is very decidedly in the ascendant. New York at large discovered Herbert Crowley only a few months ago; but, having once been discovered, he is not the sort of person easily to be forgotten. The fervor of the true artist is his; and it finds expression in sumptuously decorative designs which have been compared — although the likeness is really superficial — to a certain vein of Aubrey Beardsley; in rich-hued pastel dreams, behind the surface simplicity of which rages all the monstrous complexity with which the orchestration of modern life is instinct; in delicately whimsical little child-fables in line that are fathered by very much the same spirit that produced Stevenson's *Garden of Verses;* and in twentieth-century grotesques of the order shown here.

'I do these things,' said Mr. Crowley, 'because I have to — because my contact with people and events has bred them inside me, and they must come out. And of course the sense of humor must come out along with the rest. Humor is there — within everybody — as big and true as love or hate or desire or any other human emotion; and so fully worthy of being as finely expressed as one can express it.'

That is what Crowley does in these gargoyles. They are philosophies in bronze, commenting upon whole segments of society, yet quite without malice. Take 'Incapacity,' for instance. The face alone runs the entire emotional gamut from a child whose nurse will not stop the lollipop man who is passing to the politician who cannot stop the restrictive bills that are being passed. The Church of the Social Revolution should avail itself of these gargoyles, if only to demonstrate the genuineness of its modernity.

To keep Mr. Crowley company in the sculpture section there is Mrs. Jerome Meyers. Mrs. Meyers specializes on women — which is indiscreet, but highly diverting. Her work is always interesting, adequate, deftly executed, and modern in manner. The accompanying piece is fairly typical both of her method and her satire. The subject of it is an effusive devotee of Mr. Robinson's Romanticist, an elder sister of Mr. Don Marquis's friend, Hermione. She, too, looks out upon a world that is wonderful — simply *wonderful,* and matches her gowns and jewels to her moods and her room-furnishings to her temperament. Probably the hangings in her boudoir are mauve — with a shadow pattern.

III

As the Laird in *Trilby* so variously intimated, they do these things better in France. Paris instituted a *Salon des Humoristes* as long ago as the spring of 1907. And that Salon instantaneously and overwhelmingly captivated Paris — as things do when they are especially piquant and chic and sophisticated. There the blithest, gayest, deepest, wisest work of such artists as Forain and Willette and Steinlin and Ibels, of Guillaume, Redon, and Robida, and literally hundreds of others, rollicked gleefully forth for the delectation of the multitudes. Somehow, that is always the way. Unto him that hath shall be given! The platitudes will not be downed. For although this Salon has apotheosized certain ideals and forced the more staid and entrenched Salons to take serious recognition, as the phrase goes, of its artistic achievements, Paris was really the last city in the world that stood in actual need of such an institution. Paris, the witching, the sprightly, the saucy, the witty — Paris, which acclaimed and appreciated the mastership of a Daumier and a Toulouse-Lautrec — Paris, where to be clever is to be courted instead of to be inspected with apprehensive suspicion — Paris, where flourish regularly a half-dozen publications of the order of *le Rire* and *l'Assiette au Beurre,* in affirmation of the illustrator's right to deride mankind according to his own sweet pleasure and, if need be, to go out into the smoking-room for his inspiration in doing it — what need had Paris of an institution for the uncensored stigmatizing of affectation and folly, the disrobing of vice, the indication of the grotesque incongruities of the everyday! Why, for all its glory and its conquest, such a gallery was but as a ring on the Parisian little finger, a flower in its buttonhole.

But what chance has the American illustrator for participation in such lively and preëminently worth-while sport? Ask him — as the present writer has asked a score of illustrators — and he will tell you at voluminous length, and with a force which even a Parisian weekly might expurgate, that he has none at all. Take the case of such a well-established illustrator as J. E. Jackson. When he leaves the regular illustrative round for his metropolitan pastels he may freely express the utmost heights of his vision — and who better than he has realized that subtle green which sleeps in the sky above Manhattan when the day of toil is ending and the streets are restless with homeward-faring throngs and the air raucous with the cries of baseball extras?

Yet let him depart from the prescribed orbits in an opposite direction, and even so comparatively mild a satire as 'Beauty and the Beast' goes the normal rounds only to be shunned. Perhaps the dog was not deemed sufficiently beautiful. Yet there are many folk who would find more humor in the observation of that beast's — er, woman's — foot alone than in a volume of sketches of the *Florist:* 'We have some lovely mistletoe, miss.' *Beautiful Young Lady:* 'Thanks; I really don't need that' type.

Of course, every periodical has a right to pursue its own policy undisturbed, and editors know best to what public they wish to appeal; but at the same time, it seems prodigally slack that so much talent — one does not say genius, but undeniable and astoundingly facile talent — as exists in the ranks of our illustrators should, perforce, express itself always in echoes and embellishments.

One need not deny, either, the very patent cleverness of a good deal of the work the avowedly humorous magazines publish, to protest that the mordant, grim, relentless irony of, say, Glenn Coleman can scarcely find adequate outlet in pictorial variations upon the side-splitting themes that college youths always love chorus-girls violently and carry a little wine without due restraint, that the 'woman movement'— whatever that may be — will inevitably force hale and prosperous men into washing dishes, that young things in love simply cannot help turning down the parlor lights and kissing, while the new fashions are really too absurd and golfers use naughty words when they slice the ball, and poets always, always wear long hair because they never have enough money to meet the rapacious demands of barbers.

Yet these things of Mr. Coleman's, clothed in the curiously quaint atmosphere he so well conjures up — these forays into stuffy parks and city margins where the refuse of the ragged-edge congregate and crack grisly jokes anent their own tatters — have a very definite place in the empire of American humor. And so, equally, have the impressions of those two vivid, arresting, but sharply differentiated newspaper men, Cesare and Roth.

The restaurant scene by Cesare, here reproduced, was a mere *pièce d'occasion,* however. 'I do practically nothing,' he explains, 'that would fit into a real Salon of Humorists. As things are, such drawings are luxuries, and however much I might enjoy it, I really don't have a chance to indulge in them.'

And although Herb Roth in his crisp, tumultuous comments, manages again and again to strike from the ephemeræ of the daily news brilliant sparks, swift flashes of character and parables of mirth which, as in the cases of the Winthrop Ames caricature and the Brieux paraphrase, possess more than casual passing interest, one still cannot help wondering just how much Mr. Roth might accomplish if left entirely to his own lightning-like devices — with a Salon of Humorists waiting for the results.

And if this be the case with men who, on newspapers, are coming into constant touch with life at its liveliest, how much more should it apply to magazine illustrators whose facility is so largely devoted to depicting Estelle falling into the arms of Milton, and the King of the Wire-Tappers at the precise moment when the great detective and his trusty lieutenants burst in upon him? If the individual outlook of these illustrators could have free outlet, it would more often than not prove to be in humorous vein. And there is no time more favorable than the present for affording it outlet here in America.

Paris will have no *Salon des Humoristes* this year. Pierrot is in the trenched fields, facing the invader. But Pierrot is the last who would wish to see the carnival itself lapse. For Pierrot is immortal; and even though he die, he lives on, unconquerable.

Finally, then, we can do honor to him in the illustrator's section through Oliver Herford — not because Mr. Herford is an illustrator in the ordinary sense of the word, but because he falls into no regular classification, and so might as well go here as anywhere else. One does not think of Oliver Herford so much as an artist or a wit as in the light of an institution. He is the nearest American counterpart to Max Beerbohm. The same urbanity is his, the same poise, the same sophistication, the same naïveté, the same nice ability for doing charming and rather ticklish things without ever descending to the indelicate or offending good taste. The accompanying examples of his work are recent things; but anything else of his would have served as well. Oliver Herford ' belongs.'

IV

No age has been so multifarious as our own in playing politics through art. In literature the tendency extends all the way from Bernard Shaw to James Oppenheim — which is a long distance, any way you care to figure it. In the graphic arts it is somewhat more concentrated, and — taken on the whole — of more compelling calibre. For where a book or a play or a treatise has an excellent chance of boring you with dogmatics and repetitions and arguments, a picture simply presents its naked vision — and dares you to deny it. And, be your politics what they may, you cannot gainsay the fact that no more representative emanations exist of that tangled, restless, striving, groping, shattering, up-building, cursing, laughing, menacing, praying thing we call modernity than this little gallery of protest contains.

There are the cartoons of Arthur Young, grinning through tears of sympathy, which, ever since the Gene Field era, when they first began to appear in Chicago, have found their fundamental impulse in the social incongruities. And there are the etchings and sketches and oils of John Sloan. Keenly sensitive to his time, Sloan expresses himself inevitably in the humorous strain — and in all his humor there lives that pathos which belongs to all truly felt humor. Note the wistfulness with which he has endowed even such a denunciation of mankind's tawdriness as the accompanying drawing comprises. It is always that way with his things. And that is why John Sloan can unfold the most brutal actualities of the highways and the hidden closets of society, and still set tender chords to vibrating.

Among the younger men striving along somewhat similar lines none gives more striking promise than Stuart Davis. Bold, original, forthright, one feels that much should be before him. And although one's instinct is to be chary in praise of an ability which is still more or less potential, one yet cannot but notice the tendency toward a certain Strindbergian quality in his studies of personality that places them in the category of what Edwin Björkman has called ' pure cultures.' The more one sees of his work, the more one feels that Stuart Davis should be a decided asset to the Salon of Humorists.

And when the same motive which dominates Sloan and Davis springs, instead of from the socialistic or the ultra-realistic, from the decorative instinct, the result is a form equally important to an exhibition of this order. It is the poster at its best.

'It appears almost certain now,' laments Louis Fancher, ' that the keen interest people in this country once took in posters as works of art was merely a fad — that has gone the way of all fads. But I can't help feeling that it would n't have done so had it been properly developed. We talk about the supremacy of German posters; but we forget that German artists had to go through a long, bitter, discouraging fight before they won recognition for the high standards they finally succeeded in setting up. Here in this country, though, it 's impossible, as things are, to wage such a fight. But from personal experiences, I feel certain that the public itself, once thoroughly imbued with the poster ideal, would appreciate and demand that style of work.' Certainly, Mr. Fancher's own ' Carnival ' is not a bad argument in its favor.

And certainly the sharp, bold postures of the poster, its abrupt gestures, the simplicity of its masses of colors, the hyperbole of its statements, indicate a special sympathy with much current thought and movement.

And from posters the transition into pure fantastics is an easy one — things, for example, such as the painted groups Helena Smith Dayton models in plaster. Here is work as wholly American as Coney Island or world-series ball-games or department-store bargain-days. Whether one considers it as a parody of the new art forms or as an absolutely personal approach, it is equally interesting. There is no little tolerance manifest through all the fun and satire with which that human mélange on the ' Boarding-House Steps ' is conceived. And the same spirit accompanies Mrs. Dayton everywhere — into the restaurants and tango-halls where the out-of-towners rub elbows with the demimonde for the enrichment of waiters, along lower Fifth Avenue at that hour when the cloak and suit trade inherits the earth, into those parks where the child is indeed father to the man — wherever, in fact, the whim of the moment suggests.

In the course of these trips, too, Mrs. Dayton's feeling for types frequently expands into a genuine grasp of character. And even in her most headlong moods she never descends to downright triviality.

And triviality is the worst enemy against which the American Salon of Humorists will have to contend.

Of course, the few pictures and sculptures grouped here represent only a fragmentary glimpse even of that spirit which now is obliged to blossom sporadically. But they are sufficient to suggest some of the larger possibilities latent within that particular sort of humor that crackles beneath the cuticle of American life.

All of which may sound excessively serious; but that is the trouble with humor. One simply can't consider it without becoming serious — particularly here in America. For humor is more to us than a mere mood. It is the pith of the swift, electric atmosphere that is so distinctively our own, that capitalization of the moment which serves us in lieu of the tradition that is Europe's. It is a thing as wide as a city street, as free as a prairie, as vivid as an incandescent sign. It is as impudent as a skyscraper, as warm as a hand-clasp, as true as the shifting crowds that give rise to it while they dream and love and laugh and die.

When we fully realize this in our graphic arts, something very fresh and notable in a new way should result. Surely, it is worth while setting out toward that end.

VI

THE WAR IN ART

[*Times,* London, England (Weekly Edition), May 7, 1915.]

The Academy this year, which was opened to the public on Monday, is quite up to the average and perhaps rather better than usual. The war has not suddenly inspired British art with a new seriousness and simplicity; but no one could expect it to do that, and we shall not give ourselves the cheap pleasure of rebuking our painters because they are not new-born since August.

Some of them have painted battle-pictures, but war is a subject that has seldom brought any luck to painters. The greatest do not often attempt it, and lesser artists have not the mastery to make anything vivid or fine in design out of scenes that they have never witnessed.

Mr. H. A. Olivier's 'Where Belgium Greeted Britain' (360) represents the meeting of King George with King Albert on December 4. It is not a battle picture, but the representation of a historical event. Mr. Olivier has not attempted, like Velasquez in 'The Surrender of Breda,' to make the scene impressive by pictorial art. He aims rather at giving his picture an air of authenticity. There is nothing to excite the mind through the eye. He seems to tell us, 'This is how it happened.' But we are not convinced that it did so happen, because no one in the picture is quite lifelike enough. It is of the same character, in fact, as most coronation pictures. The right people are there, all easily recognizable, and are playing their proper parts. Those things are souvenirs of great events and must be accepted, without much criticism, as souvenirs.

Mr. Lavery's 'Wounded: London Hospital, 1915' (181) is much more a work of art. It is, in fact, one of the best pictures he has ever painted; but he would have done it better still, if he had been content to give us simply a large interior and had not been conscious of the moral and historical interest of the scene. For the one weak point in the picture is the nurse and wounded soldier in the foreground. They are not, like the rest, seen by a painter, but by a sentimentalist. They are too obviously playing their parts and over-acting them a little, so that they seem to belong to a different and inferior kind of art from the rest of the picture.

Mr. Clausen in his 'Renaissance' (143) is allegorical, and his allegory succeeds better than the realism of other painters. It is the Renaissance of France that he paints, and the whole picture is fine in color and in design except for the faces. They are always the difficulty of allegory. If too much emphasis is laid on them, their figures become too personal for allegorical types; and in this picture they are too personal and a little absurd. There is incongruity between the purely allegorical nude figure and the eminent Frenchman with the Legion of Honor, who might almost be a portrait. But we can forget this incongruity in the whole design, and that does give us a sense of the Renaissance of France.

Mr. W. L. Wyllie's 'The Fighting Line from Ypres to the Sea' (352) is a war landscape with an aëroplane. But the aëroplane is not assimilated to the landscape. It dominates everything, not as a feature in the design, but as an unusual fact; and that is the worst of war in pictures. It is nearly always merely an unusual fact, appealing too directly to the mind, like a piece of exciting news. It is not art, as exciting news is not literature. Mr. T. Mostyn in his 'Flight' (435) gives us the typical rather than the actual; but he is not quite enough of a master to make the typical impressive. These fleeing female figures are a little platitudinous, like minor poetry. They remind us of a great many other pictures, as minor poetry reminds us of other verse. That is also the fault of Mr. Richard Jack's 'Homeless' (464), though this is more a picture than most of the attempts to paint war. But, again, we feel that we have seen it before, that it belongs to the stage rather than to real life or to the world of imagination.

There is more vividness in Mr. P. W. Adam's interior, 'War' (480), a room wrecked by a shell. This is well painted, and the composition both expresses the havoc and is in itself startling and satisfactory. In the 'Retreat from the Marne' (593) Mr. John Charlton seems merely to tell us that the Germans were driven back in more confusion than they probably were. It is like the highly-colored description of a correspondent who was not present. That is also true of Mr. W. B. Wollen's 'Landrecies, August 25' (664). We have street fighting with every emphasis laid on its violence; but it is mere violence of language which may excite for a moment but soon wearies. In 'The Strongest' (973) Mr. Fortunino Matania gives us merely an illustration, but a vivid and amusing one: a Belgian or French boy putting out his tongue at a German soldier as his mother leads him by with averted face. It is effective because not exaggerated. The German is not violently brutal. He looks at the boy rather stupidly, as if uncertain whether to take any notice of him or not.

So much for the war pictures. We turn with some relief to the others. Mr. Sargent is at his best in several little pictures. He has never done anything better than his 'Tyrolese Crucifix' (198), where

light and form are so mingled that they surprise and convince us. The picture has been made straight from the reality in front of the painter, but it has all come right, except the figure of the man, where the artist's emphasis has failed, so that he is merely a little piece of dullness in a very brilliant whole.

VII

LEON BAKST'S DESIGNS FOR SCENERY AND COSTUME

GERALD C. SIORDET

[*International Studio* (John Lane Co.), November, 1913. By permission of author and publisher.]

Léon Bakst, about whom so much has been talked and written during the last few years in connection with the art of the theatre, was born in St. Petersburg in the year 1868. Passing through the academic course of art training in that city, he went to Paris to study in 1895, and on his return to Russia won such success as a painter of portraits and official pictures as to be appointed to the position of painter to the Imperial family. But a realistic subject-picture, a *Pietà*, in which the artist presented the persons of our Lord and His Mother under the guise of peasants, and attempted to depict without restraint the most violent affections of grief in the principal figures, was found so displeasing to the committee of the Academy to which it was submitted for exhibition that, though the work was hung, it was scored from corner to corner with bands of white chalk. The artist withdrew the picture: and the insult, combined with the representations of a little group of friends whose belief in his particular genius had been aroused by the success of a number of experiments in the designing of decoration and stage scenery and costume, decided him to break with official patronage and to follow his own bent. The secession of the younger school of Russian dancing, personified in the art of Nijinsky, provided him with the very opportunity he was seeking; he left Russia, staked his artistic interests in the new venture, and provided the ballets with a series of settings and costumes that have inestimably enriched the performances of the Russian dancers and have been the means of his acquiring a great artistic reputation for himself.

Yet I am not at all sure that in England, at any rate, the theatrical work of Léon Bakst has not been treated with greater solemnity than he himself would consider appropriate. The Englishman in art has always been rather like the old lady and the patent medicine —' My dear, it must be good, the advertisements speak so well of it '— and provided that the critics supply him with a few portable *sententiae* on the matter in hand he has been content to like things not so much for what they are as for the variety of terms in which they can be described. In the case of work so unavoidable as that of Bakst it is the critic's function to drape the obvious, to explain away enjoyment that might seem too indiscreet or too direct, and so to arrange things that respectability may safely become a little wild, and audacity remain still fairly respectable.

But to Bakst himself his work presents itself in a much simpler light. Art, as he says, is a plaything, and an artist's work will be good only when it has been great fun doing it. Here is the real secret of his appeal. Grant him whatever fine and farfetched qualities you will — and there is plenty enough to his credit — these designs of his charm because, behind all the intervening processes of knowledge and calculation, they reveal the enjoyment of the child, exultant in the possession of paintbox and brushes, greatly daring to draw monsters, or princesses, or cities of an enchanted world.

That they should keep the freshness and sparkle of spontaneity is the more remarkable when one considers the amount of solid learning that has gone to the designing of such a series of costumes as enrich the ballets of *Schéhérazade, Le Dieu Bleu, Hélène de Sparte,* or Signor d'Annunzio's medievalist experiments, *S. Sebastien* and *Pisanelle.* Bakst is a real student, a genuine scholar in costume. His designs are no mere archeological resuscitations of the wardrobes of the past; neither are they the summary, impressionistic stock-intrade of the quick-change artist. He is, indeed, a kind of bright, particular chameleon. He will settle into the strange, distorted glamour of the East, or the simple graces of archaic Greece, or the fierce, gay medley of the Middle Ages, and presently will bring you forth not dresses merely but *personages* who move with ease and certainty each in his own time, and yet retain the stamp of their creator.

This peculiar receptivity of mind, which at the same time recreates and rearranges, is of all qualities that most fitted to adapt itself to the art of the theatre, in which scenery and costume are most telling only when they make no attempt to conceal, rather welcome, the presence of conscious recognized artifice — in fact, when the art that makes them is considered as itself a plaything. It is hardly possible to find a single design by Bakst which is not from this point of view ' amusing.'

Of course some have greater value than others. The last exhibition of his drawings contained a number of designs which, admirable as they were as working indications of costume and color, would by themselves have carried little proof of the exuberant and at the same time fastidious power of design which, among other qualities, gives a permanent value to his more finished drawings.

One critic said of him, apropos of his drawings for *Schéhérazade* and *Le Dieu Bleu,* that he had ' rediscovered the luscious female line bequeathed by the early Orientals.' I am not sure that I know what he meant: historically the remark seems to mean nothing; yet it is very true that Bakst shows a passionate enthusiasm for the flesh, for the contours of form, for strange poise and counterpoise of limb, for furious, abandoned movement, that sets an Eastern stamp upon his art, and reminds us that he is of the nation that long ago watched King David dance before the Lord ' with all his might.'

The illustrations to this article demonstrate the extraordinary facility with which Bakst modifies treatment and design in accordance with the character of his subject. Look at the pencil drawing for the first act of *Pisanelle,* with its great three-masted ship, its bales of treasure stowed upon the quay, its crowd of detail in such little compass, the whole compact and childlike as a medieval woodcut; or the lovely, subtly simple dress of Likenion in *Daphnis and Chloe;* or the truculent swagger of the Pole from *Boris Godounoff;* of the wasted fakir, blue and yellow draped, part of the very spirit of the East. Each is of its world, and though the mind may turn to memories of the Morte D'Arthur, or the Greek vase-painters, or of that splendid Bakstian masterpiece, 'Sidonia the Sorceress,' each drawing lives by something more than the stimulus of past 5 art.

It is perhaps only natural that so versatile a master of theatrical design should have tried his hand on modern dress. Yet I cannot think that he has achieved a real 10 success. However much we may lament the fact, we live in a democratic, utilitarian age. Trousers are trousers, skirts are skirts for all the world. It is true that some words of Chaucer's 'poor parson' 15 concerning 'disordinate scantitee of clothinge' are not altogether inapplicable even to the present time: but the days when men and women made themselves picturesquely ridiculous by wearing almost nothing, or 20 trailing the 'superfluitee of their gowns in the dong and in the myre,' merely in order to furnish an advertisement of their social status, are gone to return no more. There are no more Sumptuary Laws, and, to 25 speak broadly, the dressmakers' 'matcher' may come out tomorrow in just such another costume for shape and style as her employer has been 'creating' today for the greatest lady in the land. 30

The problem, then, for the original designer is hedged about with limitations. He can do no more than ring the changes on a round of styles that can be harmonized with the thing we call a 'skirt,' 35 and when he attempts to take a flight beyond the experiments of the past he will generally land himself in an impossible situation. The most practical of Bakst's designs for modern costume are merely 40 charming adaptations of past styles. The lovely drawing, reproduced in color for this article, differs but little in idea from a creation of any well-known house, save for the arrangement of lace upon the arms 45 — a point designed to lend originality to the dress, but in reality the sole feature which in any other pose but that of the drawing itself would be impossible.

Yet, when all is said, it would be un- 50 seemly to carp in any serious spirit at the experiments of an artist to whom we owe so much pure enjoyment, and whose genius for design ranging over so wide a field finds almost nothing which it cannot at 55 once assimilate and adorn with some original feature of its own making.

VIII

THE AMERICAN ART COLLECTOR

[*Philadelphia Press*, May 4, 1915. By permission.]

The war has increased the anxiety of British art lovers as to the inroads made by American collectors upon privately-owned art works. Fearing that through fatalities and through the general financial depression caused by the war many English collections will have to be sold, a special committee of the National Gallery Trustees has been formed in London to discuss ways and means of acquiring options on such collections and prevent them from passing into the hands of Americans.

This anxiety is perhaps natural enough considering that within recent years 316 valuable paintings were shipped out of England to private and public galleries in the United States. If actually faced with the problem the British Government would probably be unwilling to permit the steady drain on its art treasures, as the Italian Government was when it passed a law forbidding the exportation of masterpieces from the country. And while no American collector will deny the British public's right to first opportunity of buying British art works, the ground upon which this committee chooses to advocate the exercise of that right is little short of offensive.

'American millionaires,' declared one art authority, testifying before the committee, 'find the collecting of old masters more amusing than other ways of spending money. It produces more social return than other ways.' Another said: 'American millionaires make collections to advertise themselves, to a certain extent, expecting to get back their money in other ways.' Said a third: 'There is a great rush for art by American millionaires who really do not care much about it.'

These charges are too absurd to require refutation. In Philadelphia alone we have the example of great collections — the Widener, the Johnson and the McFadden, for example — assembled with discriminating taste and carefully guarded from anything resembling publicity or 'social return.' It is America's pride and her hope of being the future art centre of the world, that her richest citizens have interested themselves in art and are importing the rarest masterpieces of antiquity to hang in private galleries and — as many have already done — eventually to donate whole priceless collections to the use and education of the public.

IX

THE GARDEN AS A MEANS OF ARTISTIC EXPRESSION

THOMAS H. MAWSON

[*Studio Yearbook of Decorative Art* (John Lane Co.), 1913. By permission of author and publisher.]

From the dawn of literature and art to the present day, poets have sung and artists have painted the incomparable charms of the garden. Whether by this term we conjure up to the mind a vision of parterres neat and prim, and with each portion of the design carefully balanced against every other, or, on the contrary, the rank profusion and free unrestrained growth of the wild garden with its direct tribute to the supreme beauty of Nature, we shall find that, since man's earliest ages, there has not been wanting appreciation for the incomparable possibilities of the garden on the part of those who have been leaders in art and letters in every generation.

When we add to this fact the consideration that, not only has Holy Writ placed before us a garden as the scene of many of the most sacred as well as the most stirring episodes, but that ancient mythology has almost invariably appealed to the popular mind at one point or another by means of a garden, it becomes almost impossible to conceive how the modern neglect of gardening as a means of serious art expression can have come about.

Instead of the intelligent enthusiasm which one would expect such a heritage of tradition to engender, we find today that the vast majority of people, if they trouble to define the purpose of a garden at all, would consider it merely as a place for the cultivation of individual specimens of flowering plants or shrubs for their intrinsic beauty alone, and would show no consciousness whatever for the possibilities for collective effect which it presents. Others, more in sympathy with their work,

would have us concentrate our attention on the blending and harmonizing of color masses, certainly a most laudable object in itself, but not if it is allowed to distract the attention from, and blind the vision to, the larger problem of which it is only a part.

It is not too much to say that in the majority of gardens, and in suburban gardens especially, we have more evidences of an utter lack of any kind of artistic perception than in any other class of feature capable of becoming a medium for art expression. Either an absurd effort is made to imitate the glories of Nature on half an acre of ground, and to include in this area every class of scenery, hill and vale, rock and swamp, in absurd miniature and hopeless jumble, with impossible bridges over invisible streams and little erections shiny with varnish and hideous with cheap colored glass, or, on the other hand, the ground is parcelled out into confessedly utilitarian plots for the culture of ' specimens.'

Neither course is right, for both are extremes, and extreme measures in art, as in all things, rarely point the way to perfection. Instead we must have, first of all, a clear impression of the possibilities of all the factors which go to the making of a garden, whether architecture, trees, greensward, rock, water, roads and paths, or lawns for games, as well as of their relative functions, and from these materials we must build up our picture, or rather series of pictures, for one of the greatest charms with which we can invest the garden will be that of a certain complexity which will give variety and prevent satiety. These two considerations interact on one another and cannot be considered apart, or we shall fall afresh into the errors of the gardeners of a century ago, and even earlier, who, subordinating everything to the creation of ' effects,' ended in reducing their works to a series of startling caricatures. Each walk or drive was so contrived as to bring the beholder suddenly opposite some daring creation in which sham churches or ruins and hummocky foreground and other stage scenery played a prominent part. These and other curious devices, such as sundials which squirted water at the person who approached them (from one of which the present site of the London County Council Offices obtained its name), might amuse when first seen, but, on familiarity, amusement would give place to satiety and satiety to disgust, for, of all things, the tone of a well-ordered garden should be restful, and familiarity, instead of breeding contempt, should give a greater and fuller realization of its many charms as well as adding the delights of old association.

This, then, is the garden of our dreams, a place where our highest and best instincts may find satisfaction, cut off from the jarring notes and sordid features of the outside world, and where we may find at all times coolness and brightness and a temptation to rest, and where ' retired Leisure' may 'in trim gardens take his pleasure.'

To realize such a garden we must know, first of all, what are the materials which we may legitimately use in its creation, and then, treating these as the artist views his pigments, how we may blend and use them and what limitations their physical properties will impose upon us.

Immediately we approach our task, however, we are confronted with two distinct schools of garden designers, having diametrically opposed ideas as to the methods to be employed and the results to be aimed at. The two styles they advocate may, for want of better titles, be called the ' Formal' and ' Landscape' styles. The former of these aims at a balanced and coordinated entity which shall frankly and confessedly be a work of art, made to please, and culling for its use the best from all the arts and sciences; while the latter aims at taking Nature as its guide, and avoiding, or rather consciously ignoring, every possible suggestion of conventionalization or, indeed, of design as usually understood in other arts.

Which of these two schools of garden makers we are to follow will, I think, be abundantly clear if we look into their origin. We shall then find that, whereas the former, the Formal, style of design, is of ancient origin and has been developed by that same form of evolution which has governed the production of every other class of art, and in particular in its closest relative, architecture, the latter is an upstart fashion which sprang up around a half-truth which had become a catch phrase, which was that ' All Nature is a garden fair,' and owed its opportunity to the extravagant lengths into which the

older style had been dragged by puerile imitators who had copied its forms without in the slightest understanding its spirit.

The battle of the styles was in full swing when Schiller wrote, in 1795, ' There will be found in all probability a very good middle course between the formality of the French gardening-taste and the lawless freedom of the so-called English style,' and it has been going on ever since. There are, however, strong indications that a solution of the difficulty is being found at last along the lines indicated by the writer just quoted, and that in taking from each style all that it has to teach us, acknowledging, on the one hand, Nature's preëminent and unique example, and, on the other, the claims that a style which has come down to us from remote ages, each generation adding its own vision to the conception, must have upon our respectful consideration.

We are fast coming to see that, while the Formal style is to be preferred in conjunction with architecture, the Landscape style also has its uses where Nature reigns; and so, by the use of both, or rather, of a style which makes more use of the precedent of the one mode near the mansion and more and more of the features of the other as we recede from it, we are able to blend Nature with Art in a harmonious manner.

The greatest result of this clearly indicated promise of the dawn of a truly national school of garden design which has taken place so far is the recognition accorded to the profession of Landscape Architecture, or, as the writer would prefer to have it named, ' Topographical Architecture,' the art of planning over large areas. This art, which aims more at coordinating and correlating the various units than at the designing of the units themselves, has had its professors in every generation — Haussmann in Paris, Sir Christopher Wren in London, the brothers Adam in Edinburgh, and so on, but these have had to work, one might almost say, by stealth, and rather as designers of buildings overstepping their province than as professors of a distinct branch of art, requiring for its due presentment a distinct and very liberal training.

This last phrase strikes the key-note of the whole matter with all its problems, for it is almost entirely due to the utter lack of any appreciation of the necessity for what I have called 'a distinct and very liberal training' which has resulted in the neglect of the art and the abundant possibilities of its application which have always existed and which are to be found on every hand today, unrecognized and undeveloped. While every other branch of art demands from its votaries, not only a heaven-born genius, but also a knowledge of the precedent of his art and a technical training in the use of his media, it would seem to be tacitly agreed by most people in this country that any ordinary and not very gifted individual should be able to evolve from his inner consciousness, without previous training or experience, all the qualities for the laying out of parks, gardens, boulevards, or even the artistic presentment of whole cities. The most notable, or should I say *notorious,* result of this state of things is that, in this country, practically all our public parks and gardens have been laid out by amateurs in a manner which is puerile and utterly abhorrent to any one with any artistic sense, and their architecture is chosen from the catalogues of the makers of iron buildings.

There are exceptions of course, simply because once in a century or so it happens by chance that the work falls into the hands of the right man; but the average city councilor or borough official is not chosen for his post on account of his devotion to art, but for his executive, financial, or technical ability, and to expect such a gentleman, however gifted in his own sphere, suddenly whenever called upon, like Shelley's skylark, to pour out from a full heart 'profuse strains of unpremeditated art' would strike one as utterly impossible were it not done so often.

We thus come across this strange result that, whereas in this country our splendid country seats, laid out by the great garden designers of the past, are incomparably beautiful, our public gardens, as I have already said, leave much, very much, to be desired; while in other countries, and especially in the United States of America and in France, the reverse is the case, and while the public works, like the gardens and boulevards of Paris, have a worldwide reputation, the private gardens, designed by amateurs, are on the whole inferior to ours. Exception must be made, of course, in favor of the world-famous gardens to the villas of Italy, which, however, represent the best results of that ideal arrangement only to be reached when a capable and enthusiastic practitioner works under the inspiring influence and with the practical help of a sympathetic client, himself strongly imbued with the artistic sense and able to sympathize with difficulties and rejoice when they are overcome.

Another contributing cause to the confusion of which I have complained, and which it is my object to remove, is the lack of good textbooks by competent authorities dealing with the subject of garden design. While we have a plethora of garden books, they are by amateurs for amateurs, by domestic architects for architects, or by horticulturalists on horticulture, and never, broadly speaking, since Repton's days, by landscape architects for garden designers.

And now for my confession, lest my ulterior motives should be discovered unconfessed! My chief aim, nay, almost my whole aim, in writing this article is the hope that I may influence some of the younger generation of art students, among whom the *Studio Year Book* may circulate, to make one or other of the two great sub-divisions of the profession of Landscape Architecture (Civic Art and Landscape Gardening) their life study.

It is with the latter, and in many ways the more entrancing, of these two subdivisions that we are more particularly concerned at present. Its aim is so to group and arrange the various factors which go to the making of the modern domain, and so to design and embellish them that they form a composite whole beautiful in itself, thus adding to the attractions of the individual features by providing for them a suitable setting and by harmony and contrast. That there should be any need to urge students of art to take up this work speaks volumes for the low and neglected state into which the whole art of garden design has fallen, and it is my earnest wish that the profession to which I have devoted my life should in the future be more adequately represented by men who have had a catholic art training, such as will enable them to combat the mass of misconception of the nature and functions of garden design which at present surrounds the whole subject.

There is another misconception which has tended to prevent suitable men taking up the work of garden design, due to the failure to differentiate between *garden making* and *gardening*. I would even go so far as to say that a knowledge of the sciences of horticulture and arboriculture, while extremely desirable, is not essential to the landscape architect. It is sufficient if he knows what effects are possible and what he may use under varying circumstances, for the task of materializing his designs will fall, not upon him, but upon the working gardener.

This is only true, of course, in an abstract sense, for I should always recommend that a student should have a general acquaintance with these sciences; still it serves to illustrate my point, and, anyway, there are many other subjects which are still more essential to him. Perhaps the chief of these is a knowledge of architecture and a deep and real sympathy with the aims and inspirations of its exponents; for not only will there be more or less constructional work in all his schemes, but in almost every case he will be called upon to work in collaboration with a domestic architect. This knowledge, too, will have to be of the most catholic nature, for, generally speaking, the landscape architect will be called upon to harmonize his scheme with preëxistent architecture which may be in any one of the numberless styles prevailing or in no style whatever. In the latter case there is, of course, opportunity for the exercise of genius of the highest order if the grotesque efforts of an amateur in architectural design are so to be backed up by their surroundings that defects are remedied or, at least, negatived and lack of proportion removed by the addition of balancing features.

Another requirement of the professor of garden making, which, however, must necessarily be more born than made, is the power so to interpret his vision of beauties to be to others that he fills them with his own enthusiasm for the beautiful and gains their assent to his proposals and their active coöperation. This is the most difficult task of all, but as I have dealt with it at length on many other occasions, it is unnecessary to do more than call attention to it now.

To these subjects will have to be added a knowledge in the round of road engineering, land draining, and almost every form of constructional work and estate management. It will thus be seen how many-sided his work and training will be. It is a far cry from the point at which he first stands on the vacant site, and maps out in his mind the rudiments of his scheme, to the day when he designs the finishing touches and carefully balances sun-dials, statuary, and the smaller furnishings of the garden in height, breadth and bulk against the open spaces surrounding them, or against the proportions of the vista the termination of which the feature is to mark. Between these two points, which, in time, may possibly be separated by months and even years of patient endeavor, will come a mass of questions to be decided and problems to be met which, while they will call forth the best and highest that is in him, will also prove of most absorbing interest at every turn. Nor is there the possibility of the slightest sameness in this work. Quite apart from the enormous difference between public and private gardens in spirit and intent, no two sites are the same, and every client's requirements will differ, so that originality is inevitable and will be of the best sort, that is, of that form which proceeds not from a desire to avoid sameness but which springs naturally from a proper treatment of the individual problems peculiar to the particular site under treatment.

This rapid survey of some of the more essential requirements of the landscape architect serves to show us something of the complexity, as well as of the charm, of the art of garden making. What more entrancing task could there be than one in which we are constantly employed in the creation of the beautiful, not merely with the pigments of the artist for the edification of the few who have the specialized training to feel and understand, but to be a delight, in some sort at least, to every beholder, and to be produced not in counterfeit presentment by pigments but by the manipulation of the actual objects themselves. This very fact, of course, invests the work with a special difficulty which is shared with the sculptor and which is that, while the painter or engraver selects his point of view and composes his scheme from that point alone, the garden designer and sculptor have each to create a composition which shall be equally beautiful from every point from which it may be observed.

There is, however, a reciprocal relationship between the practical and esthetic in garden design which differentiates it from every other form of art. The landscape architect is more bound by, or rather his art is more controlled by, practical and utilitarian limitations than any other branch except, perhaps, domestic architecture. Even in this instance, however, there is one great factor which is peculiar to his art and which is not shared by the domestic architect. This arises from the fact that he has to deal with two distinct classes of objects, the inanimate, which is fixed and abiding, and the animate, which is constantly changing with the seasons and even from hour to hour. The former class is represented by the architectural features incorporated with his scheme, the contours and levels of the various portions of the site, whether natural or controlled, and, to a lesser degree, the distant prospect, which may have an important function to perform in the completion of his effects. The latter class is composed of the whole available range of the native and naturalized vegetable products, from the oak to the cactus, in all their almost bewilderingly divergent forms, sizes, and esthetic qualities. We must also add to it one feature which, although really inanimate, still possesses all the qualities of variableness, otherwise almost entirely peculiar to animate nature, in a most remarkable degree. That is water, without which, in some form or other, very few landscape compositions can be deemed to be complete, and about the use and adaptation of which to the garden a whole volume might be written.

It is no light task to create a composition in which the animate and inanimate shall combine and harmonize from all points of view at all times and in every season. In some cases, of course, especially in heroic compositions in which the architecture is in the traditionally classic styles and on a large scale, the foliage effects must necessarily be kept so entirely subservient to the purely architectural portions of the scheme that only trees and 5 shrubs which may be reduced to definite and conventional form by the use of the knife and shears can be used, such as cordons, hedges, and screens of foliage. On the opposite hand, as I have pointed out in 10 one of my books, there is no sense of incongruity felt when even the tiniest of cottages is overhung by the largest trees, in fact the greater the contrast the greater the sense of protection from winter storms 15 and summer heat. Between these two extremes there is infinite gradation, and half the training of the student of the form of applied art which we are discussing will be complete when he has learned so much 20 of the laws of proportion as will enable him unerringly to decide how much of each, foliage and architecture, may be used in any class of scheme and where the mass of each should be placed.

25 From what I have said it will be seen that modern needs and modern opportunities are almost compelling the creation of what is practically a new profession and one which possesses the greatest attractions for the art student with a pronounced 30 love of architecture, arboriculture, and the allied arts, and who is filled, at the same time, with a practical enthusiasm for the betterment of the conditions under which his fellowmen labor and live. To create 35 beauty, not only of form and environment but also of mind and moral atmosphere, is a task which should inspire the best and noblest type of mind and supply food sufficient, both in quantity and quality, for 40 the greatest intellect. The student who decides to take up this work need never fear that he will not have scope for the best and the highest that is in him, or that 45 he will ever find his work pall or anything he is called upon to do lacking in intense and vital interest.

THE END

To be a reporter Horace Greely said;
"Sleep on files of paper and eat printers
ink".

A man is great if he makes you
think great things.

Charity is sometimes

The saloon is the poor man's club.
Necessity is not only the mother of invention, but also of contention.

Edison said, "99% of perspiration and 1%
of inspiration."

Emerson says it takes 3 generations to
make gentlemen.

Evidence of greatness is self-abnegation.

When the rich man rides, he rides
in chaises

When the poor man rides, he walks
by jings!

Socialism leads to liberty
Individualism leads to license.

Art is the practice of a science.

Four steps thru which ideas pass;
(1) Fool (2) Foolish (3) Eccentric (4) Acceptance

Education is proper emphasis on the correct evaluation & appraisement of real values.

Greetings in different Languages
A.S. Wassail - Be well
I. How do you stand
E. " " " find yourself.
F. " " " carry "
a. what's the word.

Maeterlink goes beyond actuists motives in his dramas.

To Reform a man give him some new ideas and something good to eat.

The Irishman said in answer to the question if life was worth living said;
"It all depends on the liver".

Lord in A.S. means provider of bread.
Lady " " " maker of ".

"Teach the young idiot how to shoot"
rather than the "idea how to spout"

Benjamin Franklin said, "If you want a thing done right, do it yourself."

When you begin to slap a hero on the back, he ceases to be a hero.

Any one who thinks for you is not your friend.

You never know a person until you dare to be silent in his presence.